CHRISTIANITY IN A REVOLUTIONARY AGE
*A History of Christianity
in the Nineteenth and Twentieth Centuries*
VOLUME IV

THE TWENTIETH CENTURY
IN EUROPE

CHRISTIANITY IN A REVOLUTIONARY AGE

*A History of Christianity in the Nineteenth and
Twentieth Centuries*

VOLUME IV

THE TWENTIETH
CENTURY
IN EUROPE

The Roman Catholic, Protestant, and Eastern Churches

By KENNETH SCOTT LATOURETTE

*Sterling Professor of Missions and Oriental History, Emeritus,
and Associate Fellow in Berkeley College in Yale University*

GREENWOOD PRESS, PUBLISHERS
WESTPORT, CONNECTICUT

The Library of Congress has catalogued this publication as follows:

Library of Congress Cataloging in Publication Data

Latourette, Kenneth Scott, 1884-1968.
The twentieth century in Europe: the Roman Catholic,
Protestant, and Eastern churches.

(His Christianity in a revolutionary age, v. 4)
Bibliography: p.
1. Europe--Church history. 2. Church history--20th
century. I. Title. II. Series.
BR475.L33 vol. 4 [BR735]   270.8s [274]
ISBN 0-8371-5704-8   72-11979

To all, both past and present,
who as his secretaries have aided the author,
these volumes are gratefully
and affectionately dedicated

Originally published in 1961
by Harper & Brothers, New York

Reprinted with the permission
of Harper & Row, Publishers, Inc.

First Greenwood Reprinting 1973

Library of Congress Catalogue Card Number 77-138141

ISBN 0-8371-5700-5 (Set)
ISBN 0-8371-5704-8 (Vol. IV)

Printed in the United States of America

CONTENTS

Chapter X

Chapter XI

Chapter XII

Chapter XIII

Chapter XIV

Chapter XV

Chapter XVI

Chapter XVII

Chapter XVIII

Chapter XIX

Chapter XX

Chapter XXI

AUTHOR'S ACKNOWLEDGEMENTS

I N THE final revision of the manuscript the author has had the benefit of comments on the original draft by a number of experts. Monsignor John Tracy Ellis read the chapters on the Roman Catholic Church, the Reverend Jacques Paul Bossière-Canton the section on the Roman Catholic Church in France and the section on Roman Catholic theology, Professor George A. Lindbeck and the Reverend Paul Murray Minus, Jr., the section on Roman Catholic theology, Professor Ernst Benz and Professor Franklin H. Littell the chapter on Protestantism in Germany, Professor W. F. Dankbaar the chapter on Protestantism in the Netherlands, the Reverend Bardwell Smith the section on Protestantism in England, and Dr. Paul B. Anderson the chapters on Russia, Greece, and the Balkans. The author is also deeply indebted to the Reverend Gustave Weigel for information on Roman Catholic theology, to Professor Claude Welch for information on Protestant theology, and to Professor Paul Minear for information on the Netherlands. To each and all of these men the author wishes to express his thanks. No work of the character of this one can be faultless, and for such mistakes and omissions as remain the author is entirely responsible, but without the assistance of these good friends the following pages would have been guilty of many more errors.

CHAPTER I

Introductory: The Revolution Is Augmented, Becomes World-wide, and Further Challenges Christianity

THE SUMMER of 1914 witnessed the beginning of a new stage in the revolutionary age. With it rather than in 1901 the twentieth century may be said to have begun. As we have often remarked, the nineteenth century can properly be regarded as having been ushered in by the close of the Napoleonic Wars in 1815. Certainly the nearly one hundred years which followed were a distinct period in the history of mankind and were characterized by developments in the revolution issuing from Western Christendom which marked them off from the eighteenth century. As we saw in our first volume, the revolution had its inception long before 1815 and reached a climax in what followed the events in France in 1789. In the ten decades after 1815 it continued and in some of its aspects was accelerated. Now and again it was punctuated by political explosions, but none of them was as shaking as the series which lasted from 1789 to 1815: no general war racked all Christendom as it had in those momentous years. Although between 1815 and 1914 the forces at work greatly altered Christendom and were beginning to impinge on the rest of the human race, among some peoples with spectacular results, compared with the quarter-century which preceded 1815 and the decades which began in 1914, from the perspective of the twentieth century the course of the revolution in the nineteenth century seemed almost peaceful. The general temper in Western Christendom—in both Western Europe and its extension in the Americas and Australasia—was one of mounting optimism and a continuation of the eighteenth-century confidence in human progress. Here and there warning voices were raised, but they were heeded only by minorities.

Then, in August, 1914, a tempest broke in Europe which within a few months either directly or indirectly engulfed all mankind. It was followed by dramatic political changes—the unseating of ancient ruling families (the Hapsburgs, the Hohenzollerns, and the Romanovs); the coming of new regimes in much of Europe, some of them democracies in the Western sense of that much abused term; the seizure of Russia by Communism in the name of a republic and professing to be inaugurating a true democracy; and the emergence into independence of nations long subject to monarchies which were now swept aside.

After what later was ominously called World War I came an uneasy pause and then World War II. In the interval Germany was captured by National Socialism and Hitler, Italy was mastered by Fascism under Mussolini, and Spain was torn by civil strife. World War II was longer and more widely destructive than World War I. It, too, was followed by dramatic changes in the map of Europe—what now came by many to be regarded as the *quondam* Christendom—and also by new regimes, some of them Communist and hostile to Christianity.

One of the most thought-provoking facts about World Wars I and II was that they centred in Europe. There Christianity had longer had a nearer approach to free course than anywhere else on the planet. The wars were fought with mechanical devices in guns, explosives, poison gas, ships, and airplanes, and by forms of organization, such as compulsory military service, which made possible total war—developed in that continent and in the larger Europe, especially the United States. As a current bit of doggerel had it:

> Two thousand years of holy mass,
> and we have come to poison gas.

To be sure, while World War I unmistakably had its inception in Europe and World War II was generally regarded as beginning there, the first rumblings of the latter conflict were the Japanese occupation of Manchuria in 1931 and the full-scale invasion of China by Japan which dated from 1937, over two years before fighting broke out in Europe. But that was evidence of the spread of the revolutionary forces which issued from Christendom.

Moreover, the invention and first use of the atomic bomb was by the United States, ostensibly a Christian nation, and the further development of atomic weapons was for several years entirely within the historic Christendom—the United States, Russia, Great Britain, and France.

Although other wars, notably some by non-Christians, such as China had known and those waged by Mongols both before and after their conversion to Islam, had been more destructive in particular areas, the two world wars of the twentieth century were more widely devastating than any of their predecessors.[1]

[1] For a thoughtful discussion see John U. Nef, *War and Human Progress: An Essay on the Rise of Industrial Civilization* (Cambridge, Harvard University Press, 1950, pp. ix, 464), *passim*.

We must hasten to point out that, by a contrast which we have often noted in the preceding volumes, although World Wars I and II centred in peoples long under the influence of Christianity, never had as much relief been given to the sufferers from war and never had such promising devices been constructed for the peaceable settlement of disputes between nations as in the half-century which followed 1914. Most of the relief came also from within what might still be called Christendom. Much of it was channeled through the Red Cross, an organization under a Christian symbol and springing from Protestantism of the Pietist-Evangelical strain. A large proportion was from frankly Christian organizations. The Popes gave great impetus to it. The League of Nations and its successor, the United Nations, owed their existence primarily to men of Christian faith derived through Protestantism. Outstanding in the creation of the League of Nations was Woodrow Wilson. Others contributed, for the League was the outcome of many dreams and efforts,[2] but it was to Wilson that the inclusion of the League in the peace settlement after World War I was primarily due, and he was impelled and sustained by a profound Christian faith.[3] If the world wars of the twentieth century had their chief centres in the historic Christendom, never from any other religion had so many movements arisen to relieve the suffering brought by war and to devise and maintain institutions for the peaceable settlement of disputes among nations as issued from Christianity in that century.[4]

Wars were only one aspect of the revolution. Other phases which began before 1914 continued and swelled to larger proportions. They, too, as earlier, occurred chiefly in what had been known as Christendom and from there radiated to other parts of the planet. They were mainly in the realm of science, in the closely associated developments in industry—the prolongation, expansion, and intensification of the Industrial Revolution—and in the changes in the structure of society with the elaboration and spread of the concomitant social theories and programmes. The fact that they originated in the region where Christianity had long had its nearest approach to free course was evidence of their indebtedness to that faith, even though some of them issued in tragic distortions of the Christian Gospel.

A full description of these developments would require many volumes. All

[2] C. Howard-Ellis, *The Origin and Structure of the League of Nations* (Boston, Houghton Mifflin Co., 1928, pp. 528), pp. 266–364; Felix Morley, *The Society of Nations* (Washington, D.C., The Brookings Institution, 1932, pp. xxii, 678), pp. 3–76; Viscount Cecil (Lord Robert Cecil), *A Great Experiment* (London, Jonathan Cape, 1941, pp. 390), pp. 63 ff.

[3] Arthur Walworth, *Woodrow Wilson* (London, Longmans, Green and Co., 2 vols., 1958), Vol. I, pp. 1–14; Vol. II, pp. 237 ff., especially pp. 418, 419.

[4] For a few examples see Conrad Hoffman, *In the Prison Camps of Germany* (New York, Association Press, 1920, pp. viii, 279), *passim;* Erik R. Berg, *Behind Barbed Wires Among War Prisoners in Germany*, translated from the Swedish by O. N. Olson (Rock Island, Ill., The Augustana Book Concern, 1944, pp. 95 ff.); *The American Christian Committee for Refugees, Ten Years of Stewardship* (1945, pp. 38), *passim.*

we can hope to do in the brief space which is ours is to hint at some of them. The knowledge of the universe associated with astronomy was enlarged in breath-taking fashion. More was found out about what had long been thought of as the Milky Way, with its spiral structure and its millions of stars, including the one of which the earth is a satellite. Thousands of similar stellar aggregations were disclosed by photography through powerful telescopes. Radio astronomy was developed. More of the composition of the stars was discerned and of the thin clouds of gas from which stars were believed to be born. Theories of the origins and histories of the stars were propounded and of the beginning and age of the universe. The principle of relativity connected with the name of Albert Einstein became an accepted assumption. Through geology, information about the history and composition of the earth was augmented, and unanswered questions about them multiplied. Both physics and chemistry had their horizons vastly expanded, with growing insight into the nature and composition of matter, the structure of the atom, the functions of electricity, and the hitherto unsuspected variations in the elements and the fashion in which they were related. The utilization of atomic energy, only in its terrifying infancy at mid-century, held untold possibilities for man's weal or woe. Much was learned about plant and animal life. Man's food supply was enlarged, partly through new varieties of grains and breeding animals. Great strides were taken in grappling with the diseases of plants, animals, and men.

What had been foreshadowed in nineteenth-century psychology became prominent. The mind and personality were explored. Psychiatry in its varying and often conflicting schools, of which those of Freud and Jung were outstanding, emerged to prominence and in some countries became a fad. Psychoanalysis and psychotherapy had their rise in a culture permeated by Christianity, but the significance of this coincidence was not clear.[5] However, disclosing as they did in the depths of the human mind irrational emotions, inheritances from man's primitive past, they made for a scepticism, a kind of anti-intellectualism, that was a further departure from the rationalism inherited from the *Aufklärung*.

Every advance in science raised additional questions, but so astounding were the revelations and achievements that confidence in the scientific approach and method largely shaped the attitudes and the basic assumptions of those caught in the revolutionary age.

Along with man's increased knowledge of his physical environment went his utilization of that environment. This meant the mechanization of much

---

[5] Of the vast literature see Ernest Jones, *The Life and Work of Sigmund Freud* (New York, Basic Books, 3 vols., 1953–1957); Sigmund Freud, *Collected Papers* (London, Hogarth Press, 5 vols., 1953–1956); *The Collected Works* of C. J. Jung, translated by R. F. C. Hull (New York, Pantheon Books, 4 vols., 1953 ff.).

of life. In the former Christendom industrialization proceeded apace. It continued in Great Britain, the first home of the Industrial Revolution. Even after the destruction wrought by the bombings of World War II it was resumed and augmented in Germany. Under Communism it made phenomenal strides in Russia. Fully as rapid was the progress of industrialization in the United States, Canada, and Australia, where "free enterprise" was combined with the expansion of government participation and control. At mid-century men were talking of "automation"—the mounting substitution of the machine for human labour. Mechanical devices wrought the expansion of transportation and communication. The nineteenth century had seen the building of railways and the invention and multiplication of steamships. To them the twentieth century added the automobile and the airplane. In time-dimensions the planet was rapidly shrinking. The world of man was becoming a neighbourhood. It was a tragically quarrelsome neighbourhood and becoming overcrowded through the rapid increase in population. Men were reaching out into space and talking confidently of flights to the moon and the planets. The electric telegraph, a creation of the nineteenth century, now much more used, was paralleled by radio and television. Far from being outmoded by these methods of transmitting ideas, the printing press became still more prominent.

After 1914 changes in the way men lived together begun by the Industrial Revolution attained even vaster dimensions. Urbanization mounted. The huge sprawling cities made for the atomization of society. They were filled with lonely individuals who felt themselves strangers and friendless in the crowds. Specialization by occupations and interests furthered a sense of isolation which was only partially compensated by membership in the ubiquitous organizations —labour unions and professional and business associations. Mechanization of the farms made possible the raising of more food by fewer man-hours, and in the more highly industrialized lands the rural population declined relative to the city populations. Urbanization and the mobility of residence which accompanied it brought continued decay of the pre-industrial patterns of life and growth of new ones. The organization of labour in the industries reached mammoth size. Government increased its functions, whether under Communism, non-Communistic socialism, or actual although unavowed socialism. The "welfare state" flourished. The capture of much of mankind by Communism was only one of the spectacular reactions against the kind of political *laissez-faire* liberalism which characterized much of the nineteenth century. Totalitarian dictatorships appeared, and even in the democracies of Anglo-Saxon provenance many heaved a sigh of relief when a strong man came to power.

Philosophies reflected the temper of the age. Early in the century Henri Louis Bergson (1859–1941) with his "creative evolution" was popular. By mid-century what were called existentialism and logical positivism were widely prevalent in the Western world. In a sense they were not new.[6] Existentialism had been foreshadowed in the ancient Greek aphorism: "Know thyself." In its manifold expressions it was concerned with man's being. At least since the seventeenth century many thoughtful souls had been troubled by a sense of homelessness in a vast universe which seemed an unfeeling mechanism. Existentialism had religious and non-religious expressions. In the nineteenth century Kierkegaard, sometimes called the father of existentialism, was profoundly Christian, while men like Friedrich Nietzsche, from an ancestry of Protestant pastors, and Franz Kafka, of Jewish stock, rejected the Christian tradition. In the decades immediately before 1914 Wilhelm Dilthey (1833–1911), son of a Reformed pastor, as a philosopher approaching history in an inclusive way from the standpoint of German Idealism, gave a further impetus to existentialism, as did also World Wars I and II. More and more, especially in Western Europe, many felt themselves caught in a complex of huge forces over which they had no control. Under these conditions, what meaning, if any, could man discover for his existence? Some Jewish thinkers, like Martin Buber, found it in religious faith. Martin Heidegger (1889——), a philosopher in a university chair, who in his early studies had prepared for the Roman Catholic priesthood but had come under the influence of Edmund Husserl (1859–1938), in his *Being and Time* (1927) displayed a dread of nothingness. His contemporary, Gabriel Marcel (1889——), was a convinced Christian. Karl Jaspers, professor of philosophy in Basel, was important. Jean Paul Sartre (1905——) in his *Being and Nothingness* (1943) came close to regarding man as the cause and foundation of his own existence.[7] The Spanish philosopher José Ortega y Gasset, while describing his approach as "vital reason," was basically existential. We will later tell of twentieth-century existential Christian theologians.

Logical positivism, a term which first appeared in 1930, was indebted to Comte and to pragmatism. It was also known as linguistic analysis and logical analysis. It made the test of truth experience—empiricism—and sought to determine the extent to which language accurately expressed experience. It could be considered another phase of the long tension between reason and faith, between natural religion and revealed religion. In the thirteenth century Aquinas had sought to resolve the tension. Somewhat similar efforts had been made in the eighteenth and nineteenth centuries. Logical positivism presented the twentieth century with the tension in a form suited to the temper of an age bemused by the achievements of a science that utilized the empirical

[6] I. M. Bockévski, *Europäische Philosophie der Gegenwart* (Bern, A. Francke, 1947, pp. 304), *passim*.

[7] James Collins, *The Existentialists. A Critical Study* (Chicago, Henry Regnery Co., 1952, pp. xi, 268), *passim;* Frederick Copleston, *Contemporary Philosophy. Studies in Logical Positivism and Existentialism* (Westminster, Md., The Newman Press, 1956, pp. ix, 227), *passim*.

methodology. Logical positivism had early centres in Cambridge University and Vienna but by mid-century was especially potent in England, Scandinavia, and the United States. It undermined the Christian faith of many.[8]

Communism, formulated by Marx, in part as a reaction against the Protestantism in which he had been reared, captured most of Eastern and much of Central Europe. Anti-Christian, it placed Christians on the defensive and in large areas where they had once been majorities reduced them to minorities.

Western Europe, in contrast with the professed confidence of Communist spokesmen in the triumph of their system, felt despair or near despair for Western civilization. The very title of Oswald Spengler's *Decline of the West,* published soon after World War I, was illuminating. Arnold Toynbee's comprehensive history of mankind, begun between the two wars and completed after the second, while more tempered and less dogmatic in its pessimism, was by no means confident of the survival of Western civilization.

In the twentieth century the revolution which began in the West spread to the entire world and wrought as great changes as it had in the region of its origin. In the preceding volume we noted the inception of these changes. After 1914 they mounted with bewildering speed. In the course of our story we shall again and again have occasion to call attention to them. Here we can merely summarize some of their features. In Asia and Africa and the adjacent islands the revolt against Western imperialism was almost universal. It spread partly by contagion from the nationalism which was a feature of the revolutionary age in the Occident and in country after country was led by men who had been educated in the West. The weakening of Western Europe by the world wars, which centred in that region, encouraged the revolt and contributed to its success. By mid-century almost all those parts of Asia that the nineteenth-century expansion of Europe had brought under the political control of Western European peoples had achieved their independence: Syria and Lebanon, India and Pakistan, Ceylon, Burma, Malaya, Vietnam, and, with the exception of Irian (West New Guinea), what had been included in the Netherlands East Indies. India, Pakistan, and Ceylon remained within the Commonwealth which had its tie in the British crown, but the association was voluntary and the designation "Commonwealth" was not preceded by the word "British." The United States had fulfilled its long-announced purpose and had granted independence to the Philippines. In Asia and its adjacent islands only such fragments as Aden, Goa, Irian, the British portions of Borneo, the Portuguese half of Timor, Macao, Hong Kong, and Okinawa remained under Western

---

[8] Copleston, *op. cit., passim;* Richard von Mises, *Positivism. A Study in Human Understanding* (Cambridge, Harvard University Press, 1951, pp. xi, 404, *passim*); Gustav Bergmann, *The Metaphysics of Logical Positivism* (London, Longmans, Green and Co., 1954, pp. x, 341), *passim;* H. Margenau and J. E. Smith, *Philosophy of Physical Science in the Twentieth Century* in *Cahiers d'Histoire Mondiale,* Vol. IV, pp. 639–667.

control. The northern shores of Africa were throwing off Western European control. Egypt, Libya, Tunisia, and Morocco had become fully independent. Persistent rebellion of non-French elements threatened French rule in Algeria. What had been the Anglo-Egyptian Sudan became independent of both Egypt and Britain. Much of Africa south of the Sahara, notably Ghana, Nigeria, the Belgian Congo, and the French possessions, was emerging from its colonial status, and unrest was increasing in several areas which were still under European governments.

Although political independence was rapidly mounting, Occidental culture was spreading and people after people were ceasing to be culturally independent. The revolution which had its source in Western Christendom was capturing all mankind. Indeed, in great areas the impact was more shattering than it was in the region of its origin. In many places minorities were dominant, as exemplified in the spread of Communism. Formulated in nineteenth-century London, through the Communist Party it took possession of Russia after World War I. Following World War II in a kind of imperialism which disavowed that term and sought to place it as a label on the policies of the Western powers, under the close direction of Moscow Communism became dominant in Estonia, Latvia, Poland, East Germany, Czechoslovakia, Hungary, Rumania, and Bulgaria. Closely allied with the Union of Soviet Socialist Republics and receiving extensive aid from it, a Communist Party seized the mainland of China. Usually taking their cue from Moscow, Communist parties were active in much of the rest of South and East Asia, notably in Japan, North Vietnam, Laos, Indonesia, Burma, and India.

In such of mankind outside the Occident as was still under the control of Westerners the revolution was advancing through the initiative of the colonial governments, the activities of Western merchants, and the Western owners of mines and plantations. But in most of non-Occidental mankind the revolution proceeded through the voluntary adoption of processes, institutions, and ideas which had their origin in the Occident. The vast majority of people were eager to acquire the material goods of life by the means through which the Occident had raised its standard of living. This meant industrialization by the methods developed in the Occident and the acquisition of the appliances invented in the Occident. It also entailed the utilization of the science which had begun in the West and the forms of education and means of the dissemination of knowledge which had been devised in the Occident. In some countries, notably Russia and Japan, outstanding additions were made to the science—and the machines created through the science—which had first appeared in the West.

In land after land was seen the revolution in the patterns of life which in the West had come through industrialization and through the adoption of the mechanical appliances and the methods that were associated with science. Cities grew. Indeed, about the middle of the century Tokyo was said to be the largest metropolitan area in the world, outstripping London and New York, earlier products of the revolutionary age. Railways were constructed, and the automobile, the airplane, the electric telegraph, the radio, and the printing press became familiar. In several countries, partly because of the methods of medicine, surgery, and public health which issued from the West, but without the birth control now become common in the Occident, the increase of population was explosive. With it came the threat of undernourishment, famine, and war.

Because of the rapid growth of the world's population, by the mid-twentieth century non-Christians were far more numerous than at any previous time. Since most of the increase was in Asia and its fringing islands, in countries (except the Philippines) where Christians had never been more than minorities, in 1961, although Asians bearing the Christian name constituted a larger percentage than in 1914, non-Christians the world over were more numerous than in the earlier year. Since the population explosion was largely due to factors originating in Christendom, in so far as Christianity was their source, that faith could be said to have been responsible for the rapidly mounting numbers of non-Christians. Here was a challenge. As we are to see, to some degree Christianity was rising to it, but it did not fully keep pace with it.

Forms of government and the associated methods of the welfare state seen in the West were widely adopted outside the Occident. The welfare state arose partly from Christian ideals, but it was prevailingly secular and in some countries anti-religious.

The demand of the masses for more of the good things of life spread by contagion from the Occident. It, too, sprang in no small degree from the hopes inspired by Christianity and the Christian emphasis upon the infinite worth of the individual. But it also became predominantly secular.

Outside the Occident the impact of the revolutionary forces issuing from the historic Christendom brought about rapid change in the inherited cultures, for millions even more drastic than in what had been called Christendom. Among primitive peoples, as in Africa, the tribe, the family, forms of social control, and ethical standards disintegrated. Among highly civilized peoples the old was giving place to the new. Thus in India caste barriers were being weakened and, so far as legislation could accomplish it, the disabilities of the depressed classes were abolished. Even before the triumph of Communism on the mainland of China Confucianism, heretofore dominant in shaping ethical standards and the family, was disappearing. Communism dealt it additional blows. The status of women was being profoundly altered. Women were being emancipated from their subjection to men and were sharing in political activities, the franchise, and employments once reserved to the opposite sex. This movement, too, first arose from impulses stemming from Christianity but later was secularized.

Religiously the effect of the revolution outside the Occident was mixed. In general, as with Confucianism, what had come from the past was weakened. Among some the inherited faiths were revived and strengthened, usually as a manifestation either of nationalism—a kind of religious statism with its patriotic reaction against the inroads of Western "materialism"—or of the insatiable religious hunger coeval with mankind. For instance, the resuscitation of Islam in the Arab world, of Buddhism in Burma and Ceylon, and of some forms of Hinduism in India was clearly indebted to nationalism. The renewed emphasis on Islam in Turkey in the 1950's came from a conviction that without religion the nation's life was being undermined, and the burgeoning of Shinto in post-World War II Japan arose from a longing for supernatural assurance and strength in a world which otherwise was meaningless.

What was happening to Christianity in the twentieth-century stage of the revolutionary age? Viewed from some angles that religion seemed to be disappearing. Indeed, the designation of the century as the post-Christian era, backed by several outstanding intellectuals, gained currency. Some, not all of them Communists, declared that mankind was outgrowing religion, as though religion, including Christianity, were an experience through which mankind was emerging, much as the individual passes through such childhood diseases as measles, mumps, and whooping cough. They could point to the fact that most of the high religions had emerged in a relatively brief span of history. The thirteen centuries between 650 B.C. and 650 A.D. had seen the careers of Confucius, Gautama Buddha, possibly Zoroaster, the great Greek philosophers, Jesus, and Mohammed. If the four centuries preceding 650 B.C. were included, the great Hebrew prophets and seers and most of the creative spirits of Hinduism would be covered. Now, so it was said, the acids of modernity were rapidly corroding all inherited religious systems.

This fate seemed especially to be in store for Christianity, for that religion had been the professed faith of the region where the revolution originated and from which it was spreading. Christianity could be said to be one of the sources and perhaps the major source of the revolution. Was it, therefore, digging the grave not only of the other religions but also of itself?

A number of facts seemed to support an affirmative answer. The two world wars of the first half of the century, centring as they did in Europe, long the chief stronghold of Christianity, militated against the faith. The hate, the falsehoods, the cruelties, and the callous slaughter engendered by them were destructive of the values most prized by the Gospel. In the obvious contradiction the commitment to the faith of many, especially youth, evaporated. Since the wars were total and all the population of a nation concentrated its efforts on the struggle, the peacetime life of entire peoples was disrupted and attendance at religious services and other activities of the churches fell off. The circumstance that the wars had their rise and had reached their most terrifying dimensions among peoples who had long been professedly Christian appeared to many to prove that the faith was impotent and, indeed, by its nature could be so perverted that it could intensify man's long propensity for conflict. As a defense it was said: "Christianity has not failed: it has never been tried." But if after centuries it had never been really tried by nations which in name adhered to it, was here not evidence of the powerlessness of the faith? So some Buddhists were saying and were advocating acceptance of their religion as a way to peace.

Similarly, as we have repeatedly noted, Communism, frankly atheistic and denouncing all religion as the opiate of the people, was given its initial and standard formulation in "Christian" England by Karl Marx, who in his youth had been a Christian. As a collaborator Marx had Engels, who had also once been a Christian and seems to have been moved to give up that faith by what he deemed its inability to right the injustices which accompanied the Industrial Revolution. Stalin, for years the ruler in Communist Russia, had much of his early education in a theological seminary and had been exposed to the Christian faith, only to reject it.

More subtle and possibly even more a threat to all religion was the widely spread secularism. It, too, was a feature of the revolution and had its origin in Western Christendom. It was compounded of a number of factors. One was the religious scepticism arising from the scientific attitude and the advances in knowledge brought by science. Secularism was not new. It had been present at least as early as the eighteenth century and had mounted in the nineteenth century. It continued and like other phases of the revolution spread throughout most of the world after 1914. Outside the Occident it had outstanding representatives among men who had been educated in the West, some of them, like Jawaharlal Nehru, in institutions on Christian foundation. Another factor was the kind of society which was born of the industrial age. As in the nineteenth century, the construction of churches did not keep pace with the growth of cities. The complexities of life distracted interest from churches that had once been the centre of the community and its activities. The factories and mines and the conditions which surrounded those who worked in them discouraged religious observances, whether in the Ruhr, Lancashire, or Tokyo.

The menace was as great a one as Christianity had ever faced. From its very beginning Christianity appeared to have very slight prospect of gaining the real allegiance of mankind. The ethical teachings of Jesus seemed beyond the capacity of human nature. Jesus Himself was born in obscurity and died on a Roman cross. In the first century His followers constituted only one, and it among the smallest, of the religions which were competing for the allegiance of the Græco-Roman world. When the majority in that world took the Christian name, with the exception of minorities their practice fell so far short of their profession that it appeared to be a denial of the power of the faith. When Christianity had not prevented the disintegration of the Roman realms, the Empire was overrun by barbarians from the North, most of them pagans, and by Arabs from the South-east who championed a new religion, Islam, which mastered about half the then Christendom and, except for the Iberian Peninsula and Sicily, reduced Christians within that half to dwindling minorities. After the northern invaders had been won to the faith and Christianity had entered deeply into the civilization of Europe, the Church, strengthened by reformers who dreamed of it as an instrument for bringing the world, or at least Europe, to full conformity to Christian standards, was captured by ambitious men who sought to use it for their selfish purposes. The Catholic and Protestant Reformations brought fresh vigour but were followed by the debilitating rationalism of the eighteenth century and the secular and at times openly anti-Christian French Revolution. The revivals in the Roman Catholic Church and the Protestant and Orthodox churches and the global expansion in the nineteenth century were paralleled by scepticism, anti-clericalism, and the drifting away of large elements in the population from all but nominal adherence to the faith.

Yet, as we have seen, in some ways the nineteenth century was the greatest century that Christianity had ever known. All the major branches of the faith experienced revitalization. It was especially marked in the Roman Catholic Church and Protestantism, particularly in the latter. Never before had Christian communities arisen in so many countries; never had Christ been as influential in the affairs of mankind when seen as a whole.

So in the twentieth century a menace which was also a challenge seemed to threaten the very existence of Christianity. But it was simultaneous with some of the most striking advances that Christianity had ever displayed. The advances were many and from the standpoint of the effect on the entire human race marked what in several ways was an even greater day than that which Christianity had known in the nineteenth century. As in the nineteenth century, the revivification spread through all the main branches of Christianity, but more through Roman Catholicism than Orthodoxy and more through Protestantism than through the Roman Catholic Church.

In Europe, the heartland of the historic Christendom, where de-Christianization appeared to be well along, fresh evidences of vitality were seen. Within some areas dominated by Communism, after initial losses the churches revived. In other areas where a Communist regime sought to curb them as obstacles to the kind of society which it was seeking to construct, the churches made a staunch resistance and displayed enhanced vigour. During the Hitler days in Germany minority elements in the churches refused to bend the knee, in contrast with such institutions as the universities (supposed citadels of free inquiry) and organized labour. In Fascist Italy Mussolini deemed it politic to make his peace with the Church, and partly on its terms. In the Roman Catholic Church were the Liturgical Movement, Eucharistic Congresses, Catholic Action, and novel efforts to reach the de-Christianized. In Protestantism came such movements as COPEC (Conference on Christian Politics, Economics, and Citizenship) in Great Britain, Iona in Scotland, Sigtuna in Sweden, *Kerk en Wereld* in the Netherlands, and the *Kirchentag* and Evangelical Academies in Germany. Creative activity was manifest in theological and Biblical studies, especially in Protestantism.

In the larger Europe—the Americas and Australasia—the United States and Canada saw many and varied expressions of vitality in the churches, and Latin America witnessed a striking growth of Protestantism.

Outside the Occident both Roman Catholicism and Protestantism continued their numerical growth. Even more significantly, their communities in these lands, although minorities, had a mounting indigenous leadership. No longer were they led almost exclusively by Occidentals. More and more they were served by their own members: Christianity was becoming more deeply rooted among more peoples than at any earlier time.

In Protestantism the Ecumenical Movement rapidly took on unprecedented proportions and had multiform manifestations. In country after country national councils of churches and national Christian councils were organized. Many unions of hitherto reciprocally independent denominations were achieved. Global organizations such as those for particular confessions and the International Missionary Council and the World Council of Churches came into being. Through Protestantism, the most divided branch of Christianity, Christians were coming together in a more inclusive fashion than at any earlier time.

Outside the churches Christianity was having a greater effect on mankind as a whole than ever before. This was seen in the impress made by Jesus on Gandhi and through him on all India, in the less potent but still important contribution in China of Sun Yat-sen, a convert, in the effects of Christianity on many less prominent but influential non-Christians, and in the Red Cross and other institutions for relief and in the creation of the League of Nations and the United Nations.

In the mid-twentieth century Christianity was far from being dominant in the life of mankind and was being as stiffly challenged as in any era. But it was more widely influential than it or any other religion had ever been. To it might be applied the words which Paul used for himself and his fellow workers: "as dying, and behold, we live."

The two volumes to which this chapter is an introduction are designed to be an elaboration of what has been so briefly summarized. The first is to be devoted to Europe, the heart of what was once called Christendom. Here we will follow the order established in the first two volumes of this series. We will begin with the Roman Catholic Church and with chapters which are the continuations of those in the second half of Volume I. Then we will deal with Protestantism, as in Volume II, country by country. Finally will come a section on Russia, Greece, and the Balkans. Because of the growing importance of Christianity outside Europe, we have assigned to that portion of the globe the final volume—half of the space given to the twentieth century, instead of the third which was all that we claimed for it in the nineteenth-century stage of our story. We will conclude the final volume with an attempt at an estimate of the significance of the story which the entire work has endeavoured to narrate.

Even in two volumes we cannot hope to give a complete account of Christianity in the crowded four and a half decades which are their theme. We must confine ourselves to the outlines and here and there the details of what seem, at the present juncture, to be the most important persons, events, and movements. Nearness may distort perspective and proportion. In each age historians must write from the vantage of their time and distinctive interests. Yet value may lie—value both for his own generation and for those which are to follow—in an account by a contemporary and a participant who must pause *in medias res*.

CHAPTER II

The Roman Catholic Church:
An Inclusive Picture

B EFORE we embark on a somewhat detailed narrative of the fashion in which the Roman Catholic Church met the challenge of the twentieth-century phase of the revolutionary age, it may be wise to remind ourselves of the manner in which that church was affected by the nineteenth-century stage of the revolution and then to give a comprehensive preview of the situations which it faced, the attitudes which it adopted, and the achievements to which it could point in the decades between 1914 and the date at which our account must pause.

In the nineteenth century, it will be recalled, the Roman Catholic Church was confronted with features of the revolutionary age which seemed to be undermining its foundations and threatening its very existence. The storm of the French Revolution subsided, but some of the forces which had produced it and many of the ideals which it embodied continued, not only in France but also elsewhere. They contributed to less spectacular political and social upheavals. In general they were anti-clerical and sought to usher the Church out of its historic control of education and marriage and to sever the traditional close tie with the state. By the more extreme among the leaders of the political movements, the Church, and especially the Roman Catholic Church, was considered the enemy of the "progress" in which they so confidently believed. The prevailing intellectual currents in Western Europe appeared to be eroding basic convictions on which the Christian faith, and especially the Roman Catholic Church, rested. Developments in the natural sciences seemed to invalidate the record of the creation of the universe, the earth, and man which was incorporated in the Scriptures that the Church declared to be authoritative. Emerging methods of historical investigation cast further doubt on the reliability of the Bible, including the accounts of the life of Christ, and by tracing the course of the Church's dogma and organization questioned the validity of beliefs and the authority of institutions which appeared to have reflected the conditions of the periods through which they had come. Thousands, among them both experts and a majority who were only superficially acquainted with the findings of contemporary scholarship, either abandoned the faith or while outwardly conforming were sceptical and at best agnostic. Philosophies were emerging which were challenging Christianity, among them the Positivism associated with the name of Auguste Comte. The Industrial Revolution and the coming of steamships, railways, the telegraph, the telephone, cheaper paper, and improved methods of printing brought vast changes in the structure of society. The patterns of community life in which the churches had had a central place were being shattered. The multitudes who knew nothing but the factories, the mines, and the burgeoning cities had decreasing contacts with the Church. For many de-Christianization was proceeding almost without their being aware of it. For others in the rising industries active antagonism to the Church was being fostered by programmes for the organization of society. The most prominent was the kind of socialism formulated by Karl Marx.

The challenge was not confined to the Roman Catholic Church. It confronted all branches of Christianity. But it was particularly acute for that church. Being more flexible, Protestantism, as we have seen, was better prepared to make an adjustment to the prevailing forces—although it might ultimately prove to be at the price of weakening or even sacrificing some central tenets of the faith. The Orthodox Church might partly by-pass the challenge by holding to its traditional emphasis on worship and the interior life. But if it was to be true to its heritage the Roman Catholic Church must meet head-on some of the forces and refuse to compromise with them. In much of the nineteenth century it stood against the separation of Church and state and the secularization of education and marriage and condemned some of the attempts at accommodation to the intellectual trends of the day. It lost ground in Latin America, the area in which it had shown the greatest geographic expansion in the sixteenth and seventeenth centuries.

Yet the Roman Catholic Church displayed an inner vitality which enabled it to come to 1914 stronger in a number of ways than in 1815. It was more centralized under the effective control of the Pope than at any other time in its history. The Pope was formally declared to have supreme administrative power and to be infallible when he spoke as the pastor and doctor of all Christians in defining doctrine regarding faith and morals to be held by the universal Church. The Roman Catholic Church was, therefore, in a better position to present a united front to the world, both in defense against its enemies and, positively, in seeking to win mankind. Although the nineteenth-century incumbents of the Holy See varied greatly in personal characteristics, all were men of high character and some were of outstanding ability. None of them handicapped their high office by moral delinquencies and nepotism, as had some of their predecessors, and within a generation after his death one was officially recognized as a saint.

In the nineteenth century the loyalty and devotion of a very large proportion of the Roman Catholic Church's children were enhanced, as was seen in the revived life in existing orders and congregations and in the emergence of more new congregations than in any preceding century. This trend was significant partly because request for entrance to an order or congregation was normally evidence of a full commitment to the Christian faith. The secular clergy displayed a marked improvement. Moreover, among a large proportion of the rank and file who did not seek membership in an order or congregation the practice of frequent Communion increased. Eucharistic Congresses were begun and multiplied and the Liturgical Movement had its inception, with its emphasis upon a more intelligent participation of the laity in the Church's central act of worship. The proclamation of the immaculate conception of the Virgin Mary was paralleled by what were believed to be her appearances. In keeping with her own origin and the angelic announcement to the shepherds at the birth of Christ, and, indeed, with the major mission of the Gospel and Christ's preaching, the appearances were to humble folk. Significant, too, was the fact that the spiritual counsellor most sought after was the peasant village priest, the Curé of Ars, and that some of the other nineteenth-century saints officially recognized and most popular were also of lowly birth. Devotion to the Sacred Heart of Jesus and to the Virgin mounted.

Although Rome condemned some of the attempts to reconcile the faith with the nineteenth-century climate of opinion, that did not mean that all efforts to meet the intellectual challenge of the age were silenced. The study of Thomas Aquinas was revived, for the system of the *Doctor Angelicus* was held to provide a solid foundation for answers to the objections to the faith which were being raised. Theological activity, while kept within the bounds set by Rome, by no means ceased. For example, much attention was given to the nature of the presence of Christ in the Eucharist and to the fashion in which the Church is His body, a continuation of His incarnation.

The Roman Catholic Church did not surrender its historic claims to the education of the young, the sanctification of marriage, the setting of standards for relations between the sexes, and the care of the unfortunate. Wherever the civil authorities permitted, it continued schools in which instruction in the faith was an integral part of the curriculum. It also insisted that marriage was a sacrament to be observed by the faithful and sought to hold its children to what it regarded as Christian principles for the family. It maintained hundreds of institutions for the indigent, the orphans, the sick, and the aged. Much of education and the care of the needy was channelled through the orders and congregations which were reinforced and the congregations which came into being in the nineteenth century.

Roman Catholics were not oblivious to the conditions brought by the Industrial Revolution. In more than one country they sought to meet the problems of the labourers in factories and mines. The encyclical *Rerum novarum* of Leo XIII formulated principles for governing the conduct of both employers and employed in the industrial age.

One of the most striking features of the Roman Catholic Church in the nineteenth century was geographic expansion. It reached a larger proportion of the globe than at any earlier time. Although the weakness in Latin America was not overcome, steps towards remedying it were taken. In other portions of the Americas the Church was much stronger in 1914 than in 1815, owing partly to the migration of millions of Roman Catholics to the United States and Canada and the success in holding them to their ancestral faith, partly to the loyalty of the French Canadians to the church of their fathers, and partly to missions to the Indians. Immigration firmly planted the Roman Catholic Church in Australia and New Zealand. Missions to non-Christians rose to unprecedented proportions. Not only was the personnel engaged in them more numerous than ever before. They were also supported financially by the voluntary contributions of more thousands of the faithful than at any previous time.

Typical of the revolutionary age was the contrast of the response in France. Here the forces and movements making for de-Christianization were more spectacular than elsewhere. Here, on the other hand, the Roman Catholic Church displayed more vitality than in any other country. More new congregations arose in France than in any other land. More expressions of the devotion of the rank and file of the faithful were seen than anywhere else. Here were the appearances of the Virgin that made Lourdes the best known of the centres of healing through faith which multiplied in the century. Here was held the first of the Eucharistic Congresses and here the Liturgical Movement had its initial radiating centre. More missionaries to non-Christians went from France than from all other countries, and the chief agency for raising funds to support missions had its inception in France.

The challenges to Christianity brought by the twentieth-century stage of the revolutionary age, noted in the preceding chapter, affected the Roman Catholic Church as they did the other branches of Christianity. De-Christianization of its traditional constituencies was as much a threat as it was to Protestantism and Orthodoxy. Both world wars engulfed lands where the Roman Catholic faith was either the prevailing religion or very strong. Germany, Italy, France, Lithuania, Poland, Austria, Hungary, and Czechoslovakia were either belligerents or deeply involved. The United States, Canada, Australia, and New Zealand, with their strong Roman Catholic minorities, were belligerents. The

Philippines, with its large Roman Catholic majority, was destructively invaded in World War II. Although Spain was a neutral in both wars, prolonged civil strife in the 1930's brought grave problems. The increase in his knowledge and the utilization of his physical environment by man also presented a challenge, though not as spectacular as that of the wars. The consequent progress of industrialization with its dissolution of the historic social structure, integrated as that had been with the patterns of Christian life and worship, threatened the hold of the Church on those who by ancestry were its children. Current philosophies—existentialism in its non-theistic aspects and especially logical positivism—undercut Christian faith. Communism and, more subtly but fully as effectively, the spreading secularism appeared to be ushering mankind into an age in which the Roman Catholic Church as well as other expressions of Christianity would be an anachronism. De-Christianization of much of Christendom, including areas where the Roman Catholic Church had been strong, seemed to be proceeding apace. Although in Latin Europe and Latin America the large majority were still baptized in the Roman Catholic Church, for millions baptism had become merely a social or cultural convention. Especially in France, among many thousands whose forebears for several generations had been subjected to a de-Christianizing environment only vague remnants of the faith persisted and some of the devout were declaring that the country had become a new mission field. The rapid progress of the revolution outside the Occident was threatening the advances which in the nineteenth century had been made there. The triumph of Communism on the mainland of China expelled or imprisoned the missionaries and for many Catholics cut the tie which connected them with Rome. The nationalism and anti-imperialism in much of the rest of Asia were accompanied by a revival of the ethnic religions and raised obstacles to the entrance of missionaries.

Yet, by a contrast which was even more striking than in the nineteenth century, the Roman Catholic Church gave proof of mounting vitality. It found expression through some of the channels which had been prominent in that century and created others. The four Popes of the period were men of ability and integrity. The ultramontanism which had contributed to strengthening the power of their office continued. Only traces of the particularism remained which had given rise to the pre-nineteenth-century semi-autonomy of some of the national churches. Something of Gallicanism survived, but more in the temper of the French Church than in administration. As in the past, the Spanish Church tended to go its own way, although not, of course, in doctrine. Orders and congregations flourished. Not as many new ones emerged as in the nineteenth century, even proportionately to the fewer number of decades, but many of the existing ones added to their ranks and expanded their activities. Among the rank and file of the membership devotion was still mounting, both in prayer and in action. The endorsement by the Pope of the bodily assumption of the Virgin Mary to heaven was greeted by a widespread satisfaction among clergy and laity which testified to the popularity of her cult. The Liturgical Movement grew rapidly and had many expressions. Eucharistic Congresses increased in numbers and attendance. Catholic Action, which had barely begun before 1914, as a channel for lay participation proliferated and assumed ever larger dimensions. In addition to Catholic Action and largely apart from it, a wide variety of organizations were developed, mostly by laity, for participation in social, economic, and political life. Roman Catholic scholars continued to be active in theology and made important contributions in that area and in Biblical studies. Roman Catholics not only maintained many schools, hospitals, and institutions for the care of orphans, the indigent, and the aged but also made extensive contributions to relieve the suffering entailed by the wars of the period. In the decades which followed 1914 the missions of the Roman Catholic Church were greatly enlarged. In spite of the disruption of much of normal life brought by the wars, most of the missionaries were still from Western Europe. Their totals were augmented by a number from the United States and Canada and by the financial contributions of the faithful in those two countries. Although de-Christianization was proceeding in France, from that land more Roman Catholic missionaries were sent than from any other country. There, too, occurred much of the theological activity of the Roman Catholic Church and in France were born novel efforts to reach the de-Christianized urban workers. Indeed, de-Christianization was spotty geographically. In extensive areas devotion to the Roman Catholic Church continued. They were mainly in a wide belt from Flanders to Venice, with other centres in Brittany, La Vendée, parts to the South-west and South of France, and in North-western Spain.

On the whole, the Roman Catholic Church moved into the mid-twentieth century stronger than in 1914. It had experienced grave losses in its traditional heartland, Western and especially Latin Europe. But even there it had a loyal body of faithful numbering millions whose devotion and spiritual life were at a higher level than a generation earlier and very much higher than in 1815. In the United States and Canada it was growing both in numbers and in quality of life. In spite of the stresses suffered under Communism in China and North Vietnam, its adherents in Asia, while minorities, were more numerous in 1960 than in 1914. In Africa south of the Sahara its adherents were mounting by leaps and bounds. Fully as significant was the fact that in Asia and Africa indigenous clergy were multiplying, and from them an increasing number were being raised to the episcopate. The Roman Catholic Church was taking deep root in people after people outside the Occident. All its children were knit together under the authority and leadership of Rome, and more and more it was embracing in its ample fold peoples of all climes and tongues and races.

Whether this growth would continue no one could clearly foresee. The fact was sobering that the Roman Catholic Church continued to suffer losses in its traditional stronghold, Latin Europe, and that Latin Europe was declining in its relative importance in the total world scene. It was in Latin Europe that most of the orders and congregations of the Roman Catholic Church had had their origin, from it the majority of missionaries had come, and in it most of the major theological systems had been formulated. There, too, was the historic seat of the head of the Church. As Bishop of Rome his residence was in that city. The periods when the Popes had lived elsewhere had been times of weakness. But Spain and Portugal had been declining for at least three centuries, in the twentieth century Italy had lost its colonial empire and politically, economically, and culturally was clearly a second-class power, and France was still retreating from the outstanding position which it had held in the seventeenth and eighteenth centuries. Moreover, in Latin Europe, although anticlericalism was not as rampant as in the nineteenth century, a large proportion of the masses were lukewarm and were drifting away from the Church, and the loyal core, while vigorous in their faith, were probably a minority. In Latin America, its largest extension outside Europe, the Roman Catholic Church was still weak, depending for its vitality upon transfusions from Europe and North America in the form of personnel. In time the expansion outside Latin Europe and Latin America might compensate or even more than compensate for the losses in these quarters. But the historian, as historian, ought not to venture a prediction.

We must now turn to the European phase of the twentieth-century story. We begin with the Papacy, for its outreach was to the entire world.

CHAPTER III

The Roman Catholic Church: The Place
of the Papacy

BETWEEN 1914 and 1960 the Papacy was faced with fully as great a combination of threats as it had known between 1789 and 1914. It had to deal with two world wars, in both of which Italy, where was its centre, was a belligerent. It was also deeply concerned with local wars, among them the devastating civil strife in Spain. It was confronted with totalitarian regimes which sought to bring the Church to heel. That of Mussolini, Fascism, embracing all Italy and with Rome as its capital, could have been as great a menace as had been that of Napoleon I, and National Socialism in Germany, directed by Hitler, could have proved even more embarrassing than the *Kulturkampf* under Bismarck. Although Communism did not capture as much of the historic heartland of the Roman Catholic Church as had the French Revolution, it was more openly and persistently anti-Christian than was that earlier movement, and the Papacy set its face like flint against it. At the same time the Papacy was confronted with other features of the revolutionary age which could bring grave losses but which also spelled opportunity—among them fluid societies in lands of rapid social change.

In at least one way the Papacy seemed in a less favourable position than it had been in 1815. Then the Pope was a secular prince as well as a spiritual leader. Through his representative, Consalvi, he participated in the Congress of Vienna. In 1914, while still claiming the powers of a territorial sovereign, in fact he could not exercise them over a square foot of land and, unreconciled, as the "prisoner of the Vatican" continued his seat in Rome only by the permission of the Kingdom of Italy. He had no place in the consultations in Paris in which the treaties were negotiated that ended World War I. Nor did he have membership in the League of Nations which came out of those negotiations. He was given no share in the counsels of the victors in World War II.

During all the stormy years which were introduced by 1914, in addition to dealing with the threats of those decades the Papacy had to keep functioning as the directing head of the Roman Catholic Church, increasingly world-wide.

In spite of what seemed as adverse a combination of threats and handicaps as it had ever known, the Papacy came to the middle of the twentieth century fully as strong as in 1914 and in some respects stronger. One reason was the ability of the men who occupied the Fisherman's chair. Another was that, deprived of its temporal power except for a settlement with the Italian Government which gave it the full control over a few acres and so ensured its independence of that regime, it could function as a spiritual and moral force. It was less entangled than at any time since the waning of the Roman Empire in the intricacies of the politics of one nation. But the enhanced power of the Papacy arose chiefly from the loyalty of the vast body of the faithful. Although still a minority of mankind as a whole and perhaps, because of the population explosion in much of Asia, traditionally non-Christian, embracing a smaller proportion of mankind than in 1914, the body of practising Roman Catholics had even more vigour and was more closely knit under the Papacy than in 1914. The Roman Catholic Church had come to 1914 on a rising tide. In the ensuing four and a half decades it did not lose momentum. As always partly on the defensive, it also, as heretofore, was intent on bringing all mankind into its fold. The triumph of ultramontanism in the nineteenth century had enabled it to face its task more nearly united administratively and spiritually than at any previous time. Unless its Pontiffs were hopelessly inept or morally corrupt, it could move ahead and augment its influence in the world. None of the four Popes after 1914 could rank with the greatest of his predecessors, but each was a man of integrity and each made distinctive contributions.

Benedict XV (1914–1922): The Pope of World War I: Election and Characteristics

The death of Pius X on August 20, 1914, less than a month after the outbreak of World War I and presumably hastened by that tragedy, left the throne of Peter vacant at a peculiarly crucial hour.

At the time Italy was still neutral, and the cardinals from the opposing sides of the conflict were able to assemble. Early in his reign, through his constitution of January 24, 1904, Pius X had forbidden the cardinals, on pain of excommunication, to permit any government to exercise a veto in future elections. Early in September, 1914, the cardinals elected Giacomo Della Chiesa. At that time Archbishop of Bologna, the new Pope took the title of Benedict, the fifteenth to hold it, in honour of Benedict XIV, who in the eighteenth century had been called from the See of Bologna to the See of Peter.

Giacomo Della Chiesa (1854–1922) was born in Genoa of ancient aristocratic stock. Although from his boyhood feeling the urge to enter the priesthood and in his early student days leading his fellows in forming a society for Catholic Action, at the behest of his father he prepared for the legal profession. Then, since his vocation to a clerical career was unshaken, still under paternal pressure, he took courses in Rome which led to a diplomatic career in the service of the Church. In the 1880's he was private secretary to Rampolla in the nunciature to Spain. There by his tact he won favour in aristocratic and intellectual circles and also engaged in the care of souls through preaching, hearing confessions, and giving himself to the poor. When, in 1887, Rampolla became cardinal and Papal Secretary of State, Della Chiesa continued in his entourage as his right-hand man. In Rome he was diligent in preaching, in hearing confessions, in organizing a third order of priests affiliated with the Lazarists, in giving catechetical instruction, and in other purely religious activities. He continued to rise in the diplomatic service. But after the accession of Pius X and the resignation of Rampolla, he was transferred from that career to the archiepiscopal chair of Bologna. He was diligent in the duties of his see—in a comprehensive visitation of the diocese, in improving the education of the seminarians, in raising the morale of the clergy, in furthering the instruction of his flock in the faith, and in leading a pilgrimage to Loreto, long famous for what was believed to be the house in which the Virgin Mary had been born and reared in Nazareth, miraculously transported to that spot. The pilgrimage also included Lourdes. In May, 1914, Della Chiesa was created cardinal.[1] It was that combination of diplomatic experience, zealous traditional piety, and skill in leadership which he brought to the Papacy. He was diminutive in stature and had a drooping left shoulder. Possessing a keen intellect and a highly retentive memory, he was vivacious, reserved, punctilious, and meticulous. He was inclined to argue, was given to satirical statements, and was choleric but without rancour. He was generous, courteous, tenacious in purpose, and vigorous in action.[2]

BENEDICT XV AND WORLD WAR I

Coming as he did to the Papal throne soon after World War I had drawn the heartland of Christendom into the throes of internecine strife, Benedict XV could not but give major attention to the problems which it presented to his church. In each warring camp were millions of the faithful. Feelings were intense and pressure was brought from each side to obtain the Papal endorsement. Benedict had to walk warily, especially after Italy cast its lot with the Entente against the Central Powers (May, 1915). Some in each camp accused him of favouring the other. That he avoided doing. He wrote to Cardinal Mercier (December 8, 1914) expressing his sorrow for Belgium's misfortunes and a few weeks later, without saying specifically whom he deemed guilty,

[1] Schmidlin, *Papstgeschichte der neuesten Zeit,* Vol. III, pp. 179–184; Peters, *The Life of Benedict XV,* pp. 3–73.
[2] Peters, *op. cit.,* pp. 94–101, 217–230; *Enciclopedia Cattolica,* Vol. II, pp. 1285 ff.

he condemned the outrages which were being perpetrated on the rights of nations—a statement which Pietro Gasparri, Benedict's Secretary of State, assured the Belgian minister referred to the violation of Belgian neutrality. Yet, diplomat that he was, Benedict succeeded in remaining on excellent terms with both Germany and Belgium.[3]

For the most part Benedict XV appealed to all the belligerents. On September 8, 1914, he asked the faithful to join him in prayer in behalf of peace. In an encyclical on November 1 of that year he pointed out the underlying moral causes of the war and urged the nations to make peace. In May, 1915, he raised his voice against what he deemed the violations by the belligerents of the principles of law and humanity. He made clear that he deplored the bitterness with which Christians in each camp were condemning their brothers in the other camp. In July, 1915, a few weeks after the entry of Italy into the war, Benedict XV called upon the warring peoples and their rulers to engage in an exchange of views for ending the slaughter and negotiating a peace in which the just aspirations of all would be considered.[4]

As the war dragged on its exhausting length, Benedict again and again spoke out in warning and protest.[5] Through his agents, notably Pacelli, the future Pope Pius XII, whom he sent to Germany, he sought to bring the belligerents to accept terms for a peace based on a moderation of the ambitions of both sides. In August, 1917, he set forth in a letter to the contending powers concrete suggestions for a settlement of the points at issue. Neither side was willing to accept it as a basis for an armistice.[6] To many it seemed to be defeatist, especially since Benedict spoke of the "useless carnage." A prayer which Benedict composed for peace and which was widely used was also characterized in some quarters as undercutting morale, and on more than one part of the fighting front its repetition was forbidden.

The Treaty of London of April 25, 1915, to which Italy was a party, provided that the Pope should not be permitted to share in the negotiations for peace. That provision was apparently inserted at the instance of the Italian representative, presumably to prevent the question of the temporal sovereignty of the Holy See from being raised. When once the armistice was signed, Bene-

[3] Premoli, *Contemporary Church History* (1900–1925), p. 40; Koenig, *Principles for Peace*, pp. 141–143; Peters, *op. cit.*, pp. 120, 121.

[4] Premoli, *op. cit.*, pp. 40–42; Schmidlin, *op. cit.*, Vol. III, pp. 196–202; Koenig, *op. cit.*, pp. 128, 129; Peters, *op. cit.*, p. 122.

[5] Schmidlin, *op. cit.*, Vol. III, pp. 202–206; Koenig, *op. cit.*, pp. 129–140, 145, 146, 151–157, 179–182.

[6] Schmidlin, *op. cit.*, Vol. III, pp. 206–218; Alfred Baudrillart, *Benoit XV* (Paris, Bloud & Gay, 1920, pp. 79), pp. 51–67; *Peace Action of Pope Benedict XV. A Summary by the History Committee of Friedrich Ritter von Lama's Die Friedensvermittlung Papst Benedict XV und ihre Verteilung durch den deutschen Reichskanzter Michaelis* (Washington, D.C., The Catholic Association for International Peace, no date, pp. 24), *passim;* Koenig, *op. cit.*, pp. 229–232; Peters, *op. cit.*, pp. 140–164.

dict XV, although not invited to join in the negotiations, asked for prayer that the peace should be just and durable.[7]

Benedict's efforts were not confined to seeking an early cessation of the war with its destruction of life and treasure and its lowering of morals. In a number of ways and through a variety of channels he endeavoured to mitigate the suffering brought by the conflict. Early in the war he asked the belligerents to arrange for the exchange of prisoners of war unfit for military service.[8] He set up in Rome an organization to serve prisoners of war, and through it, among other measures, contacts were facilitated between prisoners and hostages of war and their families and news of the missing was obtained and conveyed to their kinsfolk. It also promoted the return to their homes of civilian and war prisoners.[9] The Pope encouraged the formation of Roman Catholic agencies in Germany and Switzerland for the care of prisoners of war. He furthered the reception in neutral Switzerland of wounded soldiers unfit for further military service and of French and Germans afflicted with tuberculosis. He promoted the return to their homes of tubercular Italian patients held in Austria, of fathers of families of several of the warring armies, and of civilian prisoners unfit for military service. He backed efforts to provide inmates of prison camps with clothing, packages of food, and medicines, and to see that they had spiritual care through worship, the sacraments, and other clerical services. He also concerned himself with the spiritual care of the fighting men. He did what he could to relieve the physical lot of the civilian population in occupied territories and of child sufferers from the war. He aided the pause in fighting on Christmas, 1914, and in obtaining Sunday rest for prisoners of war. He stood out against such violations of humanity as the bombarding of unfortified towns and cities and protested the confiscation of such accessories to worship as church bells, organ pipes, and other metal objects. He denounced the German deportation of French and German civilians. After the armistice he publicly deplored the continuation of the blockade against Germany and stood for the early repatriation of prisoners of war.[10]

BENEDICT XV: ACTS NOT ARISING FROM THE WAR

Benedict XV did not permit himself to be so absorbed in the problems brought by World War I that he could not pay attention to other functions

[7] Premoli, *op. cit.*, pp. 45, 46; Lama, *Papst und Kurie in ihrer Politik nach dem Weltkreig*, pp. 9–11; Koenig, *op. cit.*, pp. 259, 260, 284–292.

[8] Schmidlin, *op. cit.*, Vol. III, pp. 218, 219; Koenig, *op. cit.*, pp. 149, 150; Peters, *op. cit.*, pp. 179 ff.

[9] Premoli, *op. cit.*, pp. 42, 43; Schmidlin, *op. cit.*, Vol. III, pp. 220, 221.

[10] Schmidlin, *op. cit.*, Vol. III, pp. 221–226; Premoli, *op. cit.*, pp. 43, 44; Paul Dudon, *L'Action de Benoît XV pendant la Guerre*, adapted from the Italian (Paris, Gabriel Beauchesne, 1918, pp. 59), pp. 29 ff.; Heuvel, *The Statesmanship of Benedict XV*, pp. 27, 50; Loewenich, *Der moderne Katholizismus*, p. 96; Koenig, *op. cit.*, pp. 156, 165, 199, 200, 213, 214, 219.

of his office. A number of his actions were significant. In his first encyclical he renewed the proscription of Modernism made by his predecessor, but he counselled restraint in making hasty accusations of a Modernist taint and thus sought to curb the extreme conservatives who were keen to scent it and reassured intellectuals. Yet he was stern against what he regarded as heresy and supported the Mosaic authorship of the Pentateuch. He reëmphasized the teaching of Thomas Aquinas and to further its study confided the supervision of the seminaries to a congregation which had charge of classical education and the universities.[11] He saw to the completion of the codification of the canon law which had been begun under Pius X. The project had been on the agenda of the Vatican Council of 1869–1870 but because of the interruption of that gathering by the Kingdom of Italy's seizure of Rome it had not been acted on. Gasparri had proposed it and Pius X had ordered it (1904) and had entrusted it to a body of consultants with Gasparri as chairman. The importance of the undertaking was clear. Canon law had grown up at various times across the centuries. Earlier compilations had contained duplications and contradictions and presented problems arising from conflicts with local customs and statutes. An entirely new codification was called for. It was designed to ensure uniformity, to discard outmoded or conflicting features, and to bring precept and practice in accord with contemporary needs. Suggestions were asked from bishops and heads of orders throughout the world. The completed *Codex Juris Canonici* was promulgated in 1917. Later in the year Benedict created a continuing commission to give authoritative interpretation to the code. The *Codex* was not binding on the Uniate churches, for their traditions differed from those of the main body of Roman Catholics. It was left to the next Pope to order (1935) the codification of the law of the Eastern Churches.[12] Here was another instance of the progressive extension of Papal authority over the entire Roman Catholic Communion.

In a variety of other ways Benedict XV exercised the powers of his office to deepen the life of the Roman Catholic Church. He approved the revision of the breviary. He encouraged the Eucharistic celebration of Lourdes, the consecration of Catholic families to the Heart of Jesus, public prayers to the Heart of Jesus, and the leadership of Italian priests in an apostolate of prayer. He extended the feast of the Archangels Gabriel and Michael to the entire Church. He approved the founding of a chair of ascetic-mystical theology in the Gregorian University in Rome as a means of nourishing the spiritual life of the clergy. He sought to improve the quality of preaching. He took the opportunity on appropriate occasions to single out particular orders and congre-

[11] Heuvel, *op. cit.,* pp. 18–20; Schmidlin, *op. cit.,* Vol. III, pp. 242–244.

[12] Heuvel, *op. cit.,* pp. 23–25; Schmidlin, *op. cit.,* Vol. III, pp. 232–235; *Twentieth Century Encyclopedia of Religious Knowledge,* Vol. I, pp. 266, 267; Peters, *op. cit.,* pp. 202–212.

gations for praise.[13] He endorsed efforts to use the press to strengthen the faith. He maintained the tradition of Leo XIII in seeking to win back to the faith the labourers in factories and mines. He encouraged Catholic Action and Catholic organizations such as the Knights of Columbus.[14]

The historic "Roman Question"—namely, that of the relations with the Kingdom of Italy on Papal political independence and territorial sovereignty —was much on the mind of Benedict XV. The issue became more acute when Italy entered the war: could the Pope preserve his neutrality? As we are to see, a solution was not reached until the reign of the next Pope. Yet the service of thousands of priests in the Italian armies lessened the tension between the Church and the state. Although it came about through universal conscription by the government, it made possible a new kind of contact between the clergy and the rank and file of Italian citizens and thus helped to lower barriers. Moreover, Benedict XV went further than Pius X in relaxing the prohibitions of Pius IX and Leo XIII on the participation of the faithful in Italian politics. He left Catholics free to vote. As a result, the Popular Party came into being, and among its avowed objectives were "the liberty and independence of the Church in the full development of its spiritual authority, liberty and respect for the Christian conscience as the foundation and stronghold of the nation, and of the popular liberties and the progressive conquests of civilization in the world."[15]

BENEDICT XV: AFTERMATH OF WAR

A popular saying declared that the Roman Catholic Church had won the war. Something was seen akin to the situation which followed the end of the French Revolution and the Napoleonic Wars. In the uncertainties of the day a quest for certainty was widespread. A reaction set in against the intellectual liberalism with its perennial questioning which had characterized much of the nineteenth century. The objective liturgy made an appeal and the claim to universalism was attractive to many who were seeking assurance in what looked like a pluralistic and meaningless world and were longing for the effective unity of mankind.[16]

Certainly the outcome of World War I ushered in not only challenges but opportunities for the Roman Catholic branch of the faith. As we are to see more at length in a chapter covering country by country the course of the Roman Catholic Church, the peace was followed by a revival of the activity

---

[13] Schmidlin, *op. cit.*, Vol. III, pp. 238–241.

[14] *Ibid.*, pp. 245, 246.

[15] *Ibid.*, pp. 258–264; Premoli, *op. cit.*, pp. 89–92; Heuvel, *op. cit.*, pp. 50–55; Friedrich Engel-Janosi in *The Catholic Historical Review*, Vol. XL, pp. 269–285; Jemolo, *Chièsa e Stato in Italia negli Ultimo Cento Anni*, pp. 565–586.

[16] Loewenich, *op. cit.*, pp. 120–123.

and influence of that church in France and Italy. Moreover, the Church's children were preponderant in nations to which the peace settlement accorded political freedom—Poland, Lithuania, and Czechoslovakia—and in the newly independent Irish Free State. They were numerous in the enlarged Jugoslavia and Rumania. Catholic political parties were important in Germany, Austria, Belgium, the Netherlands, and Hungary. Roman Catholic missions displayed a forward surge. Led by Benedict XV, in a number of ways the Holy See sought to help the Church to enter into the doors thus opened.

In much of Central Europe the post-war relief problem was acute. Here the Vatican gave or assisted in substantial relief. It also supervised the re-organization of the Roman Catholic Church made necessary by the wastage of war and the new political situation.

As we are to see, a parallel trend appeared in Protestantism. The liberalism which had progressively marked much of that branch of the faith in the nineteenth century waned. In its place came an emphasis on revelation as against the natural theology which stressed reason and man's ability. In the United States fundamentalism, less sophisticated and holding to the Bible as the infallible word of God, was widespread.

During and following the war, diplomatic relations were either renewed or established for the first time with several governments. When Benedict XV ascended the Papal throne fourteen states were represented at the Vatican by embassies or legations. On the eve of his death the number had increased to twenty-six.[17]

From the standpoint of the Roman Catholic Church, a peculiarly gratifying event was the restoration of diplomatic relations between the French Government and the Vatican. It arose out of the improvement of the status of the Church in France, of which we are to hear more in a later chapter. The rupture which was occasioned in 1904 by the unilateral act of France in breaking off diplomatic ties and in 1905 by the separation of Church and state, also at the instance of the latter, was healed in 1920–1921, likewise on the initiative of the government—although after tactful diplomatic measures by the Pope. This was in spite of the widespread dissatisfaction at Benedict's resolute neutrality during the war which in the heat of passion won him the label "the boche Pope." Among the factors making for a less unfavourable attitude was the canonization of the national heroine Joan of Arc, in 1919, with Benedict XV officiating.[18]

Early in World War I, in December, 1914, England, realizing the importance of the Holy See because of its ties with the faithful in all the belligerent

[17] Heuvel, *op. cit.,* p. 56.

[18] Premoli, *op. cit.,* pp. 121, 122; Dansette, *Histoire Religieuse en France Contemporaine,* Vol. II, pp. 500–504; Lama, *op. cit.,* pp. 171 ff.; Peters, *op. cit.,* p. 197.

countries, sent a minister to the Vatican.[19] In June, 1915, the Netherlands resumed the diplomatic relations with the Vatican which had been suspended in 1870.[20] The coming to power in Portugal in 1917–1918 of a less anti-clerical government than the one which in 1911 had separated Church and state and in 1913 had severed official ties with the Vatican brought about a renewal of relations.[21]

It was not surprising that legations were set up at the Vatican by states whose independence followed World War I and in which Roman Catholics were either a majority or a substantial element of the population. They included Hungary, Czechoslovakia, Jugoslavia, and Poland. Some Latin American countries entered into similar relations.[22]

The Vatican was not a member of the League of Nations. It was not invited to join, and although he endorsed the general idea of a league of all states Benedict was critical of that particular form of international organization on the ground that it was not founded on the Christian faith.[23]

In connexion with the peace settlement after World War I, Benedict successfully asserted the claims of his church to preserve to it the enterprises which had been conducted by German Roman Catholic missionaries.[24]

BENEDICT XV AND THE WORLD MISSION

Benedict XV was deeply interested in promoting the world mission of the Roman Catholic Church. While not unfriendly, Pius X had not emphasized that phase of his office. Papal concern was revived by Benedict. In the apostolic letter *Maximum illud,* November 30, 1919, Benedict recommended the support of missions, the creation of an indigenous clergy, and improved mission methods.[25] He encouraged the Missionary Union of the Clergy, which had been founded in 1916 in Italy to promote the support of missions. In *Maximum illud* he placed it under the Congregation for the Propagation of the Faith and expressed his desire to have it organized in every diocese of the entire Church.[26] He sought to promote the extension of the recognition of Papal authority among the Eastern Churches. To this end, by the *motu proprio* of May 1, 1917, he removed the supervision of relations with them from the Propaganda

---

[19] Premoli, *op. cit.,* p. 167; Graham, *Vatican Diplomacy,* pp. 76–78.

[20] Lama, *op. cit.,* p. 211.

[21] Premoli, *op. cit.,* pp. 181, 182.

[22] Heuvel, *op. cit.,* p. 56; Schmidlin, *op. cit.,* Vol. III, pp. 321, 322.

[23] Lama, *op. cit.,* pp. 158–171; Schmidlin, *op. cit.,* Vol. III, pp. 319, 320; Hughes, *The Popes' New Order,* p. 198.

[24] Premoli, *op. cit.,* pp. 47, 48.

[25] Schmidlin-Braun, *Catholic Mission History,* p. 566; *Acta Apostolicae Sedis,* Vol. XI, pp. 440–455.

[26] Premoli, *op. cit.,* p. 38.

and placed it under a new congregation, that of the Eastern Church. In October, 1917, he created in Rome the Pontifical Institute of Oriental Studies.[27]

Pius XI (1922–1939): Pre-Papal Career, Election, and Characteristics

The unexpected death of Benedict XV while still in his sixties brought another Papal election. The conclave was about evenly divided between two groups, but on its third day and on the fourteenth ballot the choice fell on a compromise candidate, Ambrose Damian Achilles Ratti. Achilles Ratti (1857–1939), to give him the shorter name by which he was usually known, was of Northern Italian peasant stock. His father had modest middle-class status, and a paternal uncle was a priest prominent in the Archdiocese of Milan. His education took place in that archdiocese, where he became personally known to the archbishop, and in Rome. In the Eternal City he took a doctorate in canon law and another in philosophy in the recently founded Academy of St. Thomas Aquinas, and with so brilliant a record that he was personally congratulated by Leo XIII. Returning to Milan, he first taught in the diocesan seminary and then was appointed to the staff of the Ambrosian Library, where his assignment engaged him in research, writing, and editing, and later in the reorganization of the collections. In 1914 he was placed in charge of the Vatican Library. During his residence in Milan he also had pastoral and educational duties and became intimately familiar with the *Spiritual Exercises* of Ignatius Loyola and the direction of retreats. Reared and spending much of his life at the foot of the Alps, Ratti became an expert mountaineer.

In 1918 the course of Ratti's life was radically changed. He was appointed visitor apostolic to Poland and in that post helped to put the Roman Catholic Church in a position to avail itself of the opportunities offered by the newly won independence. In 1919 he became Papal nuncio to Poland and prepared the way for the concordat which was concluded in 1925. He also paid official visits to neighbouring countries and there dealt with problems arising as aftermaths of war. He also helped to hearten the Poles in their resistance to the invasion of the Bolsheviks. In June, 1921, he was appointed Archbishop of Milan and cardinal. After less than a year in his new post he was elected Pope.[28] He chose the title of Pius, saying that he had been born under Pius IX, that Pius X had first given him office in Rome, and that he wished, as had Benedict XV, to give himself to the peace of the world. In his initial encyclical, *Ubi arcano Dei* (December 23, 1922), the new Pope declared that the remedy for the evils of the times must be "in the peace of Christ in the Kingdom of

[27] Heuvel, *op. cit.*, pp. 21, 22.
[28] Hughes, *Pope Pius the Eleventh*, pp. 1–100; Browne-Olf, *Pius XI, Apostle of Peace*, pp. 3–106; Teeling, *Pope Pius XI and World Affairs*, pp. 40–82.

Christ." That phrase, *Pax Christi in regno Christi,* was the motto of his reign.[29] As one way of attaining this goal, in 1925 he instituted the feast of Christ the King.

Pius XI opened his reign by giving his blessing *urbi et orbi* publicly, from the loggia of St. Peter's rather than in the interior, the first to do so since the occupation of Rome by the Kingdom of Italy in 1870. He thus foreshadowed the reconciliation with that state which was to be one of his achievements.[30]

Pius XI had personal characteristics which were to mark his reign. Throughful, perspicacious, an able administrator, of resolute and commanding will, sometimes short of temper, bold, courageous, he brought vigorous leadership to a post which carried with it absolute authority. A scholar by temperament, trained in the philosophy of the schoolmen, he could be counted on to further the study of Aquinas which had been stressed by his immediate predecessors. Through long experience, he was felicitous in public address and writing. He had proved himself to be a skilled diplomat under extremely trying and complex conditions. His long years as a director of souls and his familiarity with Loyola's *Spiritual Exercises* ensured his deep and mature interest in the more strictly religious aspects of the Papal See.[31] In a pontificate set in revolutionary and stormy years that saw local wars in which countries traditionally Catholic were deeply involved, the rapid spread of Communism, the domination of Italy by Fascism and of Germany by the National Socialism of Hitler, and the darkening shadows of impending World War II, Pius XI was not content merely to steer the bark of Peter safely through the tempests. He was committed to the world-wide spread of the faith and supported those who were seeking to adjust missionary methods to the rising tide of nationalism in Asia and Africa in such fashion as to plant the Church firmly in indigenous leadership. He also encouraged Catholic Action with its growing participation of the rank and file of the loyal laity in the varied apostolate of the Church.

Pius XI and the Italian Government

From the inception of his reign Pius XI was confronted with a movement which before he had been many months on the Papal throne captured political control of Italy and tested to the full his purpose of effecting a reconciliation with the Italian Government. In the internal stresses in Italy following World War I, Benito Mussolini (1883-1945), a man of vaulting ambition, a former socialist, attacked Marxist Communism and the Liberal regime then in power and created Fascism, a name derived from the *fasci,* or clubs which he organ-

29 Browne-Olf, *op. cit.,* pp. 118, 204, 205.

30 *Ibid.,* pp., 119, 120.

31 *Enciclopedia Cattolica,* Vol. IX, p. 1532; Teeling, *op. cit.,* pp. 28–39; Zsolt Aradi, *The Pope and the Man* (Garden City, N.Y., Hanover House, 1958, pp. 262), *passim.*

ized, at first largely in the industrial centres. The members wore black shirts, had as their symbol the *fasces,* or bundles of rods enclosing a battle-axe such as dignitaries of the ancient Roman Republic had adopted as emblems of office, and saluted Mussolini as *Il Duce* with the outstretched hand in the Roman manner. In October, 1922, Mussolini and his cohorts marched on Rome and King Victor Emmanuel III asked him to form a ministry. He was appointed prime minister, became in fact a dictator, restored order, suppressed strikes, undertook public works, reduced unemployment, and by the ruthless use of force silenced his critics. Until they were unseated by the debacle of World War II the Fascists and their party dominated the country.

Although Pius XI was no friend of Fascism, he came to terms with Mussolini, and the latter, earlier an atheist, deemed advisable outward conformity to the professed faith of the majority of the nation. On February 11, 1929, after months of negotiations three documents constituting the Lateran Accord were signed by Gasparri as Papal Secretary of State and by Mussolini in behalf of the King of Italy. One was a treaty by which the Pope recognized the Kingdom of Italy, surrendered his claim to the greater part of Rome, and in return was conceded full sovereignty in a small but independent Papal State embracing Vatican City and Castel Gandolfo outside Rome. The Pope was also recognized as the full owner of some of the historic churches and of other specified ecclesiastical structures in Rome, some other properties of the Church were accorded diplomatic immunity, representatives of foreign governments accredited to the Holy See were permitted free access across Italian territory, and other provisions were included to ensure the freedom of the Holy See from interference by the Italian Government. The status of "The Catholic and Apostolic and Roman religion" was reaffirmed as "the sole religion of the state." The Pope agreed also to "remain extraneous to all temporal disputes between nations and to international congresses convoked for the settlement of such disputes unless the contending parties make a joint appeal to his mission of peace." A second document assured the payment to the Pope of a sum of about one hundred million dollars as a substitute for the annual grants which the state had offered in compensation for the territories it had seized but which the Popes thus far had refused. The third document was a concordat regulating the relations between Church and state. The Pope was assured freedom of communication with the bishops and clergy of the entire Catholic world. He was to appoint all the bishops in Italy, but in each case was first to assure himself that from a political standpoint the state had no objections to the nominee. Before taking office the bishops were to swear loyalty to the state, the king, and the government. The state renounced the right of royal patronage to all benefices. The state was to continue to pay the salaries of bishops and priests, and religious instruction would be given in the state schools by teachers approved by the Church. The clergy were to be members of no political party. Numerous provisions regulated such matters as marriage and divorce and other issues which were of interest to both Church and state.[32]

The Lateran Accord eased but did not fully remove the friction between Church and state. Complete accord could scarcely be expected. Here were two powers, each believing that to accomplish its purpose it must have the shaping of the oncoming generation and cherishing conflicting convictions as to the nature of the state. Pius XI did not hesitate to criticize the Fascist conception of the state. He declared that a good Catholic could not assent to it. Before the treaties of the Lateran Pact were ratified and even while they were still under discussion and criticism of Fascism might have caused Mussolini to break off the negotiations, the Pope spoke out against some of *Il Duce's* speeches.[33]

In 1931 the issue was joined over Catholic Action. Fascists in high standing declared that in a totalitarian regime such as theirs that movement, not subject to control by the state, could not be permitted and attempted to dissolve the youth organizations connected with it. Mussolini publicly declared (June, 1931) that some sections of Catholic Action were hostile to Fascism and that destruction of Catholic associations must be undertaken in self-defense. On July 5, 1931, Pius XI replied with the encyclical *Non abbiamo bisogno*. He protested the suppression of the Catholic associations of young people and university students, denied the charge that they were used for political purposes, and renewed his prohibition that they should be employed in this manner. He denounced the Fascist objective of monopolizing the formation of youth and said that it was not possible for a Catholic to accept the Fascist assertion that the Church should confine itself to the external practices of religion such as the sacraments and that all the rest of education should belong to the state. By early in September, 1931, the conflict was resolved by what was in effect a compromise. The government's decree against Catholic Action was withdrawn and an agreement was reached which provided that Catholic Action would abstain from politics, that it would not form professional guilds, and that Catholic youth associations would refrain from athletic and sporting activities and in educational and social activities would confine themselves to those with a religious purpose. To prevent the local associations from being centres of political dissent, the organizations of Catholic youth were removed from the control of lay committees and were placed directly under the bishop

---

[32] Hayes, *Contemporary Europe since 1870*, pp. 571–578; Hughes, *op. cit.*, pp. 195–228; Teeling, *op. cit.*, pp. 121–130. English translations of the Treaty of the Vatican and the concordat are in Benedict Williamson, *The Treaty of the Lateran* (London, Burns Oates & Washbourne, 1929, pp. ix, 101), pp. 42–66.

[33] Hughes, *op. cit.*, pp. 230–235.

of the diocese. In appointing their officers the bishop was to avoid naming any one who had ever been an opponent of Fascism.[34]

PIUS XI AND THE ITALIAN INVASION OF ETHIOPIA

The invasion and conquest of Ethiopia by Fascist Italy in 1935–1936 and the eventual condemnation of Italy by the League of Nations with the application of economic sanctions by that body—futile as they proved—placed Pius XI and the Roman Catholic Church in a difficult and ambiguous position. On the one hand, in many quarters the Pope was condemned for not speaking out against a bare-faced act of imperialistic aggression, Italian Catholics with their bishops and clergy were severely criticized for joining in the public celebrations of the Italian victories, and the Roman Catholic Church was pilloried for taking advantage of the situation to set up an ecclesiastical structure for Ethiopia with the purpose of bringing that country's ancient church into communion with the Pope.[35] On the other hand, apologists for the Pope and the Roman Catholic Church pointed out that under the Lateran Accord the Pope was estopped from intervening in temporal disputes between nations unless invited by the contending parties, that more than once he had spoken out in general terms against war and on behalf of peace, that he was not a member of the League of Nations, and that during the negotiations which preceded the resort to arms he had explicitly expressed the hope that a just solution would be reached short of that act.[36]

PIUS XI: RELATIONS WITH OTHER TOTALITARIAN REGIMES

The problems presented to the Papacy by the spate of totalitarian regimes following World War I were not confined to Italy. Here was a widespread phase of the revolutionary age which could not but challenge a church which believed itself divinely commissioned to bring all men to obedience to Christ and to direct their lives with a view to their eternal salvation.

Pius XI was inevitably deeply involved in the problems presented by the coming to power in Germany in 1933 of Adolf Hitler and his National Socialist or Nazi Party. Of the Roman Catholic record in Germany we are to hear more in a later chapter. Our present concern is the attitude of Pius XI towards it and the actions taken by him.

In 1933—that is, early in the Hitler regime—the Vatican entered into a concordat with "the Third German Empire." From the side of the Holy See it

---

[34] *Ibid.*, pp. 235–248; Teeling, *op. cit.*, pp. 134–136. See an English translation of *Non abbiamo bisogno* in McLaughlin, *The Church and the Reconstruction of the Modern World*, pp. 301–330.

[35] For a forthright expression of this criticism see Ridley, *The Papacy and Fascism*, pp. 195–197. See also Binchy, *Church and State in Fascist Italy*, pp. 679, 702.

[36] Hughes, *op. cit.*, pp. 248–255.

was negotiated by Eugenio Pacelli, the later Pope Pius XII. It did not abolish the earlier concordats with Bavaria, Prussia, and Baden but, embracing all the Reich, was more comprehensive geographically than they. In the main it was favourable to the Roman Catholic Church. Rome was assured full liberty to correspond with its clergy and laity; the secrecy of the confessional was to be respected; clergy and members of orders and congregations were exempted from all civil obligations declared by canon law to be incompatible with their profession; existing diocesan divisions were to be respected; the Church was to be free to appoint to ecclesiastical posts subject only to the requirement that those thus designated be German citizens and have had at least part of their education in Germany; freedom was accorded to religious orders to exist and to own property, but with the provision that superiors resident in Germany were to be German citizens; instruction in the Catholic faith was to be given in the state schools, and by teachers approved by the bishop; and provision was made for Catholic schools of various grades. As in totalitarian Fascist Italy, the issue of Catholic Action, and especially of youth associations, was thorny. The concordat devoted a long article to it and declared that those Catholic organizations which were exclusively religious, cultural, or charitable and were subject to ecclesiastical authority were not only to be permitted but were to have the protection of law. Members of youth associations organized by the state were assured facilities for the performance of their religious duties. Clergy and members of religious communities were not to engage in party politics.[37]

In spite of the concordat, conflict between the Nazi government and the Roman Catholic Church was inevitable and could not be long delayed. Pius XI staunchly upheld the principles of his church against the Nazi programme and deeds. Only five days after the concordat was signed the state promulgated a law for the sterilization of individuals in certain categories. Pius XI soon publicly declared that the law was contrary to Christian morals.[38] The National Socialist press insisted, in contradiction of the Vatican *Osservatore Romano,* that the concordat implied Papal approval of the Nazi form of government.[39] On March 14, 1937, in the encyclical *Mit brennenden Sorge* Pius XI vigorously protested what he regarded as breaches of the concordat by the Nazis, urged the faithful to stand firm, and declared that the attempts to set up a German national church were a denial of the one Church of Christ and that the Nazi use of Christian phrases was a reprehensible distortion of their true meaning.[40]

[37] *Ibid.,* pp. 190–194; Clonmore, *Pope Pius XI and World Peace,* pp. 163, 164.
[38] Clonmore, *op. cit.,* p. 165.
[39] *Ibid.,* p. 166.
[40] *Acta Apostolicae Sedis,* Vol. XXIX, pp. 145–167; Clonmore, *op. cit.,* pp. 183, 184; Hughes, *op. cit.,* pp. 300–302. For an Italian translation of the text of the encyclical see *Le Encicliche Sociali dei Papi da Pio IX a Pio XII (1864–1956),* pp. 571–598. An English translation is in McLaughlin, *op. cit.,* pp. 336–360.

In May, 1938, Hitler visited Rome, but his restrictions on the Roman Catholic Church continued and on October 20 of that year Pius XI spoke out against the persecutions which were being inflicted on the Church and the faithful.[41]

Pius XI was also confronted by the challenge of Communism. The Bolsheviks had come to power in Russia several years before his accession to the pontificate and, anti-religious, were engaged in a severe persecution of the churches. In that persecution, as we are to see later, Roman Catholics suffered. They were also under Communist pressure in other countries, in the days of Pius XI notably in Hungary and Mexico. From the beginning of his reign Pius XI, continuing the efforts to his predecessor, had sought to bring the persecutions to an end. From time to time he spoke out forcibly. Thus, in February, 1930, in an open letter he deplored the closing of churches, the suppression of Sunday, and the compulsory declaration by factory workers of apostasy and hatred of God. In his encyclical *Quadragesimo anno,* of which we are to hear more in a moment, issued on May 15, 1931, on the fortieth anniversary of Leo XIII's *Rerum novarum,* and in which he dealt comprehensively with the social problems of the revolutionary age, Pius XI condemned Communism as a false solution, and denounced its merciless class warfare, its abolition of the private ownership of property, its open hostility to the Church and to God, and the destruction which its advocates had wrought in Eastern Europe and Asia.[42]

Communism was also a factor in the anti-clerical measures in Spain which were taken during the reign of Pius XI—an episode to which we must recur in a later chapter. On it Pius XI made public pronouncements.[43]

PIUS XI AND SOME OTHER GOVERNMENTS

Pius XI was confronted with difficulties in several other states. In France he faced *Action Française.* Here was a movement which had as its chief spokesman Charles Maurras. It advocated the restoration of the monarchy under the House of Orleans. Although he was an unbeliever, Maurras proposed that the soul of the reconstructed nation should be the Catholic Church. Pius X had intended to make public his disapproval but had died before issuing it. Benedict XV delayed for fear of the effect on France during World War I. In spite of severe criticism, in December, 1926, Pius XI formally condemned *Action Française* and forbade Catholics to join it or to read its publications. He did this, not because he objected to its political aims, for to do so

---

[41] *Enciclopedia Cattolica,* Vol. IX, p. 1536.

[42] For an Italian translation of another pertinent encyclical, *Divini Redemptoris* (March 19, 1937), see *Le Encicliche Sociali dei Papi da Pio IX a Pio XII,* pp. 600–637. An English translation is in McLaughlin, *op. cit.,* pp. 366–398.

[43] See an Italian translation in *Le Encicliche Sociali dei Papi da Pio IX a Pio XII,* pp. 545–556, of *Dilectissima nobis* (June 3, 1933).

would have been resented as interference in France's internal affairs, but because in his judgement the movement would have de-Christianized the Catholic
Church.[44] But three years earlier, in January, 1924, Pius XI had had the satisfaction of approving an arrangement with the government which gave the
Roman Catholic Church in France control over the buildings it used and full
freedom to operate them for religious purposes.[45] In December, 1925, Pius XI,
while not happy over the separation of Church and state in Chile, noted that
it had been carried through in friendly fashion.[46] However, a few weeks later,
in February, 1926, and again in November and December, 1926, he expressed
disapproval of restrictions placed by the state on the Church in Mexico.[47]
Later, in March, 1937, he urged on the Mexican clergy and laity greater holiness in life to meet the challenge.[48] In 1938 Pius XI arbitrated the conflict between Haiti and Santo Domingo.[49]

PIUS XI: CONCORDATS WITH THE NEW GOVERNMENTS

Pius XI continued the policy of Benedict XV in seeking to regularize the
relations between the Papacy and the new states which had emerged from
World War I. To this end he authorized the ratification of concordats with
Latvia (May 30, 1922), Poland (February 10, 1925), Lithuania (September 22,
1927), and Jugoslavia (July 25, 1935) and entered into a *modus vivendi* with
Czechoslovakia (February 2, 1928). Concordats were also negotiated with states
in which the war had radically altered the government—with Bavaria (January
24, 1925), Rumania (July 7, 1927), Prussia (June 14, 1929), Baden (December
12, 1932), and Austria (May 2, 1934), in addition to those already mentioned
with Italy and Germany. The terms varied from concordat to concordat but
in general placed the status of the Roman Catholic Church on a legal basis
reciprocally agreed upon and conceded that the Holy See had the exclusive
right to appoint bishops, but with prior notification to the civil government
to permit the latter to register objection to the person designated.[50] As a rule
the concordats also provided for freedom of communication with Rome, the
immunity of the clergy from military service and from fiscal obligations to
the state, the right of the Church to own property, and the autonomy of religious communities in their juridical aspects, and they contained provisions
favourable to Catholic lay organizations and Catholic education.[51] In other

---

[44] Hughes, *op. cit.,* pp. 286–291.
[45] *Ibid.,* pp. 285, 286; *Acta Apostolicae Sedis,* Vol. XVI, pp. 5–11.
[46] Hughes, *op. cit.,* pp. 291, 292.
[47] *Ibid.,* pp. 293, 294.
[48] *Acta Apostolicae Sedis,* Vol. XXIX, pp. 189–199; *Le Encicliche Sociali dei Papi da Pio IX a Pio XII,* pp. 639–654.
[49] *Enciclopedia Cattolica,* Vol. IX, p. 1537.
[50] Hughes, *op. cit.,* pp. 175–180.
[51] Marc-Bonnet, *La Papauté Contemporaine (1878–1945),* p. 104.

words, the concordats gave the formal consent of the civil governments which entered into them to the existence within their borders of a church independent of their control in important features and owing effective allegiance to a centre which was outside their jurisdiction. On some issues—for example, that of marriage—in several of the documents the Holy See felt constrained to compromise its historic claims. Yet on the whole the concordats bore witness to the continued strength of the ultramontanism which had displayed marked growth in the nineteenth century and were a far cry from the Gallicanism, the Febronianism, and the Josephism of the eighteenth century.

Pius XI: Attitude Towards Social and Economic Issues

Pius XI was keenly aware of the social and economic problems which were issuing from the revolutionary age and sought constructive solutions consonant with Christian principles. These he expressed in several encyclicals and other pronouncements.

On marriage and the family Pius XI emphatically reaffirmed what he regarded as the historic position of the Church and with specific application to some of the trends of the day. He lamented the attitude which regarded adultery and divorce as a-moral and which sanctioned "temporary," "experimental," and "companionate" marriages. He came out against birth control, with its desire to avoid the burden of child-bearing and child-rearing. He condemned abortion, even where the operation would save the life of the mother. He also objected to sterilization. Positively, he stressed the sanctity of marriage.[52]

Pius XI maintained the traditional claims of the Church to its share in the education of youth and the promotion of knowledge. He insisted that there can be no complete or perfect education which is not Christian education and that education is the business of the Church. He held that the Church, sharing as it does the teaching office of God, has the right to found schools of every kind and grade and to control the education of all its children, whether in public or private institutions. This, he said, holds true not only in religious instruction but also in every branch of learning and in every aspect which affects morals and religion. Indeed, he declared, the responsibility of the Church to educate extends to those outside her fold. He was emphatic that the family and its right to educate its children are inviolable, but that the Church has the duty to protect the children against incompetent parents.[53]

[52] Hughes, *op. cit.*, pp. 263–266. For a semi-popular treatment of the Roman Catholic attitude towards marriage, the family, and birth control, see Robert G. Brehmer, Jr., *Social Doctrines of the Catholic Church* (New York, G. P. Putnam's Sons, 1936, pp. 141), pp. 31–58. For an Italian translation of pertinent texts see *Le Encicliche Sociali dei Papi da Pio IX a Pio XII*, pp. 315, 316, 375–429.

[53] Hughes, *op. cit.*, pp. 258–260. For an important encyclical on the subject, *Divini illius magistri*

The rapid growth and increasing popularity of the cinema, one of the twentieth-century features of the revolutionary age, was of deep concern to Pius XI. In the encyclical *Vigilanti cura* (June 29, 1936) he dealt with it at some length.[54] Recognizing the importance of recreation for workers in the industries of the day and noting the appeal of the motion picture, with its music and its accompaniment of the reproduction of speech (the "talkies," as they were first called), together with the luxurious appointments and the relaxed attitude of the audience, he pointed out the power of the cinema for either good or evil. He declared that to keep the cinema wholesome rather than a school of corruption was one of the major challenges of the time, commended what was being done by individuals and governments to attain the former end, and enjoined the bishops to exert their influence with those of the faithful who were in a position to control the character of the cinema—authors, actors, and executive directors—to see that Christian standards were maintained. The bishops were urged to induce the members of their flocks annually to pledge themselves to go only to plays which did not offend Christian truth and morality. In each country, so the Pope directed, permanent national reviewing offices were to be set up and prompt, regular, and frequent lists were to be published showing which films were recommended for all, which were permitted with reservations, and which were harmful.

Pius XI was acutely alive to the progressive industrialization of society—another feature of the revolutionary age. In 1929 he took the occasion of a labour dispute in Lille to deal with the issues which it raised. He did this in a letter to the bishop of that diocese.[55] He gave a more comprehensive statement in *Quadragesimo anno* (May 15, 1931).[56] As we have said, Pius XI made the fortieth anniversary of *Rerum novarum* the occasion for an inclusive pronouncement. In it he spoke in fulsome terms of that encyclical of Leo XIII and of its effects among Roman Catholics and outside their circles. He reaffirmed the authority of the Pope to speak on social and economic problems and sought to resolve the doubts which had arisen about the correct interpretation of the encyclical. While reasserting Leo XIII's endorsement of private property, he declared that far from supporting the wealthy classes against the proletariat, as some of the critics had said, the possession of property endorsed

---

(December 31, 1929), see an Italian translation in *Le Encicliche Sociali dei Papi da Pio IX a Pio XII*, pp. 333–374. For an English translation see McLaughlin, *op. cit.*, pp. 13–109.

[54] *Acta Apostolicae Sedis*, Vol. XXVIII, pp. 249–263. See an Italian translation in *Le Encicliche Sociali dei Papi da Pio IX a Pio XII*, pp. 557–570.

[55] Hughes, *op. cit.*, pp. 270, 271.

[56] *Acta Apostolicae Sedis*, Vol. XXIII, pp. 177–228. See English translations in *Forty Years After. Reconstruction of the Social Order. Encyclical Letter of His Holiness, Pope Pius XI* (Washington, D.C., National Catholic Welfare Conference, 1936, p. 48), *passim*, and in McLaughlin, *op. cit.*, pp. 219–274. For a comprehensive analysis of the social teachings of Pius XI see Charles P. Bruehl, *The Pope's Plan for Social Reconstruction. A Commentary on the Social Encyclicals of Pius XI* (New York, The Devin-Adair Co., 1939, pp. xii, 356), *passim*.

by Leo XIII entailed obligations for its proper use. Yet misuse or non-use, so he said, did not forfeit the right to property. But Pius XI insisted that the right of ownership is not rigid and that so long as natural and divine law is observed the state has the right to regulate the utilization of property for the common good. He deplored both the excesses of the *laissez-faire* liberalism which justified the accumulation of wealth by employers while the labourers were in chronic indigence and the doctrine of the "intellectuals" that all products and profits, except those necessary to repair and replace invested capital, belonged of right to the labourers. He set forth what he believed to be the principle of the just distribution of wealth and reinforced what he held had been an objective of *Rerum novarum*—the uplifting of the proletariat. He had at heart the welfare not only of workingmen in the factories but also of rural labourers. While endorsing wage contracts, he advocated a form in which workmen would share with their employers in the proceeds of industry.

Like Leo XIII, Pius XI maintained that the wages paid to the workingmen must be sufficient for the support of themselves and their families. To complete what had been begun to attain this end, Pius XI said that a reform in the social order was essential. In it the state had a proper part, but it was not to seek to be omnicompetent and was to leave much to smaller groups and grant legal recognition to organizations of employers and employed. Strikes and lockouts, so he held, should be forbidden.

Pius XI noted the changes which had come in socialism since *Rerum novarum*—in the more violent wing in the form of Communism and in a decline of radicalism in the other wing. He condemned Communism. However, while welcoming some of the developments in the moderate wing, he maintained that basically socialism had missed the goal of human life as set forth by Christian doctrine. According to the latter, man is placed on earth to spend his life in society under an authority ordained by God that he may develop all his faculties to the praise and glory of his Creator. Socialism, on the other hand, he declared, is quite oblivious of this chief end of man and affirms that living in community is solely for the advantages which it brings to mankind. To attain this objective, so Pius XI insisted, socialism would subordinate and even sacrifice men's liberty and human dignity to ensure efficient production. Although socialism contained some elements of truth, the Pope said, it was opposed to true Christianity, and to speak of "Christian socialism" involved a contradiction in terms. He deplored the effort of socialism to rear children in its tenets, the adoption of socialism by many of the faithful, and the apostasy of many workingmen.

Yet Pius XI did not end *Quadragesimo anno* on a note of pessimism. He called on those who had left the Church to return. He welcomed the coöperation of all men of good will, including all who believed in God. He set forth what he regarded as Christian moral principles for economic and social life. He looked forward confidently to the complete renewal of society, hailed the associations of workingmen as signs of coming social reconstruction, and outlined what he believed to be the main features of a proper programme.

The world-wide economic depression which began in the United States late in 1929 and spread in the 1930's to most of the globe was of deep concern to Pius XI. In *Quadragesimo anno* he had not directly dealt with it. Now, in the encyclical *Nova impedit* (October 2, 1931) he noted with sorrow the financial crisis and the growing unemployment, called for relief of the suffering and especially of the children, and viewed with alarm the mad race of armaments.[57] The following year, as the depression deepened, the Pope returned to the subject. In *Caritate Christi compulsi* (May 3, 1932) he dealt with what he believed to have been the basic causes of the disaster—among them cupidity, militant atheism, irreligious propaganda, economic and political imperialism, and the separation of morals and religion. He called for a revival of religion, repentance, expiation, the utilization of the feast of the Holy Heart of Jesus for this purpose, and an octave of prayer and of reparation.[58]

Pius XI: Catholic Action

The rapid growth of Catholic Action which marked the twentieth century and of which we are to hear more received marked encouragement from Pius XI. He sought to make it contribute to the education of the young, to the religious instruction of the masses, to the sanctification of the family and of labour, to social improvement, and to the promotion of the Roman Catholic press.[59]

Pius XI: The Clergy and Politics

We have seen that in the struggle with Mussolini Pius XI had made it clear that he wished Catholic youth movements to keep aloof from politics. Similarly, although, as we are to see, Catholic political parties arose in several countries, Catholic Action did not have participation in politics as one of its purposes. Moreover, following the precedent of Leo XIII and Benedict XV, Pius XI urged that priests avoid aligning themselves with any political party and give themselves to their primary function, the care of souls, and withdraw themselves from the play of purely temporal passions and interests.[60]

In the encyclical *Ad Catholici sacerdotii* (December 20, 1935) commemorat-

---

[57] *Acta Apostolicae Sedis*, Vol. XXIII, pp. 393–367. See an Italian translation in *Le Encicliche Sociali dei Papi da Pio IX a Pio XII*, pp. 522–525.
[58] *Acta Apostolicae Sedis*, Vol. XXIV, pp. 177–194; McLaughlin, *op. cit.*, pp. 280–295.
[59] Browne-Olf, *op. cit.*, p. 205; *Enciclopedia Cattolica*, Vol. IX, p. 1539.
[60] Premoli, *op. cit.*, pp. 60, 61.

ing what was believed to be the nineteenth centenary of the institution of the Christian priesthood, Pius XI stressed the call of the priest to holiness and personal sanctification and the obligation of the priest to have a solid education, not only in matters ecclesiastical and in scholastic philosophy, but also in general knowledge and culture equal to that of the best-educated people of the day. He had earlier (May 24, 1931), in the apostolic constitution *Deus scientiarum Dominus,* sought so to reform ecclesiastical faculties as to broaden and deepen the education of the clergy.[61]

PIUS XI AND SCHOLARSHIP AND EDUCATION

Scholar that he was, Pius XI did much to promote education and scholarship. He furthered the formation of regional seminaries in Italy for the training of the clergy, substituting them for the seminaries of some of the smaller dioceses and thus improving the education of the priests. Through a variety of methods, organizations, and institutions he encouraged research in several branches of learning and stood for higher education through universities.[62]

PIUS XI AND THE WORLD MISSION

Pius XI was deeply committed to the world mission of the Church. His motto for his reign, *Pax Christi in regno Christi,* embraced all mankind. In many ways he gave the endorsement of his high office to the spread of the faith beyond the borders of the Occident. In 1922 he made much of the tercentenary of the founding of the Congregation for the Propagation of the Faith. In connection with that commemoration the Missionary Union of the Clergy held its international congress in Rome.[63] Pius XI called in the heads of orders and congregations and insisted that they increase their share in foreign missions. When a bishop made his periodical visit to the throne of Peter, as he was obliged to do, Pius XI commanded him to further in his diocese the missionary cause. The Pope also saw to it that the Urban College of the Propaganda for the training of personnel for missions was given a worthy site for its enlarged plant and programme. He furthered the missionary exposition of 1925 and the founding of a missionary and ethnological museum in the Lateran. He authorized the transfer of the headquarters of the Society for the Propagation of the Faith from France to Rome (1922) and placed that organization more directly under Papal supervision: what had been begun on a national scale was formally taken over as the major instrument of the entire Roman Catholic Church for the raising of funds for missions. Thus not only

---

[61] McLaughlin, *op. cit.,* pp. 170–212; *Acta Apostolicae Sedis,* Vol. XXIII, pp. 241–262, Vol. XXVIII, pp. 5–53.
[62] *Enciclopedia Cattolica,* Vol. IX, pp. 1534, 1539, 1540; Premoli, *op. cit.,* p. 68.
[63] Premoli, *op. cit.,* p. 60.

was carried forward the centralization in Rome of the direction of that church which had been marked in the nineteenth century but also practical emphasis was given by the Pope to the spread of the faith throughout the world as a major obligation of the entire Church—an emphasis which was similarly mounting among Protestants.[64]

Pius XI stressed the training of an indigenous clergy in non-Occidental lands. His creation of an apostolic delegation for China in 1922 and the appointment as delegate of the able Celso Costantini foreshadowed a more unified administration of the Roman Catholic Church in that country independent of the historic French protectorate and with greater emphasis upon a Chinese body of clergy. That same year witnessed the inauguration of an apostolic delegation for South Africa, an indication of mounting attention to an area which was predominantly Protestant. Pius XI instituted (1923) a hierarchy for the Malabar Uniates in India under indigenous bishops and clergy and erected in Tuticorin the first indigenous diocese in India of the Latin rite.[65] The encyclical *Rerum ecclesiae* (February 28, 1926) was devoted chiefly to the preparation of an indigenous priesthood. On October 28, 1926, Pius XI gave dramatic demonstration of that emphasis by officiating at the consecration of six Chinese bishops in St. Peter's—the first of that nation, with one exception in the seventeenth century, to be raised to that dignity—and the ensuing years witnessed the appointment of other non-Westerners to the episcopal office.[66] Pius XI formally approved (June, 1929) the statutes of the previously founded organization bearing the name of Peter for the formation of an indigenous clergy.[67]

Thus Pius XI gave effective recognition to the rising tide of nationalism and rebellion against Western imperialism which was a feature of the spread of the revolutionary age to Asia and Africa. The step required courage, for in the ecclesiastical imperialism which, as we have seen, marked the missions of both Roman Catholics and Protestants in the nineteenth century, many missionaries viewed with alarm the transfer of authority to clergy of the peoples among whom they served. The movement paralleled what had already been witnessed in the Russian Orthodox mission in Japan and what, as we are to see, was taking place in Protestant missions.

As part of his concern for the Church on its geographic frontiers, Pius XI exerted himself to see that the mandate to Palestine given to Great Britain did not prejudice the position of Roman Catholics as against the favour shown to the Jews.[68]

[64] *Enciclopedia Cattolica*, Vol. IX, p. 1538; Tragella, *Pio XI, Papa Missionario*, pp. 99–135, 157–159.

[65] Tragella, *op. cit.*, pp. 19–22, 26–28; *Acta Apostolicae Sedis*, Vol. XVIII, pp. 65–83.

[66] *Enciclopedia Cattolica*, Vol. IX, p. 1538; Tragella, *op. cit.*, pp. 136–151, 156.

[67] Tragella, *op. cit.*, pp. 176–181.

[68] Premoli, *op. cit.*, pp. 63, 64, 69.

In his emphasis on the world-wide mission Pius XI was reinforced both by a mounting tide of commitment among Roman Catholics to that mission and by the able Willem Van Rossum (1874–1932), a native of the Netherlands, who had been raised to the purple by Benedict XV and then appointèd by him to be Prefect (head) of the Congregation for the Propagation of the Faith. Continuing in that office until his death, Van Rossum found in Pius XI a willing sharer of his vision, and the Pope had in him a loyal collaborator who did not hesitate to make suggestions to his chief.[69]

PIUS XI: AN APPRAISAL

In Pius XI the Roman Catholic Church had one of the ablest of the Popes who served it during the age of revolution. Administrator and statesman, he was intensely aware of the multiform currents which characterized the age. He recognized their threat to the faith, but he was more impressed by their challenge than their menace. While he did not minimize the perils, he was more hopeful of their being met successfully than had been many of his predecessors. His motto, *Pax Christi in regno Christi,* gave succinct expression to the optimism which in the face of the anti-Christian forces of the day characterized his policies. Leo XIII had consecrated mankind to the Sacred Heart. Pius XI made much of Christ as King and dreamed of all mankind's being brought into the Kingdom of Christ. In this, although not in detail in the same way, he paralleled the vision of men like the nineteenth-century Anglican J. F. D. Maurice. He looked forward to the fulfilment of the vision through the Roman Catholic Church and promoted the further centralization of the direction of that church from Rome.[70] But in attaining that end he welcomed the coöperation of all men of good will and of all who believed in God. He made much of the Church as the body of Christ and thus reinforced a trend which we are to see was marked in the Roman Catholic theology of the twentieth century. While not belittling justice in human relations, he stressed charity. He was fearless in denouncing Communism and did not hesitate to speak out against what he deemed basic anti-Christian features in non-Communistic socialism. Nor would he yield to Fascism or National Socialism on issues which he regarded as essential to the Christian faith. Yet he rejoiced that the Holy See was being officially recognized by an increasing number of governments through concordats and diplomatic representation. Under him, in spite of the continued advance of the de-Christianization which had been seen in the earlier stages of the revolutionary age, the forward surge of the Roman Catholic Church which had been so notable in the nineteenth century

[69] *Enciclopedia Cattolica,* Vol. XII, p. 1028.
[70] Another example of that centralization was the institution in Rome of the Central Bureau of Catholic Organizations to coördinate the multitudinous Catholic bodies which were a feature of the twentieth century and which were working in many countries in intellectual, moral, and social fields for the peace of Christ and the Kingdom of Christ. Premoli, *op. cit.,* p. 71.

continued. During his pontificate the Roman Catholic Church made further strides towards becoming a well-disciplined minority of the faithful set in a hostile world, intent on winning that world to allegiance to Christ. An indefatigable worker, Pius XI, supported by his faith and an indomitable will, kept his hand firmly on the affairs of the Church even when in his last months progressive illness confined him to his bed.

PIUS XII (1939–1958): ELECTION AND CHARACTERISTICS

Although the reign of Pius XI had been a period of intense and varied revolution, a revolution especially marked in the traditional Christendom, compared with the reigns which immediately preceded and succeeded it, it appeared to have fallen in years of relative calm. Benedict XV had been confronted by the storm of World War I and its unquiet aftermath. Pius XI died February 10, 1939, when the lowering clouds portended World War II but it was by no means certain that they would not be dispersed. His successor had barely been inducted into his office when the tempest broke. It was much more destructive than World War I. It engulfed a larger proportion of mankind. In Italy, where the Pope had his seat, it was more devastating than its predecessor. It was followed by dramatic changes in much of the traditional Christendom and by even greater changes in Asia and Africa, areas in which the Roman Catholic Church had extensive missions. This was the world—in which the revolution was mounting and was more than ever assuming global dimensions —that Pius XI bequeathed to the next Pontiff.

The background, in both heredity and experience, of the man elected to this difficult post contrasted sharply with that of Pius XI. He was, too, of a different temperament. Eugenio Pacelli (1876–1958), who was to become Pius XII, was the first native of Rome to occupy the throne of Peter since early in the eighteenth century. He was of the aristocracy, of a family which had been in the Papal service and had been unreconciled to the occupation of Rome by the Kingdom of Italy. He received his education in Rome, early decided to enter the priesthood, and was ordained in 1899 in one of the larger and most ancient churches of that city. Although he would have preferred the life of a pastor, within two years he was appointed to the Congregation of Ecclesiastical Affairs, one of the branches of the Papal Secretariat of State. There he was under the tutelage of Rampolla, then Secretary of State, who was soon followed in that office by Merry del Val, and he in turn by Gasparri. Pacelli assisted Gasparri in the codification of the canon law. In 1917 he was appointed nuncio to Bavaria and in the same year was consecrated by Benedict XV as titular Archbishop of Sardes. He was the agent of Benedict XV in presenting the latter's peace plan to the German emperor. He served in Germany during the chaotic days which followed the defeat of that country, negotiated concordats with Bavaria and Prussia, and in November, 1929, after the conclusion of the latter, was created cardinal. A few weeks later, in February, 1930, he succeeded Gasparri as Secretary of State. Under him concordats were concluded with Baden, Germany (then under the Nazis), and Austria. Pacelli travelled widely —to Buenos Aires to an international Eucharistic Congress, to Spain, to Lourdes, to the United States, to Lisieux in France to give the Papal blessing to the basilica erected in honour of the Little Flower, and to Budapest to an international Eucharistic Congress. He had already been in England as a young man (1908). Pius XI leaned heavily on Pacelli, especially as his own health began to give way. He called him his "closest collaborator" and was said to have been assisted by him in preparing the encyclical *Divini Redemptoris* (March 18, 1937) condemning Communism and the encyclical *Mit brennenden Sorge* (March 14, 1937) protesting the actions of the Nazi government against the Church. In 1935 Pius XI appointed Pacelli Papal camerlengo, an office which carried with it responsibility for the properties and revenues of the Holy See.[71]

Pacelli came to his high office, then, with extensive diplomatic experience which, combined with travel, had given him intimate familiarity with the currents of the revolutionary age. He spoke a variety of languages. The first Secretary of State in several centuries to become Pope, unlike his five immediate predecessors he had had no experience as the administrator of a diocese. In appearance spare, aristocratic, almost fragile, in his youth in uncertain health, Pius XII brought to the pontificate a long experience in dealing with men, high intelligence, and a combination of charm and dignity in public and private address. In his personal life tending to asceticism, from boyhood he had been profoundly religious.[72] His sincere and unaffected piety was displayed, among other ways, in what was the most significant theological and devotional act of his reign, his proclamation as dogma of the bodily assumption of the Virgin Mary to heaven (November 1, 1950). This he had preceded with the consecration of the human race to the Immaculate Heart of Mary (October 31, 1942).[73] During the early years of his connexion with the Curia he had given much time to hearing confessions in a parish church and to teaching underprivileged children the catechism.[74] Like Pius XI he had a high sense of duty which urged him on in spite of physical frailty and the debilitat-

---

[71] Charles Hugo Doyle, *The Life of Pope Pius XII* (New York, Didier, 1945, pp. x, 258), pp. 2–182; *The New York Times*, October 10, 1958, p. 12; Halecki, *Eugenio Pacelli, Pope of Peace*, pp. 2–88; McKnight, *The Papacy: A New Appraisal*, pp. 218–227; Morgan, *The Listening Post*, pp. 141–158; Kees Van Hoek, *Pope Pius XII, Priest and Statesman* (New York, Philosophical Library, 1944, pp. 106), pp. 18–79; Katherine Burton, *Witness of the Light. The Life of Pope Pius XII* (London, Longmans, Green and Co., 1958, pp. vii, 248), pp. 1–115.

[72] McKnight, *op. cit.*, pp. 234–244; Morgan, *op. cit.*, pp. 149–164.

[73] *Enciclopedia Cattolica*, Vol. IX, p. 1551.

[74] Halecki, *op. cit.*, p. 22.

ing illnesses of his later years. Like him, also, he sought to make the Roman Catholic Church more catholic in the sense of being universal. He not only continued to promote its missions but also increased the non-Italian elements in its central organization. It was reported that Pius XI had contemplated devising a procedure by which the Pope would be chosen, not by the cardinals, but by the world-wide episcopate. Presumably Pius XII was more conservative. At least he was regarded as such. Yet in administration he often by-passed the inherited machinery of the Curia and depended rather on a self-chosen circle of intimates, among whom were three German Jesuits.

Pius XII and World War II

Like Benedict XV, in the early years of his reign Pius XII was confronted with a world war. When he was enthroned it was threatening and had not yet broken. In his first months in the Fisherman's chair he devoted much of his energy to efforts to avert it and to seeking a peaceful solution to the issues which provoked it. In that endeavour he had assets which were not at Benedict XV's hand. Thanks to the settlement of the Roman Question achieved by Pius XI he was not as bound to consider the policy of the Italian Government as Benedict XV had been. He had nunciatures and apostolic delegations in more of the world's capitals than had the Pope of World War I and so possessed more channels to the governments involved. What spiritual authority implemented by skilful diplomacy could accomplish he did, but with no more success than Benedict XV. In his first pontifical pronouncement, *Dum gravissimum,* made over the radio the day after his election, Pius XII clearly defined as the theme of his reign the unity of mankind and peace among the family of nations. He took as the motto for his reign *Opus justitiae pax.*[75] In May, 1939, he began negotiations looking towards peace. Through his representatives —but secretly rather than publicly—he presented to the chief governments involved a plan for peace. It was not accepted. Yet, undiscouraged, he continued to work for peace. The invasion of Poland by Germany on September 1, 1939, showed that his efforts had failed.[76]

When war had broken out in Europe, Pius XII continued his efforts for peace and sought to keep the conflict from spreading. In his encyclical *Summi pontificatus* (October 27, 1939), timed to meet the fortieth anniversary of the dedication of mankind by Leo XIII to the Sacred Heart of Jesus, he set forth the principles on which an inclusive human society should be constructed, but except for a brief and pointed reference to the overrunning of Poland he made no specific application to the concrete events of the year. He pointed out what

[75] *Le Encicliche Sociali dei Papi da Pio IX a Pio XII,* p. 661.

[76] Halecki, *op. cit.,* pp. 94–117; Morgan, *op. cit.,* pp. 161, 162; Koenig, *Principles for Peace,* pp. 582–586.

he regarded as the errors of the times and among them listed the forgetfulness of the law of human solidarity and charity issuing from the common origin and rational nature of all men, no matter what their race and nation. In the name of the commandment of love, he rejected racialism and extreme nationalism. He also denounced what he deemed the excessive authority currently given to the state and opposed to it the principle of natural international law. He opposed as an illusion of pride the belief in indefinite progress and the conviction that salvation would come to the people by external means. The sword, he held, could impose conditions of peace but could not create peace. The renewal of the earth could come only, he maintained, through an internal, spiritual power. The new birth of mankind which was needed, he declared, was the essential and maternal office of the Church, entrusted to it by its Divine Founder with the preaching of the Gospel. The spread of the Kingdom of God, to be accomplished by varied means and in diverse manners, was to be undertaken, so he said, in full faith in God. He welcomed the Eucharistic Congresses, Catholic Action, and the collaboration of the laity in the Church's apostolate. He pointed out that the calamity of war afforded a vast field for the display of Christian charity in all its forms, a charity which issued from Christian love, the very foundation of the Kingdom of Christ.[77]

In his Christmas allocution of December 24, 1939, Pius XII set forth five points which he believed to be essential to a just peace.[78] One was the independence of all nations, large and small, and reparation in case one nation had passed a sentence of death on another. A second was progressive disarmament mutually agreed upon by the nations. A third was the creation or reconstitution of international institutions which would not suffer from the imperfections and ineffectiveness of their predecessors. They would, he hoped, guarantee the fulfilment of obligations already assumed and revise and correct them in case of recognized need. As a fourth point, he called attention to conditions which would warrant an equitable and covenanted revision of treaties by peaceful methods and thus remove incentives to violent action. As his fifth and concluding point the Pope insisted that real peace was possible only on the principles which had been set forth in the Sermon on the Mount.

The suggestions thus enunciated by Pius XII touched responsive chords. On December 21, 1940, for example, after the further and disastrous progress of the war, they were underscored with hearty approval in a public letter in England which bore the signatures of Cardinal Hinsley, the head of the Roman Catholic hierarchy in that country, the (Anglican) Archbishops of

---

[77] *Acta Apostolicae Sedis,* Vol. XXI, pp. 413–453. An Italian translation of the text is in *Le Encicliche Sociali dei Papi da Pio IX a Pio XII,* pp. 669–704.

[78] Koenig, *op. cit.,* pp. 632–640. For this and other utterances during the war see extracts in Walker, *Pius of Peace,* pp. 16–71.

Canterbury and York, and the Moderator of the Free Church Federal Council.[79]

Although the Nazis resented the election of Pius XII and although in private audience with Joachim von Ribbentrop, the foreign minister of the Nazi regime, he named in detail the atrocities perpetrated on individuals in Poland, with few exceptions the Pope outwardly maintained a studied neutrality. One exception was his castigation of the Russian invasion of Finland as premeditated aggression. Another followed the violation by the Germans of the neutrality of Belgium, the Netherlands, and Luxembourg in 1940 when he sent messages of sympathy to the rulers of the three countries. Still another was his effort, fruitless as it proved, to induce Italy to keep out of the war. He would not, as some Nazis and Fascists had hoped, hail the German invasion of Russia as a crusade against Communism.[80]

With the entrance of Italy into the war on the side of the Nazis, Pius XII laboured to save Rome from the ravages of the conflict and to have it declared an open city. As the Allied advance moved northward and the Italian resistance began to crumble, the Germans, in possession, made the situation more precarious for the city and the Pope. The Pope turned a deaf ear to suggestions that he leave the city. More than once he visited in person bombed quarters, distributing financial aid and giving his blessing to the wounded and dying. Encouraged by him, numbers of the clergy sought to shield Jews from Nazi persecution. Bombings increased and Papal property suffered. The withdrawal of the German armies, June 4, 1944, ended the serious danger.[81]

Again and again in the course of the war Pius XII issued prayers for peace and called the faithful to prayer for that cause.[82]

Even more than Benedict XV in World War I, during World War II Pius XII rallied the resources of the Roman Catholic world to the relief of the sufferers. First to benefit were the Poles, as the initial victims. Then followed grants of food, funds, and clothing to the Finns, a predominantly Protestant people. Within a few days of the outbreak of the war Pius XII organized the Pontifical Relief Commission. Appeals were sent to every diocese of the Roman Catholic Church urging financial and material aid. As the Nazi tide engulfed more of Europe, agencies for relief were set up in various countries—Belgium, the Netherlands, Norway, Denmark, France, Jugoslavia, and Greece. Special attention was paid to prisoners of war. When, in June, 1940, Italy became a belligerent, an office was placed in neutral Lisbon for the purchase and reception of supplies from the United States and South America. During the German occupation of Rome, much food was brought into the city under Vatican

[79] Halecki, op. cit., pp. 135, 136.
[80] Ibid., pp. 142–147, 209.
[81] Ibid., pp. 176–206.
[82] Walker, op. cit., pp. 100–113; Koenig, op. cit., pp. 653, 654, 662–664, 666, 667, 691, 692, 718, 719, 738, 739, 763–765.

auspices, and soup kitchens and emergency ration stations were opened in the quarters of the poor. The Vatican Information Service obtained personal news of civilians and soldiers and sent it to interested friends and relatives. Millions of inquiries were received and messages transmitted to many different parts of the world. After the cessation of hostilities Pius XII exerted himself to obtain the early repatriation of prisoners of war and of displaced persons. He also stimulated relief of the misery which was the inevitable aftermath of war. He was especially interested in children. In 1944 he appointed the Pontifical Commission of Assistance which after the war continued to help refugees. In May, 1945, he created an International Committee of Catholic Charities, with headquarters in Paris, to coördinate local and national efforts for the victims of the war.[83]

PIUS XII AND THE PROBLEMS OF PEACE

Again and again in radio messages on Christmas eve and at other times, both during and after the war, Pius XII recurred to the problem of peace.[84] He approached the subject from a variety of angles. In the years immediately following the cessation of hostilities he expressed his regret that peace settlements were being delayed and that real peace was not being achieved. He reiterated what he deemed the essential foundations of enduring peace, noted the danger of vindictive self-righteousness on the part of the victors, and condemned the totalitarian state. He recommended the association of victors and vanquished in the work of reconstruction and observed that the development of atomic weapons made more urgent than ever attention to disarmament. Near the end of 1947 (December 18) he issued the encyclical *Optatissima pax,* in which he lamented the distance from true peace and laid the desperate condition of mankind to the fact that the Christian religion was not used to regulate private, domestic, and public life. In his Christmas message of that year he called attention to what he termed the martyrdom of China and to the absence of brotherhood in Europe, the "centre of the great Catholic family," and asked for prayers for peace. The message issued for Christmas, 1948, noted the threat of another world war and held that there were two errors widespread among statesmen—*si vis pacem, para bellum* (the conviction that preparation for war was the way to ensure peace), and peace at any price. He labelled all wars of aggression sin, called for education based on Christian principles to develop a public opinion which would assist in the development

[83] Halecki, *op. cit.,* pp. 207–220; Walker, *op. cit.,* pp. 72–99; *Enciclopedia Cattolica,* Vol. IX, p. 1548.

[84] *Le Encicliche Sociali dei Papi da Pio IX a Pio XII,* pp. 731–745, 747–767, 844–857, 871–883, 885–896, 907–920, 921–935, 937–985, 993–1003, 1021–1038; McKnight, *op. cit.,* pp. 262–271; O'Connor, *Catholic Social Doctrine,* pp. 110 ff.; *Acta Apostolicae Sedis,* Vol. XXXIX, pp. 601–604; Koenig, *op. cit.,* pp. 710–716, 766–776, 789–806.

of international solidarity, and declared that the violators of international law should be ostracized from civilized society. He expressed the hope that the United Nations might become the full and pure expression of international solidarity in peace.

In the radio Christmas message of 1949 Pius XII announced 1950 as a holy year, the year of God, and invited men to use it as a year of return—a return to God, a return of sinners to Christ, a return of dissident Christians to the Church, a return of the world to the design of God, and a return to an international society as the purpose of God. He hoped that the holy year would also be a year of pardon—pardon issuing from the penitence of men and the mercy of God. At the end of the holy year he ascribed the dissensions between states to hostility to the Church and spoke of the solicitude of the Church for the peace of the world.

In his radio message of the following (1951) Christmas, Pius XII returned to the subject of the contribution of the Church to the peace of the world and said that although the function of the Church was by no means exclusively political, the will of God in Christ was the basic guarantee of peace and of true liberty. He deplored the armaments race and stood for simultaneous and reciprocal disarmament. The Christmas, 1952, radio address was directed to the poor of mankind, for whom Pius XII had deep sympathy, and did not deal primarily with the problem of peace. It was concerned with the misery of men. It lamented the subordination of the individual to a vast industrial machine and the depersonalization of the modern man and declared that salvation could come only from God and could not be obtained through organization. He expressed himself as against oppression and persecution. In a discourse, not on Christmas eve, but not many days earlier, on December 6, 1953, the Pope took advantage of a national gathering of Italian Catholic jurists to speak his mind on nationalism and the international community. He entered into the thorny question of the restrictions placed by such a community on religious and moral liberty and pointed out that the Church was commissioned by its Founder to penetrate profoundly the heart of mankind. This, so he said, entailed inevitable conflict. In his Christmas eve message of 1954 he dealt with the "cold war" between the Communists and the "free world" and with the possibility of the coëxistence of fear and error with truth.

Even this imperfect digest of his advent messages will be evidence that Pius XII was fully aware of the international situation posed by the stage of the revolutionary age in which his reign fell.

Pius XII was keenly alive to the challenge presented by the utilization of atomic energy either for the destruction or for the benefit of mankind. For instance, in his Easter message of 1955 he extended his blessing not only to those who belonged to the church which he headed and to those of its members who were suffering persecution for their faith but also to "all men of good will" and all whose activity had a decisive influence for the good of humanity. He blessed the latter that they might arrange for treaties which would ensure peace and start progressive disarmament. He exhorted men of science and good will to persevere in their study of nuclear energy that it might be directed to the welfare of men. He noted the peril of radioactivity to human genes and hence to posterity.[85] In 1957 he reiterated his conviction that nuclear weapons should not be employed, and in a note on April 14 of that year to the representative of the Premier of Japan he expressed his hope that all nations would master nuclear energy for the service of men instead of expending their efforts on "a terrifying and costly march towards death." In view of the adverse attitude of Japanese public opinion at that time towards the testing of nuclear weapons in the Pacific by the United States it could be inferred that the Pope favoured the abandonment of all tests of such weapons.[86] It will be noted that not only in an earlier blanket statement but also in the specific message to the Japanese Premier Pius XII appealed to the coöperation of all men of good will. In this he followed in the footsteps of Pius XI.

Pius XII also concerned himself with other specific issues affecting peace. For instance, in encyclicals in 1948 and 1949 he dealt with the subject of Jerusalem and other places in Palestine regarded by Christians as holy. He advocated placing Jerusalem and the surrounding territory under a United Nations trusteeship guaranteeing to pilgrims free access to the holy places.[87]

As may be gathered from his discourse of December 6, 1953, Pius XII was in favour of international organizations which had hope of ensuring peace and coöperation among nations. In contrast with Benedict XV, who, as we have seen, was highly critical of the League of Nations, and with Pius XI, who publicly disparaged the League, Pius XII, although not enthusiastic about the United Nations, did not formally disapprove it. Yet in his Christmas message of 1945 he spoke out against "a musty liberalism" which "strove to create, without the Church or in opposition to her, a unity built on lay culture and secularized humanism."[88] On November 12, 1948, to delegates of the second international congress of the European Union of Federalists, he expressed the hope that the European Union would be promptly created and that the peoples of Europe would rise above "their egotistically nationalistic preoccupations."[89]

PIUS XII AND THE CHURCH AS A BOND OF HUMAN UNITY

Although he regarded its primary function as not the achievement of inter-

---

[85] *The New York Times,* April 11, 1955.
[86] *Ibid.,* May 1, 1957.
[87] *Ibid.,* May 1, 1957.
[88] McKnight, *op. cit.,* p. 271.
[89] O'Connor, *op. cit.,* p. 128.

national peace but rather the eternal salvation of souls, Pius XII deemed the Church to be a supranational divine society which with its inclusive ties made for the realization of the unity of mankind. He regarded the Church as having indivisible unity and, consistently with the traditions of his office, believed that unity to have Rome as its centre, as the seat of the Vicar of Christ.[90] To this end he supported the world mission of the Roman Catholic Church. He also, in creating new cardinals, chose them from peoples in widely different portions of the earth, thus giving to the princes of the Church a nearly global representation. In the consistory of February 18, 1946, he raised to the purple men not only from several European countries but also from the United States, Canada, five Latin American republics, Australia, Mozambique, and China. Heading the list was the Patriarch of the Armenians of Cilicia.[91]

PIUS XII AND COMMUNISM

As had his two immediate predecessors, Pius XII saw in Communism one of the most dangerous enemies of the Church. Indeed, it was even more formidable than in their reigns, for during his pontificate, as part of the aftermath of World War II, it took possession of Poland, Czechoslovakia, and Hungary, where Roman Catholics were in the majority, and of other countries, the largest of which was China, where the Roman Catholic Church was represented by minorities. In some countries in Western Europe Communist parties were active.

Pius XII regarded Communism as a major challenge to Christianity. On one occasion and another he spoke out against it, sometimes indirectly, sometimes explicitly. He excommunicated Roman Catholics who had joined with Communists in specific measures against Roman Catholic prelates. He also excommunicated those who sought to draw away the faithful into schismatic Catholic churches—as in Czechoslovakia and China. On July 1, 1949, he issued a sweeping excommunication of all Roman Catholics who were participating in Communist programmes. This included membership in a Communist Party and the circulation or reading of publications supporting Communism.[92] The Pope made it clear (September 25, 1950) that in condemning Communism he was not, as Communist critics were saying, aligning himself with capitalism, but urged that the clergy oppose the errors in both systems by maintaining the social doctrines which had been repeatedly set forth by himself and his predecessors.[93]

Pius XII also again and again expressed himself vigorously on concrete in-

[90] Allocution of December 24, 1945, in *Le Encicliche Sociali dei Papi da Pio IX a Pio XII*, pp. 847–855.
[91] Halecki, *op. cit.*, p. 233.
[92] McKnight, *op. cit.*, pp. 315, 316; Halecki, *op. cit.*, pp. 272, 273.
[93] Halecki, *op. cit.*, pp. 275, 276.

stances of Communist restrictions on the Roman Catholic Church and of Communist persecution. He gave his support to positive efforts to curb Communism and to resist Communist-inspired measures. A few examples will serve in place of what, if a complete account, would extend to many pages. In September, 1945, the Provisional Government of National Unity set up in Poland by the Communists denounced the concordat of 1925 on the ground that the Vatican had violated it. The Pope continued to recognize as legitimate the Polish government-in-exile. He backed the Polish bishops in their resistance to the Communist effort to create a Polish Catholic church independent of the Holy See. In the consistory of February 18, 1946, among those raised to the cardinalate was a Polish archbishop who had been outstanding in his resistance to the occupation.[94] In view of the mass deportations of Roman Catholic Lithuanians and the large number of displaced persons from the Baltic countries in Western Europe, in 1946 Pius XII founded the Lithuanian Ecclesiastical Institute for exiled Lithuanian priests.[95] On October 6, 1946, in an official address at the time of the trial of Stepinac, Archbishop of Zagreb and Primate of Croatia, by a Communist court under the Tito dictatorship in Jugoslavia, Pius XII came out in defense of the accused.[96] He was also deeply concerned with the pressures brought on the Roman Catholic Church in Hungary and especially in the trial and condemnation of its Primate, Cardinal Mindszenty (January, February, 1949). In an address on February 14, 1949, he excoriated the methods employed in the trial and emphatically denied the charge that the Holy See was seeking to dominate Europe. He said that while the Roman Catholic Church did not object to a form of government which was not in contrast with divine and human rights, in case of such a contrast the bishops and their flocks must oppose laws which they deemed unjust.[97] Pius XII was happy when, in 1956, the Roman Catholic Church seemed to him to have come successfully through the struggle with Communism in Poland and Hungary. In the encyclical *Laetamur admodum* (November 1, 1956) he noted with joy that Cardinal Wyszynski, Archbishop of Gniesno and Warsaw, and Cardinal Mindszenty, Archbishop of Esztergom, had been re-admitted to the dioceses from which they had been expelled.[98] In December, 1956, the Polish Government, although Communist-led, yielded on the veto power which it claimed to ecclesiastical appointments and agreed to permit religious instruction in the schools to any requesting it.[99] In Italy, where after World War II the monarchy was overturned, largely by a combined Com-

[94] *Ibid.*, pp. 243–248.
[95] *Ibid.*, p. 251.
[96] *Ibid.*, pp. 253, 254.
[97] *Ibid.*, pp. 256, 257.
[98] *The New York Times*, November 3, 1956; *Acta Apostolicae Sedis*, Vol. XLVIII, pp. 745–749.
[99] *The New York Times*, December 1 and 8, 1956.

munist and left-wing Socialist vote, Pius XII, believing that the issue between Communism and Christianity was clearly joined, called the faithful to action. While not specifically approving any one party, he urged that Catholics support only those parties which were fighting against the enemies of Christ. Catholic organizations of many kinds rose to the occasion and, aided by the parish priests, carried the campaign to the local churches. The result was the sweeping victory of the Christian Democrats and a government headed by their leader.[100]

Here was a struggle between Communism and the Roman Catholic Church which centred in Europe but extended to other parts of the globe as well—notably, as we are to see in the next volume, to China. When, in September, 1947, the Cominform (Communist Information Bureau) was organized in Warsaw by representatives of the Soviet Union and of Communist parties in several other countries to replace the Cominterm which had ostensibly been dissolved in 1943, it became an instrument not only of united Communist action and propaganda against the Western powers, and especially the United States, but also a means of countering the Roman Catholic Church. In 1949 it decided to support the formation of a Catholic church in Poland independent of the Holy See and in 1950 it created the Orginform to sow religious dissension in countries where the Roman Catholic Church was powerful and to train leaders in special schools for action against that church.[101] The contest was between two movements, each aspiring to enlist all mankind, each with comprehensive but reciprocally contradictory convictions about the nature of the universe and man, and each supported by a far-reaching organization. In the course of our narrative we shall meet it again and again.

PIUS XII AND SOCIAL AND ECONOMIC ISSUES

The issue posed by Communism was only one of several affecting the social and economic life of mankind which were dealt with by Pius XII. Like his predecessor, Pius XII was keenly alive to the changes in these areas brought by the stage of the revolutionary age in which his lot was cast.

In accordance with the long-standing position of the Roman Pontiffs, Pius XII, in an allocution on November 3, 1954, to the hierarchy assembled for the Marian year, declared that to seek to limit the Church's authority to purely religious matters was an error against which the faithful must take a firm stand. He said that social problems, whether merely social or socio-political, were of concern to the conscience and salvation of men and so were under the care of the Church. He held that the Church's power extended to the wide range of natural law, the law implanted by God in the minds of His reasoning

---

[100] Halecki, *op. cit.*, pp. 342, 344.
[101] *Ibid.*, pp. 266, 267.

creatures, and to the moral aspects of its interpretation and application. Instructions published by the Pope within the domain of moral law, so he maintained, must be obeyed, even though to some they might not seem to be in accord with reason. Among the subjects which he outlined as falling in this category were the purpose and limits of temporal authority; the relations between the individual and the totalitarian state; the complete laicization of the state, of public life, and of schools divorced from ecclesiastical control; the morality of modern war and the question of whether a conscientious person might give or withhold participation in war; and moral relationships among the nations. He condemned the tendency among Roman Catholics to think that supervision by the Church was not to be suffered by adults and that in their personal decisions no intermediary was to be placed between them and God.[102] Although not as sweeping as the Syllabus of Errors of Pius IX, the allocution had kinship with it.

Pius XII made no statement on economics and industry which was as comprehensive and which attracted as much attention as the *Rerum novarum* of Leo XIII or the *Quadragesimo anno* of Pius XI. Presumably, in view of the two documents, particularly since the second was fairly recent, he did not deem it necessary. Yet again and again he recurred to problems with which they dealt, largely by addresses on particular occasions, usually to special groups or congresses, either in Rome or, by radio, to assemblies in other cities.[103] He noted that labour, faced by a complexity of organizations, saw human life transformed into a giant automaton, in which men were only cogs. He deplored both the narrowly individualistic order which brooked no control and the totalitarian state with its contempt for the dignity of the human person. He declared that Christians had a duty to share in the solution of the problems of social justice and said that because of the new conditions brought by World War II the question was not merely one of the more equitable distribution of the products of the social economy but included as well the relations between agriculture and industry within individual nations and the manner and extent in which each nation was to share in the world market. He said that every true follower of Christ must seek to participate in improving the condition of the proletariat. He held that not only the social status of workers, both men and women, called for reform, but also the whole complex structure of society, shaken as it was to its foundations, was in need of adjustment and improvement. He believed that the establishment of associations or corporate groups would be more conducive to this end than the nationalization of industry. He appealed to the Catholics of the entire world not to be content with good in-

---

[102] *The New York Times,* November 4, 1954.

[103] See a list in Eberdt and Schnepp, *Industrialism and the Popes,* pp. 198–202. See some of the texts in *Le Encicliche Sociali dei Papi da Pio IX a Pio XII,* pp. 987–991, 1005–1019, 1039–1046, 1083–1089, and in Hughes, *The Popes' New Order,* pp. 175–182.

tentions but to seek to put them into effect and in doing so to coöperate with all who, although not of their number, were in agreement with the social teachings of the Catholic Church. He was emphatic that class struggle was not inevitable, but insisted that management and labour were linked together in a community of interest and action. He appealed for a new organization of the productive forces which would be in accord with *Quadragesimo anno*. He favoured bringing the element of partnership into wage contracts and assuring labour participation in the organization and development of the national economy. Yet this did not mean, he said, to give wage earners a share in the management of the industry in which they were employed. He opposed all-embracing socialization as the nightmare of Leviathan and stressed, as had his predecessors, the right of private property as essential to human dignity and the salvation of the soul. He did not deny that the state had the right and the duty to intervene in social and economic issues but held that a happy mean must be found between that intervention and totalitarian control. He maintained that whatever the form of government, its rulers must remember that God is the paramount ruler of the world.[104]

Pius XII did not write an encyclical on marriage or the family, but again and again he addressed himself to these subjects. He granted many audiences to the newly married and spoke to them on the state into which they had entered. He stressed the proper education of children. He urged prospective parents to dedicate themselves and their families to the Sacred Heart of Jesus. To reform society, he said, the re-Christianization of the family was necessary. While granting that abstinence to protect the health of the mother was legitimate, he denounced as immoral attempts to deprive the conjugal act of the procreation of new life. He also condemned sterilization, artificial insemination, and abortion. He sought to protect the family and to this end endorsed private property, deplored poor housing and unemployment, and stood firmly against all violation of the marriage vow.[105] He dealt with matrimonial questions in the canon law.[106]

PIUS XII: THEOLOGY AND BIBLICAL STUDIES

Outstanding as were his efforts for world peace, against Communism and totalitarianism, and for the realization of a better economic and social order, Pius XII will probably be longest remembered for his promulgations on dogma and theology.

Of these the most notable was his apostolic constitution *Munificentissimus Deus,* issued November 1, 1950, towards the close of the holy year, in which,

104 Eberdt and Schnepp, *op. cit.,* pp. 9, 14–16, 20, 29, 37, 57, 61, 63, 83, 84, 89, 106.
105 O'Connor, *op. cit.,* pp. 160–187.
106 *Enciclopedia Cattolica,* Vol. IX, p. 1550.

in the presence of a great throng of bishops and other ecclesiastics, he proclaimed as dogma to be accepted by all the faithful the bodily assumption into heaven of Mary. As, nearly a century earlier, the proclamation of the immaculate conception of Mary was held to be simply a formal pronouncement of what had been from the beginning part of the deposit of faith entrusted to the Church, so now, Pius XII believed, a rising tide within the Church called for a clear statement of what he said had been an article of faith among Catholics from the earliest times. Although, as was true of the dogma of the immaculate conception, complete unanimity had not existed among theologians, increasingly a demand was being made for unequivocal definition. Petitions had been coming in spontaneously and when the bishops were canvassed, in a fashion that had likenesses to a council of the Roman Catholic Church, the response showed an overwhelming desire for a solemn statement, an expression of Papal infallibility.[107] Here was a further stage in the emphasis by the Roman Catholic Church on the Virgin Mary, a theological expression of what had characterized the devotional life of Roman Catholics in the nineteenth century, as, indeed, it had in earlier times. It followed naturally from the Papal endorsement of the immaculate conception. In that spirit was the earlier (October 1, 1942) consecration of the human race to the Immaculate Heart of Mary[108] and the proclamation on September 9, 1953, of a special Marian year in commemoration of the centennial of the definition of the dogma of the immaculate conception. In the course of that year, on November 1, 1954, the Pope instituted the feast of the Virgin Mary.[109]

Earlier, in the encyclical *Mystici corporis Christi* (June 29, 1943) Pius XII dealt with the Church as the mystical body of Christ.[110] Here he was endorsing a strain in Roman Catholic theology which had been strikingly developed in the nineteenth century, notably by Johann Adam Möhler.[111] It was regarded as the major modern pronouncement on ecclesiology. In it Pius XII held that the Church as the mystical body of Christ is one, indivisible, visible, organically compact, and identical with the Roman Catholic Church. He said that the Church is provided with the sacraments as the means of salvation, was founded on the preaching of the Gospel and the redemption of the cross, and spread after Pentecost. He affirmed that it is directed by bishops and the Pope, and through it the faithful have a mysterious union with Christ and are saved by His blood.

Complementary to *Mystici corporis Christi* was the encyclical *Mediator Dei*

[107] *Acta Apostolicae Sedis*, Vol. XLII, pp. 753–771; *Enciclopedia Cattolica*, Vol. VIII, pp. 1516, 1517, Vol. IX, pp. 1549, 1551.
[108] *Enciclopedia Cattolica*, Vol. IX, p. 1551.
[109] *The New York Times*, October 10, 1958.
[110] *Acta Apostolicae Sedis*, Vol. XXV, pp. 193–248.
[111] Volume I, p. 379.

(November 20, 1947).[112] In it Pius XII dealt with the nature of the liturgy, the essence of the mass, the participation of the laity, and the Eucharistic sacrifice. He approved of the Liturgical Movement, the beginnings of which we have already remarked[113] and the development of which we will follow in another chapter. Yet he warned against unwise deviations.

Pius XII was aware of the intellectual currents which were a contemporary phase of the revolutionary age and which affected Biblical and theological studies. In *Divino Afflante Spiritu* (September 30, 1943) he dealt specifically with Biblical scholarship. He encouraged scientific methods of determining more accurately the original texts of the Scriptures. He also endorsed the use of the exegesis of the Fathers in interpreting the Scriptures.[114]

In *Humani generis* (August 12, 1950) Pius XII addressed himself primarily to theology.[115] He deplored the threat to Catholic doctrine posed by such movements as Modernism, neo-Kantianism, Marxism, and rationalism. He regarded as especially menacing the criticism which said that scholastic philosophy was not meeting the questions raised by modern thought. He dealt with existentialism, positivism, relativism, and universal evolution. He had in mind especially the existentialism and mysticism which were cropping up in the Roman Catholic Church under the tutelage of such French Biblical and patristic scholars as Jean Daniélou and Henri de Lubac, of whom we are to hear more in a later chapter. Yet he did not pillory specific individuals by naming them. While denying that he would have Catholic culture isolated from the surrounding climate of opinion, he frowned on what he regarded as the imprudence of Catholics who in the effort to be irenical compromised the integrity of the faith and the traditional doctrines of the Church. He condemned the views of those who on what he said was the pretense of going to the sources declared that Jesus had not founded the Church as the unique depository and interpreter of the word of God. He also came out against efforts to supplant dogma with a philosophy of religion and a dogmatic relativism and to substitute another form of philosophy for scholastic theology. He regretted what he deemed an incautious tendency to accept hypotheses of historical criticism as demonstrated conclusions. He reproved what he labelled the errors of philosophy and a new theology which viewed the authority of the Church as an impediment. He reaffirmed the emphasis of his immediate predecessors on Aquinas.

Pius XII took the occasion of the fifteenth centennial of the Council of Chalcedon to issue the encyclical *Sempiternus rex Christus* (September 8, 1951). In it he traced the history of the Council and of the part played in it by Pope

---

112 *Acta Apostolicae Sedis,* Vol. XXXIX, pp. 521–595.
113 Volume I, p. 358.
114 *Acta Apostolicae Sedis,* Vol. XXXV, pp. 297–325.
115 *Ibid.,* Vol. XLII, pp. 561–578.

Leo I and his *Tome*. He stressed the importance of the dogmatic formulations of Chalcedon and sought to warn the faithful against errors that were creeping in which compromised the unity of the person of Christ, and especially a form of kenoticism which was appearing among non-Catholics. He ended with an appeal to the dissident Oriental Christians to return to the Apostolic See.[116] Yet he encouraged the translation of the Psalter from the original texts which was being undertaken by the Pontifical Biblical Institute.[117]

Pius XII: Other Actions

Pius XII took within his comprehensive view still other phases of the life and work of the Roman Catholic Church. He encouraged Catholic Action, concerned himself with the recruiting and preparation of the clergy, and in the *Motu proprio Quotidianis precibus* (March 24, 1945) promoted the recitation of the breviary.[118] He endorsed the Pontifical Academy of Science. He announced what he regarded as finally established by archeological investigations which he had approved: the discovery of the grave of Peter under the high altar of the cathedral which bore the Apostle's name. While warning its practitioners against dangers and abuses, he endorsed psychoanalysis.[119]

Pius XII and the World Mission

If Pius XII did not stand out as prominently as Pope of the missions as had Pius XI, he was by no means oblivious to the importance of the world-wide spread of the faith and gave it his unqualified support. Down to the end of 1951 he had erected 85 new bishoprics and archbishoprics and 123 vicariates and prefectures apostolic. In areas which were regarded as the mission field, by that date he had created 37 new vicariates apostolic and 35 prefectures apostolic.[120] He threw the weight of his office on the side of an indigenous clergy and episcopate. The increase was notable in many lands but especially in China and in Africa south of the Sahara. In both areas native priests multiplied and an increasing proportion of the territory was placed under the supervision of indigenous bishops. In the first year of his pontificate, in St. Peter's, Pius XII consecrated twelve bishops representing all the continents. Among them were a Malagasy and a Ugandan, the latter the first African from south of the Sahara to be raised to that dignity since early in the sixteenth century. In his encyclicals *Evangelii praecones* (June 2, 1951) and *Fidei donum* (April 21, 1957) he called the Roman Catholic world to the support of missions, and

[116] *Ibid.*, Vol. XLIII, pp. 625–644.
[117] *Enciclopedia Cattolica*, Vol. IX, p. 1549.
[118] *Acta Apostolicae Sedis*, Vol. XXXVII, pp. 65–72.
[119] *Enciclopedia Cattolica*, Vol. IX, pp. 1549, 1551.
[120] *Ibid.*, p. 1551.

in the latter document singled out Africa as peculiarly urgent. Only a few days before his death he sent an encouraging message to an assembly of the rectors of Latin American major seminaries.[121] The number of Roman Catholics in Asia and Africa mounted. The growth was particularly striking in large portions of equatorial Africa.

PIUS XII: AN APPRAISAL

In any appraisal of the reign of Pius XII at least five facts must be borne in mind. First, like that of Benedict XV, the inception and much of the course of the pontificate of Pius XII fell in a period of a world war which centred in the historic Christendom and which dealt severe blows to most of the traditional strongholds of the Roman Catholic Church. Second, also as in the reign of Benedict XV, the political revolutions following the war shook the fabric of Christendom and confronted the Church with resolute enemies who were intent on weakening or even destroying the Church and eradicating the faith of which it was an expression. Third, Pius XII brought to his high post diplomatic rather than administrative experience and combined it with a deep piety of the traditional Roman Catholic pattern. Fourth, by background, temperament, and training Pius XII was conservative. Viewing the Roman Catholic Church as a superhuman institution designed by the Founder to be supra-national and to embrace all mankind, he was convinced that it must pursue that mission by adhering closely to its historic faith and devotional life. Fifth, during several of his later years Pius XII had severe illnesses which sapped his physical and mental energies. Although he kept indomitably at his work, he could not bring to it the creative energy of his earlier days.

Under these circumstances, the major achievements of Pius XII were steering the bark of Peter with an amazing degree of success through the storm of World War II and its aftermath and in the face of counter-currents keeping that bark on its traditional doctrinal course. Notably in affirming the bodily assumption of Mary and in *Humani generis* he held that bark firmly in the direction in which it had long been moving. In addition, he left to his church a legacy of high courage, unwavering faith, and transparently sincere piety.

With all of his sturdy adherence to the Roman Catholic faith, Pius XII was vividly aware of the many aspects of the revolutionary age. He was more openly willing, as in his Christmas message of 1944, to make room for political democracy than had been any of his predecessors. He employed the new media for mass communication, such as the radio, to speak to all the world—both to those of his church and to those outside it. In the nuclear armaments race he raised his voice again and again to warn mankind of the perils in-

---

[121] *Acta Apostolicae Sedis*, Vol. XLIII, pp. 497–528, Vol. XLIX, pp. 225–248.

volved and thus supported all men of good will who were seeking peaceful solutions.

JOHN XXIII (1948———)

The choice of the conclave of cardinals which fixed on a successor to Pius XII fell on Angelo Giusèppe Roncalli (1881———). Roncalli was born at the foot of the Alps, near Bergamo, north-east of Milan. He was one of nine children of humble farm workers. He studied in the seminary at Bergamo, took a doctorate of theology in Rome, became secretary to the Bishop of Bergamo, accompanied the latter on frequent visits to France, and acquired a fluent command of the language of that country. He was a military chaplain in World War I. Benedict XV made him an aide in the Congregation for the Propagation of the Faith and Pius XI gave him a diplomatic mission to the Middle East. Pius XII used him as Apostolic Nuncio to France and Permanent Observer for the Holy See in UNESCO. In the year 1953 he was created cardinal and appointed Patriarch of Venice. His motto, *Obediencia et pax,* was descriptive of the man. Genial, he sought to promote friendly understanding among the rival groups in Venice. At the same time he demanded obedience from his clergy.[122] In spite of his advanced age, John XXIII brought to his office marked physical vigour and the will to make important modifications in Vatican policy. With pastoral, diplomatic, and administrative experience he had broad qualifications for the chair of Peter. His unashamed loyalty to his peasant family and his early visit to a hospice of aged and retired priests in Rome brought him affectionate popularity in many quarters. Similarly he won wide approbation by a personal visit to the prisoners in one of Rome's jails. Early in his reign (January 25, 1959) he announced that he would have the canon law revised and would publish the canon law of the Oriental Churches; that he would call a synod for the city of Rome to care for its religious needs; and that he would convene an ecumenical council having among its objectives the union of all Christians, especially the Eastern Churches. The synod for the Diocese of Rome met in January, 1961. Among other measures it forbade priests to marry persons who held Communist, materialistic, or other anti-Christian principles; prohibited artificial insemination, direct sterilization, or abortion; enjoined the priests to explain extreme unction; commanded the clergy to bury the dead of the poor free of charge and to conduct funerals with dignity and without lavish decorations; encouraged the faithful to sing at religious ceremonies; declared that the Church had the right to remind the faithful of their duty at election time; and urged all Catholics to coöperate in defense of religion and of the Church.[123] By 1961 preparations were under way for the

---

[122] *The New York Times,* October 29, 1958.
[123] *Ibid.,* January 25, 27, 28, 1960.

ecumenical council. John XXIII's interest in the world-wide extension of the faith and its rootage among non-Western peoples was seen in his elevation to the cardinalate of an African, a Filipino, and a Japanese, a precedent earlier established for India and China.[124]

SUMMARY

As we have suggested, in the half-century after 1914 the Papacy faced challenges brought by the revolutionary age which, while different, were in some respects fraught with graver peril than those which confronted it in 1815. To be sure, at the dawn of the nineteenth century the storm of the French Revolution had but recently spent its force. It left behind a legacy of anti-clericalism, scepticism, and seething forces and movements which were to break out again and again in the next ten decades. Yet in retrospect, compared with what preceded and followed them, those decades seemed relatively quiet.

Now, beginning in 1914, the Papacy and the church which it headed faced more prolonged and widespread threats than had been presented to it even by the French Revolution and Napoleon. Two world wars drew into their maelstrom most of the portions of the earth in which that church had long had its chief strength. Accompanying and following the wars were vast upheavals. In the interval between the two wars, Roman Catholic Spain, although a neutral in the two global struggles, was torn by devastating civil strife in which the religious issue was prominent. Communism, more blatantly atheistic than had been the French Revolution except during a short period, captured much of Europe, including countries—Poland, Lithuania, Czechoslovakia, and Hungary—where Roman Catholics were in the majority, and infiltrated France, "the eldest daughter of the Church," and even Italy, where was the Pope's seat. More subtle but possibly more dangerous were the disintegration by mounting industrialization of the patterns of life in Western Europe with which Christianity had long been associated, the creeping secularism, and the scepticism born of the intellectual currents of the day. The menaces had their sources in Western Europe, the heartland of the Roman Catholic Church, and spread to the geographic frontiers of that church—to the Americas, Asia, and Africa.

Yet, as we have more than once noted, great though the menaces were, in the decades after 1914 the Papacy was in a better position to meet them than it had been a hundred years earlier. The triumph of ultramontanism, facilitated by the mechanical means of rapid travel and communication which were a fruit of the revolutionary age and furthered by the ability of the Pontiffs of the nineteenth century, especially those in its second half, united the Roman

---

[124] *Ibid.*, March 4, 1960.

Catholic Church more firmly under Papal direction than at any previous time. Loyalty was enhanced by the remarkable growth of religious orders and congregations which provided the Papacy with a mounting body of dedicated men and women. Among many of the laity more frequent Communion was nourishing faith.

Added to these assets was the quality of the Pontiffs who beginning in 1914 were elevated to the Holy See. All were men of more than average intelligence and ability, hard-working, devoted, and without the vices which had been a scandal in some earlier periods of the office. All were Italians, but all came to their high office seasoned by long experience and with a diplomatic background which had exposed them to conditions in other countries. Through their hundreds of visitors and their representatives throughout most of the world, the twentieth-century Popes were kept in touch with events and movements the world over. All the post-1914 Popes sought to strengthen the inner life of their church and to preserve the adherence of the faithful to the doctrines and means of salvation which they believed had been entrusted to that church by Christ. Following what they were profoundly convinced was the divine commission to their church, each of the twentieth-century Popes, and especially Popes Pius XI and XII, endeavoured to speak to all mankind and to enlist men of good will everywhere, regardless of their religious affiliation, in the promotion of peace. They addressed the world on the burning issues which involved the entire human race.

How far the voice of the Popes was heeded would be difficult to determine. One Communist leader was reported to have asked scornfully how many divisions the Pope had to support him. Even had he wished to do so, no Pope of the twentieth century could have successfully invoked a crusade as had some of his predecessors in the eleventh, twelfth, and thirteenth centuries. The force of the appeal of the Popes of the twentieth century was to the intelligence and the conscience of mankind. But they did not have as large a part as did Protestants in bringing into being such instruments for international coöperation and the peaceful settlement of disputes among peoples as the League of Nations and the United Nations or a relief agency as extensive as the Red Cross. Yet their words had a wide circulation and, at least among the loyal core of Roman Catholics, were not without effect.

The Roman Catholic Church headed by the twentieth-century Popes presented striking contrasts. On the one hand it had many aspects of a government which sought to bring under its jurisdiction all the human race. Through the Lateran Accord (1929) it gained recognition by the Italian Government of the status which it had long claimed—that of a sovereign state—although now limited to a few acres. To it came an increasing number of diplomats accredited by other governments. It had diplomatic representatives in many countries, and in several capitals, by a precedent established at the Congress of Vienna in 1815, they were the *doyens* of the diplomatic corps. In the Vatican the Popes maintained a pomp unequalled in any other court of the century. No other Christian church was headed by an ecclesiastic who exercised the prerogatives of a ruler of an independent state. A body of canon law regulated many aspects of the lives of the faithful which nineteenth- and twentieth-century civil governments sought to bring under their control. Here was much of *Romanitas,* the tradition of imperial Rome. The Popes ruled over the largest of the Christian churches and claimed that by the institution of Christ they by right had authority over all who bore the Christian name. That authority, by formal recognition of the Vatican Council (1869-1870), was held to be absolute in administration and infallible in matters of faith and morals. The conflict with counter claims of other systems was made vivid in the twentieth century by the struggle with Communism.

On the other hand, the Popes of the twentieth century could not and did not invoke armed force to support their authority. They depended upon the arm of the spirit. They and the church which they ruled extolled humility—so that by long tradition in the midst of the Papal coronation straw was burned and the new Pontiff was admonished to recall that it was the symbol that all the outward circumstance by which he was surrounded would vanish. In their private apartments the twentieth-century Popes for the most part lived abstemiously, almost ascetically. They preached love and endeavoured to promote it by deed as well as word. The church which they headed sought to promote a kind of sanctity which had self-effacing faith, prayer, and service among its distinguishing hall-marks and through canonization recognized them, often in otherwise obscure individuals, as worthy of emulation by all Christians. The Popes endeavoured to gather all men into a society which, living in faith in the God Who made Himself known in Him Who was born in a manger and suffered death on a Roman cross, was believed to encompass not only those now in the flesh but also an innumerable host of the departed.

CHAPTER IV

The Roman Catholic Church Is Reinforced by the Growth of Orders and Congregations and by Lay Organizations

A STRIKING feature of the Roman Catholic Church in the twentieth century was the growth of organizations which enlisted an increasing number of the faithful in the attempt to make Christianity effective in the revolutionary age. Some of the organizations were orders and congregations of the "religious" —those who, taking the vows of poverty, chastity, and obedience, dedicated themselves fully to the service of the Church. Others, while under the direction of the clergy, were composed primarily of laity who were engaged in "secular" occupations.

Earlier[1] we called attention to the fact that the revival of orders and the emergence of new congregations were among evidences of mounting vitality, and that in the nineteenth century not only were several existing orders and congregations renewed and strengthened but more new congregations came into being than in any preceding century. We also remarked that more of the new congregations arose in France than in any other country, and this in the face of a situation in which the Roman Catholic Church was more vigorously challenged than in any other European land.

In the first half of the twentieth century, in proportion to the span of time involved, far fewer new congregations appeared than in the nineteenth century. However, a number of the existing orders and congregations augmented their membership and established themselves in additional centres. Further, more organizations of the laity sprang up than in the nineteenth century. Indeed, in the Roman Catholic Church the twentieth century could be known as the century of the laity. For the most part the lay organizations were designed to meet specific needs and conditions emerging from the revolutionary age. In accordance with the traditions of the Roman Catholic Church, they either were under the supervision of the clergy or worked in close association with

[1] Volume I, Chapter VIII.

them. They were evidence that, as in the nineteenth century, the Roman Catholic Church, headed by the Popes, was increasingly a world-wide organization directed from one centre and supported by a body of loyal men and women recruited from every race and nation. Significantly, too, as in the nineteenth century more of the new congregations arose in France, the country in Europe where the faith was most openly and vigorously challenged, so more of the fresh organizations of the twentieth century sprang up in Western Europe, the source of the movements which were threatening the very existence of Christianity, than in any other part of the world.

GROWTH IN THE MEMBERSHIP OF THE ORDERS AND CONGREGATIONS

We cannot take the space for a detailed account of the orders and congregations of the Roman Catholic Church, but a few facts and figures may give some indication of what a complete record would disclose.

The oldest of the orders, the Benedictines, increased its members from 2,765 in 1880 to 10,356 in 1935.[2] Several new monasteries were founded and some were raised to the status of abbeys—as in Belgium, Germany, Switzerland, Portugal, England, the United States, Brazil, Venezuela, Angola, South Africa, Cameroun, China, Japan, and the Philippines.[3] A number of Benedictines who lived into the twentieth century were prolific as authors of books of devotion. More of them were in France, Belgium, Germany, and England that elsewhere.[4] Several Benedictine nuns whose lives spanned the latter part of the nineteenth and the fore part of the twentieth century were outstanding as mystics. They were found mostly in France, Germany, and the United States.[5]

The Conventuals, a branch of the Franciscans who did not come into the union of four bodies of the Brothers Minor which was achieved in the 1890's, enjoyed a revival after World War I and by mid-century were in a number of countries. For example, they were represented in France and in Central and South America in the 1940's. In 1949 they had 3,340 members in 434 convents in 32 provinces.[6] In 1948, when they held an international congress in Rome, the Capuchins, who had also remained out of the union of the 1890's, had 14,095 members in 1,126 houses in 35 provinces. The main branch of the Franciscans, that of the union, also continued to grow.[7]

The Dominicans did not prosper numerically as much as did the Franciscans. In about 1949 they had 7,661 members in 33 provinces.[8]

---

[2] *Enciclopedia Cattolica*, Vol. II, p. 1241.
[3] Philibert Schmitz, *Histoire de l'Ordre de Saint Benoît* (Les Editions de Maredsous, 7 vols., 1948–1956), Vol. IV, pp. 184, 188, 190, 199, 200, 204, 208, 209, 213–219.
[4] *Ibid.*, Vol. VI, pp. 313, 326.
[5] *Ibid.*, Vol. VII, pp. 349–352.
[6] *Enciclopedia Cattolica*, Vol. V, p. 1734.
[7] *Ibid.*, p. 1741.
[8] *Ibid.*, p. 1750.

The Society of Jesus displayed a marked growth, in spite of political storms in several countries which cost it dearly. During the revolution and civil war in Spain in the 1930's a number of the houses of the Society were burned, and in 1936, 118 Jesuits lost their lives. Yet after the restoration of order the Society revived: in 1948 a sixth province was added to the earlier five and the total membership was reported as 5,180, of whom 533 were serving in missions among non-Christians. In the neighbouring Portugal the revolution of 1910 had expelled the Jesuits, but some began secretly to make their way back and in 1933 they were permitted to renew their teaching and other activities; in 1948 they had 481 members. The Jesuits flourished in Belgium and from them extensive missions in India and the Congo were staffed. In England the Jesuits increased from 673 in 1900 to 899 in 1950. In Spanish and Portuguese America the Society also prospered, and in 1938 the seven Latin American provinces were brought together for administrative purposes into an "assistance." The outcome of World War I made possible the enlargement of Jesuit activity among Slavic peoples. For example, several Jesuits affiliated themselves with the Oriental rite to aid the Uniate churches and to seek to bring the Orthodox to submission to Rome. In Germany the restrictive legislation against the Jesuits which was part of the *Kulturkampf* was not markedly eased after that conflict had been resolved. But as an aftermath of World War I the Society was able to reëstablish itself in Germany and in 1938 it had three provinces with a membership of 1,706. World War II and the reduction of German territory which followed it brought the number down to 1,249 in 1950. In spite of vicissitudes, the total membership of the Society of Jesus rose from 15,073 in 1900 to 16,894 in 1914 and to 30,579 in 1950 grouped in 46 provinces, 9 vice-provinces, and 52 missions. Significantly, in the United States of America the Society had 11 provinces and more than a quarter of its membership.[9]

The Congregation of the Mission, better known as the Vincentians or Lazarists, which in 1909 had 3,249 members in all five continents and in the islands of the sea,[10] in 1949 had 5,299 members in 37 provinces and 456 houses.[11]

The Salesians of Don Bosco continued the amazing growth which they had displayed in the nineteenth century. When the founder died (1888) they had about 250 houses. In 1950 they had 1,076 houses—531 in Europe, 383 in the Americas, 129 in Asia, 26 in Africa, and 7 in Oceania. In that year their members numbered 16,364.[12]

The Missionaries of Our Lady of the Missions of Africa, popularly known as the White Fathers, expanded their enterprises in Africa and in 1950 as a

[9] Hubert Becher, *Die Jesuiten. Gestalt und Geschichte des Ordens* (Munich, Kösel Verlag, 1951, pp. 438), pp. 352–360.
[10] *The Catholic Encyclopedia,* Vol. X, p. 365.
[11] *Enciclopedia Cattolica,* Vol. IV, p. 291.
[12] *Ibid.,* Vol. XI, p. 870.

base for recruiting members had 85 houses in Europe and America. In that year they numbered 2,624, of whom 31 were bishops, 2,118 were priests, and 475 were brothers coadjutors.[13]

Several of the congregations which had flourished in France were driven out of the country by the hostile legislation in the decades immediately preceding 1914. Some of them won footholds in other countries and a few reëstablished themselves in France after 1914. But as a whole they did not regain the dimensions which had been theirs in the more favourable years of the nineteenth century. Although they suffered severely by the legislation in France in 1904 which closed their schools in that country, and also were dealt blows after 1914 by developments in Poland and Spain, the Brothers of Christian Schools continued and in 1932 opened their first house in Portugal.[14] The Brothers of Christian Instruction (Ploermel), founded by Jean Marie Robert de Lamennais, brother of Félicité Robert de Lamennais, expelled from France by adverse legislation, established headquarters in England and gained an entrance to Italy in 1921, to Uganda in 1926, and to Argentina in 1933.[15]

We must note that although a number of the orders and congregations attained larger dimensions after 1914 than in the nineteenth century, they did so in part through new centres opened outside Europe—to a large extent but not exclusively in the United States and Canada. Here was evidence of a slowing down of growth in Europe, but also, and fully as significantly, of the world-wide extension of the Roman Catholic Church. In this, as we shall see, the record of the Roman Catholic Church was roughly paralleled by that of Protestantism and, to a less extent, by that of the Eastern Churches.

FEW NEW CONGREGATIONS APPEAR

Although most of the more prominent orders and congregations increased their membership, very few new congregations were organized in the half-century after 1914.

For example, out of nearly four hundred women's congregations in existence in 1949, a large proportion of which were founded in the nineteenth century, only ten seem to have had their inception after 1914. Only five of these were begun in Europe and of the five two were unions of older congregations.[16] A list of women's congregations bearing the name of Francis and in existence in 1949 contained twenty-four which dated from the nineteenth century and two from before that time, but none which was started after 1914—although a few of earlier origin were given formal Papal approval after that date.[17]

[13] *Ibid.*, Vol. VIII, p. 1091.
[14] *Ibid.*, Vol. V, p. 1711.
[15] *Ibid.*, p. 1712.
[16] *Ibid.*, Vol. XI, pp. 1529–1570.
[17] *Ibid.*, Vol. V, pp. 1571–1577.

THE RAPID GROWTH OF CATHOLIC ACTION

The prominence of Catholic Action as a lay movement which we noted in Italy was paralleled in a number of other countries. It began in the nineteenth century but had its major growth after 1914. In its essence Catholic Action was not new but had precursors in many centuries which had worked for the permeation of all life by Catholic faith and principles. Yet in its organization and extension in the twentieth century it took on novel features.

In the encyclical *Ubi arcano Dei* (December 23, 1922)[18] at the beginning of his pontificate Pius XI defined Catholic Action succinctly as "the participation of the laity in the apostolate of the hierarchy." It consisted "not merely in the pursuit of personal Christian perfection," although this was included, but was an effort on the part of Roman Catholics to make their faith dominant in all phases of their lives, to seek the conversion of the world to faith in Christ, and to practice all of Christ's teachings in religious and devotional life, family life, civic life, intellectual life, economic life, and recreation. In other words, it meant the participation of the laity in ushering in the Kingdom of Christ. It embraced action by individuals and by the participation of Catholics in organizations which, suited to their age and sex and adapted to circumstances and special interests, were unified under the direction of the hierarchy. That unification was by parishes, dioceses, and nations.[19]

As Pius XI envisaged it, Catholic Action was to be essentially religious and was not to be composed of organizations with political aims. It differed profoundly from the laicization which was identical with the secularism characteristic of much of the revolutionary age. Its members were to seek to save men's souls, to train men's consciences, to spread the peace of Christ in the Kingdom of Christ, to defend the rights of the Church, and always in subordination to ecclesiastical authority. It did not attempt to supplant existing organizations of men, students, women, and workingmen if these were approved by the proper ecclesiastical officials. It aimed to implant in them a new soul, of "apostolic endeavour" rather than "social endeavour."[20]

Catholic Action was enjoined to remember that although Christ distinctly said that His kingdom is not of this world, this did not mean that He had renounced His lordship over the present life of mankind. Rather, Christ was held to have an unlimited right over all human occupations and concerns. This was regarded as including not only Roman Catholics but all men as well. Here, so it was asserted, was salvation for both individuals and society. If the rulers of this world, so those formulating Catholic Action believed, could see

---

[18] *Acta Apostolicae Sedis*, Vol. XIV, pp. 673–700.
[19] Confrey, *Readings for Catholic Action*, p. 21.
[20] *Ibid.*, pp. 16, 17; Loewenich, *Der moderne Katholizismus*, p. 129.

that they held their power not of their own right but through the command of Christ, peace and order would prevail.[21]

Although in a sense Catholic Action, enrolling as it did the laity, seemed to stand for the priesthood of all believers, this did not mean that principle as interpreted by Protestants. All Roman Catholic organizations of the laity were to be embraced in Catholic Action and coördinated through it, and the participation of all the laity in the mission of the Church was intended, but that mission, or apostolate, was always to be under the control of the hierarchy.[22] Indeed, in 1951 Pius XII refused to make Catholic Action independent of the hierarchy.[23]

Obviously both in ideal and in practice Catholic Action was multiform, embracing all aspects of life. It encouraged the Liturgical Movement, with its furthering of the intelligent participation of the laity in the central act of the Church's worship, the greater use of the missal by the laity, and the contribution of the liturgy to the promotion of holiness in the individual.[24] It bore upon the family, courtship, the choice of a mate in marriage, birth control, and all the relations between the sexes. In mixed marriages it entailed the rearing of the offspring in the Roman Catholic faith.[25] It included recreation with the choice of reading and of motion pictures. It embraced the planning and conduct of hiking.[26] It made much of the duties of citizenship. It sought to improve the life of rural populations.[27] It placed great emphasis upon education and attempted to give it Christian form and content and to free it from atheism.[28] It recognized the importance of the press, both newspapers and periodicals, and endeavoured to shape the printed word, whether in periodicals or books.[29] It included social service in its many forms, the promotion of social justice, and the reconstruction of society. It opposed both socialism and Communism.[30] It strove to enlist the faithful in efforts to win converts to the Roman Catholic Church, whether other Christians or non-Christians.[31] In an address to a great mass meeting in behalf of Catholic Action on September 7, 1947, Pius XII urged a deeper and more solid knowledge of the Catholic faith, the observance of Sunday and other holy days, the preservation of the Christian family and the Christian rearing of youth, social justice and the proper distri-

---

[21] Loewenich, *op. cit.*, p. 129.

[22] *Ibid.*, pp. 129, 130, 135.

[23] *The New York Times*, October 15, 1951.

[24] Confrey, *op. cit.*, pp. 40–365.

[25] *Ibid.*, pp. 400–518, 608.

[26] *Ibid.*, pp. 528–583.

[27] *Ibid.*, pp. 706–761.

[28] *Ibid.*, pp. 769–853; Loewenich, *op. cit.*, p. 135.

[29] Confrey, *op. cit.*, pp. 866–950; Loewenich, *op. cit.*, p. 138.

[30] Confrey, *op. cit.*, pp. 1136–1481.

[31] *Ibid.*, pp. 1011–1045; Loewenich, *op. cit.*, pp. 136 ff.

bution of wealth, and righteousness and honesty in all community life.[32]

Attempts were made in several countries, with varying degrees of success, at a comprehensive organization of Catholic Action. Thus in Italy Catholic Action was based upon parish councils which were coördinated under diocesan councils, and all were under a central council in Rome. The officers, whether of the parish or diocesan councils or the central council, were laymen, but to each body was attached an ecclesiastical assistant to ensure orthodoxy and control by the hierarchy.[33] A somewhat similar structure arose in Spain. Here were parish *juntas,* or councils, on which both men and women were represented, made up of the presidents of the several Catholic organizations of the parish and of other parishioners chosen by the pastor. The diocesan *junta* was composed of the presidents of the parish *juntas* and others appointed by the bishop. It directed Catholic Action in its relations with the family, the school, public morality, the observance of holy days, and similar concerns. It carried out the directives of the *juntas centrales* and supervised the parish *juntas.* The *junta naçional* and its secretariat were under the supervision of the primate, hierarchy, and diocesan advisors. Associated with it were a central *junta* for women's Catholic Action and a central *junta* of men. The Woman's Catholic Action was organized in 1919 by a Spanish cardinal to study and solve the problems of women, to promote their education, to protect them in industry, to assist them in obtaining a just wage, to ensure the observance of laws designed to further the interest of women and children, to organize campaigns against social vice, and to obtain respect for women and children, especially in the streets. This organization of Catholic Action was preceded in Spain by other organizations for social and moral objectives, some of which were brought together in national federations. Catholic Action sought to co-ordinate them. It held its first national congress in 1929.[34] In one degree or another this monolithic national structure was characteristic of Catholic Action in Latin lands, including Spanish America, but with the exception of France and Belgium. In these two and in Anglo-Saxon countries and Germany a less centralized organization was seen. Rather, a certain spirit was expressed in existing and new bodies and movements among particular elements.[35]

A coördination of the "lay apostolate," which included Catholic Action, was undertaken by the Holy See and with increasing success. With this in mind Pius XI created the *Actio Catholica.*[36] In connexion with Catholic Action an international pilgrimage of Christian workers assembled in Rome in May,

[32] Hermelink, *Die katholische Kirche unter den Pius-Päpsten des 20. Jahrhunderts,* p. 69.

[33] Magri, *L'Azione Cattolica in Italia,* Vol. II, pp. 85–120, 155 ff.; Guilday, *The Catholic Church in Contemporary Europe 1919–1931,* p. 189; *Enciclopedia Cattolica,* Vol. II, pp. 603–608.

[34] Guilday, *op. cit.,* pp. 333–345.

[35] *Enciclopedia Cattolica,* Vol. II, pp. 594, 598.

[36] *Ibid.*

1951. The next month it was followed by an international Catholic congress on rural life. In September, 1951, the General Council of the International Bureau of Catholic Youth assembled. In October, 1951, the first world congress of the lay apostolate was held in Rome. Soon thereafter Pius XII instituted the Permanent Committee for International Congresses for the Lay Apostolate. Under the direction of this body a second world congress convened in Rome in October, 1957, which brought together more than 2,000 from all continents and over 80 countries. Its theme was "the laity in the modern world: responsibilities and formation." The gathering had been preceded by careful preparation, which included national and continental conferences and special literature, part of it a volume, *World Crisis and the Catholic,* by several authors.[37]

In 1956 a building was erected near the Pope's summer residence at Castel Gandolfo. Over its door was a sign: "Pius XII Centre for a Better World." It arose primarily from the efforts of Riccardo Lombardi, a Jesuit, and was a gift to the Pope from Italian Catholic Action. Lombardi, a famous preacher, wished the new centre to be a training school for leaders in the "conquest of the world for Jesus." His dream was that they would help reorganize the human and social relations between class and class and individual and individual. He regarded the Roman Catholic programme as a middle way between liberalism, with its exaggerated emphasis on the individual, and totalitarianism, chiefly Communism and socialism, which sacrificed the individual to the state. Similar centres were erected in Germany and Spain.[38]

THE PROLIFERATION OF LAY ORGANIZATIONS

The decades after 1914 witnessed the proliferation of other lay movements and organizations. Many of them were local or national. We will say something of them here, but we will add more in our country-by-country survey. Others over-passed the boundaries of particular countries and were international. Several had their beginnings before 1914, mostly in the nineteenth century. A large proportion, however, dated their origin after that year, and numbers which were born before 1914 had a marked growth in the following decades.

Significantly, they flourished in some areas which were particularly subject to the currents of the revolutionary age. Indeed, many were organized to meet the challenge of that age—evidence of vitality in the Roman Catholic Church. They were especially prominent in the geographic belt which stretched from Belgium and the Netherlands to North Italy. They did not affect all the population in these regions, but they paralleled the de-Christianization which was marked among some elements. They embraced many phases of life. Several

37 *The Ecumenical Review,* Vol. X, pp. 320–327; Magri, *op. cit.,* Vol. II, pp. 143–151.
38 *The New York Times,* May 4, 1956.

were included under Catholic Action. But unlike the avowed restrictions on that movement, some had political programmes and even took the form of political parties.

STUDENTS AND OTHER INTELLECTUALS: *Pax Romana*

One of the international organizations was *Pax Romana*, for students and other intellectuals. It had its roots in France in a movement which began in 1887 and in which Albert de Mun was prominent. After 1914 it grew rapidly and held international congresses, the first of them in 1923. As an outcome of the congress in Bologna in 1925 it became a federation of national movements (*Confederatio studentium universi terrarum orbis catholica*). In a sense it paralleled the predominantly Protestant World's Student Christian Federation. After World War II it was reorganized in two movements, both international, one of Catholic intellectuals and the other of Catholic students. In 1950 the latter had seventy-four national federations in forty-six countries. The general purpose of *Pax Romana* was to proclaim the Christian message. Its motto was *Pax Christi in regno Christi*.[39]

TRADE UNIONS AND WORKERS' MOVEMENTS

In an attempt to meet the problems brought by the Industrial Revolution Christian trade unions and workers' movements arose. In some places, notably in Germany, several were interconfessional, embracing both Roman Catholics and Protestants. In other countries, especially Belgium, the Netherlands, Switzerland, and Italy, Roman Catholics and Protestants were in separate confessional organizations.

In general the Christian trade unions and workers' movements had their inception in the 1870's, 1880's, and 1890's.[40] In their early days they often met vigorous and even violent opposition from the Socialists, and particularly the Marxists. The Socialists held that the forces at work in society were basically materialistic and economic. They had as an objective public ownership and national planning, believed that the road to that goal was through class warfare and revolution, and were intent on winning the class war. They stood for the emancipation of women and against what they labelled the bourgeois family. In contrast the Christian organizations, while not underestimating economic factors and the importance of social classes, took the Christian revelation as their guide and considered of central importance the human personality and the culture of the soul. While not always standing against public ownership and national planning, in general they advocated a decentralization based

---

[39] *Enciclopedia Cattolica*, Vol. IX, pp. 1010, 1111.
[40] Fogarty, *Christian Democracy in Western Europe, 1820–1953*, pp. 186–191.

on industrial self-government. They maintained that collaboration between employers and employees was possible but could be effective only if each side came out for its own views and interests. As time passed, the Marxists and Socialists drew apart, each with its own set of organizations, and (religiously) neutralist bodies were also formed. In the last two groups some Christians had membership. After World War II, with the widening gulf between Marxists and Socialists, the latter and the Christians tended to come together.[41]

In at least some areas Christian workers' movements were stronger after World War II than after World War I. That was especially the situation in Flanders and the Netherlands. There in the mid-twentieth century the Christian unions, Roman Catholic and Protestant, probably had a majority of organized labour: they certainly outnumbered the Social Democratic unions, and the Communist-controlled unions were far behind the latter. In France and Italy Communists led, but unions under Christian Democratic leadership were potent and were ahead of the Social Democrats.[42]

The question of the relationship of the trade unions and workers' organizations to the Church was important and was not always solved in the same manner. In general the trend was for Roman Catholics and Protestants to group in frankly confessional organizations. Roman Catholic bodies often had close connexion with the clergy. As time passed, the distinction became more marked between Catholic Action and Christian Democracy. The former stressed education and the formation of personal character, in which doctrine was important. The latter was more concerned with economic and political techniques, regarded as not falling so directly within the province of the Church.

Soon after World War I a line tended to be drawn between Catholic trade unions and Catholic workers' organizations. Services connected with work, such as vocational training, were usually administered by the trade unions and those of use to workers and their families irrespective of their trade were assumed by the workers' leagues. In the Netherlands in 1916 the bishops ruled on the respective spheres of the workers' leagues and the trade unions and in 1925 the two wings were brought under one Catholic Workers' Federation. In 1921 a federation, the Christian Workers' Movement, was formed in Belgium, comprising units of both wings. Each unit had a chaplain, but in general the tie of the trade unions with the Church became tenuous. An analogous structure existed in Switzerland.

In each of the three countries—the Netherlands, Belgium, and Switzerland —the Roman Catholic worker was in a complex of organizations which in-

[41] *Ibid.*, pp. 190–193.
[42] *Ibid.*, p. 211.

cluded trade unions, coöperatives, insurance companies, political committees, and workers' leagues. In the same structure were youth organizations for both sexes and women's labour leagues. The whole had local units, diocesan or regional bodies arising out of the local units, and national committees, companies, and associations. In the Netherlands the whole workers' movement of unions and other bodies was held together by a national congress, or general council, and an executive committee. In Switzerland a comprehensive structure on a national scale was brought into being in 1943.

In Germany, France, and Italy no such inclusive structure developed and the connexion with the churches was much slighter. In Germany, as we have said, the unions embraced both Roman Catholics and Protestants, and in France and Italy they were without a confessional complexion and were Christian only in a broad sense. In Italy in 1919 the economic and social organizations were organically distinct from Catholic Action, and while the trade unions aspired to conform to Christian principles and doctrines they became a-confessional.[43]

In the global scene, in 1908 an international secretariat was founded for the Christian trade unions and was administered from Germany. In 1920, the International Federation of Christian Trade Unions came into being. In the 1920's internationals were brought together for Catholic and Protestant workers' leagues, each of which was frankly confessional.

In general the trade unions were by industries, with separate unions for clerical and supervisory workers. The workers' leagues, Church or quasi-Church, tended to reflect the ecclesiastical pattern, with parish, diocesan, and national groupings. The workers' movements, whether trade unions or workers' leagues, had to fight to gain representation in political parties and in legislative bodies. By the end of World War I they had, in general, won the battle.[44]

MOVEMENTS OF EMPLOYERS, MANAGERS, AND MIDDLE-CLASS BUSINESS MEN

Roman Catholic employers, managers, and middle-class business men were somewhat slower to form comprehensive organizations than were their employees. In the 1880's Leon Harmel, from a French family of manufacturers, whom we have already met as sharing with Albert de Mun and René de la, Tour du Pin in organizing *Cercles Catholiques d'Ouvriers*,[45] helped to bring into being a Catholic employers' association. Dissolved by the courts in a few years, it reappeared as the Social Studies Conference. Several of its members followed Harmel's example in developing welfare services, entering into joint consultation with their employees, and promoting personnel management. In

---

[43] *Ibid.*, pp. 193–203.
[44] *Ibid.*, pp. 205–208.
[45] Volume I, p. 350.

1889–1891 Harmel collaborated with a priest in organizing the Fraternal Union of Trade and Industry, made up chiefly of shopkeepers and manufacturers. Similar organizations came into being and in 1926 joined in what eventually was known as the French Christian Employers' Centre (C.F.P.C.). The year 1918 saw the organization in the Netherlands of the Christian Employers' Association and the Christian Middle Class Union. In 1915 various diocesan federations were combined in the Dutch Catholic Middle Class Union. Eventually the National Association of Catholic Employers (A.K.W.V.), based upon diocesan units, and the Federation of Catholic Trade Associations (of trade associations whose members were firms) were formed. In the 1920's several middle-class Catholic organizations of employers and engineers emerged in Belgium.

In the quarter-century which followed 1925 the Catholic employers movement spread to several countries in Europe—Switzerland, Germany, Italy, and Britain among them—and to Canada and South America. Although by the mid-twentieth century the Catholic employers' organizations did not loom as large as those with no avowed religious dynamic, and the largest employers tended to hold aloof from them, they were growing in influence. In 1924 at a meeting in Antwerp the Catholic employers inaugurated an international organization which, at first informal, prepared the way for more formal discussions in 1930–1931 and, in 1949, issued in the International Association of Catholic Employers' Organizations (U.N.I.A.P.A.C.).[46] In general, the attitude of Christian employers towards their employees changed from paternalism to collaboration. The transition was furthered by the existence of workers' unions and by their pressure on the employers.[47]

Although Roman Catholic associations of middle-class business men did not attain the proportions of those of the employers, in the Netherlands and Belgium they grew until by the mid-twentieth century they had reached substantial dimensions. In Germany the corresponding movement, which dated from Adolph Kolping,[48] suffered severely under the Nazi regime. Although after the overthrow of Hitler it made a partial recovery, in 1949 it had only 12,000 members as against 45,000 fifteen years earlier. In 1955 the International Catholic Movement for the Middle Class (I.K.M.B.) was organized with a Dutch secretariat and brought together the movements in the Netherlands, Belgium, and Germany.[49]

In the category of organizations of Roman Catholic professional men several scores of organizations were growing in the first half of the twentieth century. Among them were ones for physicians, pharmacists, engineers, journalists,

46 Fogarty, *op. cit.*, pp. 251–259.
47 *Ibid.*, pp. 234–236.
48 Volume I, pp. 348, 350.
49 Fogarty, *op. cit.*, pp. 259–261.

artists, lawyers, and teachers. The Evangelical Academies, which we are to find increasing as a phase of Protestant vigour in Germany after World War II, stimulated similar efforts among German Roman Catholics. .Some of the professional organizations were phases of Catholic Action. In 1954 the Catholic International Union of Social Service had in affiliation 27 social workers' associations, 93 schools for social workers, and 9 other training centres. Of these the majority were in Europe.[50]

ROMAN CATHOLIC FARMERS' MOVEMENTS

Organizations of Roman Catholic farmers began in the second half of the nineteenth century. Priests in Rhineland-Westphalia adopted the plan for rural credit coöperatives developed by the Protestant William Raiffeisen. In West Germany farmers' unions also appeared. In Italy friendly societies spread among the farmers and a rural credit coöperative begun by a priest stimulated the formation of others. In France priests assisted the development of credit coöperatives on the Raiffeisen pattern. A priest was the founder of the farmers' union movement in Belgium (1889), and in 1896 a (Belgian) Catholic Farmers' Union was inaugurated.

After World War I the Catholic farmers' movements grew. They continued to do so after World War II. In Belgium and the Netherlands the Catholic farmers' movement not only sought to provide better fertilizers and to reduce interest rates but also, although the clergy were less prominent in them than formerly, accentuated their educational and religious emphases. In Germany, France, and Italy, in contrast, after 1914 the avowedly Christian purpose receded, and less attention was paid to the educational and more to the economic aspects of rural life. In France the effect was to accentuate the trend towards de-Christianization. But in Germany after World War I a young farmers' movement arose which interested itself in both technological improvement and spiritual values and organized rural high schools for adult education. The Hitler regime dealt the movement severe blows, but after the Nazi collapse a new German Catholic rural movement (K.L.D.) emerged as a phase of Catholic Action and under lay leadership. In the 1950's a young Christian farmers' movement was under way and in France the young Christian farmers and the rural family movement were important.[51]

International Catholic congresses were held on rural life to raise the standards of the "spiritually and materially underprivileged rural population of the world." The third of the series met in Panama in April, 1955, and heard a message from Pius XII which called on large land-owners to pay a just wage

[50] *Ibid.*, pp. 261–263.
[51] *Ibid.*, pp. 245–250.

and contribute to the socio-economic improvement of their workers. The Pope also urged farmers to promote the coöperative movement and unite in organizations designed to improve their lot. He deplored the neglect by some governments of social legislation for the rural population.[52]

ROMAN CATHOLIC YOUTH MOVEMENTS

In addition to *Pax Romana* Roman Catholics had other youth movements which flourished in the twentieth century. As was true of a number of the organizations already noted, some of them sprang up in the second half of the nineteenth century. They arose in Germany under Kolping and in Switzerland, France, and Belgium, where they were recruited chiefly from the upper classes. However, Sillon,[53] although it fell under the displeasure of Pius X (1910), before its death set the example of extending the youth movement to all classes. Under the campaign against Modernism on the eve of World War I, some other youth movements, accused of being tainted with heresy, declined.

The Kolping movement, which had early drawn from the young craftsmen, became international, but because of its German connexions disappeared in Belgium in World War I and all but faded out in the Netherlands as a result of World War II. When, after the latter struggle, Communism became dominant in Hungary, Rumania, and Poland and non-Communist youth movements were suppressed, it vanished from those countries. But it continued in Germany, Austria, and Switzerland, still confined to craftsmen.

In Germany after World War II the Young Christian Workers' Movement was imported from Belgium and France, and *Werkmannschaft,* a revival of the pre-Nazi *Werkjugend,* also had members. After World War I a youth branch of the Catholic Commercial Union (K.K.V.) took advantage of the general unrest among youth at that time and displayed its vigour in Youth Federation congresses.

The Young Christian Workers sprang up in Belgium after World War I from beginnings that had been made by a priest, C. J. Cardijn, in Brussels in 1912. In 1925 it became affiliated with the earlier Belgian Catholic youth organization (A.C.J.B.). It spread to France in 1926, and within four years the older Catholic Action for French Youth (A.C.J.F.) was made to conform to its pattern. That pattern entailed separate Catholic youth movements for the various occupations, such as farmers, sailors, and students. In a later chapter we shall hear more of them, including *Jeunesse Ouvrière Chrétienne* (J.O.C., or the Jocists).

In Italy during the Fascist period the Italian Catholic Action Youth (G.I.A.C.) did not venture into participation in social problems. After 1945

[52] *The New York Times,* April 18, 1955.
[53] Volume I, p. 351.

a youth corps arose in the Christian Democratic movement to develop a sense of social responsibility in youth but was quite independent of the Church and not a part of Catholic Action.[54]

ROMAN CATHOLIC WOMEN'S MOVEMENTS

The twentieth century witnessed a rapid growth of Roman Catholic women's movements. The French Women's League for Catholic Action, with about 2,200,000 members in 1950, had as its purposes nourishing a more intense Christian life in the parish, encouraging teams of active parish workers and training them for missionary action among their neighbours, providing them with such facilities as they might need including books, collaborating in the re-conversion of France, defending the rights of religion, and taking responsibility in the social order. Also in France the Women's Civic and Social Union (U.F.C.S.) was founded (1925) to coördinate various Catholic women's organizations for social action. In 1945 the Austrian women's movement was begun as a constituent of the Austrian People's Party. Ten years later it took the initiative in forming the European Women's Union of similar groups in several countries.[55]

By the year 1955 the World Federation of Catholic Young Women and Girls had come into being with an alleged membership of ten millions in ninety nations and territories. The International Catholic Organization, reporting eighty million members, included the Catholic Women's Organization of thirty-six million members.[56]

THE FAMILY MOVEMENT

The twentieth century was also marked by a rapid development of organizations of families. Some had a distinctly Roman Catholic orientation and were either part of Catholic Action or closely related to it. Others, while of Roman Catholic origin or motivation, were not as frankly Christian. They were most extensive in France. There they arose partly out of the concern caused by a falling birth rate and sought to encourage large families. They were of several kinds. In 1920 they combined at a congress in Lille to support a declaration which stood for the protection of the family against public immorality and social disorganization through unemployment or other factors; the right of parents to determine their children's schooling; the right to earn, save, and inherit; the fair treatment of the family in the sphere of taxes and allowances; and political representation of the family through extra votes for fathers of families. The French family movement also sought to promote the religious

[54] Fogarty, *op. cit.,* pp. 264–281.
[55] *Ibid.,* pp. 281–284.
[56] *Worldmission Fides Service,* November 19, 1955.

life of the family, marriage guidance, coöperation among young families, and financial provision for families with a large number of children. In the early 1950's voluntary local family associations or branches of associations in France totalled about 12,000. The associations came together by departments and the departmental unions elected a national union of family associations. These unions were accorded official recognition by the state. Developments somewhat similar to those in France were seen in Belgium, Luxemburg, the Netherlands, Germany, and Italy.[57]

COMPREHENSIVE GLOBAL ACTION

By the mid-1950's the Conference of Catholic Organizations had arisen to coördinate more than thirty international bodies, largely but not entirely lay, representing different interests, activities, and occupations. Six of them had their headquarters in Rome, eight in Paris, six in Brussels, one in Belgium, two in the Netherlands, one in Italy outside of Rome, four in Fribourg, and one in Geneva. Among the organizations were the International Catholic Federation for Physical Education, the International Union of Social Studies, the World Union of Catholic Philosophic Studies, the International Federation of Catholic Youth, the International Federation of Catholic Girls' Movements, the Young Christian Workers' International, the International Federation of Catholic Men, the Catholic International Association of Girls' Protection Societies, the Catholic International Child Care Bureau, the International Conference of Catholic Charitable Organizations, the International Christian Social Union (which included the Catholic Workers', farmers', and business middle-class organizations), the Catholic International Union of Employers' Associations, the International Federation of Catholic Journalists, the International Catholic Film Bureau, and the International Catholic Association for Radio and Television.[58]

THE CHRISTIAN DEMOCRATIC MOVEMENT

In our first and second volumes we noted the emergence in the nineteenth century of distinctly and avowedly Christian parties. They sought to make the Christian conscience effective in the kind of state which was arising out of the politically liberal trends of the revolutionary age. Some were Protestant, such as the Anti-Revolutionary Party in the Netherlands. More were Roman Catholic, notably the Centre Party in Germany and the Catholic People's Party in the Netherlands. In the twentieth century such parties, and especially Roman Catholic parties, became increasingly prominent in Western Europe.

[57] Fogarty, *op. cit.*, pp. 285–293.
[58] *Ibid.*, p. 343.

Here we will speak of the Roman Catholic ones.

The strongest of the nineteenth-century Roman Catholic parties in Europe was the Centre Party in Germany. As we have seen, it arose to present a united front against Bismarck in the *Kulturkampf*.[59] It continued to be potent in both Prussian and imperial politics until after World War I. During World War I it stood for moderation and in 1917, with the Socialists, advocated a peace based on "no annexations, no indemnities." After the war, with the Socialists and the Democrats, it constituted the backbone of the Weimar Republic and was against the Communists and the National Socialists (the Nazis). It survived the Hitler landslide in the elections of March, 1933, but by the concordat of June of that year Pius XI agreed to its dissolution.[60] After World War II the elements supporting it went into the Christian Democratic Party (C.D.U), and the latter's leader, Conrad Adenauer, became the Chancellor of the German Federal Republic. In general both the Centre Party and the Christian Democratic Party took a moderate attitude on legislation in behalf of the workers in the mines and factories. Many Protestants coöperated with the Christian Democratic Party.[61]

The situation in Belgium differed from that in Germany. In the nineteenth century the Catholic Party was frankly denominational, as the Centre Party was not. It reached its height in the 1890's and concerned itself primarily with increasing the grants to the churches and to the Catholic schools. By 1914 it was modifying that policy to take account of such interests as the Christian trade unions, workers' leagues, and farmers' unions. After World War II its place was taken by the Christian Social Party. The latter attracted Roman Catholics, who constituted the majority of its members, and a minority of non-Christians. It sought support, regardless of religion, class, or economic interest, for a programme based on the Papal social encyclicals, human personality, the family, and a pluralistic view of the society.[62] In 1954 in both the upper and the lower house it had more members than any other party, although only slightly more than the next most powerful party, the Socialists.

In the Netherlands the Catholic Party, which had come into being in the nineteenth century, persisted, but with a change in programme. In 1920 the issue on which it had fought, financial equality between state and Church primary schools, was settled to the Church's satisfaction. In 1918 the bishops forbade the Roman Catholic social movements to take part in politics or to throw their weight behind any candidate. When it was revived after World War II the Catholic Party declared that it was not a church party and sought support on the basis of its programme. Few Protestants were attracted and

[59] Volume I, pp. 440, 441.
[60] Hayes, *Contemporary Europe since 1870*, pp. 396, 397, 412, 413, 584, 587.
[61] Fogarty, *op. cit.*, pp. 304–307, 313, 314.
[62] *Ibid.*, pp. 296–300, 314, 315.

though it was not subject to ecclesiastical authority the bishops endorsed it.[63]

In Austria on the collapse of the Hapsburg monarchy (1918) the Social Democrats and the Christian Socialists were in control. But they fell to fighting each other and in 1934 the latter won. A few years later the National Socialists stepped in and Austria was incorporated with Hitler's Germany (1938). After the Hitler debacle the Austrian People's Party declared that it was new and had no connexion with any previous organization. Yet it was actually Christian Democratic and was very powerful.[64]

On the Swiss scene, in 1912, Roman Catholic groups in the several cantons came together to form a Catholic party and in the mid-1950's it held two of the seven seats of the Federal Council.[65]

In Italy the emergence of a Catholic party was delayed by the unwillingness of the Popes to recognize the Kingdom of Italy, the action of the Holy See in 1867 declaring that it was "inexpedient" (*non expedit*) for the faithful to vote in parliamentary elections, and the prohibition by Leo XIII of such participation (1895). Yet the ban was gradually lifted. As the danger of socialism increased, the Vatican was more nearly inclined to allow the loyal sons of the Church to be active in politics. In 1918 Benedict XV released from clerical control not only political action but also trade unions, coöperatives, and friendly societies.[66] In 1919 a priest, Luigi Sturzo, asked Papal Secretary of State Gasparri whether the Vatican was willing to remove the bar to the participation of Roman Catholics in Italian politics. The reply was affirmative, and Sturzo set about organizing the Popular Party. It stood for free schools, government recognition of trade unions, decentralization to the advantage of regionalism, and the political education of the masses on the local level. It was strongest in the industrial North and in the national election of 1919 polled a fifth of the votes cast.[67] Not all Roman Catholics were enthusiastic about the Popular Party. Some wished it to be more emphatically Catholic and to stand for the restoration of the Papal State. Pius XI, strongly conservative, distrusted its liberal leanings and let it be known that he was against its proposed collaboration with the Socialists.[68] The triumph of Fascism spelled death for the Popular Party. In 1923 Sturzo resigned from its secretaryship and the following year went into exile. His successor, Alcide de Gasperi, after a period in a Fascist jail, was given haven as a cataloguer in the Vatican Library.[69]

The defeat of Italy in World War II and the collapse of Fascism were fol-

---

[63] *Ibid.*, pp. 300–302, 316.
[64] *Ibid.*, pp. 307–309, 341.
[65] *Ibid.*, pp. 309, 310, 341.
[66] *Ibid.*, p. 322.
[67] Einaudi and Goguel, *Christian Democracy in Italy and France*, pp. 1–18.
[68] *Ibid.*, pp. 18–20; Fogarty, *op. cit.*, pp. 323, 324.
[69] Einaudi and Goguel, *op. cit.*, pp. 21–26; Fogarty, *op. cit.*, p. 325.

lowed by the rise of the Christian Democratic Party. The way had been prepared by the increasing hostility of Pius XI to the Fascist regime and the underground opposition to Mussolini in which Catholic Action, although ostensibly non-political, shared. The Christian Democratic Party had Gasperi as leader. It also had the moral support of Catholic Action and the ecclesiastical authorities. The latter did not direct it or approve of all its policies, but they saw in it an enemy to the Communism which was rampant in post-war Italy and as such preferred it to the alternative of a more revolutionary regime.[70]

The Christian Democratic Party embraced a variety of elements not easily reconciled. In general it stood for the ideals which had inspired the Popular Party. It wished to apply Christian principles to political and social life and was opposed to the discredited pre-war bourgeois liberalism. It was willing to coöperate with Socialists and Communists in sponsoring reforms which it could endorse. Yet it was neither Communist nor socialist. It stood between these movements on the one hand and the monarchists and neo-Fascists on the other hand. It was not subservient to the Church, but it recognized God as the source of all authority, regarded the religion of the Italian people as Roman Catholic, held that the institutions of the state should conform to Christian ethics, and maintained that the state should have only an auxiliary part in education. It insisted that the democracy which it advocated could be achieved through the conscious and free participation of the people, took a middle ground between an authoritarian state and an extreme individualism, and held that the individual had social and economic as well as political rights. The Christian Democratic Party opposed Communism for the latter's materialistic view of life, its assigning all primary education to the state, its collectivization of all property, and its class conception of the state.[71]

The relation of the Christian Democratic Party to the Roman Catholic Church was fraught with problems. On the one hand, the Vatican was reluctant to come out openly for a frankly Catholic party for fear of stirring up a vigorous anti-clerical reaction. Yet the Christian Democratic Party depended for support upon civic committees organized by Catholic Action (although theoretically independent of it) as effective instruments for bringing out the vote for its candidates and was subject to pressure from the leadership of Catholic Action. Since that leadership insisted on its right to express its views on political issues, it could not be ignored in the framing of party policy.[72] Whatever the problems, in more than a decade following World War II the Christian Democratic Party was the strongest in Italy.

The picture was quite different in France. Here a large proportion of the

[70] Fogarty, *op. cit.*, p. 325.
[71] Einaudi and Goguel, *op. cit.*, pp. 28–38.
[72] *Ibid.*, pp. 84–88; Fogarty, *op. cit.*, pp. 327–329.

Roman Catholics had traditionally been at odds with the Third Republic which came to power after 1870. In spite of attempts at reconciliation and the emergence of Roman Catholics who would have been willing to coöperate as Christian Democrats, antagonism persisted and for a time was sharpened by the annulment in 1905 by legislative act of the Concordat of 1801 and the separation of Church and state. The situation was not eased by *Action Française,* with its advocacy of a monarchy and, in spite of its materialism, with its appeal to many Roman Catholics. That obstacle was not removed until the condemnation (1926) of *Action Française* by the Pope and the accompanying prohibition of membership by the faithful. In 1901 a group of Roman Catholics, among them Albert de Mun, formed what was known as Popular Liberal Action (A.L.P.). It was not officially Catholic but, rather, a-confessional. Yet it sought to protect the Church from the attacks which were being levelled against it. It opposed revolutionary socialism but stood for trade unionism; the minimum wage; old-age, sickness, and accident insurance; and legislation to protect factory workers. By the eve of World War I it had enrolled a large proportion of the Catholics of moderate views.[73] In 1924 several groups joined in the Popular Democratic Party (P.D.P.). The P.D.P. was slightly left of centre in its programme and attracted many Roman Catholics who were willing to accept the republic. It was a-confessional, for it wished to keep itself clear from Catholic Action and feared that too close a link with the Roman Catholic Church would lead many to identify it with political reaction. Its leaders had an important part in the resistance to the German occupation in World War II. It was followed, under the Fourth Republic, by the Popular Republican Movement (M.R.P.). Also a-confessional, M.R.P. appealed to a number who favoured Christian Democracy. Weaker than the Christian Democratic Party of Italy, it opposed both Communism and the groups on the extreme right. It regarded itself as a movement rather than a party and had a nation-wide organization.[74]

SUMMARY

The fifty years which immediately followed 1914 presented two rather striking contrasts in Roman Catholic organizations. On the one hand was the distinct slowing down of the emergence of new congregations of "religious" which had characterized the nineteenth century. The remarkable burst of devotion which between 1815 and 1914 had found expression in the revival of old orders and congregations and the creation of new ones was now directed into other channels. Some orders and congregations had a marked growth of

[73] Fogarty, *op. cit.,* pp. 329–332.
[74] *Ibid.,* pp. 331–339; Einaudi and Goguel, *op. cit.,* pp. 113 ff.

membership, but much of this was outside Western Europe.[75] Because of adverse conditions, several registered a decline in numbers. Very few congregations sprang into being, and by mid-century none of them had attained major dimensions. On the other hand, an amazing number of movements composed primarily of laity either appeared for the first time or increased in strength.

Outstanding was the proliferation of Catholic Action. Intended to supplement the apostolate of the hierarchy by that of the laity, it was under close ecclesiastical supervision and direction. It embraced an extensive range of activities. Its main growth was in Europe, but it spread widely among Roman Catholics in other regions. In Italy and Spain it displayed a highly integrated structure, rising in a pyramid from parochial through diocesan groups to a national body. In most lands it developed in other ways.

A bewildering number of other movements arose which enlisted Roman Catholics. All were of Roman Catholic origin and the membership of the majority was made up of Roman Catholics. Some, notably in the political scene, were a-confessional and sought to attract not only Roman Catholics but also Protestants and those of no religious faith. Among many, clerical influence was strong, but increasingly that influence waned. A large proportion had social and economic objectives, and the impact of such Papal pronouncements as *Rerum novarum* and *Quadragesimo anno* was felt. The majority either owed their origin to efforts to meet conditions brought by the revolutionary age or adjusted their programmes to deal with them. Many of the movements were trade unions and brought workers together for special objectives. Some were of employers, managers, and middle-class business men. Others were of farmers. A number were of youth, including *Pax Romana* for students. Many were of women. In the political sphere Christian Democratic movements sprang up. The more potent took the form of a Christian Democratic Party. They were conscious attempts to mobilize Christian, predominantly Roman Catholic, conviction into action to counter Communism and to embody such democratic ideals as were consistent with Roman Catholic teachings.

Whether ecclesiastically controlled, as was Catholic Action, or with a minimum of clerical participation, as were a number of other organizations and movements, this remarkable proliferation of predominantly lay movements was evidence of creative vigour in the Roman Catholic Church. Although they spread to other regions, the majority had their rise and chief development in Western Europe, where as we have again and again reminded ourselves, the forces of the revolutionary age had their origin and seemed to be making for the disappearance of the faith in its chief historic radiating centre. Indeed, most of the lay movements associated with the Roman Catholic Church in the

---

[75] In the years 1940–1954 the forty leading orders and congregations of men had an average growth of about 25 per cent. Allen, *A Seminary Survey*, p. 322.

twentieth century began in countries and regions traditionally of that faith where such forces as industrialization and the intellectual currents of the age were the most marked and upon which the wars of the century bore most heavily. They were evidence that among millions the Roman Catholic faith was so deeply rooted that it flowered into action to meet the challenges brought by the times. Yet among other millions in these very regions de-Christianization was proceeding so far that only superficial and formal traces, such as baptism, remained. In some sections the de-Christianized were in the majority, but in others the practising Roman Catholics were a majority.

As we pass to later chapters we shall find these lay movements in the Roman Catholic Church paralleled by lay emphases in Protestantism, notably, as in that church, in Western Europe but also, again as in that church, elsewhere in the world.

CHAPTER V

Worship and Devotional Life
of Roman Catholics

W HAT was happening in the worship and devotional life of Roman Catholics in Europe in the decades of storm and mounting revolution which were introduced by the events of 1914? In most ways developments which had been seen in the nineteenth century continued. They were marked by contrasts. On the one hand, millions who had been baptized in the Roman Catholic Church adhered to the faith only nominally. The corrosive currents of the revolutionary age had dissolved almost all but the name from their Christian heritage. On the other hand, for millions their faith was a living reality and they held staunchly, although with varying degrees of diligence and intelligence, to the prescribed duties of their religion. Some of the movements which either had been stressed or had had their inception in the nineteenth century mounted. Among them were an increased emphasis on the Eucharist, with frequent Communion begun in childhood, Eucharistic Congresses, the Liturgical Movement, the wider use of Gregorian music, reverence for the Sacred Heart of Jesus, and heightened devotion to the Virgin Mary. The latter was paralleled by the developments in Mariology to which we have called attention and of which we are to hear more in the next chapter.

Yet some differences set the post-1914 years off from the nineteenth century. Among thousands, probably millions, de-Christianization proceeded further than in that century. Successive generations of little or no connexion with the Church had left progressively scantier remnants of the faith. Except among Communists, less antagonism to the Church existed than before 1914. Yet that was not due to acceptance but to indifference. Christianity had all but ceased to count in the lives of multitudes. In many places anti-clericalism was less prominent than formerly, but simply because the Church as an institution seemed to count for less. In regions controlled by totalitarian and especially Communist regimes, the conflict between the state and the Church was usually, although not always, as pronounced as it had ever been in the nineteenth century.

Among the loyal millions—the practising Roman Catholics—mounting devotion among the laity went hand in hand with the growth of the lay movements recorded in the preceding chapter. The geographic coincidence was not exact, but it was close enough to suggest that the vitality in the Roman Catholic Church which found expression in "the century of the laity" had two facets: one in efforts to apply the faith to the concrete social, economic, and political situations brought by the revolutionary age, and the other in increased participation in the historic worship of the Church.

CONTRASTING AREAS OF DE-CHRISTIANIZATION AND HEIGHTENED LOYALTY

No fully accurate map can be drawn of areas of deepest de-Christianization and areas of heightened faith. For one thing, accurate statistics are lacking. For another, in·some regions both trends were seen. In general, de-Christianization was most marked in industrialized, urban, and mining districts. But striking exceptions existed. In more than one place the contrast between departure from the faith and loyalty to it was very sharp.

Most of the regions of highest observance, with Sunday attendance at mass, baptism and marriage in the Church, and confession and Communion at least once a year as the minimum, were, as we have suggested, in Western Continental Europe in a geographic belt running from the Netherlands, Belgium, and Northern France to North Italy. But beyond this belt were also sections where the proportion was high—as in North-western Spain, Brittany, La Vendée, and portions of South-eastern France. The practising Roman Catholics usually included more women than men, more older than younger people, more white-collar workers and proprietors than labourers, and more dwellers in the smaller towns and country-side than in the cities and mining districts, which had grown rapidly through the Industrial Revolution and in which the Church had not caught up with the increase in population. But some rural areas were almost de-Christianized, and in Flanders and the Netherlands, with their large cities, church attendance was high.[1] As we are to see, in Eire loyalty was marked, and in Great Britain the Roman Catholic Church grew in numbers and influence.

THE CHARACTER OF THE PRIESTHOOD

Generalizations about the character of the priesthood would be difficult to substantiate. The improvement which was seen in the nineteenth century[2] appears at least to have been maintained. The attention given by the twentieth-century Popes to the education and spiritual character of the clergy and

---

[1] Fogarty, *Christian Democracy in Western Europe, 1820–1953*, pp. 345–356, 364.
[2] Volume I, p. 356.

previously noted[3] did not sound a note of despair or even of alarm, but apparently was intended to continue an advance which was already present.

INCREASED EMPHASIS ON THE EUCHARIST: THE RAPID GROWTH OF EUCHARISTIC CONGRESSES

As we have suggested, an outstanding feature of the emphasis on the Eucharist was Eucharistic Congresses. We have seen their beginnings, in France, late in the nineteenth century and their extension to an international movement.[4] International congresses were held. The series was interrupted by World War I, but was resumed in 1922, as was fitting, in Rome. The congresses then met, as a rule biennially, in various parts of the world—in Amsterdam in 1924, Chicago in 1926, Sydney in 1928, Carthage in 1930, Dublin in 1932, Buenos Aires in 1934, Manila in 1937, and Budapest in 1938, after which they were again suspended, this time by World War II. They were attended by thousands and were accompanied by processions and other ceremonies culminating in a solemn celebration of the Eucharist. To them came pilgrimages from many countries. They were directed by an international committee and were preceded by careful preparation which included a wide use of the press and other forms of propaganda. At each congress the Pope was personally represented by a legate *a latere*. Having as one of their objectives the extension of the reign of Christ throughout the earth, the International Eucharistic Congresses were vivid illustrations of the wide extension of the Roman Catholic Church and of its claims to universality. They were also evidence of how the Roman Catholic Church was availing itself of the means of transportation and communication that were features of the revolutionary age.

Eucharistic Congresses were not merely international. On a less spectacular scale they were national, regional, inter-diocesan, diocesan, inter-parochial, and parochial. In at least one country, Italy, a continuing committee had them as its charge. They were a means of enlisting and nourishing the faith of both clergy and laity.[5]

INCREASED EMPHASIS ON THE EUCHARIST: THE MARKED DEVELOPMENT OF THE LITURGICAL MOVEMENT

We have also noted the beginnings in the nineteenth century of the Liturgical Movement.[6] In its inception it was chiefly an emphasis on the liturgy marked by scholarly study and a revival of Gregorian music. In the twentieth

[3] Chapter III.
[4] Volume I, p. 357.
[5] *Enciclopedia Cattolica,* Vol. IV, pp. 350–352.
[6] Volume I, p. 358.

century it mounted rapidly and had as a major objective the intelligent assistance of the laity at thé mass. As such it not only was a revival of the practice of the Church of the early centuries but reinforced the emphasis upon the place of the laity in making the faith effective in the revolutionary age which we summarized in the preceding chapter. Features of the Liturgical Movement were the "dialogue mass," in which the congregation said the responses, the wider use of missals by the laity, and the putting of much of the liturgy into the vernacular. In its expressions it varied, not only from country to country, but also within countries. It had many centres: several of the most important were monasteries. In some places it went beyond what was sanctioned by the hierarchy, but it did not rebel against the hierarchy. In its general purpose it received Papal endorsement. Some of its features were accorded official approval by Rome. Its aim was not primarily liturgical, in the sense of altering the forms and procedures of the liturgical services. It sought a renewal and deepening of the whole range of life of the Christian community through making more intelligent and vivid a sacramental conception of the faith and of the Church. It had theological aspects. It included a scientific study of the liturgy and a return to the historic accompaniments of the liturgy in music and art, including ornaments and altar vessels. It was also associated with Catholic Action in an effort to give spiritual content to the apostolate of the laity and to undergird and inspire the organizational forms which were devised to provide stimulus and concrete channels for that apostolate. Its vigour was evidenced by a flood of literature which issued from it and the increasing numbers of clergy and laity who were committed to it.[7]

In seeking to make the Eucharist more potent in the life of the laity, the Liturgical Movement endeavoured to reverse a long-prevailing trend. Although the laity were under obligation to attend mass and, in theory, to "assist" at it, in actual fact most of them paid little attention to what the priest was doing at the altar, or, in high mass, to the priest and the responses of the choir. The majority were too unintelligent on the liturgy (in to them an unfamiliar tongue) to follow it with comprehension. Much of it was inaudible to them. They spent the time, therefore, in their private devotions, telling their rosaries, physically present but often with their thoughts elsewhere.

In contrast, the Liturgical Movement taught that Christianity is not doctrine but life, the life of Christ in the baptized Christian. It regarded the liturgy as originally intended as a channel of the redeeming grace of God to unredeemed men. It viewed the liturgy as a collective act in which all might find inward and outward unity with Christ. It held that the sacramental mystery

---

[7] Koenker, The Liturgical Renaissance in the Roman Catholic Church, pp. 1–8. For a comprehensive bibliography see ibid., pp. 247–261.

brings the eternal into time and is the answer of God's love and grace to man's movement towards God.[8]

To the impulse given by nineteenth-century centres of the Liturgical Movement—Solesmes in France, Maria Laach (child of the Benedictine Beuron Congregation in Germany), the liturgical week in Louvain, and Maredsous (a Belgian Benedictine abbey, also sprung from Beuron)—and by a Benedictine journal in Italy,[9] Pius X had added his powerful support through his *motu proprio* of 1903, in which he stressed the singing of the Gregorian by the congregation.

Beginning in 1914 the Liturgical Movement mounted, took root in a number of centres in several countries, and radiated from them. It had precursors before that year. But in the form in which it became known in the twentieth century it has been said to date from the first liturgical week for laymen held at Maria Laach in Holy Week of 1914. There the dialogue mass was introduced in Germany. A group of laymen—lawyers, physicians, and university teachers—met and asked the abbot about ways and means for promoting the more active participation of the faithful in the mass. From there the interest spread, first among the educated and then among the working classes. Under the leadership of Idlefons Herwegen, abbot from 1913 to 1946, Maria Laach gave intellectual content to the movement, especially through a series of scholarly publications which promoted the understanding of the mass. Other Benedictine abbeys in Germany augmented the flow of literature. J. Pinsk, through his ministry to students in Berlin and numerous writings, made a notable contribution.[10]

In spite of two world wars and the Nazi regime the Liturgical Movement continued in Germany. Indeed, in some ways it was furthered by the restrictions on much of the organizational activity of the Church and by the consequent centring on the inner life and worship of the parish. An outstanding pioneer, Italian-born but educated, teaching, and writing in Germany, was Romano Guardini. He exerted a wide influence between the two wars and beyond. Translations of the missal were made, shortened editions of the breviary were issued for the laity, and simplified prayer books and hymnals were prepared for use in the dioceses. A German translation of the Psalter was published. Here as in several other countries the laity were encouraged

---

[8] Loewenich, *Der moderne Katholizismus*, p. 199; Michonneau, *Revolution in a City Parish*, pp. 26–28; James Herbert Srawley, *The Liturgical Movement: Its Origin and Growth* (London, A. R. Mowbray Co., 1954, pp. 34), pp. 12, 13.

[9] *Enciclopedia Cattolica*, Vol. VII, p. 1439; Olivier Rousseau, *The Progress of the Liturgy. An Historical Sketch from the Beginning of the Nineteenth Century to the Pontificate of Pius X* (Westminster, Md., The Newman Press, 1951, pp. xv, 219), *passim*. For a brief history of the movement and a description of the liturgy and its meaning, sympathetic with the Liturgical Movement, see Louis Bouyer, *Liturgical Piety* (University of Notre Dame Press, 1955, pp. x, 284).

[10] Koenker, *op. cit.*, pp. 12–15.

to make the responses and to join with the choir in the choral parts. In 1947 a liturgical institute was founded under the supervision of the bishops. Developments in the arts were seen. Attention was given to the theological accompaniment of the liturgy, especially to the Church as the body of Christ and to the cultic forms as the *Mysterium*. Fresh exegesis of the Scriptures came in an effort to deepen the understanding of the Eucharist. With a similar purpose a renewed study was made of the writings of the Church Fathers. Youth was attracted by the new solemnity in the celebrations of the mass, and numerous discussions and conferences helped to spread musical, artistic, and liturgical information.[11]

In Belgium and the Netherlands, where lay movements of various kinds were strong and an increasing number of recruits came for the world mission, the Liturgical Movement was prominent. A Belgian pioneer and an outstanding leader was a Benedictine, Lambert Beauduin, of the monastery of Mont César near Louvain. Formerly a secular priest who ministered to labourers, he had come to the conviction that a much more profound religious life was needed and held that it could be nourished through the liturgy. To this end he sought to stimulate in the parish clergy a greater appreciation of the liturgy as a source not only of an enhanced vitality in their flocks, but also of a deepening and enriching of their own spirits. The first liturgical week was held in Belgium in 1911, the first international liturgical congress convened in Antwerp in 1930, and the first international liturgical week was observed in Maastricht in 1946. The questions of the use of the vernacular in the liturgy and of evening masses were also prominent. The Liturgical Movement was utilized with success in winning back some persons of the de-Christianized.[12]

Austria had a radiating centre in Klosterneuburg. From here after World War I Pius Parsch was the source of publications, sermons, and conferences which popularized the Liturgical Movement. He gave practical application to the liturgical research of Maria Laach and other monasteries. After World War II and the emancipation of Austria from Nazi rule and union with Germany, the bishops took vigorous action in supervising the movement. They endeavoured to spread it beyond the places where it had been developed and to make it a regular part of the pastoral function. They issued regulations for it and sought to substitute a common order of the mass for the various prayer books and hymnals which had appeared. A liturgical commission operated in

---

[11] *Ibid.*, pp. 15, 16, 116, 117, 172, 173; Loewenich, *op. cit.*, p. 200; Bogler, *Liturgische Erneuerung in aller Welt*, pp. 15–28. On Guardini see Romano Guardini, *L'Esprit de la Liturgie* (*Vom Geist der Liturgie*), translated with an introduction by Robert d'Harcourt (Paris, Librairie Plon, 1929, pp. 277). On a distinguished work by one of the leading German liturgical scholars, see Josef Andreas Jungmann, *Missarum Sollemnia. Eine genetische Erklärung der römischen Messe* (Vienna, Herder, 2 vols., 1952).

[12] Bouyer, *La Vie de la Liturgie*, pp. 80–87; Koenker, *op. cit.*, p. 14; Bogler, *op. cit.*, pp. 41–47.

close association with the bishops' conference, and in 1946 the latter gave its approval of the *Institutum Liturgicum* which was active in producing publications and supervising the movement.[13]

Although Solesmes had perpetuated the tradition of Guéranger and was a centre for the study of Gregorian music, and in spite of distinguished work in liturgies by a number of scholars, in France the Roman Catholic Church as a whole was somewhat late in awakening to the Liturgical Movement. In the 1920's the literature issuing from Austria and Belgium began to have an effect on intellectuals among the clergy. Between the two world wars Latin-French missals and vesper books prepared by Benedictines and more or less influenced by what had been begun by Guéranger were circulated by the hundred thousand. In 1943 the *Centre de Pastorale Liturgique* was founded. Through it Jesuits, Benedictines, Dominicans, and seculars collaborated in organizing liturgical weeks, retreats, and missions, in issuing a wide variety of literature, in promoting the study of the Gregorian chant and the liturgy, and, with the approval of Rome and the French hierarchy, in translating liturgical texts into the vernacular. For years it had as its head Cardinal Suhard of Paris.[14] In the summer of 1954 in a church in Paris with a working-class congregation mass was said in a plain room, with the altar set towards the centre and the altar boy serving in a street outfit. Most of the service was in French, and the Latin portion was translated to the congregation by a priest who stood in the aisle. We will hear more of the Liturgical Movement when in our survey of France we speak of the worker-priests.

In Switzerland the absence of a liturgical movement, in the sense of an organized endeavour, and of outstanding centres for liturgical study was due partly to the linguistic diversity of the country. However, Switzerland experienced a liturgical revival, with an increased instruction of their people by the priests on the spiritual meaning of the liturgy and the study and use of Gregorian music.[15]

In Italy the Liturgical Movement was delayed in having much effect. In 1913 the periodical *Arte Cristiana* was inaugurated as an organ of a school of sacred art. But the inception of the movement in Italy is usually dated the following year. Then the first issue of the *Rivesta Liturgica* appeared, a Benedictine project. Another landmark, in 1923, was the *Bolletino Liturgico,* also a Benedictine enterprise, begun as a means of popularizing the movement. Eventually the movement took root in a number of cities, sponsored by clergy, professors, and at least one bishop and a cardinal. Translations of the missal multiplied. In several theological seminaries chairs for the study and teaching

[13] Koenker, *op. cit.*, pp. 14, 15; Bogler, *op. cit.*, pp. 48–53.
[14] Koenker, *op. cit.*, p. 16; Bogler, *op. cit.*, pp. 29–40.
[15] Bogler, *op. cit.*, pp. 54–72.

of the liturgy were established. A society and a school of sacred art were organized. World War II brought a serious reversal, with the destruction of churches and centres of study, the suspension of publications, the disorganization of parishes and parish life, vast movements of population, and the concentration of thousands on maintaining a mere physical existence. However, with the coming of peace the Liturgical Movement quickly revived and attained larger dimensions than in *ante-bellum* days. A national *Centro di Azione Liturgica* (C.A.L.) was developed, liturgical congresses and weeks were held, and various publications spread and guided the movement.[16]

Spain was backward in being stirred by the Liturgical Movement, partly because the civil war, which wrought destruction and was accompanied by much religious persecution, did not end until 1939. However, after 1939 several Benedictine monasteries became centres of liturgical study. A number of theological seminaries spread the movement among the younger clergy. Schools for training members of choirs multiplied. Translations of liturgical works were made. Editions of missals in the vernacular were published. Liturgical conferences were held. Liturgical periodicals appeared. As a phase of Spanish nationalism, the West Gothic or Mozarabic liturgy was revived and became popular. Yet the international Liturgical Movement did not awaken as much interest as in some other lands.[17]

Foreshadowings of the liturgical revival were seen in Portugal in the nineteenth century, but the Liturgical Movement as such owed its inception in that country to Antonio Coelho, a Benedictine trained in Maredsous and ordained by Mercier. On his return to Portugal in 1919 Coelho gave himself to the spread of the movement. In 1926, with the endorsement of the bishops and of leading secular and regular clergy, he began the liturgical periodical *Opus Dei* and edited it for eleven years. He also wrote a number of books. He laboured so effectively that when, in 1938, death removed him, the movement he had inaugurated continued.[18]

The Liturgical Movement did not make much headway in England, partly because "to follow the service" by the use of a missal seemed to many to smack of Protestantism and partly because the majority of the faithful were of Irish ancestry and the Irish were inclined to be subjective and individualistic and not to have the sense of a worshipping congregation essential to the movement. Yet by the 1950's some beginnings were seen.[19]

We will find the Liturgical Movement outside Europe—in Latin America,

[16] *Ibid.*, pp. 73–81; *Enciclopedia Cattolica*, Vol. VII, p. 1450.
[17] Bogler, *op. cit.*, pp. 82–90.
[18] *Ibid.*, pp. 91–96.
[19] *Ibid.*, pp. 97–100.

the United States, Canada, Australia, and various places in Asia and Africa.[20] However, its origin and its main radiating centres were in Western Europe. From there had also sprung most of the orders and congregations, the creative theology, and the missionaries of the Roman Catholic Church. There, too, was the source of most of the twentieth-century new movements, theological activity, and the majority of the missionaries. In the Liturgical Movement as in other aspects of its life the Roman Catholic Church was rising to the challenge posed by the revolutionary age in the region where that age had had its inception.

The Liturgical Movement, beginning as it did in Western Europe and flourishing in a number of countries, had several accompaniments. Common to all was the deepening of the life of the Christian community through the sacraments, and especially through the Eucharist, by a more intelligent participation of the laity. Pervading the whole was, therefore, a reaction from the extreme individualism of the nineteenth century and an emphasis upon the worshipping community and the Church as the mystical body of Christ. The parish was regarded as a unit of that body and the effort was made to have the mass in the parish church a communal offering by that unit for the entire Church. To this end mass was said in a tone audible to all, and even a working-class congregation was taught to join in repeating together the Gloria, the creed, the Sanctus, the Agnus Dei, and some of the responses. In at least one parish, in baptisms, marriages, and funerals the priest took care to explain each step of the service and the meaning of the whole, especially for the benefit of those who seldom came to church.[21]

A related development was the stress placed on the priesthood of the laity as members, along with the clergy, of the mystical body of Christ and therefore as sharing in the priesthood of Christ. This did not belittle the distinctive functions of the clergy, but the Liturgical Movement conceived of the Church at worship as the supernatural union of the baptized, the confirmed, and the ordained. Christ was regarded as the liturgist, worshipping for all, both laity and clergy, through all, and in all. Thus the layman was taught that he shared in the priestly worship of Christ. For authority for this position Pius XI was quoted.[22]

Another associated feature of the Liturgical Movement was the endeavour to promote the use of the breviary by the laity. The breviary was viewed as the prayer book of the entire Church. Families and individuals were encour-

[20] *Ibid.*, pp. 104–141; Johannes Hofinger and Joseph Kellner, *Liturgische Erneuerung in der Welt-mission* (Innsbruck, Tyrolia Verlag, 1956, pp. 455), *passim.*

[21] Michonneau, *op. cit.*, pp. 30–39.

[22] Gerald Ellard, *Men at Work at Worship* (New York, Longmans, Green and Co., 1940, pp. xvii, 307), pp. 64, 65, 69–82; Koenker, *op. cit.*, pp. 71–79.

aged to employ it in their collective and private devotions. To this end abbreviated forms of the breviary were prepared and circulated.[23]

The Liturgical Movement made much of the liturgical year. In this the *Mysterientheologie,* first developed at Maria Laach by Odo Casel, gave new meaning to the Church year as the mystical setting forth of the saving work of Christ.[24]

Other accompaniments of the Liturgical Movement were the saying of the mass by the priest facing the people, so that the laity might see what he was doing and thus share more intelligently in it; the slower and more distinct pronunciation of the liturgy, with the same purpose; emphasis upon the altar as the table of sacrifice; and afternoon and evening masses for the benefit of those who found it difficult to be present at the morning hours.[25]

If the laity was to participate intelligently, it was held that the liturgy, or at least large portions of it, must be in the vernacular. Many objected on the ground that Latin was the language of the universal Church, that Latin was necessary to Gregorian music, which was closely connected with the Liturgical Movement, and that Latin added to the sense of mystery rightfully accompanying the sacrifice of the Eucharist. Yet increasingly permission was granted for the use of the vernacular on a diocesan, regional, or national basis, but with certain portions still in Latin. This was a change from the denunciation by the Council of Trent of the celebration of the mass in the vernacular.[26]

So drastic were some of the expressions of the Liturgical Movement that severe criticism developed in conservative quarters. For instance, many were concerned with the trend, in stressing the objective character of the liturgy, towards discouraging the use of the rosary and the stations of the cross, the confession of venial sins, and private meditation. The Pope deemed it advisable to act. Two encyclicals which we have already mentioned took account of the movement—*Mystici Corporis Christi* (June 29, 1943)[27] and *Mediator Dei* (November 20, 1947).[28] The first, as we have seen, dealt primarily with the Church as the mystical body of Christ, and the second with the mass. In them Pius XII did not condemn the Liturgical Movement, but directly or indirectly he came out against some of the tendencies associated with it. In *Mystici Corporis Christi* he stressed the hierarchical structure of the Church more than the Liturgical Movement did and made more of its visible, institutional character than did the latter. He was critical of those who in emphasizing the priesthood of all believers did not, to his mind, give sufficient place to the ordained priest-

---

[23] Koenker, *op. cit.,* pp. 59–62.
[24] *Ibid.,* pp. 56–59, 104–124.
[25] *Ibid.,* pp. 53, 65, 66.
[26] *Ibid.,* pp. 138–152.
[27] *Acta Apostolicae Sedis,* Vol. XXXV, pp. 193–248.
[28] *Ibid.,* Vol. XXXIX, pp. 521–595.

hood. In *Mediator Dei* he took exception to those who criticized private masses without a congregation, and maintained that if a server was present to give the responses the mass had a social and public character. The officiating priest, he insisted, through his ordination, acted in the person of Christ and not as representing the faithful. He commended the popular piety which was frowned on by advocates of the Liturgical Movement and regretted the neglect of devotion to the Virgin and of adoration of Christ in the reserved sacrament in the tabernacle. He forbade transforming the altar into a table. However, he permitted bishops to allow the priest to make visible to the congregation some actions formerly invisible, such as the breaking of the wafer. Nor did he condemn the offertory procession in which the faithful presented to the priest the bread and wine to be changed into the body and blood of Christ. *Mediator Dei* did not apply a blanket condemnation to the vernacular, but only to its unauthorized use. Indeed, permission for the vernacular had earlier been granted on a national, regional, or diocesan basis—as in Austria in 1935 and in Bavaria in 1939.[29]

Increased Reading of the Scriptures

Associated with the mounting enlistment through the Liturgical Movement of the intelligent participation of the laity in worship was increased emphasis upon the reading of the Bible by the rank and file.

Roman Catholic translations of the Bible into the vernacular were not an innovation. Several, for example, had been made into German before Luther's famous achievement. Yet the stress placed by Protestants on translations of the Scriptures, and what, to the Roman Catholic Church, were unauthorized and heresy-begetting interpretations, had led the Holy See to be cautious in encouraging or even permitting translations. As we have seen, at least two nineteenth-century Popes had condemned the Bible societies which Protestants had organized, with their circulation of Bibles in the vernacular, even when, as was true of numbers of these editions, they were without comments.[30]

Leo XIII slightly relaxed the strictures. He charged that Protestant translations falsified the originals, but he permitted them to be employed for scholarly purposes if in their prefaces and comments they contained nothing contrary to what Roman Catholics believed. The faithful were allowed to read the Bible in the vernacular in translations approved by the Papacy, authorized by a bishop, and provided with suitable explanations. Indeed, indulgences were authorized for the regular perusal of such editions. However, the canon law continued to forbid the use of editions made by non-Catholics of the original

[29] Koenker, *op. cit.*, p. 149.
[30] Volume I, pp. 247, 276.

texts of older Catholic editions and of translations into the vernacular.[31]

In the twentieth century an extensive movement for the reading and study of the Bible developed among both clergy and laity. It began in Germany between the two world wars and spread to Belgium, France, Switzerland, Italy, Spain, and beyond Europe. Fresh translations of the Bible appeared, both from the Vulgate and from the original texts. Efforts were made to promote the reading of the Bible by the laity. Aids to understanding the Scriptures were prepared. Groups and associations arose to promote the movement. Pertinent periodicals were issued. A close connexion was sometimes made with the Liturgical Movement. Youth movements, notably J.O.C. (the Jocists) gave an important place to the study of the Bible. At first stress was placed on the letters of Paul. After World War I the entire Bible began to become familiar to the more concerned among the laity. In some parishes Bible study groups were organized. "Bible weeks" were held for the concentrated study of the Scriptures.[32]

THE PERSISTENCE AND GROWTH OF PRE-TWENTIETH-CENTURY DEVOTIONAL PRACTICES

The mounting emphasis on the Eucharist through Eucharistic Congresses and the Liturgical Movement and the stress on the reading of the Bible did not mean that the devotional practices which we saw in the nineteenth century declined. They persisted and, if anything, increased. They were found among the clergy and the laity and among the learned and the unlearned. They were another characteristic of that core of loyal Roman Catholics who held to the faith in the face of the swelling tides of the revolutionary age which were threatening Christianity.

Among those high in ecclesiastical circles and with unquestionably keen intellects were men who in their private lives held to devotional customs sometimes associated with the rank and file of the lowly of slight education. Thus Mercier, outstanding scholar and cardinal, died with a picture and relic of Thérèse of Lisieux (the Little Flower) by his side. Similarly, Pius XI had great devotion for that saint—at whose canonization, indeed, he had presided —for the Sacred Heart, and for the Virgin, and he breathed his last breath with the rosary of the Curé of Ars in his hand. In his youth he had joined the Third Order Secular of the Franciscans and as a priest had been an Oblate of Charles Borromeo. Equally marked, as we have seen, was the piety of his successor.

Emphasis upon Mary was not diminished by the Liturgical Movement with its focussing of attention on the bloodless sacrifice of the altar. If anything, it

[31] Loewenich, *op. cit.*, pp. 195, 196.
[32] *Ibid.*, pp. 196–198; Aubert, *La Théologie Catholique au Milieu du XXe Siècle*, pp. 11, 12.

increased. To this testified the endorsement of the assumption of Mary, the setting apart of a Marian year, and the institution of the feast of the Heavenly Queenship of the Virgin Mary—all acts of Pius XII.

Much attention was paid to sites connected with what were believed to have been appearances of the Virgin. Thus in 1958 the centenary of the visions of Bernadette Soubirous which made Lourdes a major centre of pilgrimage was celebrated with great pomp. After 1914 another pilgrimage centre arose in Fatima, Portugal, on a barren plateau about ninety miles north of Lisbon. It sprang from what were confidently believed to be appearances of the Virgin in 1917 to three peasant children who were tending sheep. They were preceded in 1916 by what the children reported as apparitions of a young man, the Angel of Peace, presumably the Archangel Michael. The children declared that the Virgin had warned them that because of its sins God would punish the world with another war and urged them to say their rosary every day for the end of World War I, then in progress, and for peace. At the report of the visions throngs gathered, and in 1917 a meteorological phenomenon was held to have confirmed the children's story. Two of the children, a boy and a girl, died early, in accordance, so they said, with what the Virgin had prophesied. The oldest, a girl, survived and became a nun. Sceptical civil authorities sought to persuade the children that they were either lying or had been deluded. But in 1930 the bishop of the diocese authorized the cult. In 1946 a statue of the Virgin of Fatima was crowned by a cardinal as a representative of the Pope. A large church was also erected. In 1942, on the silver jubilee of the appearances, a national celebration was held, with a message from Pius XII. Pilgrims came from many parts of the world and miracles of healing were reported.[33]

Another expression of the popular devotion to Mary was seen in the formation and spread of the Legion of Mary. Founded in Dublin in October, 1917, the Legion of Mary had the approval of Benedict XV, Pius XI, and Pius XII. Its members were to be "soldiers" or "cavaliers" of Mary Immaculate. They were to strive for their individual sanctification and were to seek the conversion of sinners and of all enemies of the Church. They engaged in many activities —among them the visitation of hospitals and prisons, and recreational centres for sailors, labourers, and members of other occupations. The movement was directed from Rome and had national and regional centres. By 1949 it had spread widely in Italy, and to Poland, Rumania, Hungary, and Japan.[34]

After 1914 examples were seen of types of piety which had been familiar in earlier centuries, evidence of the persistence of the faith in its historic forms.

[33] Finbar Ryan, *Our Lady of Fatima* (Dublin, Growne and Nolan, 1944, pp. 236), *passim;* William Thomas Walsh, *Our Lady of Fatima* (New York, The Macmillan Co., 1947, pp. ix, 228), *passim; Enciclopedia Cattolica,* Vol. V, pp. 1055, 1056.

[34] *Enciclopedia Cattolica,* Vol. VIII, pp. 1001, 1002; Guilday, *The Catholic Church in Contemporary Europe 1919–1931,* p. 163.

Thus we hear of a Capuchin, Pio da Pietrelcina, in Foggio in Southern Italy, who was said to have borne from 1918 the five stigmata of Christ in his hands, feet, and side, and to whom throngs came to make their confessions through him.[35]

WRITTEN AIDS TO THE DEVOTIONAL LIFE

Did the twentieth century see men and women emerge from the Roman Catholic Church who were outstanding examples of the devotional life? So far as the perspective of the mid-century permitted an appraisal, the answer must be no. Certainly none so caught the attention of their contemporaries as did some of earlier centuries—such as Augustine, Bernard of Clairvaux, Francis of Assisi, John of the Cross, Teresa of Avila, and Francis de Sales.

Yet the no must be qualified. If none appeared who stood out as did some of previous ages, that did not necessarily mean a waning of deep interest or of expertness in the life of the spirit. It might indicate that the life of devotion found other channels. The Liturgical Movement was one such channel. Moreover, books on the devotional life continued to pour from the press. Many were for use by the rank and file. Others were for inspiration and guidance for the minority. The aftermath of World War I brought a spiritual hunger for which many sought satisfaction in devotional literature. To meet it journals were issued, lives of the saints multiplied, and a number of solid treatises were composed or re-issued.[36] For example, a Dominican, Reginald Garrigou-Lagrange, whom we are to meet in the next chapter as a Thomistic expert, for twenty years or more taught ascetic and mystical theology in the Collegium Angelicum in Rome and was the author of books on the subject.[37] He was a warm admirer of John of the Cross. The Jesuits edited a huge dictionary designed to cover the field exhaustively; in the 1950's it was still incomplete.[38]

THE EXTENT OF THE WORSHIPPING CONSTITUENCY

What proportion of the professedly Roman Catholic population could be classified as practising? How large was the body of the faithful who were moved by the Eucharistic Congresses, who attended mass frequently enough

---

[35] Herbert Thurston, *The Physical Phenomena of Mysticism* (Chicago, Henry Regnery Co., 1952, pp. viii, 419), pp. 95–101.

[36] P. Pourrat, *La Spiritualité Chrétienne* (Paris, Librairie Lecoffre, Vol. IV, part 2, 1947, pp. xii, 680), pp. 647 ff.

[37] Among them were *Christian Perfection and Contemplation According to St. Thomas Aquinas and St. John of the Cross,* translated by M. Timotheus Doyle (St. Louis, B. Herder Book Co., 1937, pp. xviii, 470), and *The Three Ages of the Interior Life. Prelude of Eternal Life,* translated by M. Timotheus Doyle (St. Louis, B. Herder Book Co., Vol. I, 1947).

[38] *Dictionnaire de Spiritualité Ascétique et Mystique, Doctrine et Histoire,* edited by Marcel Viller, F. Cavallera, and J. de Guibert (Paris, Gabriel Beauchesne et ses fils, 1932, ff. Fascicule XXV, 1958, brought the work through "Église").

to profit by the Liturgical Movement, and who read the Bible and the devotional literature with any regularity? We have no accurate comprehensive figures which would enable us to give satisfactory answers. We can be aware of some of the forces at work which were accompaniments of the revolutionary age, and here and there we have fairly reliable statistics indicative of what a full survey might disclose.

Among the forces militating against the maintenance of religious practices, as we have again and again remarked, were the growth of cities with their shifting populations and the difficulty of keeping contact with labourers in industries and mines. Thus in Paris, with its mounting population, often only one church existed for 25,000 to 100,000 parishioners.[39] One estimate had it that in Rome and its suburbs with a population in 1951 of about 1,800,000— a total which had risen sharply since 1940—only 400,000 went to mass on Sundays. If that figure was correct, and if the aged and infants were not counted, approximately 1,000,000 Romans could be classed as non-practising.[40] In Paris not far from the same time surveys appeared to show that the proportion of practising Roman Catholics varied from parish to parish from about one in fourteen to one in five of the population. It was high for children but fell off during the working years, rose in later years, and was larger among women than men.[41] In Lens, a coal-mining centre north of Paris, not far from 1950 only between a twentieth and a seventh of the miners and labourers who constituted the large majority of the population could be reckoned as practising, while half or more of the engineers and bourgeoisie were in that category.[42] Clearly the proportion of those who called themselves Catholic and who from the standpoint of their church could be counted as practising differed from section to section even of any one large city, and from class to class. As was true among both Roman Catholics and Protestants, the labourers in the industries and mines—the products of the revolutionary age—tended to be de-Christianized; yet exceptions were to be found.

Summary

In the face of the many phases of the revolutionary age which were making for the de-Christianization of Europe between 1914 and the time these pages were penned, a striking revival was seen in the worship of a large proportion of the Roman Catholic population. In spite of two world wars, vast political revolutions which brought in a succession of regimes in most of Western Europe undreamed of in 1914, the spread of anti-Christian Communism and

[39] Michonneau, *op. cit.*, p. 98.
[40] Daniel, *Aspects de la Practique Religieuse à Paris*, p. 119.
[41] *Ibid.*, pp. 111–113.
[42] *Ibid.*, p. 115.

of the more subtle but no less corroding secularism, and the progress of industrialization, by the mid-twentieth century in large elements of the Roman Catholic constituency the level of the devotional life was higher than at the close of the nineteenth century. The rising tide was particularly marked among the laity, paralleling what was taking place through Catholic Action and through various aspects of social and political activity. The chief manifestations were the Eucharistic Congresses and the Liturgical Movement. The laity who felt their impact were led to a more intelligent participation in the central rite of the Church than at any time since the early Christian centuries.

What was seen was more a revival than a revolution. The inherited devotional practices continued the course which they had long been following. Devotion to the Sacred Heart of Jesus seems to have been unabated. The declaration of the assumption of the Virgin was an additional step in making more precise what the large majority of the faithful believed had been implicit in the truth entrusted to the Church from the beginning. The devout prized her as their predecessors had done for centuries.

The gap between the practising Roman Catholics on the one hand and their non-practising co-religionists and the de-Christianized of Roman Catholic ancestry on the other continued to widen. Many among the faithful were not content to permit the gap to remain unclosed. Here and there active efforts were put forth to win back the alienated. Some of them we are to see in our country-by-country survey. The loyal, led by the Popes, aspired to make Christ King in all ranges of life and among all men, both in the traditional Christendom and throughout the earth.

It must be noted that for the most part the new movements showing creative imagination and energy, whether in worship or in organizations, had their origin in Europe and not on the geographic frontiers of the Roman Catholic Church—the Americas, Asia, or Africa. Here was a contrast with Protestantism. As we shall see, after 1914 many fresh currents issued in Europe from that branch of the faith, but much more than in the Roman Catholic Church movements and leadership for world-wide Protestantism came from the Americas and Asia.

CHAPTER VI

The Intellectual Response of Roman Catholics

As we come to the intellectual response of Roman Catholics in Europe to the twentieth-century stage of the revolutionary age we note both similarities and contrasts with the nineteenth century.

As in the nineteenth century, much intellectual activity was seen in theology and related subjects. It took place predominantly in the historic heartland of the Roman Catholic Church, Latin Europe and the areas immediately bordering on Latin Europe, rather than in the portions of the world where that church had been planted since the collapse of the Roman Empire thirteen hundred or more years before—North-western and Central Europe, the Americas, Asia, and Africa south of the Sahara.

In contrast with the nineteenth century, no departures from the faith as defined by Rome appeared which were as marked as those of Hermes, Günther, Lamennais, Bautain, or the Modernists. Although Pius XII in *Humani generis* condemned some current trends, the censure was not as sharp as that evoked by certain movements which emerged between 1815 and 1914. Also, Protestant theology attracted more attention from Roman Catholics after 1914 than in the preceding century. To be sure, such men in the Protestant stream as Kant and Hegel had earlier been seriously dealt with, but they were philosophers, not theologians. Protestant Biblical scholarship had also had repercussions, especially in Modernism, but it was not primarily theological. In the half-century after 1914 Karl Barth, the most prominent Protestant theologian of the period, was discussed almost as much by Roman Catholic as by Protestant scholars. The "form criticism," or *Formgeschichte,* which had been developed by Protestants, also had repercussions.

We will first speak of what was taking place in theology and then, as in the corresponding chapter on the nineteenth century, go on to Biblical studies. A complete account would carry us far beyond the proper length of this chapter. We must content ourselves with brief mention of some of the major features and trends and a few of the outstanding figures.

THE RECEDING ECHOES OF MODERNISM

The Modernist movement, prominent in the closing years of the nineteenth century, had only faint echoes after the vigorous action against it taken by Pius X.[1] A late representative, Ernesto Buonaiuti, a native of Rome and a priest who for a time taught in the University of Rome, was not excommunicated until 1921, then was reconciled (temporarily as it proved), was finally excommunicated in 1924, and did not die until 1946. Most of the time he lived on in Rome, wrote,[2] and lectured. A man of great charm, deeply religious, widely read, he had many friends and disciples. He was not a Modernist of the kind represented by Loisy but wished to see the Church revived spiritually and stressed the social application of the Gospel.[3]

Baron Friedrich von Hügel (1852–1925), a layman, a friend of Tyrrell and Loisy, but regretting the extremes to which the latter went,[4] although he had feared excommunication, remained within the Roman Catholic Church. He deplored what he regarded as a shallow anti-intellectualism in much of that church in his day, but he dissociated himself from the more radical Modernists. He had warm friendships with many Protestants, gave himself more and more to spiritual counselling, and had a marked effect on influential Anglicans.[5]

For a time, as we have seen, some of the zealously orthodox, the so-called "integralists," keen to scent any suggestion of hersey, made unhappy some who were seeking to avoid Modernism and yet to take constructive account of the intellectual currents of the revolutionary age. We have also noted that in his initial encyclical Benedict XV, while reaffirming the condemnation of Modernism by his predecessor and stressing the study of Aquinas, sought to curb the excesses of the heresy-hunters.[6] Many, therefore, who wished to remain within the Roman Catholic Church and had been timid about espousing views which might bring them into conflict with the authorities, were able to breathe freely again.

EMPHASIS ON THOMISM

The Papal endorsement of the schoolmen and especially of Aquinas continued

---

[1] Volume I, pp. 380–389.

[2] See, for example, his *Il Modernismo Cattolico* (Modena, Guanda Editors, 1943, pp. 337).

[3] Valdo Vinay, *Ernesto Buonaiuti e l'Italia del suo tempo* (Torre Pellice, Liberia Editrice Claudiana, 1956, pp. 262), *passim*.

[4] Volume I, pp. 366, 367.

[5] Michael de la Bedoyère, *The Life of Baron von Hügel* (London, J. M. Dent & Sons, 1951, pp. xviii, 366); Friedrich von Hügel, *Selected Letters 1896–1924*, edited with a memoir by Bernard Holland (London, J. M. Dent & Sons, 1927, pp. vii, 396); Friedrich von Hügel, *Essays and Addresses on the Philosophy of Religion* (first series, London, J. M. Dent & Sons, 1921, pp. xix, 309; second series, London, J. M. Dent & Sons, 1926, pp. ix, 287); Lester Vallis Lester-Garland, *The Religious Philosophy of Baron F. von Hügel* (London, J. M. Dent & Sons, 1933, pp. vii, 115); Arthur Hazard Dakin, *Von Hügel and the Supernatural* (New York, The Macmillan Co., 1934, pp. xii, 273).

[6] *Acta Apostolicae Sedis*, Vol. VI, pp. 576, 577.

to be reflected in theological thought and writing. Out of the large number whose thought was expressed in print we may select four. The choice does not necessarily mean that they were the most important. But through their books they came into a certain prominence and were widely read. Each in his own way contributed to the effort to approach through Aquinas the intellectual and religious problems presented by the revolutionary age.

One of the four, the Dominican Reginald Garrigou-Lagrange, we have already met as a specialist on ascetic and mystical theology. Born in 1877, in 1909 he became a professor in the Collegium Angelicum in Rome and there did most of his work. He wrote several commentaries on sections of the *Summa Theologica* of Aquinas.[7] In addition he was the author of the seven-volume *Cursus Theologiae,* which obviously reflected the Thomistic approach.[8]

A second Thomistic scholar who also wrote voluminously was a layman, Jacques Maritain (1882——). He was born in Paris, the son of a Burgundian lawyer, a nominal Roman Catholic, and a liberal Protestant mother. He was baptized by a Protestant clergyman but had little if any religious rearing. While a student in the Sorbonne, specializing in biology, he fell in love with a fellow student, a Russian Jewess, whom he married (1904). Both were sceptical and searching. Both were greatly impressed by Bergson. They attended Bergson's lectures and were members of an intimate group which met with that philosopher. Maritain became his earnest disciple. Through Léon Bloy (1846-1917), an author who had come to a warm faith in his youth and was a precursor of a French Roman Catholic literary revival of which we are to hear more in the next chapter, Maritain and his wife were introduced to the Roman Catholic Church and in 1906 were baptized. Their spiritual director, a Dominican, drew their attention to the *Summa Theologica* of Aquinas. To Maritain Aquinas came as a revelation—a demonstration that philosophy was not incompatible with Christianity. He gave himself to the study of the *Doctor Angelicus* and of Aristotle— to whom Aquinas was deeply indebted. He became a teacher of philosophy. Although still a warm admirer of Bergson, he was convinced that the latter's system did not have adequate answers to the questions raised by the revolutionary age. He found them, rather, in Aristotle and Aquinas. His first published book, on Bergsonianism, appeared soon after 1914. Other books rapidly followed, at first

---

[7] Among them were *De Beatitudine de Actibus Humanis et Habitibus. Commentarius in Summam Theologicam S. Thomas Ia IIae qq. 1–54* (Turin, R. Berruti & Co., 1951, pp. 485); *The One God. Commentary on the First Part of St. Thomas' Theological Summa,* translated by Bede Rose (St. Louis, B. Herder Book Co., 1943, pp. viii, 736); *Grace. Commentary on the Summa Theologica of St. Thomas Ia IIae qq. 109–14,* translated by the Dominican Nuns, Corpus Christi Monastery, Menlo Park, Calif. (St. Louis, B. Herder Book Co., 1952, pp. xi, 535); *God. His Existence and His Nature. A Thomistic Solution of Certain Agnostic Antinomies,* translated from the fifth French edition by Bede Rose (St. Louis, B. Herder Book Co., 2 vols., 1934–1936); *Predestination,* translated by Bede Rose (St. Louis, B. Herder Book Co., 1939, pp. xiv, 382); *La Synthèse Thomiste* (Paris, Desclée de Brouwer, 1947, pp. 739).

[8] (Turin, 1943–1951).

on philosophy and theology and then also on politics. Maritain lectured extensively in Europe and America. From 1945 to 1948 he was French ambassador to the Vatican. Then he became a member of the faculty of Princeton University. In his day he was often called the greatest living Roman Catholic philosopher.

Basic to the teaching and writing of Maritain was the conviction that Western Europe had gone wrong in following Descartes's stress on rationalism and in making a sharp disjunction between reason and faith. He believed that the Kantian approach was not adequate, even though it pointed out some of the limitations of reason. He maintained that in the synthesis of faith and reason effected by Aquinas, the bringing together of reason with the Christian Gospel, lay the hope of the world.[9]

A Dominican, Antonin Gilbert Sertillanges (1863–1948), was one of the outstanding interpreters of Aquinas. Although he lived to a great age, his mind remained alert to the end. He centred his work on creation, and his conception of creation had a marked influence on the development of Thomism. He was familiar with modern science, as was Maritain, but unlike the latter, who was largely self-trained in theology, he was more nearly in the historic Roman Catholic tradition.[10]

A fourth Thomistic scholar was another Frenchman, Étienne Gilson (1884 ———). Historian and philosopher, a layman, he was born in Paris and educated at the Sorbonne. He was taken prisoner in World War I and used the months of captivity for reflection. He taught in Lille, Strasbourg, the Sorbonne, and the Collège de France. He was the organizer and for a time director of the Pontifical Institute of Medieval Studies in Toronto. In his youth he became familiar with Descartes and the Cartesian philosophy. He was introduced to both Descartes and Aquinas by a disciple of Auguste Comte. He brought, therefore, to his study of Aquinas a background of the modern philosophy which was deeply indebted to Descartes. He ranged widely over the schoolmen and pointed out the striking differences among them. He adhered to Aquinas. He held that Aquinas, in approaching Aristotle from the angle of the Christian revelation, had made of philosophy what it should be: rational and so enlightened by Christian faith that it became true philosophy. He held that the modern divorce of philosophy and

---

[9] Charles A. Fecher, *The Philosophy of Jacques Maritain* (Westminster, Md., The Newman Press, 1953), pp. xiv, 361), *passim*. For a list of Maritain's books see Jacques Croteau, *Les Fondements Thomistes du Personnalisme de Maritain* (Éditions de l'Université d'Ottawa, 1956, pp. 267), pp. 254, 255. On Léon Bloy see Albert Beguin, *Léon Bloy: a Study in Impatience*, translated by Edith M. Riley (New York, Sheed and Ward, 1917, pp. vii, 247), and *Léon Bloy, Pilgrim of the Absolute. Selections by Raïssa Maritain and Jacques Maritain*, translated by J. Coleman and H. E. Binssa (New York, Pantheon Books, 1947, pp. 358).

[10] Among the books by Sertillanges are *Saint Thomas Aquinas and his Work*, translated by Godfrey Anstruther (London, Burns Oates & Washbourne, 1933, pp. ix, 150); *La Philosophie de S. Thomas d'Aquin* (Paris, Aubier, Éditions Montaigne, rev. ed., 2 vols., 1940); *La Philosophie Morale de Saint Thomas d'Aquin* (Paris, Aubier, Editions Montaigne, new ed., 1946, pp. iii, 433); *Les Grandes Thèses de la Philosophie Thomiste* (Paris, Bloud & Gay, 1928, pp. 247).

theology did violence to philosophy. Viewing German Idealism as springing from that divorce and regarding Idealism as dead, he was profoundly convinced that Thomism was the philosophy of the future, the answer to the prevailing existentialism and Marxism.[11]

Some others of whom the limitations of space prevent more than a bare mention but who made notable contributions to the study of scholastic thought include Joseph Geyser (1869–1948), the central figure in the revival of Thomism in Germany,[12] Franz Ehrle (1845–1934), Martin Grabmann (1875–1949), and Maurice de Wulf (1867–1947).

Varied Attempts to Take Account of the Contemporary Scene

Among Roman Catholic theologians were many who deplored what they regarded as a ghetto mentality, the effort to remain aloof from the revolutionary world and to approach theology in ways which had long been employed. While honouring Aquinas, they sought to regard him, as Mercier said, quoting Lacordaire, not as a barrier restricting further thought, but as a light-house, a beacon illuminating and guiding in the voyage to untried seas. Such, indeed, was the attitude of several Thomists, among them Maritain. Rudolph Otto and Kierkegaard were read by some theologians and, as we are to see, Karl Barth had a marked impact.[13] Many shared in the efforts to chart a course in the stormy seas of the twentieth-century stage of the revolutionary age. They did not always agree among themselves. None who came to prominence ventured as far from what was permitted by Rome as had Lamennais and the Modernists. Yet some sailed so close to the limits set by the Papacy that they brought down on themselves the thinly veiled censure of *Humani generis.*

Humani generis, it will be recalled, condemned what it viewed as erroneous applications of the theory of evolution. It did not forbid scientific research into or discussion of the theory but held that inquiries into the origin of the human body as coming from preëxistent and living matter must not counter the Church's teaching that souls are created immediately by God. It also cautioned against the assumption that after Adam true men existed on the earth who did

---

[11] For a brief summary of Gilson's teaching see Anton C. Pegis, *A Gilson Reader. Selected Writings of Étienne Gilson* (Garden City, N.Y., Hanover House, 1957, pp. 358), pp. 7–19. For a bibliography of Gilson's writings see *ibid.,* pp. 348–351, and J. Maritain and others, *Etienne Gilson, Philosophe de la Chrétienté* (Paris, Éditions du Cerf, 1949, pp. 295), pp. 14–21. Two of Gilson's important works, showing his approach, are *The Philosophy of St. Thomas Aquinas,* a translation of *Le Thomisme,* by E. B. Bullough (St. Louis, B. Herder Book Co., 1941, pp. xv, 372), and his Gifford Lectures, *l'Esprit de la Philosophie Médiévale* (Paris, J. Vrin, 2 vols., 1932), translated by A. H. C. Downes as *The Spirit of Medieval Philosophy* (New York, Charles Scribner's Sons, 1940, pp. ix, 490).

[12] *De Katholieke Encyclopaedie,* Vol. XI, p. 748.

[13] Aubert, *La Théologie Catholique au Milieu du XXe Siècle,* p. 51; Loewenich, *Der moderne Katholizismus,* p. 287.

not have him as their ancestor or that Adam represented collectively a certain number of parents.

Several Roman Catholic intellectuals attempted to make their peace with evolution. Thus a Jesuit, Pierre Teilhard de Chardin (1881–1955), a distinguished geologist and paleontologist, presented an interpretation of evolution which was not materialistic or mechanistic and which against a purely naturalistic conception of the world opposed what he regarded as the Christian view. Yet Rome considered his position unorthodox and forbade him to teach or to put his controversial books into print.[14]

Pierre Lecomte du Noüy (1883–1947), a distinguished French scientist who from agnosticism had come to Christian faith, put forward a view of evolution which regarded the life of the spirit as being the crown of that process.[15]

The climate of opinion in the Western world stressed evolutionary development in ideas, institutions, religion, and dogma. In *Humani generis* Pius XII sought to check what he regarded as the danger to Christian thought in a relativism which emphasized that development at the expense of a doctrine considered by the Church divinely revealed. He was supported by theologians who viewed religious truths as having the immutability of mathematical abstractions.[16]

The mounting emphasis upon the laity which we noted in the last two chapters and which found expression in the Liturgical Movement, Catholic Action, and various organizations was reflected in theology. That emphasis was in part born of the temper of the times with its trend towards democracy in one or another form. It also arose out of recognition of the fact that many of the historic constituency of the Roman Catholic Church were being de-Christianized through movements arising from the revolutionary age. Here and there efforts were made to define the position of the laity in theological terms. They were stimulated by the world conference on the apostolate of the laity which convened in Rome in October, 1951, with delegates from seventy-two states and thirty-eight international organizations.

Two men were especially prominent in formulating a theological basis for the movement, G. Philips of Louvain[17] and the Dominican Yves M.-J. Congar

---

[14] Louis Cognet, *Le Père Teilhard de Chardin et la Pensée Contemporaine* (Paris, Portulan chez Flammarion, 1952), *passim;* Teilhard de Chardin, *Le Phénomène Humain,* translated by Bernard Wall as *The Phenomenon of Man* (New York, Harper & Brothers, 1959, pp. 318); *Time,* December 14, 1959.

[15] Mary Lecomte du Noüy, *Lecomte du Noüy, De l'Agnosticisme à la Foi* (Paris, La Colombe, Éditions du Vieux Colombier, 1955, pp. 251), *passim.* Among Lecomte du Noüy's books were *Biological Time* (London, Methuen & Co., 1936, pp. x, 180); *L'Avenir de l'Esprit* (New York, Brentano's, 1943, pp. xviii, 308); *La Dignité Humaine* (New York, Brentano's, 1944, pp. 331); and *Human Destiny* (New York, Longmans, Green and Co., 1947, pp. xix, 289).

[16] Aubert, *op. cit.,* pp. 50, 51.

[17] G. Philips, *Le Rôle du Laïcat dans l'Église* (Tournai, Casterman, 1954, pp. 248).

of France.[18] They reacted against what had long been customary—to regard the function of the laity as being to kneel before the altar, to remain seated before the pulpit, and to contribute from their purses. They held that assigning this role to the laity had arisen from experience with heretical movements in the Middle Ages led by laymen and with the Protestant Reformation with its emphasis on the priesthood of all believers. They pointed out that notable lay movements had been loyal to the Roman Catholic Church and cited as an outstanding example that of Francis of Assisi, a layman. They sought to define on the basis of Scripture the sense in which the laity could properly be said to share in the priesthood of the faithful and to make clear the respective roles in that priesthood of the hierarchy and the laity. They believed that the recent practice of the Roman Catholic Church needed reforming, but not in the Protestant sense, and enthusiastically welcomed as steps in that direction such movements as Catholic Action and the new emphasis on the reading of the Bible. They would have endorsed the phrase of another of the clergy that "neither are the clergy at the service of the laity nor the laity at the service of the clergy. Both together are to serve the Church."[19]

Of somewhat similar import was what was called kerygmatic theology. It had its radiating centre in Jesuits in Innsbruck. Outstanding among them were Josef Jungmann (1889——) and Hugo Rahner (1900——). They sought to formulate a theological structure which, while essentially the same as that historically taught by the Church, would be so shaped as to meet the needs of non-theologians, among both the clergy and the laity. Its aim would be to help them proclaim the eternal Gospel in terms which could be comprehended by the children of the revolutionary age and which would speak to their needs. They wished to present Christian dogma less in its metaphysical aspects than in its religious significance as the joyous message of salvation, good news for a distraught humanity.[20] We have already met Jungmann as active in the Liturgical Movement. Through kerygmatic theology he was striving from another angle to accomplish what that movement had as an objective—the bringing of all the faithful into an intelligently worshipping community.

Slightly earlier a French Jesuit, Yves de Montcheuil (1900–1944), who died in World War II, was seeking so to present the historic faith of the Church as to make it obviously germane to the concrete needs of the rank and file of his fellow countrymen.[21] He was endeavouring to meet the challenge of existentialism.

[18] Yves M.-J. Congar, *Jalons pour une Théologie du Laïcat* (Paris, Éditions du Cerf, 2nd ed., 1954, pp. 683). An English translation, by Donald Attwater, is *Lay People in the Church. A Study for a Theology of the Laity* (London, Bloomsbury Publishing Co., 1957, pp. xxxii, 447).

[19] Aubert, *op. cit.*, p. 55.

[20] *Ibid.*, pp. 47, 48.

[21] *Ibid.*, p. 45. See, for example, Yves de Montcheuil, *Aspects de l'Église* (Paris, Editions du Cerf, 1949, pp. 169), a semi-popular brief treatment of the Church delivered in 1942–1943 in lectures for the intellectuals.

Somewhat similarly, the German Romano Guardini (1885——) wrote for thoughtful laymen faced with the perplexities of their times. Several of his books were composed during World War II, to aid those who were troubled by the questions which that conflict raised about man, God, and the meaning of life and of history. The fact that some of his writing was translated was evidence that it appealed to an even larger constituency than that in Germany.[22]

The two world wars and the rapid changes in the hurrying decades stimulated Roman Catholic thinkers to deal with the philosophy of history. Could men be hopeful of the outcome, or must they view the future of mankind and of civilization as did some secular writers, among them Spengler and Toynbee, with either complete or ambiguous pessimism? Here opinion was divided, as it was among Protestants.

Some, with kinship to the social gospel in the United States and Ritschlianism on the Continent, were optimistic. Basing their theology on the incarnation, the assumption by the Son of God of human nature, on the statement, recorded in Genesis, that God viewed His created world as good, and on the invitation to man to collaborate with God in His creative work, they held that prevenient grace would bring man to a stage where he would be free from ignorance and disease. They viewed the expansion of Christianity in the Western world and the progress of science as stages in the advance of humanity towards a community of love in God. Through the incarnation the body of Christ was being developed. These convictions were finding expression through Catholic Action and the institution of the feast of Christ the King, with the vision of the reign of Christ in all the ranges of man's life—among nations, families, professional groups, and industry. The scientific research and the proletarian revolutions of the day were viewed as preparations essential to the spread of the Gospel throughout the earth.[23]

On the other hand, there were those who espoused an eschatological theology incorporating a pessimistic outlook. It was pessimistic in the sense that it did not view the achievements of science and the revolutions of the age as signs of the effective coöperation of man with God in bringing in the reign of Christ. Some of the eschatological theologians were mission-minded and held that the nations of the world were being converted. Yet they regarded the Church as *in via* towards a promised land, and believed that what was to be anticipated was not

---

[22] Romano Guardini, *The Faith and Modern Man,* translated by Charlotte E. Forsyth (New York, Pantheon Books, 1952, pp. vii, 166); Romano Guardini, *Welt und Person. Versuche zur christlichen Lehre von Menschen* (Würzburg, Werkbund-Verlag, 1950, pp. 158); Romano Guardini, *The Last Things. Concerning Death, Purification after Death, Resurrection, Judgment, and Eternity,* translated by Charlotte E. Forsyth and Grace B. Branham (New York, Pantheon Books, 1954, pp. 118); Romano Guardini, *Der Herr. Betrachtungen über die Person und das Leben Jesu Christi* (Würzburg, Werkbund-Verlag, 1949, pp. xi, 656), translated by Elinor Castendyk Briefs as *The Lord* (Chicago, Henry Regnery Co., 1954, pp. xi, 535).

[23] Aubert, *op. cit.,* pp. 65–67.

a gradual mastery by Christ of the present world but the glorious return of Christ. Christians, so they held with Paul, were strangers and pilgrims in this present world, and men, even when born anew in Christ, could not build the Kingdom of God. They maintained that the coming of that Kingdom was a pure act of God's grace which was to be greeted humbly and was not even partially the fruit of human civilization.[24]

A theology of history was being developed, among others by the French Jesuit Jean Daniélou (1905——). Daniélou had kinship with eschatological theology in that he held that history has in it no visible determinism but in it God has been working out a plan which He has made through His grace and which He will faithfully carry through. Man, so Daniélou maintained, can do nothing to thwart that plan. Human freedom has no part in it, for God will carry it through though man is faithless to his obligations to God. Amid all the tragedies and revolutions of the age, Daniélou held, the Christian conviction is that the City of God is being built, even when we cannot perceive it, because God is faithful to His promise, in spite of man's misuse of his liberty. Marxist optimism, so Daniélou said, was shallow and naïve because it failed to take into account the terrifying element of human freedom.[25] History, as he conceived it as taught in the Scriptures, is the realization of God's plan. In the accomplishment of that plan "everything happens at its appointed hour." The Christian insight, he goes on to say, is that the second advent of Christ is always imminent but may be delayed much longer than the early Christians anticipated. The conversion of the nations would be extended over many centuries. But the second advent was sure.[26]

Henri de Lubac (1896——), also a French Jesuit, while holding that "this world is good and will be saved" and that the hope of peace upon the world and "the unity of all peoples in the service and praise of Jehovah" is not a dream but rests upon the word of God, declared that "the Church realizes full well that she will never triumph completely over evil."[27]

[24] *Ibid.*, pp. 67, 68.

[25] Daniélou, *Advent*, pp. 10–15.

[26] Jean Daniélou, *The Salvation of the Nations*, translated by Angeline Bouchard (New York, Sheed and Ward, 1950, pp. 118), pp. 70–81; Jean Daniélou, *Théologie du Judéo-Christianisme* (Paris, Desclée, 1958, pp. 457); Jean Daniélou, *Origene* (Paris, La Table Ronde, 1948, pp. 310), translated by Walter Mitchell as *Origen* (New York, Sheed and Ward, 1955, pp. xvii, 343); Jean Daniélou, *Advent*, translated by Rosemary Sheed (New York, Sheed and Ward, 1951, pp. v, 181); Jean Daniélou, *Sacramentum Futuri. Études sur les Origines de la Typologie Biblique* (Paris, Beauchesne, 1950, pp. xvi, 265); Jean Daniélou, *Platonisme et Théologie Mystique. Essai sur la Doctrine Spirituelle de Saint Grégoire de Nysse* (Paris, Aubier, Éditions Montaigne, 1944, pp. 339); Jean Daniélou, *God and the Ways of Knowing*, translated by Walter Roberts (New York, Pantheon Books, 1957, pp. 249); Jean Daniélou, *Bible et Liturgie. La Théologie Biblique des Sacraments et des Fêtes d'après les Pères de l'Église* (Paris, Éditions du Cerf, 1958, pp. 477).

[27] Henri de Lubac, *Catholicism. A Study of Dogma in Relation to the Corporate Destiny of Mankind*, translated by Lancelot C. Sheppard from the 4th French edition (London, Burns Oates & Washbourne, 1950, pp. xix, 283), pp. 74, 138.

This contrast in the Roman Catholic philosophy of history was paralleled in Protestant thought. It found vivid expression in the attempt to formulate the Christian hope in the Assembly of the World Council of Churches which convened in Evanston, Illinois, in 1953.

Still another attempt to make the Roman Catholic Church speak to the revolutionary age was through a Christian existentialism. Here an outstanding figure, Gabriel Marcel, has already been mentioned.[28] Gabriel Marcel (1889——), son of an agnostic French diplomat, educated in the University of Paris, in his early manhood was much impressed by Coleridge, Schelling, Bergson, and Royce. In 1928 he became a Roman Catholic. Seeking for himself and for others to make Christianity speak to the needs of his age, he developed a Christian existentialism. He accepted existence as actual and physical in the original sense of that word and not as a metaphysical abstraction, and from there worked out his philosophy.[29]

Humani generis was in part directed, not against Marcel as an individual, but against a tendency which Pius XII thought that he discerned to discount Aquinas and scholastic theology and to place undue stress upon existentialism. It had also in mind trends represented by Daniélou and de Lubac, although neither of them was mentioned by name.

Michael Schmaus (1897——), regarded by some as the outstanding German Roman Catholic theologian of the 1940's and 1950's, covered the full field. He also dealt with eschatology and the philosophy of history. He sought to interpret the doctrines of the Church in terms of contemporary thought and to bring consistency into the teachings of the Bible, the Church Fathers, and the decisions of the councils by attempting to discern their intention in terms of the problems to which they addressed themselves.[30] In this purpose he had much in common with many European Roman Catholic theologians of the day. They were loyal to the Church but exercised much freedom—a latitude which was not shared by most of the contemporary Roman Catholic theologians of the Americas.

---

[28] Chapter I. See also Roberts, *Existentialism and Religious Belief*, pp. 277 ff.

[29] For a statement of his position see his Gifford Lectures: Gabriel Marcel, *The Mystery of Being* (London, Harvill Press, 2 vols., 1950–1951). For treatments of him see *De Katholieke Encyclopaedie*, Vol. XVII, p. 229; A. A. Leite Rainho, *L'Existencialisme de M. Gabriel Marcel* (Lisbon, Uniãa Gráfica, 1955, pp. 143); Friedrich Hoefeld, *Der christliche Existenzialismus Gabriel Marcels. Eine Analysis der geistlichen Situation der Gegenwart* (Zürich, Zwingli Verlag, 1956, pp. 174); Étienne Henri Gilson, *Existentialisme Chrétien Gabriel Marcel* (Paris, Plon, 1948, pp. 325); and Paul Ricoeur, *Gabriel Marcel et Karl Jaspers. Philosophie du Mystère et Philosophie du Paradox* (Paris, Éditions du Temps Présent, 1948, pp. 455).

[30] Michael Schmaus, *Katholische Dogmatik* (Munich, M. Hueber, 5 vols. in 7 parts, 1953–1959); Michael Schmaus, *Von den letzten Dingen* (Münster, Regensburg, 1948, pp. 735); Johann Auer and Hermann Volk, editors, *Theologie in Geschichte und Gegenwart. Michael Schmaus zum sechzigsten Geburtstag dargebracht von seinem Freunden und Schülern* (Munich, K. Zink, 1957, pp. xxx, 956).

THE CHURCH: THE MYSTICAL BODY OF CHRIST

Much was made of the Church as the mystical body of Christ. This, as we have seen, was not a new emphasis. For example, in the nineteenth century Johann Adam Möhler of Tübingen had stressed it in *Die Einheit in der Kirche*.[31] Again and again twentieth-century Roman Catholic writers returned to the theme. This concern was in part a reaction against the individualism of the nineteenth century and it also countered the existentialism of the twentieth century. Both Catholic Action and the Liturgical Movement helped to create an interest in the Church as the community of the faithful. The emphasis upon the Eucharist, whether through the Eucharistic Congresses or the Eucharistic Movement, centring as it did upon the actual presence of Christ, tended to call attention to the Church as the *corpus Christi mysticum*. A renewed attention to ecclesiology followed. But many theologians, believing that too much was being made of the visible and hierarchical structure of the Church centralized under the infallible primacy of the Pope, stressed the Church as invisible, embracing all men of good will, mysteriously united by grace in the heavenly Christ.[32]

This view was strong between the two world wars. To it Karl Adam (1870 ——), long on the Tübingen faculty, gave an impulse by a notable book, translated into English as *The Spirit of Catholicism*.[33] In this book Adam expressed conviction that the Church is permeated by Christ, is organically united with Him, and is His body. The dogmas, morals, and worship of the Church, so he held, are stamped with the name of Christ, and the purpose of the Church is to make the Christian a second Christ, or Christ-like. Through the sacraments, he went on to say, and especially the sacrament of the altar, the faithful are incorporated in Christ. The authority of the Church, clearly, he declared, belongs only to Christ and is exercised in His name, for the Church came into being with the incarnation, when the Eternal Word became flesh. As Adam envisioned it, the Church is a community and is not the product of the faithful but in its unity embraces all redeemed humanity. Yet he insisted that the Church is a visible organism and the Pope is the continuing guarantee of its unity and is, indeed, the embodiment of that unity. The Pope rules *ex sese,* from himself, so Adam maintained, and is not dependent on individual bishops, the whole episcopate, or the rest of the faithful, but is the pastor to whom alone the sheep of the Divine Pastor are committed. Adam frankly recognized that the Church as seen in history had never been perfect but had always been in need of reform, but that was of the very nature of revelation, because grace and truth are conveyed to men through earthly vessels.

[31] Volume I, p. 379.
[32] Aubert, *op. cit.,* pp. 86–90.
[33] *Ibid.;* Karl Adam, *The Spirit of Catholicism,* revised edition, translated by Justin McCann (New York, The Macmillan Co., 1936, pp. xi, 272).

Maurice de la Taille (1872–1933) also made a notable contribution to the emphasis on the Church as the mystical body of Christ.[34] He had a marked influence on the Belgian Émile Mersch (1890–1940), who did much to bring fresh emphasis on the Church as the mystical body of Christ.[35]

Somewhat similarly, Henri de Lubac declared that the Church is both a universal and a visible community which cannot be divided. But, he said, it is not a this-worldly reality such as lends itself to exact measurement and analysis, but, as the Roman catechism called it, "a mystery of faith."[36] He developed that view in a historical survey of the Catholic Church in the Middle Ages.[37] In seeking to expound theology for the laity, Congar contributed a widely circulated short book on the Church.[38]

We have seen that Pius XII in the encyclical *Mystici Corporis Christi* endorsed the conception of the Church as the mystical body of Christ. In doing so, he silenced the opposition to it which some theologians had expressed. Yet he also, by identifying the Church with the Roman Catholic Church, discouraged any trend to emphasize the invisible character of the Church as contrasted with the visible ecclesiastical institution of which he was the head as the Vicegerent of Christ.

MARIOLOGY

In the period when emphasis was being placed on the Virgin Mary through the Papal pronouncement on her bodily assumption to heaven and what were believed to be additional appearances, notably in Lourdes and Fatima, it was to be expected that Mariology would be prominent in Roman Catholic theology.

We have already seen something of the honour paid Mary by the Popes of the twentieth century. In addition to the many titles by which she had been known through the ages, Benedict XV, Pius XI, and Pius XII either by implication or directly hailed her as co-Redemptrix. In 1918, in his apostolic letter *Inter sodalica,* Benedict XV said that she suffered and all but died along with her Son: "thus for the salvation of men she abdicated the rights of a mother towards her Son and in so far as it was hers to do, she immolated the Son to placate God's justice, so that she herself may justly be said to have redeemed

---

[34] *De Katholieke Encyclopaedie,* Vol. XXII, p. 810.

[35] Émile Mersch, *La Théologie du Corps Mystique* (Bruges, Desclée de Brouwer, 4th edition, 2 vols., 1954); Émile Mersch, *The Whole Christ. The Historical Development of the Doctrine of the Mystical Body in Scripture and Tradition,* translated by John R. Kelly (Milwaukee, The Bruce Publishing Co., 1938, pp. xvi, 623).

[36] Henri de Lubac, *The Splendour of the Church,* translated by Michael Mason (New York, Sheed and Ward, 1956, pp. xii, 289), pp. 4, 56.

[37] Henri de Lubac, *Corpus Mysticum: l'Eucharistie et l'Église au Moyen Age. Étude Historique* (Paris, Aubier, 2nd ed., 1949, pp. 373), *passim.*

[38] Marie-Joseph Congar, *Esquisses du Mystère de l'Église* (Paris, Éditions du Cerf, new ed., 1953, p. 79). For a more technical work by Congar see his *Vrai et Fausse Reformé dans l'Église* (Paris, Éditions du Cerf, 1950, pp. 648).

together with Christ the human race." At the end of the holy year of 1933 Pius XI publicly addressed Mary as co-Redemptrix. He had earlier declared, in the encyclical *Miserentissimus Redemptor* (1928), that by "giving us Christ the Redeemer, and by rearing Him, and offering Him at the foot of the cross as Victim for our sins . . . and by her most singular grace, became and is affectionately known as Reparatrix." He spoke of himself as confident of Mary's intercession with Christ, "Who alone is Mediator of God and man and Who willed to associate His mother with Himself as the advocate of sinners." In his encyclical *Mystici Corporis Christi* (1943) Pius XII spoke of Mary as "corporally the mother of our Head" who "through the added title of pain and glory became spiritually the mother of all His members," and said that it was she who by her prayers "obtained the grace that the Spirit of our Divine Redeemer, already given to the Church on the cross, should be bestowed through miraculous gifts on the newly founded hierarchy at Pentecost." He also said that she continued to show for the mystical body of Christ "the same mother's care and ardent love with which she clasped the infant Jesus to her warm and nourishing breast." These statements confirmed the earlier action of the Congregation of the Holy Office (1913) in praising the practice of adding to the name of Jesus the name "of His mother the blessed Mary as our co-Redemptrix" and in granting an indulgence (1914) for a prayer in which Mary was referred to as "co-Redemptrix of the human race."[39]

Pius XII was especially devoted to the Virgin Mary. We have seen that it was he who in the apostolic constitution *Munificentissimus Deus* (November 1, 1950) defined as dogma the bodily assumption of Mary. In a multiplicity of other documents and discourses he gave evidence of his emphasis upon Mary. For example, he spoke of her as the patroness of the Christian family, on the eve of World War II appealed to her for peace, again and again during that war authorized prayers through her for peace, and declared her to be the patroness of several cities, of the various dioceses of the Philippines, of Ceylon, and of Italian cyclists. He sent greetings to a large number of national Marian congresses, which were evidences of the rising popular devotion to Mary.[40]

With such emphasis on Mary by the Popes and in popular devotion, we need not be surprised that theologians paid attention to her. Because of the limitations of space a few examples out of many must suffice.

Daniélou gave a large place to the Virgin. He commented on the fact that

[39] Paul F. Palmer, *Mary in the Documents of the Church* (Westminster, Md., The Newman Press, 1952, pp. xxii, 129), pp. 90–100.

For an historical survey, not polemical, but with a distinctly Protestant slant, by a Waldensian scholar, see Giovanni Miegge, *The Virgin Mary. The Roman Catholic Marian Doctrine,* translated from the Italian by Waldo Smith (Philadelphia, The Westminster Press, 1955, pp. 196). See also Loewenich, *Der moderne Katholizismus,* pp. 219–281.

[40] Domenico Bertetto, compiler, *Il Magistero Mariano di Pio XII. Edizione Italiana di Tutti i Documenti Mariani di Sua Santità Pio XII* (Rome, Edizioni Paoline, 1956, pp. 1015), pp. 184, 187, 208, 210, 220–225, 236–238, 241–245, 276, 277, 296, 323, 347, 348, 398–402, 445, 612 ff.

she was coming "more and more into view in contemporary Catholic life," and not from an addition to Scripture but "from the mind of the Word of God Himself as it came to be more clearly understood over the centuries by the faith of the community." He maintained that in her all the aspirations, inspirations, and graces of the Old Testament were summed up and that she not only had a decisive part in the birth of Christ but also continued to play a leading part in preparing for every subsequent coming of Christ, for "He has come but not yet wholly come." Just as Mary was in Israel before Christ came, he said, "so she is present to the nations which are still in darkness," and the "nations which do not yet know Christ" have had "special protection and preparation." She is the prevenient grace, Daniélou declared, the grace which prepares for the grace where it has not yet come. As "we are still living in the time before the true Church" of which the "Church as she now is only is a figure," Mary's "presence fills the space between Pentecost and the day of judgement, in exactly the same way as she filled the space between the Ascension and Pentecost." She "is still at work in the Church preparing it for its final glory." Her manifestation, he was convinced, was still growing, as was shown by her frequent appearances in the preceding hundred years—as in Lourdes, La Sallette, and Fatima. Since Mary is the "spouse of the Holy Ghost" and through her presence the Holy Ghost was poured out at Pentecost, he believed that the increasing frequency of her appearances gave hope for "a new descent of the Holy Ghost, a new Pentecost."[41]

Louis Bouyer (1913——), of the French Oratory, said that the terms "co-Redemptrix" and "co-Mediatrix" could mean either too much or too little and that, therefore, the Church hesitated to use them. Strictly speaking, he said, God-made-man is the only Redeemer and Paul had said (I Tim. 2:5) that "there is one mediator between God and man, the man Christ Jesus." Yet he maintained that Mary coöperated in the work of redemption accomplished on Calvary.[42]

The Italian Domenico Bertetto (1914——) in a larger work outlined the history of Mariology in the Bible in the ante-Nicene and post-Nicene fathers and in medieval and modern theology and piety and expounded the beliefs which constituted Mariology. Mary, so he held, is co-Redemptrix, the dispenser of all the graces, and the *auxilium Christianorum*. Her mediation does not detract from the mediatorial function of Christ.[43]

As recently as 1941 some questions concerning Mary had not yet been fully resolved by the Pope when he spoke infallibly. Roman Catholic theologians

---

[41] Daniélou, *Advent,* pp. 101, 109, 112, 117, 119, 120.

[42] Louis Bouyer, *Le Trône de la Sagesse. Essai sur la Signification du Culte Marial* (Paris, Éditions du Cerf, 1957, pp. 296), *passim.*

[43] Domenico Bertetto, *Maria nel Domma Cattolico. Trattato di Mariologia* (Turin, Società Editrice Internazionale, 2nd ed., 1955, pp. 724), *passim.*

were still divided on the extent of her place in the work of redemption and as the "mediatrix of all the graces."[44]

UNRESOLVED ISSUES IN THEOLOGY

Not only were some features of the work and place of Mary still under discussion by Roman Catholic theologians, but on several other issues no common mind had emerged and the Pope had not spoken authoritatively.

One of the questions had been debated in the nineteenth century. It had to do with the manner in which the mass was a sacrifice.[45] The doctrine that the mass was a sacrifice was not challenged. All agreed that one victim was offered and that the number of separate daily offerings was mounting. One view was that since a real death had occurred on Calvary, the mass was only a mystical immolation. Another view had it that each mass was a real sacrifice and that in every mass Christ is the Victim, but without the qualities which His risen body has in heaven. Maurice de la Taille put forward an interpretation which he believed to have been found in the Fathers: as Christ at His institution of the Eucharist offered a sacrifice of a Victim Who was to be immolated on the morrow, so now in the mass a sacrifice is offered of a Victim immolated once for all on Calvary. He believed that the mass repeats mystically the sacrifice on Calvary, but in an unbloody manner.[46]

As may be discerned from what we have sketched in this rapid summary, most of the creative activity in Roman Catholic theology in the four decades which followed 1914 was in France and Germany. In France it displayed much freedom and was widely discussed by lay folk, especially among the *petite bourgeoisie*. The theological ferment in West Germany after World War II was greater than that in France, and the German laity were much more concerned than were the French laity. Yet less was known of it outside the country than was the discussion in France.

BIBLICAL STUDIES

The attention to Biblical studies and to archeology as throwing light on the Scriptures continued the growth it had shown in the nineteenth century.[47] It paralleled the increasing emphasis in the twentieth century upon the reading of the Bible by the laity.

The Biblical Commission (*Pontificia Commissio de re Biblica*), founded in Rome in 1902 by Leo XIII, continued. Its members made themselves familiar with what was being done in Biblical studies not only by Roman Catholics but

[44] W. J. McGarry in *Religion and the Modern World*, p. 36.
[45] Volume I, p. 393.
[46] McGarry, *op. cit.*, p. 37.
[47] Volume I, pp. 395, 396.

also by Protestants. It published Biblical studies, passed on questions raised by Roman Catholic scholars, and advised on what studies and approaches were permitted.[48]

Albert Lagrange (1855–1938), the Dominican who had pioneered in founding (1890) the centre of Biblical studies in Jerusalem, carried on work in that city. As we have seen,[49] in the course of the agitation against Modernism he had been suspected of sympathy with it, had been recalled to France, but had made his full submission to Pius X and with the latter's approval had returned to his work in Jerusalem. There he kept at his studies and writing until an advanced age. In his later years he wrote commentaries on New Testament books. He was aware of the theories advanced by Protestant scholars and was not afraid to employ the critical methods of the historians of the revolutionary age. Believing firmly in the divine inspiration of the Scriptures, he differentiated inspiration from revelation and accepted some of the findings of contemporary specialists. For example, while maintaining that Moses was the author of the legislation which bore his name, Lagrange conceded that in the form in which it appeared in the Pentateuch that legislation bore the marks of redaction by other hands. He did not accept literally the creation stories of Genesis and took account of archeological discoveries which shed light on them. He was careful to remain within the bounds permitted by the ecclesiastical authorities. In his studies of the Gospels he held that Matthew, written by the apostle of that name, was composed in Aramaic and more satisfactorily than Luke reproduced the discourses of Jesus; that Mark most closely preserved the teaching of Peter; that Luke was the best historian of the four and that his order was to be preferred to the others; and that the Fourth Gospel was written by the beloved disciple, assumed on the part of his readers the information given in the three earlier Gospels, and more nearly penetrated the thoughts of Jesus than did the others.[50] He was an unquestioned master of the sources and the pertinent languages, and even some of the more extreme among Protestant specialists viewed with respect his commentaries on the New Testament. The *Revue Biblique Internationale,* published by l'École Pratique d'Études Biblique and founded by him, continued his work. The Dominican school in Jerusalem which Lagrange inaugurated made a notable translation of the Bible into French which began

48 *Enciclopedia Cattolica,* Vol. IV, p. 61.

49 Volume I, p. 396.

50 F. M. Braun, *l'Œuvre du Père Lagrange. Études et Bibliographie* (Freiburg in Switzerland, 1943, pp. xv, 342), gives a bibliography of Lagrange's writings. See also *Père Lagrange and the Scriptures,* by various authors, on the fiftieth anniversary of his ordination, translated from the French by Richard T. Murphy (Milwaukee, The Bruce Publishing Co., 1946, pp. 216); and Francis J. Schrader, *Père Lagrange and Biblical Inspiration* (Washington, D.C., The Catholic University of America Press, 1954, pp. xii, 47). Lagrange's views of the Gospels and of the story which they tell are comprehensively given in Marie Joseph Lagrange, *The Gospel of Jesus Christ,* translated by members of the English Dominican province (London, Burns Oates & Washbourne, 2 vols., 1938).

to appear in 1948 and was finished in 1956. Some of the translation was by Ronald de Vaux and Stanislas Lyonnet and by laymen as well as priests.

A distinguished younger contemporary of Lagrange, Lucien Cerfaux (1883——), long on the faculty of the University of Louvain, devoted himself chiefly to the New Testament. Like Lagrange, he was quite aware of the developments in Biblical scholarship among Protestants, especially those in Germany. We are to hear more of them later. They included *Formgeschichte* ("form criticism") with Martin Dibelius as one of its early exponents and the "de-mythologizing" of which Rudolf Bultmann was the outstanding exponent. Cerfaux faced them frankly and summarized them fairly. He also pointed out what seemed to him to be the weaknesses in *Formgeschichte* and especially in the theories of Bultmann. Here, as in other aspects of the study of the New Testament, Cerfaux felt free to employ the critical apparatus of the day but reached different conclusions from those arrived at by the more radical of the Protestant scholars.[51] Cerfaux produced numerous learned articles and short treatises rather than many large volumes. For example, recognizing that Lagrange had written an extensive and detailed commentary, he contented himself with a more popular lecture on Paul's Epistle to the Romans. He insisted on the integrity of the letter as we now have it and, contrary to the conjectures of Protestants who suggested that it belonged to some other epistle of Paul, held that Chapter 16 with its extensive salutations was directed to Christians in Rome.[52] He wrote a book on New Testament theology[53] which was hailed as a milestone in modern Roman Catholic exegesis. Partly because of Cerfaux and the number of scholars whom he trained, Louvain was ranked by some along with Jerusalem as one of the two main centres of twentieth-century Roman Catholic Biblical study.[54]

Yet distinguished works on the Bible appeared as well in other places. Thus the Jesuit Jules Lebreton (1873——), who for many years lectured in the Catholic Institute of Paris, wrote as the summary of his teaching a substantial work on the life and teaching of Jesus.[55] Intended, as were his lectures, for a Christian clientele, it aimed at confirming their faith. He was thoroughly familiar with the hypotheses of *Formgeschichte,* but while saying, as did the exponents of the latter, that the Gospels represented the catechetical teaching of many years before they were reduced to writing, he held that the Church bears witness to Christ rather than, as some Protestants maintained, that the mind of

---

[51] *Recueil Lucien Cerfaux. Études d'Exégèse et d'Histoire Religieuse de Monseigneur Cerfaux . . . Réunies à l'Occasion de son Soixante-dixième Anniversaire* (Gembloux, Éditions J. Duculot, S.A., 2 vols., 1954), Vol. I, pp. 353–367.

[52] L. Cerfaux, *Une Lecture l'Épitre aux Romains* (Tournai, Casterman, 1947, pp. 139), *passim.*

[53] L. Cerfaux, *Le Christ dans la Théologie de Saint Paul* (Paris, Éditions du Cerf, 2nd ed., 1954, pp. 435).

[54] Aubert, *op. cit.,* p. 15.

[55] Jules Lebreton, *The Life and Teaching of Jesus Christ Our Lord,* translated from the French (London, Burns Oates & Washbourne, rev. ed., 2 vols., 1935).

the early Church created the Christ as Messiah and Son of God. The Jesuit Joseph Bonsirven (1880——) was a specialist on the New Testament and particularly on Palestinian and rabbinic Judaism.[56] Rudolf Schnackenburg (1914 ——), in a meticulously learned work on the Johannine epistles, maintained that they as well as the Fourth Gospel were written by John the disciple.[57] Another German, Viktor Warnach, also in a careful and comprehensive study, described *Agape* as central in the Gospel.[58] Interestingly, a book with a similar title and theme by a Protestant scholar had recently appeared.[59] Ronald Arbuthnott Knox (1888–1957), son of an Anglican bishop, reared an Evangelical, moving into Anglo-Catholicism and then, in 1917, becoming a Roman Catholic,[60] made a widely used translation of the Bible into modern English and also a semi-popular commentary on the New Testament for English readers. Heinrich Joseph Vogel (1880——) was outstanding as a textual critic.[61]

Several features characterized Roman Catholic Biblical scholarship in the twentieth century. Much of it was aware of tendencies within the corresponding studies of Protestants. The wide vogue of *Formgeschichte* among the latter had its effect. Roman Catholics did not carry *Formgeschichte* as far as did many Protestants, but they granted that it threw light on the way in which the Scriptures, and especially the Gosepls, arose.[62] They dealt with it frankly and did not shut their eyes to the applications to the Scriptures made by Bultmann. For example, two Jesuits, René Marlé and Leopold Malevez (1900——) wrote on him.[63] Some Roman Catholics seemed more intent on refuting Wellhausen, Harnack, and Loisy than on stressing the religious message of the Bible. Like many Protestants, Roman Catholic Biblical scholars sought to utilize the findings of the archeology of the nineteenth and twentieth centuries to portray the cultural environment of the Biblical figures and narratives. They were concerned with the Mosaic origin of the Pentateuch, the synoptic problem, and the chronology of the Pauline epistles, but increasingly they viewed the Bible as a whole and endeavoured to search out and set forth its meaning for the faith.

[56] Joseph Bonsirven, *Les Judaïsme Palestinien au Temps de Jésus Christ: sa Théologie* (Paris, Gabriel Beauchesne et ses fils, 2 vols., 1934, 1935); Joseph Bonsirven, *Exégèse Rabbinique et Exégèse Paulinienne* (Paris, Beauchesne et ses fils, 1939, pp. 405); Joseph Bonsirven, *l'Évangile de Paul* (Paris, Aubier, 1948, pp. 364).

[57] Rudolf Schnackenburg, *Die Johannesbriefe* (Freiburg i. B., Herder, 1953, pp. xx, 299), *passim*.

[58] Viktor Warnach, *Agape. Die Liebe as Grundmotiv der neutestamentlichen Theologie* (Düsseldorf, Patmos-Verlag, 1951, pp. 756), *passim*.

[59] Anders Nygren, *Agape and Eros. A Study of the Christian Idea of Love*, translated by A. G. Hebert (New York, The Macmillan Co., 2 vols., 1937–1939).

[60] R. A. Knox, *A Spiritual Aenead* (London, Longmans, Green and Co., 1918, pp. 263), *passim*.

[61] See his *Übungsbuch zur Einführung in die Textgeschichte des Neuen Testamentes* (Bonn, P. Hanstein, 1928, pp. 32) and *Textus Antenicaeni ad Primatum Romanum Spectantes* (Bonn, P. Hanstein, 1937, pp. 4, 39).

[62] Aubert, *op. cit.*, p. 19.

[63] René Marlé, *Bultmann et l'Interprétation du Nouveau Testament* (Paris, Aubier, Éditions Montaigne, 1956, pp. 205); L. Malevez, *Le Message Chrétien et le Mythe. La Théologie de Rudolf Bultmann* (Paris, Desclée de Brouwer, 1954, pp. 167).

They held that the Bible is the record of God's revelation, that the New Testament cannot be understood without taking account of the Old Testament, and, similarly, that the Old Testament needs the New Testament to disclose its import and the exegesis of Genesis must have the Revelation of John in mind. Some commentators made much of Old Testament figures and events as types to throw light on Christ, baptism, the Eucharist, and the Church. They studied afresh the use of the Scriptures by the early Christian Fathers. Students of Biblical theology viewed the Scriptures as *Heilsgeschichte,* the record of God's acts for the salvation of men.[64]

Roman Catholic scholars had a large part in deciphering and interpreting what were known as the Dead Sea Scrolls. These ancient documents were first brought to the attention of specialists in 1947. They had been discovered by Bedouins. More came to light in succeeding years. Found in caves at Qumran not far above the Dead Sea and only a few miles from Jerusalem, they were the literary remains of a Jewish religious sect—either Essenes or akin to the Essenes—who had there led a community life and had disappeared centuries before, the victims of Roman troops. The manuscripts included portions of the Old Testament and for them provided Hebrew texts of an earlier date than any heretofore in possession of modern scholarship. They also contained documents which threw light on the beliefs of the sect. They enlarged the world's knowledge of the setting in which Christianity emerged. Given wide publicity, they spawned many theories, especially of possible connexions with Christ and the beginnings of Christianity. Although by the early 1960's when these lines were penned not all the documents had been deciphered and edited, an enormous literature had already arisen.[65] To it Roman Catholics, Protestants, Jews, and writers of no religious faith contributed. The Dominican Ronald de Vaux (1903 ——) of l'École Biblique of Jerusalem was on the ground when the first discoveries came to light. He was a translator of some of the books of the Old Testament in the French version which we have noted and was the author of an important study of Old Testament institutions.[66] He early saw the importance of the find, did excavations on the site of the community, gave careful study to the documents, and wrote extensively on them.[67] Oher Roman Catholics were also attracted and added to the literature. Andrew Dupont-Sommer (1900——),

---

[64] Aubert, *op. cit.,* pp. 21–28.

[65] See especially the standard summary account, Millar Burrows, *The Dead Sea Scrolls,* including the excellent bibliography on pp. 419–435, and Millar Burrows, *More Light on the Dead Sea Scrolls. New Scrolls and New Interpretations, with Translations of Important Recent Discoveries* (New York, The Viking Press, 1958, pp. xiii, 434).

[66] Ronald de Vaux, *Les Institutions de l'Ancien Testament* (Paris, Éditions du Cerf, Vol. I, 1958).

[67] Burrows, *The Dead Sea Scrolls,* pp. 32, 34, 54, 56, 57, 59, 63. For a partial bibliography see *ibid.,* p. 424.

a Sulpician who later left the Church, and Joséf Tadeusz Milik (1922——) were especially prolific.[68]

CHRISTIAN ETHICS

What was called by Roman Catholics moral philosophy came in for treatment in compilations, some large and some small, of the historic teachings of the Church. Many of them appeared in more than one edition, thus testifying to their usefulness.[69]

Yet many Roman Catholic thinkers maintained that the revolutionary age made necessary, if not basic alterations in traditional moral principles, at least fresh approaches. They realized that the vast changes in social and political structures and the concern for sociological problems demanded of Christians reconsideration of ethics. They held that moral theology should not be the reduction of Christian ethics to legalistic obligations. The emphasis upon *Agape* which we have noted stressed the importance of taking as a standard the love which Christ had shown in accomplishing the redemption of man. In conferences, some of them of younger theologians at Louvain, such themes were discussed as the destiny of man, freedom of the spirit, and the encounter of man with grace.[70]

ROMAN CATHOLICS AND PROTESTANT THEOLOGY

Roman Catholic theologians were acutely aware of major developments in Protestant theology. Many welcomed what they regarded as the reaction from the humanistic liberalism of the decades immediately preceding World War I to an approach to historic Christian beliefs. The Johann-Adam-Möhler Institut in Paderborn was a major enterprise which was devoted primarily to the study of Protestant theology. Some Roman Catholic theologians, among them the head of the Institute Catholique of Paris, had views of grace more nearly in accord with Luther and Calvin than their pre-twentieth-century predecessors. In the later years of the nineteenth century nearly all Roman Catholic theologians had described faith as a kind of intellectual pre-condition to the supernatural life. They regarded faith as a belief in doctrines rather than as trust in the love of

---

[68] See bibliographies in *ibid.*, pp. 424, 425, 429, 435.

[69] Among the larger of the compendiums on moral theology were *Opera Moralia Sancti Alphonsi Mariae de Ligorio. Theologia Moralis,* by Leonardi Gaudé (Graz, Akademische Druck—U. Verlagsanstalt, 4 vols., 1954), based on the work of the famous eighteenth-century Italian saint; Arthur Preuss, *A Handbook of Moral Theology. Based on the Lehrbuch der Moraltheologie by Antony Koch* (St. Louis, B. Herder Book Co., 3rd ed., 5 vols., 1925–1933. The first edition was published in 1918); Henry Davis, S.J., *Moral and Pastoral Theology* (London, Sheed and Ward, 2nd ed., 4 vols., 1936. The first edition was published in 1935); Arthurus Vermeersch, S.J., *Theologiae Moralis* (Rome, Gregorian University, 4th ed., 3 vols., 1947, 1948. The first edition was published in 1925).

[70] Aubert, *op. cit.*, pp. 80 ff.

God. In post-1914 Roman Catholic theological circles in Europe faith was thought of as a total commitment which includes trust and obedience as well as intellectual assent.[71]

Karl Barth, of whom we are to hear much in later chapters, especially attracted Roman Catholic thinkers. The book which first brought Barth to wide attention, *Der Römerbrief* ("The Epistle to the Romans"), with its "theology of crisis," found a reading with Roman Catholics. When the multi-volume *Die kirchliche Dogmatik* began to appear, it had almost as many Roman Catholic as Protestant purchasers. Indeed, of its total sales by the mid-1950's—about five thousand—Barth said that nearly half had been to Roman Catholics. Some of the most extensive treatments of Barth were by Roman Catholics. Hans Urs von Balthasar wrote an understanding book in which he discussed the relation between Barth's theology and Roman Catholic theology. He pointed out both the kinship and the differences.[72] Henri Bouillard, a French Jesuit, had a three-volume work on Barth.[73] Barth himself wrote a preface to *Rechtfertigung: die Lehre Karl Barths und seine katholische Besinnung,* by Hans Küng, a priest and a fellow Swiss. Küng said that every positive element in Barth's teaching on justification was in harmony with theology as taught by Roman Catholics.[74] Barth early entered into controversy with the Jesuit Erich Przywara (1889———). The latter made much of *analogia entis* ("analogy of being").[75] Holding that he was in accord with the *constitutio dogmatica de fide catholica* of the Vatican Council, he maintained that God is separate from all that is external to Him, yet that there is nothing external to Him which is not in its essence and existence derived from Him and that the entire creation is without exception the similitude of His own Being and yet is in no way necessary to Him. God and creation, he insisted, are like each other and yet even in this resemblance are completely unlike. This, he said, was what was meant by *analogia entis.*[76] Barth declared that *analogia entis* was a non-Christian invention and because of it no Christian could become a Roman Catholic. Yet Bouillard said that *analogia entis* was not even mentioned by Aquinas, that it was peculiar to Przywara's

[71] George A. Lindbeck to the author, December, 1959.

[72] Hans Urs von Balthasar, *Karl Barth: Darstellung und Deutung seiner Theologie* (Cologne, Jakob Hegner Verlag, 1951, pp. 420).

[73] Henri Bouillard, *Karl Barth: Ouvrage Publié avec le Concours du Centre National de la Recherche Scientifique* (Paris, Aubier, 3 vols., 1959). They first appeared in 1957 as *Karl Barth, Genèse et Évolution de la Théologie Dialectique,* in one volume, and *Karl Barth: Parole de Dieu et Existence Humaine,* in two volumes.

[74] On this and other aspects of Roman Catholic treatment of Barth see G. H. Tavard, a Roman Catholic, in *The Christian Century,* Vol. LVI, pp. 132, 133; and George A. Lindbeck, in *The Ecumenical Review,* Vol. XI, pp. 334–340.

[75] Erich Przywara, *Analogia Entis. Metaphysik. I. Prinzip* (Munich, J. Kövel & F. Pustet, 1932, pp. xvi, 154); Erich Przywara, *Polarity, a German Catholic's Interpretation of Religion,* translated by A. C. Boquet (London, Oxford University Press, 1935, pp. xii, 150).

[76] Przywara, *Polarity,* pp. 30, 31.

personal philosophy and, as Barth understood the term, had been generally rejected by Roman Catholic theologians.[77]

SUMMARY

The half-century which followed 1914 was marked by much intellectual activity among Roman Catholics, partly to take account of the currents sweeping across the world in the age of revolution. It sought to meet these currents constructively and so far as possible took advantage of them to give a fresh understanding of the deposit of faith which was held to have been entrusted to the Church and was basically unalterable. Departures from that faith as defined by the councils and the Popes were not as marked as in the nineteenth century. Although they showed flexibility, Roman Catholic theologians and Biblical scholars hewed more nearly to the line than did some of their precedecessors. Encouraged by the Popes, much emphasis was placed on Aquinas and scholastic philosophy and theology. With it went the study of Aristotle, Plato, and Augustine for their bearing on Thomism. Yet Aquinas was taken by many not as a strait jacket but as a guide in meeting the challenges of the age. Accommodations were made to the evolutionary hypothesis. In an era of the common man and of democracy in its varied forms, efforts were put forth to interpret the faith for the rank and file of the laity: theologians and scholars, in setting forth the Church as the body of Christ, sought to include the laity in the priesthood which ideally comprised all the members of that body. Here and there in contrast with earlier centuries were laymen, notably Maritain, Gilson, and Marcel, who made substantial contributions to theology. In an age when men were poignantly aware of being swept along in vast movements, fresh efforts were put forth to understand how God works in history and to formulate a theology of history in accord both with the Christian revelation and with the course of events in the past and present. The mounting popular devotion to Mary with the Papal declaration of the bodily assumption of the Virgin to heaven stimulated Mariology and the endeavour to put it into theological terms and to relate it to the acts of God as recorded in the Scriptures. Much attention was paid to the Bible. Translations for the laity were produced and fresh scholarly approaches were made. The latter took account of the critical methods developed by secular historians and by Protestants in their approach to the Scriptures. Numerous commentaries were written. Scholars strove to avoid being so engrossed in technical studies of authorship and texts that they missed the religious import of the Bible. In the treatment of moral theology some attempts were made to break away from legalistic formulations and to emphasize such basic principles as the love exhibited by God in Christ and in the imitation of Christ. Less of

[77] Tavard, *op. cit.*

anti-Protestant polemic was seen than in earlier centuries. More attempts were made to deal with Protestant scholarship dispassionately and even sympathetically, but without surrendering the essential differing convictions of the Roman Catholic branch of the faith.

Significantly, as we pointed out at the beginning of this chapter, most of the outstanding scholarship was in areas which had once been included in the Roman Empire—either in Latin Europe or regions bordering on Latin Europe which had been within the Roman limes. In spite of some hopeful exceptions in North America, it was still to be proved that the Roman Catholic Church, which in many ways was the heir of the Roman Empire and bore the indelible imprint of *Romanitas,* could be genuinely universal in stimulating minds reared in other cultural traditions to creative thought on Christian themes.

CHAPTER VII

The Country-by-Country Course of the Roman Catholic Church

As in Volume I, we must follow the description of developments in the Roman Catholic Church under the Papacy and a comprehensive account of various aspects of the course of that church in Europe in the four and a half decades after 1914 with a survey of the record of that branch of the faith in the several countries of Europe.

We shall see that the contrast continued to be marked between the forces emerging from the revolutionary age which were adverse to Christianity and the vitality in the Roman Catholic Church which gave rise to movements, some of them fresh, not only to counter those forces but also to permeate the life of each country with the Christian faith. In the first half of the twentieth century both facets of the picture were accentuated.

On the one hand, among large segments of the traditional Roman Catholic population de-Christianization proceeded further than in the nineteenth century. "De-Christianization" may carry inaccurate connotations. It seems to indicate that at one time the nations which we are to survey could be called Christian. It is true that outwardly the large majority of their populations had conformed to some aspects of the faith. They were baptized and went to mass on the great festivals of the Church, or perhaps more frequently. For the most part they were married and buried from the church. Yet for an undetermined proportion of the population adherence to the faith meant little. The high ethical demands of Christ were honoured more in the breach than in the observance and appreciation of the real character of the nominally accepted religion was very slight. Except in the most superficial fashion, vast multitudes had never been "Christianized" and so could not properly be said to be "de-Christianized." Yet for many in the post-1914 decades even that outward conformity to the faith continued to fade. Open antagonism still existed, particularly among Communists, but, more alarmingly, to thousands Christianity seemed too inconsequential to warrant vigorous dissent. They might have their children baptized as a social convention but entertained no purpose of having them instructed in the faith of the church of which that sacrament was supposed to have made them members.

On the other hand, as the preceding chapters must have shown, the twentieth century witnessed the permeation of millions of the population of Europe by the Roman Catholic faith. The Liturgical Movement enlisted the intelligent participation of the laity in the central rite of the Church. Eucharistic Congresses increased the loyalty of the devout to the sacrifice of the mass. Devotion to Mary mounted. More was made of the priesthood of the laity. Catholic Action engaged thousands in one form or another of the "apostolate of the laity," and a variety of organizations brought the faithful together for common purposes in economic, social, and political life. Even more than in the nineteenth century the loyal were directed by a hierarchy which was headed by the Pope, and in the post-1914 decades that office was filled by able and hard-working men.

France: Generalizations

In our country-by-country survey we begin with France, where, as in the nineteenth century, the contrasts were more striking than in any other land. On the one hand de-Christianization was more obvious than anywhere else in Western Europe. Yet more than elsewhere new movements arose from within the Roman Catholic Church to counteract it. As in the preceding century, more missionaries went from France to plant and nourish the faith outside the Occident than from any other country.

France: The Setting

A combination of factors complicated the course of the Roman Catholic Church in France in the half-century after 1914. That church was still staggering from the blows dealt it under the Third Republic, which culminated in disestablishment in 1905 when the country was catapulted into World War I. A large part of the war was fought on French soil and in it thousands of the flower of the youth of France perished. Victory was followed by a breathing space of less than a generation. In 1939 France was engulfed in World War II. In its course much of the country was occupied by enemy forces, and the Third Republic came to an inglorious end. After a little less than six gruelling years France was again among the victors and the Fourth Republic came into being. It proved inept, the French colonial possessions in Asia and French predominance in Tunisia and Morocco were lost, and an exhausting war was waged to preserve French authority in Algeria. The Fourth Republic had all but crumpled when Charles de Gaulle came to power (1958) and set up the Fifth Republic. Under him a large part of the remaining colonial empire became independent or, autonomous, was associated with France in an inclusive commonwealth. Yet, in spite of the successive blows, unstable governments, and costly and futile attempts to maintain intact the colonial empire acquired in the nineteenth century, France reached the mid-century mark fairly prosperous.

FRANCE: ADJUSTMENT OF THE ROMAN CATHOLIC CHURCH
TO THE SEPARATION OF CHURCH AND STATE

As we saw in an earlier volume,[1] since the 1870's chronic tension had existed between the Roman Catholic Church and the Third Republic. Attempts at reconciliation failed. The Associations Act of 1901 was followed by the suppression of many religious orders and congregations and by the closing of thousands of schools maintained by them. In 1904 all teaching congregations were ordered dissolved within ten years. This meant too the end of the schools taught by them. In 1905 the concordat of 1801 was annulled by the state. State support of the clergy was terminated, and church edifices were declared to be the property of the state. Through voluntary associations Roman Catholics were permitted to use the church buildings, but Pope Pius X denounced the law of separation and condemned the associations authorized by that act.

The immediate effect of disestablishment was shock. The number of young men preparing for the priesthood fell off by about 50 per cent. Voluntary contributions for the support of public worship and of ecclesiastical institutions did not immediately fill the vacuum caused by the withdrawal of state aid.

Yet the Roman Catholic Church was now freed from control by the state, could fix the boundaries of its dioceses, and could control its clergy. The Pope could name the bishops without consulting the state. A law passed in January, 1907, sought to ease the conditions for the use of church structures.

Other factors complicated the situation. The Papal condemnation of Modernism was followed by efforts of the zealous to smell out all suggestions of heresy. What was called "integral" Catholicism had "integralists" as its champions. The "integralists" were profoundly convinced that men were so corrupted by original sin that they were not able to discover truth by their own efforts but must accept truth as objective, given by God, transmitted by the Church, not susceptible to new developments, and to be guarded by authority. They adhered rigorously to scholasticism, viewed all liberalism in religion or in politics as anathema, and regarded Leo XIII as too lenient. Repeatedly they called the attention of the hierarchy to what they regarded as deviations from strict orthodoxy.[2] The "integralists" brought much unrest in the Roman Catholic Church in France until they were curbed by Benedict XV.[3] The adverse attitude of Pius X towards Sillon which gave the blow to that movement also disturbed many who had hoped through it to offset the secularist trends. Yet Sillon's founder, Marc Sangnier (1873–1950), was never personally condemned. He was

---

[1] Volume I, pp. 408–414.
[2] Dansette, *Histoire Religieuse en France Contemporaine*, Vol. II, pp. 462–468; Brugerette, *Le Prêtre Français et la Société Contemporaine*, pp. 306–327.
[3] Brugerette, *op. cit.*, pp. 327–335.

considered the founder of French Christian Democracy and after World War II was regarded as its symbol.[4]

In spite of the handicaps, by 1914 the Roman Catholic Church in France had begun to make its adjustment to the separation of Church and state. For example, between 1906 and 1914 it constructed twenty-four new churches in Paris alone, half of them in the suburbs of that rapidly growing metropolis.[5]

FRANCE: REVIVAL OF THE ROMAN CATHOLIC CHURCH DURING AND IMMEDIATELY AFTER WORLD WAR I

An accompaniment and early sequel of World War I was a surge of fresh life in the Roman Catholic Church in France. A contributing factor was the record of the clergy in the armed forces. The clergy of the pertinent age groups were subject to call to the colours along with other young men. A limited number were appointed chaplains but as such, along with their fellows who carried weapons, faced the perils of combat. Out of the 32,699 priests mobilized, 4,618 were killed.[6] The discipline, courage, and patriotism of the clergy who served as common soldiers elicited praise, even from rabid anti-clericals. The behaviour of the soldier-priests disproved the charge of effeminacy which had long been brought against them, especially since 9,378 were awarded the *croix de guerre*, 1,533 *médailles militaires*, and 895 the Legion of Honour, and 10,414 were mentioned in the dispatches.[7] Many of the officers, including some of the generals, notably Marshal Foch, were devout and unabashed Roman Catholics. By their courage and patriotism they won respect for their faith.[8] In regions invaded by the German armies the clergy ministered to their flocks, both spiritually and physically, helped to keep up morale, and sought to protect the church buildings and to restore those damaged or destroyed. Bishops and clergy led in prayers for victory and peace.[9] In what was called the *Union Sacrée,* in the face of the common peril a truce was declared between clericals and most anti-clericals.[10]

In the years which immediately followed World War I the condition of the Roman Catholic Church continued to improve. For a time several of the theological seminaries were thronged with young men, many of them with enviable war records. Even the war years saw an influx of boys into the seminaries.[11] Fi-

[4] Volume I, p. 352; Dansette, *op. cit.,* Vol. II, pp. 397–436.
[5] Dansette, *op. cit.,* Vol. II, p. 379.
[6] Palmer, *The Catholic Church in France,* p. 29.
[7] Gwynn, *The Catholic Reaction in France,* pp. 21, 22.
[8] *Ibid.,* pp. 36–42.
[9] *Ibid.,* pp. 26–32; Brugerette, *op. cit.,* pp. 429–495.
[10] Guilday, *The Catholic Church in Contemporary Europe 1919–1931,* p. 90.
[11] Gwynn, *op. cit.,* pp. 48–52.

nancial support began to improve. Voluntary contributions, made necessary by the cessation of state aid after 1905, did not quickly take up the slack but showed an increase which varied from region to region.[12] We have already noted the favourable impression made on the French public by the canonization of Joan of Arc (1919) and we have called attention to the renewal of diplomatic relations between France and the Vatican (1920–1921).[13] The issue of the use of the church buildings was eased. The law of 1905 provided that the structures, now the property of the state, would be available for public worship, rent free, by voluntary associations of the faithful. Although Pope Pius X had denounced this arrangement, in 1920 Rome intimated that it would withdraw its opposition. However, the French cardinals, supported by most of the French archbishops and bishops, remained intransigent. Eventually, on January 18, 1924, Pius XI, in the encyclical Maximam, authorized the bishops to found diocesan associations.[14] The associations were predominantly lay, but each was to have the bishop as president. They were to have the full right of administering the buildings used for worship. Not all the bishops were satisfied. Indeed, in 1928 Cardinal Andrieu, Archbishop of Bordeaux, a staunch "integralist," publicly excoriated the arrangement as substituting the authority of the laity for that of the Pope and the bishops. Yet in general the question ceased to be acute—or rather, became acute in new ways. Some bishops, indeed, were eventually of the opinion that the separation of Church and state had worked to the advantage of the Church. But a few felt that the Church was acquiring too much power and that a new wave of anti-clericalism might arise. Late in 1959, after long and bitter debate, the National Assembly voted to give state financial aid to Roman Catholic schools. Some Socialists, anti-clerical, wished a concordat with the Holy See which would limit the power of the Church.[15]

Both during and after the war an effort was made to set up a Roman Catholic press to offset the anti-clericalism of some existing papers. The Maison de la Bonne Presse was formed which syndicated articles and news for distribution among French newspapers. It supported La Croix, a distinctly clerical organ begun in 1880 by the Augustinians of the Assumption, which in 1883 had become a daily. Provincial dailies and several hundreds of weekly and monthly reviews were conducted by loyal Roman Catholics. In North-western France Ouest Éclair, a daily which first appeared in 1899, was committed to the Republic, and had a priest, Trochu, and a layman, Desgrées du Lou, as its outstanding figures, had a wide circulation.[16]

12 Ibid., pp. 52–57.
13 Chapter III.
14 Acta Apostolicae Sedis, Vol. XVI, pp. 5–11.
15 Brugerette, op. cit., pp. 656–666; The New York Times, December 24, 1959.
16 Gwynn, op. cit., pp. 115–142.

POLITICALLY DIVIDED FRENCH ROMAN CATHOLICISM: *Action Française*

Politically French Roman Catholics continued to be divided. After World War I some of the younger priests, especially those who had served at the front, were much attracted to democratic movements and to organizations of workers which we mentioned in an earlier chapter. They were opposed to Communism but were committed to one or another programme for the improvement of society.[17]

A movement which for a time enlisted the support of numbers of the clergy was *Action Française*. *Action Française* had its inception late in the 1890's and was virulent in its attack on Dreyfus and those who supported him. It was prominent in the years after World War I. Intensely nationalistic, it sought the rejuvenation of France and the achievement of internal order through the restoration of the monarchy under the House of Orleans. It also advocated, as a basis for a stable society, the renewal of the establishment of the Roman Catholic Church in close alliance with the crown. The chief organ of the movement was *L'Action Française*, which eventually became a daily journal. The outstanding leader was Charles Maurras (1868–1952). Although he himself was probably an atheist, Maurras saw in the Roman Catholic Church an indispensable support to the kind of France he envisaged. Wielding a vigorous pen, he attracted much attention.[18] He was aided by Léon Daudet (1867–1942), also skilled as a writer.[19]

Roman Catholic opinion on *Action Française* was divided. The "integralists" and the majority of the Benedictines endorsed the movement. The Jesuits were opposed. The withdrawal of the support of many of the clergy contributed to the defeat of Maurras to election to the National Assembly in 1923 and 1925. As we have seen,[20] Pius X contemplated a condemnation, Benedict XV hesitated for fear of the effect during the throes of World War I, but in December, 1926, Pius XI forbade the faithful to join the movement and in January, 1927, the Holy Office placed *L'Action Française* and some of Maurras's books on the Index.[21] Cardinal Andrieu, Archbishop of Bordeaux, had already (August 23, 1926) condemned *Action Française*. Maurras declared that the Papal action was due to the pressure of a German clique on Pius XI. Although critics were not lacking among Roman Catholics, for the most part the faithful complied with the commands of Rome. A few of the French clergy remained recalcitrant. One, Cardinal Billot, eventually (September, 1927) was allowed to resign from his high post and lived in retirement until his death.

Action Française continued but with waning influence. In 1937 the head

---

[17] Brugerette, *op. cit.*, pp. 667–679.

[18] Léon Daudet, *Charles Maurras et Son Temps* (Paris, Ernest Flammarion, 1930, pp. 169); *The Encyclopædia Britannica*, Vol. XV, p. 110.

[19] *The Encyclopædia Britannica*, Vol. VII, pp. 70, 71.

[20] Chapter III.

[21] *Acta Apostolicae Sedis*, Vol. XVIII, pp. 529, 530.

of the House of Orleans broke with it. After World War II Maurras was condemned to life imprisonment for collaborating with the Germans. His sentence was shortened and he died, an old man, in comparative obscurity. Yet it is said that, while rejected in France, his writings had contributed to the growth of Fascism in Italy.[22]

FRANCE: THE GROWTH OF CATHOLIC ACTION

The growth of Catholic Action was a feature of the post-1914 Roman Catholic Church in France. Here, as in several other countries, the first half of the twentieth century was marked by a striking increase in what was called the apostolate of the laity. Much of this was sketched in an earlier chapter.[23] In France, as in the Roman Catholic Church as a whole, many welcomed the development. Here was a return to a tradition of the first Christian centuries. In the strong drift towards secularism in the revolutionary age—indeed, ever since the Renaissance and particularly in the nineteenth century—the tendency had been to consider the laity as having a passive role. The revival in the nineteenth century had first affected the clergy, and the Church could be said to have become "clericalized." But there were exceptions, and these were the foreshadowing of the notable changes after 1914.[24]

In France Catholic Action was said to have become significant in 1927 with the conjunction of a spiritual or mystical movement, the apostolate of the laity, with attempts to make the faith effective in various aspects of the environment.[25] Much of Catholic Action was indebted to the A.C.J.F. (*Association Catholique de la Jeunesse Française*). The A.C.J.F. had been organized in 1886. It had been mainly under the direction of young middle-class intellectuals, and its members were mostly from the middle class. At first largely on the defensive and conservative socially and politically, it gradually moved in the direction encouraged by Popes Pius X and Benedict XV of *ralliement,* namely, coöperation with the Republic, a policy sponsored by Leo XIII. It did not follow the line of *Action Française* but, enlisting a minority of the laity under lay direction and with clerical advice, and adopting the motto *piété, étude, action* ("piety, study, action"), it sought to encourage the improvement of the individual and the carrying of Christian principles into social issues. However, it failed to enlist members of the working class and was too intellectual for many of the younger generation.

---

[22] Brugerette, *op. cit.,* pp. 678–705; *Die Katholieke Encyclopaedie,* Vol. L, pp. 393, 394; Gwynn, *op. cit.,* pp. 93–98; Dansette, *op. cit.,* Vol. II, pp. 563–613; Guilday, *op. cit.,* pp. 95–101; Leo Ward, editor, *The Condemnation of the "Action Française"* (London, Sheed and Ward, 1928, pp. 79).
[23] Chapter III.
[24] Dansette, *Destin du Catholicisme Français (1926–1956),* pp. 81–84.
[25] *Ibid.,* p. 85.

In the 1920's, 1930's, and 1940's, at the outset largely by the example of Cardijn, the Belgian priest who had founded J.O.C. (*Jeunesse Ouvrière Chrétienne*) among labourers, a youth movement proliferated which was organized by occupations and sexes. Among others, it was represented by J.O.C. (the Jocists), J.O.C.E. (*Jeunesse Ouvrière Chrétienne Féminine*), J.A.C. (*Jeunesse Agricole Chrétienne*), J.A.C.F. (*Jeunesse Agricole Chrétienne Féminine*), J.E.C. (*Jeunesse Étudiante Chrétienne*), J.E.S.F. (*Jeunesse Étudiante Chrétienne Féminine*), and J.M.C. (*Jeunesse Maritime Chrétienne*). In the same period, i.e., between the two world wars, such other bodies sprang up as F.N.C. (*Fédération Nationale Catholique*), L.F.A.C. (*Ligue Féminine d'Action Catholique*), F.N.A.C. (*Fédération Nationale d'Action Catholique*), M.I.C.I.A.C. (*Mouvement d'Ingénieurs et de Chefs d'Industries d'Action Catholique*), and M.F.R. (*Mouvement Familial Rural*).[26]

The rapid proliferation of youth movements entailed problems. An attempt was made to coördinate them through the A.C.J.F. This led to the alteration of the latter's structure. Some of its unspecialized local units recruited from middle-class youth tended to disintegrate and disappear. The A.C.J.F. also had difficulty in bringing to a common mind occupational groups as disparate as those which it sought to draw together. They might outwardly conform to the ideal of participating in civic affairs in a democratic and republican state and subscribe to the policy of Pius XI in his attempt to promote international concord, but they would do so without enthusiasm. Then, too, not all the bishops and parish priests were cordial to movements which did not fit easily into the familiar ecclesiastical structure.[27]

In France Catholic Action brought a transformation of the purposes of some older groups and movements. These represented a pre-World War I mentality, that of defending Roman Catholic institutions and traditions. Catholic Action and the youth movements had as their major objective the "apostolate"—the capturing for the Gospel of classes which were being de-Christianized. To further the transformation, in 1929 Pius XI appointed to the Archbishopric of Paris Jean Verdier (1864-1940), Superior General of Saint Sulpice, and soon raised him to the cardinalate. That appointment was made partly for the purpose of giving a social orientation to the Church in France and improving the preparation of the clergy, but it also had as its object the creation of a French Catholic Action. Verdier sought to overcome the coolness of the French episcopate, and in 1931 at his instance the Assembly of the Cardinals and Archbishops authorized a structure for Catholic Action in France. The *Fédération Nationale Catholique* was soon nominally united with it, and several other

[26] *Ibid.*, pp. 85–105; Hoog, *Histoire du Catholicisme Social en France 1871–1931*, pp. 196–205, 282.

[27] Dansette, *Destin du Catholicisme Français (1926–1956)*, pp. 104–108.

organizations were brought under it. The effort at coördination was attended by friction, especially as the central committee of *Action Catholique* set up subcommittees on political action, education, and religion which seemed to some to be usurping functions of associated specialized bodies. The Boy Scout movement, of foreign origin, had appeared in France before World War I and was organized nationally in 1920, and the Girl Guides achieved a similar organization in 1923. Both were regarded as part of Catholic Action.[28]

During World War II Catholic Action and its problems of organization were quiescent, but with the coming of peace they re-awakened. Efforts were put forth to revive the specialized branches and to solve the problems of coördination. Some of the branches appeared not to be much interested in the apostolate—the permeation of their environment with Christianity—but to have more secular objectives. The attempt was made, especially by the Assembly of Cardinals and Archbishops, to ensure the emphasis upon the apostolate. In the mid-1950's, however, several of the branches remained feeble and enlisted only small minorities of the groups they were designed to serve.[29]

FRANCE: THE CHALLENGE OF DE-CHRISTIANIZATION

In the decades which followed 1914 and especially in the years after World War II, many French Roman Catholics became vividly aware of the threat of the progressive de-Christianization of large elements in the nation. The vigour of their faith was seen in the varied programmes, several of them quite new, which were devised to meet the challenge, and in the devotion which was shown in seeking to make them effective.

Comprehensive statistics or comparative figures to record the advance or recession of de-Christianization in France were unobtainable. Not long after World War I general agreement existed that practising Roman Catholics were only a minority of the population. Estimates of the size of that minority varied from five to ten millions, or from an eighth to a quarter of the population. One estimate which did not include Alsace Lorraine (restored to France after World War I) or Paris put the number of practising Roman Catholics at ten millions and said that perhaps another sixteen or seventeen millions kept in touch with the Church by occasional attendance at mass and that seven or eight millions, although possibly baptized in infancy, had no regard for religious observances. This was out of a total of thirty-four millions.[30] In 1943 French Roman Catholics were shocked by a book by Henri Godin and Yvan Daniel entitled *La France: Pays de Mission?* which said that at least a fourth of the population of

---

[28] *Ibid.*, pp. 108–118.

[29] *Ibid.*, pp. 372–430.

[30] Gwynn, *op. cit.*, pp. 2, 3. See also, on the progress of de-Christianization, Charles Guignebert, *Le Problème Religieux dans la France d'Aujourd'hui* (Paris, Garnier Frères, 1922, pp. xvi, 322), pp. 296 ff.

France was atheist and that the entire working class suffered from almost total lack of religion. It maintained that of the adult population of the country only a tenth were practising Roman Catholics.[31]

The degree of de-Christianization varied from section to section, from parish to parish, between the sexes, by age groups, and from class to class. Although the decay of religion was due partly to the vast shifts of population from rural areas to cities and industrial centres where conditions of life made difficult the maintenance of Christian morals and attendance at church services and where the erection of churches did not keep pace with the growth of the urban areas, many rural parishes were said to be practically pagan.[32] In a very good urban parish, one observer declared, only a quarter of the professed Christians were practising, and in several others the proportion was only 6 or 7 per cent.[33] Paris, so a careful study in the early 1950's disclosed, was really made up of several cities. In parishes which might be described as no man's lands, slums with shifting populations, the number of practising Roman Catholics was very small.[34] In the parishes, the survey showed, the proportion varied from one in fourteen to one in five. In general, women were more faithful than men. Observance of religious duties fell off after adolescence and remained low between the ages of twenty and forty or forty-five. It was highest among the wealthy and the middle classes and lowest among the poor and the labourers.[35] In Lens, a coal-mining centre in the North of France, in the fore part of the 1950's about two-thirds of the engineers were practising Roman Catholics, about half of the students and bourgeoisie and two-fifths of the farmers were in that category, while only about one-fourteenth of the miners and one-twentieth of the non-mining labourers could be classed as practising.[36] Regions of high observance were Brittany, La Vendée, Flanders, the Basque regions, and in some cantons in Franche-Comté and Haute-Savoie.[37] Yet even within these regions marked variations were seen. For instance, in Brittany in considerable areas less than 30 per cent. of the population were practising Roman Catholics and in an approximately equal proportion of the region the percentage was 85 or more.[38] Some villages could be called indifferent in religious matters; only a few women attended mass, but the men received the last sacrament and the village council voted, without the request of the priest, a sum to repair the roof of the church.[39] In still other

---

[31] See a translation of the second part in Ward, *France Pagan?*
[32] Daniel-Rops in *Problèmes du Catholicisme Français*, pp. 27 ff.; Gwynn, *op. cit.*, pp. 9–13.
[33] Daniel-Rops, *op. cit.*, pp. 27 ff.
[34] Daniel, *Aspects de la Pratique Religieuse à Paris*, pp. 111–113.
[35] *Ibid., passim.*
[36] *Ibid.*, p. 115.
[37] Boulard, *Rencontres 16 Problèmes Missionnaires de la France Rurale*, Part I, pp. 18, 19.
[38] Lebret, *La France en Transition*, p. 44.
[39] Boulard, *op. cit.*, Part I, pp. 24 ff.

parishes most of the population had no touch whatever with the Church.[40] The scene varied from time to time.[41] Around 1930 only about 8 per cent. of the labourers in factories and mines, so it was said, were practising Roman Catholics.[42]

Part of the challenge was immigration. Many thousands came from Spain and Italy, bringing with them the attitudes which prevailed in those lands—not always favourable to the faith. Hundreds of thousands of Moslems moved in from Algeria.

Both a cause and a symptom of the de-Christianization of France was the shortage of clergy. One set of figures seemed to indicate that the number of priests had risen fairly steadily from 11 to every 10,000 of the population in 1806 to about 16 in 1868, had fallen sharply after 1890, and was about 10.5 in 1948. To put it another way, in 1810 there were 31,870 priests, or one to every 913 of the population; in 1871-1875, before the anti-clericalism of the Third Republic had begun to be strongly felt, priests totaled 56,500, or one to every 639 of the population; by 1948 the body of priests had fallen to 42,486, or one to every 913 of the population. These figures seem to have counted only seculars. If regulars were included, the total in 1948 was about 51,000, or about 12.1 for each 100,000 of the population.[43] A survey begun in 1947 showed that the preceding years had seen an increase in the number of practising laity in all classes of society, but that priests to minister to them were lacking. It was said that in 1904, 4,772 parishes were without priests and that in 1950, 15,416 parishes were vacant. These figures, however, were deceptive, for many parishes had suffered from depopulation. Some had only 50 to 70 inhabitants and 14,418 parishes had less than 300 people. A better parochial organization, it was held, would leave few parishes with more than 300 without a priest.[44] The proportion of priests varied greatly from diocese to diocese.[45]

The class origins of the priests changed. During the larger part of the nineteenth century most of the clergy came from the peasantry, probably because entrance to the priesthood brought enhanced social prestige. As the economic level of the farmers was lifted, fewer of their sons entered seminaries. By 1948 most of the students in the seminaries were from the middle classes and in some dioceses an increasing proportion came from the working classes. As a rule scions of the upper classes who entered the priesthood became regulars.[46]

As was to be expected from the prolonged governmental restrictions on orders

[40] *Ibid.*, pp. 27 ff.
[41] On conditions about 1940 see Gabriel le Bras, *Introduction à l'Histoire de la Pratique Religieuse en France* (Paris, Presses Universitaires de France, 1942, pp. 128), pp. 108 ff.
[42] Somerville, *Studies in the Catholic Social Movement*, p. 127.
[43] Boulard, *Essor ou Déclin du Clergé Français*, pp. 78, 79.
[44] *Ibid.*, pp. 13, 19-22.
[45] *Ibid.*, tables opposite pp. 30, 40.
[46] *Ibid.*, pp. 117, 130-134.

and congregations, the numbers of regulars fell off after 1905. Beginning in 1913 the totals of regulars began slowly to mount. However, after 1905, with disestablishment, seculars showed a decline which became especially marked after 1913.[47] The influx to the seminaries which followed World War I proved to be a passing phenomenon.

Although in the 1950's a remarkable spiritual rebirth was deemed to be in progress in France, with an awareness on the part of many of the faithful of the problems peculiar to the age, the secular clergy were held, by and large, to be inadequate in vision and in an understanding of the real problems of the day. They were regarded by one observer as insufficiently prepared for the new situations presented by the times; they blamed de-Christianization upon such factors as the cinema, socialism, and Freemasonry and did not discern the underlying forces which were playing upon the family and the collective life of the community.[48]

That recruits to the secular priesthood continued to appear and were trained in seminaries gave evidence of devotion among both clergy and laity. The withdrawal of state financial aid by the action of the government in 1905 meant that the stipends of the clergy, already meagre for the rank and file, and the maintenance of the seminaries must come from a laity unaccustomed to such demands. In entering the priesthood, moreover, a young man would have to face the prospect, not only of an income often less than that of an unskilled factory labourer, but also of service in a parish most of whose members were indifferent or openly scornful and hostile. However, the financial burden was lightened by mass stipends and other fees charged by the clergy for their services and by the fact that existing church buildings, being the property of the state, were kept in repair by public funds. Moreover, an inter-diocesan fund aided some of the poor dioceses.[49]

FRANCE: RISING TO THE CHALLENGE OF DE-CHRISTIANIZATION

French Roman Catholics were not content to permit the challenge of de-Christianization to go unanswered. The vitality of the faith in France was shown by the fashion in which many rose to the occasion. Some of the methods employed were traditional. They included instruction of the children, pastoral care through the maintenance of the ministration of the sacraments, and the labours of the historic orders and congregations. Others were novel, and efforts at adaptation to the conditions of the day. Not all practising Roman Catholics joined in these efforts. Yet a substantial number, both of clergy and of laity, engaged in them.

[47] *Ibid.*, p. 232.
[48] Lebret, *op. cit.*, pp. 156–158.
[49] Gwynn, *op. cit.*, pp. 53–56.

A marked revival was seen in religious orders and congregations—for example, among the Benedictines. It was notable in the growth of the Cassinese Congregation. Called the *Reforme de Subiaco,* from the cave in which Benedict began his austere life, it sought to revive the primitive Benedictine observances. Begun in 1851 and recognized by Pius IX in 1872, in 1950 it had six provinces, 35 abbeys and priories, and 1,750 monks, and in the 1950's was expanding in France at the rate of about an abbey a year. The Dominicans were aiding in an intellectual revival, and the Franciscans were engaged more and more in preaching. The Cistercians were growing. Many able youth from the upper classes were attracted to these and other orders and congregations.

To meet the challenges of the day, both de-Christianization and others, the episcopate achieved better coördination. The Assembly of Cardinals and Archbishops took on increasing responsibilities, thus lightening the load of the Archbishop of Paris, on whose shoulders fell much of the burden of supervising the French Church and Catholic Action. Since in that Assembly the bishops had been represented only in a secondary manner through provincial assemblies convened by each archibishop, in 1946 a new secretariat—of the bishops—was created, and in accordance with Papal permission (1947) in 1951 a plenary assembly of the entire episcopate convened, the first in a series which numbered successors in 1954 and 1957. The assembly of 1951 brought into being permanent commissions charged with specific assignments—among them Catholic Action, youth, the catechism, the industrial workers, the rural problem, and social work.[50]

In other ways the episcopate was active in seeking to meet the challenges. Resolutions passed by the bishops with appeals to the faithful and public utterances, collective and by individual bishops, gave evidence of an awareness of the social and economic factors which entered into the changing scene.[51] Vigorous efforts were put forth, especially after World War II, to improve religious education. The mounting Biblical, liturgical, and theological studies were made to serve the purpose of the apostolate. Cathechists were trained. By 1956, on the initiative (1942) of the Assembly of Cardinals and Archbishops, about sixty-four dioceses had instituted special offices for religious education. In 1947 a national centre was begun to coördinate these efforts and in 1951 an episcopal commission was charged with the catechism. The attempt was made to create a uniform national catechism. The zeal for religious education had as its purpose both the re-Christianization of youth and the training of the laity to share in the apostolate.[52]

In Paris scores of additional churches and chapels were erected, largely at the instance of Cardinal Verdier assisted by Canon Tousé, vicar general of the archdiocese. This was in the 1930's. Yet in 1950 Paris was said to have only one

[50] Dansette, *Destin du Catholicisme Français* (1926–1956), pp. 449–451.
[51] Deroo, *l'Épiscopat Français,* pp. 34–61.
[52] Dansette, *Destin du Catholicisme Français* (1926–1956), pp. 447, 448.

church to every 25,000 to 100,000 parishioners.[53]

An effort to bring back to the faith the class where de-Christianization had proceeded furthest, the labourers in mines and industries, was made by the worker-priests. It attracted much attention. The term "worker-priests" (*prêtres-ouvriers*) was applied to priests who sought to win the de-Christianized labourers by becoming identified with them in their occupations, sharing their toil and their day-by-day life.[54]

The worker-priests had no single origin, but their main source was the Paris Mission (*Mission de Paris*), begun by Emmanuel Caelestinus Suhard (1874–1949), who succeeded Verdier as Archbishop of Paris in 1940. Suhard had long taught in a seminary and had been a cardinal since 1935. Of the Paris Mission we are to hear more in a moment. The designation "worker-priest" is of uncertain coinage and seems to have been used in the nineteenth century. As it was employed in France in the period of which we speak it could have been applied to Loew, a Dominican who worked as a docker in Marseilles in 1941 with the purpose of being a missionary to his fellow employees. When, in 1942, the Germans demanded 800,000 Frenchmen for labour in Germany, twenty-five priests were secretly appointed by the ecclesiastical authorities to go with them, as labourers, to serve clandestinely as chaplains, especially to the seminarians and members of Catholic Action. Their experience of becoming intimate with the needs of the working class helped to stimulate the mission of worker-priests in time of peace.

After World War II the number of worker-priests increased fairly rapidly. In 1949 they numbered about fifty. They were in various centres and a dozen of them were regulars—Capuchins, Dominicans, Franciscans, and Jesuits. When, in 1951, the Holy See forbade the recruitment of additional members, the total was approximately ninety, in about a score of dioceses. Most of them were from the bourgeoisie and at least one was from a rural area where the faith was strong.

The adjustment to the life of the working classes required courage of no mean order. Some worker-priests were reported to be insufficiently prepared theologically. Several bishops were said to have been unconvinced of the importance of the project and to have been unwilling to release their best priests for it, with the result that only the poorly trained and emotionally unstable were permitted to engage in it. Much greater was the problem of full identifica-

---

[53] *Ibid., op. cit.*, pp. 617, 618; Michonneau, *Revolution in a City Parish*, p. 98.

[54] Out of the large literature see Dansette, *op. cit.*, pp. 165–305; *Documents des Prêtes Ouvriers* (Paris, Éditions de Minuit, 1954, pp. 290), *passim;* Claudio Cesa, *Apostolato Cattolico e Condizione Operaia. Testimonianze e Documenti sui Preti Operai* (Florence, Edizioni de Silva la Nueva Italia, 1955, pp. 155), *passim;* Die Arbeiterpriester. Dokumente (Heilbronn a. N., E. Salzer, 1957, pp. 227), *passim;* Henri Perrin, *Tagebuch eines Arbeiterpriesters* (Munich, Kösel-Verlag, 1955, pp. 352), *passim;* R. F. Byrnes in *Foreign Affairs*, Vol. XXXIII, pp. 327–331; *Information Service*, December 11, 1954.

tion with those whom the worker-priests sought to serve. Priests, and therefore unmarried, they did not have the family responsibilities of many of those among whom they worked. Although they had a prophetic spirit appropriate to the period of liberation from Nazi rule, were critical of compromises made by the Church, and condemned a society which rejected the Gospel, they were optimistic about the resources of the faith to work changes, had confidence in the power of the virtue inherent in the masses to renew society, and, at least at the outset, did not share in the conviction of the inevitability of the class struggle which characterized the rank and file of the men among whom they lived. They were plunged into a proletarian society marked by dire poverty, insecurity, sexual promiscuity, and unstable home life. The leadership in that segment of society was largely from the Communist Party and the C.G.T. (*Confédération Générale du Travail*), which was prevailingly Socialist but with Communist infiltration.

Some of the worker-priests zealously identified themselves with the aspirations of the working class. In that identification they tended to dissociate themselves from the ecclesiastical structure, parish life, and even such movements as Catholic Action and the C.G.T.C. (*Confédération Générale des Travailleurs Chrétiens*). They supported the Communist-sponsored peace movement which was launched by a meeting in Warsaw in 1948 and the Stockholm appeal of 1950, and similar projects for the abolition of atomic arms. Some held office in the C.G.T. Several joined in the popular, Communist-encouraged protest (May, 1952) against the coming of General Ridgway to France.

Because of the long hours and the physical fatigue of their daily labour, the worker-priests had difficulty in keeping up their meditation and their reading of the breviary. Although they were permitted to say mass in the evening, they lacked time for the sacerdotal care of souls.

These problems bore most heavily on the worker-priests in Paris. They were not as pressing in some of the provinces. For example, in a mining district in Pas-de-Calais three Jesuits shared loyally in the life of the miners, brought some of them into effective touch with the local clergy, and were active in evangelization. In Marseilles the Dominican Loew was given a regular parish in 1945 and attracted some from the cosmopolitan population of the port.

What were known as the worker-vicars, in a broad sense a part of the worker-priest movement, had the support of Suhard. They were priests attached to specific parishes and, living in parsonages, were not subjected to the irregular life in the rooming-houses in which many of the worker-priests were domiciled. However, they did not achieve the hoped-for correlation of their mission with that of the parish.[55]

A movement which superficially seemed to have kinship with the worker-priests project but was quite distinct was the Little Brothers of Jesus. It arose

[55] Dansette, *Destin du Catholicisme Français (1926–1956)*, pp. 212, 213.

from the inspiration of the life of Charles de Foucauld (1850–1916). A scion of the French nobility, in his youth an army officer, Foucauld had already achieved fame as an explorer in North Africa when, from complete scepticism, he was converted, became a Trappist, left the Trappists to follow an even more austere regimen, and lived as a hermit and missionary in the Sahara until killed by Tuaregs.[56]

Before his death Foucauld had thought of inaugurating a congregation which would give itself to evangelism, but the actual founder of the Little Brothers of Jesus was R. Voillaume, who was moved to take the step by reading a biography of Foucauld. Begun in 1933, within twenty years the congregation had about 180 members. Following their example, the Little Sisters of Jesus sprang up with a similar rule, and the Little Sisters of the Sacred Heart came into being, the latter as a purely contemplative congregation. The Little Brothers of Jesus lived in communities in various parts of the world. They sought by sharing the poverty of those among whom they lived and by supporting themselves by labour—in France agricultural labour—to witness by their lives to the love of Christ among those in whose toil they participated. As Foucauld had through his life of ascetic contemplation borne witness among the Tuaregs, so the Little Brothers of Jesus, instead of living apart from the world as contemplatives had traditionally done, desired to give their witness among the de-Christianized. They said mass in the morning and used their evenings for prayer, silence, and the reception of visitors. In 1955 they had ten centres in France. For the most part the worker-priests criticized them for not joining in the class struggle but instead taking a position of non-violent resistance.[57]

Antagonism developed in Rome to the worker-priests and to the movement which they represented. In 1947 the Holy See had become sufficiently uncertain about the experiment to send a questionnaire to determine the extent of the hostility. It found so little that in 1949 the *Osservatore Romano,* an organ of the Vatican, published an article commending the effort. In 1951, believing that the devotion of the worker-priests could be better expended through the traditional channels of the parish, Rome forbade the extension of the movement by recruiting new members. News reached Rome that Marxist publications were being read in the seminary in Limoges which was training clergy for the Paris Mission. A few of the worker-priests were defecting from the clerical status. In

[56] René Bazin, *Charles de Foucauld, Hermit and Explorer,* translated by Peter Keelan (London, Burns Oates & Washbourne, 1923, pp. v, 356), *passim;* Georges Gorrée, *Sur les Traces du Père de Foucauld* (Paris, La Colombe, Éditions du Vieux Colombier, new ed., 1953, pp. 355), *passim;* Michel Carrouges, *Soldier of the Spirit. The Life of Charles de Foucauld,* translated from the French by Marie-Christine Hellin (London, Victor Gollancz, 1956, pp. xiv, 300), *passim;* Anne Fremantle, *Desert Calling. The Life of Charles de Foucauld* (London, Hollis & Carter, 1950, pp. xii, 343), *passim.*

[57] R. Voillaume, *Seeds of the Desert: the Legacy of Charles de Foucauld* (Chicago, Fides Publishers Association, 1955, pp. xii, 368), *passim;* Dansette, *Destin du Catholicisme Français (1926–1956)*, pp. 213–217; *Time,* April 23, 1956.

1953 the Cardinal Prefect of the Congregation of Seminaries and Universities forbade seminarians to be workers' apprentices in any industry. Later in the year Rome ordered the Limoges seminary closed. It deemed the movement which it represented a menace to the Church in questioning its traditional forms. Each bishop was to recall his clergy engaged in the worker-priest movement, and the heads of the orders who had men engaged in it were gradually to withdraw them. Some of the French hierarchy, including three cardinals, believed the suppression of the worker-priests to be disastrous and held that Rome had not been sufficiently informed. However, when the three protested in person to Pius XII, they were informed that the decision must stand. The Pope outlined as a substitute that secular priests who replaced the worker-priests be chosen by their bishops, receive an adequate preparation in doctrine and the spiritual life, give themselves to manual labour only for three hours a day, not become members of secular organizations, such as labour unions, and live in community with other priests. Clearly these conditions would make impossible employment such as the worker-priests had undertaken. Finally, in September, 1959, the Congregation of the Holy Office made public a decision that any work in the factories or in instruction yards was incompatible with the life and obligation of the priesthood.

The decision presented the worker-priests with a difficult choice. They believed the hard alternative was the abandonment of the working class with which they had cast their lot or disobedience to their ecclesiastical superiors. Some chose the latter, others the former.[58]

Although their numbers were never large, the worker-priests were given so much publicity by the press that they and the Papal condemnation of their methods attracted wide attention, both in France and in other parts of the world. Here was a bold experiment in approaching de-Christianized labourers. It was of importance to both Roman Catholics and Protestants. In one form or another the problem to which the worker-priests addressed themselves was growing in prominence wherever the revolutionary age was making its effect felt. In France much of the Roman Catholic press defended them and deplored the action of the Vatican as surrendering the working class to non-Christian forces.

The Paris Mission (*Mission de Paris*) was so intimately associated with the worker-priests that it is difficult to separate the two. As we have seen, it arose from the initiative of Cardinal Suhard; in January, 1944, Suhard was convinced that with World War II an old world had passed and a new one had come into being. The Church, so he said, could either withdraw from that new world and let it go its disastrous way, without God and without law, or seek to transform it. In addition to the worker-priests, Suhard had the Paris Mission employ

58 Dansette, *Destin du Catholicisme Français (1926–1956)*, pp. 264–292.

such methods as the cinema, chaplaincies to the firemen, efforts to reclaim prostitutes, and scientific research.[59]

Henri Godin (1906–1944) had much to do with stimulating the formation of the Paris Mission and the development of the worker-priest movement. Born of a poor family in a rural village, he early decided to become a priest. He was ordained in 1933 and served for a time in a parish. Wishing to give himself to the unemployed poor, he joined the *Fils de la Charité*. The *Fils de la Charité* had been begun by Jean Émile Anizan (1853–1928), a Lazarist caught in the anti-Modernist wave, by which he and some of his colleagues were deposed for "social Modernism." On leaving the Lazarists he espoused the cause of the poor and founded a new congregation (approved by the Holy See in 1934) to evangelize the working class and to combine the religious life with the demands of a parish.[60] But Godin came to the conviction that to devote himself to the poor he must be even poorer, left that congregation, and became the French organizer of the J.O.C. While serving in the army in World War II he made friends with anti-clericals, Communists, and atheists. After the war he devoted himself to the Parisian proletariat. As the main author of *La France: Pays de Missions?* he helped French Roman Catholics to see the state of the de-Christianized.[61]

Somewhat distinct from the Paris Mission was the Mission to France (*Mission de France.*) It was begun in July, 1941, by the Assembly of Cardinals and Archbishops during the throes of World War II and the German occupation and sought to prepare missionaries for the de-Christianized dioceses. To that end an inter-diocesan seminary was opened at Lisieux under the direction of the Sulpicians, who had long had experience in theological education. By 1954 it had graduated nearly four hundred priests who served in varied ways—some in urban and some in rural parishes. In 1952 it was moved from Lisieux—situated as it was in a diocese with conservative tendencies—and placed in Limoges, in the centre of de-Christianized regions which its graduates were designed to evangelize. It was closed here by order of the Vatican but finally set up in Potigny (Yonne) in a very de-Christianized area under the leadership of the oldest French cardinal. Moreover, in the De-Christianized rural areas the J.A.C., a child of Catholic Action and the rural equivalent of Jocism, played much the role that the latter had in the cities.[62] In 1943, also in the war years, a former Dominican, Dominique Epagneul, inaugurated the *Frères Missionnaires des Campagnes,* to reach the rural areas. In 1954 the members numbered 108, largely on the plateau of Brie, east of Paris. A group of Benedictines, led by Fr. de Féligonde, founded a new congregation of monks dedicated to parish work in

[59] *Ibid.*, pp. 127, 135–137; Daniel-Rops, *op. cit.*, p. 37.

[60] *Enciclopedia Cattolica*, Vol. V, p. 1255.

[61] Ward, *France Pagan?*, pp. 3–62.

[62] Dansette, *Destin du Catholicisme Français (1926–1956)*, p. 258; Daniel-Rops, *op. cit.*, p. 37; Ward, *op. cit.*, p. 55; David Watmough, *A Church Renascent. A Study in Modern French Roman Catholicism* (London, S.P.C.K., 1951, pp. xviii, 125), p. 72; Bishop, *France Alive*, pp. 133–152.

an underprivileged quarter of Paris. The Premonstratensians or Nobertines (canons regular) strove to reach de-Christianized parishes through teams of from three to six priests living in community.[63]

A fresh effort to win the de-Christianized working classes was associated with the name and work of George Michonneau. Placed in charge of a parish in Paris which served a pagan proletariat, he attempted to make the Christian minority active in winning their neighbours. He held that they must seek to create a Christian atmosphere that would revolutionize the character of the parish. Among other devices he held meetings in homes and district missions. He also employed some of the devices of the Liturgical Movement.[64]

In their attempts to penetrate with the Christian faith the new society which was emerging in the revolutionary age after World War II and so to halt de-Christianization, some Roman Catholics went further towards social radicalism than the ecclesiastical authorities would countenance. "Christian progressives," while opposing the atheism of the Communists, endeavoured to coöperate with the latter in changing the world. Towards the close of 1947 they came together in the U.C.P. (*Unions des Chrétiens Progressistes*). The Assembly of Cardinals and Archbishops of France condemned them (1954). The Youth of the Church (*Jeunesse de l'Église*), begun in 1936 by clergy and laity, sought to work out a form of the apostolate which would be adapted to the sociology of the working classes. It came under suspicion, and one of the major publications issuing from it was placed on the Index.[65]

Somewhat similar, with service to the underprivileged as their purpose, were the Companions of Emmaus. They were initiated soon after World War II by the Abbé Pierre (1912———). From a wealthy family of Lyons and educated by the Jesuits, at the age of eighteen he chose a life of strict asceticism and after three years entered the secular clergy. Active in the resistance movement against the Germans during the war, for a time he served as a deputy in the National Assembly. He made his home in the slums and his house became a refuge for the destitute. Under his leadership the Companions of Emmaus, also known more picturesquely as the Ragpickers of the Lord, organized shanty camps on the eastern fringe of Paris to enable the houseless and abandoned, through self-help, to erect houses. They stirred the government to action. Their movement spread to Belgium, Argentina, Brazil, Chile, Uruguay, Canada, and Japan.[66] They were

[63] Daniel-Rops, *op. cit.*, p. 28. On the rural areas see Henri Bordeaux, *Barrage Spirituel. Le Prêtre dans les Campagnes de France* (Paris, P. Téqui, 1956, pp. vi, 196), *passim;* Jacques P. Bossière to the author, December, 1959.

[64] Michonneau, *Revolution in a City Parish*, pp. 99 ff.; G. Michonneau, *The Missionary Spirit in Parish Life* (Westminster, Md., The Newman Press, 1952, pp. viii, 194), *passim;* Bishop, *op. cit.*, pp. 89–132.

[65] Dansette, *Destin du Catholicisme Français* (1926–1956), pp. 225–238.

[66] *The New York Times*, March 28, 1954, January 27, 1956; *The Christian Century*, Vol. LXXX, p. 1027; *Information Service*, June 11, 1955.

partly paralleled by the somewhat older Goodwill Industries, maintained by Protestants in the United States.

In a quite different category, but as an example of the effect of Christianity in reinforcing a purpose of selfless living, was Simone Weil (1909–1943). The daughter of agnostic Jewish parents, brilliant as a student of philosophy, she had already identified herself with factory workers when, in 1941, she came in touch with a Dominican and thought of seeking baptism. Although possessed by a strong sense of God and giving herself with rare devotion as a labourer in the fields and, in London, helping with the French war effort while voluntarily observing the food rationing imposed in the occupied zone in her mother country, she did not believe it to be her vocation to identify herself with the Church.[67]

France: Growing Social Concern in Roman Catholic Circles

After 1914 Roman Catholics became more and more concerned about the social issues brought by the revolutionary age. Their concern was heightened by the growth of Communism and its triumph in Russia after World War I. Conferences (*Semaines Sociales*) had been held before 1914 for the discussion of the problems raised by industry and the multiplication of workers employed in it. After World War I they were continued. The one in 1920 took up the relations of capital and labour, especially in light of the Russian Revolution and the social troubles in France in 1919–1920.[68] Others followed annually, concentrating on specific issues.[69] Cardinal Suhard declared that the growth of the working class had reached the point where alterations were needed in the ways in which the Church dealt with the issue. After World War II the French hierarchy gave increasing attention to social problems.[70]

Leaders in the Roman Catholic Church were not content with discussion. They either took the initiative or supported measures to improve the lot of the labourers. Thus A.C.J.F. and former members of Sillon contributed to the passage of legislation in 1919 which fixed the eight-hour day and forbade night work in bakeries.[71] In 1928 Roman Catholics with a deep interest in social conditions proposed in the Chamber of Deputies a programme for agrarian reform. They worked for laws to protect labourers who were minors and to establish workingmen's compensation. In 1929 they espoused the cause of forced labour in the colonies.[72]

During the emergency of World War II and the German occupation the

---

[67] Simone Weil, *Waiting for God*, translated by Emma Crawford (New York, G. P. Putnam's Sons, 1951, pp. 227), *passim*.
[68] Villain, *l'Enseignement Social de l'Église*, Vol. III, pp. 37–47.
[69] Hoog, *Histoire du Catholicisme Social en France 1871–1931*, pp. 223, 280.
[70] Villain, *op. cit.*, Vol. III, pp. 77–83.
[71] Hoog, *op. cit.*, p. 248.
[72] *Ibid.*, p. 282.

episcopate stood out against the violation of human rights. Facing possible retaliation by the leaders of the occupation, the Assembly of Cardinals and Archbishops through Cardinal Suhard protested (1942) against the anti-Semitic measures. The previous year the theological faculty and the Archbishop of Lyons, Cardinal Gerlier, had raised their voices against the persecution of the Jews. In 1942 Gerlier again spoke his mind. Other protests were made in 1943. Measures were taken to aid suffering Jewish families and Jewish children.[73] The episcopate opposed the mobilization of men and especially of women for forced labour in Germany. It also condemned the German massacres of French men and boys and the German execution of hostages. Measures were taken to serve the inmates of prison camps.[74]

After World War II Louis Josep Lebret (1897——), a Dominican, formerly a marine officer, led in studying the structure of society to see in what degree, if at all, it conformed to Christian ideals.[75] His counsel was sought by the governor of Sao Pãulo, in Brazil, to help in planning for the rapidly growing capital of that state.

It was also after World War II that Édouard Leclerc, as a Christian vocation, built up a number of retail grocery stores which through careful management sold to the public at prices considerably lower than had been customary and at the same time paid higher wages to employees than was usual.[76]

FRANCE: LAY ORGANIZATIONS OF LABOURERS AND EMPLOYERS

We have already said something[77] of the many Roman Catholic lay organizations not directly a part of Catholic Action which proliferated in Europe after 1914 and have noted that they were numerous in France. They witnessed to the active concern of French Roman Catholics for the issues brought by industrialization.

We must not take the space to give the story of these bodies in any detail.[78] They began late in the nineteenth century and grew rapidly after World War

---

[73] Guerry, L'Église Catholique en France sous l'Occupation, pp. 33–65.

[74] Ibid., pp. 66–92, 93–106, 128–136.
On measures by the French episcopate during the occupation see also Jacques Marteaux, L'Église de France devant la Révolution Marxiste (Paris, La Table Ronde, Vol. V, no date, pp. 660), Vol. I, pp. 463 ff.

[75] Louis Joseph Lebret, La France in Transition. Étapes d'une Recherche Collection de Sociologie Religieuse (Paris, Éditions Ouvrières Economie et Humanisme, 1957, pp. 167).

[76] Frontier, Vol. I, pp. 24–26 (Spring, 1960).

[77] Chapter IV.

[78] Among the books dealing with the subject, in addition to Fogarty, Christian Democracy in Western Europe, 1820–1953, to which we have repeatedly referred, are Gaston de Marcieu, Les Syndicats Catholiques du Commerce et de l'Industrie (Paris, La Vie Universitaire, ca. 1921, pp. 160). Jean Guerin-Long, Les Syndicats Chrétiens en France et Principalement en Provence (Cannes, Guiglion, 1922, pp. 169), Paul Ardoin, Le Syndicalisme Ouvrier Chrétien en Provence 1884–1935 (Marseilles, Imprimerie de la Société du "Petit Marseillais," 1936, pp. 175), and Gwynn, op. cit., pp. 143–160.

I. Many of them were local and were grouped by occupations and sex. For example, in 1936 fifty-one Christian unions existed in Provence. In Marseilles they included, among others, a union of electricians, another of metallurgists, two of garment workers, and one of women accountants. We also hear of several of railway employees.[79] In 1919, in the burst of idealistic activity which followed World War I and growing out of an international gathering of trade unions, the *Confédération Française des Travailleurs Chrétiens,* or C.F.T.C. (French Confederation of Christian Trade Unions), was brought into being. When, in 1920, it held its first national congress, it represented 578 unions. Some of these were in regional confederations. The total membership was about 140,000. This, however, was less than the membership of similar unions in Belgium, the Netherlands, and especially in Germany (reported as 1,250,000), which were represented at an international congress at The Hague in 1920.[80] It was also small compared with the combination of Socialist-Communist unions which in 1921, before it broke down, had 2,000,000 members and even in the slump after 1921 enrolled 600,000.[81] Yet, in 1950, it was able to poll 1,172,000 votes as against the 2,392,000 votes for the *Confédération Générale du Travail* (C.G.T.), which had a Socialist-Communist tinge.[82] In 1926, as we have noted, French Catholic employers, who had been organizing in the previous century, formed what in the 1950's was known as the *Centre Français du Patronat Chrétien,* or C.F.P.C. (French Christian Employers' Centre).[83]

French Roman Catholics Organize for Political Action

No one party in France drew Roman Catholics together for political action as effectively as did the Centre Party and then the Christian Democratic Union Party in Germany, the Christian Democratic Party in Italy, and similar parties in Belgum and the Netherlands. That is not surprising. The prolonged antagonism of a large proportion of French Roman Catholics to the Third Republic and the popularity among many Roman Catholics of the monarchist *l'Action Française* worked against the consolidation of the Roman Catholic vote under any one party. As we have seen, Popular Liberal Action (A.L.P.), the Popular Democratic Party (P.D.P.), and the Popular Republican Movement (M.R.P.) attracted some of the Roman Catholic vote but were never a majority, even of Roman Catholics.[84] The *Parti Démocratique Populaire* (P.D.P.) advocated a decentralized government with professional and family representation but by 1928 had only about 37,000 members in units in perhaps half of the

[79] Ardoin, *op. cit.,* pp. 147–149.
[80] Marcieu, *op. cit.,* pp. 99–116.
[81] Fogarty, *op. cit.,* p. 209.
[82] Paul Vignaux in *Problèmes du Catholicisme Français,* p. 125.
[83] Fogarty, *op. cit.,* p. 252.
[84] Chapter IV.

departments. It was amalgamated with the *Mouvement Républicain Populaire* (M.R.P.), which in part grew out of the resistance movement against the Germans, was initiated by a student in Lyons, and was organized in 1944. In the election of 1945 the M.P.R. polled about a fourth of the votes.[85] In the 1950's it obtained and increased national subsidies for parochial schools.[86] Many who voted with the M.R.P. did so not from Christian conviction but as an alternative to Communism.[87]

FRANCE: COMPETITION BETWEEN THE ROMAN CATHOLIC CHURCH AND COMMUNISM

In the years which followed World War II Communism became potent in France and Roman Catholics set themselves to meet it in two ways—by seeking to coöperate with Communists and by combatting Communism.

Several attempts were made at collaboration without sacrificing Christian ideals. One was through the *Mouvement Populaire des Familles* (M.P.F.). An outgrowth of the Jocists, M.P.F. was born in the late 1930's. It sought the welfare of the family and the community and included bachelors and widows. Its members were labourers with small incomes. It arose from Christian concern, but both militant Roman Catholics and rank-and-file Communists were welcomed. In the post-World War II years it aided homeless families, through self-help, to find homes. It established communal laundries, printing shops, and home service. It was intent on improving living conditions for the labourers and thus on undercutting the class hatred and the urge to class warfare which fed Communism.[88]

Another such effort, but with a different programme, was the Boimondau Community. Its founder was a devout Roman Catholic who had for a time prepared for the priesthood but had left the seminary because he felt that he had no vocation. He became a workman, knew extreme poverty, and conceived the idea of making possible a more human, balanced life for labourers. It was in the 1940's that he succeeded in setting up a community which gained its livelihood through the manufacture of watch casings. They held in common the means of production and stimulated one another to acquire a better education. The membership embraced Communists, Roman Catholics, and Protestants. The basic ethical assumptions were Christian. Similar communities arose elsewhere in France.[89]

---

[85] Louis Biton, *La Démocratie Chrétienne dans la Politique Française* (Angers, H. Siraudeau et Cie, 1934, pp. 170), pp. 58–65; Einaudi and Goguel, *Christian Democracy in Italy and France*, pp. 107 ff.

[86] *The Christian Century*, February 1, 1956, p. 134.

[87] Vignaux, *op. cit.*, pp. 137, 139.

[88] Bishop, *France Alive*, pp. 37–56.

[89] *Ibid.*, pp. 153–172.

Communism was combatted openly. Although, realizing the hold that the Roman Catholic Church had on a large proportion of the people of France, some Communists sought to minimize the differences between their ideology and Christianity and claimed that Communism was religiously tolerant, Roman Catholics were not wanting who pointed out the basic antagonism between their faith and Communism and maintained that the two were irreconcilable. From the standpoint of the Roman Catholic Church, as the Popes made clear to the faithful, compromise was impossible.[90]

FRANCE: INTELLECTUAL ACTIVITY IN ROMAN CATHOLIC CIRCLES

In the intellectual world French Roman Catholics displayed marked activity. Whether it was greater or less than in the nineteenth century would be difficult to ascertain, for dependable standards of measurement could not be easily set up and applied. That it was striking was clear.

In the realm of philosophy and theology as much has already been said as our space will permit.[91] The several distinguished figures to which we have called attention—such as Maritain, Gilson, Marcel, Daniélou, and De Lubac—would have commanded respect in any land or period. In Biblical scholarship Lagrange, Lebreton, and De Vaux were evidence that French Roman Catholics were facing open-eyed the challenges of the day and were making positive contributions. Earlier in this chapter we noted the extensive daily and periodical press, local, provincial, and national, maintained by Roman Catholics.

Beginning in the 1920's an association of French Roman Catholic intellectuals (*Centre Catholique des Intellectuels Français*) met annually in Paris to discuss theological, philosophical, and cultural problems. Annually a pilgrimage was made at Pentecost to Chartres. It sometimes had 12,000 student participants. For three days conferences were held at which the Papal nuncio and the Cardinal Archbishop of Paris might speak. Many conversions followed.

Among French men of letters some Roman Catholics stood out. To be sure, the existentialist novelist André Malraux (1902——) while in his teens gave up the Roman Catholic faith and entered upon an unsuccessful quest for a satisfying religion.[92] Albert Camus (1913–1960), very widely read in the 1950's, was clearly non-Christian. But shortly before and between the two world wars authentically Roman Catholic writers appeared, some of them sharing popularity with Malraux. Outstanding in his popular appeal, François Mauriac (1885——),

---

[90] G. Fessard, *La Main Tendue? Le Dialogue Catholique-Communiste est-il Possible?* (Paris, Éditions Bernard Grasset, 1937, pp. 244), *passim;* R. P. Daniélou, *Dialogues* (Paris, Le Portulan, 1948, pp. 192), pp. 31–65.

[91] Chapter VI.

[92] *Time,* July 18, 1955, pp. 24–30.

novelist, poet, dramatist, and critic, won the Nobel prize for literature.[93] Georges Bernanos (1888–1948), novelist and essayist, was a man of prodigious vitality and striking contrasts—gay and vituperative, tender and violent.[94] Paul Claudel (1868–1955), a poet whom admirers compared with Dante, at eighteen had a deep religious experience which led him to see the world as the work of God and from which came his purpose to sing of that work with joy.[95] Slightly older than Claudel, Charles Péguy died in 1914, but his poetry continued to be read after that year. Engaged in stormy crusades, unconventional in his poems, uncompromising, his short career (he was born in 1873) strewn with broken friendships, he inspired much of Roman Catholic youth. In his earlier years he wavered between Christian faith and unbelief and after his conversion, because of family impediments, he abstained from mass.[96] The priest Louis le Cardonnel (1862–1936) was noted for his religious poetry.[97] The novelist Léon Bloy (1846–1917) had done most of his writing before 1914. He was called the predecessor of Bernanos. He and his family were chronically destitute and, an angry and pitiful visionary, he took poverty and suffering as his themes.[98] These were only leading lights among a numerous galaxy.

France: Summary

We have given so much space to the course of the Roman Catholic faith in France since 1914 partly because in that country the challenge of the currents of the revolutionary era, with the resulting de-Christianization, had long been acute and partly because the contrasting vigour of the Roman Catholic Church continued to be marked.

Here the prolonged struggle between the anti-clerical forces and the Church had, in 1905, less than a decade before World War I, issued in disestablishment, apparently a body blow to the Church. Here the bulk of the labourers in the industries and mines which were a symptom of the changing age were progressively drifting away from the Church. Even large sections of rural France, once solidly committed to Christianity, were being de-Christianized. France, too, was bled white by the two world wars and in the second war fell victim to alien occupation.

Yet in France in a variety of ways the Roman Catholic Church displayed creative vitality. The faithful rose to the financial support of the Church and

---

[93] Robert J. North, *Le Catholicisme dans l'Œuvre de François Mauriac* (Paris, Éditions du Conquistador, 1950, pp. xlvi, 183), *passim*.

[94] Hopper, *Spiritual Problems in Contemporary Literature*, pp. 229, 230; Brémond and others, *Manuel de la Littérature Catholique en France*, pp. 127, 128. See Bernanos's *The Diary of a Country Priest*, translated by Pamela Morris (New York, The Macmillan Co., 1937, pp. 298).

[95] Hopper, *op. cit.*, pp. 235–238; Brémond, *op. cit.*, pp. 24–26.

[96] Wilder, *Modern Poetry and the Christian Tradition*, pp. 132–137.

[97] Brémond, *op. cit.*, p. 32.

[98] *Ibid.*, pp. 112, 113; Wilder, *op. cit.*, pp. 130, 131.

its institutions. Catholic Action was outstanding. Novel and courageous attempts were being made to reach the de-Christianized. Each world war was accompanied and followed by fresh efforts to meet the emergency. Although the Church was not re-established, reconciliation was effected between it and the state. The Liturgical Movement, with its purpose of reviving the intelligent participation of the laity in the central rite of the Church, had some of its major developments in France. Fresh translations of the Bible were made, also with the object of reaching the rank and file. Theological and Biblical studies flourished and philosophers arose who made their learning ancillary to the Church. As in the nineteenth century and as we are to see in the next chapter, more Roman Catholic missionaries went from France than from any other country. In no other land was the contrast quite as marked between the corroding effects of the revolutionary currents on the Roman Catholic Church and the vitality in that church which sought not only to stem the corrosion but also to spread the faith throughout the world.

ITALY: THE SETTING

We have already seen[99] something of the setting in Italy in which the Roman Catholic Church lived in the four and a half decades immediately after 1914. In both world wars Italy was a belligerent. In the first it was on the side of the victors. In the second it threw in its lot with the Germans, largely fell under their control, and was invaded by its enemies. After World War I for a little over two decades (1922–1943) Italy was dominated by Mussolini and his Fascists. When Mussolini was eliminated and the Fascist Party outlawed, the House of Savoy abdicated, after vainly attempting to govern Italy under the revived constitutional monarchy. Italy then (1946) became a republic. The republic was confronted with rival parties. For a time it seemed that Communists in collaboration with Socialists would dominate the government. But the Christian Democratic Party, which had most of the Roman Catholic vote, although in a minority in the National Assembly which was called (1946) to draft a constitution, was able through the coöperation of small liberal groups and right-wing Socialists to form an anti-Communist cabinet and to bring into being a democratic republic. Thereafter the Christian Democratic Party, although not without its factions, was the strongest in the country. In the late 1950's the Communists lost in voting strength, even in some of the industrial centres in the North.

ITALY: THE ROMAN CATHOLIC CHURCH AND THE STATE

In the near-half-century which followed 1914, as we have noted, relations be-

99 Chapter III.

tween the Roman Catholic Church and the Italian Government fairly steadily improved. By the Lateran Accord (1929) the Papacy at last recognized the Kingdom of Italy, accepted compensation for the sequestered Papal States, was accorded full sovereignty over Vatican City and Castel Gandolfo, and was assured the right to appoint all the bishops in Italy. Roman Catholic marriage was made legal and sufficient. Religious orders were safeguarded. The state also agreed to pay the salaries of the bishops, renounced the right of patronage to the benefices of Italy, and agreed that religious instruction should be given in all state schools by teachers approved by the Church. Friction developed over the direction of youth activities—whether it should be entirely through the Fascist state or shared with the Church—but a compromise was reached (1931) which eased the tension.[100] Moreover, in some respects the interests of the Papacy and Mussolini coincided. Both were opposed to Freemasonry and Communism, both looked with disfavour on the Popular Front republic in the struggle in Spain— the Pope because it had Communist elements and Mussolini because it was a serious threat to the ideology of Fascism and was unfriendly to him.[101]

The Roman Catholic Church was much more sympathetic with Christian Democracy than with Fascism. Christian Democracy appeared in Italy in organized form in 1919, soon after World War I. As we have noted,[102] it found expression at first through the Popular Party, led by Luigi Sturzo (1871-1959), a Sicilian priest. Sturzo had come to Rome as secretary of Catholic Action. He sought to base the Popular Party on Papal encyclicals and advocated radical reforms, especially in agriculture. In the days just after World War I when the trend in many countries was towards democratic idealism, the Popular Party flourished, especially among the peasants and in the South, and became a force with which to reckon. In the election of 1919 it attracted a fifth of the votes.[103] Benedict XV smiled on it.

Under the Fascist regime the Popular Party dwindled. Pius XI, a conservative, looked on it with disfavour for its espousal of reforms, its refusal to make an issue of the Roman Question, and its unwillingness to become openly confessional. In 1923 Sturzo resigned as secretary of the party, was followed in that post by Alcide de Gasperi, and left the country in 1924, a voluntary exile.

---

[100] Chapter III. Of the extensive literature on the relations of the Fascist regime and the Papacy, see Ridley, *The Papacy and Fascism's Crisis, passim;* John Hearly, *Pope or Mussolini* (New York, The Macaulay Co., 1929, pp. 256), *passim;* Wilfrid Parsons, *The Pope and Italy: Concerning the Recent Vatican Settlement* (New York, The America Press, 1929, pp. 134), *passim;* Binchy, *Church and State in Fascist Italy, passim;* S. William Halperin, *The Separation of Church and State in Italian Thought from Cavour to Mussolini* (University of Chicago Press, 1937, pp. ix, 115), pp. 87–108; and Jemolo, *Chièsa e Stato in Italia negli Ultimo Cento Anni,* pp. 589–686.

[101] Hales, *The Catholic Church in the Modern World,* pp. 267–269.

[102] Chapter IV.

[103] Einaudi and Goguel, *Christian Democracy in Italy and France,* pp. 8–18. On Sturzo and his convictions see Santo Ballia, *Chièsa e Stato nel Pensiero di L. Sturzo Presentazione del F. della Rocca* (Turin, Società Editrice Internazionale, 1956, pp. 187), *passim.*

The Popular Party was suppressed in 1926. Yet it maintained an underground resistance.[104]

After the fall of Mussolini and with the coming of peace the Popular Party, as we have remarked,[105] was reborn as the Christian Democratic Party. Its first leader was De Gasperi. Several different elements were included within it, but its guiding purpose was the application of Christian principles to political and social life. Although it said boldly that the religion of Italians was Catholic and that the state must conform to Christian ethics and had only an auxiliary right in the education of youth, it disavowed control by the ecclesiastical structure of the Roman Catholic Church. Yet it had closer relation with that church than the Popular Party had possessed, and the clergy and Catholic Action supported it. That support had dangers: the chronic anti-clericalism might charge the party with being a tool of the Church and thus alienate many voters. The Christian Democratic Party opposed both Marxism and the secularized liberalism of the bourgeoisie. It wrote its ideals into the constitution of the Republic.

The Christian Democratic Party was strongest in the North, in spite of the fact that there industrialism had created seed beds for socialism and Communism. But its moderate leftist policies on such issues as state ownership, permission for labour to organize, and land reform attracted many who reacted both against conservatism and against the extreme radicalism of the Communists and the more advanced Socialists. At the outset it was weakest in the South, but it later made gains in that region.

The Christian Democrats continued to be the strongest party, but again and again, to retain power, they collaborated with other groups. Sturzo returned to Italy, but while he was not restored to a position of power in the party's leadership, in 1952 he was made senator for life.[106]

ITALY: CATHOLIC ACTION

After what was earlier said,[107] we need no extended account of Italian Catholic Action. It was in part the outgrowth of movements, such as *Gioventù Cattolica Italiana*, the *Federazione Universitaria Cattolica Italiana*, the National Congress of Catholics, the *Opera dei Congressi*, and the *Unione Popolare*, which had their rise in the nineteenth century.[108] The year 1908 saw the organization of a woman's movement, the *Unione fra le Donne Cattoliche d'Italia*.[109] The *Unione Popolare* was especially strong, with parish groups.

[104] Einaudi and Goguel, *op. cit.*, pp. 18–26.
[105] Chapter IV.
[106] Einaudi and Goguel, *op. cit.*, pp. 27–96; Leicester C. Webb, *Church and State in Italy, 1947–1957* (Melbourne University Press, 1958, pp. x, 60), *passim.*
[107] Chapter IV.
[108] Volume I, pp. 417, 418.
[109] Civardi, *Compendio di Storia dell' Azione Cattolica Italiana*, pp. 140–143.

In 1915, early in World War I, a council (*La Giunta Direttiva dell' Azione Cattolica*) was created to coördinate the activities of these movements to meet the challenge of that struggle. Late in 1918 a woman's youth organization (*Gioventù Femminile Cattolica Italiana*) was added. During or soon after World War I several movements arose related to the *Unione Popolare* and in the socio-economic sphere. They included a Federation of Labour (*Confederazione Italiana dei Lavoratori*), a Confederation of Coöperatives (*Confederazione Cooperativa*), and the National Secretariat for Professional Unions (*Segretariato Nazionale delle Unioni Professionali*).[110]

The impetus given by Pius XI brought fresh vigour to Italian Catholic Action. In 1922 a Central Council of Catholic Action (*Giunta Central dell' Azione Cattolica*) was set up. It headed the structure, to which we earlier called attention, of diocesan councils (*giunte diocesane*)and parish councils (*consigli parrocchiali*). Not far from the same time the Italian Federation of Catholic Men (*Federazione Italiana Uomini Cattolica*) was instituted. It held annual congresses. In 1925 the Catholic Institute for Social Activity (*Instituto Cattolico di Attività Sociali*) was begun to carry on the Economic-Social Secretariat that had been inaugurated in 1919.[111] In spite of the conflict with Mussolini, Catholic Action continued under the Fascist regime, but with functions more strictly in the religious sphere, in a narrower sense of that word.[112]

Pius XII brought changes in Italian Catholic Action. Instead of reserving its direction to the Pope, as Pius XI had done, he transferred it to a representative of the Italian episcopate. Under the stress of World War II centralized supervision became so difficult that it was temporarily replaced by regional and local direction by the episcopate.[113]

With the end of World War II, Italian Catholic Action resumed and broadened its activities. In connexion with it, partly to parallel the General Confederation of Italian Labour (C.G.I.L.), the Christian Association of Italian Labour (*Associazioni Cristiane dei Lavoratori Italiani*)—the A.C.L.I.—was instituted. Professional unions of various occupations followed. A Papal commission of bishops appointed in 1946 gave new statutes for Italian Catholic Action which revived the national, diocesan, and parochial structures and with an enlarged lay participation and direction. Annual conferences (*Settimane Sociali*—"Social Weeks") were held, akin to similar ones in France, which centred on specific concerns: labour, the rural problem, social security, professional organization, school and society, the population problem, and the family in the changing social context. Associations for occupational and professional groups, among them physicians, lawyers, teachers, pharmacists, and artists, were

---

[110] *Ibid.*, pp. 145–157; Magri, *L'Azione Cattolica in Italia*, Vol. I, pp. 333–398.
[111] Civardi, *op. cit.*, pp. 177–195; Magri, *op. cit.*, Vol. I, pp. 399–550.
[112] Civardi, *op. cit.*, pp. 197–232.
[113] *Ibid.*, pp. 242–246; Magri, *op. cit.*, Vol. II, pp. 3–36.

either revived from pre-Fascist days or organized for the first time. A vast network of local civic committees sprang up. Although not a part of Catholic Action, they were a phase of organized Roman Catholic effort. In 1952 Pius XII renewed the episcopal commission for the direction of Catholic Action. Catholic Action paid special attention to education and to catechetical instruction.[114]

The proliferation of Catholic Action was possible only because of the participation and often the initiative of laymen. Although a large proportion of the Italian populace, nominally Roman Catholic, were secularized, by the contrast which we have seen in France and will find in many another country, thousands of men as well as women were ardent practising Catholics. Among them were not only humble folk but also intellectuals distinguished in their several professions and occupations.[115]

ITALY: EDUCATION AND THE INTELLECTUAL LIFE

The years which followed 1914 witnessed improvement in religious education and in the share of Roman Catholics in the intellectual life of Italy. Under the Fascist regime instruction in religion was introduced into the primary schools as early as 1923 and anti-religious propaganda was sternly repressed. Following the Lateran Accord instruction in the Roman Catholic faith was made obligatory in the secondary schools as well.[116] In December, 1921, the Catholic University of the Sacred Heart was opened in Milan. From at least the second half of the nineteenth century a dream had been cherished, led by Amitori Fanfani, of creating in Italy a university committed to the Roman Catholic faith to offset the secularism which characterized existing universities. The purpose was to raise up a loyal elite who would penetrate the intellectual circles of the nation and bring the Christian message to all the highly educated. To accomplish this purpose it would be necessary to have the members of the faculty of the university of such scholarly stature as to win the respect of specialists in their respective fields. Now a beginning was made towards the realization of that dream.[117] The first rector, Agostino Gemelli (1878——), a Franciscan, in his youth had been a materialistic Socialist and a physician. Converted, he continued his scientific studies, especially in experimental psychology. He was also committed to the revival of scholastic philosophy.[118]

---

[114] Civardi, *op. cit.*, pp. 245–269; Magri, *op. cit.*, Vol. II, pp. 47–108.

[115] For a few of them see the personal reminiscences of Luigi Sturzo in his *Spiritual Problems of Our Times* (New York, Longmans, Green and Co., 1945, pp. ix, 182), pp. 138–152.

[116] Guilday, *The Catholic Church in Contemporary Europe 1919–1931*, p. 183.

[117] Francesco Ogliati, *L'Università Cattolica del Sacro Cuore* (Milan, Società Editrice *Vita e Pensiero*, Vol. I, 1955, pp. xxiii, 499).

[118] *De Katholieke Encyclopaedie*, Vol. XI, p. 499.

ITALY: THE LITURGICAL MOVEMENT

As we earlier noted, the Liturgical Movement was tardy in making itself felt in Italy. It is usually said to have begun in 1914 with the inception of the *Rivista Liturgica*. Even World War II did not entirely halt the Movement and after the coming of peace it was renewed. Stimulated by the encyclical *Mediator Dei* and led by Cardinal Lecaros in the Archdiociese of Bologna, numbers of bishops encouraged the Movement in their dioceses. Several Benedictine monasteries became radiating centres.[119]

ITALY: THE CONTINUED THREAT OF DE-CHRISTIANIZATION

Although the Roman Catholic Church made substantial gains in Italy after 1914, the threat of de-Christianization continued, even though its forms were somewhat different from those of the nineteenth century. Communism was a menace, especially after World War II. In the late 1950's it and the Marxist Socialists together were outnumbered at the polls only by the Christian Democrats. More subtle and perhaps more serious was the burgeoning of cities, especially Rome, Under urban conditions, as in most of Europe, a large proportion of the populace drifted away from the Church. In 1951, for example, out of a population of 1,800,000 in the Eternal City more than half were said to be non-practising.[120] Here as elsewhere the contrast was marked between the de-Christianizing forces of the revolutionary age and the mounting vigour in the post-1914 Roman Catholic Church.

SPAIN: THE SWING OF THE POLITICAL PENDULUM
AGAINST AND FOR THE ROMAN CATHOLIC CHURCH

Spain after 1914 experienced political unrest, revolutions, and civil strife, interspersed with periods of calm which, with important variations, were reminiscent of the nineteenth century and which were features of the revolutionary age. A neutral in World War I, Spain profited by the markets which her position gave her. After the war, that advantage passed and economic depression came, with unemployment and agricultural distress. The situation was aggravated by a costly war to put down uprisings in Northern Morocco, an area which had been allotted to Spain before 1914. A rising tide of criticism, directed against the government, led the King, Alfonso XIII, to call Primo de Rivera to head the administration (1924). Primo de Rivera suspended the constitution and headed a dictatorship with the motto "Country, monarchy, religion." Strikes, riots, and mutinies followed. In 1930 Primo de Rivera resigned, the constitution was restored, and in the local elections (1931) the Republicans were overwhelm-

[119] Chapter V; Bogler, *Liturgische Erneuerung in aller Welt*, pp. 73–81.
[120] Daniel, *Aspects de la Pratique Religeuse à Paris*, p. 119.

ingly in the majority. Alfonso XIII fled, and Niceto Alcalá Zamora headed the "provisional government" of the Second Spanish Republic. The First Spanish Republic, it will be remembered, had lasted from 1873 to 1875. The Second Republic had a longer life, from 1931 to 1936.

In the National Assembly elected in June, 1931, a constitution was adopted, Church and state were ordered separated, the property of the Church was nationalized, the Jesuits were expelled, the clergy were deprived of all government support, and orders and congregations were taxed. The concordat which had governed relations with the Holy See since 1851 was abrogated. The constitution declared that the state had no religion and provided for liberty of conscience and freedom of worship. Education was to be wholly in the hands of the state, and instruction was to be entirely lay. A leading official declared that "Spain has ceased to be Catholic." Yet a number of bishops advised the faithful not to form a Catholic party and counselled submission to the Republic as the lawful government and as such ordained by God. However, the primate of Spain, Cardinal Seguray Saenz, Archbishop of Toledo, came out in open opposition to the Republic and was expelled from the country. The Pope also spoke against the separation of Church and state and the bishops forbade the faithful to send their children to state schools.[121]

The Second Republic did not at first strictly enforce its anti-clerical measures. Conservatives formed the C.E.D.A. (Spanish Confederation of the Autonomous Rightists) and held the balance of power in the Moderate Republican majority. The "Popular Front" was formed by Radicals, Socialists, and Communists. In 1936 it won a majority of the seats in parliament. Communists and Anarchist extremists, although a small minority, burned churches and monasteries, killed priests, and terrorized "reactionaries."[122]

Civil war followed, from 1936 to 1939. The Falange, composed of a number of elements, including the C.E.D.A., led by Francisco Franco (1892——), a professional soldier, championed the conservative forces against the Popular Front. Franco received aid from Mussolini and Hitler. The Roman Catholic Church was clearly with him. Russian Communist help was given to the Popular Front. Assistance also came to the latter from the French Government, the Labour Party in Great Britain, and sympathizers in the United States. In the heat of the struggle the Republican government did not permit Roman Catholic worship in most of such territory as it controlled. Churches and monasteries were destroyed. Bishops, priests, and members of religious orders were murdered. Many of the laity were killed for adhering to the faith. Indeed, some regarded the years of the civil war as spanning the worst persecution that the Church had

---

[121] Guilday, *op. cit.,* pp. 348–350; Descola, *Histoire de l'Espagne Chrétienne,* pp. 327–330; Mendizabal, *The Martyrdom of Spain,* pp. 162 ff.; Hughey, *Religious Freedom in Spain,* pp. 117–131; Peers, *Spain, the Church and the Orders,* pp. 126–162.

[122] Hayes, *Contemporary Europe since 1870,* pp. 619, 620; Descola, *op. cit.,* p. 331.

experienced in Spain. Franco gradually prevailed and by April 1, 1939, was in full control of the country. The war was said to have cost Spain a million killed, wounded, or exiled, and an untold amount of property.[123] Franco thereupon instituted a dictatorship which lasted beyond the date when these lines were penned.

SPAIN: CONTRASTS BETWEEN DE-CHRISTIANIZATION AND ROMAN CATHOLIC VIGOUR

In Spain, as in other countries in European lands which were regarded as traditionally Roman Catholic, a striking contrast was seen between de-Christianizing trends on the one hand and vigour in the Roman Catholic Church on the other.

In the mid-twentieth century the overwhelming majority of the population of Spain were baptized as Roman Catholics and, if asked, would call themselves Catholics. Even many avowed Communists retained a belief in God.[124] Outwardly a close alliance existed between the Roman Catholic Church and the Franco regime. In 1953 a concordat was entered into by that government and the Holy See, partly renewing the one of 1851.[125] Through it, among other provisions, the state recognized the Roman Catholic Church as a perfect society and guaranteed it the full exercise of its spiritual power and of its public worship; said that the Catholic religion was the only one of the Spanish nation; gave the Holy See the right to make public in Spain its actions relating to the government of the Church and to communicate freely with the bishops, clergy, and faithful; held to the historic right of patronage but gave the Pope a voice in the selection of the bishops; conceded to the Church the right to acquire, possess, and administer every form of property; maintained marriage as defined by canon law; provided for instruction in the faith; guaranteed the Church's authority to establish new parishes and fix parish boundaries; and recognized the competence of ecclesiastical courts in causes governed by canon law.

Yet the alliance of the Church and the Franco government was one of convenience and many of the clergy, both high and low, were restive under it. For example, late in the 1950's friction arose in Catalonia over the attempt of the state to interfere with Catholic Boy Scouts, an issue complicated by the movement in that section for greater local autonomy.[126]

Nor did the alliance prevent the progress of what in effect was de-Christianiza-

---

[123] For vignettes of the civil war by an observer, see John Langdon-Davies, *Behind the Spanish Barricades* (New York, Robert McBride and Co., 1936, pp. viii, 275), *passim*. Hughey, *op. cit.*, pp. 132, 133, gives a hint at the involvement of the Roman Catholic Church. See also Peers, *op. cit.*, pp. 163–176.

[124] Peers, *op. cit.*, pp. 183, 184.

[125] Atilio Garcia Mellid, *La Constitucion Cristiana de los Estados y el Concordato Español* (Madrid, Editora Nacional, 1955, pp. 309), *passim*. For the document itself see *ibid.*, pp. 279–306.

[126] *The New York Times*, February 13, 1959.

tion. In Spain, as in other lands, the scene differed from area to area and from class to class. For instance, the Basque country, south of the south-eastern corner of the Bay of Biscay, tended to remain loyally Roman Catholic. Yet even here the picture was mixed, with strong Socialist elements and Basque nationalism.[127] In Andalusia, in the extreme South, church attendance was lower than in what had once been Castile. In Barcelona in the mid-1950's, slightly less than 1,600 priests, secular and regular, were found to minister to a population of more than 2,250,000, and the vocations were insufficient adequately to recruit the clergy.[128] Here was a phenomenon characteristic of the revolutionary age—a city which had expanded in numbers and been altered in its patterns of life beyond the ability of the Church to supply clergy and buildings and adjust its methods to the changing situation. Also an accompaniment of the age was the declining number of practising Roman Catholics among the workers in industries. In the mid-1950's *Ecclesia,* the organ of Catholic Action of Spain, declared that the overwhelming majority of Spanish workers were non-practising. It listed as reasons poverty and the infiltration of Anarchists, Socialists, and Marxists into the trade unions.[129] Although the full significance is not clear, the numbers of the "religious"—members of orders and congregations—seem to have shown a fairly steady decline (a decline which had also characterized the nineteenth century) from an estimated 92,727 in 1809 to 50,993 in 1902, to 49,231 in 1928, and to 44,965 in 1931.[130] Among intellectuals, antagonism to the Roman Catholic Church or scepticism and indifference were potent. For example, in the mid-1950's it was said by a priest who was devoting himself to them that of about 50,000 university students in Madrid only approximately 1,000 were loyally Roman Catholic,[131] and this in spite of the prominence given to the Roman Catholic faith by the Franco government in all levels of education, from primary grades through the universities.[132] Among the intellectuals Positivism and Krausism (the panentheism, or spiritual eclecticism which had the University of Oviedo as a radiating centre), prominent in the nineteenth century, were waning. More influential were the writings of Unamuno and Ortega.

Miguel de Unamuno y Jugo (1864–1936), a layman, a university professor, and deeply religious, was not anti-Christian, but he did not fit into traditional Roman Catholic patterns and was classed as an anti-clerical. He was described as the epitome of the Spanish spirit, both intensely individualistic and universal. Part of his life exiled for his political opinions, he wrote prodigiously and was widely read in Spain as well as abroad. He was a master of the mystical and

[127] Mendizabal, *op. cit.,* pp. 20, 21.
[128] *World Around Press* (Mimeographed), April 12, 1956.
[129] *The New York Times,* January 25, 1954.
[130] Peers, *op. cit.,* p. 206.
[131] The source of this information, while direct, must remain anonymous.
[132] See a hostile account, but with extracts from the official documents, in R. Lopis, *La Sainte-Siège et France* (Paris, Société Universitaire d'Éditions et de Libraire, no date, pp. 79), *passim.*

classical literature of Spain, learned sixteen languages in order to be able to read the literature of other peoples in the original, and was profoundly influenced by Kierkegaard when the "gloomy Dane" was as yet scarcely known outside his own country. Unamuno was written about extensively and was variously interpreted as a Catholic heart at war with the Protestant spirit, a Protestant-like aberration, an atheist subject to a Chateaubriandesque conversion, and more religious than his books. He bridged the transition between the nineteenth and twentieth centuries and was deeply impressed with the tragic aspects of the age in which he lived.[133]

José Ortega y Gasset (1883–1955) was born in Madrid, the son of a distinguished journalist. Precocious, after several years of study in Germany he returned to Spain aflame with the purpose of bringing his native land into the main current of European life. Before he was thirty he had become the outstanding philosopher of the Spanish-speaking world, taking the leadership from Unamuno. As teacher of metaphysics in the University of Madrid, orator, writer, founder of what became the most influential newspaper in the country, *El Sol,* and of the journal and publishing house *Revista de Occidente,* and translator of leading writers of contemporary Europe, he sought to influence the political and intellectual life of the nation. He aroused controversy by the vigour and often the paradox of his expression. A conservative in politics, he had a share in the creation of the Republic but became disillusioned with it and held that "mass man" was not competent to achieve true democracy. Yet he would not side with the opponents of the Republic in the civil war. Desperately ill, he left the country (1936). He returned in 1945 but was not permitted to resume his professorship, and the Franco government attempted to keep him out of the public eye.

Ortega reacted against the neo-Kantianism of his student days in Germany and became an existentialist. He seems to have been much impressed with Dilthey and Heidegger. He distrusted the approach to reality through reason which characterized much of Western thought, including Aquinas. He therefore fell afoul of the Thomists. He did not discard reason but protested against "pure physico-mathematical reason" and held that it made of man and life a thing. He maintained, rather, that reason should be subservient to life. Man,

---

133 One of Unamuno's most widely read books was *The Tragic Sense of Life in Men and in Peoples,* translated by J. E. Crawford Flitch (London, Macmillan and Co., 1926, pp. xxxv, 332), written on the eve of World War I. See also his *L'Agonie du Christianisme,* translated from the unpublished Spanish text by Jean Cassou (Paris, F. Rieder et Cie, 1926, pp. 162), *passim.* In it he speaks of Christ as on the cross not dead but in agony, said that agony is struggle, and pointed out that Jesus declared that he had not come to bring peace but a sword. Yet he also said that Christ's kingdom was not of this world. A large number of his essays are in *Ensayos* (Madrid, Publicaciones de la Residencia de Estudiantes, 7 vols., 1916–1918). For a more extensive bibliography and a thoughtful interpretation, see François Mayer, *L'Ontologie de Miguel de Unamuno* (Paris, Presses Universitaires de France, 1955, pp. xii, 133). For a summary account by a specialist see J. A. Mackay in *The Twentieth Century Encyclopedia of Religious Knowledge,* Vol. II, pp. 1129, 1130.

he insisted, could be understood only through history, for the individual was constantly being shaped by the past and was laying his plans for the present and future in what he sought to learn from the past. Ortega, therefore, made much of the philosophy of history. Like Spengler and Toynbee, he viewed history as moving in great cycles. He took a pessimistic view of the contemporary scene and repudiated Roman Catholicism on the ground that it was a betrayal of true Christianity. He was not a Protestant but he never classed himself as in the anti-Christian camp. Speaking little of God, he did not regard Christ as of decisive importance, but he had a stern sense of duty which may have been derived from his neo-Kantian years.[134]

In contrast with the wide circulation enjoyed by the writings of Unamuno and Ortega, activity in theological studies, while increasingly marked in the 1940's and 1950's, was chiefly confined to clerical circles and did not reach many of the intelligentsia.

Against these threats to its historic hold on Spain, the Roman Catholic Church presented a strong resistance, both in traditional and in new ways. Numbers of Roman Catholics, especially in high ecclesiastical quarters, regarded Spain as the one remaining bulwark of the faith against the corrosive currents of modernity. Culturally, more than in France, the Roman Catholic faith was still part of the national tradition, even though for the majority its hold was largely nominal. Much of personal piety existed and fresh studies were made of the great Spanish mystics such as John of the Cross and Teresa of Avila. The integralist reaction provoked by Modernism long persisted. It was reported that for a number of years a lay organization called *Integristas* said a rosary every evening for the "conversion" of Pius XI.[135] The hierarchy was slow to accept the social and economic principles of *Rerum novarum* and *Quadragesimo anno,* and the workers and peasants tended to regard the Church as allied with the monarchy, the dictatorships, the army, the big landowners, and the business men. Women were a conservative force and were reported to be the main strength of the Church.[136]

Novel movements and trends were under way, evidence that the Roman

---

[134] See an interesting summary and appraisal by David White in *Religion in Life,* Vol. XXV, pp. 247–458. For the writings of Ortega see his *Obras Completos* (Madrid, Revista de Occidente, 6 vols., 1946–1947). For English translations see his *Man and Crisis,* translated from the Spanish by Mildred Adams (New York, W. W. Norton and Co., 1958, pp. 217); his *Man and People,* translated by Willard R. Trask (New York, W. W. Norton and Co., 1957, pp. 272); his *Revolt of the Masses* (London, G. Allen and Unwin, 1932, pp. 204); his *Toward a Philosophy of History* (New York, W. W. Norton and Co., 1941, pp. x, 273); and his *Mission of the University,* translated by Howard Lee Nostrand (London, Routledge and Kegan Paul, 1946, pp. 81). Among the works on Ortega, see Miguel Oromi, *Ortega y la Filosofía: seis Glosas* (Madrid, Esplanadian, 1953, pp. 358), and José Sanchez Villaseñor, *Ortega y Gasset, Existentialist: a Critical Study of His Thought and Its Sources,* translated by Joseph Small (Chicago, Henry Regnery Co., 1949, pp. viii, 264).

[135] *The New York Times,* September 19, 1956.
[136] *Ibid.*

Catholic Church in Spain had continuing vitality. We have already seen something of the development of Catholic Action, with its centralized and comprehensive organization.[137] Catholic Action is said to have had its beginning in Spain in 1868 in an effort to combat the trend towards secularism. The attempt gave birth to branches in many parts of the country but they did not last long. During the latter part of the century various associations of laity came into being for specific purposes which in the next century would have been counted as phases of Catholic Action. A nation-wide structure and a clear definition of Catholic Action were achieved in the decade after World War I. In 1922 the episcopate inaugurated a campaign to create a university to train youth in administrative and social political science, to multiply Catholic primary schools, and to systematize Catholic Action in labour unions. In 1919 Woman's Catholic Action (La Acción Católica de la Mujer) was begun by Cardinal Guisasola to study and solve feminine problems, to educate women, to assist them in obtaining a just wage, and to obtain the enforcement of legislation for the protection of women and children. A similar organization for men (Acción Católica de Caballeros) sought to create a better spirit between employers and employees and to develop programmes for meeting problems in agriculture, industry, and commerce. Numbers of other organizations were instituted—some for women, some for men, others for youth, still others for students, some for employers, and a variety for specific functions, such as fighting public immorality and furthering religious pilgrimages. The first national Congress of Catholic Action met in 1929.[138]

This proliferating Catholic Action suffered severely during the civil war. Moreover, under the Franco regime some phases of it were either curtailed, driven into exile, or suppressed.[139] Yet in the early 1950's the bishops showed an increasing awareness of the problems to which Catholic Action was addressed, including the disaffection of the working classes. In their pastorals they urged improvement in the living conditions of labour.[140] In the late 1940's and the 1950's a Dominican, González Menendez-Reigada, as Bishop of Córdoba, worked a transformation in that ancient Andalusian city. At his initiative and under his direction over 5,000 model homes were erected to house the poverty-stricken denizens of the sordid slums, and new industries were encouraged to give employment to the ambitious poor.[141]

Another indication of vitality in the Roman Catholic Church in Spain was the changing character of the priesthood. Although much ignorance and narrowness were found among the clergy, in the twentieth century the average quality

137 Chapter IV.
138 Guilday, The Catholic Church in Contemporary Europe 1919–1931, pp. 326–346.
139 Fogarty, Christian Democracy in Western Europe, 1820–1953, p. 95.
140 The New York Times, January 25, 1954; Information Service, December 22, 1951.
141 The Catholic World, March, 1958.

was said to be rising. Many of the younger priests were aware of the economic, social, and political problems of the contemporary world. In 1956 so many of them sided with the workers in the strikes in the Basque country that their bishop, of an older generation, transferred about 200 of them from their parishes.[142]

In 1928 a new congregation, the *Opus Dei* (with the formal title *Sociedad Sacerdotál de la Santa Cruz*) was founded by a wealthy high-born priest, José Maria Escrivá de Balaguer. Although its main strength was in Spain, by 1960 it had spread to forty-two lands. The inner circle took the vows of poverty, chastity, and obedience. Others followed a discipline like the third orders of older movements. None wore a distinctive garb. All normally continued at their trades and professions and there strove to be exemplary Christians. Recruited from the social and intellectually elite, they endeavoured to promote the religious life, partly through retreats, and to prepare a more cultured clergy. They conducted a university in Pamplona. By 1957 several members were holding key positions in the government.[143]

The Liturgical Movement, as we have hinted,[144] made marked headway in Spain, especially after the civil war. Yet it met with resistance in many conservative quarters. Even the encyclical *Mediator Dei* did not at once break down the opposition. The liturgical commissions formed in response to the Papal request had to contend with numerous variations from the standard liturgy which had the sanction of long usage. But among the young secular priests enthusiasm for the Liturgical Movement developed. Montserrat, the great Benedictine pilgrimage centre in Catalonia, visited annually by more than half a million visitors, endeavoured to make it a means of deepened devotion among those who flocked to it. Eucharistic Congresses also spread the Movement. The Movement enjoyed a marked expansion after the establishment of domestic peace by Franco.[145]

PORTUGAL

Portugal came to the year 1914 under the strongly anti-clerical republic which had been created in 1910. As we have noted,[146] in 1911 Church and state were separated; in 1913 relations with the Vatican were severed, the teaching of the catechism in the schools was forbidden, and only priests who had been educated in Portugal were permitted to officiate in the churches.

In 1916 Portugal entered World War I on the side of the Allies and sent an

---

[142] *The New York Times,* September 19, 1956.
[143] *Ibid.,* September 19, 1956, March 7, 1957, April 25, 1960. For the life of one of the early members, Isadore Zorzano, see Daniel Sargent, *God's Engineer* (Chicago, Scepter, 1954, pp. 191).
[144] Chapter V.
[145] Bogler, *Liturgische Erneuerung in aller Welt,* pp. 82–90.
[146] Volume I, p. 425.

army to fight on the Western front. The strain added to the burdens of the already unstable republic, ruling as it did an impoverished land. In an attempt to bring the country out of its near-anarchy and bankruptcy, in 1926 General Antonio Carmora seized power, had himself elected president and, re-confirmed in that office by successive controlled elections, retained the post until his death in 1951. In 1928 he called to his assistance the extremely able Antonio de Oliveira Salazar, who had once planned to become a priest and was then professor in the University of Coimbra. As minister of finance Salazar restored the nation's credit. As prime minister he carried through (1933) a new constitution which made of Portugal a "unitary and corporate republic." The government became practically a dictatorship with the party *Uñiao Nacional* dominant.

Under Salazar relations with the Roman Catholic Church improved. Diplomatic ties with the Vatican were resumed. In 1940 a concordat was signed which regulated the status of the Church in Portugal and the Portuguese colonies. By it the Roman Catholic Church was recognized as a lawful body with juridical status, its property was restored to it (except some used for public purposes and treated as national monuments), it was allowed to maintain private schools, in the state schools religious instruction was to be given under conditions approved by the ecclesiastical authorities, church marriages were recognized if registered with the proper officials, and divorce was forbidden for those married in the Church. Exemption from taxation was accorded to churches, theological seminaries, and ecclesiastics in the performance of their duties.[147]

Yet, as in Italy and Spain, friction was not absent between the Roman Catholic Church and the political dictatorship. In 1958 high ecclesiastical officials complained that the state was disregarding basic human rights in its treatment of workers and pleaded for more freedom for Catholic Action on behalf of labour.[148]

The corrosive currents of the revolutionary age, reinforced by the years of anti-clerical rule, left their mark. Although 95 per cent. of the population were technically Roman Catholics, in 1956 only 30 per cent. were regarded as practising. The shortage of priests was acute. In the South, where traditionally the parishes had been served by regulars, the expulsion of a large proportion of the orders and congregations had made for lack of pastoral care, and de-Christianization was marked.[149]

But indications of vitality were observable. The pilgrimages to Fatima did much to revive the faith and no lack of clergy was seen in the diocese in which

---

[147] Richard Pattee, *Portugal and the Portuguese World* (Milwaukee, Bruce Publishing Co., 1957, pp. vii, 350), p. 321.
[148] *The New York Times,* February 23, 1959.
[149] Bolshakoff, *New Missionary Review,* 6th year of issue (1958), Nos. 11–12 (12–13), pp. 9–11.

Fatima was situated. Under the Salazar regime monasticism was revived and in the 1950's the Benedictines were erecting at Singeverga, in the North, buildings of what they hoped would become the mother house of the restored Portuguese congregation of their order.[150] As we have seen,[151] the Liturgical Movement first spread to Portugal through Antonio Coelho, a Benedictine who had studied in Belgium. Before Coelho's early death (1938) liturgical congresses and weeks had been held, periodicals furthering the Movement had been initiated, books had been written on the subject, and translations of missals were being circulated. The Singeverga abbey became the chief continuing centre. It also gave stimulus to the use of Gregorian music.[152]

BELGIUM

In Belgium the Roman Catholic Church flourished, in spite of the German invasion and occupation in both World War I and World War II, the destruction of life and property during the two conflicts, the rapid progress of industrialization, the accompanying growth of cities, and the influx of the intellectual currents which were aspects of the revolutionary age. Material prosperity, very marked, was both an asset and a liability to Christianity.

Indications of de-Christianization were not wanting. They were particularly noticeable in the cities and industrial centres in the Walloon South. Although the overwhelming majority of the population were baptized in the Roman Catholic Church, the proportion of non-practising Catholics increased after World War I, especially in the French-speaking regions and in the big cities.[153] Moreover, in proportion to the population the number of clergy declined.[154]

Yet in the main the Roman Catholic Church in Belgium was vigorous and from it issued fresh life which strengthened many pre-1914 movements and gave rise to new ones. The Church came to the fateful year of 1914 in a healthy condition. Church and state were reciprocally independent. The state had no control over the appointment of bishops or pastors. Nor could it prevent the clergy from corresponding with their superiors or publishing the latter's messages. The state paid the salaries and pensions of a large proportion of the clergy. Those not so supported, hundreds in number, taught in diocesan colleges or served as chaplains in convents and charitable institutions. Roman Catholics were a force in the government and had controlled it since 1884. The University of Louvain, the most widely known of the Belgian universities, was an institu-

[150] *Ibid.*
[151] Chapter V.
[152] Bogler, *op. cit.*, pp. 91–96.
[153] Guilday, *op. cit.*, pp. 42, 43. Fogarty, *op. cit.*, p. 348, estimates for the early 1950's that in French-speaking Belgium about 35 or 40 per cent. of the Roman Catholics were regular churchgoers, with more women than men and more than their share of older people, and says this was about the average in France.
[154] Guilday, *op. cit.*, p. 11.

tion of the Church. The teaching of religion in the public primary schools was compulsory—although pupils might be exempted from it if their parents formally protested. In schools supported and controlled by the Church, religion was, of course, part of the curriculum. Many of the laity went to retreat centres conducted by the orders and congregations. Daily communion was on the increase, especially among children.[155] But most of the parish clergy were from rural districts and had a limited education. Young men from the bourgeoisie or the more cultivated families who entered the priesthood usually joined one of the orders, especially that of the Jesuits.[156]

During World War I an outstanding contribution to the nation was made by Désiré Joseph Mercier (1851-1926). We have called attention to the fashion in which he had brought about the Higher Institute of Philosophy at Louvain, in a quite original attempt to achieve a synthesis of Thomistic philosophy with the experimental sciences.[157] A brilliant scholar and teacher, with a wide-ranging knowledge which commanded the respect of experts, an able organizer of proven capacity in the face of the opposition of conservatives within the university and the Church, and a man of deep piety with a concern for individuals as well as for masses of men, Mercier was the choice of Rome for the Archbishopric of Malines. The appointment was made in 1906. As Archbishop of Malines Mercier was the primate of the Belgian Church. He was soon (1907) created cardinal. From his youth severely disciplined and indefatigable and a leader with vision and charm, in his high office he continued to exemplify those traits. Although on state occasions enjoying the pomp which he deemed belonged to the Church of Christ, in his private life he was an ascetic, a Franciscan tertiary. He gave pastoral attention to hundreds of individuals, many of them humble. He wrote prodigiously on a variety of subjects. Faithful and sincere in his private devotions, he sought to raise the level of the devotional life of his clergy. He also enjoined the clergy not to become embroiled in political parties. He prized the Gregorian music and did much to beautify and solemnize the liturgy in the Belgian churches.

During World War I, when Belgium was invaded and most of it occupied by the Germans, Mercier sturdily remained with his flock. Completely fearless, he denounced the atrocities of the conquerors and brought them to the attention of the world. In successive pastoral letters, to the indignation of the German authorities, he minced no words in declaring the alien rule illegitimate and in counselling resistance. The Germans sought to exile him but were unsuccessful. He protested against the military reprisals of the Germans, the imprisonment of his clergy, and the deportation of Belgians to forced labour in Germany. He was at least partly responsible for the eventual return of many of the deported.

155 Guilday, op. cit., pp. 8-10, 14, 27, 28.
156 Gade, The Life of Cardinal Mercier, pp. 115-117.
157 Volume I, p. 390.

He helped in the distribution of the relief which came from abroad.

In the years which remained to him after the coming of peace, in addition to helping in reconstruction, Mercier founded the Association of Catholic Youth (*Association de la Jeunesse Catholique*) and its offshoot, the Catholic Youth Worker (*Jeunesse Catholique Ouvrière*), and organized the International Union for Social Studies (*Union Internationale d'Études Sociales*). He sponsored the temperance movement and was appointed by the Pope as the protector of temperance work throughout the world. He was the central figure in the Malines Conversations (1921–1926) between Roman Catholics and Anglo-Catholics which sought the reconciliation of the Roman Catholic Church and the Anglicans. Although they did not accomplish their purpose, on his death bed Mercier gave his pastoral ring to the leader of the Anglican group, Lord Halifax.[158]

In spite of the two world wars, the Higher Institute of Philosophy begun by Mercier continued, and that in the face of the destruction wrought by the invaders in Louvain early in the first of the struggles. It enlarged its curriculum and sought to fulfill the dream which had inspired it.[159]

We have already said[160] something of the organizations which sprang up in Belgium to meet the challenge of the economic and social movements of the revolutionary age. They were especially prominent in the occupations which flourished as Belgium became more and more industrialized. Some were aspects of Catholic Action and were closely connected with the clergy and parish life. Others were primarily lay, but were Catholic in membership. Even a complete list would carry us far beyond the proper limits of this chapter. We must content ourselves with a few examples. The Young Christian Workers (*Jeunesse Ouvrière Chrétienne*, the J.O.C.) had their origin in 1912 through the initiative of Joseph Cardijn, appointed in that year to be a curate in Brussels. Put in charge of several women's organizations, he gathered a group of girls from the factories and workshops in the city. He stimulated them to self-help in the circumstances in which they found themselves. His enquiry method with its "see, judge, act" formula was developed to aid them in remedying bad conditions. Interrupted by World War I, with the coming of peace the movement was resumed, primarily for young men, and in 1921 it took the name by which it was later known. It was accorded the right to enter the parishes and quickly

---

[158] Gade, *op. cit., passim;* Charlotte Kellogg, *Mercier, the Fighting Cardinal of Belgium* (New York, D. Appleton and Co., 1920, pp. viii, 249), *passim;* Cardinal Mercier, *Cardinal Mercier's Own Story* (New York, George H. Doran Co., 1920, pp. xviii, 441), *passim; The Voice of Belgium, Being the War Utterances of Cardinal Mercier* (London, Burns Oates, no date, pp. 330), *passim;* Jesus Guia y Azevedo, *El Cadinal Mercier ó la Conciencia Occidental* (Mexico, Polis, 1952, pp. 119), *passim.*

[159] L. de Raeymaeker, *La Cardinal Mercier et l'Institut Supérieur de Philosophie de Louvain* (Louvain, Publications Universitaires de Louvain, 1952, pp. 275), pp. 177–227.

[160] Chapter IV.

mushroomed. In 1925 it held its first national congress and then had a membership of between 15,000 and 20,000. In that year it affiliated itself with the Catholic Association of Belgian Youth (*Association Catholique de la Jeunesse Belge,* the A.C.J.B.), an organization dating from late in the nineteenth century with which all the Catholic youth organizations in the country were related. A girls' section was formed.[161] The Young Christian Workers helped to strengthen its members against the de-Christianizing influences of industrial communities. Coming, as many of them did, from rural or village backgrounds where they had been given Christian nurture, when immersed in their new surroundings they tended to drop their connexion with the Church and to abandon the moral standards of their rearing. Yet by the late 1920's the J.O.C., prospering though it was, had not reached a tenth of those it was designed to serve.[162]

The *Boerenbond,* or Farmers' Union, founded in 1890 by two laymen and a priest, was consolidated and centralized during World War I and expanded after 1918. Although it had no religious test for membership, it remained essentially a Roman Catholic organization and rejected the suggestion that it become a-confessional. It was especially strong in the Flemish section of the country. It organized coöperative societies for a wide variety of purposes, such as buying farm implements, livestock, feed, and fertilizers, selling products in foreign markets, and issuing insurance. It had agricultural schools, lecture tours, technical advisers, and experiment stations. Following the failure of its central bank in the world-wide financial depression of the 1930's, the *Boerenbond* was reorganized, its central committee no longer had a majority of clergymen, and more autonomy was given to its technical services.[163]

In the nineteenth century the Socialists captured the industrial workers and at the outset of the twentieth century the Christian labour unions were able to attract only a minority of that element of the population. However, in the course of the first four decades after 1914 the latter increased their strength, both numerically and in influence. In 1930 they enrolled slightly more than a fourth of the trade union members of the country.[164] In 1951 they had more than half of the trade union membership and had many more in coöperatives, compulsory insurance, and women's organizations than the Socialists. By that year J.O.C. and the corresponding girls' organization, the J.O.C.F., enrolled more than four times as many as the Young Socialist organizations. What became the Christian Workers' Movement was tightly organized on a national scale. Of it the Con-

[161] Fogarty, *op. cit.,* pp. 57, 272–274; Somerville, *Studies in the Catholic Social Movement,* pp. 119–125.
[162] Guilday, *op. cit.,* pp. 12, 13; Somerville, *op. cit.,* pp. 114, 115.
[163] Guilday, *op. cit.,* pp. 18–20; Fogarty, *op. cit.,* pp. 246, 248; Somerville, *op. cit.,* pp. 106, 107.
[164] Guilday, *op. cit.,* pp. 18, 19; Somerville, *op. cit.,* pp. 114, 115.

federation of Christian Trade Unions was one of the components.[165]

We have noted that Belgian Roman Catholics were powerful politically.[166] Various elements normally coöperated with what after World War II became the Christian Social Party. One of them, the Catholic Union, was formed in 1921 and included the Federation of Catholic Clubs and of Constitutional and Conservative Associations, the *Boerenbond,* the Federation of the Middle Classes, and the Christian Workers' Movement. The Flemish and Walloon wings at times came into conflict, for the former were intent upon winning a larger voice in the nation's affairs and more autonomy for their section of the nation. What had been the Christian Socialist Party had as its chief figure a Dominican, George Albert Rutten (1875–1952), who doffed the dress of his order to live with the workmen. Mercier supported Rutten and the latter won a seat in the upper house.[167]

We have also mentioned the prominence of Belgium in the Liturgical Movement.[168] Although it was later in making itself felt than in some other countries, by the mid-twentieth century the Belgian Liturgical Movement had assumed large proportions. At the outset it was stronger in the French-speaking South than in the Flemish North, but it was in Antwerp that the first international liturgical congress convened (1930).[169]

The religious temper of a large proportion of the population was made evident when in 1919 Mercier celebrated a mass of thanksgiving for the freeing of Belgium and consecrated the country to the Sacred Heart. The ceremony took place in the presence of the king and queen, ministers of state and members of the upper and lower houses, and a throng of many tens of thousands. The words of consecration were repeated by the entire assembly.[170]

LUXEMBURG

The grand-duchy of Luxemburg, the small, independent country bounded by France, Belgium, and Germany, and with a population of about 300,000 in the mid-1950's, must be dismissed with only a brief notice. Predominantly Roman Catholic, it was given its own bishop in 1870. It was occupied by the Germans in World Wars I and II and during the latter struggle many of the population were deported by the Nazis for forced labour. Partly agricultural and with important mines and industries, Luxemburg presented the familiar problems of the revolutionary age. Here, as in Belgium, the proportion of practising Roman

---

[165] Fogarty, *op. cit.,* pp. 188, 202, 217, 220, 221.
[166] Chapter IV.
[167] Fogarty, *op. cit.,* pp. 297–300; Gade, *op. cit.,* pp. 232; Gestel, *Het Religieus-Socialisme,* pp. 320–339; *De Katholieke Encyclopaedie,* Vol. XXI, p. 294.
[168] Chapter V.
[169] Bogler, *op. cit.,* pp. 41, 42; Guilday, *op. cit.,* p. 15.
[170] Guilday, *op. cit.,* p. 7.

Catholics was fairly high. Here, too, were Catholic youth movements, labour organizations, and coöperatives similar to those which we have noted in Belgium. Priests led a movement to fight alcoholism which dated from the nineteenth century. The Christian Social Party, although not having a majority, was the largest in the Chamber of Deputies. A trend towards de-Christianization was seen in the winning of adherents by Socialism and Communism. Under the Nazi regime the Church was greatly restricted and various Roman Catholic organizations were either banned or curbed. However, after the coming of peace and the restoration of independence they revived, but with modifications. For example, Catholic Action was separated from some of the lay organizations. Yet church attendance and the sacramental life were slow in coming back to their pre-war proportions.[171]

THE KINGDOM OF THE NETHERLANDS (HOLLAND)

In Holland, or, officially, the Kingdom of the Netherlands, the Roman Catholic Church flourished in the twentieth century. Here the forces of the revolutionary age made themselves felt, notably in the growth of cities and the drift towards secularism. During World War II normal life was disrupted by the German occupation and much damage was done in the fighting, spectacularly in the bombing and burning of Rotterdam. As the war went on, the ruthlessness of German rule mounted. Mass deportations were made for forced labour in Germany. The population increasingly suffered from cold and hunger. With peace, recovery came quickly. At the time of the separation of Belgium from Holland, it will be recalled, about a million Roman Catholics remained in the Netherlands under the House of Orange. They were mostly in the South.

The numbers of Roman Catholics grew. Because of unfavourable economic conditions in the South, in the nineteenth century their proportion of the total population of the country declined and was about 35 per cent. in 1909 as against 38.99 per cent. in 1839.[172] In the twentieth century the proportion rose and in 1950 was said to be 37 per cent.[173] In the mid-twentieth century the stronghold of the Roman Catholics was still in the South. There and in the South-east they constituted a majority.[174]

Those of the population of the country reporting no religious affiliation were 1,144,600 in 1930 and 1,641,300 in 1947, an increase much larger proportionately than that of the population as a whole. A slightly higher percentage of Roman

---

171 E. Donckel, *Die Kirche in Luxemburg von den Anfängen bis nur Gegenwart* (Luxemburg, Sankt Paulus-Druckerei, 1950, pp. 248), pp. 184–212; Fogarty, *op. cit.*, pp. 8, 111, 230, 291, 294.

172 Volume I, p. 431.

173 *The Encyclopædia Britannica*, 14th ed., Vol. XI, pp. 659, 660. Another set of figures, apparently that of the Roman Catholic Church, makes the proportion 40 per cent. at about the same time.—*De Katholieke Encyclopaedie*, Vol. XVIII, p. 510.

174 *De Katholieke Encyclopaedie*, Vol. XVIII, map opposite p. 481.

Catholics than Protestants reported non-affiliation.[175] In the mid-twentieth century it was said that non-practising Roman Catholics, if measured by abstention from Easter Communion for seven years, amounted to 23.6 per cent. of those formally of that faith. As was to be expected, the proportion was highest in the large cities—42 per cent. in Rotterdam, 38.7 per cent. in Amsterdam, and 30.7 per cent. in The Hague.[176]

Yet, as we have found in other countries, in spite of the indifference of a large minority of its professed adherents, the Roman Catholic Church gave evidence of marked vitality. It was potent in the political scene. For example, in 1948, although it had declared itself non-confessional, the party still bearing the name "Catholic" and endorsed by the bishops had the largest representation in the second chamber—32 out of 100 seats—and was ahead of the second largest, Labour, which had 27 seats.[177] As we have noted,[178] Roman Catholic labour was highly organized. In 1919, in the revolutionary wave which immediately followed World War I, it and the Catholic Party helped to defeat the Communist effort to take over the country.[179] In 1923 and 1925 the Catholic Workers' Federation (*R. K. Werliedenverbond in Nederland*) brought together all the multiform aspects of the Catholic Workers' Movement. During World War II it was driven underground but after the war it revived.[180] It included trade unions, a youth movement, and a women's movement, was organized by parishes and dioceses, had central councils which concerned themselves with religious, moral, cultural, social, and economic issues and activities, and public health, and embraced an insurance society, a housing institute, a sanatorium and rest homes, a leader training centre, and a press. It gave legal assistance, maintained coöperatives, a coal purchase society, a sickness fund, and a savings bank, and aided workers preparing for the priesthood.[181] Corresponding to the *Boerenbond* of Belgium was the Catholic Farmers' and Market Gardeners' Union (*Katholieke Nederlandse Boeren-en-Tuindersbond—*K.N.B.T.B.). In 1953 it had 48 per cent. of all organized farmers.[182] A Catholic Employers' Movement existed which included the Federation of Catholic Trade Associations, whose members were firms. Middle-class elements (shopkeepers and craftsmen) organized. The St. Adalbert Association for cultural and social purposes enrolled

---

[175] Fogarty, *op. cit.,* pp. 355, 357.

[176] *De Katholieke Encyclopaedie,* Vol. XVIII, p. 510. See approximately the same figures in Fogarty, *op. cit.,* p. 350.

[177] *The Encyclopædia Britannica,* 14th ed., Vol. XI, p. 668; Rogier, *Katholieke Herleving,* pp. 607, 608.

[178] Chapter IV.

[179] Somerville, *op. cit.,* p. 96.

[180] Fogarty, *op. cit.,* pp. 193–203. See especially the charts on pp. 199, 200. W. G. Vershuis, *Beknopte Geschiedenis van de Katholieke Arbeidersbewegung in Nederland* (Utrecht, Dekker & van de Vegt, 1940, pp. 127), pp. 55 ff.

[181] Fogarty, *op. cit.,* pp. 197, 198.

[182] *Ibid.,* p. 250.

about 3,000 from the intellectual professions.[183] Social work developed, partly as an outgrowth of a Catholic women's movement. For example, in 1920 and 1921 schools for training in it were organized.[184]

In industrial and political issues the differences between Christians, both Roman Catholic and Protestant on the one hand and Socialists on the other, were less pronounced than in the latter part of the nineteenth century. For a time Socialists hoped for a combined Christian and Socialist labour party. Soon after World War II the Catholic People's Party was weakened by the secession of right-wing elements who formed the Catholic National Party (*Katholieke Nationale Partij*—K.N.P.) and by a movement of Catholic workers to vote for the Labour Party. However, after the election of 1952, when the Catholic People's Party had suffered from the centrifugal movements, efforts were made to heal the breach and in 1954 the Dutch bishops reproved those of their flocks who had joined the Labour Party. In general, 90 per cent. of the entire Roman Catholic adult population, and not simply the practising elements, voted for the Catholic parties.[185]

Since the Dutch episcopate took a conservative attitude towards the Liturgical Movement, only slow progress was made. However, about 1950 a project was under way for the condensation of the breviary to be used by the laity and nuns. Advances were made in other aspects of the Movement.[186]

The question of state subsidies to denominational schools, a thorny issue inherited from the nineteenth century, was settled in 1920. By a concession won in 1889 by a coalition of Roman Catholics, Protestants, and Conservatives the state made financial grants to confessional schools. However, the grants from the central government were not equal to those to the public schools, and the communes, while assisting the latter, gave no aid to the confessional schools. The adoption of universal suffrage brought to power the elements which favoured placing the two kinds of schools on a financial equality and in 1920 a measure was passed to that effect. Roman Catholic education achieved a further gain when in 1923 the Catholic University of Nijmegen was opened. Significantly, it enrolled a large number from the worker classes.[187]

The prestige of the Roman Catholic Church was enhanced when, during World War I, diplomatic relations were entered into with the Holy See. At first regarded as temporary, after the war they were given continuing status.[188]

The vigour of the Roman Catholic Church in the Netherlands found additional expression in the world-wide spread of the faith. In 1953 missionaries from

[183] *Ibid.*, pp. 253–261.
[184] Rogier, *op. cit.*, p. 399.
[185] Fogarty, *op. cit.*, pp. 294, 358, 380, 387–390.
[186] Bogler, *op. cit.*, pp. 42–44; Rogier, *op. cit.*, pp. 520–528.
[187] Premoli, *Contemporary Church History (1900–1925)*, pp. 195, 196; Rogier, *op. cit.*, p. 612.
[188] Premoli, *op. cit.*, p. 198.

Holland were surpassed in numbers only by those from France and Belgium and showed an increase of 137 per cent. in twenty years, a larger growth percentage-wise than that by the Roman Catholics of any other country except Ireland and in figures more even than that land. The achievement was the more remarkable in view of the fact that the two decades spanned World War II, with the destruction and foreign occupation which accompanied that struggle. Extensive efforts were also made to reach out in evangelism in the Netherlands.[189]

Switzerland

As in the Netherlands, so in Switzerland Roman Catholics constituted only a minority but a very substantial minority of the population. Although at mid-twentieth century Roman Catholics were approximately the same percentage of the population as in the Netherlands, because of the smaller population of Switzerland their total in that country was only about half that in the Netherlands. At least partly because of immigration, Roman Catholics increased in numbers more rapidly than Protestants—172 per cent. as against 152 per cent. between 1850 and 1930.[190] They still formed a majority of the population in some cantons, but because of the religious freedom granted in the nineteenth century Protestants were found in what were previously Roman Catholic cantons and Roman Catholics were also in what had been solidly Protestant regions.[191]

As in several other countries of Western Europe, after 1914 lay organizations of Roman Catholics for economic, social, and political purposes multiplied. In 1943 the Swiss Christian Trade Union, organized in 1907, was embraced in a more inclusive structure, the Swiss Christian Social Workers' Movement. The latter included religious and social bodies which were organized by occupations, age, and sex (such as manual workers, clerical workers, women, and youth); and a services committee under which were such activities as publishing, films, education, employment, a savings bank, coöperatives, legal aid, insurance, a burial fund, a war relief fund, and a holiday home.[192] However, Roman Catholic unions did not enroll as large a proportion of the workers of their faith as the corresponding ones in the Netherlands and Flanders.[193] A Catholic Farmers' Union was founded in 1942 and was closely affiliated with the Conservative (Catholic) People's Party.[194] That party was formally constituted in 1912. Owing to the adoption of proportional representation in 1919, it increased

---

[189] Rogier, *op. cit.*, pp. 515–520, 558–562.
[190] *De Katholieke Encyclopaedie*, Vol. XXV, p. 537.
[191] See map in *ibid.*, opposite p. 498.
[192] Fogarty, *op. cit.*, pp. 201, 207.
[193] *Ibid.*, p. 211.
[194] *Ibid.*, p. 247.

in importance in the national scene. In 1943 it had two of the seven seats of the Federal Council. Within it a group arose which championed social legislation and which by the 1940's had won seats in the Federal Assembly.[195]

As we have seen,[196] although Switzerland could not be said to have the Liturgical Movement in an organized form, it experienced a liturgical revival. The revival spread from several centres and in various forms.[197]

In proportion to their numerical strength, the Roman Catholics of Switzerland did not have as large a share in the spread of their faith outside the Occident as did their brethren in the Netherlands or Belgium. Yet in 1921 the Society of Bethlehem was formed as a national congregation for missions.[198] Moreover, between 1933 and 1953 the number of Swiss priests serving abroad more than doubled.

In the domestic scene, in 1941 the Society for Interior Missions supported 227 parishes and centres for pastoral care, 8 Italian missions, 10 French and German centres, 5 student centres, and 18 schools and asylums.[199]

In both World War I and World War II Switzerland maintained her neutrality. Many Swiss Roman Catholics sought to relieve the distress of the victims of the war, partly by gifts of money and food, and also by caring for prisoners interned in their country.[200]

Swiss Roman Catholicism of the twentieth century was producing scholars. For example, Charles Journet (1891——), professor in Fribourg i. S., was the author of a major work, in which he dealt comprehensively with the various aspects of the Church and addressed himself to such questions as heresy, schism, the possibility of salvation outside the Church, and the problem of the imperfections of the Church in history. He devoted a large section to the position of Barth.[201]

The Swiss Church was strengthened by renewed diplomatic relations between the state and the Holy See. Broken off in 1873, they were resumed in 1920. During World War I the Pope had had a representative in Switzerland to aid in administering relief.[202]

GERMANY: THE SETTING

The setting in which the Roman Catholic Church was involved in Germany after 1914 was sharply divided into periods by political developments. From the

---

[195] *Ibid.*, pp. 309, 310, 314.
[196] Chapter V.
[197] Fogarty, *op. cit.*, pp. 54–72.
[198] *De Katholieke Encyclopaedie*, Vol. XXV, p. 498.
[199] Schwegler, *Geschichte der katholischen Kirche in der Schweiz*, p. 331.
[200] Premoli, *op. cit.*, pp. 202, 203.
[201] Charles Journet, *L'Église du Verbe Incarné. Essai de Théologie Spéculative* (Paris, Desclée de Brouwer et Cie, 2 vols., 1939–1951). The first volume, revised, was published in 1955).
[202] Schwegler, *op. cit.*, p. 330.

summer of 1914 to the autumn of 1918 Germany was engaged in World War I. The years were marked by growing strain and suffering. After initial military successes came complete defeat and near-prostration. As a consequence of defeat ancient hereditary thrones toppled. The Hohenzollerns were ousted from Prussia and from their imperial position in the Reich. In Bavaria the Wittelsbach dynasty was deposed and was followed by a republic. In Baden the family that had ruled for eight centuries was supplanted by a republic. The King of Saxony abdicated and a republic took the place of the monarchy. Württemberg was the scene of a similar revolution.

What was known as the Weimar Republic (from the city in which it was organized) was substituted for the Hohenzollerns as the government of the nation. It was confronted with a combination of problems which, unsolved or only partly solved, spelled its doom. Germans smarted under the accusation of the victors, written into the peace treaty and to which they had no choice but to subscribe, that they were responsible for the war. Impoverished by the long strain of the war and near starvation from the Allied blockade, they were loaded with a burden of reparations which they could not hope to pay for a generation, if ever. They had a rankling sense of having been betrayed into surrendering on the basis of President Wilson's Fourteen Points and then of having seen those points flouted in the treaty dictated by their conquerors. Inflation wiped out their currency. As if these handicaps were not enough, in 1929 and the early 1930's the world-wide financial depression hit their tottering economy.

Under these circumstances the Weimar Republic was seized by the National Socialists—the Nazis—led by Adolf Hitler (1889–1945). In 1933 it gave way to what was called the Third Reich (the first having been the Holy Roman Empire, from 962 to 1806, and the second the Hohenzollern Empire, from 1871 to 1918). Under it Hitler created a dictatorship with himself as *Führer* supported by the National Socialist Party, the only one which was permitted. The several states—Prussia, Saxony, Bavaria, and the others—were made into administrative districts of the Empire. Drastic action was taken against the Communists and the Jews. The latter were all but exterminated. Opposition was crushed. The new regime was totalitarian and required unquestioning conformity. Youth were organized and indoctrinated in its principles. *Mein Kampf,* written by Hitler, was its authoritative book. Hitler, although himself nominally a Roman Catholic, sought to bring the churches to heel. National Socialism, as he interpreted it, displayed some of the aspects of a rival religion.

The Nazi regime rode on the tide of seeming success. In effect it tore up the humiliating Treaty of Versailles. The country appeared to be prospering financially. Unemployment dropped. Employers were making profits. Territorial gains were achieved. The Rhineland, de-militarized by the Treaty of Versailles, was occupied by Hitler's troops and re-militarized (1926). In 1938 Austria was annexed. Sudetenland in Czechoslovakia was seized (September, 1938)—on the ground that its population was predominantly German. In March, 1939, what remained of Czechoslovakia was occupied and Lithuania was frightened into ceding Memel, a city of which Germany had been deprived by the Treaty of Versailles.

The Hitler regime culminated in tragic World War II. Precipitated by the Nazi invasion of Poland (September, 1939) made possible by the Russo-German non-aggression pact of the preceding month, its opening weeks witnessed the partition of Poland by the two huge neighbours. Early in 1940 Russia took part of Finland. The year 1940 was marked by the German occupation of Denmark, Norway, the Netherlands, Belgium, Luxemburg, and much of France. Italy entered the war in 1940 and made gains in the Eastern Mediterranean. Russia seized Lithuania, Latvia, Estonia, and much of Rumania. Greece was invaded, first (1940) by Italy and then (1941) by Germany. Jugoslavia was invaded and divided (1941). In the meantime Japan continued the advance into China which it had begun in 1931 and resumed in 1937. Conflicting ambitions led to a Russian-German break. In June, 1941, Hitler launched a lightning invasion of his quondam ally. With Italy, Finland, Hungary, Slovakia, Rumania, Bulgaria, Albania, and Croatia on his side, for a time he seemed to have every prospect of success. By the end of 1941 his armies had driven far into Russia. In December of that year Japan by a sudden attack on Pearl Harbour destroyed or crippled much of the American fleet. The United States immediately declared war on Japan, followed by Great Britain, the Netherlands, Australia, New Zealand, Canada, and several Latin American countries. Germany, Italy, and their Axis associates declared war on the United States. Japan quickly overran the Philippines, Hong Kong, Singapore, Malaya, Indochina, Indonesia, and Burma and threatened India. For a time in 1942 the German advance continued. Then, in the latter part of 1942, the tide began to turn. The German armies were halted in Russia and were driven out of North Africa, and Japan was beginning to be repulsed in the Pacific. In 1943 the Italian Government surrendered and the German armies, which now occupied the peninsula, were slowly driven back. That year witnessed the beginning of the retreat of the German armies from Russia and the "round the clock" bombing of German railways, cities, and munition-manufacturing centres. In 1944 the Allies landed large forces in France and by the end of the year had freed most of that country of the Nazis. In 1945 the Russians moved relentlessly westward, the other Allies marched northward and eastward, Hitler shot his mistress and himself, and on May 7, 1945, the Germans surrendered. In mid-summer of that year Japan was brought to her knees and occupied.

Following the collapse of the Nazi regime Germany was left prostrate, with her territory more curtailed than after World War I and with what was left to her divided. Alsace-Lorraine was restored to France, Eupen and Malmédy to Belgium, and the Sudetenland, with its large German element, to Czechoslovakia. Austria was again independent and much of Germany's eastern territory was divided between Russia and Poland. West Germany, occupied by Great Britain, France, and the United States, became the German Federal Republic (in 1949) and in 1952 was given almost complete self-government and joined NATO (the North Atlantic Treaty Organization). East Germany, occupied by Russia, was made into the German Democratic Republic, modelled on the Russian Communist pattern. Berlin, set in the midst of East Germany, was occupied by Great Britain, France, the United States, and Russia—the eastern portion under Russia and the western portion under the other three powers.

The German Federal Republic made an amazing economic recovery. By 1960 its destroyed cities had been largely rebuilt, its industries were flourishing, and it was expanding its foreign trade. The German Democratic Republic was much slower in repairing the damage wrought by the war.

GERMANY: THE ROMAN CATHOLIC CHURCH AND THE STATE

What were the relations between the Roman Catholic Church and the state in the successive stages of Germany's tumultuous post-1914 course?

During World War I the Centre Party, predominantly Roman Catholic, continued to be important. In 1917 it joined with the Social Democrats and the Progressive People's Party in counselling peace. Under the Weimar Republic the Centre Party persisted. Not all Roman Catholics supported it, for many objected to its advocacy of that form of government, and some Protestants voted with it. The Bavarian members separated from it and organized a distinct party.[203]

With the Republic came a partial separation of Church and state. The constitution guaranteed religious liberty and the right of property. Each church was given complete control over its affairs without interference by the state and named its officials and clergy without the collaboration of the government. Bishops and parish priests could be appointed freely by the ecclesiastical authorities. No restrictions were placed on monastic orders or congregations of religious.[204] The state still provided some of the support of the clergy, but this was regarded as compensation from ecclesiastical property confiscated in 1803. Some parishes were maintained by ancient endowments. Others, without such

[203] John K. Zeender, *The German Center Party during World War I. An Internal Study,* in *The Catholic Historical Review,* Vol. XLII, pp. 441–468 (January, 1957); Guilday, *The Catholic Church in Contemporary Europe 1919–1931,* pp. 108, 109; Rovan, *Le Catholicisme Politique en Allemagne,* pp. 187–207.
[204] Premoli, *Contemporary Church History (1900–1925),* pp. 161, 162; Schmidlin, *Papstgeschichte der neuesten Zeit,* Vol. III, p. 280; Cazelles, *Église et État en Allemagne de Weimar aux Premières Années du IIIe Reich,* pp. 82–128.

sources of income, were dependent on church taxes collected by the state, and they varied.[205] Diplomatic relations were maintained with the Holy See and concordats favorable to the Church were concluded with Prussia, Bavaria, and Baden.[206] A struggle developed over religious instruction in the schools. The constitution made it obligatory but did not prescribe its exact nature. The Centre Party wished it to be frankly Christian and to be given according to the denominational affiliation of the pupils. The Socialists succeeded (1923) in having the teaching based upon religious morality, without specifying the kind of religion. During the Weimar Republic Roman Catholics, profiting by the ruin of many of the propertied classes and the favourable rate of exchange, bought back many monastic properties which had been secularized centuries earlier. Between 1919 and 1927 they founded over 700 new religious houses.[207]

Some Roman Catholic leaders early became aware of the incompatibility of National Socialism and Christianity. Thus in 1930 the Bishop of Mainz supported a parish priest who had declared in a sermon that no Catholic could belong to the party and that members of the party would not be given the sacraments. On February 12, 1931, the eight bishops of Bavaria pointed out what they deemed the false doctrines of National Socialism and forbade Catholic priests to be associated with the movement.[208]

For a time, however, some Roman Catholics supported Hitler. They viewed him as a hopeful alternative to Communism and believed that the responsibilities of office would temper his more extreme views. The Centre Party enabled him to obtain control of the Reichstag (March, 1933). Von Papen, esteemed a good Catholic, had made him vice-chancellor. The excommunication against the party leaders was lifted. Von Papen negotiated a concordat with Rome, an achievement which had not been possible under the Weimar regime.[209] That document, it will be recalled, seemed to grant all that the Roman Catholic Church wished.[210] Some Roman Catholics in Von Papen's circle formed an organization, the Eagle and the Cross, and dreamed of a German Christian empire under National Socialist leadership.[211] In his earlier years Hitler had declared that National Socialism was not anti-religious or anti-Christian but was based upon "real Christianity" and that he desired both Roman Catholics and Protestants to live together in peace in the common struggle against the "power

[205] Guilday, *op. cit.*, pp. 107, 108; Cazelles, *op. cit.*, pp. 129–153.
[206] Guilday, *op. cit.*, p. 106; Cazelles, *op. cit.*, pp. 182–212.
[207] Premoli, *op. cit.*, p. 163. On the Roman Catholics and the schools late in the 1920's see *Kirchliches Handbuch*, Vol. XVII, pp. 83 ff. On the increase in monastic houses see Drummond, *German Protestantism Since Luther*, p. 260.
[208] D'Harcourt, *The German Catholics*, pp. 3–16.
[209] Hales, *The Catholic Church in the Modern World*, pp. 270, 271; Cazelles, *op. cit.*, pp. 230–244; D'Harcourt, *op. cit.*, pp. 80–96, 107–136.
[210] Chapter III. See a translation of the text in *The Persecution of the Catholic Church in the Third Reich*, pp. 516–522.
[211] Bendiscioli, *Nazism versus Christianity*, p. 152.

which is the deadly enemy of any Christianity."[212]

However, friction between the National Socialist regime and the Roman Catholic Church mounted. Ominous for the future was the compulsory dissolution (1933) of the Centre Party. All the other parties were also destroyed—with the exception of the National Socialist Party. The latter was left with no rivals. Some Roman Catholics who had been prominent in the Centre Party or had belonged to Christian trade unions were persecuted.[213] The Nazi state increasingly espoused policies which the Roman Catholic Church could not but denounce. In return, it brought increasing pressure on that church which in time became thinly veiled or open persecution.

The "real" or "positive" Christianity endorsed by Hitler had its chief exponent in Alfred Rosenberg. Rosenberg called himself a Christian but declared that Christianity had been corrupted by the Jews and that it should be emancipated from its Jewish elements, including the Old Testament.[214] "Positive" Christianity was set forth in a slightly less radical form by the "German Christians." They sought a revival of religion to undergird the National Socialist state. They were against anything they considered un-German, were anti-Jewish, and desired to overcome denominational differences and unite all Germans in service for the public weal in one national church which would fulfil what they deemed the "eternal longing of the German people."[215] They had the support of Hitler. As a totalitarian regime, the National Socialists insisted upon controlling all aspects of the nation's life, including the education of youth.

The Roman Catholic Church could not assent to the teachings of Rosenberg or the "German Christians." Its leaders felt themselves constrained by their faith to protest against the persecution of the Jews, the sterilization measures of the state, and the efforts of the government to get complete control of youth, the schools, and the press. The bishops again and again protested. Sometimes they spoke out collectively in pastoral letters warning the faithful of the threat of the government measures. At least one of these was suppressed by the state.[216] Others voiced their criticism in sermons or in pastoral letters. One of the most fearless was Michael von Faulhaber (1869–1952). Scholar, Cardinal Archbishop of Munich, in pastoral letters and sermons he denounced in no uncertain terms the treatment of the Jews, the theories of the German Christians, and various

---

[212] Micklem, *National Socialism and the Roman Catholic Church*, p. 2.

[213] Bendiscioli, *op. cit.*, p. 147. See a Roman Catholic attack on the Centre Party and the Papal policy in Wilhelm Maria Genn, *Halt! Katholizismus und Nationalsozialismus* (Munich, Frz. Eher Nacht, G.M.b.h., no date, pp. 96), *passim*. See also an attack on "political Catholicism" and the Centre Party in Emil Ritter, *Der Weg des politischen Katholizismus in Deutschland* (Breslau, Wilh. Gottl. Korn, 1934, pp. 312), *passim*.

[214] Micklem, *op. cit.*, pp. 15–23, 38–52.

[215] *Ibid.*, pp. 38–52. For a Roman Catholic writing in favour of a "national Catholicism" in which Protestants and Roman Catholics would rise above their differences as Germans, see Konrad Hentrich, *National Katholizismus* (Hamburg, Hanseatische Verlagsastalt, 1934, pp. 40), *passim*.

[216] Bendiscioli, *op. cit.*, pp. 168 ff.; D'Harcourt, *op. cit.*, pp. 189–202.

actions of the Nazis. He upheld the religious values of the Old Testament, noted the debt of Christianity to the Jews, and pointed out that the conversion of the Germans to Christianity had made a nation of that once divided people.[217] Clemens August Graf von Galen (1878–1946), appointed Bishop of Münster in 1933 and created cardinal shortly before his death, was outspoken in his denunciation of the writings of Rosenberg and of the activities of the Gestapo.[218] As we have seen, in 1937 Pius XII, in the encyclical *Mit brennenden Sorge,* protested against the Nazi government's measures against the Church.[219]

Yet the National Socialist regime did not heed the protests but stepped up its persecution of the Roman Catholic Church. The persecution was heightened after Germany became involved in World War II, with the obvious purpose of stamping out all internal resistance to the government with its possible weakening of the prosecution of the war. In this, as we shall see, the state paralleled what it was doing to the Protestants.

Again and again the government violated the terms of the concordat. Although in that document it had promised to accord full freedom to the Holy See to communicate with the bishops and other members of the Roman Catholic Church, when on Palm Sunday, 1937, *Mit brennenden Sorge* was read from the pulpits of most of the parish pulpits, twelve printing establishments which had put the document into type were closed, parish and diocesan publications which had reproduced the encyclical were suspended for three months, and many individuals who had circulated it were arrested. The state had also sought to stop the printing of the encyclical of 1929 on the Christian education of youth. Most of the pastoral letters of the German bishops could be conveyed to the faithful only through surreptitious channels. Far-reaching measures were taken against the Roman Catholic press.[220] The concordat had assured the Roman Catholic Church that existing denominational schools could be maintained and new ones established and that Catholic charitable, cultural, religious, social, and professional organizations would be permitted. Yet by 1939 most Roman Cath-

---

[217] Bendiscioli, *op. cit.,* pp. 153–155. See a sermon by Faulhaber in *The Persecution of the Catholic Church in the Third Reich,* pp. 538–543. See especially some of his sermons in Michael von Faulhaber, *Judaism, Christianity, and Germany,* translated by George D. Smith (New York, The Macmillan Co., 1934, pp. ix, 116), *passim.*

[218] *De Katholieke Encyclopaedie,* Vol. XI, p. 207.

[219] For the text of the encyclical see Simon Hirt, editor, *Mit brennenden Sorge. Das päpstliche Rundschreiben gegen den Nationalsozialismus und seine Folgen in Deutschland* (Freiburg im Breisgau, Herder, 1946, pp. 102), *passim.* As other examples of Roman Catholic criticisms see Heinrich Portmann, editor, *Bishop Graf von Galen Spricht. Ein apostolischer Kampf und sein Widerhall* (Freiburg im Breisgau, Herder, 1946, pp. 112), *passim;* Konrad Hofmann, editor, *Zeugnis und Kampf des deutschen Episkopats. Gemeinsame Hirtenbriefe und Denkschriften* (Freiburg im Breisgau, Herder, 1946, pp. 84), *passim;* Max Müller, *Das christliche Menschenbild und die Weltanschauungen der Neuzeit. Zwei Vorträge gehalten in der katholischen Studentenseelsorge zu Freiburg im Breisgau am 30 Juni und 5 Juli, 1939* (Freiburg im Breisgau, Herder, 1945, pp. 63), *passim;* Philip Dessauer, *Das Bionome Geschichtsbild. Hintergründe und Konsequenzen einer Geschichtsideologie* (Freiburg, Herder, 1946, pp. 51), *passim.*

[220] *The Persecution of the Catholic Church in the Third Reich,* pp. 59–81.

olic schools and youth organizations had been suppressed, and that in spite of protests. The alleged reasons were that they interfered with the national effort, now that Germany was at war. Terrorization was also employed, some of it by patently illegal methods which the police made no effort to check.[221] The provision in the concordat for instruction in the Catholic faith in the schools was also violated. Obstacles were put in the way of such instruction and instead no effort was spared to instill in youth the principles of the "German Christians."[222] Likewise in contradiction to the express provisions of the concordat, organizations of adult Roman Catholics were destroyed, among them Catholic labour unions, and efforts to obtain funds for Catholic charities were hindered.[223]

In addition to the overt violations of the concordat other measures were taken adverse to the Roman Catholic Church. Apostasy was encouraged. Thousands were officially recorded as having left the Church.[224] Accusations were brought against members of religious orders of sending currency out of the country against the law. Convictions followed with imprisonments and fines. The press gave them wide publicity. Charges were made that clergy and members of religious orders and congregations were guilty of sexual irregularities. Such offenses were relatively few and in most cases the ecclesiastical authorities had taken prompt and stern measures against the guilty. Yet the press made much of them.[225] In a wide variety of other ways the Roman Catholic Church was defamed as unpatriotic and anti-social, and the Hitler youth organizations were used to undermine the faith. Increasingly the National Socialists sought to make of their beliefs a religion which would be a substitute for Christianity and in doing so at times they adapted Catholic symbols—such as a Nazi demonstration taking the trappings of a public procession honouring the Eucharist. Many priests were killed.[226]

With the downfall of Hitler and the National Socialists and the emergence of the German Federal Republic and the German Democratic Republic the Roman Catholic Church faced sharply contrasting conditions. In East Germany, ruled by the Communists, the situation was increasingly adverse to Christianity. However, here the traditional affiliation of the large majority of the population had been with Protestantism and Roman Catholics were in the minority. We will, then, reserve our account of developments there for the chapter on Protes-

---

[221] *Ibid.*, pp. 82–162.

[222] *Ibid.*, pp. 163–186.

[223] *Ibid.*, pp. 187–205.

[224] See some figures in *ibid.*, pp. 226–231.

[225] *Ibid.*, pp. 295–325; D'Harcourt, *op. cit.*, pp. 169–177, 217–224.

[226] *The Persecution of the Catholic Church in the Third Reich*, pp. 327 ff. For other accounts of the persecution of the Roman Catholic Church see K. Trossmann, *Hitler und Rom* (Nuremberg, Sebaldus, 1931, pp. 208); John Mason Brown, *Hitler's First Foes. A Study in Religion and Politics* (Minneapolis, Burgess Publishing Co., 1936, pp. v, 118); Micklem, *op. cit.*, pp. 84–237, where a year-by-year account is given for 1933–1938. For one of the martyred priests see Lilian Stevenson, *Max Josef Metzger, Priest and Martyr* (London, S.P.C.K., 1952, pp. 147).

tantism in Germany. In West Germany, under the German Federal Republic, conditions were almost the reverse. Here the Roman Catholic Church was relatively stronger than in the nineteenth century. By the census of 1950 it had 45.2 per cent. of the population as against 50.7 per cent. counted as Protestant and 4.1 per cent. "others." Within the German borders as they were between the two world wars Roman Catholics had been approximately a third of the population.

In the German Federal Republic the Christian Democratic Union (*Christliche demokratische Union*—C.D.U.) became the majority party. In a sense it was the successor of the Centre Party. But more nearly than the latter it was a-confessional. Although predominantly Roman Catholic in membership it was joined by many Protestants. It had liberal tendencies but was far from being on the extreme left. It was proud of its record of increasing the budget for social security and it stood for full employment. It was closely allied with the Christian Social Union, a Bavarian party which was an expression of the particularism in what had once been an independent kingdom.[227]

GERMANY: ASPECTS OF ROMAN CATHOLIC LIFE AND THOUGHT

A striking feature of post-1914 Germany was the vigour of the Roman Catholic Church. Through all the vicissitudes of the stormy decades which immediately followed 1914 that church persisted. It came to the half-century mark with a record of creative vitality in spite of the stresses brought by World War I, the National Socialists, and World War II with their near-interruption of some phases of church life.

Several of the manifestations of vitality we have touched upon in earlier chapters. We have hinted at the growth of Catholic Action, of trade unions and workers' organizations, in many of which Roman Catholics and Protestants joined, of youth movements, and of a farmers' organization. We have noted that the Liturgical Movement had more than one of its main centres in Germany and that it continued to mount after World War II. We have called attention to the activity in theology and Biblical sudies, which, although not as outstanding as in France, was prominent.

We must now attempt a few examples which will at least give some indication of what a full account would disclose. Comparative studies by years of the proportion of Roman Catholics who could be called practising seem not to be available. However, in the early 1950's between 55 and 60 per cent. of baptized Roman Catholics were said to be attending mass with some degree of regularity, a higher ratio than in France and Italy. As elsewhere, more women than men were in that category, but no great contrast appears to have existed between the

---

[227] H. G. Wieck, *Die Entstehung der CDU und die Wiedergründung des Zentrums im Jahre 1945* (Düsseldorf, Droste Verlag, 1953, pp. 227), *passim;* Fogarty, *Christian Democracy in Western Europe, 1820–1953,* pp. 25, 121, 306, 307, 341; Rovan, *op. cit.,* pp. 253, 254, 264–289.

upper and lower income groups.[228] During the period of the Weimar Republic Roman Catholics were found in a wide variety of organizations. Some had their origin before World War I. For example, the movement which counted Ketteler and Kolping among its pioneers and Franz Hitze as a worthy successor[229] continued. Hitze lived until 1921. He it was who organized the Roman Catholic labour movement in Germany. In 1890 he founded the *Volksverein für das katholische Deutschland* (People's Union for Catholic Germany) and made it a means for social organization and education. In spite of "integralist" critics, he was a major force in leading German Roman Catholics from a narrow confessionalism and clericalism to a realistic facing of the problems brought by the industrial age. Most of his activity was in the highly industrialized Rhenish-Westphalian region. As a young priest he had served there and had seen the distress and injustice which accompanied the coming of the machine. Stirred to the depths of his being, he had sought to arouse his fellow believers to the need and initiated practical measures to remedy the situation. Partly from him came Catholic trade unions. He had a large part in writing clauses into the constitution of the new republic.[230] Following his tradition, his friend and disciple Heinrich Brauns (1868–1939), a priest, served as minister of labour from 1920 to 1928 and promoted social legislation. He so won the coöperation of the trade unions and employers' associations that he laid a firm foundation for German social policies which survived until the Hitler regime and served as precedent for post-Hitler programmes.[231]

The trade unions and employers' associations were only one facet of the organizational structure of Roman Catholic lay activity which dated from the pre-1914 years and burgeoned under the Weimar Republic. There were societies of mothers, of rural labourers, of store clerks, of school teachers, of waiters in hotels and restaurants, and to aid discharged prisoners. About 90 per cent. of the Roman Catholic university students belonged to one or another organization which sought to encourage observance of Sunday duties, the frequent reception of the sacraments, attendance at retreats, and lecture courses on the faith. They were affiliated with the *Akademische Bonifatius-Einigung,* which, in turn, was an auxiliary of the Society of St. Boniface *(Bonifatius Verein).*[232] The Society of St. Boniface, as we have seen,[233] had as its primary purpose the spiritual and educational care of Roman Catholics in predominantly Protestant areas. On the eve of the Hitler regime, the *Volksverein für das katholische Deutschland*

---

[228] Fogarty, *op. cit.,* p. 348.
[229] Volume I, pp. 439, 440.
[230] Moody, *Church and Society,* pp. 422–431.
[231] *Ibid.,* pp. 430–432.
[232] Guilday, *op. cit.,* pp. 115–118; Delattre, *La Vie Catholique en Allemagne,* pp. 71–83, 128–135; Loewenich, *Der moderne Katholizismus,* pp. 137–140; *Kirchliches Handbuch,* Vol. XVII, pp. 108–111.
[233] Volume I, p. 441.

counted about 500,000 members, largely workingmen, in about 4,500 local units. They were provided with literature of various kinds, and the local units were encouraged to discuss subjects that were suggested by Papal utterances. The *Caritas-Verband,* in which the many societies and institutions engaged in charitable undertakings were coördinated, in 1930 enrolled about 600,000 members and had branches in each diocese. From its headquarters at Freiburg in Breisgau and a branch office in Berlin it served refugees, offered courses on social work, gathered statistics, obtained Catholic guardians for Catholic children, and carried on extensive correspondence with diocesan and local units. Catholic Action flourished and was furthered by the great concourses assembled in the *Katholikentag.* The *Winfriedbund* was introduced in a number of dioceses. A great outpouring of Roman Catholic literature was seen.[234]

With the dissolution of most of these and other Roman Catholic organizations in the years of National Socialism the Roman Catholic Church in Germany concentrated much of its life in the parishes. When religious instruction was prohibited in the schools, it was given by parish priests in voluntary classes. The classes were said to have enrolled a majority of the Catholic children. Although the study of theology did not carry with it, as previously, exemption from military service, vocations to the priesthood were reported to have increased during the years of persecution.[235]

Yet during the National Socialist regime, culminating as it did in World War II, the Roman Catholic Church could not but suffer severely. Many priests and theological students died in concentration camps, others were killed while in the army, numbers did not return from prisoner-of-war camps, and still others died of starvation or disease in areas invaded by the Russians. Thousands of former members of Catholic youth organizations perished in the fighting. In the pressure for man-power in the later phases of the war, untold numbers of fifteen- to seventeen-year-old boys were mustered into the army and many of them, normally sources of recruits for the priesthood, were killed. In the bombings thousands of church buildings were destroyed or damaged. All this meant a severe shortage of clergy and of physical equipment when peace at last came.[236]

The difficulties were accentuated by the vast movements of population brought by the war and its aftermath. The bombings forced the evacuation of millions from their accustomed environment. An agreement among the victors which fixed the eastern border of Germany at the Oder and Neisse rivers forced even more millions to move from their homes in what was now Polish and Russian territory. That action cost the lives of between three and four millions, and of the eleven millions who survived about half were Roman Catholics. In addi-

234 Guilday, *op. cit.,* pp. 115–127; Delattre, *op. cit.,* pp. 38–43, 103–128.
235 Guriàn and Fitzsimons, *The Catholic Church in World Affairs,* pp. 208–210; *Kirchliches Handbuch,* Vol. XX, pp. 81 ff.
236 Guriàn and Fitzsimons, *op. cit.,* pp. 210–213.

tion were hundreds of thousands of displaced persons and fugitives from the Russian zone of occupation to West Germany. The physical plight of the refugees posed the government and the churches with problems of the first magnitude: food, shelter, and employment. More than three-fourths of the Roman Catholics directly affected found themselves in what had been predominantly Protestant territory and their church, already hampered by losses in its body of clergy, could not at once provide them with spiritual care. At least two millions were in the traditionally Protestant Russian zone, where Communist rule presented additional handicaps. Similarly, thousands of Protestants were now in areas which had been prevailingly Roman Catholic.[237]

Both confessions rose to the challenge. Of the Protestant achievements we will say more in a later chapter. As an organ of Roman Catholic action, the *Bonifatius Verein,* still suffering from the Hitler era, was revived and put forth heroic efforts for material and spiritual help for the new *diaspora.* Through *Caritas* physical relief was given to many thousands, some of it sacrificially contributed by the impoverished German Roman Catholics and much of it sent from abroad, including tons of food from the Vatican.[238]

In the years which followed 1945 a number of the pre-Hitler Roman Catholic organizations were renewed. Among them, as we have just said, was the *Bonifatius Verein.* Another, of somewhat similar purpose and also founded in the nineteenth century, was the *Borromäus Verein.* Begun in 1845 to produce and distribute Roman Catholic literature, it had its headquarters at Bonn. Among the stimuli which gave rise to it were the *Gustav Adolf Verein,* founded in 1832 on the bicentennial of the death of Gustavus Adolphus to promote the circulation of Protestant literature, some of it among Roman Catholics; the popularity of such books as Strauss's *Leben Jesu;* and the continued spread of the teachings of Hermes, in spite of their condemnation by Rome. It prospered and published books, pamphlets, and periodicals. In connexion with it was the *Vereinigung des katholisches Buchhandels* (Association of the Catholic Book Trade). During World War I the *Borromäus Verein* produced books, pamphlets, and other literature in great quantities for the troops and prisoners of war. After World War I its membership at first shrank, then again mounted. The depression of 1929 cost it dearly. Although it suffered from the adverse conditions of the National Socialist regime, it revived after 1945 and was hailed as the most effective of its kind in the Roman Catholic world.[239]

The Christian trade unions of pre-Hitler days were not renewed. They had included both Roman Catholics and Protestants and in the 1920's had about 1,250,000 members. In 1928, 452,000 of these were of clerical workers, more

[237] *Ibid.,* pp. 213, 214.
[238] *Ibid.,* pp. 214, 221, 222.
[239] Wilhelm Spael, *Das Buch im Geisteskampf. 100 Jahre Borromäusverein* (Bonn, Verlag des Borromäus Vereins, 1950, pp. 403), *passim.*

than in the Socialist, liberal, or independent unions. In Rhineland-Westphalia, including the highly industrialized Ruhr, they had from 40 to 45 per cent. of all manual labourers.[240] But they were dissolved by the National Socialists. After World War II, owing largely to American and British influence and to the fraternizing of the members of the several unions in concentration camps, labour joined in forming non-denominational or religiously neutral trade unions. To this some Roman Catholics objected, but numbers of leading Roman Catholic trade unionists supported the policy. However, the Catholic Workers' Movement, with about 200,000 members in the early 1950's and closely related to Catholic Action, gave an opportunity for Roman Catholic labourers to coöperate in influencing the trade unions. Moreover, in 1955 the German Christian Trade Union Movement (*Christliche Gewerkschafts-bewegung Deutschlands*— C.G.D.) was organized by Roman Catholics and Protestants.[241]

The Roman Catholic schools dissolved under the Third Reich were only partly restored after Hitler's downfall. In a few of the states (*Länder*) of the German Federal Republic, as in Bavaria, South Würtemberg, and Rhineland-Pflaz, denominational schools could be conducted where parents desired them. Yet by the fundamental law of the Federal Republic Church-supervised instruction in all schools was provided. In the Federal Republic all the high schools and universities were state or municipal institutions. None was Roman Catholic. But several universities had Roman Catholic theological faculties.[242]

Under the German Federal Republic the Roman Catholic periodical press that the Nazis had suppressed enjoyed a rapid revival. Some pre-Hitler reviews reappeared. Diocesan and parish papers, and journals of the various Catholic organizations and of the orders, congregations, and missionary societies together by the mid-1950's had a circulation of over nine million.[243]

AUSTRIA

When, as a result of World War I, the Hapsburg empire was broken into its main components, Austria became a federal republic, predominantly German in language and nationality and with the large majority of its citizens Roman Catholics. As we have seen, in 1938 Hitler annexed it to his Third Reich. It shared in the defeat of Germany in World War II. Then, with a population of about seven millions, it was once more made a federal republic. Like Germany, it was occupied by Britain, France, Russia, and the United States, each of the four having its own zone. In 1955 through a treaty with the four powers Austria regained full autonomy.

---

[240] Fogarty, *op. cit.*, p. 208.
[241] *Ibid.*, pp. 223–226; Guriàn and Fitzsimons, *op. cit.*, pp. 222, 223.
[242] Guriàn and Fitzsimons, *op. cit.*, pp. 224, 225.
[243] *Ibid.*, pp. 225, 226.

The record of the Roman Catholic Church subsequent to 1914 was one of contrasts—as in so many other lands. Soon after the outbreak of World War I Austria experienced a revival of religion and the governor of the Tyrol consecrated that province to the Sacred Heart. However, with defeat and the setting up of the republic, the Socialists came to power. They were said to be largely Jewish and Masonic. In 1919 an elementary school programme was adopted by the government which made participation in religious exercises purely voluntary. Within a few months a government took over in which the Christian Socialists, representing the conservative elements and supported mainly by the peasants, landowners, and bureaucrats and army officers of the old regime, gained control. A Roman Catholic priest, Ignaz Seipel (1876–1932), headed them and in 1922 he became chancellor. Under him an anti-socialist majority ruled the country and saw Austria through the worst of its post-war suffering. Seipel retired in 1929. Under his leadership the Roman Catholic forces rallied and regained morale. Yet the movement away from Christianity continued. In 1922, 9,268 persons formally renounced the Roman Catholic faith. The next year the corresponding figure was 22,888.[244]

The strong man who followed Seipel was Engelbert Dollfuss (1892–1934). He too led the Christian Socialists. He entered public life as the leader of the Farmers' Association (*Bauernbund*). He dreamed of making Austria a corporate state based upon Roman Catholic principles as outlined in Papal encyclicals, especially *Rerum novarum* and *Quadragesimo anno*. He had to face the German nationalists, who were strong among the middle classes in Vienna and who favoured close coöperation or even union with Germany. But his chief opponents were the Social Democrats, who were the majority in Vienna. Civil war broke out in 1934 between the Social Democrats and the Dollfuss regime. Dollfuss was victorious and the Social Democratic Party was declared illegal. The Roman Catholic Church was granted special privileges. Facing a strong movement to annex Austria to Germany, Dollfuss dispensed with meetings of the *Nationalrat* (Parliament). He was assassinated by the Austrian Nazis.

Dollfuss was followed by Kurt von Schuschnigg. Schuschnigg had been educated by the Jesuits, had been a leader of Catholic youth in the Tyrol, and was pro-clerical. He too professed to be guided by *Rerum novarum* and *Quadragesimo anno* and to be seeking to build a Christian corporate state. A union was formed between the Christian Socialists and some other elements to form the *Vaterländische Front*.[245]

With the annexation of Austria by the Third Reich (1938), a step which the majority of the Austrians seem to have favoured, the policies of the Hitler

[244] Premoli, *Contemporary Church History (1900–1925)*, pp. 144–147.
[245] Moody, *op. cit.*, pp. 478–486; Edward Quinn, *The Mission of Austria* (London, The Paladin Press, 1938, pp. vii, 138), pp. 81–112.

regime were extended to that country. During World War II the Roman Catholic Church faced the restrictions with which we have become familiar in Germany.

With the coming of peace, the Roman Catholic Church did not recover as quickly as in Germany. In the first year after the defeat of Germany 400,000 were said to have left the Church. One estimate had it that in 1950 only 25 per cent. of the population were practising Roman Catholics and that, while in the Tyrol and Vorarlberg the masses were still loyal, the currents of the revolutionary age had not yet made their full force felt in these mountain provinces. In that year true Catholic Action was reported to be lacking, Roman Catholic schools received no state subsidies, almost every diocese suffered from a lack of clergy, in the Archdiocese of Vienna alone 1,500 pastorates and chaplaincies were vacant, and the immediate hope appeared to be for assistance by foreign seculars.[246]

World Wars I and II with the interval of National Socialism greatly reduced the vigorous intellectual life which had marked Austria in the latter part of the nineteenth century. Some of the thought which had sprung from it was anti-Christian, or at least indifferent to the faith. Some of the notable Christians were Franz Brentano (1838–1917), a Roman Catholic priest and philosopher, who could not accept Papal infallibility, gave up the priesthood, and for more than two decades was on the philosophical faculty in Vienna; Brentano's pupil Edmund Husserl (1859–1938), whose phenomenology contributed to existentialism and logical positivism; Sigmund Freud (1856–1939), with his wide and profound effect on psychoanalysis; and Friedrich Jodl (1849–1914), a distinguished teacher of ethics. On the Roman Catholic side was the controversial and many-sided Richard Kralik von Meyrswalden. Der Brenner, a review begun in 1910, had liberal, Protestant, and Roman Catholic contributors.[247] In Austria, too, the Roman Catholic social movement had shared in the ferment of thought on economic and social issues. It had been critical of modern capitalism. In spite of opposition from the hierarchy, some Roman Catholics had wished a rapprochement with socialism.[248] Although intellectual activity continued after 1914, the National Socialist period, World War II, and the uncertainty and disputes between the occupying powers which followed that conflict gradually put a damper on it.

The social and political pattern of Austria was inevitably altered by World War II. The Christian trade unions came through the struggle with greatly reduced memberships. They revived, but by the mid-1950's the Socialists outnumbered them five to one. In addition, in 1953 about 11 per cent. of the mem-

---

[246] De Katholieke Encyclopaedie, Vol. XIX, p. 303.
[247] Albert Fuchs, Geistige Strömungen in Österreich 1867–1918 (Vienna, Globus-Verein, 1949, pp. xxxv, 320), passim.
[248] Somerville, Studies in the Catholic Social Movement, p. 74.

bers of the Austrian Manual and Clerical Workers' Union were in the Christian Democratic section. The Christian Democratic Party, predominantly Roman Catholic in membership, was non-confessional and stood against the possible effort of any ecclesiastical body to affect its policies. In that it was reinforced by the official attitude of the Roman Catholic Church, which publicly disavowed any participation in politics and forbade the clergy to hold office.[249]

We have seen that after World War II the Liturgical Movement flourished and that the bishops sought to make it a regular part of parish life.[250] When after the war the bishops met to reconstitute an episcopal conference independent of Germany, they were of the opinion that the Liturgical Movement in its original sense should not be revived but that its purpose should be renewed and that, while having certain centres, it should be considered a regular part of the life of every parish. Provision was made for the production of appropriate literature, both to aid instruction from the pulpit and to supply missals to fill the gap brought by the war.[251]

HUNGARY

Hungary had an even more chequered post-1914 history than Austria. On the collapse of the Hapsburg empire, in October, 1918, Count Michael Károlyi made himself head of a provisional government and soon proclaimed Hungary an independent republic. However, the Croats and Slovaks separated themselves from it and the Rumanians invaded the country. In March, 1919, when it was clear that the victorious Allies intended to back the claims of Jugoslavia, Czechoslovakia, and Rumania, Károlyi resigned and Béla Kun, a Jewish journalist, a convinced Communist, took charge. He attempted to turn back the tide of Slovak and Rumanian invasion, failed, and fled (August, 1919), and Budapest was occupied by the Rumanians throughout the latter part of that year. The conservative Admiral Nicholas Horthy and Count Stephen Bethlen formed a government, the Rumanians withdrew, and a general election (January, 1920) confirmed the authority of the two men. Horthy was made regent, and in April, 1921, Bethlen began a decade as premier and dictator. Horthy, a Protestant, held power with a succession of premiers into World War II. By the Treaty of Trianon (1920), which was part of the post-World War I settlement made by the Allies, Hungary lost Slovakia, Transylvania, Croatia, and the Banat and was left a land-locked predominantly Magyar country of about eight millions. Nominally a constitutional monarchy, under Horthy Hungary was an aristocratic state and the great landed holdings for the most part remained intact. In World War II Hungary took the side of the Axis and in 1940 was

---

249 Fogarty, *op. cit.*, pp. 208, 212, 314, 315.
250 Chapter V.
251 Bogler, *Liturgische Erneuerung in aller Welt*, pp. 48, 49.

192 *The Twentieth Century in Europe*

given a portion of Transylvania. In consequence, after the tide turned against the Axis, Hungary was occupied by the Russians and was loaded with a heavy indemnity. The retreating Germans and their supporters and the Soviet troops stripped the country of much of its movable wealth. In November, 1945, a republican constitution was adopted with Ferenc Nagy as premier. Backed by the Russians, in May, 1947, the Communist minority gained control, and in 1949 Hungary became "a republic of workers and working peasants" with a Communist constitution and a single party (Communist), and came within the Russian orbit. In October, 1956, a revolt broke out and a coalition government was set up under Imre Nagy. Within two weeks Russian troops moved in, abducted Imre Nagy, and instituted a puppet regime. About 200,000 Hungarians fled the country. After careful investigation the United Nations condemned the Russian intervention (September 14, 1957).

As we have noted,[252] the Roman Catholic Church in Hungary entered the twentieth century closely associated with an aristocratic land-owning society. It enrolled about two-thirds of the population. The bishops were selected by the state. The workers in the rising industries were largely under the influence of the anti-clerical Social Democrats. But the Church afforded opportunity to enterprising youth to rise above a lowly social status, and some of its higher posts were filled by men of peasant stock.

On the eve on 1914 an awakening had begun in the Roman Catholic Church. Its outstanding figure was Ottokar Prohászka (1858–1927), who, created Bishop of Székesfehéruár in 1905, was the founder of a revival in Hungarian Catholic literature and the pathfinder in Hungary of Christian Socialism. In 1916 he proposed to an assembly of the large landowners that part of their estates be distributed among veterans and returning emigrants. Before World War II a scholarly priest, Sander Giesswein, following the principles of Prohászka, put forward a programme for winning the alienated workers.[253]

Under the Horthy regime the Roman Catholic Church shared in the aristocratic reaction against the radical government of Béla Kun. It continued to hold hundreds of thousands of acres, and the largest of the landed estates were in the hands of Roman Catholics. But the ratio of Roman Catholics in the lower economic and social strata was much higher than that of the non-Catholic population. In 1919 and again in 1923 the bishops offered a portion of the ecclesiastical holdings to further land reform. Prohászka, who presided at the National Assembly in 1920, distributed among the peasants a large proportion of the land attached to his see. At the outset of the Horthy era the Party of Christian Union was the most powerful and had Prohászka as its head. Among the opposition were the Christian Social and Economic Party, in which Roman Catholic priests

252 Volume I, pp. 444, 445.
253 Moody, *op. cit.*, pp. 675–680.

and laymen were active, and the Christian People's Party, founded by Miklós Griger, a priest. The Christian Party obtained state aid for the erection of churches, the maintenance of church life, and the care of children and the poor. In the inter-war years, although practising Roman Catholics were a minority, a formal adherence to the faith became fashionable and fresh indications of life were seen. The Boy Scout movement developed through Roman Catholic schools, new congregations were founded, one of them the Social Mission Society, begun by Prohászka, intellectual activity among Roman Catholics increased, much of the national literature was permeated with Catholic ideals, through the Jesuits the Catholic Young Men's Peasant Federation (K.A.L.O.T.) and the Catholic Young Women's Peasant Federation (K.A.L.A.S.Z.) came into being, and mass pilgrimages to shrines of the Virgin Mary drew increasing throngs. K.A.L.O.T. opened colleges for peasants and demanded land reform.[254]

During the German occupation which began in March, 1944, to hold Hungary in the war, leaders of the Roman Catholic Church came out actively against Nazi measures. They organized to rescue victims of the anti-Semitic persecution, both those of Jewish faith and Christians of Jewish blood. Protestants cooperated. Many priests and nuns were killed in their efforts to save Jews and still more were sent to prison and concentration camps. In 1944 Joseph Mindszenty, then Bishop of Veszprém, was imprisoned for rescuing Jews and condemning the prolongation of the war.[255] When the Russian armies moved in, the large majority of the village priests stood by their flocks, often at the risk of their lives. Vilmos Apor, the Bishop of Gyor, was killed in his effort to protect women who had taken refuge in his residence.[256]

Communist rule brought a series of crises to the Roman Catholic Church and a marked alteration of status. Land reform through division of the large estates entailed a change in the economic status; the Church lost a large part of the holdings that had constituted its endowment, and each bishopric, chapter, and other ecclesiastical unit was permitted to retain only about 100 acres. The state ceased to collect church taxes but contributed to the support of the clergy. Various Roman Catholic organizations were disbanded, including the K.A.L.O.T. With three exceptions the Roman Catholic periodicals and daily papers were suppressed. One of the three was later proscribed and the other two were restricted. Roman Catholic publishing houses and printing establishments were expropriated. To obtain control of the oncoming generations, the Communists nationalized all but a few of the church's schools. Religious instruction was permitted, but only to those children whose parents requested it of the local soviet. Such requests brought official suspicion on those who made them.

---

[254] *Ibid.*, pp. 685–694; *De Katholieke Encyclopaedie*, Vol. XIII, p. 485.
[255] Moody, *op. cit.*, pp. 691, 697.
[256] *Ibid.*, p. 697.

Catholic Action was put under strict surveillance. In September, 1950, 59 orders and congregations with more than 10,000 members were dissolved and their houses were taken over by the state. Although vocations for the priesthood increased, all but four theological seminaries and the Academy of Theology were closed. Numbers of wayside crosses and chapels were destroyed. Many priests were removed from their parishes.[257]

An incident which attracted world-wide attention was the arrest and condemnation to life imprisonment of Cardinal Mindszenty. Mindszenty was of peasant birth and by sheer ability and devotion had risen rapidly in the hierarchy. In 1944 he was appointed Bishop of Veszprém, the largest diocese west of the Danube. The following year he was promoted to be Archbishop of Esztergom and Prince Primate of Hungary. In 1946 he was created cardinal. He was fearless in denouncing government measures which he deemed injurious to the faith. In 1947 he proclaimed the Year of the Holy Virgin and placed Hungary under her protection. More than four million worshippers were said to have come to her shrines, and that in spite of Communist opposition. Although, led by him, the bishops declared that they accepted democracy, and he had never commented on economic nationalization or condemned land reform, on December 26, 1948, he was arrested. The following year he was convicted of political treason. The revolution of 1956 released him and he took refuge in the American legation. In 1951 Jozsef Grosz, Archbishop of Kalocsamwas, was sentenced to death on similar charges but the penalty was commuted to life imprisonment. Grosz was also released by the uprising of 1956.[258]

In the main, the Hungarian Roman Catholic Church stood firm against the Communist persecution. The state induced a small proportion of the clergy to coöperate with it. It set up the Government Church Bureau to reorganize the Church and placed one of these priests by the side of each bishop and removed many pastors who refused to conform. Yet churches were said to be crowded and the numbers taking Communion to have increased. Moreover, between 1957 and 1960 the government reported that it had not only subsidized the churches to the extent of $3,520,000 but also spent $2,200,000 on church building and restoration and within the past two years erected 44 new churches. Most of this aid was given to the Roman Catholic Church as the largest religious body in the country.[259] However, under the adverse conditions such renewals of life as the

[257] *Ibid.*, pp. 701–719; *The Statesman's Year Book*, 1958, pp. 1111, 1112; Shuster, *In Silence I Speak*, pp. 131–150, 176–213; Gsovski, *Church and State behind the Iron Curtain*, pp. 88–104.

[258] Moody, *op. cit.*, pp. 698–714; *The Statesman's Year Book*, 1958, p. 1111; Halecki, *Eugenio Pacelli, Pope of Peace*, pp. 256–259; Shuster, *op. cit.*, pp. 1–86; Gsovski, *op. cit.*, pp. 106–109. On Papal encyclicals on events in Hungary, i.e., *Luctuosissimi eventus* (October 28, 1956) and *Datis nuperrimus* (November 5, 1956), see *Acta Apostolicae Sedis*, Vol. XLVIII, pp. 741–744, 748, 749.

[259] Moody, *op. cit.*, pp. 717–719; Shuster, *op. cit.*, pp. 150–156. See John XXIII's protest against the reorganization movement in *The New York Times*, May 18, 1959. On church repair and building see *The New York Times*, February 2, 1960.

Liturgical Movement could not make much if any impact. Nor could the Hungarian Church share substantially in the world-wide spread of the faith.

JUGOSLAVIA

Jugoslavia, through which as a result of World War I the South Slavs were united in one state, was divided religiously and by history. Serbia, in the South, was predominantly Orthodox. We are to recur to it later in this volume. In the North, Croatia, with its capital in Zagreb, was prevailingly Roman Catholic.

During World War II Jugoslavia was overrun by the Germans. Croatia was made a puppet state and Serbia was placed under the nominal rule of an Italian prince. During the German and Italian occupation, for political reasons numbers of Orthodox were forcibly converted to Roman Catholicism, in spite of the teaching of the Pope and the bishops that conversion must not come from external pressure but from free conviction.

When, after the war, the Germans and Italians were expelled and Jugoslavia was once more united, this time under the dictatorship of the Communist Tito, an anti-Roman Catholic reaction assumed violent proportions. By the end of 1949 thousands of places of worship had been abandoned and hundreds of Roman Catholic priests had been murdered, were in prison or concentration camps, had sought refuge in exile, or had disappeared. In October, 1946, Aloisius Stepinac (1898–1960), Archbishop of Zagreb and Primate of Croatia, was tried and sentenced to sixteen years of labour on the charge of having collaborated with the invaders. Yet during the occupation Stepinac had saved many Jews and Orthodox from death or concentration camps. He was freed in 1951 and was created cardinal in 1953. But the government refused to permit him to resume his functions and confined him to his native village.[260]

CZECHOSLOVAKIA

One of the fragments of the Hapsburg empire which emerged from World War I as an independent nation was Czechoslovakia. It was made up of the former Bohemia, Moravia, Slovakia, Carpathian Ruthenia, and a part of Silesia. With its somewhat diverse racial composition, it became a republic with Thomas G. Masaryk as its first president.

In 1938 Hitler annexed Sudetenland, predominantly German, and Poland and Hungary seized portions, thus reducing the country by about a third of its area and population. In 1939, subsequent to a reorganization of what remained of Czechoslovakia into a federal union of Czekia (Bohemia and Moravia), Slovakia, and Carpatho-Ukrainia, Hitler sent in troops which took possession of the country. Czekia became a German protectorate, Slovakia, with a priest,

[260] Halecki, *op. cit.*, pp. 252–255; *De Katholieke Encyclopaedie*, Vol. XXII, p. 472; *The New York Times*, February 11, 1960.

Joseph Tiso, as its head, became a puppet state, and Carpatho-Ukrainia was given to Hungary. After the defeat of Hitler, Russia took possession of Carpathia-Ruthenia, and the remainder of the former Czechoslovakia regained its independence with its pre-war constitution. However, in 1948 the Communists seized control and a constitution of their making was adopted. It set up what was called the People's Democratic Republic.

From the standpoint of the Roman Catholic Church, when in 1918 it became independent Czechoslovakia presented a varied picture. Bohemia and Moravia were predominantly Roman Catholic, the result of the missions which after the Thirty Years' War and under Hapsburg rule all but eliminated the flourishing Protestantism. Through much of the nineteenth century and especially in the later decades, among intellectuals and workingmen the tide was running against the Roman Catholic Church.[261] One reason was a nationalistic ferment against a church imposed by the Hapsburgs and staffed in many cases by bishops who were foreigners. Slovakia, over two-thirds Slovak by race, was more slowly penetrated by the currents of the revolutionary age and was more loyally Roman Catholic. Carpatho-Ukrainia, on the extreme east, was peopled mainly by Ruthenians, who were predominantly peasants and were Uniates by religion.

Under these circumstances the response to Christianity which the coming of independence precipitated was also diverse. In Bohemia and Moravia, with their Czech majorities, the pre-1914 trends issued in movements both away from Rome and, in reverse, towards the Roman Catholic Church. The movements away from Rome included the growth of Protestantism, of which we are to hear more in a later chapter, a practical repudiation of Christianity under the spell of Marxist socialism, mainly among the workers in the modern industries, and the emergence of a Catholic Church independent of the Papacy. Political independence was quickly followed by violence against Roman Catholic symbols. Statues of the Virgin were pulled down and destroyed and crosses were removed from many classrooms. The iconoclastic wave included desecration of statues of the saints, sacred pictures, and monuments in cemeteries. About three hundred churches were expropriated and scores of shrines were pillaged. Many priests were attacked.[262] Although Masaryk chose as the national motto "Christ not Caesar," he had renounced the Roman Catholic faith in which he had been reared.

As part of the nationalistic movement, in 1919–1920 the Czechoslovak Church came into being. In 1919 a number of Roman Catholic priests associated themselves in the *Jednota katolického duchovenstva* (Association of Catholic Clerics). They were led by Xavier Dvorák and Bohuslav Zahradnik. They asked Rome for the abolition of patronage, the election of bishops by the clergy, the erection

---

[261] Volume I, pp. 446, 447.
[262] Nemec, *Church and State in Czechoslovakia*, pp. 123, 124; Premoli, *op. cit.*, pp. 238, 239.

of a patriarchate for Czechoslovakia, adequate financial support for the priests, a liturgy in the vernacular, the reform of the breviary, a democratic constitution for the episcopal courts, permission to wear a beard and dispense with ecclesiastical garb, and freedom to marry. Benedict XV refused to accede to the demands. A large proportion of the petitioning priests acquiesced, but a minority persisted and were excommunicated. The recalcitrants led the Czechoslovak Church. It adopted a Unitarian theology. In September, 1920, the government gave it legal status and assisted it financially. The adherents took possession of several churches, and a number of parishes were established, most of them in Bohemia. At one time, in 1921, the adherents of the Czechoslovak Church were said to number 1,388,000. An attempt to unite with the Serbian Orthodox Church did not succeed. The movement gradually spent its force and in 1930 the membership was reported to have shrunk to 853,000.[263]

The emergence of the Czechoslovak Church was not the only feature of the new order in Czechoslovakia which troubled the Roman Catholic Church. The constitution of the state, adopted in 1920, guaranteed liberty of conscience and religious belief. When, in 1920, a census was taken which included the statement of religious affiliation, several hundred thousand, most of them in Bohemia and workers in the industries, declared they had no religion. In 1930 only 75 per cent. of the population were registered as Roman Catholics as contrasted with an estimated 95 per cent. in 1914. Against the protest of the Vatican, the anniversary was officially celebrated of the burning of John Hus, whom the Roman Catholic Church regarded as an arch heretic and the Czechs esteemed as a national hero.[264]

Within a few years the Roman Catholic Church adjusted itself to the new situation and staged a partial recovery. In February, 1928, a *modus vivendi* was entered into by the government and the Vatican which, among other provisions, said that no part of Czechoslovakia was to depend on a bishop whose see was outside the boundaries of the country and that no diocese in the country should extend beyond those boundaries; that orders and congregations in Czechoslovakia should not be dependent upon superiors in other countries, and that if dependence was upon a supervisory office of the entire order or organization, the local representative should be a citizen of Czechoslovakia; that all bishops and other ordinaries should be Czechoslovakian citizens and that before naming them Rome would obtain assurance from the government that no political reason existed against the choice; and that all members of the hierarchy would swear allegiance to the state. Regular diplomatic relations with the Holy See were established.[265]

[263] Nemec, *op. cit.*, pp. 124–130; Premoli, *op. cit.*, pp. 239, 240; Siegmund-Schultze, *Die Kirchen der Tschechoslowakei*, pp. 175–185.
[264] Nemec, *op. cit.*, pp. 130–136.
[265] *Ibid.*, pp. 137, 138.

Under the Republic Roman Catholics were active in politics. Before 1914 Catholic workers' organizations and Catholic political parties had been created. After 1918 Jan Srámek, a priest who had earlier formed the Christian Social Party in Moravia and still earlier had helped to bring into being Christian workers' trade unions, became prominent in the government and was the major figure in the People's Party, the chief political organ of the Roman Catholics. Another priest, Andrie Hlinka, was outstanding in the Slovak People's Party, which stood for the national interest of Slovakia. Still another of the clergy, Bohumil Stăsek, sought to bring the Czech and the Slovak People's parties together and, wishing to implement *Quadragesimo anno,* endeavoured to have the Roman Catholics adopt a new social and economic action programme. He was in parliament and after the Nazi occupation of his native land was sent by the invaders to the concentration camp at Dachau and emerged with broken health.[266] In addition to political action, non-political Roman Catholic organizations multiplied, especially among students and other young people.[267]

With World War II the Roman Catholic Church in Czechoslovakia entered upon a prolonged time of troubles. The German occupation brought persecution. The archbishops and bishops stood staunchly by the Czechoslovak Republic. Srámek became the prime minister of the government-in-exile in London. Shrines which were centres of pilgrimage attracted thousands. There preachers exhorted to loyalty to the nation. Orel, a Roman Catholic athletic organization, staged celebrations which were attended by throngs. The Nazi authorities retaliated by forbidding pilgrimages and sending the officers of Orel to concentration camps. The publication of Roman Catholic journals was stopped and some of their editors were imprisoned. Nearly all Roman Catholic lay associations were disbanded. Many scores of the clergy were arrested and 73 were said to have died in jail. The total number of priests sent to concentration camps was reported to have been 260, and 58 died there. Priests executed totalled eight, and seven died under torture. One of the effects of the Nazi measures was to increase the loyalty of many of the population to the Roman Catholic Church as a stalwart bulwark against the Germans.[268]

The defeat of the Germans, followed as it was in 1948 after a brief respite by the Communist regime, had as a sequel a persecution which was more prolonged than that at the hands of the Nazis. Persecution did not start immediately and, although Communist influence was strong, in the interval between 1945 and 1948 the Roman Catholic Church made something of a recovery. Yet because of Communist pressures the government took action limiting the Church.[269]

[266] Moody, *Church and Society,* pp. 643–648.
[267] Nemec, *op. cit.,* p. 131.
[268] *Ibid.,* pp. 151–163, 190–194; Moody, *op. cit.,* pp. 648, 649.
[269] Nemec, *op. cit.,* pp. 197–220; Moody, *op. cit.,* pp. 653, 654.

With the coming of full Communist rule persecution became as intense as in Nazi days.[270] Although the new constitution guaranteed freedom of conscience, the claims of the Roman Catholic Church and of the totalitarian state under frankly atheistic Communist rule could not but clash. Pleading canon law, the bishops forbade the clergy to serve in any capacity in political or state organizations—although the government had asked the priests to join the Communist Party and had said that their refusal to serve on the Central Action Committee would be regarded as an unfriendly act. All Roman Catholic publications were gradually suppressed on the alleged ground of a shortage of paper. Devotional works, especially those having to do with the Eucharist and the Virgin Mary, were classified as "immoral." Text-books, particularly the ones on history, were revised in such a way as to eliminate references to the constructive achievements of the Church. Almost all Roman Catholic schools were suppressed, and in the few permitted, teachers and pupils were required to take Marxist courses. Roman Catholic organizations were disbanded, including Mojzes, made up of Catholic students in Slovakia. The Roman Catholic Church was deprived of its landed property.

The state increasingly took measures to make the Church subordinate to its purposes. In 1949 a Bureau for Church Affairs was instituted under which were put relations of the state with all the churches—Roman Catholic, Protestant, and Orthodox. In an attempt to infiltrate the Roman Catholic Church the government gave an annual subsidy to the Church to help in the support of priests and offered to increase the incomes of clergy who coöperated with the state. The government also sponsored a Catholic People's Party and endeavoured to set up what it called Catholic Action. Although Archbishop Beran of Prague wrote to the clergy in the name of the episcopate that collaboration with any who restricted the liberty of the Church meant excommunication and that participation in the Communist-inspired Catholic Action would entail ecclesiastical sanctions, some of the clergy went along with the regime. In June, 1949, a congress of "patriotic" priests and laity convened in Prague and pledged its loyalty to the People's Democratic Republic. Rome added its condemnation of the schismatic Catholic Action. In 1950 diplomatic relations with the Vatican were broken off. The seizure of monasteries soon followed on the ground that they were centres of the espionage and subversive activities of the Vatican. Some of the inmates were placed in what in effect were concentration camps. Attempts were made by the state to control the appointments of clergy to parishes and to supervise their activities. All theological seminaries were abolished and in their stead

---

[270] The ensuing paragraphs are taken from an extended account of the persecution in Nemec, *op. cit.*, pp. 177 ff.; Ludvik Nemec, *Episcopal and Vatican Reaction to the Persecution of the Catholic Church in Czechoslovakia* (Washington, D.C., The Catholic University of America Press, 1953, pp. ix, 94), *passim;* Gsovski, *op. cit.*, pp. 20–61; Zubek, *The Church of Silence in Slovakia*, pp. 25 ff.; Guriàn and Fitzsimons, *The Catholic Church in World Affairs*, pp. 197, 198.

theological faculties controlled by the state were set up in Prague (primarily for Bohemia and Moravia) and in Bratislava (mainly for Slovakia). At one time seven bishops were under arrest and five others under house arrest.

The number of "patriotic priests" who coöperated with the state increased fairly rapidly and included all university professors of theology in Prague and Bratislava and some others in high positions. They recognized the Pope's authority in faith and morals but repudiated his administrative authority. The state appointed from among them men to administer the affairs of the Roman Catholic Church and arrested or placed under police guard in their residences bishops who refused to comply with the government's directions.

By the early 1950's the Roman Catholic Church in Czechoslovakia had a somewhat ambiguous position. It could not be called schismatic or an independent national church, for it was still under bishops who had been appointed by the Holy See. But it had in it many priests who were regarded by the state as "patriotic" and who had been given their posts by the quite secular state Bureau of Church Affairs. From the standpoint of Rome such priests had been validly ordained but were now excommunicated.

At best the relations of the Roman Catholic Church and the state did not satisfy either. The government sought to deprive the Church of its leaders. The clergymen Joseph Tiso, who had been President of the Slovak Republic, was tried and hanged (April 18, 1947). Some of the bishops and other high ecclesiastical leaders were condemned for "conspiracy" against the state. Prayer in the schools was discontinued and crosses were removed from the walls of classrooms. Instruction in religion was made elective and placed outside regular school hours. Teachers and students were enrolled in Communist youth organizations and cultural activities. Interned religious were subjected to "reeducation" in Communism. Yet, to the annoyance of the state, the Roman Catholic Church persisted. About three-quarters of the population counted themselves as members. To take the place of imprisoned priests and interned religious, the bishops trained laymen to give instruction in the catechism. But, as in Hungary, the Liturgical Movement could make little or no headway and no missionaries were sent to expand the frontiers of the Church.

As we are to find true of the larger bodies of Uniates in other areas under Communist rule, the Uniate minorities in Czechoslovakia were induced "voluntarily" to move into the Orthodox Church which their ancestors had left centuries earlier, also under political constraint.

POLAND

In Poland the Roman Catholic Church was profoundly affected by the political changes of the twentieth century. Overwhelmingly Roman Catholic, during the political disunity which had been forced on them in the eighteenth and nineteenth centuries the Poles had come to regard that faith as associated with their nationalistic aspirations. Political unity and independence were regained as a result of World War I and a republican form of government was adopted. Within the first few weeks of World War II Poland was overrun by the Germans and the Russians. It was then divided between Germany and Russia. The Nazis annexed outright half of their portion and made the other half into a "protectorate," with Cracow as its capital. In characteristic Nazi fashion, thousands of Jews and many Poles were killed by "gas chambers" and firing squads. Both Russians and Germans subjected their respective portions to ruthless exploitation. Poles who escaped from the invaders set up a government-in-exile, first in Rumania and then in England. After the break between Hitler and Stalin and the German invasion of Russia and after the Russians had driven the Germans out of Poland, with the assent of Great Britain and the United States the U.S.S.R. entered into a treaty with a provisional Polish government (not the one in exile in England). Russia was given about 70,000 square miles of what had been the eastern portion of Poland since World War I and in return permitted Poland to take possession of about 39,000 square miles of the eastern portion of Germany.

Although Great Britain and the United States had given their consent to the recognition of the provisional Polish government on the condition that free and unfettered elections be held as a prelude to a permanent regime, in the elections held in presumed fulfilment of that promise in January, 1947, a Communist minority, reinforced by secret police and terrorist methods, seized control. In the constitution of 1952 of the Polish People's Republic the Russian pattern was followed.

In 1956 mounting restlessness found expression in workers' and students' riots. As a result, anti-Stalinist nationalist and "liberal" elements became dominant in the Communist Party and Wladyslaw Gomulka rose to power. A Communist, Gomulka had been imprisoned for some years for "Titoist variations" from Moscow orthodoxy. In the 1957 elections the Communists held slightly more than half of the seats in the *Sejm*, the governing assembly of the country, with Peasants next, a few Democrats, and a substantial minority of non-party members, including several Roman Catholic writers and social workers. Following the 1956 revolution, a greater degree of freedom of speech and of worship existed than in any Communist country and reforms in education were introduced. Outwardly friendy relations with Russia were maintained.

Under these striking changes in the political complexion of Poland, the Roman Catholic Church went through a succession of vicissitudes. In the Poland which emerged after World War I the overwhelming majority of the population were Roman Catholics. A considerable minority, but mostly in the eastern regions ceded to Russia in 1945, were Orthodox, and much smaller minorities were Mariavites[271] and Protestants. Of the Roman Catholics, according to the census of 1921, 17,368,352 were of the Latin rite and 3,032,636 were Uniates who dated their connexion with Rome from 1596. In addition, Protestants numbered 1,014,577, and 2,849,020 were Jews.[272]

The years between World Wars I and II were, on the whole, favourable to the Roman Catholic Church. Socialists and Freemasons were prominent in the early days. Missionaries from the United States from the Polish National Catholic Church attempted to build up a National Catholic Church which would be independent of Rome. Roman Catholics themselves were divided on what policies to adopt under the new order. Some wished the state to have the appointment of bishops and in other ways to control the Church. Others advocated the separation of Church and state. Many maintained that ecclesiastical property confiscated by Germany, Russia, and Austria should be returned to the Church.[273] Yet the constitution adopted in 1921, while guaranteeing freedom of conscience and religion, declared that "the Roman Catholic creed, being the creed of the majority of the people, shall have a preponderating authority in the state among other religions which shall enjoy equal treatment."[274] In 1918, in response to a request from Poland, the Pope sent an apostolic visitor to Poland and Lithuania. He was none other than Achille Ratti, later to be Pope Pius XI. In 1925 a concordat was signed. Among other features it provided that bishops and archbishops should be appointed by the Pope, but not before the President of Poland had an opportunity to express objections of a political nature, and that prelates must take an oath of loyalty to the state and require their clergy to respect the government. It also regulated religious education in schools and universities, the property rights of the Church and clergy, patronage, and the exercise by the state of criminal jurisdiction over the clergy. It granted full freedom to Roman Catholics to organize societies, associations, and Catholic Action. The concordat required religious instruction in primary and secondary schools by teachers appointed by the state but with the condition that any teacher to whom the hierarchy objected would be suspended. Where children of a minority group numbered as many as twelve, instruction could be given in their faith at the expense of the state if the parents so desired.[275]

Efforts were made to provide better pastoral care for the faithful and to further Roman Catholic higher education. At the time of independence the portion of the country formerly held by Russia was suffering from a lack of clergy. Regulars were sent in to help fill the gap. To ensure a continuing flow of clergy, theological faculties were maintained in five universities. In addition, in 1922

271 Volume I, p. 287.
272 Guilday, The Catholic Church in Contemporary Europe 1919-1931, p. 202.
273 Premoli, Contemporary Church History (1900-1925), pp. 227, 228.
274 Guilday, op. cit., pp. 200, 201.
275 Acta Apostolicae Sedis, Vol. XVII, pp. 273-287.

the Catholic University of Lublin was opened, partly to train clergy and partly as a centre of Roman Catholic intellectual life.[276]

In several other ways the years between the two world wars seemed to be a springtime for the Roman Catholic Church. A number of associations of the faithful sprang up. The Catholic League flourished. A seminary was founded at Lublin (1923) to prepare missionaries to Russia. A national unit of the Missionary Union of the Clergy was inaugurated and grew rapidly. The second president of the Republic, Stanislas Wojciechowski, although elected by the parties of the left, was a practising Roman Catholic and outspoken in his advocacy of the faith.[277] The Catholic University of Lublin became a radiating centre of vigorous thought. Its faculty dealt not only with theology but also with social problems. Stephan Wyszynski (1901———), later primate of Poland, paid much attention to them. A Catholic school of social science arose in Poznan. August Hlond (1881–1948), a Salesian of Don Bosco, cardinal and primate of Poland, formed a council to deal with current social issues.[278]

Yet natonalistic Poland was in turn plagued by the nationalistic ambitions of minorities within its borders. Thus in Galicia the Ruthenian Uniates, numbering about 3,000,000, fearing absorption into the Latin rite of the Polish majority, tended to move towards the Orthodoxy of their Ukrainian neighbours and staged riots.[279]

During the Hitler era the German-occupied portions of Poland were the scene of a severe persecution of the Roman Catholic Church. Numbers of the clergy were imprisoned, others were deported to Germany, still others were confined to concentration camps, and not a few were shot outright. Hlond himself was interned. Hundreds of thousands of the laity were deported. Crucifixes were removed from the schools and no religious instruction was permitted. Monasteries and houses of nuns were expropriated or closed. Various organizations for Catholic Action and associations and societies for charitable work were dissolved, the school of social science at Poznan was abolished, and church periodicals were suppressed. Church funds were confiscated, many church buildings were shut, church services frequently lapsed, few of the dying could be given extreme unction, and confessions were heard and Communion was administered clandestinely, if at all. To keep the faith alive, many infants were baptized by their parents.[280]

In the face of the German measures, the Roman Catholic faith survived.

[276] Premoli, *op. cit.*, p. 229.

[277] *Ibid.*, pp. 229, 230.

[278] Moody, *Church and Society*, p. 599.

[279] Premoli, *op. cit.*, pp. 209, 210.

[280] *The Persecution of the Catholic Church in German-Occupied Poland, Reports Presented by H. E. Cardinal Hlond, ·Primate of Poland, to Pope Pius XII, Vatican Broadcasts and Other Reliable Evidence* (New York, Longmans, Green and Co., 1941, pp. x, 123).

Underground resistance was carried on within Poland itself, in addition to what was done by Poles in exile. Even though it provoked the Germans to still sterner measures, opposition was maintained. In it the Polish Christian Labour Party and the Christian Democratic Party collaborated with other groups in the underground government.[281]

For a time after the expulsion of the Germans recovery was begun and a working arrangement was entered into with the new regime which held some promise of a better day. In July, 1945, Hlond returned from his German internment as head of the administration of the Roman Catholic Church. He consecrated new bishops, re-opened theological seminaries, revived the Roman Catholic press, and had the pleasure of seeing the Catholic University of Lublin once more a fact. The transfer of millions of Poles from the portion of the country in the East ceded to Russia to that in the West from which the Germans were being deported confronted Hlond with the major challenge of providing adequate pastoral care for the newly acquired region. He and his clergy made heroic efforts to meet it.[282]

However, difficulties were not long in developing with the Communist-controlled Polish People's Republic. They continued to mount. Very early (September 12, 1945) the government unilaterally abrogated the concordat of 1925. Instead it entered into an accord with the Polish hierarchy (February 16, 1950) whereby the latter agreed to teach respect for the law and temporal authority, oppose the anti-Polish trends of the German clergy in the "regained territories," offer no resistance to the state's extension of the system of collective farms, and comply with the requirements of the state with the provision that in faith, morality, and ecclesiastical jurisdiction the supreme authority in the Church was the Pope. On its side, the state promised, among other things, to recognize the right of the Church to teach religion in the schools according to curricula determined jointly by the school authorities and representatives of the hierarchy, to permit public religious ceremonies and pilgrimages, to give freedom to monastic orders and congregations, and to allow, but always subject to law, Catholic societies, charitable and catechetical activities, and Catholic publications. This accord seemed to some of the faithful to be a compromise but was welcomed by others.[283] Moreover, the constitution of the Polish People's Republic enacted in 1952, while not recognizing the Roman Catholic creed as that of the majority of the people as did its predecessor of 1921, and while separating the Church from the state, guaranteed freedom of religion and conscience.[284]

---

[281] Moody, *op. cit.*, p. 623.

[282] Gsovski, *Church and State behind the Iron Curtain*, pp. 175, 176, 208–214.

[283] *Ibid.*, pp. 197–208; Tobias, *Communist-Christian Encounter in East Europe*, pp. 399, 410–413; Szuldrzynski, *The Pattern of Life in Poland. XVI. The Situation of the Catholic Church*, pp. 8, 16–24; Naurois, *Dieu Contre Dieu?*, pp. 156 ff.

[284] Gsovski, *op. cit.*, pp. 176, 177; Naurois, *op. cit.*, p. 199.

But very soon the state began violating its accord and restricting the activities of the Roman Catholic Church. Early in 1950 it assumed control of *Caritas,* the organization through which the Church, with help from abroad, chiefly the United States, had administered very extensive relief to the sufferers from the war.[285] That same year the government nationalized the church lands and created a fund from which it proposed to support the clergy, to maintain and rebuild churches, and to carry out charitable and social welfare services.[286] Complaints were voiced that contrary to the accord the state was liquidating the church schools, was removing religion from the public schools, and was strangling the Catholic press.[287] The Society of Children's Friends (*Towarzystwo Przyjaciol Dzieci*—T.P.D.), favoured by the government, operated schools of various grades which sought to inculcate in youth loyalty to the state, Marxist ideology, and atheism.[288] Theological faculties in the universities were abolished and in their place two theological academies were set up, one for Protestantism and the Polish Catholic Church, and the other for the Roman Catholic Church. Although public worship was permitted, political meetings on Sundays at which attendance was compulsory, Sunday excursions, and work brigades kept many away from church services.[289] In 1953 the government convicted and punished a number of civilians and clergy on the charge that they were carrying on espionage for the Vatican and the United States. It also decreed (February 9, 1953) that no appointment to an ecclesiastical office should be made without its approval and that all appointees must take an oath of loyalty to the state.[290] The animosity to the Vatican arose from the latter's well-known opposition to Communism, its failure to recognize the Polish People's Republic, and its continued relations with the Polish government-in-exile in London.

The government made determined efforts to induce the clergy and laity to break with Rome and to create a Polish Catholic Church independent of the Vatican. It succeeded in enrolling about 1,700 priests out of a total of about 11,000 of the clergy as "patriotic." They were brought into the Commission of Priests Fighting for Liberty and Independence (Z.B.O.W.I.D.). What was called the Main Commission of Intellectuals and Catholic Activists (*Glowna Komisja Intelektualistow i Dzialaczy Katolickich*) was begun in 1950. It brought together clergy and laity, sponsored the peace campaign which was part of the world-wide Communist propaganda, and sought the collaboration of Roman Catholics with the government. Another organization, the Catholic Social Club (*Klub Katolicko-Spoleczy*—K.K.S.), had six parliamentary deputies and endeavoured

[285] Gsovski, *op. cit.,* pp. 190–197; Szuldrzynski, *op. cit.,* pp. 13–16; Naurois, *op. cit.,* pp. 173, 174; Tobias, *op. cit.,* pp. 387, 398.
[286] Gsovski, *op. cit.,* pp. 194–197.
[287] *Ibid.,* pp. 204, 205; Naurois, *op. cit.,* pp. 199, 200.
[288] R. F. Starr in *The Catholic Historical Review,* Vol. XLII, p. 307.
[289] A. S. Cardwell in *The Christian Century,* Vol. LXXIII, pp. 232, 233 (February 22, 1956).
[290] Gsovski, *op. cit.,* pp. 214–224; Naurois, *op. cit.,* pp. 201–205.

to reconcile the dialectical materialism of Communism with Christianity.[291]

In September, 1953, the government took a further step in its campaign towards bringing the Roman Catholic Church to conformity with its wishes. It arrested Cardinal Wyszynski, had him confined to a monastery, and forbade him to exercise the functions of his office. The hierarchy, presumably at the state's request, chose the Bishop of Lodz as their chairman and a few months later issued a pastoral letter which, while outwardly conforming to Papal statements, actually supported the programme of the state in condemning atomic warfare and urging international peace and voluntary disarmament.[292]

The "liberalizing" of the Communist programme which followed the riots of 1956 had as one of its features the easing of restrictions on the Roman Catholic Church. Cardinal Wyszynski was restored to his diocese; the government retreated from its demand for veto power over the church appointments, accepted the nominations made by the Vatican in 1951 for the five dioceses in the former German territory incorporated into Poland after World War II, and promised freedom of religious instruction for those who desired it. In return the Roman Catholic Church accepted the Communist regime.[293]

How far the 1956 relaxation of the restrictions on the Roman Catholic Church in Poland was due to the uprising in Hungary in that year is not entirely clear, but a natural presumption is that the synchronization was more than accidental. Pius XII in his encyclical *Laetamur admodum* (November 1, 1956) greeted with joy as "the rising of a dawn of peace based on justice" (attributing it to the prayers of many, especially of boys and girls), the release of Cardinals Wyszynski and Mindszenty, and their readmission to their posts.[294]

Although the uprising in Poland was not met by a Russian-administered blood bath as was that in Hungary, by 1959 the Roman Catholic Church was beginning to face a renewal of strictures on its freedom.[295]

LITHUANIA

The post-1914 history of Lithuania, like that of so many other European countries, was varied and troubled. Geographicaly and politically but not racially, Lithuania was closely connected with Poland. For about four centuries before 1795 it was united with that country. In 1795, in the third partition of Poland, it was annexed by Russia.

In the nineteenth century the Lithuanians shared with the Poles in some of the uprisings against Russian rule. As a result of the revolutionary year of 1905 for a time Lithuania gained partial autonomy. During World War I the Ger-

[291] Starr, *op. cit.*, Vol. XLII, pp. 297–306; Naurois, *op. cit.*, p. 210.
[292] Starr, *op. cit.*, Vol. XLII, pp. 320, 321; Naurois, *op. cit.*, pp. 223–233, 248.
[293] *The New York Times*, December 1 and 8, 1956; *The Statesman's Year Book, 1958*, p. 1339.
[294] *Acta Apostolicae Sedis*, Vol. XLVIII, pp. 745–748.
[295] *The New York Times*, November 2, 1959.

mans occupied the country, and the destruction and requisitions were heavy. As a result of that war independence was gained (1918) but for some years friction continued with neighbouring governments, especially Poland. In 1939 the Russians moved in, and in 1940 Lithuania became one of the republics of the U.S.S.R. The German invasion (1941–1944) during World War II was accompanied by much devastation. The German collapse was followed by reincorporation into the U.S.S.R., again as one of the latter's constitutent units.

The Lithuanians, said to number about 2,400,000 in 1950, were overwhelmingly Roman Catholic. In the brief period of independence Roman Catholics were prominent in the government and the Roman Catholic Church made significant progress in seizing the opportunity brought by the new order. In the assembly of 1922 which gave the country a constitution over half the delegates were Christian Democrats. In 1927 a concordat was signed with the Holy See.[296] On the whole it was favourable to the Church. Rome was to choose the bishops but was to give the president the privilege of registering objections on political grounds and the bishops were to take an oath of loyalty to the Republic of Lithuania. The state was to subsidize ecclesiastical seminaries. The teaching of religion was compulsory in the public schools, the religious authorities were to set up the programme and choose the texts, and the bishops could withdraw from any instructor the permission to teach. The clergy had as one of their functions the registration of births, baptisms, marriages, and burials. In 1926 the Diocese of Samogita was made the Archdiocese of Kaunos (Kovno), and four suffragan sees, all created in that year, were placed under it. The constitution of 1928 was favourable to the Church. That of 1938 was somewhat less so. In 1940 four seminaries were preparing men for the priesthood and the University of Kaunos had a Roman Catholic theological faculty.[297]

Obviously the second German occupation, the incorporation of Lithuania into the U.S.S.R., and the renewal of Russian Communist mastery which were phases of World War II brought reverses to the Roman Catholic Church in Lithuania.

RUMANIA

Rumania, emerging from the last traces of Turkish rule and becoming fully independent in 1878, managed to retain that status in the first half of the twentieth century, but with varying fortunes and shifting boundaries. For siding with the Allies in World War I it was rewarded with territories on its northern and eastern borders. In 1938 the democratic constitution of 1923 was abolished and Rumania became totalitarian. In 1940 part of the country (Bessarabia and

---

[296] *Acta Apostolicae Sedis*, Vol. XIX, pp. 425 ff.; Prunskis, *Comparative Law, Ecclesiastical and Civil, in the Lithuanian Concordat, passim.*
[297] *De Katholieke Encyclopaedie*, Vol. XVI, p. 642; Prunskis, *op. cit.*, p. 134.

Northern Bukovina) was seized by Russia, and another portion, in Transylvania, was transferred by Russia and Germany to Hungary. Joining in the German attack on Russia in 1941, Rumania was further humiliated. Russian armies invaded the country and late in 1947 its king abdicated and the "People's Republic" was set up. The Communists came into control and in 1952 a constitution modelled on that of Russia was adopted.

Religiously, a large majority of the population were Orthodox, but on the eve of World War II a substantial minority were Roman Catholics divided between the Latin rite and Uniates. The Roman Catholics of the Latin rite were mostly Hungarians, Poles, and Germans. In 1927 a concordat, ratified in 1929, was concluded with Rome. In 1930 an additional bishopric was created for the Uniates. But with the coming to power of the Communists it was cancelled (1948) and in 1950 the Papal nuncio was expelled. Under Communist rule about 700 Roman Catholic priests of both rites were arrested and deported, many priests and laymen were condemned to forced labour, and monasteries were dissolved. In 1948 the Uniates were compelled to join the Orthodox Church from which their ancestors had come.[298] Their five bishops were arrested. Four of the six bishoprics of the Latin rite were suppressed and later the two remaining bishops were arrested for refusing to accept the Church Statute. In 1951 an effort was made by the government, in part successful, to bring into being a national Catholic Church administratively independent of Rome.[299]

RUSSIA

In Russia the course of the Roman Catholic Church had never been easy. In the pre-1914 Empire Roman Catholics, as we have seen, were predominant in Poland and Lithuania. They were also minorities in Latvia and Estonia. A few were found in other parts of the realm and for them a hierarchy existed. An archbishop, with his seat at Mohilev, on the lower Dniester on the southwestern border, had jurisdiction over a vast region which stretched across European Russia and Siberia except for the territory included under the Vicariate Apostolic of Vladivostok.[300]

The coming of Communist rule in 1917 brought a succession of crises. The persecution launched by the Communists, of which we are to hear more in a later chapter, included Roman Catholics among its victims. Uniates of the Byzantine rite were more severely dealt with than those of the Latin rite. All foreign priests were compelled to leave the country. In 1923 fifteen priests and prelates were condemned for resisting the government's confiscation of church

---

[298] De Katholieke Encyclopaedie, Vol. XXI, pp. 95, 96; Acta Apostolicae Sedis, Vol. XXI, pp. 441–454.

[299] Gurián and Fitzsimons, The Catholic Church in World Affairs, p. 197.

[300] Ammann, Abriss der ostslawischen Kirchengeschichte, p. 629; Graham, Vatican Diplomacy, pp. 353, 363.

property. Some of the episcopal sees fell vacant. In spite of the fact that it had supported an extensive programme of famine relief, the Papacy was denounced by the Russian radio as the chief enemy of the U.S.S.R.,[301] partly because the Pope was outspoken against Communism and the persecutions in Russia, notably in encyclicals in 1930 and 1937.[302] Pius XI founded a Russian college in Rome and encouraged the Slavonic liturgy. By 1950 the college had trained a number of priests who ministered to the Russian refugees in other lands.[303] When, in World War II, the Pope attempted to give help to the prisoners of war held by Russia he was refused and declared to be pro-Fascist.[304] At the time of the occupation of Eastern Poland by the Russians (1939) Metropolitan Szeptckyj of the Ruthenian Uniates remained at his post and in 1940 convened a diocesan synod. He continued to hold on when the Germans came and sought to win the dissidents to Rome. He died in 1944 after the Russians had reëntered.[305] During the German occupation of White Russia and Volhynia an attempt was made to resume jurisdiction over the Uniates in that region. Jesuits, Redemptorists, and Capuchins came to serve them, conforming to their rite. The hope was cherished, illusory as it proved, that here a door would open for reaching more of Russia.[306] In 1950 the resurgent Russians were suppressing the Uniate church in Galicia and Podcarpathia and had taken over a monastery of Uniate Basilians and given it to another Christian body.[307]

In the mid-1950's, in addition to the Roman Catholics in Poland and Lithuania, some of that faith survived in Latvia, and worship according to the Latin rite continued in Odessa and Leningrad. However, the Roman Catholic minority in Estonia had been liquidated.[308] Moreover, a chapel and a priest were permitted in Moscow, but purely to serve members of the foreign legations and embassies. One of the incumbents also took the opportunity to minister clandestinely to Russians.[309] In at least one centre Jesuits were studying Russian, and in other ways, including the Russian College in Rome, priests were preparing to revive their church in Russia if and when the opportunity should come.

[301] Ammann, *op. cit.*, p. 663; Lama, *Papst und Kurie*, pp. 368–375; *De Katholieke Encyclopaedie*, Vol. XXII, pp. 165, 166; Graham, *op. cit.*, pp. 355, 356, 364; McCullagh, *The Bolshevik Persecution of Christianity*, pp. 99–281.

[302] Ammann, *op. cit.*, p. 629; *Acta Apostolicae Sedis*, Vol. XXII, pp. 153, 154, Vol. XXIX, pp. 65–139. On persecutions in Russia, see *First Victims of Communism. White Book on the Religious Persecution in the Ukraine, translated from the Italian* (Rome, Analecta O.S.B.M., 1953, pp. 115), by Ukrainian Catholic priests resident in Rome. See also *Through God's Underground. The Adventures of "Father George" among People under Soviet Rule as Told by Gretta Palmer* (London, Hollis & Carter, 1949, pp. ix, 226).

[303] Ammann, *op. cit.*, p. 631; *De Katholieke Encyclopaedie*, Vol. XXII, pp. 165, 166.

[304] Ammann, *op. cit.*, p. 629.

[305] *Ibid.*, pp. 631, 632.

[306] *Ibid.*, p. 631.

[307] *Ibid.*, p. 667.

[308] *De Katholieke Encyclopaedie*, Vol. XXII, p. 166.

[309] George Bissonnette, *Moscow Was My Parish* (New York, McGraw-Hill Book Co., 1956, pp. 272), *passim*.

SCANDINAVIA

In the overwhelmingly Lutheran Northern countries (Denmark, Iceland, Norway, Sweden, and Finland) the Roman Catholic Church had taken the occasion of the relaxation of restrictions on dissent in the nineteenth century to win small minorities. In 1914 it was adding to their numbers and had organized them under vicariates apostolic and prefectures apostolic.[310] After 1914 Roman Catholics continued to increase, partly among the intelligentsia. In Norway, for example, the distinguished novelist Sigrid Undset (1882–1949) became a convert (1925). Numerous schools were conducted in which Catholic instruction was given.[311] The Liturgical Movement made headway as a means of nourishing the faith of the often widely scattered adherents.[312] Denmark contained by far the largest number of Roman Catholics of any of the Northern countries. At mid-twentieth century Norway had 4,900,[313] Sweden about 18,000 (of whom only about 6,000 were of Swedish stock and the others were immigrants from Poland and Lithuania),[314] and Finland 2,100, served by 22 priests, of whom only one was Finnish.[315] In 1953 the vicariates apostolic of Denmark, Norway, and Sweden were raised to the Dioceses of Copenhagen, Oslo, and Stockholm.

IRELAND

During the period which followed 1914 Ireland presented a scene of civil strife, acute in the early years and waning as time went on. The long struggle over home rule reached an acute stage soon after 1914. In 1912 the House of Commons passed a home rule bill which applied to all the island, including the predominantly Protestant Ulster. The House of Lords rejected it. The Ulsterites organized an army and were determined to set up a separate government if the bill became law. In September, 1914, a few weeks after the outbreak of World War I, the bill was passed but with another act which provided that it would not come into force until after the coming of peace. More extreme Irish nationalists staged a revolt in 1916 which proved abortive. In 1919–1921 more violence followed, chiefly in the form of guerilla warfare. The British Government attempted to cut the Gordian knot by granting (1921) what amounted to dominion status to the Irish Free State, embracing twenty-six counties and with its capital at Dublin, and semi-dominion status to six counties and two county boroughs in Northern Ireland with the centre in Belfast. Unrest continued, including clashes between moderates and extremists in the Irish Free State, insistence in the South that Ulster be included in the Irish Free State, and the demand

310 Volume I, p. 450.

311 Premoli, *Contemporary Church History (1900–1925)*, pp. 205, 206.

312 Bogler, *Liturgische Erneuerung in aller Welt*, pp. 101–103.

313 *De Katholieke Encyclopaedie*, Vol. XVIII, p. 840.

314 *Ibid.*, Vol. XXV, p. 506.

315 *Ecumenical Press Service*, March 6, 1959.

for more independence. By stages the Irish Free State became (1935) the Republic of Ireland (Éire) and severed its ties with Great Britain: an act of Parliament in 1948 which came into force in 1949 severed the last constitutional bond with the British crown. However, the connexion between Northern Ireland and the United Kingdom was continued, largely because of the insistence of the predominantly Protestant population of Ulster. Yet extreme nationalists persisted in agitating for the incorporation of Ulster in Éire.

Religiously the two portions of Ireland were strikingly but not entirely different. In 1946 Éire, with a population of about 3,000,000, had 2,786,033 Roman Catholics, 124,829 in the Church of Ireland, 23,870 Presbyterians, 8,355 Methodists, and 12,020 others.[316] Northern Ireland, with a population (1946) of 1,370,921, had 471,460 Roman Catholics, 410,215 Presbyterians, 353,245 in the Church of Ireland, 66,639 Methodists, and 69,362 others.[317] Éire was, accordingly, almost solidly Roman Catholic, while Northern Ireland, with not quite half as many people and the more prosperous part of the island, was approximately two-thirds Protestant and a third Roman Catholic. The North of Ireland Protestants were firm on maintaining their independence from Éire.

The religious loyalties of each the two uneven divisions of Ireland had back of them a long history.[318] They were associated with competing cultural and racial inheritances. To the Irish Roman Catholics their church was identified with their national aspirations, a symbol and bond of their long struggle, fraught with a rankling sense of oppression by the English overlords. The Ulsterites, on the other hand, feared discriminatory measures if the overwhelming and ardently Roman Catholic Éire were to gain the upper hand. The Presbyterians, mainly Scottish by ancestry, had long memories of oppressive legislation of their forebears by the former English and Anglican government. Now the Anglicans made common interest with them.

In Ireland the Roman Catholic Church was spared the impact of some of the challenging forces of the revolutionary age. In the Republic of Ireland industrialization did not take as large strides as in some other parts of Western Christendom. Nor were the intellectual currents that characterized the age as potent as in many other lands. The island was not subjected to the invasions that troubled many other countries. Civil strife, while prolonged, was not as acute as in Spain. Socialism was not as prominent as in numbers of other places and Communism was only a slight threat.

The Republic of Ireland prided itself on its religious tolerance and its Roman Catholic character. Its constitution acknowledged the Roman Catholic Church as the "guardian of the faith professed by the great majority of the citizens,"

[316] *The Statesman's Year Book,* 1958, p. 1155.
[317] *Ibid.,* p. 120.
[318] Volume I, pp. 451–454.

but it also guaranteed freedom of conscience and explicitly recognized the (Anglican) Church of Ireland, the Presbyterian Church, the Methodist Church, and the Society of Friends. The first president, Douglas Hyde, was a Protestant. In 1926 more Protestants were employed by the state and in the learned secular professions they were more numerous than their proportionate strength in the country would have warranted.[319]

The vigour of the Roman Catholic Church in the Republic of Ireland was displayed in a number of ways. Retreats multiplied, especially among the workers in Dublin. The third Order of Franciscans, confraternities encouraged by the Dominicans, and sodalities of the Virgin flourished. Roman Catholic publications had an enormous output. Catholic Action had many expressions. The Catholic Truth Society not only produced and distributed a large body of popular doctrinal and apologetic literature but also maintained an orphanage, a class for deaf mutes, sailors' clubs, savings banks, and restaurants for the poor. In 1923 the Rescue Society of Ireland was inaugurated to combat efforts to win Roman Catholics to Protestantism. The League of the Kingship of Christ sought to inculcate Catholic principles in public life. By 1930 the Pioneer Total Abstinence Society, founded in 1899 to resist the rampant alcoholism, enrolled over 300,000.[320] The Legion of Mary, begun in 1921 in Dublin by a layman, Frank Duff, primarily for the laity, with an organization modelled on the ancient Roman military legion, sought "the sanctification of its members by prayer and active coöperation in Mary's and the Church's work of crushing the head of the serpent and advancing the reign of Christ." It attempted seemingly impossible tasks. Among its achievements in its first decade were bringing into existence 130 branches in Éire and other countries, a hostel in Dublin to rehabilitate "down and out men," and two other enterprises, also in Dublin, for derelict women.[321]

Roman Catholic power in Éire was shown in the insistence of the hierarchy on control of aspects of life which they believed properly fell within the domain of the Church. Thus they effectively resisted a plan which in seeking to lower the rate of infant mortality would have created a state programme for health service to women and children. They did so on the ground that it would infringe upon the rights of parents and suggested that instead of a nationalized medical service the government provide maternity hospitals and other institutional facilities and give financial aid to large families. Consistently with the Roman Catholic policy in other lands, the hierarchy opposed teaching methods of birth control. The bishops, appointed by Rome, stood against nationalistic movements to give priests and laity a voice in the administration of the Church and to

---

[319] Guilday, The Catholic Church in Contemporary Europe 1919–1931, pp. 154, 158; Blanshard, The Irish and Catholic Power, pp. 50–55.
[320] Guilday, op. cit., pp. 161–163.
[321] Ibid., pp. 163, 164.

reduce the authority of the episcopate over the priests. Roman Catholic influence was responsible for legislation, enforced by a board, which established a state censorship of literature and excluded from Éire books and publications deemed injurious to morals. Censorship was also exercised over the radio and cinema. The Roman Catholic Church succeeded in discouraging public non-denominational schools and came close to approximating the ideals set forth by Pius XI for the education of youth. With a few exceptions, primary and secondary education was in ecclesiastical hands, and government funds contributed to the support of both Roman Catholic and Protestant schools. Marriage, in accord with Roman Catholic belief, was reserved to the Church and divorce was frowned upon.[322]

The Roman Catholic Church in Ireland produced many devout souls. Such a one was Matt Talbot (1856–1925). Born in a humble home of deeply religious parents, in his teens he became an alcoholic. Then, in his late twenties, he took the pledge of total abstinence, kept it, and in his thirties joined the Third Order of St. Francis. He was a faithful workman, lived voluntarily in poverty, remained unmarried, was generous with his wages to those in need, and was indefatigable in attending mass and in prayer. His admirers proposed his name for canonization.[323]

Another saintly life was that of John Sullivan (1861–1933). Born in a prominent and wealthy family to a Protestant father and a Roman Catholic mother, Sullivan was baptized a Protestant and for a time was a barrister. He was received into the Roman Catholic Church in 1896, joined the Jesuits in 1900, became a priest, for a time taught boys, but was better known as an ascetic, a man of prayer, and a spiritual director. Many cures were attributed to his prayers during his lifetime and to his intercession after his death.[324]

Very different from the other two, more a churchman than a saint, was John Healy (1841–1918), who died as Archbishop of Tuam, Metropolitan of the West of Ireland. A man of robust physique, with marked gifts as an author and orator, an ardent controversialist who once entered the lists with Newman, in his early manhood Healy taught theology in St. Patrick's College, Maynooth. In 1884 he became Bishop of Macra and Coadjutor Bishop of Clonfert, and in 1903 he was appointed Archbishop of Tuam. Greatly interested in education, he stood for more opportunities for university training for his Irish co-religionists. He also was deeply versed in the early history of Christianity in his island and wrote on it.[325]

[322] Blanshard, *op. cit.,* pp. 48–167.

[323] Frei Henrique Golland Trindale, *Matt Talbot, Worker and Penitent* (Paterson, N.J., St. Anthony Guild Press, 1953, pp. ix, 126), *passim.*

[324] Fergal McGrath, *Father John Sullivan, S.J.* (New York, Longmans, Green and Co., 1941, pp. vii, 285), *passim.*

[325] P. J. Joyce, *John Healy, Archbishop of Tuam* (Dublin, M. H. Gill and Son, 1931, pp. xvi, 330), *passim.*

A striking feature of the Roman Catholic Church in Ireland was its contribution to the spread of the faith. Much of this was by emigration—chiefly to Great Britain, the United States, Canada, Australia, New Zealand, and South Africa. To a large extent the emigrants and their children remained loyal. More significant was the degree to which they supplied the clergy for their church in the lands to which they went, not only to their fellows of the Irish *Diaspora* but also to those of other national backgrounds. In the preceding volume we saw this in the United States, Canada, Australia, and somewhat less in New Zealand and South Africa. It was said in 1931 that nearly 3,000 Irish priests and over 5,000 Irish sisters were serving abroad in English-speaking lands. The Irish were increasingly represented in Roman Catholic missions outside the Occident. That same year an incomplete list gave as labouring among non-Christian peoples 385 priests, 259 teaching brothers, and 1,063 sisters. They were in several places in Africa, the Philippines, and India. In 1958 there were 1,149 priests in Africa alone. In 1916 the Maynooth Mission to China was founded.[326]

ENGLAND

We have seen[327] that in England in the nineteenth century the Roman Catholic Church was recruited from three sources—descendants of the families which had held to the faith through all the vicissitudes since the Protestant Reformation, conversions (mainly from Anglicans and stimulated by the Anglo-Catholic movement), and immigration, chiefly from Ireland. At the outset of the century Roman Catholics had been handicapped by discriminatory legislation and by widespread popular prejudice. But by 1914 the legislation had been removed and the prejudice, while not extinct, had waned. Yet, as elsewhere in the Occident, the faith faced the challenges of the revolutionary age. The challenges were not so much open antagonism as indifference, widespread scepticism arising from the intellectual currents of the day, and new patterns of life which made difficult the observance of religious practices and instruction in the faith.

In spite of impediments arising from the revolutionary age, the Roman Catholic Church in England came to the mid-1950's stronger than in 1914. The improvement was both numerical and in quality of life.

The numerical growth was through the natural increase of the Roman Catholic population, conversions, and immigration. In the 1950's conversions were said to number from 11,000 to 12,000 a year and were partly through intermarriage, partly through youthful enthusiasm in university days, and partly in late youth. They included a fairly steady but small trickle from the clergy of the Church of England:[328] in the 1950's from twenty to thirty Anglican priests a

[326] Guilday, *op. cit.*, pp. 160, 161; J. T. Ellis to the author, July, 1959.
[327] Volume I, pp. 454–458.
[328] Mathew, *Catholicism in England*, pp. 258, 259.

year were received. To aid them and others to whom the adjustment brought financial difficulties the Converts' Aid Society was supported. By the mid-1950's the Roman Catholic Church was the second largest denomination, next to the Church of England. It was estimated to comprise about one-tenth of the population of England. In Sunday attendance it surpassed both the Anglicans and the Nonconforming Protestants.[329] Another estimate gives the number of Roman Catholics in England and Wales in 1949 as 2,650,000, or about 6 per cent. of the population, but this was said to be an increase of 275,000 in ten years as against a growth of less than 550,000 in the entire population in the decade. At mid-century the Roman Catholics were beginning to move into the suburbs and not to be as closely confined as formerly to the heart of the urban areas.[330] Still another set of figures said that about 30 per cent. of the baptized Roman Catholics were non-practising and that about 3,000,000 could be counted as practising.[331]

A noticeable leakage was seen in the Irish immigration. Coming from Ireland where church attendance was part of the normal way of life and plunged into great cities where the swirling currents of the revolutionary age made difficult conformity to the inherited customs, many lost their faith.[332] One estimate had in that within a year of their arrival between 60 and 80 per cent. of the immigrants ceased to make their Communions.[333]

Evidence of the identification of the Irish immigration with the industrial areas and as low-income workers is the fact that politically after 1918 the Irish voted almost solidly with the Labour Party. Earlier they had sided with the Liberals, but with the rapid growth of the Labour Party they transferred their allegiance.[334]

From Ireland came many of the priests. Trained at Maynooth to be pastors, few of them were raised to the episcopate.[335] This was in striking contrast with the overseas record of clergy of Irish stock. There a very large proportion of the hierarchy were either from Ireland or had an Irish ancestry. The Roman Catholic Church in England by no means depended entirely on Ireland for its clergy. More and more of its priests were recruited and educated in England. Nor during the first half of the twentieth century did it suffer from a dearth of clergy as much as did the Church of England. Between 1939 and 1949 the number of priests rose from about 5,330 to about 6,200, or at almost twice the rate of increase of the total body of the faithful.[336]

Various orders and congregations contributed to the life of the Roman Cath-

[329] Peter Rowley in *The Catholic World*, April, 1959, pp. 32–38.
[330] Beck, *The English Catholics, 1850–1950*, p. 436.
[331] E. I. Watkin, *Roman Catholicism in England from the Reformation to 1950* (London, Oxford University Press, 1957, pp. xi, 244), p. 229.
[332] Peter Rowley, *op. cit.*, pp. 32–38.
[333] J. V. Kelleher in *Foreign Affairs*, Vol. XXXV, p. 493.
[334] Beck, *op. cit.*, p. 288.
[335] *Ibid.*, pp. 289, 290.
[336] *Ibid.*, p. 436.

olic Church in England. Most of the great orders and congregations of men had been reëstablished or established in England before 1914 and had been growing before that year. They included the Benedictines, the Franciscans, the Dominicans, the Cistercians, the Carmelites, the Oratorians, the Rosminians, the Passionists, the Redemptorists, and the Salesians of Don Bosco. Numbers of women's congregations had either been introduced into England or had originated there before 1914. Most of them enjoyed a significant growth after that year. In 1950 England had 70 orders and congregations of men with about 2,360 priests and over 140 congregations of women in 1,075 houses.[337]

The orders and congregations produced remarkable individuals who in one way and another made major contributions to the life of the Roman Catholic community. Several exerted an influence beyond the borders of their church. To single out some for special mention seems almost invidious. Yet mention can be made of the Dominican Bede Jarrett (1881–1934). Born in England, the son of a member of the Indian Civil Service, he was baptized as Cyril Beaufort Jarrett by Bertrand Wilberforce, the Dominican grandson of William Wilberforce, and was educated in schools of his faith. At seventeen he joined the Dominicans and took the name of Bede. He graduated from Oxford in 1907 with a brilliant "first" in history and completed his university studies at Louvain. As contemplative, scholar, preacher, and author he had a large share in the growth of his order in England in the twentieth century. He had experience in a London parish. In 1916 he was made provincial of the English branch of his order. In that office he extended the work of the Dominicans in England, Wales, and Scotland, had the joy of seeing them reëstablished in a house at Oxford after the lapse of nearly four centuries, and promoted missions abroad. By his sermons and his books he left his impress on many who were not of his order or even of his church.[338] Another of the Order of Preachers, Joseph Vincent Mary McNabb (1868–1943), was born in Ireland, had his higher theological training in Louvain, served as prior of more than one house in England, taught theology, wrote many books, some of them on the devotional life, and was notable as a preacher and lecturer.[339]

John Chapman (1865–1933), son of an Anglican archdeacon and planning to take orders in the Church of England, became a Roman Catholic in 1890 and was ultimately fourth Abbot of Downside. Downside was a Benedictine abbey which had been founded in 1605 in Douai for English monks, and there had long maintained a school. Driven out by the French Revolution, the monks had taken refuge in England. There, not far from Bath, they had a foundation which

---

[337] *Ibid.*, pp. 442–474.

[338] Kenneth Wykeham-George and Gervase Mathew, *Bede Jarrett of the Order of Preachers* (London, Blackfriars Publications, 1952, pp. viii, 168), *passim*.

[339] Walter Gumbley, *Obituary Notices of the English Dominicans 1555 to 1952* (London, Blackfriars Publications, 1955, pp. xii, 216), pp. 173–175.

conducted a large school for boys from which came bishops, archbishops, and other leaders, lay and clerical. Chapman's *Spiritual Letters,* published after his death, were evidence of his deep religious faith.[340]

English Roman Catholics had an increasing place in education. In the nineteenth century they had already served extensively in schools on the elementary, secondary, and higher levels and for both sexes. Men's orders and congregations, secular priests, and congregations of women participated. After 1914 many new schools were founded and the laity had a mounting share in administration and teaching.

During much of the nineteenth century Rome had frowned on having the youth of the church go to Oxford and Cambridge because of the supposed undermining of their faith. Several of the bishops, led by Cardinal Manning, had joined in the distrust. Some thought was given to the creation of a Catholic university. In the 1890's and especially in the twentieth century the policy changed. The ban against Oxford and Cambridge was lifted by Rome in 1896 and houses were founded at both Cambridge and Oxford by orders and congregations. Many Roman Catholics attended the ancient foundations and the University of London and still more enrolled in the new "provincial" universities. For the latter chaplains were appointed to give their time exclusively to students. In the twentieth century, under the legislation of which we are to hear more in a later chapter, grants from the government were made to denominational schools but were insufficient to meet the rising costs.[341]

English Roman Catholics had an increasing role in various aspects of the life of the nation. There were Roman Catholics in both houses of Parliament and in several leading posts in the diplomatic service. They had a hand in the periodical press. *The Tablet,* founded in 1840, continued into the twentieth century. For many years it was under ecclesiastical control and for a time was the mouthpiece of the head of the hierarchy. In 1936 it was sold to laymen and, while it remained loyal to the faith, the scope of its articles and reviews broadened. A large number of periodicals were maintained for special purposes, such as missions and the clergy. *The Catholic Herald,* begun in 1884 to further social reform as an organ of Catholic industrial democracy, in 1934 passed to new ownership and became a weekly which dealt with world news from the Roman Catholic standpoint. The Catholic Truth Society, dating from 1884, continued into the twentieth century, with its primary objects missionary, apologetic, and propagandist.[342]

In the field of literature the twentieth century added to such nineteenth-century Roman Catholics as Coventry Patmore (1823–1896) and Francis Thomp-

[340] *The Spiritual Letters of Dom John Chapman, O.S.B., Fourth Abbot of Downside,* edited by Roger Hudleston (New York, Sheed and Ward, 1935, pp. xiv, 330).
[341] Beck, *op. cit.,* pp. 291–409.
[342] *Ibid.,* pp. 482–514.

son (1859-1907), G. K. Chesterton (1874-1936), who was admitted to the Roman Catholic Church in 1922; the genial, tempestuous humorist, essayist, and historian Hilaire Belloc (1870-1953), French by birth but Oxford by training and naturalized in 1902, who served in Parliament and stood for social reform; Maurice Baring (1874-1945), converted in 1909; Ronald Knox (1888-1957), brilliant and charming son of an Anglican bishop, first an Anglican and then a Roman Catholic priest, a master of light verse and author of a felicitous translation of the Bible; the historian and essayist Christopher Dawson (1889——), converted after his early youth; and the novelists Evelyn Waugh (1903——), received into the Roman Catholic Church in 1930, and Graham Greene (1904——). The list could be greatly lengthened.[343]

True to their long-standing tradition, Roman Catholics made major contributions to twentieth-century England in care of the sick, the poor, underprivileged youth, and the aged. They began in the nineteenth century as soon as the anti-Roman Catholic legislation was relaxed. They continued after 1914. The twentieth-century emphasis on Catholic Action augmented their efforts.[344]

At the head of its hierarchy the Roman Catholic Church in England had a succession of able men as Archbishops of Westminster who maintained the high standard set by their predecessors of the nineteenth century. Francis Bourne (1861-1934) held the post from 1903 until his death. Born in Clapham, famous for the Anglican "sect" of that name, the son of a convert and reared in the faith, in his middle teens he decided to enter the priesthood. He had part of his theological training at St. Sulpice, in Paris, and part in Louvain. Ordained priest in 1884, after brief experience in parishes, in 1889 he was appointed rector of the diocesan seminary in Southwark. In 1896 he was created Titular Bishop of Epiphania and named Coadjutor to the Bishop of Southwark with the right of succession. The next year the latter died and Bourne became Bishop of Southwark. Six years later (1903), on the death of Herbert Vaughan, he was translated to Westminster. In 1911 he was made cardinal. As head of the English hierarchy Bourne stood staunchly for the rights of his church as he understood them. This was true in the many controversies over the legislation, proposed or enacted, for education and the place of religion in the schools. Presumably here lay the reason why he was never invited to the Malines Conversations between Mercier and the Anglo-Catholics, an omission which led to his dignified protest to the Belgian cardinal. He was an able administrator and under him his church continued its progress.[345]

Bourne's successor, Arthur Hinsley (1868-1943), was of a different tempera-

---

[343] *Ibid.*, pp. 515-558. For a life of Knox see Evelyn Waugh, *Monsignor Ronald Knox* (Boston, Little, Brown and Co., 1960, pp. 358).

[344] Beck, *op. cit.*, pp. 559-584.

[345] Ernest Oldmeadow, *Francis Cardinal Bourne* (London, Burns Oates & Washbourne, 2 vols., 1940-1944), *passim*.

ment and from a contrasting background. Born in Yorkshire and educated in England and in the English College in Rome, for years he was a teacher and a parish priest in England. From 1917 to 1928 he was Rector of the English College in Rome and regarded his position as an opportunity to train secular priests to work for the conversion of England. In 1927 he was appointed Visitor Apostolic to Africa and in 1930 was created Titular Archbishop of Sardis and Apostolic Delegate to Africa. In that post he travelled indefatigably and did much to promote the rapid growth of his church south of the Sahara. He was Canon of St. Peter's in Rome in 1934-1935. Then, much to his dismay and against his protests, the Pope commanded him to become Archbishop of Westminster. He was given the red hat in 1937. He took up his duties almost a stranger to his clergy, fellow bishops, and English conditions. Serving as he did during most of World War II and the bombings of London, he faced unusual problems as well as those normal to his office. In contrast to Bourne, who by nature was reserved and maintained the dignity of a great prelate, Hinsley took time at the outset to visit his clergy informally and individually to become acquainted with them. What by many was regarded as his most distinct achievement was "the Sword of the Spirit," a movement which he launched and in which he was the leading figure. He inaugurated it in August, 1940, as "a campaign of prayer, study, and action" with the "fundamental aim" of restoring in Europe "a Christian basis for both public and private life, by a return to the principles of international order and Christian freedom." While making clear his loyalty to his church as, in his conviction, the one divinely appointed centre of Christian unity, and holding firmly to the five peace points of Pius XII, he sought the coöperation of Christians who were not of his communion and appeared on the public platform with Anglicans, notably the Archbishop of Canterbury and the Bishop of Chichester, and with Nonconformist leaders. Yet he also let it be known that the movement was Roman Catholic, was under episcopal control, and that full membership was open only to Roman Catholics. But he hoped that similar movements would arise in other churches.[346]

Hinsley was followed by Bernard W. Griffin (1899-1956). A native of Birmingham, during the thirteen years (1943-1956) that he was Archbishop of Westminster Griffin resumed much of the tradition of Bourne and did not reach out to other communions as Hinsley had done.

Griffin, in turn, was succeeded by William Godfrey (1889——). Born in Liverpool, educated in Rome, like Hinsley he had been Rector of the English College in that city (1930-1938). But, Apostolic Delegate to England from 1934 to 1954, he came to the English primacy with a better knowledge of the country

[346] John C. Heenan, *Cardinal Hinsley* (London, Burns Oates & Washbourne, 1944, pp. viii, 242), *passim*.

than had Hinsley. As chargé d'affaires in Poland in 1943 he also had first-hand experience of conditions on the troubled Continent.

WALES

We have noted[347] that in Wales the Roman Catholic Church was represented in the nineteenth century by a relatively few families who had held to the faith since pre-Reformation days and by immigrants from Ireland. In 1916 Wales was made into an ecclesiastical province with an archbishop and two dioceses. That step was taken in recognition of Welsh nationalism and of the fact that Wales was a distinct country. The first archbishop was English, but the second was Welsh. Wales was predominantly Protestant. In 1935 it had about 103,311 Roman Catholics—approximately 4 per cent. of the population. The number had grown in the past few decades, with the opening of new parishes and the erection of churches. Some of the increase was through conversions. Orders and congregations of men and women were represented and progress was made in recruiting and training a Welsh clergy.[348]

SCOTLAND

Like Wales, Scotland's Roman Catholics in the twentieth century were in part members of families which had been of that communion since before the Reformation, but more were immigrants from Ireland and their descendants. The Irish were mostly in Glasgow, the second largest city on the island of Great Britain. In 1947 Roman Catholics twenty years old or more were estimated to number 472,600, or about 14.55 per cent. of the adult population and nearly a quarter of the total church membership of the country. They were mostly in the industrialized Clyde Valley. They had about doubled and the number of priests had trebled since 1893. The growth had been so marked that in 1948 the Diocese of Glasgow was created an archdiocese and was given two suffragan sees. In 1947 the Archdiocese of Glasgow had over 100,000 in Catholic schools, subsidized by the state on an equal basis with other schools. A variety of social services and philanthropic activities were carried on, following the customary pattern in countries where the Roman Catholic Church was given freedom to minister to human need. In general they were only for members of that church.[349]

SUMMARY

As we look back over this long chapter certain general trends become apparent. Features which characterized the revolutionary age in the nineteenth cen-

[347] Volume I, p. 458.
[348] Donald Attwater, *The Catholic Church in Modern Wales. A Record of the Past Century* (London, Burns Oates & Washbourne, 1935), pp. xiii, 235), pp. 129 ff.
[349] Highet, *The Churches in Scotland To-day*, pp. 35–37, 74, 75, 229.

tury and which constituted a challenge to Christianity continued. Some were augmented. Industrialization mounted, and with it the cities. Through the industrial society more and more millions were in an environment which at times was hostile to Christianity and nearly always made difficult the maintenance of Christian worship and morals for those caught in its toils. A second trend was the continuation of intellectual currents, reinforced by new ones, which threatened to undermine the faith. A third trend was the threat of war, which broke out in two world struggles that centred in Western Europe—the historic Christendom—and which in the mid-1950's cast a shadow of a possible third holocaust. The second of the wars had been more destructive than the first, and the third, if it came, promised to be more disastrous than either of its predecessors. In addition to the general wars a number of civil wars wrought widespread devastation in several countries. A fourth trend was the heightened menace of socialism, at best religiously neutral and often anti-Christian, and of atheistic Communism. The latter had captured control over more than half the area and approximately half the population of Europe and was a force with which to reckon in some other countries. A fifth trend was the waning hold of the Roman Catholic Church on large elements in its former constituencies. This was most marked in the lands mastered by the Communists, but it was apparent in several others. Only in the Netherlands, Great Britain, and Ireland did the Roman Catholics grow after 1914 in proportion to the total population. In some countries the percentage of practising Roman Catholics seems to have declined.

Yet, by contrast, as a sixth trend, the Roman Catholic Church was more closely knit and the great body of the practising faithful, clergy and especially laity, were more actively loyal than in the nineteenth century and possibly than in any century since the early days in the Roman Empire. In a great variety of organizations, many of them designed to meet the special problems brought by the revolutionary age, and an increasing proportion of them more lay than clerical, practising Roman Catholics were rising to meet constructively the challenges of the day, to win back the de-Christianized, to permeate all society, and to spread the faith throughout the world.

The chief centres of this vitality were, in general, where they had been for many centuries. They were in Latin Europe and on its fringes. From Latin Europe had issued most of the great theological thinkers, the large majority of the orders and congregations, the chief currents of fresh vitality in worship both of the community and of the individual, and the overwhelming proportion of the missionaries who had carried the faith to other lands. That continued to be true. In this area the Liturgical Movement arose, the main Eucharistic Congresses were held, most of the fresh theological thinking developed, and the Roman Catholic expressions of Christian democracy were organized. Here, too, Catholic Action originated and had its largest expansion. The outstanding losses were in Central Europe, where Christianity was fighting for its life against Communism. Fewer significant movements had sprung from the Roman Catholic Church in that region across the centuries than in Latin Europe. Yet even here at the mid-twentieth century the Roman Catholic Church was far from moribund. It was presenting a stubborn resistance to an aggressive and resourceful enemy which was in the saddle politically and was seeking to obliterate it.

CHAPTER VIII

The Share of European Roman Catholics in the World-Wide Spread of the Faith

I N SPITE of the many challenges of the revolutionary age in their home countries and of the fact that all these countries with the exception of Switzerland had been involved as active participants in World War I or World War II, or both, after 1914 the Roman Catholics of Western Europe continued to supply by far the majority of the missionaries for the world-wide spread of their faith. That record was the more remarkable in view of the occupation by foreign armies during part of the period of the soil of the countries from which came most of the missionaries and the extensive destruction wrought by the invaders. Ireland and Spain had managed to keep aloof from deep involvement in both wars, but both had been troubled by civil strife and Spain had been badly racked by it. Yet it was said that in 1957, of the 10,812 priests who were serving as foreign missionaries, 2,210 were from France, 2,123 from Belgium, 1,082 from Ireland, 1,053 from the Netherlands, 627 from Italy, 441 from Germany, 356 from Great Britain, 321 from Switzerland, and 175 from Spain. Only 206 were from the United States and 366 from Canada.[1] Another set of figures has some discrepancies from the preceding but seems to show a marked increase in the two decades between 1933 and 1953.[2]

From either list it must be apparent that the bulk of personnel to assist the growth of the Roman Catholic Church outside Christendom was from Western Europe and from approximately, although not precisely, the areas in which we have noted the major activity in Christian democracy, Catholic Action, the Liturgical Movement, Christian labour and farmers' organizations, and other evidences of vigorous life.

As to the financial undergirding, comprehensive figures were lacking. It was clear that by the 1950's the Society for the Propagation of the Faith obtained more than two-thirds of its income from the United States, but while

[1] *Worldmission Fides Service*, Vol. IX, p. 6.
[2] Allen, *A Seminary Survey*, p. 296.

From	Priests Serving Abroad 1933	Priests Serving Abroad 1953	Increase (Per Cent.)	Decrease (Per Cent.)
France	3,373	3,505	4	
Belgium	1,106	2,289	107	
The Netherlands	941	2,289	137	
Italy	1,251	1,382	10	
Ireland	314	1,001	219	
Germany	954	847		11
U.S.A.	373	829	122	
Spain	860	779		9
Canada	285	709	149	
England	241	560	124	
Switzerland	159	362	128	

this was distributed among the several agencies sending missionaries, so far as estimates could be obtained it accounted for only about a fifth of the total expenditure. The other four-fifths was raised by the various orders and congregations which engaged in missions outside Christendom. Presumably a large part of the four-fifths was contributed in Europe.

Here was a striking contrast with Protestant missions outside Christendom. As we are to see later, both in this and the next volume, after World War I and especially after World War II an increasing majority of Protestant foreign missionaries and of the funds which supported them were from the United States of America.

As we have noted,[3] under Pius XI and Pius XII Rome was very active in promoting the world-wide spread of the faith, partly owing to the Popes'[4] initiative and partly through extremely able leadership in the Congregation for the Propagation of the Faith. In 1922 the headquarters of the Society for the Propagation of the Faith were moved from France to Rome, so that the Pope could directly supervise the organization which was raising more money for foreign missions than any other in the Roman Catholic Church.[5] In 1950, as a vivid demonstration of the leadership of Rome, an International Missionary Congress was held in the Eternal City.[6]

As we are to recount in the next volume, owing partly to policies adopted in Rome, increasingly the staffs of the Roman Catholic Church outside the Occident—whether priests, lay brothers, or sisters—were recruited from the

[3] Chapter III.

[4] On Pius XII see Celso Costantini, *S.S. Pio XII Grande Pontefice Missionario* (Rome, 1956, no publisher given, pp. 47), *passim*.

[5] Éduard E. F. Descamps, *Histoire Générale Comparée des Missions* (Paris, Librairie Plon, 1932, pp. viii, 760), p. 518; Delacroix, *Histoire Universelle des Missions Catholiques*, Vol. III, pp. 137, 138.

[6] Delacroix, *op. cit.*, p. 154.

faithful in those lands and supervision was entrusted to bishops from the peoples to whom they ministered. At the mid-twentieth-century mark the Roman Catholic Church was more firmly rooted in more countries and peoples than ever before.

The growth of the indigenous as well as the European staffs of the Roman Catholic Church outside Christendom can be vividly summarized in a few figures. In territories dependent on the Congregation for the Propagation of the Faith the secular and regular priests numbered 18,028 in 1933 and 23,961 in 1949. In 1947, of approximately 16,000 priests in Asia about 11,000 were Asiatics, and of about 12,000 in Africa roughly 2,000 were Africans. At mid-century, of about 17,000 sisters in Asia only 4,000 were from the Occident (not included were 2,000 foreign and 4,000 native sisters in China in 1950). In Africa 4,500 of the 14,000 sisters were Africans. Of the 8,000 brothers in the regions under the Propaganda 3,700 were sprung from the soil.[7]

7 *Ibid.*, pp. 405 ff.

CHAPTER IX

Roman Catholic Efforts for Christian Unity: The European Phase

A FEATURE of the record of the Roman Catholic Church in the twentieth century was the variety of efforts to achieve Christian unity.

THE IDEAL AND THE PRE-TWENTIETH-CENTURY RECORD OF CHRISTIAN UNITY

The history of Christianity through the centuries has been punctuated by a striking contrast between ideals and realities. On the one hand Christians have had before them the "new commandment" of Christ, remembered as given to the disciples at the Last Supper: that they love one another as He had loved them. The record goes on to state that after they had left the Upper Room Christ prayed that all who believed in Him might be one, as the Father was in Him and He in the Father. Christians have been both inspired and rebuked by that command and that prayer and again and again have sought to attain to them. Yet from the very first generation of the Church Christians have been divided, often bitterly. Indeed, divisions multiplied and were never as numerous as in the twentieth century. The very attempts to bring about unity frequently, indeed usually, were provocative of division. The same thing was true of the first of the Ecumenical Councils, at Nicaea, in the fourth century, and of a large proportion of those to which Roman Catholics gave that designation. Moved by the dream of making the ideal actual, the Roman Catholic Church brought into one great ecclesiastical structure a larger proportion of those who bore the Christian name than did any other of the branches of Christianity. But the Roman Catholic Church did not succeed in drawing all of its children into a unity of love. The fashion in which its adherents lined up on opposite sides of the world wars of the twentieth century was tragic evidence of that failure. The chronic rivalries and jealousies of the great orders and congregations of "religious"—those who presumably were fully committed to the faith—provided additional proof of the inadequacy of that approach to Christian unity.

Although thoughtful Roman Catholics were sadly aware that their church had brought to its members only outward conformity in doctrine and communion, they continued to strive to attract to its fold all who called themselves Christians. We have seen the statement of Pius XII which identified the body of Christ with the Roman Catholic Church. We have also recorded, both in this and previous volumes, the sincere labours in the nineteenth and twentieth centuries to bring all Christians to acknowledge the authority of the Pope and draw them into communion with Rome. Here and there successes were registered, partly in accessions of individuals from one or another form of Protestantism, and partly in the adherence of individuals and groups from the Eastern Churches, sometimes as Uniates and sometimes by full conformity to the Latin rite.

However, with the rapid growth of Protestantism, by the mid-twentieth century Roman Catholics constituted a smaller proportion of those who bore the Christian name than they had at the dawn of the nineteenth century and even in 1914.

TWENTIETH-CENTURY *Rapprochement* OF ROMAN CATHOLICS AND PROTESTANTS

One of the striking features of the twentieth century was the new approaches towards bringing to a reality the ideal of Christian unity. We have seen something of this in Protestantism and are to see even more when, in the next volume, we describe the phenomenal growth of the multiform Ecumenical Movement which issued from Protestantism. Here and there, notably in Western Europe, Roman Catholics and Protestants were reaching out in attempts to bridge the gulf that had so long separated them, not in the spirit of controversy but of fellowship and reciprocal understanding. Here was adventuring in unexplored ways towards a deeper and a higher unity than had been experienced through any existing ecclesiastical body. Only minorities were as yet involved, but never since the emergence of Protestantism had as much friendly intercourse existed between Roman Catholics and Protestants.

The reasons for the *rapprochement* were probably at least three. One was consciences sensitive to the obvious contrast between the existing divisions and the kind of love which ideally should bind together all disciples of Christ. A second was the challenge of the revolutionary age. In Europe especially Roman Catholics and Protestants were confronted with the anti-Christian movements emerging in the erstwhile Christendom—whether widespread secularism or militant Fascism, Nazism, and Communism. Latterly Communism was the most obvious threat. A third factor was the Protestant-inspired and led Ecumenical Movement. Many Roman Catholics noted it and a number made it an object of special study.

The majority of Roman Catholics and Protestants were as yet uninvolved in the efforts at better relations between the two branches of the faith. They were either only slightly aware or entirely unaware of them. Many of those who were aware were highly critical. In the Roman Catholic fold the integralists were adamant against any seeming compromise of the Roman Catholic position.[1]

Improving relations between Roman Catholics and Protestants and the search for unity had many expressions. We cannot hope even to name them all in the brief compass to which we must confine our account. We can, however, give a few examples, selected almost at random, noting particularly those in Europe. Indeed, most of them were in Europe.

THE UNA SANCTA MOVEMENT IN GERMANY

The Una Sancta movement must obviously be included. It had its origin and centre in Germany. Before and after World War I among both Protestants and Roman Catholics were some who longed for a union of all Christians. In Germany Friedrich Siegmund-Schultze (1885——), a Protestant, had begun a quarterly in 1913 to further the mounting efforts among Protestants towards Christian unity. He was reinforced by Friedrich Heiler (1892——) who, reared a Roman Catholic, had become a Protestant in 1919 and had begun a Protestant third order of the Franciscans.[2] After World War I both men became prominent in the Una Sancta movement. The chief driving force in creating it was a Roman Catholic priest, Max Josef Metzger (1887-1944). A chaplain in the German army in World War I, he returned a convinced pacifist and devoted himself to promoting world peace. He is said to have been the first German after the war to give public addresses in Paris. To attain peace among the nations he endeavoured to further peace among the churches. To this end he founded (1928) the Una Sancta Brotherhood. He had earlier (1919) begun the Society of Christ the King of the White Cross for service to the poor, the outcast, and the disinherited. Imprisoned by the Nazis in 1939, he was freed for a time, urged Pius XII to endorse the Una Sancta and suggested a general council as a step towards unity. He was active in the resistance to the National Socialists, sought to bring about peace in World War II, but was arrested, convicted, and executed by the Hitler regime.[3]

Metzger's work was continued by Matthias Laros under the name of the

---

[1] Wylie, New Patterns for Christian Action, p. 15.

[2] Rouse and Neill, A History of the Ecumenical Movement, 1517–1948, pp. 635–637; De Katholieke Encyclopaedie, Vol. XIII, p. 23, Vol. XXI, p. 821; Weigel, A Catholic Primer on the Ecumenical Movement, p. 31.

[3] Loewenich, Der moderne Katholizismus, pp. 355, 356; Max Josef Metzger, Gefangenschaftsbriefe, edited, with an introduction, by Matthias Laros (Augsburg, Kyrios-Verlag, 1947, pp. 282), passim; Lilian Stevenson, Max Josef Metzger, Priest and Martyr (London, S.P.C.K., 1952, pp. 149), passim; Weigel, op. cit., pp. 31, 32.

Una Sancta with headquarters at Meitingen near Augsburg. It flourished after World War II and had groups in many different places. It did not seek to make converts to the Roman Catholic Church but had confidence that if Christians would really love one another God would show them the way to more visible unity. The distinguished Roman Catholic theologian Karl Adam (1876——), in public addresses in a Protestant church in Stuttgart, thought that he was in accord with the mind of the Pope when he suggested that Protestants might be encouraged to return to the Roman Catholic Church if the liturgy were put into the vernacular, the cup were given to the laity, and the clergy were permitted to marry.[4]

Metzger's dream was also perpetuated by Thomas Satory, a Benedictine, of Niederaltaich Abbey in Bavaria. He edited *Una Sancta,* to which both Roman Catholics and Lutherans contributed, and held annual conferences attended by Roman Catholics and Protestants in which understanding fellowship was facilitated, but without compromising the convictions of the participants.[5]

Rapprochement between Roman Catholics and Protestants in Germany was facilitated by the use of each other's churches during and after World War II. In the general destruction wrought by enemy bombings so many church buildings were damaged or obliterated and such migrations occurred that Roman Catholics permitted Protestants to hold services in their churches and Protestants extended similar courtesies to Roman Catholics.[6]

ATTITUDES OF ROME

Some of the aspects of the Una Sancta movement were frowned on by Rome. On the eve of the first meeting of the General Assembly of the World Council of Churches in Amsterdam, the Holy Office issued (June 5, 1948) a *monitum* ("admonition"), calling attention to the section in the canon law which forbade clergy and laity to participate in mixed congresses of "Catholics and non-Catholics" where matters of faith were discussed unless leave was obtained from the Holy See. The faithful were also reminded that canon law estopped them from taking part in common services of worship.[7] Although timed to warn Roman Catholics against joining in the Amsterdam gathering, the *monitum* was officially interpreted as directed to German Roman Catholics and as applying specifically to the Una Sancta movement. A further instruction (*Ecclesia Catholica*) of the Holy Office admonished Roman Catholics not to exaggerate their failings or to play down the guilt of the Protestant Re-

---

[4] Loewenich, *op. cit.,* p. 356; Karl Adam, *One and Holy,* translated by Cecily Hastings (New York, Sheed and Ward, 1951, pp. vii, 150).

[5] Avery Dulles in *America,* January 24, 1959.

[6] Loewenich, *op. cit.,* p. 356.

[7] *Acta Apostolicae Sedis,* Vol. XL, p. 257; Weigel, *op. cit.,* p. 37; Loewenich, *op. cit.,* pp. 356, 357.

formers.[8] In September, 1948, Pius XII took the occasion of the *Katholikentag* to warn the faithful against compromising the teachings of their church by dwelling on the similarities with other confessions.[9]

In spite of these restrictions the Una Sancta movement continued, but in small groups for conversation between Roman Catholics and Protestants and with the purpose, as least from some on the Roman Catholic side, of winning converts and not of achieving a higher synthesis of what was held by the two branches of the faith.[10] Yet such conversations, whether through the Una Sancta circles or under other auspices, served to remove misunderstandings of the others' position on points at issue. Moreover, on at least one Corpus Christi Day, in Munich, Lutheran pastors, on invitation from the Roman Catholic authorities, took part in the public procession which followed the Blessed Sacrament.[11]

Although not a part of the Una Sancta movement, in the 1950's a group of about twenty-five, roughly half Roman Catholics and half Protestants, met annually under the patronage of the Archbishop of Paderborn for discussion of theological and historical topics. There, in 1957, an institute was inaugurated for the study of ecumenical questions, including Protestant theology.[12] It was named for Johann Adam Möhler, whom we have met as an irenic nineteenth-century advocate of Christian unity.[13]

THE MALINES CONVERSATIONS

We have already mentioned the Malines Conversations, but because of their importance a slightly longer notice seems appropriate. They arose out of Anglican seconded by Roman Catholic initiative. In the 1890's Charles Wood, later the second Viscount Halifax, a staunch Anglo-Catholic, had taken the lead and was joined by a French priest, Fernand Portal, in seeking to gain the recognition by Rome of the validity of Anglican orders.[14] Although Rome acted adversely, Halifax was not discouraged. When Cardinal Mercier sent a cordial reply to the appeal of the (Anglican) Lambeth Conference (1920) "to all Christian people," Portal and Halifax called on Mercier. As a result meetings took place at intervals between December, 1921, and October, 1926. Several Anglicans and Roman Catholics, eminent for their scholarship, shared in them. Rome approved and the Archbishop of Canterbury gave guarded recognition. At the fourth conversation Mercier read a plea for uniting the Church

[8] *Acta Apostolicae Sedis*, Vol. XLII, pp. 142–147.
[9] *Ibid.*, Vol. XL, pp. 417–420.
[10] Loewenich, *op. cit.*, pp. 358–360.
[11] Wylie, *op. cit.*, pp. 10–14.
[12] Weigel, *op. cit.*, pp. 33, 34; Avery Dulles, *loc. cit.*
[13] Volume I, p. 379.
[14] Volume I, p. 304.

of England with Rome as a uniate body with a patriarch. The death of Mercier, followed by that of Portal, contributed to the end of the venture. The encyclical *Mortalium animos*, January, 1928, while not mentioning it by name, was regarded as a condemnation of the enterprise. Shortly afterward the *Osservatore Romano*, presumably speaking for the Vatican, said that the series would not be resumed.[15]

The Approach Through Prayer

Less controversial approaches were through prayer. The Octave of Prayer, observed yearly during January 18–25, arose from both Protestant and Roman Catholic leadership. It went back to the Evangelical Alliance and in the 1890's was taken up by Anglicans in the United States and England. In the 1890's Leo XIII called for prayer in the days between Ascension and Pentecost for the "reconciliation of our separated brethren." The January octave was approved by Popes Pius X, Benedict XV, and Pius XI. In France at least it was observed by both Roman Catholics and Protestants.[16]

Another movement for prayer was associated with the January octave and centred around Paul Couturier (1881–1953).[17] Couturier was born in Lyons, of a middle-class, deeply religious family. He entered the priesthood and served in various capacities. His commitment to the cause of Christian unity seems to have dated from contacts with Russian Orthodox who became refugees in France after the Communist seizure of power in their native land. He came in touch with them in Lyons in 1923 and did what he could to aid them. The experience widened his horizons and stimulated his interest in Christian union. That concern was deepened by a familiarity with the January Octave of Prayer, which came to him through Belgium. Couturier promoted the octave at Lyons and enrolled in it Metropolitan Eulogios, who represented the Ecumenical Patriarch in the latter's capacity as head of the Orthodox of the dispersion. He devoted the rest of his life to enlisting Christians of the severed branches of the Church in the prayer for unity. He believed that true unity must be based on love, love as seen in the heart of Christ. He was convinced that as Christians of the various communions shared in prayer, spiritual unity would be realized. He rejoiced to see Roman Catholics, Orthodox, Anglicans, and Protes-

[15] Rouse and Neill, *op. cit.*, pp. 297–299. From a Roman Catholic standpoint see Jacques de Bivort de la Saudée, *Anglicans et Catholiques, Problème de l'Union Anglo-Romain* (Paris, Librairie Plon, 1949), *passim*. For documents see *The Conversations at Malines 1921–1925* (New York, Oxford University Press, 1927, pp. 95); G. K. A. Bell, editor, *Documents on Christian Unity 1920–4* (New York, Oxford University Press, 1924, pp. xx, 382), pp. 349–365; G. K. A. Bell, editor, *Documents on Christian Unity. Third Series, 1930–1948* (New York, Oxford University Press, pp. xii, 300), pp. 21–32.
[16] Congar, *Chrétiens Désunis*, pp. lx–xi; Loewenich, *op. cit.*, pp. 361, 362.
[17] Maurice Villain, *L'Abbé Paul Couturier, passim*.

tants joining in the January octave. To aid in the octave he issued tracts and suggested prayers. He arranged for conferences in Lyons and stimulated them in other centres. He brought into being inter-confessional groups for fellowship, discussion, and prayer. He stimulated "ecumenical conversations," made contacts with the Protestant communities of Taize (of men) and Grandchamp (of women), came in touch with the Lutheran pastor Gunnar Rosendal, who in Sweden was promoting prayer for Christian unity, and became familiar with the World Council of Churches before and after its official institution. He carried on an enormous correspondence, both within and outside his church. For a few weeks in 1944 he was imprisoned by the German Gestapo but survived to continue his mission after World War II. A loyal son of the Roman Catholic Church, in his prayers and his efforts he sought to embrace all Christians in Christlike love.

The Approach by Union with Rome

Another avenue of approach was that of seeking frankly the union of all Christians with the Roman Catholic Church. That was the objective of the Unitas Association, founded in Rome in 1945. Its president was a Jesuit, Charles Boyer, of the Gregorian University. Its central committee was in Rome and it had groups in a number of countries which were organized by diocesan units. Formal membership was restricted to Roman Catholics, but it had many friends in other communions. Its quarterly publication, *Unitas,* was issued in Italian, French, and English.[18]

In Belgium the Benedictine Priory of Union was founded in 1926 in Amay and transferred to Chevetogne in 1939. Its inaugurator was the Benedictine Lambert Beauduin. At first its objective was the union of the Eastern Churches with Rome, but in time that was broadened to embrace all bearing the Christian name. The title of its quarterly review, *Irenikon,* expressed its attitude towards those of other communions.[19]

Roman Catholics and the Ecumenical Movement

The Ecumenical Movement clearly called for official action by Rome. It was of Protestant origin but in one form or another attracted some of the Eastern Churches and, chiefly through the Young Men's and Young Women's Christion Associations, many Roman Catholics and Orthodox who were affiliated as individuals and without breaking their connexions with their respective

---

[18] Weigel, *op. cit.,* pp. 30, 31. See a brief comprehensive statement with an appeal to the "dissidents" to "return" to the Roman allegiance in Charles Boyer, *One Shepherd. The Problem of Christian Reunion,* translated by Angeline Bouchard (New York, P. J. Kenedy and Sons, 1952, pp. xvi, 142).

[19] Weigel, *op. cit.,* p. 30.

churches. The most prominent of the ecumenical bodies was the World Council of Churches, formally organized at Amsterdam in 1948. It arose from the fusion of the Universal Christian Council for Life and Work and the World Conference on Faith and Order, both post-World War I developments. The World Council of Churches had as members churches which enrolled the overwhelming majority of the Protestants of Europe and a substantial majority of the Protestants of the rest of the world. It also was joined by some of the Old Catholic and Eastern Churches.

In general the attitude of Rome towards the Ecumenical Movement was one of not unfriendly interest, but also of frank refusal to participate. To be officially represented would seem to imply recognition of other ecclesiastical bodies as true churches on an equality with the Roman Catholic Church. This would appear to surrender the conviction cherished by that church of being the body ordained by Christ as the true Church, His body, and of adherence to it as the divinely instituted means of Christian unity. Moreover, Roman Catholics pointed out the difference in the connotations of the words "ecumenical" and "ecumenism" as used by their church and the adherents of the Ecumenical Movement. To their mind true Christian ecumenism could be realized only through the Roman Catholic Church.[20]

Some of the chief expressions of this position will serve to make clear the attitude of the Holy See. Rome was invited to be represented at the initiation of Life and Work. Söderblom, who was the chief early leader, insisted that if that movement was to be genuinely ecumenical, it must not be limited to Protestants but all Christian churches should be asked. Accordingly a letter was sent in February, 1921, raising the question as to whether Rome would welcome an invitation to send delegates to the first meeting of the Universal Christian Council for Life and Work, to be held in Stockholm in 1925. The letter made it clear that the proposed coöperation among the churches did not entail any compromise of the ritual or dogma of any of the participants but was simply a common effort, in love, to help relieve the suffering of mankind. Gasparri, as Papal Secretary of State, replied (April, 1921), expressing Benedict XV's thanks for the letter but saying nothing about the invitation. The silence was interpreted as a refusal and no formal invitation was sent.[21] In preparation for the first meeting of the World Conference on Faith and Order a deputation visited Rome in 1919 and presented an official invitation to be represented at the meeting, which was to be held in Lausanne in 1927. They were received in audience by the Pope. He was most cordial but made it clear

---

[20] See a statement of this position, with extensive bibliographies, in Edward Francis Hanahoe, *Catholic Ecumenism: the Reunion of Christendom in Contemporary Papal Pronouncements* (Washington, D.C., The Catholic University of America Press, 1953, pp. 182), *passim.*

[21] Rouse and Neill, *op. cit.,* pp. 539, 540; Weigel, *op. cit.,* p. 35.

that the well-known conviction of the Roman Catholic Church that the unity of the Church of Christ could be attained only through recognizing the authority of the chair of Peter made it impossible for him to accept. He went on to say that he earnestly desired that the conference might lead the way to reunion with the visible head of the Church.[22] Undiscouraged, Charles H. Brent, a chief instigator of Faith and Order, went to Rome in 1926 with a similar purpose and received the same courtesy and the same answer.[23] On July 8, 1927, on the eve of the Lausanne meeting, the Holy Office declared that Roman Catholics must not take part in or further "congresses, meetings, lectures, or societies which have the scope of uniting into a religious confederation all who in any sense whatever call themselves Christians."[24]

A few months later, on Epiphany, January 6, 1928, Pius XI issued an encyclical, *Mortalium animos,* which dealt with the Ecumenical Movement as far as it had developed at that time. He prohibited the faithful from taking any part in it. He gave as his reasons the implicit denial by the Movement that the *una sancta* already existed in the visible form of the Roman Catholic Church; the implication by the Movement that union could be achieved without unity of doctrine; and the fact that the Roman Catholic Church was regarded by the Movement as one of many branches of the Church of Christ rather than identical with it. This, he held, entailed relativism in dogma, indifferentism in ecclesiology, and "modernism" in theology.[25]

On June 5, 1948, as we have seen, slightly less than three months before the first Assembly of the World Council of Churches, the Holy Office came out with a *monitum* noting that, contrary to canon law, without the permission of the Holy See "Catholics" had participated with "non-Catholics" in congresses in which matters of faith had been discussed. The *monitum* strictly forbade laity and clergy to take part in such congresses without that permission or to convoke them. It specifically mentioned "ecumenical" congresses as falling within that category.[26] We have also called attention to the fact that on December 20, 1949, the Holy Office amplified the assistance to be given to "dissident" Christians in conversations between them and Roman Catholics. Some forms were permitted but were required to be only with the permission and under the supervision of the appropriate bishop, and each bishop was required to report annually on them to the Holy Office.[27]

Yet with official permission Metzger attended the Lausanne meeting and

[22] Rouse and Neill, *op. cit.,* pp. 414–416; William Adams Brown, *Toward a United Church* (New York, Charles Scribner's Sons, 1946, pp. xvi, 264), pp. 59, 60.

[23] Alexander C. Zabriskie, *Bishop Brent, Crusader for Christian Unity* (Philadelphia, The Westminster Press, 1948, pp. 217), p. 146; Weigel, *op. cit.,* p. 35.

[24] Weigel, *op. cit.,* p. 35.

[25] *Acta Apostolicae Sedis,* Vol. XX, pp. 5–16; Weigel, *op. cit.,* p. 36.

[26] *Acta Apostolicae Sedis,* Vol. XL, p. 257.

[27] *Ibid.,* Vol. XLII, pp. 142–147.

unofficial Roman Catholic observers were present at the Oxford meeting of Life and Work in 1937 and at the Edinburgh meeting of Faith and Order that same summer. In 1952, at the Lund conference of Faith and Order, with the consent of the Vicar Apostolic of Sweden four were present as "observers." Two unaccredited but official observers attended the North American study conference of Faith and Order at Oberlin in 1957. As reporters for the press Roman Catholics were present at the first and second assemblies of the World Council of Churches, at Amsterdam in 1948 and Evanston in 1954, and at the Lund and Oberlin meetings of Faith and Order.[28] These facts speak for both the interest of Roman Catholics in the Ecumenical Movement and the willingness of the leaders of the Movement to have them at its major gatherings.

Roman Catholics paid more and more attention to the Ecumenical Movement, as is seen in a vast flood of publications.[29] Several journals dealt with it and the issues which it raised. Among them were *Irenikon* and *Unitas.* Another was *Istina,* from a Russian word for "truth." It was an organ of a French centre of studies by that name, a Dominican enterprise. Dealing primarily with the Russian Orthodox Church, it also concerned itself with Orthodoxy in general and the Ecumenical Movement. The same centre published a monthly, *Vers l'Unité Chrétienne,* which began in 1948.[30] It contained both articles and a wide range of documents, not only on the World Council of Churches, but also on various movements for unity among Protestants.

Many books appeared which, while in no way compromising the Roman Catholic position, sought to deal fairly with Protestantism. Such a one was *The Catholic Approach to Protestantism,* by an Assumptionist, George H. Tavard, giving a rapid survey of Roman Catholic-Protestant relations, the main tenets and divisions of Protestantism, and the Ecumenical Movement, and pointing out what he believed to be the basic weaknesses of Protestantism.[31] Another book, endeavouring to base its statements on Papal pronouncements and putting forth what its author believed to be full truth as held by the Roman Catholic Church, rejoiced that the time of bitter controversy had come to an end, gladly acknowledged that all who believed in Christ as God and Saviour were Christians, held with the Popes in calling them "brethren," although "dissident brethren," recognized them as belonging to the faith, and pointed out that Protestant churches, while not really churches as Roman Catholics understood that term, preserved some features of the Gospel.[32] Similarly Aubert, a distinguished Church historian in Louvain, came out with

---

[28] Weigel, *op. cit.,* pp. 44, 45.

[29] W. A. Visser 't Hooft in *The Ecumenical Review,* Vol. VIII, pp. 191–197.

[30] *Istina* (Boulogne-sur-Seine, Centre d'Études Istina, 1954 ff.).

[31] George H. Tavard, *The Catholic Approach to Protestantism,* translated from the French by the author (New York, Harper & Brothers, 1955, pp. 160).

[32] Gregory Baum, *That They May Be One. A Study of Papal Doctrine (Leo XIII–Pius XII)* (Westminster, Md., The Newman Press, 1958, pp. ix, 181).

an understanding and not unsympathetic popular account, for Roman Catholic readers, of the Eastern and especially the Protestant churches and of the Ecumenical Movement.[33] Significantly, Aubert's book was one of a series, *Collection Irenikon,* and had a preface by Beauduin.

A frank but kindly statement of the Roman Catholic position on ecumenism was made by the Dominican Congar, who was a specialist on the Ecumenical Movement.[34] He, too, regarded the "dissident brethren" as Christians and by their baptism related to the Catholic Church—although he saw difficulties in saying, as did some, that they belonged to her soul but not to her body. He recognized closer kinship with the Eastern Churches and was willing to recognize them as churches. But, while not giving them that designation and preferring to call them confessions, he held that Protestant bodies preserved in varying degrees remnants of the Christian heritage. He was outspokenly critical of Life and Work, partly on the ground that it was created by a "modernist" and was without adequate doctrinal undergirding. He looked with less disfavour on Faith and Order but viewed it as mainly inspired by Anglicanism, and Anglicanism, he believed, had lost much of its Catholic heritage by infusions of Protestantism. Gustave Thils gave a comprehensive and sympathetic survey of the theological and ecclesiastical issues presented by the Ecumenical Movement and pointed out what seemed to him to be weaknesses and unresolved problems.[35] He pleaded for greater understanding by Roman Catholics of the beliefs of Protestants. Louis Bouyer maintained that the Roman Catholic Church was necessary for the full realization of the positive aspects of Protestantism.[36] An English lay Roman Catholic sought to point out areas in which Roman Catholics and Protestants could coöperate in meeting the challenges of the age.[37]

PROTESTANT RESPONSES

From time to time Roman Catholics and Protestants engaged in conversations in an effort to clarify the convictions which they held in common and the issues which divided them.[38] Many Protestants sought to join in conversation with Roman Catholics by unilateral contributions. Some were irenic, others controversial. A few samples must suffice. A Swedish Lutheran, K. E.

[33] Roger Aubert, *Problèmes de l'Unité Chrétienne. Initiation* (Chevetogne, Éditions de Chevetogne, 1953, pp. 123).

[34] Congar, *op. cit.*

[35] Gustave Thils, *Histoire Doctrinale du Mouvement Œcuménique* (Louvain, Em. Warny, 1955, pp. 260), *passim.*

[36] Louis Bouyer, *Du Protestantisme à l'Église* (Paris, Éditions du Cerf, 2nd ed., 1955, pp. x, 251).

[37] John M. Todd, *Catholicism and the Ecumenical Movement* (London, Longmans, Green and Co., 1956, pp. xiv, 111).

[38] See one such in Canon Cristiani and Pastor Rilliet, *Catholiques, Protestants. Les Pierres d'Achoppement* (Paris, Librairie Arthème Fayard, 1955, pp. 189).

Skydsgaard, had a thoughtful, comprehensive study.[39] A group of Germans, among them members of a movement which stressed the Eucharist and sought the deepening of the spiritual life in German Protestantism through the Communion and a disciplined life of prayer and Bible reading, were responsible for a coöperative volume.[40] A Dutch Reformed scholar came out with a study based on extensive research in the material dealing with the Ecumenical Movement and Christian unity and critical of the Roman Catholic Church.[41] A professor in the University of Geneva gave a somewhat controversial approach to a suggested conversation with the Roman Catholic bishop of that diocese.[42] A German Protestant pleaded for a unity of love between Roman Catholics and Protestants which would overpass their differences.[43]

ROMAN CATHOLICS AND THE EASTERN CHURCHES

With all this concern for Christian unity between Protestants and Roman Catholics, the latter did not forget the Eastern Churches and prayed and worked to bring them into union with the See of Peter.

THE MID-TWENTIETH-CENTURY STATUS OF
ROMAN CATHOLIC-PROTESTANT RELATIONS

In spite of all the efforts, in the first half of the twentieth century no large numbers of the "dissident brethren" found their way to the Roman communion. Here and there individuals made the change and small groups came over from one or another of the Eastern Churches. But no mass movements were seen. Indeed, some Roman Catholics wondered whether better results might be achieved if individuals were kept waiting until they could bring with them the groups of which they were a part. Shifts of population due to the exigencies of the times softened the historic geographic boundaries: Protestants were found in traditionally Roman Catholic territories and Roman Catholics in historically Protestant communities. But in the main the demarcations fixed in the seventeenth century remained intact. Roman Catholics who optimistically looked for large accessions from Protestantism were disappointed, nor, in Europe, did any large numbers of Roman Catholics become Protestants. The

---

[39] K. E. Skydsgaard, *Katolicism och Protestantism. Gemenskap och Splittring* (Lund, C. W. K. Gleerups Forlag, 1954, pp. 241), translated by Axel C. Kildegaard as *One in Christ* (Philadelphia, Muhlenberg Press, 1957, pp. vii, 220).

[40] Hans Asmussen and Wilhelm Stählin, editors, *Die Katholizität der Kirche. Beiträge zum Gespräch zwischen der evangelischen und der römisch-katholischen Kirche* (Stuttgart, Evangelisches Verlagswerk, 1957, pp. 392).

[41] H. Van der Linde, *Rome en de Una Sancta. Het Oecumenisch Vraagstuk en de Arbeid van Rome voor de Hereniging der Kerken* (Nijkerk, G. F. Callenbach N.V., 2nd ed., 1948, pp. 382).

[42] Franz-J. Leenhardt, *L'Église et le Royaume de Dieu. Réflexions sur l'Unité de l'Église et sur le Salut de Non-Catholiques* (Geneva, Éditions Labor, 4th ed., no date, pp. 87).

[43] George Donatus, *Es Gibt kein Zurück* (Stuttgart, Schwabenverlag, 1953, pp. 201).

shifts of large bodies of Uniates to their ancestral Orthodox connexions were under political duress rather than from religious conviction. The changes in religious allegiance were chiefly away from Christianity to secularism or to Communism.

Although no marked gains were made in Europe by either the Roman Catholic Church or Protestantism at the expense of the other, it may well have been that never since the rupture of the sixteenth century had the relations between the two branches of Christianity been as nearly free from strain as in the twentieth century. Here and there persecutions were seen. They were largely of Protestants by Roman Catholics in areas, chiefly in Spain and Italy, where Protestants were small minorities and their presence was regarded as an alien and dangerous intrusion. In Northern Ireland the Protestant majority often made life difficult for Roman Catholics. Much prejudice, suspicion, and antagonism still existed, heightened by reciprocal ignorance. Yet, even though only among minorities, chiefly the clergy, more effort was made by both Roman Catholics and Protestants at an intelligent and sympathetic understanding of the others' beliefs and practices than at any previous time. The kind of love which is of the essence of true Christian unity was only here and there realized, but more of it seems to have existed than before. The common menace of secularism and Communism which characterized the revolutionary age was undoubtedly one cause of the change, but no slight impelling motive was the perennial prodding of consciences made sensitive by a faith which had at its centre wondering response to divine and entirely undeserved love with the dream that all its recipients would sometime be one in a united witness to the world of that kind of love.

Yet the realization of the unity which had been traditionally envisioned seemed as remote as ever. Not only were the vast majority of Protestants still unwilling to assent to the authority of the Pope, but Roman Catholics as much as and perhaps more than ever stressed that authority as indispensable to the Church of Christ. Moreover, the place of Mariology in the Roman Catholic Church, emphasized by the proclamation of the bodily assumption of the Virgin Mary and added to the nineteenth-century affirmation of her immaculate conception, presented a mounting barrier to Protestant accord. In the 1950's ecclesiastical unity seemed fully as far off as ever.

CHAPTER X

The Protestant Phase in Europe:
By Way of Introduction

As we move from the record of the Roman Catholic Church in Europe in the four and a half decades after 1914 to that of Protestantism in Europe in the same period, we do well to make the transition by a comparison of the responses of these two branches of Christianity to the revolutionary age in those momentous years. We will first point out the similarities and then the contrasts.

SIMILARITIES IN RESPONSE

In both the Roman Catholic Church and Protestantism striking similarities were seen in the effects upon each and in the responses each made to the revolution in which they were set; what was true in the nineteenth century continued to be true of the stage ushered in by World War I.

First and most obvious was the fact that beginning with the summer of 1914 the revolution quickened its pace and dealt additional blows to Christianity. So severe were the blows that many observers declared that mankind was entering the post-Christian era. To those whose attention was focussed solely on Europe and upon the aspects of the age which were adverse to Christianity much seemed to bear out this appraisal. Europe was the heart of the historic Christendom. As we have repeatedly reminded ourselves, a combination of forces which arose in Western Christendom and in part from Christianity threatened extinction to the religion which had contributed to them. Continued industrialization, the disruption of old patterns of society, the growth of cities, intellectual questionings arising from the scientific approach, and the spread of socialism, especially in its Marxist Communist form, were accompanied either by the fading out of the faith in millions of lives or by frontal attacks on it. So far as could be determined, the Roman Catholic Church and Protestantism suffered about equally. We have seen the progress of de-Christianization in traditionally Roman Catholic populations. We shall find it in not far from the same proportions among historically Protestant peoples.

Another feature of the revolutionary age which affected both branches of the faith was the continued trend towards the separation of Church and state. It was most marked in countries which were captured by Communism, but was seen too in lands not so dominated. In Communist governments the separation arose from antagonism to Christianity. In some others antagonism was not the cause. Yet everywhere it was a symptom of the secularization of a society which had once been called Christian.

Anti-clericalism was not as marked as in the nineteenth century, though in some countries it was still seen. As in the nineteenth century, it was not as prominent in Protestant as in Roman Catholic lands. In France, where anti-clericalism was as pronounced in the nineteenth century as in any country, by the middle of the twentieth century it had all but disappeared. However, the decline was due not so much to a more favourable attitude towards the Church as to the waning importance of the Church in politics. Christianity had still to be reckoned with as a factor in the politics of several countries. In some its influence grew—as in the German Federal Republic, Belgium, Italy, and probably the Netherlands. But this does not seem to have carried with it a correspondingly enhanced power of the clergy. It was achieved more through lay initiative. As such it was evidence of a growing impact of the faith through the main body of the laity.

In Western Europe the great majority of the population were still baptized, either as Roman Catholics or as Protestants. For many, perhaps for most, the rite was perpetuated as a social convention and had all but lost its religious connotation. Indeed, in some Protestant circles where infant baptism had formerly been supported voices were being raised against administering the sacrament to individuals until they were old enough to request it, or in favour of baptizing only infants whose parents and godparents were prepared to take their responsibilities seriously. Yet that attitude was an indication, not of a loss of vigour in Christianity, but of a mounting sensitiveness among earnest Christians to the importance and significance of baptism.

The questioning of the propriety of infant baptism where that sacrament was not considered to be more than a social convention was indicative of another feature of the revolutionary age in Europe which was common to both Roman Catholics and Protestants: the growing contrast between practising and non-practising Christians. Among thousands who were baptized the traces of the Christian heritage in morals and in maintaining specifically religious customs were fading. Among other thousands Christian moral standards were maintained and faithfulness in church attendance and in other religious duties was marked.

Associated with adherence to Christian obligations was a mounting emphasis upon the laity. We have seen that in the Roman Catholic Church the post-1914 period was known as the century of the laity. Through Catholic Action, the Liturgical Movement, the reading of the Bible, and a variety of organizations the rank and file of the faithful laity were becoming far more active than in the nineteenth century. Much was said of the priesthood of the laity, although care was taken to distinguish it from the priesthood of the clergy. We are to call attention to a parallel trend in Protestantism. Particularly on the Continent, the laity were more active, and in fresh channels, than they had been for many years.

In both the Roman Catholic Church and Protestantism the life of prayer was strong. In each it manifested itself in a variety of ways and often through inconspicuous and saintly individuals and small groups.

Both the Roman Catholic Church and Protestantism shared in the geographic expansion of the faith. As we are to see in our global pilgrimage, Christianity continued the growth outside the historic Christendom which had been accelerating since the fifteenth century and particularly in the nineteenth century. That growth was still by the migrations of traditionally Christian peoples and by missions among non-European folk. Through both branches of the faith Christianity became more deeply rooted among more peoples than ever before in its history. In most lands outside Europe, the Americas, Australia, and New Zealand, Christians were minorities, usually very small minorities. But except where they were countered by Communism they were growing minorities and increasingly were served by clergy who were of their own people. Moreover, Christianity was having a wider influence on mankind as a whole than at any previous time. Even where its adherents were few, often it was having effects on the collective life of the non-Christians which were quite out of proportion to its numerical strength.

As we have said again and again and are to remind ourselves repeatedly, for the Roman Catholic Church and Protestantism in Europe and elsewhere, the characterization of the age as post-Christian was an over-simplification. It did not take account of the vitality in both branches of the faith nor did it see the basic philosophical and theological questions propounded by the contrasts in the evidence for and against that designation. Although Western Christendom was the major source of the revolution which was engulfing all mankind and which everywhere was threatening and in vast areas was undermining all religion, the Christianity, Roman Catholic and Protestant, of that region was displaying more vigour than was any other of the forms of Christianity or any other religion.

DIFFERENCES IN RESPONSE

Similar though the responses of the Roman Catholic Church and Protestantism were to the revolutionary age in Europe in the four and a half decades after 1914, the two exhibited marked differences.

One contrast was the share which each had in the geographic expansion of the faith. From the Roman Catholics of Western Europe still came the overwhelming majority of missionaries who were planting and nourishing the churches of their communion in Asia and Africa. Although their fellow believers in the Americas—mostly in the United States and Canada—supplied a growing proportion of the personnel and particularly of the financial undergirding of the missions, the Roman Catholics of Europe continued to bear the main burden of the propagation of their branch of the faith. By contrast, after World War I and especially after World War II the majority of the Protestant missionaries and of the funds which supported them were from the United States, with substantial contributions from Canada and somewhat smaller ones from Australia and New Zealand.

Why that difference and what its significance would be difficult if not impossible to determine. Did it mean that the Roman Catholic Church in Europe had better resisted the corrosion of the revolutionary age and the wars which punctuated it than had Protestantism? Or was it that the Roman Catholic Church had not succeeded in transmitting its vitality to its children outside Latin Europe, the historic centre of its creative power, and that Protestantism had done so with such distinction that on its American frontiers it was more vigorous than on its native soil? In the mid-twentieth century Protestant missionaries still went from Western Europe, even from Germany, although that country had been wasted by two wars and had not fully recovered from the Hitler nightmare. But Roman Catholic missionaries went from France, which had suffered fully as severely, and in much greater numbers than German missionaries of either branch of the faith and more than from any other country. French Roman Catholic missionaries were several times more numerous than were Roman Catholic missionaries from the United States, and that in spite of the fact that by the 1950's in the United States the Roman Catholic Church had nearly the numerical strength which it had in France.

Again, in the twentieth century as in the nineteenth, creative intellectual activity was finding greater expression in fresh ways in European Protestantism than in the Roman Catholic Church in Europe. Even more than in the nineteenth century Roman Catholic scholars were being influenced by what Protestants were doing in theological and Biblical studies. Protestants were showing the effects of the impact of Roman Catholic theology, but it was the theology of the early Christian centuries and of the schoolmen rather than of the nineteenth and twentieth centuries. In this realm also more was appearing in the Protestantism of the United States than in Roman Catholic circles in that country.

Fully as striking a difference was in the Ecumenical Movement. Through that movement in its manifold expressions Protestants were reaching out in quite novel channels towards the realization of the dream of Christian unity that was inherent in the faith. In the coördination of their efforts they were paralleling the ultramontane trend in the Roman Catholic Church that had been a feature of that church in the nineteenth century and continued into the twentieth century. Yet they were doing so in a manner which was without precedent and which was congenial to the Protestant heritage. Moreover, as the Roman Catholic Church had long been wooing the Eastern Churches and by the Uniate device had drawn large segments into its fellowship, Protestants were attracting to the Ecumenical Movement entire Eastern Churches and also thousands of individuals from the Eastern Churches and the Roman Catholic Church—but without asking them to sever their ties with their ancestral communions. The geographical headquarters of most of the ecumenical bodies with a global outreach were in Europe and much of the initiative and leadership was from the Continent and the British Isles. Yet here, too, the United States and Canada were having a prominent share in both ideas and leadership. Again the contrast with the Roman Catholic Church was marked, for the Popes and a large majority of the cardinals were Europeans and since the sixteenth century all the Popes had been Italians.

In an earlier volume we pointed out that the nineteenth century could be called the Protestant century. That same designation could be given to the twentieth century. If as criteria we take geographic spread, the degree to which the faith became rooted on its frontiers, the number of new movements to which the faith gave rise, and the effect on mankind as a whole, in the twentieth as in the nineteenth century Protestantism was clearly in the van of the human scene. The Eastern Churches were losing ground before the onslaught of a militant Communism and the attrition of rising nationalism and a resurgent Islam. In Asia and Africa taken as a whole Roman Catholics outnumbered Protestants, but that was because the former were building on foundations laid from one to three centuries before the coming of Protestant missionaries. Percentage-wise, in most of Asia and Africa and the islands of the Pacific the numerical increase of Protestantism was greater than that of the Roman Catholic Church. The proportionate disparity of the growth of Protestantism as against the Roman Catholic Church in these areas was not as marked as in the nineteenth century. Especially in the years which immediately followed World War II in some regions, notably in portions of Africa south of the Sahara, Roman Catholics were outstripping Protestants. Yet the generalization still held true. In Latin America, where before 1914 Protestantism had barely won a foothold, in the four and a half decades which followed that year it was having a phenomenal numerical increase, largely through conversions from a nominal Roman Catholicism. In the United States, in which, thanks to immigration, the Roman Catholic Church had shown major growth in the nineteenth century, so far as figures could be obtained the movement of Roman Catholics into Protestant churches probably far outstripped the conversions from Protestantism to Roman Catholicism. In its rootage among non-European peoples through indigenous leadership Protestantism was making substantial progress. So, too, was the Roman Catholic Church. Indeed, with the emphasis placed by the Holy See on that aspect of its missions, in this respect in the decades just before the mid-twentieth century Roman Catholics may have been outstripping Protestants. They were certainly putting more money into training an indigenous clergy than were the latter. As to new movements, Protestantism was clearly ahead of all other branches of Christianity. Almost none were emerging from the Eastern Churches. As we have seen, in the Liturgical Movement, Catholic Action, lay movements, and theology the Roman Catholic Church was displaying marked creativity. But Protestantism was giving birth to even more novel features in an attempt to meet the challenge of the revolutionary age. Here the evidence of the Ecumenical Movement, fresh currents in theology and in Biblical studies, and greater lay activity in new ways were convincing. In placing the imprint of Christianity upon mankind as a whole outside the bounds of the churches, Protestantism was having a larger share than the Eastern Churches and even the Roman Catholic Church. That had been seen in the nineteenth century in such achievements as the abolition of the African slave trade and Negro slavery in the Americas and in the Red Cross. In the twentieth century it was apparent in the creation of the League of Nations and the United Nations, largely from Protestant initiative or by individuals from a Protestant background. Further contributions of Christianity through Protestantism were made by such figures as Gandhi and Sun Yat-sen, outstanding in shaping the revolutions in their respective countries.

Yet it must also be said that here, as in so many other aspects of the revolutionary age, the effects of Christianity were ambiguous: the Gospel could be warped to contribute to movements which were antagonistic to Christianity. Communism was given form by Marx and Engels, one-time Protestants. Stalin had much of his early education in an Orthodox theological seminary. Hitler and Mussolini were nominally Roman Catholics. But even in the negative distortion of what came from the Gospel, the vitality of Protestantism may have been in part responsible. It was as a reaction against that branch of the faith that the revolutionary ideology was devised which by the mid-twentieth century had captured a third of mankind.

THE MAIN OUTLINE OF THE TREATMENT OF PROTESTANTISM IN EUROPE AFTER 1914

In the ensuing chapters we will summarize the course of Protestantism in Europe in the decades after 1914 in the manner which we employed in covering the Protestant story in Europe in the nineteenth century. Ours will be a country-by-country treatment. For the sake of continuity we will follow the geographic order used in the earlier volume and before passing on to the Orthodox Churches in Eastern Europe we will attempt a summary of the main features common to Protestantism in Europe and of the share which European Protestantism had in the world-wide spread of the faith.

CHAPTER XI

Protestantism in Storm-Tossed Germany

How did Protestantism fare in twentieth-century Germany? In our coverage of the Roman Catholic Church in that country we have summarized the setting in such fashion that we need not repeat it here. Would Protestantism survive in the drastic changes which the revolutionary age wrought in the political, economic, and ideological structure of the country? As we saw in our first and second volumes, Protestantism was closely associated with the state. It was fragmented into churches, *Landeskirchen*, which reflected the territorial divisions. Each *Landeskirche* was controlled by the state and financed by it. Most of the states were ruled by secular princes, and the prince was the administrative head of the Church in his domain. Although in the nineteenth century most of the population of Protestant affiliation were baptized and confirmed, and although in some areas the percentage who had conformed to those rites had risen, many parishes were too large to be given adequate pastoral care. A large proportion of the laity were passive and did not attend church except for baptisms, confirmations, marriages, and funerals. The Social Democrats, strong among the labourers in the mounting industries, were critical of the Church and often hostile. Now came World War I with its defeat and the suffering brought by the war effort and the enemy blockade. After a surge in religious faith at the outset of the war, as the conflict lengthened a reaction took place and for a time subsequent to the armistice Communism seemed about to take over. The moral sag consequent to war was also painfully evident. Youth especially was affected and a movement of young people (*Wandervögel*) which began before the war and mounted after it tended to revolt against all conventional restraints. Many youths were also attracted by a variety of cults which to them had the charm of novelty—such as anthroposophy, nature mysticism, and Oriental faiths.[1] Then came the Weimar Republic, the run-away inflation, involvement in the world-wide economic depression, and the National Socialist regime under Hitler with its restrictions on the churches. World War II followed, far more destructive and exhausting than

[1] Gerhardt, *Ein Jahrhundert Innere Mission*, Vol. II, p. 209; Schweitzer, *Das religiöse Deutschland der Gegenwart*, Vol. I, pp. 208–238; Means, *Things That Are Caesar's*, pp. 97–120.

World War I. Great losses of territory resulted. Vast shifts of predominantly Protestant populations and a divided Germany ensued, with Communism in control in the prevailingly Protestant German Democratic Republic. These vicissitudes bore even more heavily on Protestantism than on the Roman Catholic Church, because they affected the Protestant portions of the country more profoundly than the Roman Catholic sections and because Protestantism did not have the undergirding of centralized direction that was given the Roman Catholic Church through the Holy See. Moreover, Protestantism, especially Lutheranism and the united churches which embraced both Lutherans and Reformed, by tradition was more controlled by the princes. Now the princes had disappeared.

Yet Protestantism had a number of assets as it faced the succession of crises. It had long been an accepted part of the life of the majority of Germans. The awakenings of the nineteenth century had enhanced its vitality, partly through Pietism, partly through revived Lutheranism, and partly through such movements as the Inner Mission.

PROTESTANTISM UNDER THE WEIMAR REPUBLIC

World War I tended to shut off the Protestants of Germany from their fellow Protestants in other countries. Not long after the armistice fellowship was renewed, although at times with difficulty. German Protestants deeply resented the charge that their country was responsible for the war. They sought to present the German case. Late in 1914 Adolf Deissmann, a distinguished New Testament scholar, began a weekly publication, which continued to the end of 1921, setting forth to the neutrals the German side.[2] German and British churchmen differed publicly and sharply on the alleged accountability of Germany for the war.[3] On the eve of the war Nathan Söderblom, Archbishop of Uppsala and primate of the Church of Sweden, had been indefatigable in seeking to mobilize the churches to prevent the conflict. During the war he was equally active in efforts to bring the churches together to suggest ways of ending the conflict. As soon as possible after the war, he stimulated the World Alliance for Promoting International Friendship through the Churches into holding a conference (October, 1919) at Oud Wassenaar in the neutral Netherlands near The Hague, in which churchmen from various countries discussed controversial issues. A delegation came from Germany. The German delegation, one of whom was Deissmann, allayed some of the tensions with the British, French, and Italian delegations by personal admissions that the infringement of Belgian neutrality by their government had been iniquitous. The conference helped to remove German indignation over the treatment of

---

[2] Schuster, *Das Werden der Kirche*, p. 521.
[3] Hogg, *Ecumenical Foundations*, pp. 166, 170, 171.

their missions by the Allies by affirming that missions were supranational and that the freedom of all Christians to carry the Gospel to all the world was essential to the Church's message.[4] Germans were present at the Universal Christian Conference on Life and Work in Stockholm in 1925. Moreover, the German churches were well represented at the World Conference on Faith and Order in Lausanne in 1927 and Germans were prominent on the programme.[5]

Difficulty was encountered in resuming fellowship in the Protestant missionary enterprise. Most of the German missions were in British territories or in German possessions which were taken over by the Allies. They were badly disrupted by the war, and while extensive aid was given to German personnel by funds collected in Britain and the United States, and British societies attempted to fill provisionally the vacuum created by the deportation of the Germans, the German societies were aggrieved by the exclusion of German missionaries from their posts and by what they viewed as the un-neutral attitude of John R. Mott, the chairman of the Continuation Committee of the (Edinburgh) World Missionary Conference of 1910. But the secretary of the Continuation Committee, J. H. Oldham, did much to induce the victorious Allies to exempt German missionary properties from confiscation and to pave the way for their restoration to the German societies. Oldham helped to preserve freedom for missions and religion in Africa. Some months passed before the German missionary leaders fully understood and appreciated what Oldham had achieved. Yet Germans came unofficially to an international missionary conference at Crans, in Switzerland, in 1920, and financial aid went from Protestants in the United States to straitened German missionaries. Germans were not present at the Lake Mohonk meeting at which the International Missionary Council was organized (1921), but through the Council assistance was given to German missionaries, the return of German missionaries to their posts was facilitated, and provision was made for carrying on former German missionary enterprises until the Germans could resume responsibility for them. In 1928 Germans were present at the meeting of the International Missionary Council in Jerusalem and reconcilation could be considered as completed.[6]

The Weimar Republic saw a change in the relation of the *Landeskirchen* to the state. The disappearance of the princes and their replacement by republics brought a partial separation of Church and state. In the body which drafted the constitution of the Weimar Republic various views were represented. The Social Democrats, numerous but divided, wished to have Church and state

[4] Rouse and Neill, *A History of the Ecumenical Movement, 1517–1948*, pp. 530–532.

[5] *Faith and Order. Proceedings of the World Conference, Lausanne, August, 1927* (Garden City, N.Y., Doubleday, Doran and Co., 1928, pp. xiii, 541), pp. 43–53., 280–282, 476–478, 528, 529.

[6] Hogg, *op. cit.*, pp. 174, 186, 187, 191, 192, 194–196, 203, 208, 227–230, 252.

completely separated and to have religion declared to be a purely private matter. The Centre Party was able to carry the day. It regarded the Church as essential to society. It was eager to have reduced or cancelled the power of the state to name ecclesiastical officers and wished Church and state separated, but it desired that the churches have juridical status.[7] As a result the outward façade of ecclesiastical life and structure was altered, but the basic operations continued much as before. The Weimar constitution of 1919 freed the churches from control by the state and granted full religious liberty. Henceforth the churches were not state institutions. No teacher was required to give instruction in religion and no student was compelled to submit to it. Yet normally, except in the secular schools, religious instruction went on, and in the traditional confessions. The theological faculties of the universities were maintained by state support, as were the other faculties. The state continued some financial assistance to the churches in the form of interest on church property secularized during the Napoleonic Wars. The tax for the support of the Church persisted, and although an individual could easily take the necessary legal steps to be freed from it, relatively few did so. For several of the *Landeskirchen* the state was the collecting agency. Chaplains were still provided for the army and the prisons. The churches retained their full legal privileges. The high days of the ecclesiastical year were accorded formal recognition.[8] Moreover, many of the pastors and their flocks were not reconciled to the fall of the monarchy or to the Weimar Republic. For example, some continued to celebrate the Kaiser's birthday.

A number of Germans took advantage of the new conditions formally to dissociate themselves from the Protestant churches. For some time before World War I a few had been doing so. In 1910 the total for that year was about 12,000. After the war the number suddenly mounted and then fell off. In 1919 it was 229,778, in 1920 it was 305,584, in 1921 it was 246,000, and in 1923 it shrank to 111,000.[9] The fact that the large majority of the professedly Protestant population retained their church connexion does not necessarily imply strong conviction. For many it probably arose from such indifference to the faith that they were not disposed to go to the trouble of taking the legal steps to sever the tie. The rank and file of the historically Protestant laity still conformed to the ancestral patterns but had little active part in the life of the churches.

Yet, even though only among a minority, enough vigour was present in the Protestant churches to institute fresh measures to meet the new conditions. The

---

[7] Cazelles, *Église et État en Allemagne de Weimar aux Premières Années du IIIe Reich*, pp. 65–78.

[8] *Ibid.*, pp. 79–143; Schuster, *op. cit.*, pp. 520, 521; Stephan and Leube, *Die Neuzeit*, pp. 418, 419; Drummond, *German Protestantism Since Luther*, pp. 258, 259.

[9] Drummond, *op. cit.*, p. 260 n.; Gerhardt, *op. cit.*, Vol. II, p. 259.

Kirchentag which met at Stuttgart in 1921 strengthened the ties created in the nineteenth century for consultation and action by the *Landeskirchen*.[10] What was called the *Deutschen evangelischen Kirchenbund* (German Evangelical Church Federation) was founded and the following year it was formally inaugurated with a membership of more than twenty *Landeskirchen*. Each of the member bodies retained its full independence.[11]

The relative freedom from state control stimulated movements for modifying some features of church life and administration. Even during the war, at the four hundredth anniversary of the Reformation (1917) one pastor sought to bridge the gulf between Lutheran and Roman Catholic doctrine and was rebuked by Protestant authorities. In that year another pastor advocated a return to the Catholic Church, but distinguished between "Catholic" and "Roman Catholic." The High Church Union (*Hochkirchliche Vereinigung*) which he inaugurated published a periodical, *Die Hochkirche,* eventually edited by a lay convert from the Roman Catholic Church. The Union advocated the creation of an episcopate with apostolic succession, making more of the Eucharist, and the founding of brotherhoods. It split in 1924. One wing remained strictly Lutheran and the other sought *rapprochement* with the Anglicans, Orthodox, and Roman Catholics.[12] It did not attract a large following. In most of the *Landeskirchen* the title of bishop was adopted, but the holders of the office were not in the apostolic succession and were installed but not consecrated. The largest of the *Landeskirchen,* that of Prussia, did not use the designation.[13]

A phase of what might be called a Protestant high-church or liturgical movement was the Evangelical Brotherhood of St. Michael. Founded at Marburg in 1931, it was composed of clergy and laity and sought a renewal of spiritual life within German Protestantism. It advocated the full restoration of Eucharistic worship and the daily prayer and hymnology of the early Christian centuries. Its members pledged themselves to lead a disciplined life of prayer, meditation, Bible study, reception of the Communion, and fellowship. It was the nucleus of the larger Berneuchen Movement and continued through the political changes of the ensuing decades. In 1951 it had convents in Switzerland, Austria, Transylvania, and Alsatia.[14] The Berneuchen Movement, so called from a village in Brandenburg where a conference met from which it grew, combined Lutheranism with contributions from anthroposophy and the youth

10 Volume II, pp. 85–88.
11 Hermelink, *Geschichte der evangelischen Kirche in Württemberg,* p. 466; Drummond, *op. cit.,* p. 262.
12 Drummond, *op. cit.,* pp. 260, 261.
13 *Ibid.,* p. 263.
14 *Twentieth Century Encyclopedia of Religious Knowledge,* Vol. II, p. 993; Schweitzer, *op. cit.,* Vol. II, pp. 259–277.

movements. Its members believed that God works through the liturgy and sacraments and therefore stressed them as more than human expressions of faith.[15]

Each of the *Landeskirchen* found it necessary to adapt itself to the new conditions brought by the outcome of the war and by the Weimar Republic. In doing so several found themselves confronted by hostile civil regimes. Not only Social Democracy but also Communism was rampant. Moreover, in the adjustment various currents and counter-currents were seen. Some tended to democratize the churches. Others were fearful of an upsurge of the masses and a liberalizing of the structures of the churches. The high-church advocates, usually a minority, made their voices heard. By 1925 the reconstruction of the *Landeskirchen* had been largely accomplished. Women were accorded the vote in ecclesiastical affairs and the functions and powers of the synods were clarified.[16] The structure differed from *Landeskirche* to *Landeskirche* and we need not here go into the several variations.[17] In some of the states movements sprang up or were continued which sought to bring together Protestants of similar convictions. Thus in the South the Free Folkchurch Union (*Freie Volkskirchliche Vereinigung*) arose at the close of the period. We hear of an association of high-church convictions, also in the South.[18]

Several of the pre-war movements persisted. The Inner Mission had a notable continuing life. World War I with its defeat and wide suffering brought a compelling challenge. The Weimar Republic was a welfare state and the question early arose as to whether it would leave room for voluntary agencies. The Social Democrats were bent on creating an inclusive structure which would not permit private bodies to parallel it. However, the Centre Party stood staunchly for such organizations, both Roman Catholic and Protestant. The Centre Party won its point and the Inner Mission continued.

The Inner Mission was reorganized and reached out in a variety of undertakings in spite of the impoverishment of many in its supporting constituencies and of the mounting costs and skyrocketing inflation. It carried on a *Volksmission*—an attempt to reach with the Gospel the many who, largely de-Christianized, in spite of their baptism were as yet really untouched. To that end it employed the press and public speech in evangelization, apologetics, and other means of deepening such Christian life of the nation as still existed. Through special missioners, Bible study circles, and addresses it endeavoured to win those whom it touched to commitment to Christ. Evangelists went from village to village in vans especially constructed for that purpose. *Landeskirchen*

---

[15] Piper, *Recent Developments in German Protestantism*, p. 135.

[16] Schuster, *op. cit.*, pp. 526, 527; Hermelink, *op. cit.*, pp. 466, 467.

[17] *Kirchliches Jahrbuch, 1921*, pp. 435 ff. On the situation in Württemberg see Hermelink, *op. cit.*, p. 476. On that in the Old Prussian Union see Schuster, *op. cit.*, p. 527.

[18] Hermelink, *op. cit.*, p. 467.

were stimulated to similar efforts. The apologetic took account of such current challenges as depth psychology, Sigmund Freud, existentialism, phenomenology, Keyserling's *Reisetagebuch eines Philosophen* (*The Travel Diary of a Philosopher*), the pessimism of Oswald Spengler's *Der Untergang des Abendlandes* (*The Decline of the West*), anthroposophy, and the mystical and romantic German racism and religion which were to bear striking fruit under the National Socialist regime. A leader in the apologetics of the Inner Mission was Helmuth Schreiner (1893——). He headed a centre from which substantial literary work issued. Societies for apologetics existed in several other places. Pastors and Christian physicians were brought together for the application of psychoanalysis and psychotherapy in their professions.[19]

The programme of the Inner Mission included welfare work for youth, the crippled, transients, and prisoners, and what in the United States was known as Travellers' Aid. The adoption of children was furthered. Men and women were trained to assist in some of these activities. By 1931 it had connexions with 650 Protestant schools for youths of both sexes. Alcoholism and prostitution were fought. German refugees from Russia were aided in their re-settlement in South America. Measures to improve public health were adopted. Legal counsel was provided for those who needed it. Invalids and the aged were part of the Inner Mission's concern. Wholesome films for the burgeoning cinemas were produced.[20] The Evangelical School Association was organized (1926) and in 1929 became independent of the Inner Mission. The Inner Mission addressed itself to housing, a problem rendered more acute by the war. Even before the war about 200,000 new dwellings were needed to care for the shifting and growing population. From 1914 to 1918 building was neglected because of the concentration of the nation's resources on the war effort. After the war returning soldiers, the immigration of Germans made homeless by the transfer of territories to the victors, and the shortage and spiralling costs of building materials presented an almost impossible challenge. In the early 1930's the world-wide depression brought additional obstacles. Yet at least a million dwellings were urgently needed. Assisted by funds from various sources the Inner Mission did what it could to ease the national burden.[21]

In 1926 the first Continental Congress for Inner Mission and Service was held in Amsterdam, with representatives from thirteen nations. It dealt with welfare problems, apologetics, and efforts to reach the masses with the Gospel. The fact that it met was proof that Continental Protestantism was vigorous and was rising to the challenges of the revolutionary age. An address by Karl Barth on "Church and Culture" helped to bring dialectical theology to bear

[19] Gerhardt, *op. cit.*, Vol. II, pp. 224–282; Schweitzer, *op. cit.*, Vol. II, pp. 227–243.

[20] Gerhardt, *op. cit.*, Vol. II, pp. 283–329; *Kirchliches Jahrbuch, 1925*, pp. 176–212, *1929*, pp. 128–169; Schweitzer, *op. cit.*, Vol. II, pp. 211–226.

[21] Gerhardt, *op. cit.*, pp. 330–348.

upon the situation and thus to point up the relation of that rising school of thought to the social problems of the day.[22]

The effort to reach the masses of nominal but indifferent Protestants and to bring them to an intelligent commitment to the faith was not confined to the Inner Mission. Many who were either lightly connected with the Inner Mission or entirely uncommitted to it saw in the loosing of the state tie with the *Landeskirchen* an opportunity to make the latter more vital. The Pietists were especially concerned. They inaugurated *Innerkirchliche Evangelisation*. That movement had several centres in more than one of the states and gave rise to periodicals which promoted it. It was critical of the *Volksmission* of the Inner Mission on the ground that the latter did not speak clearly of conversion but held to baptismal regeneration and used pastors of liberal theology who themselves were not really awakened.[23] In 1925 it created the *Christenbund*, dedicated to uniting all organizations and bodies, including the free churches, which stood for the knowledge of Jesus Christ the crucified and risen Who had given Himself as a sacrifice for all men and Whose coming again would bring in the Kingdom of God. It did not wish to create an Evangelical party but sought to permeate the existing churches and looked askance at sects which taught perfectionism and faith healing.[24] It had as a radiating centre conferences which bore the name of Gnadau and which had been held at Pentecost since the 1880's.[25]

Comprehensive measures were devised to nurture the rising generation in the faith. In addition to the pre-confirmation classes much energy was expended on confessional schools in which religious instruction in the tenets of the parents was given. National associations of parents and of teachers made for concerted action. Determined efforts were made to obtain favourable legislation and regulations and to prevent or modify hostile measures.[26]

In spite of the efforts by the Inner Mission and the Pietists to enlist a larger proportion of the population in the active life of the churches and to further Christian instruction through the schools, the Weimar Republic seems to have witnessed a fairly steady numerical decline in Protestantism. One indication is the number of confirmations. In 1920 those in all the *Landeskirchen* totalled 808,911. In 1924 the corresponding figure was 777,065, in 1929 it was 647,265, and in 1930 it was 447,695. The decrease was about evenly distributed over the various parts of the country.[27] A somewhat similar, although not as striking, recession was seen in the number taking the Communion. In 1920 it was

[22] *Ibid.*, p. 252.
[23] *Kirchliches Jahrbuch, 1922*, pp. 232–237, *1923*, pp. 210–220.
[24] *Ibid.*, *1926*, pp. 295–312.
[25] *Ibid.*, *1924*, p. 249, *1928*, p. 277.
[26] *Ibid.*, *1924*, pp. 340 ff., *1926*, pp. 431 ff.
[27] *Ibid.*, *1927*, p. 221, *1932*, p. 231.

11,481,129, in 1925 it was 10,761,416, and in 1930 it was 10,241,818. Percentage-wise it also fell off. In 1920 those making their Communions were 30.12 per cent of the Protestant population, in 1925 the percentage was 28.47, and in 1930 it was 25.79.[28] Although in the country as a whole those who formally separated themselves from the Protestant churches were not as numerous in the later as in the early 1920's, in Berlin the numbers taking that step mounted. For Protestants, in a metropolis where their branch of the faith was predominant, the total rose sharply from 27,621 in 1925 to 59,255 in 1930. For the Roman Catholic minority the increase was even more striking—from 2,741 in 1925 to 6,794 in 1930. In both confessions more men than women left the Church.[29] The Berlin record may have been symptomatic of what was happening in the cities as urbanization progressed. Nation-wide figures indicate that the loss was partly offset by the numbers who affiliated themselves with the Church after having been separated from it. They rose from 6,911 in 1920 to 18,439 in 1930 in contrast with the formal demission of the faith by 305,584 in 1920 and 215,160 in 1930.[30]

Another criterion by which the vigour in Protestantism could be measured was the number of young men studying theology and seeking ordination. The totals of young men enrolled in the theological faculties of the universities and in the theological schools in Bethel and Elberfeld showed a striking increase. In 1911 the number was 2,663, in 1926 it sank to 2,089, but in 1928 it rose to 3,517, and in 1931 it was 6,731.[31] But if Old Prussia is typical, those going on from university or theological school to ordination declined. In 1890 the total there was 329, in 1900 it was 295, in 1910 it was 150, in 1920 it was 200, and in 1930 it was 134.[32]

The shift from one faith to another was not great. Proportionately it was much larger from the Roman Catholic Church to Protestantism, for although Roman Catholics were fewer than Protestants, far more of them became Protestants than moved from Protestantism to the Roman Catholic Church. The numbers showed very little variation from year to year. In 1925, 13,591 Roman Catholics became Protestants and 6,938 Protestants became Roman Catholics. In 1929 the corresponding totals were 14,984 and 8,474, and in 1930 they were 16,302 and 9,190.[33] Another set of figures gives the same totals for the transition from Roman Catholicism to Protestantism but much fewer in the reverse direction—1,878 in 1925, 1,783 in 1929, and 1,971 in 1930.[34] Very

28 *Ibid., 1932*, p. 233.
29 *Ibid.*, p. 252.
30 *Ibid.*, p. 250.
31 *Ibid.*, p. 255.
32 *Ibid.*, p. 262.
33 *Ibid.*, p. 243.
34 *Ibid.*, p. 241.

few Jews became Protestants and a still smaller number of Protestants adopted Judaism. In 1920 the number of Jewish converts to Protestantism was 452 and in 1930 it was 212. In the corresponding years the Protestants who transferred their allegiance to Judaism totalled 82 and 55 respectively.[35]

German Protestants were slower to organize for political action and in labour unions than were Roman Catholics, as was to be expected from the traditional attitude of the Lutheran majority. The Centre Party was in theory a-confessional and enrolled a few Protestants. However, it was predominantly Roman Catholic.[36] Stoecker, whom we met in an earlier volume,[37] had attracted only a small minority of Protestants. He died in 1908 and before World War I his movement had practically disappeared. His successors associated themselves for a time with the National Socialist Party but broke with it in the 1920's. Their anti-Semitism was not on racial grounds, as was that of Hitler, but for economic reasons.[38] An Evangelical Workers' Movement had begun before 1914 and was the strongest of the united efforts for Protestant action in the political sphere, but World War I dealt it severe blows and it regained its strength much more slowly than did its Roman Catholic counterparts.[39]

Yet Protestants were by no means inactive in addressing themselves to the social issues emerging from the industrialized age. Their leaders were very conscious of the drift of workers away from the faith. In addition to what the Inner Mission was doing, we hear of conferences of professional church social workers, of a school for social work, of a Protestant social conference, of meetings of the Church Social Association (*Kirchlich-sozialen Bund*), and of the Association of the Protestant Labour Unions of Germany (*Gesamtverband Evangelischer Arbeitervereine Deutschlands*). In 1931 the latter had a membership of 96,319. In addition, in 1930 the inter-confessional Christian miners' union had 792,827 members.[40]

In the ferment which followed World War I some Protestants, led chiefly by pastors, formed the Association of Religious Socialists of Germany (*Bund religiöser Socialisten Deutschlands*). It was an effort to meet the economic, especially the industrial, conditions of the revolutionary age. The movement was found in both the North and the South. It sought to have socialism renounce Marx and follow Christ. It enrolled only minorities, some of them labourers but most of them intellectuals, and in time developed divisions. The influence of Karl Barth, already strong, tended to discourage the movement, for the Barthian trend at that time was to deny that from the revelation of

[35] *Ibid.*, p. 247.
[36] Fogarty, *Christian Domocracy in Western Europe, 1820–1953,* p. 313.
[37] Volume II, pp. 123, 124.
[38] Fogarty, *op. cit.*, p. 303.
[39] *Ibid.*, pp. 182, 215; van Gestel, *Het Religieus-Socialisme,* pp. 33–39.
[40] *Kirchliches Jahrbuch, 1931,* pp. 353 ff.

God in Christ principles could be deduced which were applicable to human society.[41] An outstanding formulator of religious socialism was a pastor, Georg Wünsch (1887——); under him it opposed both Marxism and National Socialism. Later he weakened in his attitude towards the Nazis and after Hitler's collapse was not permitted to teach.[42]

During the Weimar Republic German Protestant efforts to plant the faith among non-Occidental peoples made a partial recovery from the blows dealt them by World War I. In 1921 German Protestant missions had less than half the dimensions of 1914. The forced exodus of most of the missionaries during the war with the necessity of finding financial support for them was eventually largely relieved by the absorption of the majority by church staffs or in schools in Germany, but for some years it proved a heavy financial burden. As we have seen, delay was experienced in restoring the mission properties in former enemy territories and in areas occupied by the Allies. The rapidly mounting costs, especially in terms of the inflated German currency, placed an additional load on the societies. Although the incomes in German marks of at least some of the missionary societies rapidly increased—a tribute to the loyalty of their constituencies—they did not keep pace with the soaring costs. Because of the post-war slump of giving in the United States the aid given by the Lutherans of that land during and immediately after the war fell off.[43] By the mid-1920's the British Government made it possible for missionaries of approved German societies to go to British possessions and mandates. Delay was experienced in obtaining a similar permission in French, Belgian, and Portuguese territories.[44] Gradually recovery was achieved and contributions mounted. When in 1928 the centennial was celebrated of the largest of the German bodies, the Rhenish Missionary Society based upon congregations in Westphalia and the lower Rhine Valley where the Pietist tradition was strong, the rejoicing in the constituency was general.[45] However, the world-wide depression of the early 1930's brought reverses on the eve of the even greater challenges of the Hitler regime. Contributions declined, missionaries scheduled to sail were kept at home, and in some of the countries where the missionaries were labouring the governments found it necessary to reduce their subventions, and curtailment of the budgets of schools operated by missions followed.[46]

[41] Gestel, *op. cit.*, pp. 33–72.

[42] Georg Wünsch, editor, *Reich Gottes, Marxismus, National Sozialismus. Ein Bekentnis religiöser Socialisten* (Tübingen, J. C. B. Mohr [Paul Siebeck], 1931, pp. iv, 116). See also Georg Wünsch, *Der Zusammenbruch des Luthertums als Sozialgestaltung* (Tübingen, J. C. B. Mohr [Paul Siebeck], 1921, pp. 70).

[43] *Kirchliches Jahrbuch, 1921*, pp. 241–250, *1924*, pp. 93 ff.; Schweitzer, *op. cit.*, Vol. II, pp. 370–385.

[44] *Kirchliches Jahrbuch, 1926*, pp. 244 ff.

[45] *Ibid., 1929*, pp. 170 ff.

[46] *Ibid., 1931*, pp. 382 ff., *1932*, pp. 452 ff.

During the period of the Weimar Republic a step was taken which was to prove of great assistance to German Lutheranism in the years ahead. In the nineteenth century the General Evangelical Lutheran Conference had been created. At first it embraced only Lutherans in Germany but before the end of the century it had been extended to Scandinavia. Now, in 1923, at a meeting in Eisenach the Lutheran World Convention was organized. It held a world assembly in Copenhagen in 1929 and one in Paris in 1935. In 1947 it was to be transformed into the Lutheran World Federation.[47] Here was one result of a heightened Lutheran confessional consciousness.

PROTESTANTISM IS TESTED BY THE THIRD REICH

Beginning in 1933 Protestantism was subjected to the most acute testing that it had experienced since the sixteenth and seventeenth centuries. In those centuries a resurgent Roman Catholic Church and a series of conflicts culminating in the Thirty Years' War (1618–1648) had threatened the very existence of Protestantism. In the eighteenth century the *Aufklärung* and the wars of the French Revolution and Napoleon with the resulting political changes wrought reverses, but not as severe as those in the hundred years after Luther. With the arrival of the Third Reich a series of events brought to German Protestantism a succession of crises which threatened, if not its extinction, at least a great reduction of its influence in Germany and in the total world scene. First came National Socialism with the Nazi effort to bring every aspect of the nation's life under a fanatical regime which in fact if not openly was anti-Christian. World War II followed in which the sacrifices, the concentration of the entire energy of the people on the aims of the *Führer* and his henchmen, the destruction wrought by enemy bombings, and the ensuing exhaustion, more nearly complete than that brought by World War I, left the country prostrate. Defeat was followed by occupation by the victors, the loss of large areas, chiefly Protestant, with the forced evacuation of millions to what was left of Germany, and the division of the country between the German Federal Republic, in the West, and the German Democratic Republic, in the East. The latter was ruled by a Russian-imposed Communist government which subjected the churches to slow strangulation.

German Protestantism seemed ill prepared for the testing. It had been dealt severe blows by World War I and the shifts in government which followed. In the post-war years it had been confronted by National Socialism and Communism. Before 1914 a large proportion of the labourers in the industries and mines which were features of the revolutionary age had been drifting away.

[47] Rouse and Neill, *A History of the Ecumenical Movement, 1517–1948*, pp. 615, 616.

After that year they had been more and more alienated. Confirmations and attendance at Communion fell off.

Yet German Protestantism was probably better equipped to meet the challenges of the second quarter of the twentieth century than it had been to deal with those which confronted it at the outset of the nineteenth century. Then, except for the Pietist awakenings, it appeared to be somnolent and, because of the _Aufklärung,_ lacking in inner conviction. In the nineteenth century, awakening after awakening, both Pietist and through a revived Lutheran confessionalism, had brought it renewed vigour. Its intellectuals had wrestled valiantly with the problems brought by the intellectual currents of the day and in their responses had led the Christian world. It was by no means a moribund Protestantism which faced the next stage of the revolutionary age. Although, by that contrast which we have repeatedly seen, large elements in the population were further de-Christianized—if they could be said ever to have been Christian—and those who had their attention focussed only on that aspect of the scene spoke glibly of the post-Christian era, German Protestantism showed a quite amazing vitality which was manifested in both old and new ways.

The testing to which Protestantism was subjected in Germany under the Third Reich had two sources. The major one was National Socialism, led by the nominal Roman Catholic Hitler. The other, which reinforced the first and was utilized by it, was religious movements and was from men of Protestant background. Both illustrated what we have more than once seen, the contributions of Christianity through the warping and perversion of its central message to the threatened destruction of the faith. The first and the second were so inter-related that they can be treated together.

The second had two main branches. Both were sprung from the intense nationalism which was a feature of the revolutionary age. In Germany nationalism had been strengthened by such men of Protestant affiliation as Fichte and Hegel.[48] It was heightened by the experience of World War I with the sense of frustration brought by defeat and the rankling conviction of the injustice of the terms imposed by the victors.

The more extreme of the religious challenges was what was called collectively the German Faith Movement. We have already met it in our account of the Roman Catholic Church under the Nazi regime. Into it a number of currents entered.[49] Several had their beginnings in the nineteenth century and

---

[48] Frey, _Cross and Swastika,_ pp. 50–54.
[49] Douglass, _God among the Germans,_ pp. 30–86; Frey, _op. cit.,_ pp. 150, 151. For brief accounts of some of the movements see Means, _Things That Are Caesar's,_ pp. 163–198; Andrew J. Krzesinski, _National Cultures, Nazism and the Church_ (Boston, Bruce Humphries, 1945, pp. 128), _passim._

even earlier. Liberal Protestantism was the source of some. In the post-World War I years others arose.[50] Notable, because he and Hitler for a time made common cause, was that indebted to Alfred Rosenberg (1893–1946).[51] Common to all was a theory of race. It emphasized the Germans as a race and gloried in what it regarded as the achievements of the German people. It made much of folk religion and insisted that in Germany this religion must be congenial to the German spirit and an expression of it. The adherents of the German Faith Movement varied in their attitude towards Christianity. Some would hold to it, but only in so far as it was true to the "German soul." Most of them would preserve some contributions from Christ, but they would all reject anything that they contended came through Judaism. In 1933 a number of the currents coalesced under the leadership of university professors who drew up the Eisenach declaration affirming their allegiance to the German faith—"rooted in the divine reality of our Germanic origins"—and asking Hitler, as Führer of the Third Reich, to give that faith official recognition.[52]

The second main branch of the religious movements affiliated with National Socialism was that of the German Christians. More explicitly, it was *Die Glaubenswegung Deutscher Christen* (The Faith Movement of German Christians). Led by a pastor, Joachim Hossenfelder, the German Christians sought to give a religious foundation to National Socialism. Combining with other elements, the German Christians endeavoured to parallel the National Socialist Party with a united Protestant church which would be the soul of the Third Reich. That church, so they said, was to be frankly Aryan, to correspond with the German spirit as seen in Luther, and to hold to Christ as neither Aryan nor Jew but as the Son of God. The intention was to give it a tight organization from the parish to the national level.[53] The dream of a *Reichskirche* bringing into a national unity all the *Landeskirchen* was not new. In the nineteenth century some had cherished it. Bismarck opposed it. The particular expression given it by Hossenfelder and the German Christians had distinctive features, but precedent existed for the controlling purpose of one united Protestant church for all Germany.[54]

For a brief time a united Protestant church allied with the National Socialists seemed possible. Hitler became chancellor on January 30, 1933. In April, 1933, the German Christians met in Berlin and demanded that the *Landeskirchen* be drastically reorganized into a single *Reichskirche,* a people's church.

[50] Schweitzer, *op. cit.,* Vol. I, pp. 324–336.

[51] Douglass, *op. cit.,* pp. 30–46. A widely known book was Alfred Rosenberg, *Der Mythus des 20 Jahrhunderts. Eine Wertung der seelisch-geistigen Gestaltkämpe undserer Zeit* (Munich, Hoheneichen-Verlag, 129–132 editions, 1939, pp. xxi, 712).

[52] Douglass, *op. cit.,* pp. 58–60.

[53] *Ibid.,* pp. 87–106; Duncan-Jones, *The Struggle for Religious Freedom in Germany,* pp. 32–34; Frey, *op. cit.,* pp. 151–155.

[54] Ernst Benz to the author, April, 1960.

It would be a race church in which non-Aryans would be excluded from office. Many pastors were at first attracted, for here seemed to them to be a hopeful thrust against the atheistic Communism which was a major threat. The German Christians did not deny the universality of Christ but said that each *Volk* must express their loyalty to Him in ways which were in accord with their genius. The leaders of the *Deutschen evangelischen Kirchenbund* (German Evangelical Church Federation) took steps looking towards the reorganization of the churches with a more centralized national structure. They suggested as *Reichsbishop* to head the new structure Friedrich von Bodelschwingh, of the great group of institutions at Bethel.

But division soon arose which split the Protestant forces from top to bottom. As early as January, 1933, a group of pastors met and formulated a declaration which boldly said that the Church was called into existence by God, that in it Christ is the living power, that the state is ordained by God to curb man's sinful passions, that no specific form of the state is Christian, that Christians must obey God rather than men, that when the state seeks to dominate the consciences of men it has become anti-Christian, that when political parties assume the form of religion they do violence to the state, and that Christians must resist both the deification of the state and any party which seeks absolute control over the individual.[55]

The issue was sharply drawn over the choice of a *Reichsbishop*. In opposition to Bodelschwingh the German Christians put forward Ludwig Müller. Müller, a former army chaplain, was heart and soul for Hitler and was supported by Hossenfelder. In May, 1933, representatives of the *Landeskirchen* confirmed the choice of Bodelschwingh as *Reichsbishop*. Their action was endorsed by the council of the *Deutschen evangelischen Kirchenbund*. Hitler, as chancellor, backed the appointment of a state commissar to dominate the Evangelical Church of Prussia. The commissar dismissed pastors for hostility to the government. Through elections in which Hitler gave his support to the German Christians, synods were chosen by popular vote. One, that of Prussia, elected Müller as bishop of the Prussian *Landeskirche*. The other, professedly national, elected him *Reichsbishop*. As *Reichsbishop* Müller had in theory much the authority over the *Reichskirche* that Hitler had over the state, but always subordinate to Hitler. The *Reichskirche*, the German Evangelical Church, created in September, 1933, the month of Müller's election, was dominated by the

55 Duncan-Jones, *op. cit.*, pp. 37–39. For documents giving aspects of the dispute see *Die Bekenntnisse und grundsätzlichen Ausserungen zur Kirchenfrage des Jahres 1933*, edited by Kurt Dietrich Schmidt (Göttingen, Vanderhoeck & Ruprecht, 1934, pp. 200), *passim*. Also for documents see *Kirchliches Jahrbuch, 1933–1944*, pp. 4–35. An account, valuable chiefly for its documents, especially from the side of the state, is Andreas Duhm, *Der Kampf um die deutsche Kirche. Eine Kirchengeschichte des Jahres 1933/1934 dargestellt für das evangelische Volk* (Gotha, Leopold Klotz, no date, pp. 361). For a summary of the church struggle between 1933 and 1945 see *Kirchliches Jahrbuch, 1945–1948*, pp. 414–445.

German Christians. Yet in its constitution it declared that its foundation was the Gospel of Jesus Christ as revealed in the Holy Scriptures and as expressed in the confessions of the Reformation, and that by these its mission was defined and limited. The German Christians also obtained control of several of the *Landeskirchen,* notably those of Prussia, Mecklenburg, Thuringia, and Hesse.[56]

Müller attempted to quiet opposition and ensure unity by withdrawing as protector of the Faith Movement of German Christians and ordering (December 4, 1933) officials and their assistants in the national ecclesiastical structure to abstain from membership in church political parties, federations, groups, and movements. A few days later the Faith Movement of the German Christians declared itself dissolved as a church party but continued as a movement to reform the church on Aryan principles. But before the end of the month Hossenfelder resigned both as its leader and as Bishop of Brandenberg.[57]

Opposition to the measures initiated by the German Christians continued to mount and was not pacified by the steps which were taken to conciliate it. The Pastors' Emergency League (*Pfarrernotbund*) had brought together various pastors' brotherhoods and was closely associated with the Young Movement of the Reformation. Members of the Pastors' Emergency League, largely made up of younger men, had early begun taking exception to the race prejudice and what they regarded as the heathen theology introduced by the German Christians. On November 19, 1933, they read from their pulpits a denunciation of the government of the *Reichskirche* for tolerating such attitudes. They declared: "We refuse to earn the reproach of being dumb dogs. We owe it to our congregations and to the Church to resist the falsification of the Gospel. We emphatically recognize the Holy Scripture of the Old and New Testaments as the unique test of our faith and life and the confessions of our fathers as the reformed explanation thereof." About 3,000 pastors supported the movement. The resistance was especially strong in Westphalia. It was also outspoken in Bavaria, Württemberg, Hanover, Oldenburg, and Hamburg. Many of the laity and of the older clergy were roused. So violent was the storm that the German Christians had to bow before it. The December measures of Müller and the resignation of the particularly opprobrious Hossenfelder followed.[58]

Yet Müller only seemed to yield. He took vigorous measures to muzzle the opposition. On December 19, 1933, he ordered the incorporation of the flourishing Evangelical youth movement into the Nazi *Hitler-Jugend.* The Evangelical youth societies had about 400,000 members over eighteen years of age and the *Hitler-Jugend* about 700,000 or 800,000. The resulting fusion constituted a

[56] Duncan-Jones, *op. cit.,* pp. 42–51; Douglass, *op. cit.,* pp. 180–231.
[57] Douglass, *op. cit.,* pp. 108, 109, 229–231.
[58] Duncan-Jones, *op. cit.,* pp. 58–60.

formidable support of the National Socialist regime—another example of the effort to mould the rising generation to its purposes which characterized the programme of more than one totalitarian regime in the revolutionary age.[59] Müller also forbade pastors to preach or write on the church controversy.[60] Far from being silenced, the Pastors' Emergency League, grown to about 4,000, held a meeting in Halle and framed a protest which on January 7, 1934, was read from its pulpits to crowded congregations.[61] Hitler now intervened. He called a meeting of representatives of the German Christians and of the opposition (January 25, 1934), with the result that the leaders were induced to express themselves as solidly behind Müller and Hitler. To reinforce the action Martin Niemöller was arrested by the secret police and released after examination and the confiscation of the documents of the Pastors' Emergency League.[62]

Martin Niemöller (1892——) had been coming forward as a leader of the opposition. He was the son of a pastor, a staunch Lutheran. During World War I he served in submarines and rose to the command of one of them. After the war, his marriage, and a period of uncertainty he decided to enter the ministry. Handicapped by dire poverty and burdened with a growing family, he struggled through his university theological course and after a curacy and ordination became manager of the Inner Mission for Westphalia. From that post, in 1931 he became head pastor of the Dahlem parish in a wealthy suburb of Berlin.[63] At first he supported Hitler as a promising alternative to chaos or Communism but soon differed from the Führer's religious policies and became a fearless and eloquent critic prominent in what became known as the Confessing Church (Bekennende Kirche). From his pulpit he spoke out boldly against the movement to form a national church which would be deconfessionalized and condemned the measures against the Confessing Church.[64]

The Confessing Church began to take form on January 3 and 4, 1934, in a meeting of a synod at Barmen, in Westphalia, in which 320 elders and preachers and 167 representatives of congregations gathered. They were chiefly from the Reformed tradition, which more than Lutheranism had stood for the independence of the Church from control by the state. Karl Barth, then teaching at the University of Bonn, made a notable address, and the Barmen gathering adopted a statement which pointed out what it deemed the errors that were being introduced into the Church. The government promptly dismissed Barth

[59] Ibid., p. 68; Douglass, op. cit., pp. 163–169.
[60] Duncan-Jones, op. cit., p. 69.
[61] Ibid.
[62] Ibid., pp. 70, 71.
[63] Martin Niemöller, From U-Boat to Pulpit, translated by D. Hastie Smith (Chicago, Willett, Clark & Co., 1937, pp. viii, 223), passim; Miller, Martin Niemoeller, pp. 9–73.
[64] "God is My Fuehrer." Being the Last Twenty-eight Sermons by Martin Niemöller, Vicar of Berlin-Dahlem, translated by Jane Lynburn (New York, Philosophical Library and Alliance Book Corporation, 1941, pp. 294), passim.

from his post, but, undiscouraged, on February 19 the dissidents held a "free Evangelical synod" in the Rhineland which adopted the Barmen declaration, and the following month a synod convened in Berlin. A few weeks later a synod of the Confessing movement, representing a majority of the pastors of Westphalia, set up a structure which they insisted was the constitutional church of that region. On April 22 the Confessing movement held in Ulm, in Württemberg, the most widely representative gathering which it had yet convened and declared itself to be the "constitutional Evangelical Church of Germany." Not long afterward the Lutheran church in Hanover, under the leadership of Marahrens, refused incorporation into the *Reichskirche*. Late in May, 1934, representatives of United, Reformed, and Lutheran churches gathered in Barmen as the Synod of the Confessing Church and called all those who adhered to the historic confessions of the Reformation to reject what they insisted was the betrayal of these confessions by the German Christians and the government. [65]

A distinction must be recognized between the Confessing and the confessional elements in the church struggle. The Confessing Church (*Bekennende Kirche*) led in the active resistance and was made up chiefly, although not entirely, of men from the Old Prussian Union and the Reformed churches, in which Calvinistic influence was present and at times strong. In it the lay element, not disposed to be docile under clerical domination, was potent. Marahrens, on the other hand, did not belong to the *Bekennende Kirche* but was a spokesman for the staunch Lutherans who held by the historic Lutheran confessions. They maintained that the form of church government was relatively unimportant so long as the confessions were left intact. Few of the old-line Lutherans went into the active resistance, and many of them were critical of fellow Lutherans who coöperated with the Reformed and Union men in drawing up a statement of faith, as at Barmen, for to their mind that compromised true Lutheran doctrine. The cleavage went back to nineteenth-century

[65] Duncan-Jones, *op. cit.*, pp. 74–82. See a translation of the declaration, with favourable comments, in *The Significance of the Barmen Declaration for the Œcumenical Church* (London, Society for Promoting Christian Knowledge, 1943, pp. 44). For documents on various aspects of the struggle see *Die Bekenntnisse und Grundsätzlichen Ausserungen zur Kirchenfrage. Band 2. Das Jahr 1934*, edited by Kurt Dietrich Schmidt (Göttingen, Vanderhoeck & Ruprecht, 1935, pp. 192), *passim*. For documents also see *Kirchliches Jahrbuch, 1933–1944*, pp. 36–83, and Duhm, *op. cit.*, pp. 283–309. See also Günther Koch, *Die christliche Wahrheit der Barmer Theologischen Erklärung* (Munich, Chr. Kaiser, 1950, pp. 60), *passim*. For a sympathetic treatment of the Confessing Movement by an eminent Swedish Lutheran churchman, see Anders Nygren, *The Church Controversy in Germany. The Position of the Evangelical Church in the Third Reich*, translated by G. C. Richards (London, Student Christian Movement Press, 1934, pp. ix, 115), *passim*. See also Rudolf Grob, *Der Kirchenkampf in Deutschland. Kurze Geschichte der kirchlichen Wirren in Deutschland von 1933 bis Sommer 1937* (Zürich, Zwingli Verlag, 1937, pp. 111), *passim*; Herman, *It's Your Souls We Want*, pp. 3–187; Herman, *The Rebirth of the German Church*, pp. 31 ff.; Niemöller, *Die evangelische Kirche im dritten Reich*, pp. 23–30, 115 ff.

disputes and even earlier, and made for continued friction in efforts at Protestant coöperation in the post-Hitler era.

Müller was not slow in enacting measures countering the Confessing Church. Early in August a synod of the *Reichskirche* under his direction required all pastors to take an oath of loyalty to Hitler as the *Führer* of the German people and state. The standing committee of the Confessing synod insisted that the actions of the Berlin synod were illegal and unorthodox and singled out the oath for especial condemnation. The administration of the *Reichskirche* endeavoured to incorporate the *Landeskirchen* of Württemberg and Bavaria into that body but was met by the determined and public refusal of their bishops. Yet on September 23, 1934, in the Protestant cathedral in Berlin Müller was formally installed as primate of the *Reichskirche*. Soon Theophil Wurm (1868-1953), the Bishop of Württemberg, was placed under house arrest and Hans Meisner, Bishop of the Bavarian church, was ordered deposed. A popular revolt against these acts broke out in Württemberg and Bavaria and on October 20 the Confessing synod, meeting in Dahlem, set up organs for the government of the Evangelical Church of Germany, which it insisted was the only legal church, and called upon the parishes, pastors, and elders to refuse compliance with the instructions of the *Reichskirche*.[66]

For a time the resistance seemed about to win. The two bishops were released from house arrest. The state professed to grant full religious freedom.[67] By the end of March, 1935, while continuing to hold the title of *Reichsbishop* and to draw the salary of the office, Müller had ceased to be an effective force. The provisional government of the Evangelical Church of Germany issued to its parishes (February, 1935) a manifesto against what it condemned as the new heathenism of the German Faith, the German Christians, and other movements which it adjudged dangerous. On March 11 the document was read from scores of pulpits.

The issue was now sharply drawn between the Nazi regime and the opposition. The state reduced the church tax in Prussia and hundreds of pastors were either placed under house arrest, imprisoned, or consigned to concentration camps. But pastors announced from their pulpits the names of the victims and in June, 1935, the Confessing synod convening in Augsburg, consolidated the organizaton of the Evangelical Church of Germany and called on the government to release the imprisoned pastors and to restore free speech, free publication, and free assembly. To prevent appeal to the civil courts, for they were proving independent in ecclesiastical cases, the state transferred the latter to

66 Duncan-Jones, *op. cit.*, pp. 82–91.

67 See a collection of documents, assembled to support this contention, in *Religionsfreiheit. Amtliche Dokumente. Wörte führender Manner*, edited by *Gotthilf Herrmann* (Zwickau, Saxony, Johannes Herrmann, 6th ed., pp. 120), *passim*.

the Ministry of Cultus. The Ministry of Church Affairs was also created. Under its head and backed by Hitler it sought to exercise dictatorial control over the Church.[68]

Before long a division appeared in the ranks of the opposition. Many Lutherans, by tradition more submissive to the state than the Reformed, were more disposed than the latter to coöperate with the regime. In 1936 they set up the Council of the Evangelical Lutheran Church in Germany (*Lutherrat*) to represent Lutheran interests.[69] Some of the Lutherans endeavoured to collaborate with the committees appointed by the Ministry of Cultus for the administration of the Protestant churches.

The Confessing Church synod, meeting at Bad Oeynhausen on February 17, 1936, refused to recognize the committees. It also insisted on the right of the Church, given as it said by God, to educate all baptized children and protested against the state's programme of the schools as leading to the substitution of a false faith for Christian teaching. Holding to its course, the state continued its arrest of pastors. In June, 1937, the police broke up the theological college which had been created secretly in Berlin by the Confessing leadership to train candidates for the ministry. Yet other centres for the preparation of the opposition ministry were secretly carried on. Among them was one in the Wupperthal, in which the instructors were in daily peril from the secret police. Financial pressure was exerted on the pastors to bring them to heel, and voluntary collections were forbidden through which the *Bekennende Kirche* sought to be independent of the church tax. The opposition continued their public protests—in a statement on August 29, 1937, in which the issue was clearly set forth between "political claims and the claims of the living God," and a week later in a declaration that their pastors would not consent to financial control by the state, to the curb on theological teaching, to the prohibition of reading out the names of those who had left the Church, or to the prevention of offerings aside from those ordered by the state. The second declaration also asked for prayers for the persecuted.[70]

The conflict between the Confessing Church and the National Socialist state came to a dramatic climax in the imprisonment, trial, and consignment to a concentration camp of Niemöller. As an outspoken and fearless representative of the *Bekennende Kirche* in an influential pulpit in the capital, he was a

---

[68] Duncan-Jones, *op. cit.*, pp. 97–128; Keller, *Church and State on the European Continent*, pp. 306–312. For documents in the struggle see W. Jannasch, editor, *Deutsche Kirchendokumente. Die Haltung der Bekennenden Kirche im Dritten Reich* (Zürich, A. G. Zollikon, 1946, pp. 116), *passim; Die Bekenntnisse und Grundsätzlichen Ausserungen zur Kirchenfrage. Band 3. Das Jahr 1935,* edited by Kurt Dietrich Schmidt (Göttingen, Vanderhoeck & Ruprecht, 1936, pp. 340), *passim;* and *Kirchliches Jahrbuch, 1933–1944,* pp. 84–109. For excerpts of letters from imprisoned pastors see Charles B. Macfarland, *"I was in Prison" The Suppressed Letters of Imprisoned German Pastors* (New York, Fleming H. Revell Co., 1939, pp. 112), *passim.*

[69] *Twentieth Century Encyclopedia of Religious Knowledge,* Vol. II, p. 683.

[70] Duncan-Jones, *op. cit.*, pp. 126–147.

chronic thorn in the flesh to the Hitler regime. More than once he had been arrested and questioned but had always been released. Now, on July 1, 1937, he was imprisoned. For months he was held without a trial. Finally, on February 7, 1938, he was brought into court and on March 2 a mild sentence was imposed and he was freed. But the secret police promptly seized him and whisked him off to prison and then to a concentration camp. The incident attracted wide attention not only in Germany but also in other lands, and protests came from prominent Protestant churchmen in several countries. But not until the end of World War II and the collapse of the National Socialist regime was Niemöller released.[71]

In the months between the arrest and trial of Niemöller and the outbreak of World War II the struggle continued between the National Socialist government and the opposition. The state raised increasing obstacles to voluntary collections for the support of the protesting churches and of the Inner Mission and foreign missions and also continued its prohibition against training young men for the ministry of the recalcitrants. The issue of the oath of allegiance of the clergy to the *Führer* was prominent.[72] In Advent, 1938, instead of a synod the *Bekennende Kirche* convened a *Kirchentag* in Berlin. It issued a statement deploring the mounting persecution, the measures taken against Christians of Jewish blood, and the restrictions on the Christian education of youth.[73]

MOUNTING PRESSURES DURING WORLD WAR II

The involvement of Germany in World War II was inevitably accompanied by increasingly stringent measures against all dissent which would in any fashion compromise national unity in what became a life and death struggle. Under the exigencies of the war, largely apart from any hostility to Christianity or the *Bekennende Kirche,* the Protestant churches had their ministry, worship, and other functions sharply curtailed. The German Christians were staunchly with the government. Under the pressure of the common danger many critics of the ecclesiastical policies of the state rallied to its support. Among them were such leaders of the Lutheran opposition as Marahrens. In the invasion of Russia numbers saw a holy war against a Godless Communism.[74] Soon after the outbreak of hostilities the *Vertrauensrat* was formed with Marahrens as the head to give leadership to the supporting churchmen during the war.[75] The pre-war effort was continued to eliminate from the theological faculties all open opposition to National Socialism. The situation varied from university

[71] *Ibid.,* pp. 149–154; Miller, *op. cit.,* pp. 135–160.

[72] *Kirchliches Jahrbuch, 1933–1944,* pp. 185, 201–210, 238–263.

[73] *Ibid.,* pp. 273–275. On the chronology of the struggle from 1933 through 1939 see Niemöller, *op. cit.,* pp. 53–60.

[74] Keller, *Christian Europe Today,* p. 73; Drummond, *German Protestantism Since Luther,* p. 273.

[75] *Twentieth Century Encyclopedia of Religious Knowledge,* Vol. I, p. 459.

to university. In some universities the theological faculties were maintained with government supervision to see that nothing adverse to the state was taught. Candidates for the ministry of the *Bekennende Kirche* were not permitted to enroll in them nor could they hope for appointment to parishes.[76] In Württemberg the state refused to collect church taxes. Many of the *Bekennende Kirche* worshipped in houses, barns, and forests.[77] Forty-five per cent. of the Protestant clergy were called to military duty, leaving the care of the parishes to the old and the physically infirm. State and party gatherings were set at hours which interfered with church services. After 1940, as the stress of shortages in many essential materials became acute, no paper was permitted to be used for the printing of Bibles, and after 1941 other religious publications were suspended on the same ground. The ministrations of the chaplains were limited to the army and navy and were hampered by the shortage of clergy. The air force had no chaplains. Inner Mission activities were impeded.[78] Religious instruction of the youth and confirmation became more difficult. As the war dragged on, large displacements of population put obstacles in the way of normal parish life. The handicaps were enhanced by enemy bombings, with the destruction or serious damage of many church buildings.

Yet the Protestant churches displayed marked vigour, partly through the *Bekennende Kirche* and partly through other channels. Although Marahrens and some other bishops in June, 1941, sent a message to Hitler praying God's assistance to him in creating a new order for all Europe under his leadership,[79] the *Vertrauensrat* courageously spoke out against such actions of the state as euthanasia, the reduction of the Church in Poland to the status of a private society, the expropriation of church funds, and the persecution of the Jews.[80] The Inner Mission, greatly handicapped by the Nazis, continued and stood out courageously and at times effectively against the official euthanasia of the physically and mentally chronically ill. A notable instance was the successful resistance to the proposal to kill the inmates of the great institutions at Bethel,[81] which still had one of the Bodelschwinghs as its head.[82] In many places the religious education of children was continued in the schools,[83] and in parish

---

[76] Keller, *Christian Europe Today*, p. 80. Ernst Benz to the author, April, 1960.

[77] Drummond, *op. cit.*, p. 273.

[78] *Twentieth Century Encyclopedia of Religious Knowledge*, Vol. I, p. 459; Fritz Klinger, editor, *Dokumente zum Abwehrkampf der deutschen evangelischen Pfarrershaft gegen Verfolgung und Bedruckung 1933–1945* (Nuremberg, no date, pp. 125), *passim;* Herman, *It's Your Souls We Want*, pp. 209 ff.

[79] Drummond, *op. cit.*, p. 273. On the chronology of the struggle, 1939–1945, see Niemöller, *op. cit.*, p. 49.

[80] *Twentieth Century Encyclopedia of Religious Knowledge*, Vol. I, p. 459; Niemöller, *op. cit.*, p. 49.

[81] Volume II, pp. 107, 108.

[82] Gerhardt, *Ein Jahrhundert Innere Mission*, Vol. II, pp. 349–401.

[83] *Kirchliches Jahrbuch, 1933–1944*, p. 384.

after parish women aided in the maintenance of the work of the Church, and other measures were devised to fill the gaps brought by the depletion of the numbers of the clergy.[84]

A legacy of the war years to Protestantism was the heroism of those who witnessed to their faith in prisons and concentration camps. Some of the sufferers survived and their stories heartened those who heard them. Prominent among them was Niemöller, who lived to share with audiences in Europe and elsewhere the enrichment of spirit which came to him during his years of confinement.[85] Many perished, relatively unknown, but a few left behind them letters and other writings which soon became classics. Prominent among the latter was Dietrich Bonhoeffer (1906–1945).[86] The son of a professor of psychiatry and neurology, he inherited a tradition of scholarship, culture, and Christian faith from both his father's and mother's side. He was a great-grandson of the Church historian Karl August von Hase[87] and was reared in a home of liberal religious humanitarianism. Friendly, charming, at fourteen he decided to give himself to the ministry and theological scholarship. He studied under some of the outstanding German theologians of his day, was much influenced by Karl Barth, and had a period in Union Theological Seminary in New York City. A brilliant career opened before him and in 1930 he became a lecturer in theology at the University of Berlin. When, in 1933, Hitler came to power Bonhoeffer quickly saw the menace of National Socialism to the Christian faith and refused to compromise. He left Berlin, was a pastor in London, and became an ardent advocate of the Ecumenical Movement. In 1935 he returned to Germany. Forbidden by the Gestapo to preach or speak, he directed an illegal church training school in which he endeavoured to have a community life embodying genuine Christian brotherhood. The school was closed by the Gestapo in 1940. For a time, through the kindness of American friends, he was in the United States, but he felt constrained to return to Germany. Arrested by the Gestapo in 1943, he was in various prisons and concentration camps and was executed on April 9, 1945, shortly before the Allied victory would have brought him release. In the months of confinement he was a tower of strength to his fellow prisoners. Sustained by his faith and love of

[84] Ibid., pp. 390, 391, 465; Herman, The Rebirth of the German Church, pp. 78 ff.

[85] Martin Niemöller, Dachau Sermons, translated by R. H. Pfeiffer (New York, Harper &. Brothers, 1946, pp. 97), passim.

[86] See a brief account of his life by G. Leibholz in Dietrich Bonhoeffer, The Cost of Discipleship, translated by R. H. Fuller (New York, The Macmillan Co., 1953, pp. 199), pp. 9–28. Some of his writings have been put into English, among them Ethics, edited by Eberhard Bethge, translated by Neville Horton Smith (London, S.C.M. Press, 1955, pp. xv, 342). His Gesammelte Schriften, edited by Eberhard Bethge, is being published (Munich, C. Kaiser, 2 vols., 1948, 1959). See also John D. Godsey, The Theology of Dietrich Bonhoeffer (Philadelphia, The Westminster Press, 1960, pp. 299), passim, based on solid scholarship.

[87] Volume II, pp. 24, 47, 57.

God, he had a poise and a radiance which brought solace to many. The prison letters of others who were not as prominently remembered as Bonhoeffer were also preserved and published, evidence of the vitality of their faith in the darkest hours and an inspiration to many in the difficult post-war days.[88]

In general, with the exception of the Roman Catholic Church, the Protestant churches, and especially the *Bekennende Kirche,* came through the National Socialist era more nearly free from Nazi control than any other set of institutions. It has been said that only 5 per cent. of the Protestant pastors were Nazis. In this their record was less compromising than that of the Roman Catholic Church. Outspoken as the latter eventually became in its opposition, for a time through the concordat of 1933 it sought accommodation to the Hitler regime. Under that policy numbers of its priests joined the National Socialist Party. The *Bekennende Kirche* came out in opposition to the Nazis earlier than the Roman Catholic Church. When, because of the friendliness of the National Socialists to Rosenberg and the German Faith movement, the Roman Catholic leadership denounced policies to which it could not consent, priests withdrew from the party. They suffered severely, for the Nazis held that that act was more reprehensible than criticism by those who had never been party members. The *Bekennende Kirche* came through the Nazi years with a far better record of continuous resistance to the National Socialist madness than did the universities and the labour movements. We must note, moreover, that Pietism, prominent in the awakenings in the seventeenth, eighteenth, and nineteenth centuries, was a waning force, and the minorities committed to it had little or no share in the resistance to National Socialism. Some Pietists, indeed, tended to conform.[89]

VIGOUR UNDER THE GERMAN FEDERAL REPUBLIC

Following the collapse of the Hitler regime Protestantism displayed decided vigour under both the German Federal Republic in the West and the German Democratic Republic in the East. The challenges which confronted it in both regions were staggering. In Western Germany Protestantism faced the secularization of large elements of the population and did not have a substantial

---

[88] See, for example, Helmut Gollwitzer, Käthe Kuhn, and Reinhold Schneider, editors, *Dying We Live. The Final Messages and Records of the Resistance,* translated by Reinhold C. Kuhn (New York, Pantheon Books, 1956, pp. xxi, 285), *passim,* which includes Protestants, Roman Catholics, and a few without Christian faith. For an account by Hans Lilje (1899——), in his youth prominent in the Student Christian Movement and the World's Student Christian Federation, later Lutheran bishop in Hanover, outstanding in the resistance to the Nazis, arrested in 1944, released by the German defeat, and later a leader in EKD and the Lutheran World Federation, see Hans Lilje, *The Valley of the Shadow,* translated with an introduction by Olive Wyon (Philadelphia, Muhlenberg Press, 1950, pp. 128), *passim.* It contains not only Lilje's experience but also something of others who did not survive.

[89] F. H. Littell to the author, April, 1954, March, 1960.

majority of the population as it did before the division of the country: the separation from East Germany, where Protestants far outnumbered Roman Catholics, reduced its previous relative strength in the Western zone. The vast shifts of population brought by the war increased the number of Protestants in prevailingly Roman Catholic areas, thus augmenting the problems of pastoral care, and introduced Roman Catholics into what had been Protestant territories. Thousands of refugees from the East and from areas from which Germans had been displaced by transfers of territory constituted a major problem. The moving of the eastern border of Germany westward with the forcible evacuation of the German population from East Prussia, Pomerania, and Silesia, long prevailingly Protestant, all but destroyed Protestantism in those areas. In the German Democratic Republic a Communist regime raised more and more obstacles to the churches, both Protestant and Roman Catholic, which bore especially heavily on the Protestant majority. In both West and East Germany Protestantism, like Roman Catholicism, had to contend with the destruction wrought by enemy bombings, and with dire impoverishment, physical exhaustion, and spiritual disillusion which followed the prolonged strain of the war and the final defeat. The military occupation by the victors also brought problems.

As Protestantism rose to meet the emergency, the leadership was chiefly from the opponents of the Nazi regime. That leadership soon took decisive action which placed its stamp upon a reorganized German Protestantism. The German Christians, compromised by their coöperation with the discredited Nazi regime, were soon removed from ecclesiastical office. In August, 1945, a gathering in Treysa in which Bishop Wurm and Niemöller were prominent organized Die Evangelische Kirche in Deutschlands (The Evangelical Church in Germany), usually known under its initials as EKD or EKiD.[90] EKD was a loose federation of the Landeskirchen rather than a union, and of the Free Churches only the Moravians were included. The other Free Churches had relations with EKD through the more inclusive Committee of the Christian Churches, which had Niemöller as its head and through which they as well as the Landeskirchen coöperated.[91] At the Treysa meeting Hilfswerk was begun as an agency of EKD to deal with the relief of suffering and with other problems of the new day.[92] The Treysa gathering condemned the centralized state church of the Nazi regime and adopted the form of unity freely entered into by the Confessing synods of Barmen, Dahlem, and Augsburg.[93] As a

[90] Kirchliches Jahrbuch, 1945–1948, pp. 8 ff.
[91] Hans Lilje in World Dominion, Vol. XXXV, p. 17.
[92] Kirchliches Jahrbuch, 1945–1948, p. 15.
[93] Ibid., pp. 15–17.

distinct organization the *Bekennende Kirche* was no longer needed and passed out of existence.

In October, 1945, the council (*Rat*) of EKD, meeting in Stuttgart with Bishop Wurm as its chairman, restored the fellowship with Protestants in former enemy countries which had been jeopardized by the war. The World Council of Churches, then in process of formation, was welcomed through its general secretary, W. A. Visser 't Hooft, and representatives were present from the Missouri Lutheran Synod, the Federal Council of the Churches of Christ in the U.S.A., the French Reformed Church, the Dutch Reformed Church, the Church of England, and the Council of Swiss churches. The Council, speaking for EKD, although calling attention to the contribution which the Allies had made through the Treaty of Versailles to the rise of the National Socialists, did not seek to excuse or condone the atrocities perpetrated in World War II by the German forces in occupied lands or the mass murders of German and Polish Jews. But it pleaded for a united effort of the Christian forces of the world to establish relations between peoples on the basis not of revenge and retribution but of forgiveness and trust and thus to seek to counter the alienation from God and the hostility to Christ which twice in a generation had brought disaster to peoples and states originally founded on Christian principles.[94]

Partly in connexion with EKD significant developments took place in German Protestantism. Since EKD was a federation and not a centralized structure as the *Reichskirche* of National Socialists was designed to be, the several *Landeskirchen* whose autonomy had been threatened were rebuilt, and on Confessional lines.[95] Now that the common menace of the National Socialist regime was removed, the unity displayed in the common resistance tended further to disintegrate: the historic confessional differences threatened to dissolve the unity of EKD. To preserve their distinctive witness the Lutherans came together under the *Verfassung der Vereinigten Evangelischen-Lutherischen Kirche Deutschlands* (VELKD) (Constitution of the United Evangelical Church of Germany), formulated over the year end of 1946–1947. Fear was expressed that it might disrupt EKD, but working arrangements between the two were devised.[96] The Reformed had their own alliance and deplored the movement to make the Augsburg Confession the doctrinal basis of EKD.[97] The Prussian Union of Lutherans and Reformed of nineteenth-century origin,[98]

[94] *Ibid.*, pp. 19–29. See other actions in *ibid.*, *1954*, pp. 55 ff. For other expressions of confession and repentance see Herman, *The Rebirth of the German Church*, pp. 125 ff.
[95] *Kirchliches Jahrbuch, 1945–1948*, pp. 108–158.
[96] *Ibid.*, pp. 448, 449.
[97] *Kirchliches Jahrbuch, 1950*, pp. 313 ff.
[98] Volume II, pp. 75 ff.

the *Evangelische Kirche die altprussischen Union* (EKapU), was revived[99] and became the largest member of the *Evangelische Kirche der Union* (EKU) (Evangelical Church of the Union), which drew together it and similar bodies. EKU was without a creed and so was looked at askance by the Lutherans.[100] Yet the Evangelical Church of Bremen, which had been the only one of the *Landeskirchen* to hold aloof, in 1952 acceded to EKD.[101] Moreover, EKD reached across the political barrier which separated West from East Germany and maintained partial fellowship with its brethren in the Communist zone.[102] The separation of Church and state achieved under the Weimar Republic was renewed, but, as under that regime and under Hitler, the various state governments, as a matter of convenience, were the collecting agencies for the church tax. The church tax amounted to a small percentage of an individual's income, and much of it was paid in connexion with the general income tax collected through employers.

The various free churches which were not included in EKD continued and some of them grew rapidly, but they still enrolled only minorities. Among them were the Methodists, the Baptists, the Mennonites, the Old Catholics, the Lutheran Free Churches, and Jehovah's Witnesses. Jehovah's Witnesses suffered severely under the National Socialist regime but revived after World War II and by 1954 claimed half a million members in Germany. The New Apostolic Church, which sought to restore the government of the Church by the Twelve Apostles and expected the early return of Christ, by the mid-1950's had enrolled 229,000 strongly disciplined members.[103] We also hear of the Church of the Kingdom of God, a split from Jehovah's Witnesses, of Swiss post-World War I origin, which in the late 1940's was said to have 50,000 adherents in Germany. The Seventh Day Adventists grew in numbers. The *Christengemeinschaft* (Christian Community), a development from anthroposophy, proscribed by the Nazis but revived after their fall, had its centre in Stuttgart.[104]

Hilfswerk, an early creation of EKD, had a rapid expansion. Inspiring it was the purpose not only of relieving the widespread distress which followed the war but also of seeking to reach the thousands who were alienated from the Church and to meet basic social conditions which were a fruit of the revolutionary age. The leaders recognized gratefully the service long performed

---

[99] *Kirchliches Jahrbuch, 1951*, pp. 43 ff.
[100] *Kirchliches Jahrbuch, 1957*, pp. 197 ff.; C. E. Schneider in *The Christian Century*, Vol. LXXIV, p. 988.
[101] *Kirchliches Jahrbuch, 1953*, pp. 5–7.
[102] *Ibid.*, pp. 159 ff.
[103] *Kirchliches Jahrbuch, 1945–1948*, pp. 471–473; F. H. Littell in *The Ecumenical Review*, Vol. VI, pp. 274, 275.
[104] Kurt Hutten, *Sehe, Grübler Enthusiasten. Sekten und religiöse Sondergemeinschaften der Gegenwart* (Stuttgart, Im Quell-Verlag der Evang. Gesellschaft, 1950, pp. 293), pp. 34–36, 64, 65, 121 ff.

by the Inner Mission but held that it was chiefly confined to care for the poor and the sick. They dreamed of attacking the social problems of the day and of having the Church take on the responsibility rather than delegating the task, as formerly, to the Inner Mission. They also sought to enlist a large body of laity.[105] *Hilfswerk,* accordingly, became a phase of that movement of lay participation in the life of Protestantism which was a prominent feature of the post-World War II years, especially in Germany and the Netherlands, was stressed by the World Council of Churches, and was akin to what we have met in the Roman Catholic Church of these decades. The laity had been prominent in nineteenth-century Protestantism in the British Isles and North America and to a certain extent on the Continent of Europe, but now, in a variety of ways, of which *Hilfswerk* was one, they had a mounting share in German Protantism. All non-Roman Catholic ecclesiastical bodies, the Free Churches as well as EKD, joined in supporting *Hilfswerk* in the most inclusive, so it was said, Protestant effort in Germany since the Reformation. *Hilfswerk* was de-centralized, with committees of the *Landeskirchen,* of the Free Churches, and of the churches in exile, all coördinated by a committee in Stuttgart. At the outset it addressed itself primarily to relief of the widespread need, including the refugees from the many regions in Central and East Europe, and to the rebuilding of destroyed churches and the crippled church life. It raised substantial funds by collections in Germany, and that in spite of the destitution of the immediate post-war years. It also received help from abroad in both money and goods, given not directly by one denomination to another but through an ecumenical agency with headquarters in Geneva.[106] As the years passed remarkable contributions were made to the care of refugees, including the thousands who continued to come to the German Federal Republic from the German Democratic Republic, to hundreds of youths among the refugees, to Germans who remained in Central Europe, to homeless foreigners, to churches in East Germany, to the rebuilding of churches destroyed by the bombings, to care for students, and to the restoration of the life of the congregations. Coöperation increased between *Hilfswerk* and the Inner Mission and late in the 1950's the two were formally united. The Inner Mission had survived under Hitler but had been greatly handicapped. After World War II it was revived.[107] Some of the institutions long connected with the Inner Mission continued, notably the congeries at Bethel. Several new ones were created, not directly under *Hilfswerk* or the Inner Mission. Among them were thirteen youth villages, conducted by Protestants through the Young Men's Christian

---

[105] *Kirchliches Jahrbuch, 1945–1948,* pp. 389–391.

[106] *Ibid.,* pp. 391–413.

[107] *Ibid., 1957,* pp. 209–245. On early relief through the churches see Herman, *The Rebirth of the German Church,* pp. 200 ff.

Association but inspired by Boys' Town in the United States, an institution inaugurated by a Roman Catholic priest. They were for youths cast adrift by the war. They trained boys in various handicrafts and drew their financial support from the government, churches, and private gifts. In them the Mennonite Central Committee and the Brethren were especially active. For years, indeed, the former was the third largest relief agency.[108]

The collective voice of EKD did not leave to *Hilfswerk* the entire task of seeking to bring the conscience and voice of Protestantism to bear upon the social and political issues of the day. *Hilfswerk* was too engrossed in the appalling magnitude of the tasks which were its immediate concern to pay much attention to other phases of the purpose for which it was originally conceived. More than once EKD spoke out on public questions. It opposed the rearming of West Germany (although Protestant opinion on this was divided), compulsory military service for conscientious objectors, and the kind of propaganda which would provoke enmity between governments. It was silent on the question of the inclusion of West Germany in a military alliance, but it expressed itself on the issue of atomic weapons and on the moot question of the disposition of the Saar Valley.[109] In one of its synods it made "the Church in the world of labour" its main theme.[110]

In the effort to enlist the laity and to apply Christian principles to various aspects of the life of the laity Protestants were quick to take advantage of the freedom in West Germany which followed World War II. One of the most spectacular developments was the multiplication of Evangelical Academies. They arose from the attempt to promote conversation between the Church and the world. Back of them was the conviction that the Protestant churches in Germany had not addressed themselves sufficiently to the wide range of problems which confronted the laity in the revolutionary age and had not given guidance to their members in the application of the Christian faith to their daily occupations. To be sure, Protestantism had long said that every Christian should think of his daily work as a divine vocation, but it had been of little or no help to the laity in the practice of that principle. During the National Socialist period a beginning had been made, but under the restrictions of the Nazi regime no freedom existed for an extensive prosecution of such a programme. Now, in a comparatively fluid situation when the Church was the only major institution to come through the Nazi era intact and with the prestige which accrued to Protestantism from the resistance of the *Bekennende Kirche*, a unique opportunity was seen to fulfil the dream. Here was a challenge to a kind of evangelism which would penetrate all society.

[108] The author's personal observation in 1954.
[109] *Kirchliches Jahrbuch, 1954*, pp. 62, 63; *1957*, pp. 72–97; *Information Service*, May 28, 1955.
[110] *Kirchliches Jahrbuch, 1955*, p. 77.

The initial Evangelical Academy was the creation of a pastor, Eberhard Müller, at Bad Boll, in Württemberg, in the autumn of 1945. By 1957 Evangelical Academies numbered eighteen, five of them in the German Democratic Republic. Some were the property of one or another of the *Landeskirchen*. They were coördinated through a directors' association with headquarters at Bad Boll. Bad Boll was also the seat of an association of the directors of similar centres for the laity in all Western Europe, for several came into being, some entirely independent of the German example and others inspired by it. In 1959 they were said to number sixty in twelve countries.

By "academy" was not meant an educational institution with courses of study leading to degrees, but a place for conferences, usually of two to five days' duration. The conferences were designed to reach groups, mostly intellectuals and workers, otherwise on the fringe of the Church or entirely untouched by it. Their purpose was in part to help to a Christian orientation those who had been demoralized by National Socialism and left morally and spiritually adrift by the collapse of the Nazis. To one conference came physicians, to another teachers, to another lawyers, to another farmers, to another workers on railroads, to another journalists, and to still another students. Each was encouraged to discuss the bearing of the Christian faith on the particular occupation or profession of those in attendance and on the problems confronted in daily living. The conferences could enroll only minorities and were directed to the elite rather than the masses. The churches were not solidly committed to the Evangelical Academies, for some in ecclesiastical posts were more intent on restoring the traditional character and functions of the churches than in reaching out into society. Several of the Evangelical Academies were independent of the *Landeskirchen* and were more ecumenically minded than was much of the leadership of the latter. How far if at all the Evangelical Academies affected national life as a whole would be difficult to determine. Some who had been in the Academies formed guilds which published magazines to carry further the discussions begun in them.[111]

The Evangelical Academies were not the only Protestant agencies which sought laity who were partly or entirely estranged from the Church. The Gossner Mission, begun in the nineteenth century,[112] whose members were centres of support for the Confessing Church during the Hitler era and some of whom had been imprisoned or had lost their lives during those years, saw a challenge in the classes who had fallen victim to Nazism and might succumb

---

[111] *Kirchliches Jahrbuch, 1945–1948*, pp. 368–388; M. Frakes in *The Christian Century*, Vol. LXXVI, pp. 288–290; T. Luckmann in *Christianity and Crisis*, Vol. XVII, pp. 68–70; F. H. Littell in *The Christian Century*, Vol. LXXVI, p. 1092; Weber, *Signs of Renewal*, pp. 5–11; Eberhard Mueller, *Die Welt ist anders geworden* (Hamburg, Furche-Verlag, 1953), *passim;* F. H. Littell, in *The Emory University Quarterly*, Vol. XV, pp. 49–53, March, 1959.

[112] Volume II, p. 115.

to Communism, and sought to bring the Gospel to them. One of its pastors donned working clothes and as a labourer in a factory became a creator of Christian comradeship. The Gossner Mission conducted international work camps, had a school in Berlin to train teachers of religion for the Eastern zone, and operated three trailer churches to serve areas wasted by the war.[113] In 1949 the *Evangelische Social Akademie* was begun at the instance of the *Evangelische Aktionsgemeindschaft für Arbeitersfragan* (Evangelical Action Association for Labour Problems). It established a centre at Haus Friedewald, a castle in a rural community, to which it brought trade union leaders for periods of one to eight weeks to train them in economics, sociology, and Christian theology with the purpose of inducing labour to take intelligent Christian responsibility for society. One of the Gossner pastors was connected with it. It published a monthly journal and also sought to bring students and labourers together to break down class differences.[114]

Another movement, primarily lay in leadership and for the purpose of enlisting the laity and dealing with phases of the revolutionary age, was the *Kirchentag.* The name was old in Protestant circles,[115] and Roman Catholics had had the *Katholikentag* both in the nineteenth century and currently.[116] Yet the post-World War II *Kirchentag* was not a replica of either but a fresh creation. Its originator and continued inspiring leader was Reinold von Thadden-Trieglaff (1891——). Of the East Prussian aristocracy, from a family which had long been a centre of earnest and joyous Pietism and of a circle to which Bismarck owed much of his Christian faith,[117] Reinhold von Thadden-Trieglaff was a layman who had an extensive education in the law, had been in government service, and had been chairman of the German Student Christian Movement and a vice-chairman of the World's Student Christian Federation.[118] As the administrator of an area which included Louvain during the German occupation in World War II he had won the gratitude of that city by refusing to carry out orders of the government involving injustice to the citizens. Later, as a prisoner in Russia, his health had suffered greatly. He was deeply concerned for the Protestant Church and saw it facing an atheistic state or slowly undermined by religious indifference or open hostility. Unless the tide was turned, he believed, more and more unwillingness to pay the church tax would develop and increasing resignations from the Church could be expected. While in a camp in Siberia he conceived the *Kirchentag* as stemming

---

[113] A mimeographed statement on the Gossner Mission, January, 1959.
[114] Information gathered by the author through a visit in April, 1954.
[115] Volume II, pp. 18, 85, 86, 105, 106, 109, 116.
[116] Volume I, pp. 349, 435, 438; Volume IV, Chapter VII.
[117] Volume II, pp. 73, 119, 120.
[118] Werner Hühne, *Thadden-Trieglaff. Ein Leben unter uns* (Stuttgart, Kreuz-Verlag, 1959, pp. 247), *passim; Who's Who in Germany*, p. 1156.

from love of the Church, and as not seeking to replace the simple preaching of the Gospel but giving visible form to the community of Christians, encouraging the laymen to be missionary, and applying the Christian faith not only to the winning of individuals but also to the "burning East-West problem, the possibility for real peace, the racial question, the pressing need for social reform, and the recovery and development of a democratic civic consciousness." Not the individual by himself, but only the Christian community, so he said, must be called upon. It "must not only want to go to heaven; it must also desire the world to be brought under the rule of Christ."[119]

The first *Kirchentag* of this new pattern was held in the summer of 1949 in Hanover. Called the *Evangelische Woch* (Evangelical Week) it gave itself to Bible study and to such problems as the Christian answer to the political situation and the crisis in the human community. Niemöller preached a memorable sermon. A constitution was adopted for the continuation of the *Kirchentag* as a means of preparing the laity for their service in the world.[120] The second *Kirchentag,* the first mass meeting, convened in Essen in the heart of industrialized Westphalia in August, 1950, was concerned with "the whole human being" rather than "saving the human soul," addressed itself to such questions as preserving the freedom, the family, and the faith of the labourers, and made much of Bible study, the great music of the Church, and the Communion.[121] The *Kirchentag* of 1951 met in politically divided Berlin, with the theme "in spite of all we are still brothers," and that of 1952 in Stuttgart under the theme "choose life." The *Kirchentag* of 1953 was in Hamburg, nominally a predominantly Protestant city but where church attendance averaged only about 2.5 per cent. of those who paid church taxes. It concerned itself with the place of the laity in the Church, the relations of children and their elders, the intercourse of the German people with other peoples, the use of money, and the problems of the rural village and of the city. Thousands came in special trains from East Germany.[122] The Hamburg *Kirchentag* was followed by the organization of a *Kirchentag* for the city itself in an effort to penetrate the circles which paid the church tax but were estranged from the Church. This was largely through groups called *"Kirchentag* families" meeting one evening a month in private houses and discussing such questions as Christian responsibility in industry and commerce, the Christian and war, and conscientious objection to military service. By 1957 six other cities had a local *Kirchentag.*[123] In 1954 the *Kirchentag* convened in Leipzig, in the German Democratic Re-

---

[119] Reinold von Thadden-Trieglaff in *The Ecumenical Review,* Vol. IX, pp. 410–418; Causton, *Kirchentag Calling,* pp. 15–18.
[120] *Kirchliches Jahrbuch, 1949,* pp. 58–68.
[121] *Ibid., 1950,* pp. 13 ff.; Causton, *op. cit.,* pp. 7, 8.
[122] *Kirchliches Jahrbuch, 1953,* pp. 15 ff.; Causton, *op. cit.,* pp. 18, 19.
[123] *A Monthly Letter about Evangelism,* March, 1957.

public, and was attended by 400,000 or 500,000 from both the West and the East zones and from a number of foreign countries.[124] The 1956 Kirchentag was in Frankfurt-am-Main. The meeting of the 1959 Kirchentag was in Munich and was marked by the hospitality of Roman Catholics in a city in which they were in the large majority. The East German Government permitted only 1,000 of its citizens to attend, but delegations came from east of the Iron Curtain from Czechoslovakia, Hungary, Poland, and Russia. Delegations were also present from most Western European countries and from Asia, Africa, the Americas, Australia, New Zealand, Japan, and Greenland. At the final service 370,000 were said to be present.[125] An outgrowth of the Kirchentag was a Studententag for students. The third in the student series was held in Heidelberg in August, 1954, with the theme Das Reich Gottes und das Reich der Deutschen ("The Kingdom of God and the realm of the Germans").[126] From the beginning the Kirchentag had close contacts with the Ecumenical Movement and especially the World Council of Churches. It proved contagious and similar gatherings sprang up in a number of other lands, among them South-west France, Scotland, Alsace, and even distant Sumatra.[127]

In the Kirchentag, as in the Evangelical Academies, was a movement paralleling that in the Roman Catholic Church in Europe to enlist the laity. The movement took different forms in the two branches of Christianity, but it was clear evidence of a vigour which was endeavouring to counter the de-Christianizing phases of the revolutionary age. In neither was it defensive or a rearguard action. Rather it sought to capture the once nominally Christian society for Christ and to make Christ King of the new society which was emerging. There might be despair of attaining that goal in the present age and belief in Christ as the hope of the world in an eschatological end of an age in which the powers of darkness seemed dominant. But in both Protestant and Roman Catholic circles the confident hope was cherished that, if not in history, then beyond history Christ would be acknowledged as Lord.

Active as German Protestantism was in seeking to enlist the laity and through them to penetrate the common life with Christian principles, it is not surprising that like the Roman Catholics it created labour unions and engaged in political action. After World War II several Protestant workers' organizations existed. At times Protestants joined with Roman Catholics in non-confessional unions. An Evangelical Action Committee made up of representatives of Protestant workers' groups endeavoured to make possible joint action on

---

[124] Kirchliches Jahrbuch, 1954, pp. 20 ff.
[125] F. H. Littell in The Christian Century, Vol. LXXVI, pp. 1046, 1047; Ecumenical Press Service, August 18, 1959.
[126] Kirchliches Jahrbuch, 1954, pp. 43-55.
[127] Thadden-Trieglaff, op. cit., p. 410.

issues which concerned them all.[128] Protestants also constituted themselves a section of the Christian Democratic Union, a party in which Roman Catholics were strong, and took positive stands on political issues.[129]

The concern for enlisting the laity did not eclipse efforts to recruit and train clerical leadership for German Protestantism and thus both to fill the gaps caused by war casualties and to prepare pastors who could meet the challenges of the new stage of the revolutionary age. For a time after 1945 the number of theological students increased rapidly. It reached a peak in 1949–1950 and then fell off steadily and sharply. In contrast with 1934, an early year of the Nazi rule, the clergy of 1950 had a smaller proportion of young men and a larger proportion of those in middle life.[130] Theological faculties in the universities were, as formerly, supported by the state. In addition, several *Kirchliche Hochschülen* (Church Colleges) were maintained for theological training, among them one in connexion with the great institutions at Bethel where practical was combined with theoretical training in ministering to the unfortunate.[131] The *Kirchliche Hochschülen* dated from the Nazi period and were begun by the *Bekennende Kirche* as a substitute for the theological faculties in the universities, then filled by German Christians who coöperated with the National Socialists, and when the universities were closed to Confessing students. What may be described as preparatory theological education was given in some other schools, among them one in the buildings of an ancient Cistercian foundation at Maulbronn in Württemberg.[132] Some of the *Landeskirchen* had *Pastoralcollegs*. Here was an innovation which sprang from the conviction that the theological training in the universities prepared students for research rather than the pastorate. The *Pastoralcollegs* stressed subjects which would be more germane to what was required in the parish. The first was in Neuendettelsau. The *Pastoralcollegs* were an advance over the seminaries which had been maintained in the nineteenth century. The latter were largely for men without university training and did not have high academic requirements. From the scholarly standpoint the *Pastoralcollegs* were held in more esteem.[133]

The entire scope of the preparation for the ministry was given careful study by EKD. Two examinations were still required.[134] The first included the Old and New Testaments, Church history and the history of doctrine, systematic

---

[128] Fogarty, *Christian Democracy in Western Europe, 1820–1953*, pp. 224, 225.

[129] As in *Kirchliches Jahrbuch, 1954*, pp. 71 ff., *1955*, pp. 17 ff., *1957*, pp. 72–97.

[130] *Ibid., 1953*, p. 406, *1954*, p. 372.

[131] *Ibid., 1945–1948*, pp. 474–482.

[132] Gustav Lang, *Maulbronn. Führer durch das Kloster* (Brackenheim, Georg Kohl, new ed., 1953, pp. 63), pp. 16, 59.

[133] *Kirchliches Jahrbuch, 1950*, pp. 91, 92.

[134] Volume II, p. 99.

theology, and practical theology. As formerly, Greek, Latin, and Hebrew were stressed. Between the first and second examinations training in the work of the ministry was acquired through a period as an assistant (vicar) in a parish, seminars on preaching, service as a catechist, or helping in a school. Eight semesters were regarded as the minimum for theological training, the problem of adequate financial support for the student was faced, and the importance of a community life for theological students was emphasized.[135] As a further aid to the theological student in preparing for the practical aspects of his future ministry in the changing environment, a *Dienstjahr* ("service year") was begun, in Württemberg in 1948, in which experience was had with *Hilfswerk* or the Inner Mission.[136] In the growing shortage of clergy by the late 1950's a few laymen were being admitted to the ministry as "non-academic pastors" without theological training but after periods of special instruction. In addition, some laymen were being recruited to take over much of the work of the parishes. The farming areas were less the source of the clergy than formerly. We shall observe a similar shortage in several other countries.[137]

Pietism did not loom as prominently as in the nineteenth century. No Pietist awakenings were seen on a scale comparable to those of the ten decades which followed the Napoleonic Wars. Yet in some areas, especially in Westphalia and Württemberg, Pietism continued as an important phase of Protestantism. In Württemberg it displayed great variety. Most of those touched by it remained in the *Landeskirchen,* but some were outside them. Pietism seems to have perpetuated itself chiefly among those who were reared in it and not to have made many fresh converts. Yet the European Alliance, partly an outgrowth of the Evangelical Alliance and predominantly Pietist, was reorganized in 1952, held an annual study conference, and promoted a week of prayer.

In addition to Pietism, within the *Landeskirchen* or among their constituencies were a number of movements, some of them new and others old. Several of the latter were renewed after the Nazi years. Among the new ones was the *Oekumenische Marienschwesternschaft* (Ecumenical Sisterhood of Mary), with headquarters at Darmstadt. Lutheran, it arose from a Bible class, but the decision to begin it was stimulated by an air raid in September, 1944. Its members did all the work of the community, including the construction of its physical plant. Its motto was "Christ is my life, death is my gain." In its chapel a perpetual vigil of prayer was maintained.[138] A revival of private confession was seen in Lutheran circles. It was symptomatic of a growth in individual pastoral care[139] and seems also to have been related to a growing liturgical

[135] *Kirchliches Jahrbuch, 1953,* pp. 58–61, *1954,* pp. 151, 152, *1955,* pp. 89–92.
[136] *Ibid., 1950,* pp. 89–91.
[137] *Ecumenical Press Service,* October 2, 1959.
[138] Arthur Kreinheder, letter to the author, September 1, 1954.
[139] *Time,* September 14, 1959.

movement. A form of ministry which was becoming widespread not only in Germany but elsewhere in Europe and on the other side of the Atlantic was carried on by telephone. Men and women in need of advice or consolation or contemplating suicide were encouraged to call on the telephone. The service was introduced in Berlin and spread to other cities. It evoked a wide response.[140] The Young Men's Christian Association revived after the downfall of the Nazis. However, a method of reaching the youth favoured by most of the *Landeskirchen* was organizations within the parish as part of the parish programme. While still strongly Pietist, the Young Men's Christian Association was said to be less so than formerly. It reached out to several different groups: refugees, displaced persons, labourers in industry, students, rural youth, and the youth villages of which we have spoken.[141]

Not only did the destruction of church buildings by the bombings call for extensive construction of churches, but the vast shifts of population, including the refugees, demanded new churches if the traditionally Protestant were to be held to the faith. Need also existed to aid in providing housing for the refugees. A movement arose, the *Baugemeinde* (Building Association), to unite efforts, especially in West Germany, for the accomplishment of this purpose. It first had headquarters in Frankfurt-am-Main. The initial general meeting of its members was in Stuttgart in 1952. There an executive committee was elected further to coördinate what was being done in several of the states.[142] The *Evang. Baugemeinschaft*, sponsored by *Hilfswerk*, was also important.

The *Gustav Adolf Verein*, founded in 1832 to give spiritual care to Protestants of the *Diaspora* in predominantly Roman Catholic territories,[143] celebrated its centennial on the eve of the Hitler era. Under that regime it continued and aided the Protestant Church in Austria after the annexation of that country (1938) and in the Sudetenland subsequent to the seizure of that region (1939). It also concerned itself with Germans moved by Hitler into areas in the East during World War II.[144] The territorial rearrangements which followed that war cut off from the operations of the *Gustav Adolf Verein* some of the regions with which it had been concerned and confronted it with new challenges in the vast displaced populations. Reorganization was accomplished to meet the changing conditions, and the name was altered to the *Gustav Adolf Werk*. Efforts to make the new structure an official organ of EKD came to naught and problems were encountered in relations with the strictly confessional

---

[140] *A Monthly Letter about Evangelism*, March, 1959.
[141] Robert Miller, representing the International Committee of the YMCA, in conversation with the author, May 3, 1954.
[142] *Kirchliches Jahrbuch, 1950*, pp. 89 ff.; *1952*, pp. 438–441.
[143] Volume II, pp. 111, 112.
[144] *Kirchliches Jahrbuch, 1955*, pp. 310–317.

Martin Luther Bund and with the *Lutherischen Weltdienst* (Lutheran World Service), founded in Hanover in 1952. A division of organization between the West and the East zones became necessary. But the adjustments were made and the *Gustav Adolf Werk* carried on its ministry in both zones and among the *Diaspora* in Central Europe.[145]

The German Protestant minorities in countries outside Europe came within the concern of EKD. Niemöller was put in charge of what might be called the foreign affairs of EKD and in that capacity interested himself in congregations of German Protestants in various parts of the world which had had connexions with the *Reichskirche* (DEK) of the National Socialist years. Under the new political conditions several of the congregations which had existed disappeared, but many remained. Niemöller visited some of them and furthered relations with them. The large Lutheran population in Brazil was especially important.[146]

The provision for the religious education of Protestant youth varied from state to state. In general, religion was a normal part of the curriculum of the schools. Confessional schools, Protestant and Roman Catholic, were numerous, and in them instruction in the tenets of the respective churches was a part of the curriculum. In some of the state schools no teacher could be required to give religious instruction. In others teachers were appointed of the same confession as the students, and the religious instruction was in accordance with the prevailing background of the pupils. In still others it was non-confessional and in such phases of the subject as were common to all. In at least one state the religious instruction in the state or folk school was given by the regular teachers, by the clergy, or by catechists. Related to the lay movements were efforts to bring parents and teachers together for consultation, and for that purpose periodic national conferences were held under Protestant auspices. Protestant religious instruction was also extended to the vocational schools, enrolling as they did a large proportion of the school population. Programmes were formulated for adequate preparation of the teachers.[147] During the Nazi regime many became teachers of religion to defame Christianity, but in the German Federal Republic all teachers of religion were required to be certified by the churches to be sure that they were sympathetic and informed.

How far these many measures were preventing the progress of de-Christianization in the historically Protestant elements of the population and were winning back those who had been alienated would be difficult or impossible to determine. Some observers said that church life was most vigorous in the cities and was declining in the rural districts. Others were of precisely the

---

[145] *Ibid.*, pp. 320–356.
[146] *Ibid., 1950*, pp. 333–371, *1955*, p. 332.
[147] *Ibid., 1955*, pp. 237–280.

opposite opinion. In general it was clear that church attendance was better in the villages than in the cities. Yet the revolutionary age was working changes in the villages. Movement of population to the cities, the introduction of machinery into agriculture, and the coming of refugees to many communities were adverse to traditional church patterns. Conditions varied from section to section. Statistically, some growth was seen in the number of congregations but with the exception of a few states the total of those who formally left the Church slightly exceeded that of new entrants. Neither was large in proportion to the population.[148] As in much of Western Europe, whether in Roman Catholic or Protestant areas, the large majority of the population were baptized and a substantial percentage—even in Berlin about two-thirds—were confirmed, but the average attendance at services was low and many never took Communion after the one received at confirmation.

Some contributions came to Protestantism in West Germany from refugees and from those who survived the Russian prison camps and, escaping or released, returned home. In addition to the great impulse given by Reinhold von Thadden-Trieglaff, who was a refugee from East Prussia and had suffered in a Russian cantonment, numbers of others from East Prussia, that centre of Pietism, brought fresh vigour to the religious life of EKD. As one among a number with similar experiences, a former prisoner in Russia, Helmut Gollwitzer, by his account of the deepening of his spiritual life in the midst of his hardships helped to reinforce the faith of many.[149]

From the Protestant standpoint, the relations with the Roman Catholics varied from time to time and from group to group. The emergency brought by the bombings which led to the use of each other's buildings for worship was only temporary. With its passing that kind of association declined. On the Protestant side *Die Sammlung* paralleled in part the Una Sancta movement of the Roman Catholics. It was made up of pastors, laymen, and women, most of whom had been active in the resistance to Hitler. Its members deplored what they deemed the reciprocal misjudgements in both branches of the faith which accompanied and followed the Reformation and longed to have the churches of the Reformation find their place in the one Catholic and Apostolic Church. They held annual gatherings over which a pastor presided.[150]

The share of German Protestantism in the world mission of the Church inevitably suffered from the vicissitudes of the post-1914 decades. In both world wars German missionaries were shut out from colonial areas held or captured by their enemies. The inflation and impoverishment which accom-

---

[148] *Ibid., 1957*, pp. 247–251, 273–276.
[149] Helmut Gollwitzer, *Unwilling Journey. A Diary from Russia*, translated by E. M. Delacour and Robert Fenn (Philadelphia, Muhlenberg Press, 1953, pp. 316), *passim*.
[150] *The Commonweal*, Vol. LXIX, pp. 229, 230.

panied or followed these struggles made heavy inroads on the incomes of missionary agencies. Following 1945 partial recovery was achieved, but relative to the entire Protestant world enterprise German Protestants did not have as large a role as in the nineteenth century. During World War II complete collapse was prevented by the heroism of missionaries and by assistance from the International Missionary Council through the Orphaned Missions Fund, gathered from Protestants in neutral or enemy countries and evidence of a Christian fellowship which transcended warring lines and national boundaries.[151] In 1946 formal contacts were renewed between the German and other Continental missionary agencies. In 1947 Germans were present at a more inclusive gathering, that of the International Missionary Council at Whitby, in Ontario. Five years later they were hosts to the same body at Willingen. The societies of pre-war years were revived and sought to adjust themselves to the conditions brought by the rising nationalism in Asia, Africa, and the fringing islands, with the attendant self-consciousness of the churches in those lands. Of this we are to hear more in our final volume. The outstanding leader in the post-1945 years was Walter Freytag (1899–1959), who, among other contributions, headed an institution for missionary scholarship.[152] In general in the post-World War II years the missionary societies tended to draw nearer to the churches. Originally they had been quite independent of the Landeskirchen, but the gap began to be narrowed. Each Landeskirche had a missions conference, and through their central council the missions coöperated with EKD by means of a joint committee. The missionary societies were still distrustful of the theological faculties of the universities as not being orthodox and made few appointments from their graduates.

MOUNTING RESTRICTIONS AND STALWART RESISTANCE IN
THE GERMAN DEMOCRATIC REPUBLIC

The German Democratic Republic was in the zone occupied by the Russians after World War II. Slightly smaller in square miles than the German Federal Republic, it was less highly industrialized and had a population which was only a little more than a third that of the latter. It surrounded Berlin, but that city was divided into a Western and Eastern section, the one under the Western powers and the other under Russia. Since it was in the Russian zone, the German Democratic Republic had a Communist regime. Economic recovery was much slower than in the West and a fairly steady migration, mostly clandestine and often numbering many thousands a month, moved from the East to the West, partly because of more prosperous conditions in the latter

151 Latourette and Hogg, World Christian Community in Action, passim.
152 Kirchliches Jahrbuch, 1945–1948, pp. 321–351, 1953, pp. 336–378.

and partly from objection to Communism and the longing for greater personal liberty.

Religiously the German Democratic Republic had a predominantly Protestant population. True to the pattern which, with variations, was common to all lands under Communist rule, restrictions were placed on the churches. In spite of stalwart resistance, they continued to mount. Even to enumerate all the measures which the state took to bring the Protestant Church to heel would lengthen these pages beyond all proper limits. Space can be given to only a few, and they not necessarily in chronological or logical order. As in any totalitarian state a source of conflict with the Church was over the shaping of youth. An attempt was made to crush youth movements, including those associated with the Church, which were not under the control of the state and the Communist Party.[153] Religious instruction in the schools was permitted and was made the responsibility of the churches. However, it was voluntary for pupils and could be given only on the written request of parents. Teachers whose salaries were paid by the state who were willing to undertake that instruction at the request of the churches became fewer and the necessity arose of preparing men and women catechists to fill the gap.[154] In 1956 the civil authorities in East Berlin decreed that religious instruction should not be permitted in schools beyond the elementary level. Pastors and catechists who gave it were required to be friendly to the "workers' and peasants' state" and their permits were to be renewed for only three months at a time and could be withdrawn whenever the headmasters so decided. The headmasters were accorded control over extra-school events and other extra-curriculum activities, and this authority was applied to preparation for confirmation.[155] The government attempted to make a formal dedication of youth (*Jugendweihe*) to the purposes of the state a substitute for confirmation.[156] The prime minister was emphatic that the state was to be built on atheism. Weddings, funerals, and the naming of children were often in the atheistic spirit. Baptisms, confirmations, and church weddings declined. The number of children applying for religious instruction fell off. Many pastors engaged in secular employment to supplement their salaries. Obstacles were placed in the way of repairing old churches and constructing new ones. Economic discrimination was practised against active Christians.[157] Obstacles were placed in front of theological education. Theological faculties—both teachers and students—were subsidized by the state, and the civil authorities accused the professors of disseminating views

---

[153] *Kirchliches Jahrbuch, 1952*, pp. 196, 197.
[154] *Ibid., 1950*, pp. 387–391.
[155] *Ecumenical Press Service*, March 16, 1956; *Kirchliches Jahrbuch, 1956*, p. 159.
[156] *Kirchliches Jahrbuch, 1956*, p. 185, *1957*, pp. 151–158.
[157] *Theology Today*, Vol. XVI, pp. 381; *Time*, November 2, 1959.

contrary to the interests of the German Democratic Republic. The Church attempted to erect an institution comparable to the Church High Schools (Colleges) in the Western zone which would be independent of the state, but was frustrated. A marked shortage of clergy developed.[158] In January, 1956, leading representatives of the Railway Mission were arrested on the charge that they were espionage agents of the enemies of the German Democratic Republic.[159] The Francke Foundation founded at Halle by the Pietist of that name early in the eighteenth century, which had preserved its Christian character even under the Nazis, was gradually taken over and secularized by the East German regime. Symbolic of the change was the fact that it no longer printed Bibles and hymnals.[160] Many workers in the Protestant Church were imprisoned on the charge that they were subversive to the interests of the state.[161]

Against these and other pressures and attacks the Protestant Church presented sturdy resistance. In this it had an outstanding leader in Otto Dibelius (1880——), Bishop of Berlin. The son of a civil official, as a young man he had been active in seeking to win those of his own age who were being alienated from the Christian faith. He had been present at the World Missionary Conference in Edinburgh in 1910 and had been caught up in the early stages of the Ecumenical Movement. During the Nazi years he was a leader in the Bekennende Kirche. He was prominent in the formation of EKD and became the chairman of its council (Rat). He was instrumental in effecting the union under EKD of the Protestant Church in West and East Germany and fearlessly led EKD in its struggle with the government of the German Democratic Republic. He continued his contacts with Christians of other lands and was elected one of the presidents of the World Council of Churches.[162]

In East Germany the members of EKD had open before them three possible courses. They could conform, they could come out in open opposition and become martyrs, or they could recognize the authority of the political regime but seek to defend the oppressed and to present to the civil officials their position on controversial issues. In general, the leaders of the Protestant forces in the Eastern zone adopted the third course. They believed that no early hope was warranted of throwing off the Russian power except through total war, that by temperament the German people could not be expected to support protracted guerrilla warfare, and that it and underground resistance move-

158 Kirchliches Jahrbuch, 1952, pp. 229 ff., 1956, pp. 189, 190; Ecumenical Press Service, October 2, 1959.
159 Kirchliches Jahrbuch, 1952, pp. 144–147.
160 Information Service, May 12, 1956.
161 Ibid.; F. H. Littell, mimeographed letter, December 1, 1957.
162 Fred D. Wentzel, editor, Day Is Dawning. The Story of Bishop Otto Dibelius Based on His Proclamations and Authentic Documents (Philadelphia, Christian Education Press, 1956, pp. xv, 222), passim.

ments would be futile and might help to provoke total war—a disaster of inconceivable magnitude in the atomic age. They advocated and practised, therefore, appeal to the courts and other legally established agencies, trusting that even if what they believed to be justice was denied or only partially granted they would have had opportunity to give testimony to their faith and to bring their cause before the authorities and the public. They held that even in prison witness to the Gospel could be borne to other prisoners and that secret policemen, spies, informers, and other minions of the state were human beings in spiritual need and by Christian example might be helped. Moreover, they trusted that God reigns, that in some way He would use their efforts for His purposes, and that He could be counted on for strength even behind iron bars or in a Siberian prison camp. The Church continued to claim the support of the state but without accepting conditions for its reception. It held on to its lands, refused to register its meetings with the police, and sought to carry out its programme until prevented by the police. So far as permitted it provided relief for the unfortunate. By these measures, as the one free institution, it endeavoured to continue its testimony to the Gospel.[163]

To a limited degree and often at great cost the Protestants in the German Democratic Republic maintained this attitude. Theirs was clearly, as was repeatedly said, the Church under the cross. They succeeded in carrying on what were in effect five Evangelical Academies and in part under that name.[164] They attended the *Kirchentag,* sometimes in large numbers, and, although the civil authorities prevented the holding of another of the gatherings in the Eastern zone, the notable one at Leipzig was permitted. Church services and Christian instruction were regularly maintained, although often with difficulty. Voluntary contributions mounted. Dibelius again and again set forth the position of the Church to the officials of the German Democratic Republic, and statements giving the position of the Church were read by pastors from the pulpits.[165] Some youths who were seeking to keep the faith did so by the ethically dubious expedient of outwardly professing to accept the Communist position with which they were being indoctrinated, for only thus could they obtain advanced education and employment. Yet numbers of outside observers held that the Protestant Church was more vital in the East zone than in the West zone, for in the latter little or no obloquy or persecution attended a Christian profession.

CREATIVE SCHOLARSHIP

What was done in Germany by Protestants in the four decades following

[163] Charles C. West in *Religion in Life,* Vol. XXIV, pp. 17–29.
[164] *Kirchliches Jahrbuch, 1945–1948,* p. 382; Weber, *Signs of Renewal,* p. 8.
[165] For a few examples see *Kirchliches Jahrbuch, 1950,* pp. 110 ff.

1914 to take account of the intellectual currents of the revolutionary age? In those stormy years when the trends which had developed in the eighteenth and nineteenth centuries continued, at times reinforced, when new challenges were presented by National Socialism and Communism, and when orderly study was often made difficult or impossible by war, did German Protestantism hold the leadership in theological thought and Biblical and historical scholarship which it had achieved in the nineteenth century? That it was not as outstanding as in those halcyon years was unmistakable. Some of the most widely influential contributions were by citizens of countries which remained neutral in both world wars. The Swiss were especially prominent, for although some of them, of whom Barth has already appeared in our story, had part of their careers in Germany, it was in their native land that most of their creative writing and teaching was done. From Sweden also issued books which were widely read. Although the United States became a belligerent in each of the global struggles, it was late in entering them and escaped enemy invasion and bombing. In it one of the outstanding German theologians, Paul Tillich, found haven and did most of the writing which brought him renown, and among its sons were several who became well known outside as well as within its borders. However, in spite of exhaustion and defeat in the two wars, the Hitler interlude, and the occupation by the victors, Germany continued to be the home of much of the Protestant effort to think through the Christian faith and to present it in terms which would be intelligible and convincing to the generations who were shaped in the first half of the twentieth century. Books produced in the years of stress were widely read, and after World War II students from abroad again flocked to the German theological faculties. If their numbers were not as great as in the nineteenth century, they were significant; through these channels German Protestant thought made itself felt in other lands. As had been true earlier, the universities were the chief germinating centres of that thought.

As we proceed with our story we shall see that some trends in theology and Biblical studies were common in much of the Protestant world. To them German scholars contributed, but without dominating them. They arose, rather, from an awareness of the challenges presented by the twentieth-century stage of the revolutionary age, challenges which, although varying in detail from country to country and region to region, were world-wide.

CHANGING THEOLOGY

Protestant theology in Germany could not but be affected by the stage in the revolutionary age which was introduced by World War I. The long agony of that conflict, the suffering which followed it, the tragic Messianism of the Hitler era with what might be called its *Ersatz* religions, the spread of Communism, partly by conquest and partly by infiltration, the exhausting efforts of World War II with the prostration, loss of territory, foreign occupation, and political division which followed, then the amazing economic recovery in the German Federal Republic inevitably had repercussions on theological thought. Moreover, that thought was paralleled by philosophical currents.

An early climate of opinion was the passing of the optimistic liberalism characteristic of the nineteenth century with its achievement of German political unity and its rising industrial and commercial prosperity. German Idealism, which had accompanied that optimism and had expressed itself in a variety of forms, was weakened. It survived, but as a minority movement and in modified expressions. Bewilderment and pessimism were fertile ground for existentialism, both in its German formulations by Martin Heidegger and Karl Jaspers and in its foreign expressions: the writings of Kierkegaard enjoyed a vogue. In some quarters the revival of scholastic philosophy and theology in the Roman Catholic Church had repercussions. During the Hitler years an answer had to be given to movements which were then popular. The scientific discoveries and theories were a challenge, as their predecessors had been in the nineteenth century.[166] Karl Barth exerted a momentous influence; the dialectic theology and the theology of crisis with their despair of human reason and effort, their consciousness of human frailty and sin, and their emphasis upon revelation and grace which were associated with his name were inescapable. "Dialectic" was not new in Christian theology. Abelard had embodied it in his *Sic et non* (*Yes and No*) by stating the reasons for and against Christian doctrines. Hegel presented a phase of it, with the thesis and the antithesis resolved in a higher synthesis. Kierkegaard had his "either, or," where the answer came not by human reason but by revelation. As we shall see, Barth gave fresh emphasis to it—although he denied arguing for dialectic theology. The theology of crisis, associated with dialectic theology and often, with the latter, called neo-orthodoxy, accepted the central convictions of the sixteenth-century Reformers of what God did through Jesus Christ for man's salvation but endeavoured to present them in terms which would be intelligible to twentieth-century man. It stressed the sovereignty of God, His self-revelation in Jesus Christ and the Bible, and the Church as the vehicle for His Holy Spirit in His self-communication. It made much of the crisis of human life and held that through preaching men are confronted with their sinfulness and the necessity of decision to reject or accept the Gospel. Relations between God and man were described as paradoxical: man is both believer and unbeliever, sinner and forgiven, and Jesus Christ is both God and man. Exponents of the dialectic, crisis, and neo-orthodox theology differed widely among themselves.

[166] See a useful summary of some of this setting in Horton, *Contemporary Continental Theology,* pp. 85 ff.

The movement was multiform, and not universally accepted. But it had wide vogue in Germany and elsewhere in Protestantism, and especially in circles which under the tragedies of the age reacted against the optimistic liberalism and the confidence in human ability of the nineteenth century.

We can take the space to mention, and that only briefly, the thinkers who stood out most prominently in the theological developments in these kaleidoscopic years.

First we must speak of Martin Buber (1878——), whose *Ich und Du* (*I and Thou*), although slight in physical dimensions, both in the original and in translation was widely read in Christian circles.[167] Buber was a Jew, born in Vienna of scholarly ancestry. Much of his life was spent in Germany, but in 1938, during the anti-Semitic campaigns of the Nazis, he became an exile and taught in the Hebrew University of Jerusalem. An ardent Zionist, he helped to contribute cultural and religious motivation to that movement. He was the author of many books, but the most widely influential was the one we have mentioned. It held that God, the Thou, can be addressed but not expressed, that God is transcendent and is not set in the context of time and space, that God is never It, but always Thou, and that through the initiative of Thou man becomes real. His effect was particularly noticeable on Karl Heim, of whom we are to say more in a moment. Franz Rosenzweig (1886-1929) collaborated with Buber.[168]

The name of Rudolf Otto (1869-1937) was closely associated with Marburg, where he was professor of theology and taught from 1917 (he had previously been on the faculties of Göttingen and Breslau). He wrote a number of books but was best remembered for his *The Idea of the Holy,* which went into many editions, both in German and in translation.[169] In *The Idea of the Holy* Otto

[167] Martin Buber, *Ich und Du* (Leipzig, Inset Verlag, 1923, pp. 137), translated by Ronald Gregor Smith as *I and Thou* (Edinburgh, T. & T. Clark, 1937, pp. xiii, 120).

[168] Franz Rosenzweig, *Bücher der Kündung verdeutscht von Martin Buber gemeinsam mit Franz Rosenzweig* (Cologne, Jakob Hegner, new ed., 1958, pp. 778).

[169] Rudolf Otto, *Das Heilige: über das Irrationale in der Idee des Göttlichen und sein Verhältniss zum Rationalen* (Gotha-Stuttgart, F. A. Perthes, 1924, pp. viii, 228), translated by J. W. Harvey as *The Idea of the Holy: An Inquiry into the Non-rational Factor, in the Idea of the Divine and Its Relation to the Rational* (New York, Oxford University Press, 1928, pp. xix, 239). Among Otto's other works were *West-ostliche Mystik: Vergleich und Unterscheidung* (Gotha, L. Klotz, 1926, pp. xiii, 397), translated by Bertha L. Bracey and R. C. Payne as *Mysticism East and West. A Comparative Analysis of the Nature of Mysticism* (New York, The Macmillan Co., 1932, pp. xvii, 262), which had principally to do with Hindu and Christian mysticism, the latter especially as seen in Luther and Schleiermacher, and which carried further some of the positions in *The Idea of the Holy; Die Gnadenreligion Indiens und das Christentums Vergleich und Unterscheidung* (Gotha, L. Klotz, 1930, pp. v, 109), translated by Frank Hugh Foster as *India's Religion of Grace and Christianity Compared and Contrasted* (New York, The Macmillan Co., 1930, pp. 143); the earlier *Naturalistische und religiöse Weltansicht* (Tübingen, J. C. B. Mohr, 1904, pp. 296), translated as *Naturalism and Religion* by J. A. Thomson and M. R. Thomson (London, Williams and Norgate, 1907, pp. xi, 374); and *The Kingdom of God and the Son of Man. A Study in the History of Religion,* translated by Floyd V. Filson and Bertram Lee Woolf (London, Lutterworth

did not seek to be anti-intellectual or anti-rational, but he maintained the autonomy and validity of a particular way of knowing. He stressed elements not included in ethical and rational concepts. While criticizing Schleiermacher's emphasis upon "feeling," he made much of what he called the "numinous" and the *mysterium tremendum,* the "wholly other," and held that where concept fails it is possible to have real knowledge of a Being Who is above knowledge and transcends personality and declared that communion with Him can be had. He was a student of mysticism, both Christian and non-Christian, and especially of Hinduism. He went on to say that Christianity is a religion of redemption and salvation. He was interested in the entire range of religion but was a convinced Christian and held Christ to be the crown of Hinduism.

Three theologians, younger than Buber and Otto, very nearly the same age, were Friedrich Gogarten (1887——), Emanuel Hirsch (1888——), and Paul Althaus (1888——). Gogarten had a spiritual and intellectual pilgrimage which displayed marked variety and the influence of a number of thinkers. He studied under Troeltsch and taught theology at Jena, Breslau, and Göttingen. He supported the German Christians and opposed the *Bekennende Kirche.* Differing from Troeltsch, he sought through German Idealism a faith to support reason. He denounced what he deemed the *Kultur-Protestantismus* of his day. For a time he was enamoured of Luther and Kierkegaard and endorsed Barth. Later he turned against their "supernaturalism" and came more nearly to the position of Buber. In doing so he was clearly an existentialist. He wished not to make Christian thought easy of acceptance by the modern mind but to enable modern thought to know what the Christian faith entailed. In his position on "orders," an historic Lutheran doctrine, Gogarten held that, although man is sinful in his political life as elsewhere, the state is necessary to prevent anarchy and through it God keeps our world in existence until the Last Day. Therefore the Christian, although free in his private life to serve in the spirit of love, is bound to honour and obey the state as he would his father and mother. After the Nazis came to power Gogarten modified this view to make the ethics of the state depend on the will of the *Volk* (nation), and this change gave ground for his acquiescence in the totalitarian rule of Hitler.[170]

Press, 1938, p. 406), from *Reich Gottes und Menschensohn: ein religionsversichtlicher Versuch* (Munich, Beck, 1934, pp. vii, 348).

[170] Horton, *op. cit.,* pp. 108–110; *Twentieth Century Encyclopedia of Religious Knowledge,* Vol. I, p. 466. Some of Gogarten's works are *Glaube und Wirklichkeit* (Jena, E. Diederichs, 1928, pp. 195); *Ich glaube an den dreieinigen Gott: ein Untersuchung über Glauben und Geschichte* (Jena, E. Diederichs, 1926, pp. 212); *Illusion: eine Auseinandersetzung mit dem Kulturidealizmus* (Jena, E. Diederichs, 1926, pp. 145); *Die religiöse Entscheidung* (Jena, E. Diederichs, 1924, pp. 97); *Entmythologisierum und Kirche* (Stuttgart, F. Vorwerk Verlag, 1953, pp. 103), translated by Neville Horton Smith as *Demythologizing and History* (London, S.C.M. Press, 1955, pp. 92); *Die Verkundigung Jesu Christi: Grundlagen und Aufgabe* (Heidelberg, L. Schneider, 1948, pp. 545); *Verhängnis und Hoffnung der Neuzeit. Die Säkularizierung als theologisches Problem* (Stuttgart, F. Vorwerk Verlag, 1953, pp. 220); *Der Mensch zwischen Gott und Welt* (Heidelberg, L. Schnei-

Hirsch, a Lutheran, covered a variety of fields—the history of modern philosophy and theology, Biblical studies, especially the Gospels, contemporary theological issues, and the practical application of the Christian faith. He wrote voluminously under the Weimar Republic, the Third Reich, and after World War II. Professor at Göttingen from 1921 to 1945, he took a theological position which reinforced the German Christians and the Nazis. Like Gogarten, his conception of the "orders" made room for working with the state as the expression of the Volk and ordained by God, sinful though it was. But he insisted that neither Volk nor race should be deified. In a view which appeared to coincide with that of the Nazis he made a clean break between the Old and New Testaments. Indeed, he became an apologist for Aryan Christianity. Although not rejecting the Old Testament, he held that it must always be interpreted in the light of the New Testament.[171]

Althaus, who was a chaplain in the German army in World War I and later taught at Rostock and Erlangen, covered theology, ethics, and the New Testament. His major work, on systematic theology, was largely written during World War II and was based on his lectures in Göttingen, Rostock, and Erlangen. In it, although a Lutheran, he took independent positions. For example, while freely accepting the historical method of Biblical study, he came out for angels as real beings and not poetry; believing profoundly in the incarnation, he held that the virgin birth of Christ is not essential to that doctrine; he stood for the bodily resurrection of Christ and the empty tomb as against the theory that the accounts of the resurrection appearances were based on visions; and he was critical of some phases of Lutheran orthodox Christology. He differed from the dialectical theology of Barth and from Karl Heim.[172] He sided neither with the Nazis nor with the Bekennende Kirche but, like Hans Lilje,

der, 1952, pp. 482). For a summary of Gogarten's views of "orders" and the state see Nils Ehrenström, Christian Faith and the Modern State: An Ecumenical Approach, translated by Denzil Patrick and Olive Wyon (Chicago, Willett, Clark & Co., 1937, pp. vi, 158), pp. 71–76.

[171] For brief interpretations and statements see Twentieth Century Encyclopedia of Religious Knowledge, Vol. I, p. 514; Horton, op. cit., pp. 120–126; and Ehrenström, op. cit., pp. 76–80. A pamphlet giving some of Hirsch's views on the issue of Christianity, the Volk, and the state is Deutsche Volkstum und evangelische Glaube (Hamburg, Hanseatische Verlagsanstalt, 1934, pp. 42). Works showing Hirsch's major interests in theology include Kierkegaard-Studien (Gütersloh, C. Bertelsmann, 2 vols., 1933); Schöpfung und Sünde in der natürlich-geschichtlichen Wirklichkeit des einselen Menschen: Versuch einer Grundlegung christlicher Lebensweisung (Tübingen, J. C. B. Mohr, 1931, pp. vi, 130); Hilfsbuch zum Studium der Dogmatik; die Dogmatik der Reformatoren und der altevangelischen Lehrer quellemässig und verdeutsch (Berlin, W. de Gruyter, 1951, pp. xii, 446); Lutherstudien (Gütersloh, C. Bertelsmann, 2 vols., 1954); Geschichte der neueren evangelischen Theologie im Zusammenhang mit der allgemeinen Bewegungen des europaischen Denkens (Gütersloh, C. Bertelsmann, 5 vols., 1949–1954).

[172] Paul Althaus, Die christliche Wahrheit: Lehrbuch der Dogmatik (Gütersloh, C. Bertelsmann, 2 vols., 1947, 1948). Among other works by Althaus are Forschungen zur evangelischen Gebetsliteratur (Gütersloh, C. Bertelsmann, 1927, pp. x, 279); Die letzten Dinge, Lehrbuch der Eschatologie (Gütersloh, C. Bertelsmann, 6th ed., 1956, pp. xvi, 370); Grundriss der Ethik (Gütersloh, C. Bertelsmann, 2nd ed., 1953, pp. 174). See also Horton, op. cit., pp. 138–143.

was one of the Lutheran Confessionals who were passive resisters.

Althaus had much to say on eschatology and so aroused controversy. Here he sought to support the prevailing disillusionment with the eighteenth- and nineteenth-centuries doctrine of progress. He held that the second coming of Christ is the end towards which all history moves and brings with it the fulfilment of history and the transformation of the world. But since the second coming means the death of this world, the millennial reign of Christ before the final consummation is not to be expected. The world is not gradually to grow better, Althaus held, but to the end evil will be present, both in the Church and in the milieu in which the Church is set. As every man must act under the pressure of the possibility that each day may be his last, so Christ's second coming may come at any moment. It will be followed by the triumph of Christ in all the universe and in eternity, for God stands above time and is the end of time.

In the years which followed 1914 and brought so much of tragedy to Germany, it is not surprising that German theologians gave much attention to eschatology and despaired of seeing improvement in human society within history. In this they reflected, as did such massive works as Spengler's *The Decline of the West* and Toynbee's *A Study of History,* the widespread pessimism in Western Europe which was in striking contrast with the confident optimism of the Marxist Communism centred in Soviet Russia. Much of theological as well as other thought in the United States, while less hopeful than in the nineteenth century, retained, somewhat sobered, a degree of optimism. In the gatherings associated with the Ecumenical Movement in the post-1914 years the two views, those of Continental Protestantism and those still widespread in the United States, were often in sharp contrast.

Eschatology was also prominent in the theology of Karl Heim (1874–1957). Reared in a deeply religious family where the sermons of the Pietists Johann Christoph Blumhardt and Ludwig Hofacker were read on Sunday afternoons,[173] in his student days in Tübingen Heim was caught up in the strongly Pietistic student Christian movement and was much impressed by Hudson Taylor of the China Inland Mission and by a former missionary to Africa. After writing a prize essay on "Faith and History" (which hinted at the interest he was later to develop in eschatology) and serving as an assistant in a parish, he became a travelling secretary of the German Christian Student Union and as such visited the German universities and technical schools, encouraging the little groups of Christian students in their efforts to reach their fellows. Through that assignment he became involved in the recently organized World's Student Christian Federation and was deeply impressed by its organizer, John R. Mott. Through these contacts he met the Pietist Baron Paul Nicolai, who

[173] Volume II, pp. 67, 68.

was seeking to reach Russian students, and with his help visited Russian universities.

Because of his background and his experience with students and moved by a word of Spurgeon,[174] Heim felt himself called to a career of writing to seek to present the Christian faith in a convincing fashion to those throughout the world who were caught in the intellectual currents of the revolutionary age. He therefore sought to make himself familiar with those currents, especially in the realm of the natural sciences, and to show that those persuaded of their truth could also honestly maintain a belief in God and the Christian Gospel. To this purpose he gave most of the rest of his life. For a time between the two wars his books were said to be more widely read, especially by youth, than any others in the field of religion except those of Barth.

Heim maintained his contacts with the world-wide spread of the faith. Attendance at the meeting of the World's Student Christian Federation in Peking in 1922 gave him an opportunity to see something of East Asia and especially of Japanese Buddhism, and membership in the German delegation at the International Missionary Council's enlarged meeting in Jerusalem in 1928 enabled him not only to keep in touch with the global enterprise represented by that organization but also to visit the Middle East.

In 1914 Heim was appointed to the chair of dogmatics in the newly founded Protestant theological faculty of the University of Münster in Westphalia. World War I brought an interruption during which he served as military chaplain in an internment camp for Germans in Denmark. In 1920 he was called to a chair of theology in Tübingen after a contest between liberals who wished Rudolf Otto and those who saw in Heim support for the Pietism which was strong in Württemberg. He spent the rest of his teaching life in Tübingen and made that city his residence after his retirement. During the Hitler era he opposed the German Christians and came more and more into conflict with National Socialism both through his writings and by his preaching in a church close to the university. Yet he was able to continue and survived the collapse of Germany in World War II.[175]

Heim's theology was profoundly influenced by the Pietism in which he had been reared and to which he remained committed. Both his philosophy and his theology were summed up, so he said, in the words of Paul: "[In Christ] are hid all the treasures of wisdom and knowledge."[176] He kept abreast of the philosophical, theological, and scientific thought of the changing years and made himself master of much of it, but his purpose was so to know the intel-

---

[174] Volume II, pp. 331, 332.

[175] Heim's autobiography is in his *Ich gedenke der vorigen Zeiten: Erinnerungen aus acht Jahrzehnten* (Hamburg, Furche-Verlag, 1957, pp. 320).

[176] *Ibid.*, p. 111; Colossians II:3.

lectual climate in which they lived as to be able to confront his hearers and readers with the necessity of deciding for Christ. He endeavoured to show how the current solutions offered to the mystery of life had failed to solve the basic human problem. He made much of the transcendence of God, Who is not confined to the three-dimensional world of human experience but Who, by way of analogy, is in what may be called a fourth dimension and Who can be known only as He reveals Himself. This, so Heim said, He has done in Jesus Christ. Heim found in the "I and Thou" of Martin Buber a convenient expression of God's relation to men and saw in God the "Thou" who comes to men. In the Nazi period he spoke of Jesus as *Führer* ("Leader"), using the term which was claimed for Hitler. He believed Jesus to be the Saviour from sin. Sin he held to be associated with the warfare between a personal super-human evil will—Satan—and God. Satan is bent on de-throning God and Gethsemane shows that we cannot be sure of the outcome, but he acts only as God permits, for God is sovereign and triumphed in the resurrection. The Church, Heim believed, is the form in which Christ continues in the world. The victory which He won on Calvary, so Heim maintained the New Testament teaches, was confirmed by God in the resurrection and the ascension, and Christ is now the invincible Lord of history. The cosmic drama is to be consummated in the public seizure of power by Christ, the general resurrection, and the termination of the age of birth and death when all the fruits of history are to be gathered in God's eternal kingdom. The end of history will come in history, Heim insisted, and in that coming the time-form in which man's history has been enacted will end and the meaning of time will be fulfilled in God's eternity.[177]

---

[177] For interpretations of Heim and summaries of his position see Horton, *op. cit.*, pp. 127–141; E. L. Allen, *Jesus Our Leader: A Guide to the Thought of Karl Heim* (London, Hodder and Stoughton, 1948, pp. 45); and Francis Burger, *Karl Heim as Apologeet* (Francker, T. Wever, 1954, pp. 204, a doctoral dissertation of the Free University of Amsterdam).

Among Heim's works are *Glaube und Leben: gesammelte Aufsätze und Vorträge* (Berlin, Furche-Verlag, 3rd ed., 1928, pp. 757); *Jesus der Herr: die Führervollmacht Jesu und die Gottesoffenbarung in Christus* (Berlin, Furche-Verlag, 1935, pp. 218, 4th ed., 1955, pp. 207); *Spirit and Truth: the Nature of Evangelical Christianity*, translated by Edgar P. Dickie (London, Lutterworth Press, 1935, pp. 201); *Der christliche Gottesglaube und die Naturwissenschaft II. Die Wandlung im natur-wissenschaftlichen Weltbild* (Hamburg, Furche-Verlag, 1951, pp. 271), translated as *The Transformation of the Scientific World View* (New York, Harper & Brothers, 1953, pp. 262); *Jesus der Weltvollender: der Glaube an die Versöhnung und Weltverwandlung* (Berlin, Furche-Verlag, 1937, pp. 268); *God Transcendent: Foundation for a Christian Metaphysic,* translated by Edgar Primrose Dickie (London, Nisbet, 1935, pp. xix, 242) from *Glaube und Denken: philosophie Grundlegen einer christlichen Lebensanschauung* (Berlin, Furche-Verlag, 3rd ed., 1934, pp. 250); *Der evangelische Glaube und das Denken der Gegenwart* (Berlin, Tübingen, Hamburg, Furche-Verlag, 6 vols., 1934–1952); *Glaube und Denken: gesammelte Aufsätze und Vorträge: mit einer Einführung über Sinn und Ziel meiner theologischen Arbeit* (Berlin, Furche-Verlag, 3rd ed., 1928, pp. 757); *The Church of Christ and the Problems of the Day* (New York, Charles Scribner's Sons, 1935, pp. viii, 172); *Die Bergpredigt Jesu für die heutige Zeit ausgelegt* (Tübingen, Furche-Verlag, 3rd ed., 1949, pp. 72); *Die christliche Ethik: tübinger Vorlesungen nachgeschreiben und ausgearbeitet von Walter Kreusburg* (Tübingen, Katzmann-Verlag, 1955, pp. 292); *Der christliche Gottesglaube und*

Georg Wobbermin was slightly older than Heim and represented a quite different view in theology, but while his mind was formed and much of his significant writing was before 1914, he had marked influence after World War I. Born in Stettin in 1869, he studied in Halle and Berlin, taught for a short time in Breslau, succeeded Troeltsch in Heidelberg, and then had a chair of systematic theology in Göttingen. A warm admirer of Schleiermacher, he had as his slogan "back to Schleiermacher and from Schleiermacher forward." Influenced by William James as well, he used the religio-psychological method. He developed a philosophy of religion in which he moved away from Ritschl's dislike of metaphysics. He fought the battle of Christian theism against Haeckel and the naturalistic left. He was also critical of the crisis theology of Barth, which would separate Christianity from other religions, and on the other hand of Otto, who, he believed, neglected the uniqueness of Christianity. He disagreed with Troeltsch. In other words, he sought to unite philosophy and religion, employing what he deemed the fruitful suggestions of psychology, and in such fashion as to support the Christian faith amid the conflicting currents of his day.[178] The still older Reinhold Seeberg (1859–1935), who was best remembered for his massive history of dogma with its Lutheran slant, in its second edition published on the eve of 1914,[179] under the Weimar Republic came out with a comprehensive work on theology.[180]

Werner Elert (1885–1954) was of a slightly younger generation and represented the revived Lutheran orthodoxy. He and Althaus had much in common. He was professor of historical and systematic theology at Erlangen from 1923 to his death and his best remembered work was in the field of Lutheran dogmatics. He also wrote on Lutheran ethics.[181]

A new voice in German Protestant theology and a phase of the ecumenical temper which was increasingly prevalent was that of Friedrich Heiler (1892——). Reared in a devout Roman Catholic family and himself deeply religious from childhood, Heiler early came in touch with Roman Catholic Modernist and contemporary Protestant literature. He was particularly im-

---

die Naturwissenschaft, I, Grundlegung (Tübingen, Furche-Verlag, 1949, pp. 282), translated by N. Horton Smith as Christian Faith and Natural Science (New York, Harper & Brothers, 1953, pp. 256).

[178] Wobbermin's views were most comprehensively expressed in his Systematische Theologie nach religionpsychologischer Methode (Leipzig, J. C. Hinrichs'sche Buchhandlung, 2nd ed., unrevised, 3 vols., 1925, 1926). A free translation of the second volume of that work, by Daniel Sommer Robinson and Theophil Menzil and approved by Wobbermin, is The Nature of Religion (New York, Thomas Y. Crowell Co., 1933, pp. xvi, 379).

[179] Lehrbuch der Dogmengeschichte (Leipzig, A. Deichert, 2nd ed., 3 vols., 1908–1913).

[180] Reinhold Seeberg, Christliche Dogmatik (Erlangen, H. Deicherts'sche Buchhandlung, 2 vols., 1924, 1925).

[181] Werner Elert, Der christliche Glaube: Grundlinien der lutherischen Dogmatik (Hamburg, Furche-Verlag, 1956, pp. 574); Werner Elert, Das christliche Ethos: Grundlinien der lutherischen Ethik (Tübingen, Furche-Verlag, 1949, pp. 595), translated by Carl J. Schindler as The Christian Ethos (Philadelphia, Muhlenberg Press, 1957, pp. xi, 451).

pressed by Nathan Söderblom[182] and while in Sweden at a conference called by the latter (1919) he took the Communion at a Lutheran altar. Yet he wished not to identify himself with any one branch of Christianity, whether Roman Catholic, Protestant, or Eastern, but thought of himself as an ecumenical Christian—an evangelical Catholic. Beginning in 1920 he held a chair at Marburg in the history of religion. He sought in a variety of ways to promote the unity of Christians, and his major books had that as their objective. He was particularly remembered for writings on prayer and worship. He was most widely read in the interval between the two world wars.[183]

After World War II a number of younger men began coming to the fore in theology. Several had been in the Confessing Church or otherwise had shared in resistance movements in the Nazi years. In general they were exponents of the dialectical or crisis theology, but their views displayed wide variety. By mid-century when this narrative must pause, some had not reached their full maturity, and their literary output had not attained the dimensions of those of several of their older contemporaries and immediate predecessors. We will mention the ones who by late in the 1950's had become most prominent and will do so in alphabetical order to avoid any appearance of expressing judgement on their relative importance.

Hans Asmussen (1898———) served in World War I and was dismissed from his pastorate by the German Christians. A Lutheran, he was an adviser to the *Bekennende Kirche,* and was on the faculty of the clandestine theological seminary maintained by that body in Berlin. From 1945 to 1949 he was on the chancellery of EKD and in the latter became Dean of Kiel in the Church of Schleswig-Holstein. In his writing he had a pastoral interest—seen in his works on the Epistle to the Romans and the Epistle to the Galatians, and in his handbook on pastoral care.[184]

Hermann Diem (1900———) was a pastor in Württemberg who theologically was close to Barth, was a leader in the Confessing Church, was concerned with practical theology and church organization, and was prominent in organizing

---

[182] Volume II, pp. 179–181.
[183] Among his best-known works were *Das Gebet: eine religionsgeschichtliche und religionspsychologische Untersuchung* (Munich, E. Reinhardt, 5th ed., 1923, pp. 622), translated by Samuel McComb and J. Edgar Park as *Prayer: a Study in the History and Psychology of Religion* (New York, Oxford University Press, 1932, pp. xxviii, 376); *The Spirit of Worship: Its Forms and Manifestations in the Christian Churches with an Additional Essay on Catholicity, Eastern, Roman, and Evangelical* (London, Hodder and Stoughton, 1926, pp. xvi, 214); *Der Katholizismus: seine Idee und seine Erscheinung* (Munich, E. Reinhardt, rev. ed., 1923, pp. xxxviii, 704); *Urkirche und Ostkirche* (Munich, E. Reinhardt, 1937, pp. xx, 607).
[184] *Twentieth Century Encyclopedia of Religious Knowledge,* Vol. I, p. 86; Hans Asmussen, *Der Römerbrief* (Stuttgart, Evangelisches Verlagswerk, 1952, pp. 371); *Theologisch-kirchliche Erwägungen zum Galaterbrief* (Munich, C. Kaiser, 2nd ed., 1935, pp. 205); *Die Seelsorge: ein praktisches Handbuch über Seelsorge und Seelenführung* (New York, Commission for World Council Service of the American Committee of the World Council of Churches, 4th ed., no date, pp. xxiv, 230).

the *Kirchlich-theologische Arbeitsgemeinschaft für Deutschland,* in the *Kirch-lich-theologische Sozietat* in Württemberg, and in the *Gesellschaft evangelische Theologie.*[185] A controversialist, he was a specialist on Kierkegaard and had a major work on systematic theology.[186] He also wrote shorter books and pamphlets on the contemporary scene.

We have already met Helmut Gollwitzer (1908——) and noted his experiences as a prisoner of war in Russia. In 1950 he became professor of systematic theology in Bonn. His small book on the death and resurrection of Jesus as narrated by Luke was more a set of meditations than a treatise in theology.[187]

Walter Künneth (1901——) studied in Erlangen and Tübingen and became dean in Erlangen in 1944 and professor in 1946. A conservative Lutheran, in addition to a book on the theology of the resurrection he wrote an account of the struggle between National Socialism and Christianity which traced the roots of the conflict to the secularism of the nineteenth century and which suggested a new approach to the subject.[188] He had a wide influence in the 1950's.

Edmund Schlink (1903——), at one time a pastor in Hesse, taught in Giessen and in the *Kirchliche Hochschule* in Bethel and latterly was professor of dogmatics in Heidelberg. He had been associated with the Confessing Church and was active in the Ecumenical Movement. His theological approach was seen in the address which he gave in 1954 at the Assembly of the World Council of Churches on the Christian hope. It embodied a view on eschatology which was widespread in Germany.[189]

Helmut Thielicke (1908——), who was banned by the Nazi regime from his professorship at Heidelberg because of his connexion with the Confessing Church and was a member of the resistance to Hitler, in 1945 was appointed professor of systematic theology and religious philosophy at Tübingen and was rector of the university in 1951. He was active in the Evangelical Academies.[190] His theological position was reflected in the dedication of one of his

---

[185] *Twentieth Century Encyclopedia of Religious Knowledge,* Vol. I, p. 338; *Who's Who in Germany,* p. 230.

[186] Hermann Diem, *Philosophie und Christentum bei Sören Kierkegaard* (Munich, C. Kaiser, 1929, pp. viii, 368); *Die Existenzdialektik von Soeren Kirkegaard* (Zollikon-Zürich, Evangelischer Verlag, 1950, pp. xi, 207); *Dogmatik: ihr Weg zwischen Historismus und Existenialismus,* Vol. II of *Theologie als kirchliche Wissenschaft,* translated by Harold Knight as *Dogmatics* (Edinburgh, Oliver and Boyd, 1959, pp. 375).

[187] *Who's Who in Germany,* p. 402; Helmut Gollwitzer, *Jesu Tod und Auferstehung nach dem Bericht des Lukas* (Munich, C. Kaiser, 2nd ed., 1951, pp. 119).

[188] *Who's Who in Germany,* p. 680; Walter Künneth, *Der grosse Abfall: eine geschichtstheologische Untersuchung der Begegnung zwischen National Socialismus und Christentum* (Hamburg, F. Wittig, 1947, pp. 319).

[189] *Twentieth Century Encyclopedia of Religious Knowledge,* Vol. II, p. 1000; *Who's Who in Germany,* p. 1017; Edmund Schlink, *Der Mensch in der Verkündigung der Kirche: eine dogmatische Untersuchung* (Munich, C. Kaiser, 1936, pp. xii, 331); *Theologie der lutherischen Bekenntnisschriften* (Munich, C. Kaiser, 1946, pp. 434).

[190] *Who's Who in Germany,* p. 1160.

books to Althaus,[191] and his opposition to the Nazis by the dedication of another to Bishop Theophil Wurm.[192] He, a Lutheran, and Gollwitzer, of the *Bekennende Kirche,* were the most talked about in the 1950's. The titles of some of his other books give some indication of the scope of Thielicke's interests.[193] He was familiar with current trends, as was seen in his attention to psychotherapy, and he sought to present the Christian message to men shaped by the secularism of the day. He was also profoundly convinced of the demonic in the world about him and supported his belief in the existence and activity of malevolent spiritual powers by references to the Bible.

Heinrich Vogel (1902——), the son of a clergyman and himself for many years a pastor, was associated with the Confessing Church, was director of the *Kirchliche Hochschule* in Berlin founded in resistance to the Nazis, and was three times imprisoned. After the war he was professor of dogmatics and ethics in the University of Berlin and in the *Kirchliche Hochschule* in that city.[194] He was a contributor to *Zwischen den Zeiten,* a journal founded by Barth, and in a large volume on systematic theology expressed views which might have been anticipated from that connexion.[195]

Hans Joachim Iwand (1899——), also associated with the *Bekennende Kirche,* director of its preachers' seminar in East Prussia (1935–1937), and pastor in Dortmund (1937–1945), after World War II was successively professor in Göttingen and Bonn.[196]

Heinz-Dietrich Wendland (1900——), educated in theology and philosophy

---

[191] Helmut Thielicke, *Geschichte und Existenz: Grundlegung einer evangelischen Geschichtstheologie* (Gütersloh, C. Bertelsmann, 1935, pp. xv, 369), solidly based on the Bible.

[192] Helmut Thielicke, *Der Glaube der Christenheit: unsere Welt vor Jesus Christus* (Göttingen, Vanderhoeck & Ruprecht, 1955, pp. 475).

[193] Helmut Thielicke, *Fragen des Christentums an die moderne Welt: eine christliche Kulturkritik* (Geneva, Oekumene Verlag, 1945, pp. 263); *Tod und Leben: Studien zur christlichen Anthropologie* (Tübingen, J. C. B. Mohr, 1946, pp. 225); *Theologische Ethik* (Tübingen, J. C. B. Mohr, 2 vols., 1951–1958); *Geschichte und Existenz; Grundlegung einer evangelischen Geschichtstheologie* (Gütersloh, C. Bertelsmann, 1935, pp. xv, 369); *Theologie der Anfectung* (Tübingen, J. C. B. Mohr, 1949, pp. vii, 269), made up of several essays on various topics, such as demythologizing, religious conditions in Germany, and Marxism, and critical of natural theology; *Der Glaube der Christenheit. Unsere Welt vor Jesus Christus* (Göttingen, Vanderhoeck & Ruprecht, 2nd ed., 1955, pp. 475); *"Ich aber sage euch." Auslegungen der Bergpredigt in Stuttgarter Gottesdiensten* (Stuttgart, Quell-Verlag der Evang. Gesellschaft, 4 vols., 1946–1948); *Der Nihilismus: Enstehung, Wesen, Überwindung* (Pfullingen, G. Neske, 2nd ed., 1951, pp. 214); *Die Lebenangst und ihre Überwindung* (Gütersloh, C. Bertelsmann, 1957, pp. 232); *Offenbarung, Vernunft und Existenz. Studien zur Religionsphilosophie Lessings* (Gütersloh, C. Bertelsmann, 3rd ed., 1957, pp. 171); *Das Bilderbuch Gottes. Reden über die Gleichnisse Jesu* (Stuttgart, Quell-Verlag, 1957, pp. 320); *Das Leben kann noch einmal beginnen: ein Gang durch das Bergpredigt* (Stuttgart, Quell-Verlag, 4th revised ed., 1958, pp. 245).

[194] *Twentieth Century Encyclopedia of Religious Knowledge,* Vol. II, p. 1154; *Who's Who in Germany,* p. 1200.

[195] Heinrich Vogel, *Gott in Christo: ein Erkenntnisgang durch die Grundprobleme der Dogmatik* (Berlin, Lettner-verlag, 1951, pp. xxxi, 1071).

[196] Hans Joachim Iwand, *Glaubensgerechtigkeit nach Luthers Lehre* (Munich, A. Lempp, 1941, pp. 93). *Who's Who in Germany,* p. 558.

in Berlin and Heidelberg, was professor of theology at Kiel and then at Münster. He specialized in the New Testament and social ethics and particularly in the relation of Christianity to Communism.[197]

SHIFTING APPROACHES TO BIBLICAL STUDIES

The post-1914 years were marked by striking changes in Biblical scholarship. Here, as in the nineteenth century, the Germans broke new paths which to a greater or less degree were followed by many Protestant scholars in other countries. Sometimes they were counter to the movements in theology, at other times diverged from them, and at still others reinforced them. The major directions were set by *Formgeschichte* and by one who accepted the main thesis of *Formgeschichte* but was clearly distinct, Rudolf Bultmann. Both stirred up controversies and by the close of the 1950's the trend in many places was to follow them in part but to go beyond them. Here were attempts to apply the historical methods of the contemporary revolutionary age to the Bible.

Formgeschichte, usually called in English form criticism or, more properly, the history of form, had to do with the literary form of the documents in which the previous oral tradition was crystallized. It arose from the conviction that the historical accounts in the Biblical records were preceded by shorter or longer periods of oral transmission and that the varied forms seen in the writings preserved in the Bible reflected the different channels through which the material had been handed down by word of mouth and also the situations in which the writing was done and the purposes governing it. The method had already been applied to secular literature. It was now diligently employed in the study of the Scriptures.

Hermann Gunkel (1862–1932) was a pioneer in utilizing *Formgeschichte* in Old Testament studies. He taught Old Testament in Berlin, Giessen, and Halle. He was associated with Johann Franz Wilhelm Bousset (1865–1920), who specialized in the New Testament and long taught at Giessen, and with Rudolf Bultmann (1884——), and the three edited a series of monographs by various authors which published the results of research in the field.[198]

---

[197] His interest in the first is shown by his *Die Briefe an die Korinther: übersetzt und erklärt* (Göttingen, Vanderhoeck & Ruprecht, 5th ed., 1948, pp. 176), and in the second by his *Die Kirche in der modernen Gesellschaft: Entscheidungsfragen für das kirchliche Handeln im Zeitalter der Massenwelt* (Hamburg, Furche-Verlag, 2nd ed., 1958, pp. 285).

[198] *Forschungen zur Religion und Literatur des Alten und Neuen Testaments* (Göttingen, 1903 ff.). Among the important books by Gunkel were *Ausgewalte Psalmen übersetz und erklärt* (Göttingen, Vanderhoeck & Ruprecht, 4th ed., 1917, pp. x, 258); *Das Märchen im Alten Testaments* (Tübingen, J. C. B. Mohr, 1917, pp. 179); *Einleitung in die Psalmen: die Gattungen der religiösen Lyrik Israels*, completed by Joachim Begrich (Göttingen, Vanderhoeck & Ruprecht, 1922, pp. ciii, 509). Gunkel edited *Die Schriften des Alten Testaments in Auswahl neu übersetzt und erklärt*, by various authors (Göttingen, Vanderhoeck & Ruprecht, 7 vols., 1910–1915), and was one of the editors of *Die Religion in Geschichte und Gegenwart: Handwörterbuch für Theologie und Religionswissenschaft* (Tübingen, J. C. B. Mohr, 6 vols., 1927–1932).

Formgeschichte created more stir when applied to the New Testament, and particularly to the Synoptic Gospels. Its advocates held that scholarship could not be content with identifying the written sources of the three first Gospels, for between their composition and the events and sayings which they recorded an interval elapsed in which oral tradition had been the means of transmission. They maintained that the Gospels were made up of separate units, and that their form in those books did not necessarily preserve the sequence of events in the life of Jesus or His exact teachings but was determined by the situation in the early Church at the time the writing was done. They held that from the Gospels could be ascertained the setting in the Church which influenced the form; thus light would be shed on the early Church. Much depended, they maintained, on what was taught the converts, for it was that instruction which familiarized the neophytes with the record which the Church valued and wished to transmit to them. To a large degree the preaching, they declared, which employed the sayings of Jesus and the incidents in His life had as its purpose the winning of converts. The specialists in *Formgeschichte* did not agree among themselves as to how far the Gospels gave an authentic picture of Jesus. In general they reacted against the attempts of the preceding genera-tion to discover the Jesus of history and were convinced that no biography of Him was possible in the sense in which that word was usually understood. They believed that narratives of the passion were the first to take shape and that the form in which the sayings and deeds of Jesus were set down were coloured by the conviction that He was Christ and Lord. Those who differed from the exponents of *Formgeschichte*—and they were numerous—declared that justice had not been done to the role of eyewitnesses, to the historical sense and honesty of the early Christians, or to the fact that within two decades or less of the crucifixion and resurrection what had been transmitted orally had begun to be put into writing.

The chief pioneer in applying the methods of *Formgeschichte* to the New Testament was Martin Franz Dibelius (1883-1947). A pupil of Harnack and Gunkel, he taught in Berlin from 1908 to 1915 and at Heidelberg from 1915 to his death.[199] His approach was reverent and he was intent upon finding out what Jesus said and did and what happened in the crucifixion and the resur-rection and thus to make Jesus more intelligible and compelling to his con-temporaries. Believing that what was remembered of the sayings and deeds of Jesus could not be fitted into a reliable chronological pattern but was chosen by early Christian preachers out of much more extensive recollections which circulated orally, he endeavoured to ascertain the purposes which de-termined the choice and to suggest how far those purposes modified the

[199] *Twentieth Century Encyclopedia of Religious Knowledge*, Vol. I, p. 336.

forms eventually committed to writing. He held that a sufficient number of the sayings of Jesus had been preserved, such as aphorisms and parables, to give a clear picture of what Jesus had taught and much could be known of what he did and of the main facts of his death and resurrection. He was convinced that Jesus and the first Christians looked for the early consummation of the age in a decisive act of God, but he also maintained that the teachings of Jesus had continuing validity, both in their demand upon men for unwavering and complete commitment to God and confidence in God and in detailed principles for action. He wrote extensively, at times at length and frequently in shorter books for which he hoped wide circulation among non-specialists.[200]

Rudolf Bultmann (1884——) provoked more widespread dissent than Martin Dibelius. He was a landmark in twentieth-century New Testament studies, much as Ferdinand Christian Baur had been in the nineteenth century.[201] He studied in Tübingen, Berlin, and Marburg and from 1921 until his retirement was on the faculty of Marburg. He sought, as did many others of his generation, and, indeed, of many preceding generations from the beginnings of Christianity, to show the pertinence of the Gospel to the contemporary climate of opinion and to state it in terms which would speak to men of his day. To accomplish this purpose he felt himself constrained to determine what the enduring features of the original Gospel were, to seek to separate them from the aspects of the world view in which they had first found expression and which were not congenial to the outlook of the twentieth century, and to relate them to current frames of thought.

To ascertain what the Gospel was at its outset Bultmann employed the principles of *Formgeschichte*. He did so in the belief that the pure objectivity aimed at by many scholars was impossible. He maintained that no student of the records of Jesus could stand outside the stream of history but was caught up in it and could not come at his quest as though he were a neutral observer fully detached from what he was seeking. This did not, he maintained, entail

---

[200] Of the extensive bibliography of the writings of Dibelius, the following may indicate something of his areas of concentration: *Die Formgeschichte des Evangeliums* (Tübingen, J. C. B. Mohr, 1919, pp. 108), translated by Bertram Lee Woolf as *From Tradition to Gospel* (New York, Charles Scribner's Sons, pp. xv, 311); *Die Botschaft von Jesu Christi* (Tübingen, J. C. B. Mohr, 1935), translated by Frederick C. Grant as *The Message of Jesus Christ: the Tradition of the Early Christian Communities* (New York, Charles Scribner's Sons, 1939, pp. xx, 192); *Aufsätze zur Apostelgeschichte* (Göttingen, Vanderhoeck & Ruprecht, 1951, pp. xxx, 192), translated by Mary Ling and Paul Schubert as *Studies in the Acts of the Apostles* (London, S.C.M. Press, 1956, pp. ix, 228); *Die Briefe des Apostels Paulus*, by Hans Lietzmann and Martin Dibelius (Tübingen, J. C. B. Mohr, 2 vols., 1913); *Der Brief des Jakobus*, edited by Heinrich Greeven (Göttingen, Vanderhoeck & Ruprecht, 1957, pp. viii, 240); *Geschichte der urchristlichen Literatur* (Berlin, Walter de Gruyter & Co., 2 vols., 1926); and *Paulus*, edited and completed by Georg Kümmel (Berlin, Walter de Gruyter & Co., 1951, pp. 155), translated by Frank Clarke as *Paul* (Philadelphia, The Westminster Press, 1953, pp. 172).

[201] On Baur see Volume II, pp. 48-50.

a stultifying relativism but had the nature of a dialogue with history, a highly personal encounter with it. He believed that to discover what Jesus taught, did, and suffered as pictured in the Synoptic Gospels—the fullest accounts and least subject to interpretation such as was found in the Fourth Gospel—it was necessary to strip off successive layers: the elements of Hellenistic origin and those embodied in the Aramaic tradition of the oldest Palestinian Christian community. Even then, he said, the results were debatable. Moreover, so he held, Jesus was not teaching a system of general truths, but was Himself imbedded in the concrete situation in which He lived. Yet Bultmann regarded the authenticity of the main body of the sayings attributed to Jesus to be sufficiently established to permit a dependable account of Him and His message. He saw as central in the teaching of Jesus the Kingdom of God, its immediately impending irruption, and the necessity of decision to get ready or to keep ready for it.

The world view in which the records of Jesus were made, in which Jesus concurred, and by which the New Testament writings were shaped was, Bultmann declared, alien to the twentieth-century mind. It regarded the universe as in three stories—this world, heaven above where are God and the angels, and the region beneath, or hell. The New Testament had a picture of the last judgement with a miraculous intervention of transcendent beings which now seemed absurd to many.

To make the Gospel relevant to the twentieth-century man, Bultmann held, de-mythologizing was imperative—discarding the myths of the New Testament language and confronting contemporaries with the scandal of the Gospel, the crucifixion and the resurrection, and calling men to decision. To him myths were means of speaking about transcendence in terms of this world. The New Testament myths, he insisted, were alien to the scientific mind of the twentieth century. Bultmann did not say that the world view of the revolutionary age was perfect, but he held that it was the world view of his day. Christians must, he maintained, translate the New Testament view of the eternally valid Gospel into the prevailing view of the present, even though that might entail constructing new myths.

In de-mythologizing Bultmann gave an interpretation of the Gospel in terms of the widely prevalent existentialism. Here he found Heidegger useful. That truth is existential, as Bultmann interpreted it, means that it is not speculative but comes to man in the midst of his world, and that man recognizes his own finiteness and his need of God's saving act. We must speak, so Bultmann declared, not of Christology but of soteriology, as Paul's theology was not speculative about God in Himself but was always concerned about God in His relation to man. A man who complains that he cannot see meaning in history and therefore in his own history, Bultmann said, is to be admonished not to look around him in universal history, but to search his personal history. In a man's own present, so Bultmann maintained, lies the meaning of his story, and he cannot see that meaning as a spectator but only in his responsible decisions. "In every moment slumbers the possibility of being the eschatological moment," he said: each must awaken it.[202] The salvation of which the *kerygma* —the proclamation of the Gospel—speaks, Bultmann insisted, is always present and is not fixed at any one point in the past but constantly occurs in the preaching of the Word: it is ever reaching man. This does not deny that the crucifixion occurred in a particular year, but says that it is now valid through faith. The resurrection means that the historic Jesus was raised in an eschatological event. Grace is God's eschatological deed and faith means, not experience, but obedience, a free act of decision.[203]

Dissent from Bultmann was widespread. During the stress of World War II discussion was quiescent but with the coming of peace it awakened. Criticism was especially vocal in Pietist circles, notably in Württemberg with its strong Pietist tradition, and in Lutheran confessionalism. Among the accusations were that Bultmann had made of the Bible the word of man and not the Word of God, that he had denied the bodily resurrection, and that his treatment of the Fourth Gospel departed from fact for he had said that its author had expanded a pre-Christian compilation of revelation discourses and had combined it with a document narrating the "signs" which are the framework of much of that Gospel to illustrate the theme of the Redemptor-Revealer. The Bishop of Württemberg came out (January, 1951) with a pastoral letter of warning against de-mythologizing (*Entmythologisierung*), and in 1952 the General Synod of the United Lutheran Church (VELKD) took somewhat similar action.[204]

---

[202] Rudolf Bultmann, *The Presence of Eternity: History and Echatology,* the Gifford Lectures, 1955 (Edinburgh, University Press, 1957, pp. ix, 170), p. 155.

[203] Of the extensive writings of Bultmann the following may be named as typical and important: *Jesus* (Berlin, Deutsche Bibliothek, 1926, pp. 204), translated by Louise Pettibone Smith and Erminie Huntress Lantero as *Jesus and the Word* (New York, Charles Scribner's Sons, 1958, pp. 226); *Theologie des Neuen Testaments* (Tübingen, J. C. B. Mohr, 1948-1953, pp. xi, 608), translated by Kendrick Grobel as *Theology of the New Testament* (New York, Charles Scribner's Sons, 2 vols., 1951-1955); *Das Evangelium des Johannes* (Göttingen, Vanderhoeck & Ruprecht, 13th ed., 1953, pp. 563); *Die Geschichte der synoptischen Tradition* (Göttingen, Vanderhoeck & Ruprecht, 1931, pp. 408); *Glauben und Verstehen* (Tübingen, J. C. B. Mohr, 2 vols., 1933-1952), the earlier part translated by J. C. Greig as *Essays, Theological and Philosophical* (London, S.C.M. Press, 1955, pp. xi, 337); and *Das Urchristentum im Rahmen der antiken Religionen* (Zürich, Artemis-Verlag, 1949, pp. 261), translated by R. H. Fuller as *Primitive Christianity in Its Contemporary Setting* (London, Thomas and Hudson, 1956, pp. 240).

Among the many writings about Bultmann see Karl Barth, *Rudolf Bultmann, ein Versuch, ihn zu Verstehen* (Zollikon-Zürich, Evangelischer Verlag, 1952, pp. 56); Paul Althaus, *Das sogenannte Kerygma und der historische Jesus: zur Kritik der heutigen Kerygma-Theologie* (Gütersloh, C. Bertelsmann, 1958, pp. 52); John Macquarrie, *An Existential Theology: a Comparison of Heidegger and Bultmann* (London, S.C.M. Press, 1955, pp. xii, 252); Gustaf Wingren, *Theology in Conflict: Nygren, Barth, Bultmann,* translated by Eric H. Wahlstrom from *Theologiens Metodfråga* (Philadelphia, Muhlenberg Press, 1958, pp. xiii, 170).

[204] *Kirchliches Jahrbuch, 1951,* pp. 185-221, *1953,* pp. 62-77.

The towering figures in *Formgeschichte*—Gunkel, Martin Dibelius, and Bultmann—did not exhaust the list of outstanding German Biblical scholars in the four decades which followed 1914. Mention of a few may serve further to show that the tumultuous years did not halt creativity in a field in which the nineteenth century had witnessed notable German contributions. Thus Wilhelm Michaelis (1896——) wrote a comprehensive introduction to the New Testament[205] which was said to have been in the traditional nineteenth-century style and not to have taken sufficient account of *Formgeschichte*. Martin Albertz (1883——), who was arrested three times under the Hitler regime and spent two and a half years in prison, and after the fall of the Nazis was professor of theology in the University of Berlin and in the *Kirchliche Hochschule* in Berlin-Zehlendorf, wrote on the New Testament.[206] Gerhard von Rad (1901——), who taught successively in Leipzig, Jena, Göttingen, and Heidelberg, wrote on the Old Testament.[207] In the 1950's many regarded him as the world's outstanding living Old Testament theologian. Emanuel Hirsch dealt with the New Testament as well as theology.[208] Gerhard Kittel (1888–1948) specialized on the Jewish background of the New Testament and held that the Jewish elements prevailed over the Hellenistic elements in the making of the New Testament books.[209] He was chiefly remembered for his initiation (1933) of the standard *Theologisches Wörterbuch zum Neuen Testament.*[210] After his death it was continued by Gerhard Friedrich (1908——), who, beginning in 1947 after military service, lectured in the *Kirchliche Hochschule* in Bethel.[211] Most of the writing of Adolf von Schlatter (1852–1938), a scholar of Swiss birth, was done before 1914. From 1893 to 1898 he was professor of systematic theology in Berlin, but beginning in 1898 he held a chair of New Testament exegesis in Tübingen.[212] Karl Ludwig Schmidt (1891–1956) worked on the literary sources for the history of Jesus.[213] Martin Noth (1902——)

---

[205] Wilhelm Michaelis, *Einleitung in das Neue Testament: die Entstehung, Sammlung, und Überlieferung der Schriften des Neuen Testaments* (Bonn, BEG-Verlag, 1946, pp. xi, 410). See also his *Die Gleichnisse Jesu: eine Einführung* (Bamberg, Furche-Verlag, 3rd ed., 1956, pp. 272), which is one of several books by him that appeared after 1914.

[206] Martin Albertz, *Die Botschaft des Neuen Testaments* (Zollikon-Zürich, Evangelischer-Verlag, 2 vols., 1947–1957).

[207] Among his books is *Gesammelte Studien zum Alten Testament* (Munich, C. Kaiser, 1958, pp. 312).

[208] Emanuel Hirsch, *Das Vierte Evangelium in seiner ursprünglichen Gestalt verdeutscht und erklärt* (Tübingen, J. C. B. Mohr, 1936, pp. 466); *Studien zum vierten Evangelium (Text, Literarkritik Entstehungsgeschichte)* (Tübingen, J. C. B. Mohr, 1936, pp. vii, 190); *Frühgeschichte des Evangeliums* (Tübingen, J. C. B. Mohr, 2 vols., 1941–1951).

[209] *Twentieth Century Encyclopedia of Religious Knowledge,* Vol. I, p. 627.

[210] Published by W. Kohlhammer (Stuttgart, 6 vols., 1933–1959).

[211] *Twentieth Century Encyclopedia of Religious Knowledge,* Vol. I, p. 446.

[212] *The New Schaff-Herzog Encyclopedia of Religious Knowledge,* Vol. X, p. 239.

[213] Karl Ludwig Schmidt, *Der Rahmen der Geschichte Jesu: literarkritische Untersuchungen zur ältesten Jesusüberlieferung* (Berlin, Trowitsch & Sohn, 1919, pp. xviii, 322).

specialized on the Old Testament.[214] So did Albrecht Alt (1883——)[215] and Johannes Meinhold (1861–1937),[216] although most of the latter's writing was before 1914.

STUDIES IN THE HISTORY OF CHRISTIANITY

The history of Christianity did not provoke the widespread and heated discussion that marked the course of theological and Biblical scholarship in the decades which followed 1914. Yet, as in these other areas, the stormy four decades which began with the outbreak of World War I witnessed much German research and writing in that field. Several of the men who had won distinction in the relative quiet of the years which immediately preceded the tempest lived to see the beginning of the next stage of the revolutionary age and some of them continued to publish. With notable exceptions, most of their attention was confined to Germany and the Church of the first few centuries. Thus Karl Holl (1868–1926), a friend of Harnack, left unfinished an edition of Epiphanius which was completed by Hans Lietzmann. A collection of his writings was issued shortly after his death.[217] Hans Lietzmann (1875–1943) did some of his writing before 1914 but much of the work for which he was best remembered was after that year. Struggling up from dire boyhood poverty, he taught in Bonn and Jena and succeeded Harnack in Berlin. He specialized on the beginnings of Christianity. That led him into New Testament studies, but his major contributions were in a slightly later period.[218] Also primarily on the early Church through the time of Constantine and Ambrose were Hans Freiherr von Campenhausen (1903——) of Heidelberg, Hermann Dörries (1895——) of Göttingen, and Walther von Loewenich (1903——). Franz von Schubert (1859–1931), whose specialty was the early Middle Ages,[219] also wrote on Luther and had a survey of Church history. Heinrich Hermelink, who

---

[214] For example, he wrote *Das Buch Josua* (Tübingen, J. C. B. Mohr, 2nd ed., 1953, pp. 151); *Geschichte Israels* (Göttingen, Vanderhoeck & Ruprecht, 1950, pp. viii, 395); and *Gesammelte Studien zum Alten Testament* (Munich, C. Kaiser, 1957, pp. 306).

[215] As in his *Kleine Schriften zur Geschichte des Volkes Israel* (Munich, C. H. Beck, 2 vols., 1953——).

[216] As in his *Einführung in das Alte Testament* (Giessen, A. Töpelmann, 1919, pp. viii, 316).

[217] Karl Holl, *Gesammelte Aufsätze zur Kirchengeschichte* (Tübingen, J. C. B. Mohr, 3 vols., 1928–1932).

[218] Hans Lietzmann, *Geschichte der alten Kirche* (Berlin, Walter de Gruyter & Co., 3 vols., 1932–1938, translated by Bertram Lee Woolf as *The Beginnings of the Christian Church* (New York, Charles Scribner's Sons, 3 vols., 1950); *Messe und Herrenmahl: eine Studie zur Geschichte der Liturgie* (Bonn, A. Marcus und Weber's Verlag, 1926, pp. xii, 263), translated with appendices by Dorothea H. G. Reeve, introduction and supplementary essay by Robert Douglas Richardson (Leiden, E. J. Brill, 5 parts, 1953–1958); *Petrus und Paulus in Rom: liturgische und archäologische Studien* (Berlin, W. de Gruyter & Co., 1927, pp. viii, 315). These are only a few of Lietzmann's many publications.

[219] Hans von Schubert, *Geschichte der christlichen Kirche in Frühmittelalter* (Tübingen, J. C. B. Mohr, 1921, pp. xxiv, 808).

lived and worked to an advanced age, and some of whose works have been utilized in our pages, made his major contributions on the nineteenth and twentieth centuries. The revival continued of the study of Luther which had been notable in the nineteenth century. Among those who specialized on Luther and the Reformation were Ernest Friedrich Wolf (1902——), who was successively professor in Bonn, Halle, and Göttingen; Gerhard Ritter (1888——), who was imprisoned by the Gestapo in 1944 and was released on the approach of the Russian army; Heinrich Bornkamm (1901——), who taught at Giessen, Leipzig, and Heidelberg; and Franz Lau (1907——). Martin Schmidt (1909——) wrote chiefly on the Ecumenical Movement and some features of English Protestantism. Ernst Benz (1907——) of Marburg also had a wide ecumenical interest and in his prodigious literary output ranged widely geographically, chronologically, and ecclesiastically. Karl Ferdinand Müller (1911——) edited with Walter Blankenburg a liturgical handbook.[220]

SUMMARY

The stage of the revolutionary age which began in the summer of 1914 brought striking challenges to German Protestantism. Currents which had threatened it in the nineteenth century continued. Among them were the adverse intellectual movements and the industrialization with the growth of cities and of an urban proletariat which, as in other countries, tended to drift away from the Church and to be susceptible to anti-Christian movements. In addition Germany suffered defeat in two world wars. The second left it prostrate, exhausted, with many of its cities in ruins, its territory divided and occupied by the victors. Large segments of what had been Germany were transferred to Poland and the inhabitants forced to move into what was left of their country. In the Russian zone a Communist regime was set up which imposed mounting restrictions on the Church. In these changes Protestantism suffered more than the Roman Catholic Church, for they were in areas long predominantly Protestant. Moreover, between the two wars came the Hitler era with measures that bore heavily on the faith. Sobering though they were, the challenges to Protestantism in Germany in the post-1914 decades were not more staggering than some earlier periods had seen—notably the Thirty Years' War and its aftermath, the *Aufklärung,* the French Revolution, and the Napoleonic Wars. They were of a different nature but they were a no greater threat to the faith than had been the earlier ones.

By the end of the 1950's it was clear that Protestantism, while suffering losses, was far from moribund and was rising to the challenge in both old and

[220] Karl Ferdinand Müller and Walter Blankenburg, editors, *Leiturgia Handbuch des evangelischen Gottesdienstes, mit einen Geleitwort der lutherischen liturgischen Konferenz Deutschlands* (Kassel, J. Stauda-Verlag, 4 vols., 1954–1959).

novel ways. The churches had been disestablished, but only a small minority of people had taken the step of formally disassociating themselves from them; the large majority continued to pay the church tax. As with Roman Catholics, so with Protestants, most of the children were baptized and, although the observance of that rite fell off sharply in the Russian zone after World War II, the majority were confirmed. The attendance of Protestants at church services left much to be desired, especially in the cities, and in the latter parishes were far too large to be given adequate care by their clergy, but comprehensive statistics were not available for comparison with the nineteenth century. Whether the record was worse or better was not known. The great Pietist awakenings which had done much to revitalize Protestantism in the nineteenth century were not repeated, but, while declining, Pietism was not dead. Lutheran confessionalism continued to display the vigour which it had shown in the hundred years after 1815. In spite of the conformation of the majority of Protestants to the ecclesiastical structure imposed by the National Socialists, resistance was sturdy and after the collapse of the Hitler regime those who had led in it took the initiative in bringing into being EKD, the Evangelical Church in Germany. EKD, a federation, included the large majority of Protestants in both West and East Germany. Within that federation the several *Landeskirchen* were revived after the Hitler interlude, on a national scale the Lutherans drew together in the United Evangelical Church of Germany (VELKD), and the bodies made up of unions of Lutherans and Reformed associated themselves in the Evangelical Church of the Union (EKU). To meet the widespread spiritual and material needs of the country the Inner Mission was reinforced, both during the Weimar Republic and after 1945, and subsequent to World War II *Hilfswerk* was created in connexion with EKD. Two very striking new movements were the Evangelical Academies and the *Kirchentag*. Both were attempts to enlist the laity and had much of lay leadership. They paralleled what was seen in the Roman Catholic Church and similar developments in Protestantism in several other countries. Larger than their Protestant counterparts elsewhere, although they enrolled many thousands they were still what might be called "creative minorities" and did not reach directly the bulk of the population. A variety of other movements, some old and some of post-World War II origin, were expressions of vitality and of attempts to meet the challenge of the revolutionary age. Among them were efforts to reach the industrial workers, emphasis on liturgy and on private confession, organizations for the re-building of churches destroyed or damaged during World War II, for the erection of new churches, for service to Protestants displaced by World War II, and for the reinforcement of Protestant minorities in prevailing Roman Catholic areas. The recruitment and education of clergy continued. During the Hitler years the opposition maintained clandestine institutions. After 1945 theological education was partly, as heretofore, through faculties in the universities, partly through new institutions, *Kirchliche Hochschülen,* and partly through other institutions, some new and some old. Yet the numbers of clergy were never sufficient to meet the pastoral needs of the population. After World War II the Communist regime in the German Democratic Republic imposed increasingly serious handicaps on the churches within its borders and most of the revivals of old movements and the creation of new ones were in the German Federal Republic. Yet some observers were of the opinion that in the East zone the "Church under the cross" was displaying more vigour than the Church in the West zone, where restrictions by the state were not imposed and full religious freedom prevailed.

In meeting the intellectual challenge of the post-1914 stage of the revolutionary age German Protestantism had an important share, although not as outstanding as in the nineteenth century. In theology a marked reaction occurred against the liberalism of the decades which immediately preceded World War I. That holocaust and the even more destructive one which followed and which bore especially heavily on Germans disclosed to millions of thoughtful souls the tragic contradictions in human nature and in Christendom, the presence of baleful forces, and the failure of Western man to achieve the ideal civilization to which many liberals and socialists had confidently aspired. In Protestantism, especially but not exclusively in Germany, the multiform kind of theology known as dialectic, crisis, or neo-orthodox became current, with its recognition of man's sin and helplessness and of the work of God for man's salvation in revelation, the incarnation, the cross, the resurrection, and the Holy Spirit. In Biblical studies *Formgeschichte* ("form criticism") was the vogue and, in circles in which Bultmann was outstanding, attempted to speak to contemporary man by disengaging the eternal Gospel from the historical *milieu* of the first century and by an approach congenial to those shaped by the existentialism of the day.

Here, obviously, was vitality, although, as in the Roman Catholic and much of the Protestant world, multitudes who by ancestry were Christian were but little affected by it and were being captured by secularism or Communism or both.

CHAPTER XII

Protestantism in Scandinavia

I N THE four and a half decades which followed 1914 Protestantism in Scandinavia did not display the dramatic vitality that had marked its course in
the nineteenth century. No awakenings comparable in vigour to those of that
century were seen. Leaders there were who became international figures, but
their characters had been shaped before World War I. A few specialists in
theology made contributions which had more than local recognition, but none
created such stir as had Kierkegaard. Much the same could be said of culture
outside ecclesiastical circles and of those who attracted attention because of
their attack on traditional Christianity. No musicians so captured the imagination of the Western world as had Grieg, no dramatists had as wide vogue
as Ibsen and Bjornsen, and no sceptic was quite as internationally provocative
as Brandes. The revolutionary age continued and brought with it mounting
challenges to Christianity, partly through the increase of industrialization, the
growth of cities, the further decay of the old patterns of urban and rural life,
the advance of secularization, and the spread of Marxist ideas. Yet the Lutheran churches were still established, almost all the population were baptized,
a large proportion were confirmed, and although church attendance declined,
vigour was not lacking. That vigour was seen chiefly in the continuation of
movements of pre-twentieth-century origin, but it also found expression in
new ways and in leaders in thought and action. Although dissent slightly increased, Scandinavians continued to be more nearly solidly Protestant and
Lutheran than was true of other regions.

DENMARK

Like the rest of Scandinavia, Denmark was caught in the currents of the
revolutionary age as they accelerated after 1914. The two world wars could
not but affect it. During the first it remained officially neutral but suffered
from restrictions, largely on its exports and imports, imposed by the belligerents. It profited by the defeat of Germany in the restoration to it of North
Schleswig, taken from it by Prussia and Austria in 1864. But it was afflicted

by the world-wide depression of the 1930's. Then came deep involvement in World War II. At the outset the Danish Government declared itself neutral. In less than a year, in April, 1940, the Germans occupied the country. The British countered by moving into the Faeroe Islands and Iceland. Iceland had become autonomous in 1918 but had retained a tie with Denmark through a common monarch and a common citizenship. In 1944 it took the occasion of the German occupation of Denmark to sever its remaining bond with that country. As the war took its weary way, tension between the Danes and the Germans mounted. Danes increased their resistance and in August, 1943, the pretense of peaceful coöperation ended, the German army assumed control, the king was interned, and much of the Danish navy was scuttled. Because the Danish police were regarded by the Germans as untrustworthy, in 1944 they were sent to German concentration camps and lawlessness and terror became widely prevalent.

The Church of Denmark played an important part in the resistance. Its leaders were moved not only by patriotism but also by the conviction that National Socialism and Christianity were irreconcilable. A few pastors sought to collaborate through the National Socialist Pastoral Society, organized in 1942, but its members numbered less than a dozen. In contrast the bishops came out for liberty of preaching and against the anti-Jewish policy of the Nazis and the cruelties practised by the forces of occupation. Some of the clergy were arrested and tortured, at least one of the bishops hid some members of the resistance in his cellar and to escape arrest slept in a different place each night, and in January, 1944, Kaj Munk (1898–1944), a pastor, a brilliant dramatist, poet, and preacher, who in his youth had been profoundly influenced by the Inner Mission and Grundtvig and who had been fearless in his denunciation of the occupation, was arrested by the Gestapo and shot. Other pastors were sent to German concentration camps.[1] For a time after the liberation some hope was entertained that because of the Church's outstanding share in the resistance and the sobering effect of the war a revival in Christian faith would be seen. That hope was not realized. Two years after the coming of peace a leading Danish churchman reported that the faith of those at the heart of the congregations had been strengthened but that animosity to the Church was mounting in secular circles.[2]

Even apart from the world wars, political, economic, and social changes associated with the revolutionary age were seen. In 1915 a new constitution was promulgated which instituted a two-chamber parliament, abolished the

[1] Paul Borchsenius, *L'Église, Âme de la Résistance,* translated from the Danish by Roger Petterson, adapted by Ch. Durand-Pallot (Geneva, Éditions Labor et Fides, written in Stockholm, 1944, pp. 99), pp. 37–61, 80–96; Kaj Munk, *Four Sermons,* translated by John M. Jensen (Blair, Neb., Lutheran Publishing House, no date, pp. 36), *passim.*

[2] A. M. Jorgensen in Leiper, *Christianity Today,* pp. 25–27.

privileged suffrage of the landlords and wealthier classes, and granted equal voting rights to women. Land reform in 1919 broke up some of the large estates and increased the number of small proprietors. Representing industrial and agricultural labourers and small landowners, the Social Democrats grew in power, compulsory accident insurance was adopted, and other aspects of a welfare state appeared. Cities grew: in the 1950's Copenhagen, by far the largest, had between a sixth and a fifth of the population of the country.

In spite of the stress of the world wars and the slower but basically more persistent changes wrought by the continuing forces of the revolutionary age, some of the important nineteenth-century movements were vigorous. One was Grundtvigianism. Although waning as an organized movement it still influenced the attitudes of many. After 1914 a great church was erected in Copenhagen in Grundtvig's memory. Folk schools were maintained on Grundtvig's principles which embodied distinctive educational ideals. Here and there, especially in the villages, were voluntary Grundtvigian associations, really "free churches," which had their own buildings.[3] The Inner Mission, largely the result of the awakenings of the nineteenth century, continued to be potent. It maintained schools and several scores of itinerant preachers. Like the Grundtvigians its adherents remained within the state church. Indeed, in the 1950's about a third of the clergy were said to be in sympathy with it.[4] The Grundtvigians and those committed to the Inner Mission agreed in their emphasis on the sacraments, but the latter, unlike the former, who made much of culture and held that a man was first a man and later a Christian, stressed personal salvation by faith and strict moralism, with abstinence from intoxicating drinks, card-playing, dancing, and theatre-going. They had prayer houses for informal meetings. In contrast with the Grundtvigians, who were chiefly among the prosperous farmers, the highly educated, and the townsfolk, the Inner Mission was strongest on the west coast of Jutland and among the lower-income elements of the population.[5] The Luther Mission, whose adherents were sometimes called the Bornholmers, from the island where it originated, continued. It did not separate from the national church but had its own prayer houses and folk schools.[6] Many of the clergy followed a middle way, with Mynster and Martensen for precedents.[7]

The Church of Denmark, Lutheran, was still closely tied to the state and controlled by it. Much of its financial support came through the state, and one of the cabinet ministers was charged with its supervision and in part with its direction. Subject to state control as it was, the Church of Denmark was a

[3] Siegmund-Schultze, *Die Kirche in Dänemark*, pp. 55, 97, 98, 150, 151.
[4] *Ibid.*, pp. 54, 98, 99; the author's personal observation, March, 1954.
[5] The author's personal observation, March, 1954.
[6] Siegmund-Schultze, *op. cit.*, pp. 58, 59; Volume II, pp. 147, 148.
[7] Siegmund-Schultze, *op. cit.*, p. 99; Volume II, pp. 135, 136, 143, 144.

folk church, the church of the nation. Boards, or councils, elected by the constituencies, had a large share in the management of parish affairs. They were accorded permanent status in 1912 and among other functions participated in the choice of pastors.[8] In the 1950's, following long tradition, the overwhelming majority of the population were baptized and confirmed in the Church of Denmark. Although a civil confirmation ceremony growing out of the anti-Christian secularism of Georg Brandes[9] was legally permissible, only a small minority availed themselves of it. Instruction in the Christian faith was given both in the folk schools and by the pastors in pre-confirmation classes. The law permitted only teachers belonging to the national church to give instruction in religion in the primary schools.[10] The instruction was required to be in accord with the teachings of the Church of Denmark, but parents might have their children exempted if they so desired, and a teacher who felt that he could not conscientiously coöperate was not required to do so. Provision was made for excusing pupils from school for pre-confirmation classes by their pastors during the hours which the latter asked for it.[11]

How far did the instruction in school and for confirmation issue in a full Christian commitment and active participation in the life and worship of the Church? That the vast majority of the population became acquainted with the main tenets of the Christian faith as held by Lutherans was clear. That to some degree the life of the nation was modified was probable and in the nearly half a century which followed 1914 little active dissent or anti-clericalism was seen. However, the divorce rate was high, and in Copenhagen in the mid-1950's about two-fifths of the children were said to be born out of wedlock.[12] Late in the 1950's about half the marriages were by civil and not by church ceremonies. Church attendance varied with the section of the country. In the 1950's only between 1 and 2 per cent. of the population of Copenhagen attended church with any degree of regularity and in the rural districts from 5 to 7 per cent. were estimated to do so.[13] If a larger proportion had wished to come, the existing church buildings, at least in Copenhagen, were entirely insufficient to accommodate them and clergy were too few for adequate pastoral care. Thus in Copenhagen in 1957 in the metropolitan boroughs there was only one seat in a church to every seventeen inhabitants and in the suburbs, growing as they were, only one seat to every thirty of the population. The metropolitan boroughs had one pastor for every 3,900 and the suburbs one for

---

[8] Andersen, *Survey of the History of the Church in Denmark,* p. 73.
[9] Volume II, p. 149; Siegmund-Schultze, *op. cit.,* p. 95.
[10] *Church News from the Northern Countries,* December 23, 1957.
[11] *Ibid.,* June 30, 1959, October 29, 1959.
[12] Information obtained by the author in March, 1954.
[13] *Ibid.;* Margaret Frakes in The Christian Century, Vol. LXXV, pp. 1020–1022 (September 10, 1958); *Church News from the Northern Countries,* November 27, 1959.

every 4,400 of the population.[14] Yet in that same year in Copenhagen only 1,252 children were named without baptism (only 7.3 per cent. of those baptized), and only 1,104, mostly men, formally withdrew from the national church.[15] Obviously here was no extensive antagonism, but a willingness to conform to what was at least a social convention. Yet if Christian life was to be nourished, better provision for worship and pastoral oversight were imperative.

Efforts were not lacking to remedy the situation. In 1896 *Det Koebenhavnske Kirkefond* (the Copenhagen Church Fund) was instituted in succession to a slightly earlier (1890) purely laymen's enterprise to increase the number of church buildings in the capital.[16] Funds came originally purely from private subscription and latterly partly from the state. For years the new churches were chiefly in the poorer sections of the city and some of them had kindergartens to care on weekdays for the children of working mothers.[17] In 1957 the Danish Government made a substantial grant to aid in the erection of new churches, with the provision that the subsidy was not to exceed half the cost, that at least a quarter must come from private subscription, and that the remainder might be granted by the state as a loan. This would enable more building to be done in the rapidly growing suburbs of Copenhagen and the Copenhagen Church Fund sought to take advantage of the opportunity.[18] It was said that the post-1914 years were the greatest period of church building since the twelfth and thirteenth centuries.[19] In the mid-1950's a device was instituted for the pastoral care of the residents of the housing developments in the cities: in 1956, for example, a clergyman was appointed to a new block of apartment houses in Aalborg, in the north of Jutland. Recognition was given to the fact that those moving into such areas were spiritually rootless and the hope was cherished that in time churches could be erected for them.[20]

Although the proportion of the population actively associated with the national church was small, that minority sought to aid the country in a variety of ways. Lay initiative and participation were prominent, parelleling what we have found in Germany, in much of Roman Catholic Europe, and, as we shall see, elsewhere. Missions were carried on for the taxi drivers and street-car employees. Christian unions were organized in the telegraph and postal serv-

[14] *Church News from the Northern Countries,* January 28, 1958.
[15] *Ibid.*
[16] Siegmund-Schultze, *op. cit.,* pp. 91, 92; *Kobenhavns Kirkesag 1890–1915. Festskrift udgivet af Kirkefondets Forretningsudvalg* (Copenhagen, G. E. C. Gad, 1915, pp. 278); Andersen, *op. cit.,* p. 69.
[17] Observation by the author, March, 1954.
[18] *Church News from the Northern Countries,* January 18, 1958, November 22, 1958.
[19] Andersen, *op. cit.,* p. 77.
[20] *Church News from the Northern Countries,* September 7, 1955.

ices and for longshoremen and members of some other occupations.[21] Refuges for Magdalenes and for homeless men were maintained. The Church Cross Army, corresponding to the Salvation Army and with several hundred members, both men and women, had centres in a number of cities for rescue of the wayward, street preaching, missions in the slums, and the distribution of literature. The Blue Cross, for the promotion of temperance, was active. In 1931 a comprehensive organization for the coördination and promotion of church philanthropies was formed. Several hundred deaconesses ministered in hospitals. Homes for the aged were maintained and care was given to the indigent ill. Pre-school children were provided with kindergartens, and during summer vacations thousands of city children were sent to the country as guests in private families or in camps. In the 1930's Niels Dahl of Lisolund led a movement which sought to counter Fascism and Communism by a "Christian revolution" centring about a free church where Christ would be a living reality and brotherhood would be the only creed.[22] An organization was supported to provide churches and pastoral care for Danes in foreign lands.[23] Foreign missions were continued. In proportion to the population the missionaries were not as numerous as those of Norway and Sweden but were more numerous than those from Germany. In 1957 they totalled 280 as compared with 967 from Norway, 1,568 from Sweden, and 975 from Germany.[24]

Movements in Protestantism in other countries made an impact upon Danish Protestantism. Dialectic theology with Barth as its outstanding representative and the de-mythologizing of which Bultmann was the chief formulator had advocates but also aroused opposition. The "Oxford Groups," later to be called "Moral Rearmament," of American origin and of which we are to hear more in this and the next volume, attracted both adherents and critics.[25] "Youth for Christ," also of American provenance and for young people in their teens, had its World Congress in Copenhagen in 1957.[26] Under the inspiration of the German example, a *Kirchentag* was held which in 1958 attracted about three thousand.[27] Danish Protestants were caught up in the Ecumenical Movement and were represented in the first assembly of the World Council of Churches in Amsterdam in 1948.[28] Danish churchmen also coöperated with Europe's Evangelical Alliance.[29]

---

[21] Siegmund-Schultze, *op. cit.*, p. 91.

[22] *Ibid.*, pp. 91, 166–169; Koch, *Danmarks Kirke gennem Tiderne*, pp. 238, 239; Horton, *Contemporary Continental Theology*, pp. 158, 159.

[23] Koch, *op. cit.*, p. 239.

[24] *Occasional Bulletin from the Missionary Research Library*, December 8, 1958, p. 29.

[25] Koch, *op. cit.*, pp. 236, 237.

[26] *Church News from the Northern Countries*, March 21, 1957.

[27] *Ibid.*, September 30, 1958.

[28] Koch, *op. cit.*, p. 239.

[29] *Church News from the Northern Countries*, November 25, 1957.

High-church tendencies were not as marked in Denmark as in Sweden, but in the 1950's communities were seen of women living according to the rules of poverty, chastity, and obedience and observing the canonical hours of prayer. Such designations were heard as "Daughters of Mary" and "Ecumenical Little Sisters."[30] In 1959 several of the churches in Copenhagen followed the example of the cathedral in introducing old liturgical elements in their services in accordance with the recommendation of the Church Music Group and with an effort at the active participation of the laity.[31]

Although the overwhelming majority of the population were baptized and confirmed in the national church, several other churches were represented. Of these the largest was the Roman Catholic Church. Of the Protestant bodies the Baptists enrolled more than any of the others, with the Methodists next and the Irvingites third. The Seventh Day Adventists grew rapidly.[32]

While the Danish theologians and Biblical scholars of the twentieth century did not attract as much attention outside their country as had Kierkegaard and Grundtvig of the preceding hundred years, they were by no means lacking and in keenness of intellect would bear comparison with any of their contemporaries in other lands. To single out some for mention seems almost invidious, but as examples note may be made of K. E. Skydsgaard (1902——), whose lectures on a comparison between Roman Catholicism and Protestantism[33] made him the natural choice of the Lutheran World Federation to head its Inter-Confessional Institute which first centred on a study of Roman Catholic theology; Bent Noack, who maintained that the Fourth Gospel does not presuppose the Synoptic Gospels but rests independently on oral tradition;[34] Paul Georg Lindhart (1910——), brilliant and provocative theologian and Church historian; and Hal Koch (1904——), eminent Church historian and educator, whose wife was the able and successful minister of church affairs of the Socialist government.

ICELAND

The population of Iceland grew in the twentieth century, but by 1957 it was only 166,831. So small was it that in our world-wide survey we can devote only a brief paragraph to the island. Autonomy and the final severing of the remaining political connexion with Denmark, in 1918 and 1944 respectively, did not essentially change the status of Christianity. The Lutheran Church

---

[30] The Christian Century, Vol. LXXVI, p. 704.

[31] Church News from the Northern Countries, June 30, 1959.

[32] Siegmund-Schultze, op. cit., p. 76.

[33] Ja og Nej. Till Forstaaelse af Forholdet mellem Katholicisme og Protestantisme, translated as One in Christ by Axel C. Kildegaard (Philadelphia, Muhlenberg Press, 1957, pp. 220), passim.

[34] Bent Noack, Zur johannischen Tradition: Beiträge zur Kritik an der literakritische Analyse des vierten Evangelium (Copenhagen, Rosenkilde og Baggar, 1954, pp. 170).

continued to be tied to the state, and in the census of 1950 only 1,454 were counted as dissenters and 2,242 said that they had no religious connexion.[35] Most of the clergy were trained in the theological faculty of the university which was founded in 1911 and a few went abroad for further study. Tensions existed between the older clergy, conservative, and the younger ones, affected by currents from other lands, but by the mid-1950's they had lessened. In 1934 changes in the form of public worship were effected which made possible larger variety than previously. As in many countries, the shift of population from the rural districts to the towns and cities made for a falling off in church attendance, but the attitude towards Christianity was one of indifference rather than hostility. Early in the century spiritualism, with its alleged communication with the dead, had a wide vogue and many of the clergy were friendly to it. Before 1960 it was waning among the clergy but a large proportion of the laity were still attracted by it. Yet in the 1950's new churches and a new cathedral were being erected.[36]

NORWAY

For Norway and its church even more than for Denmark World War II brought striking developments. Like the other Scandinavian countries, during World War I it maintained its neutrality and endeavoured to do so on the outbreak of the second global struggle. However, in April, 1940, Germany launched a surprise attack. In spite of the lack of military preparedness, in contrast with Denmark Norway offered military resistance. After sixty-two days that was crushed. The king and his cabinet, unreconciled, took refuge in London and there conducted a government in exile. The Germans substituted a government with which the name of Vidkun Quisling, a Norwegian, was associated and maintained it by their bayonets. On the defeat of Germany it collapsed and in May, 1945, the government recognized by the majority of the nation was restored to power.

The Church of Norway took a leading part in the resistance to the German rule. By long tradition it was tied closely to the state, and the Germans through the government which they set up endeavoured to utilize it for their purposes. Since all Norwegians unless belonging to another religious body were automatically members of that church and since by the constitution the king was its head, the Germans saw in it either a powerful support for their regime or a dangerous rival and sought to bring it to heel. At the time of the invasion the Church of Norway was torn by violent dissensions, largely on attitudes towards the intellectual currents associated with the revolutionary age. Con-

---

[35] *The Statesman's Year Book, 1959*, p. 1106.

[36] D. F. Siegmund-Schultze, editor, *Die Kirche in Island* (Leipzig, Leopold Klotz, 1937, pp. 35), pp. 24–35; *Church News from the Northern Countries*, December 23, 1957, May 26, 1959.

fronted by the common danger the conflicting groups united against the hated alien. They had a leader in Eivind Berggrav (1884-1959). A man of marked vigour of mind and character, Berggrav was from the theologically liberal wing of the church, had been a teacher, pastor, and editor of the periodical *For Kirke og Kultur* (*For Church and Culture*), and bishop of the diocese which covered the northern part of the country. On the eve of World War II as president of the World Alliance for Promoting Friendship through the Churches he had sought by personal approaches to various European governments to prevent the outbreak of that struggle. At the time of the German invasion he was Bishop of Oslo, the most important see of Norway (he was appointed in 1937), and while there, under the stresses of the years, moved towards conservatism.

Although Hitler had assured the Norwegians of complete religious liberty, by the end of September, 1940, the dissolution of the existing government and its parties and the substitution of the Quisling minority made abundantly clear the purpose to incorporate Norway into the National Socialist structure. The Church was commanded to conform to the new order and to give it its blessing. Thereupon the church leaders rose above their controversies and on October 25, 1940, the seven bishops and ten clergymen from all the contending parties, headed by Berggrav, signed a manifesto which announced the organization of the Christian Council for the Church of Norway. Following various acts of the Nazis against recalcitrants in the population, on January 15, 1941, the bishops sent a letter to the minister for Church and education of the Quisling regime protesting against the acts of that government as contrary to the law of God and coming out as the spokesmen of the nation's conscience. In spite of the government's effort to suppress it, the letter was widely circulated. Berggrav also preserved an eloquent silence when urged to endorse the Nazi invasion of Russia as a crusade against Bolshevism.

In February, 1942, the Quisling cohorts took possession of the cathedral at Trondhjem (Nidaros) during the Sunday morning service, and its dean, who attempted to hold services, was dismissed from his office and arrested. The entire episcopate—seven in all—sent in their resignations as state officials, but retaining their spiritual status as bishops, and were supported by all but a small minority of the clergy. Most of the clergy also resigned their posts under the state but continued as pastors. The Christian bodies not part of the Church of Norway rallied to them. The government retaliated by dismissing all but one of the bishops and the clergy who stood by them. The clergy continued to use the church buildings and to hold services. The latter were thronged—evidence of the appreciation of the populace of the stand against the Nazi regime. On Easter Sunday, 1942, a letter was read from the pulpits of the churches stating the position of the clergy and protesting against measures of the government, including the effort to indoctrinate the children with Nazi principles.

The government sought to set up an ecclesiastical structure to take the place of the dismissed bishops and clergy, but with only slight success. Berggrav and several members of the Christian Council for the Church of Norway were arrested and sent to a concentration camp. Berggrav was later released from the camp but kept under house arrest. In the summer of 1942 bishops and clergy who were still at liberty formed a Provisional Church Council. In November of that year the Provisional Church Council, reinforced by members of other denominations, issued a sharp protest against the anti-Semitic measures of the Quisling regime, and prayers were said in the churches on behalf of the Jews. A further letter of protest against Nazi actions was read from the pulpits as a New Year's message on January 17, 1943. Efforts to conscript theological students and younger pastors for compulsory labour were also protested. The bishops of the Church of Sweden stood staunchly by their Norwegian brethren.[37]

As the occupation continued, the resistance of the Norwegian majority was intensified and with it the restrictive measures of the Nazi regime were heightened. The government closed the theological faculty of the university and *Det Teologiske Menighetsfakultetet* (The Congregations' Theological Faculty). To meet the need for pastors and in defiance of the government abridged courses in theology were improvised. The properties and funds of the missionary societies were confiscated, including those of the largest, the Norwegian Missionary Society, and the latter's secretary was imprisoned.[38]

With the defeat of Germany in the spring of 1945, the Nazi regime collapsed and the king and his government, returning from England, were restored to power. With their coming Christianity resumed its pre-war course without striking changes. The features of the revolutionary age which had been present before the interruption were still present, acting more slowly than the war and the German invasion, but with more continuing result. The growth of population and the movement from the rural districts towards the cities were marked and with them came a mounting mechanization and a secularization of life. Little or no outspoken hostility to Christianity was heard. The Church of Norway was supported and governed by the state, religious instruction in the tenets of Christianity was given in the schools, and the large

[37] J. L. Mowinckel, *The Fight of the Norwegian Church* (New York, Arnesen Press, 1943, pp. 10), *passim;* *The Norwegian Church Struggle* (no author given, London, Hodder and Stoughton, 1943, pp. 68), *passim;* Eivind Berggrav, *With God in the Darkness and other Papers Illustrating the Norwegian Church Conflict* (London, Hodder and Stoughton, 1943, pp. viii, 109), *passim;* Hansson, *Stat og Kirke,* pp. 70 ff.; Bjarne Höye and Trygve M. Ager, *The Fight of the Norwegian Church against Nazism* (New York, The Macmillan Co., 1943, pp. 180), *passim;* Hoffmann, *Les Églises du Nord dans la Crise Mondiale,* pp. 41–139.

[38] *The International Review of Missions,* Vol. XXXIV, p. 70, Vol. XXXV, p. 7.

majority of the population were baptized and confirmed.[39]

The major developments in the quarter-century between the outbreak of World War I and the German occupation must be quickly summarized. The theological strife between liberals and conservatives which became acute on the eve of 1914[40] persisted for some years. The *Menighetsfakultetet* flourished and became permanent, founded as it had been in 1908 in protest against the appointment to the university theological faculty of J. Ording, who represented the school of Ritschl and Hermann. The liberal pastors who in 1913 formed the Progressive Norwegian Ministerial Group (*Norske Presters Fremskritisgruppe*) were countered by the Brotherhood of Pastors Loyal to the Church's Confession (*Bekjennelsestro Presters Broderkrets*), which, organized in 1919, stood for "the faith of the congregation" and made much of the Apostles' Creed, using Grundtvigian ideas.[41] In that year one of the *Menighetsfakultetet* offered as a way to peace the acceptance by the liberals of the Apostles' Creed "word for word," but they refused on the ground that that statement of faith reflected a particular historical situation and must not be permanently binding on "evangelical Christians." The conflict waxed still warmer, with a large proportion of the active church members among the laity siding with the conservatives. Bitter words were uttered on both sides. In 1925, to offset the state's Practical Seminary, headed by a liberal rector appointed in 1916, the *Menighetsfakultetet* organized its own Practical Theological Seminary. In 1929 it began its periodical *Tidsskrift for Teologi og Kirke* to counter the liberal *Norsk Teologisk Tidsskrift*. Each camp had extremists and the efforts of irenic moderates to effect peace appeared to fail. One of the more radical, Kristian Schjelderup, gave up historical Christianity, espoused a general religion, and regarded Jesus as simply a religious genius. The government refused him a pastorate, and when he was elected president of the Norwegian Students' Christian Alliance (*Norske Studenters Kristelige Forbund*) in 1924 the conservative students withdrew and formed the *Norges Kristelige Studenterforbund*, which soon enrolled more members than the older organization and extended its activities to the high schools.[42] The conflict, as we are to see, particularly in the next volume, was paralleled by similar ones in Protestantism in other lands.

The 1920's witnessed much hostility to the Church in some labour circles and an increase in self-government in the church. In 1920 provision for elective parish councils was made which came into effect in 1922. Each council was given a voice in nominating three candidates for its vacant pastorate from

[39] On the relations of Church and state from 1914 to 1940 see Hansson, *op. cit.*, pp. 19–70.
[40] Volume II, pp. 164, 165.
[41] Molland, *Church Life in Norway*, p. 104.
[42] Molland, *op. cit.*, pp. 102–111; Hansson, *op. cit.*, pp. 32 ff.; Siegmund-Schultze, *Die Kirche von Norwegen*, pp. 90–92.

whom the king through the appropriate ministry, the *Kirkedepartementet,* made the selection. The councils also proposed candidates for the episcopate.[43]

In the 1930's the theological dissensions were eased and fresh life was seen, partly because many were wearied by the unhappy and weakening strife and partly because new movements entered from abroad. The dialectic or crisis theology began to make itself felt and, espoused by many of the younger men on both sides, dealt blows to the older liberalism and formed a bridge between the warring camps. The years 1930–1934 were marked by awakenings. In 1934 the Oxford Groups centred on Norway and won the adherence of many who, some pastors and some previously indifferent, earnest in their new experience, remained with the Church of Norway and brought vitality to numbers of parishes. In 1929 the Progressive Norwegian Ministerial group disbanded. The attempt of Schjelderup (1928) to found a National Association for Broad-minded Christianity met with slight response and in 1933 was abandoned. Although when, in 1937, Berggrav, labelled as a liberal, was transferred to the Diocese of Oslo an outstanding conservative protested, the appointment was confirmed by an overwhelming majority of the votes of the parish councils of the diocese. Berggrav had long been working to bring the conflicting parties together to present a united front to an unfriendly Labour Party, and his leadership was soon to be effective in the tragic and successful struggle with the Nazis.[44] After what for a time had been a stormy debate and initial crushing opposition, in 1938 legislation was enacted which made possible the ordination of women.[45]

The attitude of the rank and file of the population towards the Church was ambiguous. On most Sundays attendance at the services was poor. As in many other countries, the day was used more for recreation than for worship. Thousands took the occasion to pour out of the cities by auto, railroad, on foot, or, in winter, on skis. In the rural districts regular church-going was not as common as a generation earlier. Yet on the high days of the church year the churches were full, and especially on the Sundays which were set aside for confirmation. The rite was administered after instruction, in most of the country given once a week to children who often came long distances.[46]

In spite of the quickenings early in the 1930's the great awakenings which marked the course of the nineteenth century—those associated with the names of Hans Nielsen Hauge and Gisle Johnson, the repercussions from Grundtvig, and the ones of the 1890's—were not repeated. But their fruits were still seen in the many prayer houses where those who inherited their convictions con-

---

[43] Molland, *op. cit.,* p. 108; Hansson, *op. cit.,* p. 32; Siegmund-Schultze, *Die Kirche von Nor-wegen,* p. 105.
[44] Molland, *op. cit.,* pp. 112–114.
[45] Hansson, *op. cit.,* pp. 64–70.
[46] Siegmund-Schultze, *Die Kirche von Norwegen,* pp. 114–116.

vened, and in such organizations as the Norwegian Lutheran Inner Mission Society (which in 1891 succeeded the Luther Foundation), the Western Inner Mission Association, the Norwegian Lutheran China Mission Association, three missionary societies for seamen, and the Norwegian Missionary Society.[47] In the mid-1930's about a quarter of a million were said to be members of one or another of the missionary societies.[48] The lay movement which had been given an impetus by the awakenings persisted. As early as 1906 some lay preachers of the Western Inner Mission Association and the Norwegian Lutheran China Mission Association began advocating Communion administered in the inner circles of believers by men who were not ordained. In 1913 the *Storting* (Parliament) cancelled the penalties for such "private Communions."[49]

After the expulsion of the Germans the pre-war structure of the Church and the various societies and movements were quickly restored. For a time the tribulations and the courageous resistance in which the Church had been prominent seemed to have brought a marked revival. The dissensions between liberals and conservatives were quieted, concord appeared to prevail, and the controversial Kristian Schjelderup, who had had a striking religious experience and had served as pastor and preacher to his fellow prisoners in a concentration camp, was accepted by all circles and in 1947 was made a bishop.[50] Yet conservatives still challenged him on theological issues, among them his questioning of eternal punishment in hell.[51] But the strains between the constituencies of the prayer houses and the pastors were lessened, and many of the latter became associated with the prayer houses. The tensions which had put the two theological faculties at variance subsided and changes were within them rather than between them.[52] The Norwegian Lutheran Inner Mission Society, the Western Inner Mission Association, the Norwegian Missionary Society, and other organizations and institutions for domestic and foreign missions and action were revived. A list in 1952 showed fully fifty of them. The majority had been begun between 1842 and 1914, but several had been initiated after 1914 and to them were added a few after World War II.[53] Among them were a large training school for deaconesses, another for deacons, a mission to Buddhists, another to Moslems, another to Tibet, a Christian labour union, the

[47] Volume II, pp. 155–163.
[48] Siegmund-Schultze, *Die Kirche von Norwegen*, p. 152. On the Western Inner Mission Association in the years between 1918 and 1940 see *Det Vestlandske Indremisjonsforbund gjennom 50 år* (Bergen, Det Vestlandske Indremisjonsforbund, 1948, pp. 249 ff.).
[49] Molland, *op. cit.*, pp. 97, 98.
[50] Siegmund-Schultze, *Die Kirche von Norwegen*, p. 117.
[51] *Church News from the Northern Countries*, November 25, 1957, December 23, 1957.
[52] Information obtained in Norway in March, 1954.
[53] *Årbok for den Norske Kirke, 1952*, pp. 78–116.

extensive Oslo Inner Mission,[54] and the Norwegian Mission for the Homeless.[55] More than 90 per cent. of the population of Norway were regarded as members of the Church of Norway, but in the 1950's about thirty other churches were represented.[56] Of them the ones with the most adherents in 1946, beginning with the largest, were the Pentecostals,[57] the Lutheran Free Church, the Methodists, the Baptists,[58] the Roman Catholics, and the Seventh Day Adventists. The most striking growth since 1931, both proportionately and in actual numbers, was first by the Pentecostals, who owed their inception to T. B. Barrett, of English birth, a Methodist product of the Welsh revival who became a Pentecostal in New York in 1906; next by the Seventh Day Adventists; and third by the Roman Catholics. We shall meet the flourishing Pentecostal and Seventh Day Adventist movements in a number of other countries. Both were of American origin. The older dissenting Protestant bodies, notably the Lutheran Free Church, the Methodists, and the Baptists, increased more slowly; indeed, the Methodists lost ground between 1920 and 1946.[59]

As was true in most of Western Europe in the post-1914 and especially the post-World War II decades, church attendance in Norway declined. A survey made in 1957 disclosed that the percentage of the population going to the Church of Norway on Easter was 5.8 and on ordinary holy days 2.7.[60] One of the problems was the large size of the parishes and the small number of clergy. The percentage ranged on ordinary Sundays from 3.83 in parishes with 3,000 or under to 1.91 in parishes of 5,000 or more.[61] Moreover, after the entrance of more young men into the ministry in the years which immediately followed World War II than could be given pastorates, late in the 1950's theological students fell off sharply. In the autumn of 1959 only twenty young men were newly enrolled in the two theological faculties. Difficulty was being encountered in finding assistant pastors, applicants for the difficult posts in the northern part of the country, and men trained in theology for the staffs of religious organizations and teaching posts in the growing schools.[62]

[54] Stephan Tschudi, *Hundre År in Kamp mot nod. Oslo Indremisjon 1855–1955* (Oslo, Land og Kirke, 1955, pp. 175), *passim*.

[55] Oscar Lyngstad, *Landeveiens Folk i Norge. Kort Oversikt over Omstreifernes Historie og Norsk Misjon blant Hjemlose* (Oslo, Land og Kirke, 1947, pp. 86), pp. 53 ff.

[56] *Årbok for den Norske Kirke, 1952,* p. 149.

[57] Nils Bloch-Hoell, *Pinsebevegelsen* (Oslo, Universitetsforlaget, 1956, pp. viii, 459), *passim;* Du Plessis, *A Brief History of Pentecostal Assemblies.*

[58] *Baptist Work in Denmark, Finland, Norway, and Sweden,* pp. 49–61; Franks, *European Baptists Today,* pp. 52–57.

[59] *Årbok for den Norske Kirke, 1952,* p. 149.

[60] *Church News from the Northern Countries,* September 20, 1957.

[61] *Årbok for den Norske Kirke, 1958,* pp. 105, 106.

[62] *Church News from the Northern Countries,* October 29, 1959.

The situation was not as grim as these figures might seem to indicate. Here as elsewhere in many lands in the former Christendom, especially in Europe and Latin America, sharp contrasts were seen between what appeared to be a waning of the faith on the one hand and marked vigour on the other. We can take the space to mention only a few of the indications of that vitality in Norway. Although the average church attendance was low, in 1957 about half the population had been to church at least once during the preceding year, about three-fourths of the parents taught their children to say evening prayers, and fully half listened to a Sunday church service over the radio.[63] After a dearth of building materials in the immediate post-World War II years, an easing of the shortage was accompanied by the erection of a number of new churches, especially but not entirely in the growing outskirts of the cities. In the ten years which followed 1945, 29 new churches were dedicated and 20 more were under construction. New livings totalling 184 had been established. Most of the buildings were financed by the municipalities.[64] In 1957 an active, well-organized programme of evangelism was undertaken in which the laity were prominent in visiting the indifferent or hostile. It was akin to the Tell Scotland movement, of which we are to hear in a later chapter. In 1951 four chapel boats were put into service to minister to isolated communities.[65] After several years of careful preparation the Norwegian Church Academy was founded in 1956 with purposes resembling those of the Evangelical Academies in Germany and what we are to find in several other countries, notably in the Netherlands.[66] Attempts, not unsuccessful, were made to establish conversation between representatives of the Church on the one hand and leaders in politics and in the labour unions on the other[67]—the latter reminiscent of what we saw in Germany. Some opposition was raised to the tie between Church and state. The clergyman who advocated severing the bond did so on the ground that the connexion led to doctrinal laxity and to a church which was tolerant of a wide diversity of theological opinions and teaching rather than holding to strict Lutheran confessionalism.[68] However, in the 1950's public opinion in general was counter to the separation of Church and state. The Socialists, who until 1920 had had it as a plank in their platform, now did not wish it, for through the connexion the state could continue to control the Church. Those in the Church who were critical of the awakenings were against the divorce, for it might mean that the elements touched by the revivals would break with

[63] *Ibid.*

[64] *Årbok for den Norske Kirke, 1954*, pp. 51, 54, 55, *1956*, p. 71; *Church News from the Northern Countries*, November 5, 1955, March 21, 1957.

[65] *Church News from the Northern Countries*, December 18, 1956, March 21, 1957, November 25, 1957; Herman, *Report from Christian Europe*, p. 5.

[66] *Church News from the Northern Countries*, November 23, 1956, March 21, 1957.

[67] *Ibid.*, June 30, 1959.

[68] *Ibid.*, January 28, 1958.

the Church, and those committed to the revivals wished the tie retained, for in their opinion it insured that the masses had at least a smattering of Christianity and thus were more likely to be converted than if they were completely ignorant of it.[69] The Education Act of 1959 passed by a Parliament in which Labour had the majority continued the association of Church and state. The schools were required, as in the past, to give instruction in Christianity, and in accord with the Lutheran Confession and through textbooks approved by the bishops and representatives of the theological faculties. However, the pastors, vicars, and bishops were no longer *ex officio* members of the supervisory boards.[70]

Although no theologian or Biblical specialist emerged who made a deep impression on Protestant thought outside Norway, able scholars in the field of religion were not lacking. The one with the widest reputation was Sigmund Olaf Plytt Mowinckel (1884——), whose extensive writings on the Old Testament circulated not only in Norwegian but also in German and to a less extent in English. Norway had a notable share in the Protestant world mission. In 1947 the total of foreign missionaries from its various societies was 967. In proportion to the Protestant population this was larger than that of any country on the continent of Europe with the possible exception of France.[71]

SWEDEN

In Sweden, by far the largest of the Scandinavian lands in area, population, and wealth, the contrasts in the status of Christianity were more striking than in any of the others. As in the others, the church of the overwhelming majority was Lutheran and was supported and controlled by the state. Sweden maintained its neutrality in the two world wars which followed 1914, but the forces of the revolutionary age in some respects proved more corrosive to the faith than in Denmark, Iceland, or Norway. Church attendance fell off both in cities and in rural districts and the proportion of those baptized and confirmed declined, although it was still much more than 50 per cent. of the population. Complaints were heard of widespread sexual laxity and of a high incidence of illegitimate births. As was true in the nineteenth century, a large percentage of those touched by the awakenings, although for most of the period still members of the Church of Sweden, were in dissenting bodies. The Church of Sweden, having kept the apostolic succession in contrast with its sister Scandinavian state churches, developed high-church tendencies more than the

[69] Information given the author in Norway, March, 1954.

[70] *Church News from the Northern Countries*, April 28, 1959.

[71] *Occasional Bulletin from the Missionary Research Library*, December 8, 1958. In 1960 the total in active service was said to be 811. *Church News from the Northern Countries*, March 24, 1960.

others. Swedish churchmen, particularly Nathan Söderblom, were accorded a larger place in the Ecumenical Movement than were those of other Scandinavian lands, and the scholarship of Sweden had much wider repercussions upon Protestantism as a whole than did that of Denmark, Iceland, or Norway. Sweden presented a particularly striking example of the contrast between de-Christianization and the vigour of the faith which we have repeatedly noted in the former Christendom. We can best give a picture of post-1914 developments in Swedish Christianity by high-lighting these contrasts by specific examples.

The decline in observance of church customs was vividly seen in Stockholm, the capital and largest city of Sweden. There in 1957 on the average only 1.3 per cent. of the population attended services of the Church of Sweden on Sunday mornings and 2.1 per cent. were present at services some time during the week. In the years 1940–1945, 91 per cent. of the newly born were baptized, while in the years 1951–1956 the percentage dropped to 86. Yet on the heartening side was the fact that more than twice as many took the Communion in Stockholm in 1956 than sixteen years earlier.[72] On the whole, however, the figures indicated a more serious deterioration than in Oslo and Copenhagen.

In Sweden as a whole the situation was not as bad as in Stockholm, but it was sobering. An extensive study showed that about 1950 in Stockholm and much of the centre of the country the average attendance at the main service of the Church of Sweden on Sundays was less than 2.5 per cent. of the population, that in the North and part of the South it was between 2.5 and 5 per cent., that in a few sections, mostly in the South, it was between 5 and 7.5 per cent., and that only here and there, mostly in the South-west, was it over 7.5 per cent. Attendance at Communion in the same period gave much the same picture. It disclosed that those taking Communion one or more times a year were 5 per cent. or less of the population in Stockholm and most of the North, and that in only scattered areas in the South and South-west was the proportion more than a fourth.[73] In every diocese the statistics disclosed a fairly steady falling off of attendance at the morning service after 1927. However, in several dioceses the proportion of the population taking Communion was mounting. The decline in attendance was more marked in the cities than in the rural parishes—a condition paralleled in other lands among both Roman Catholics and Protestants and evidence of the effect of urbanization. The proportion of the population who had never taken Communion since confirmation was in no classification less than half and in the larger cities was two-thirds. But in cities of medium size all but 3 per cent. of the inhabitants had been confirmed and in the larger cities and smaller towns all but 11 per cent. had

[72] The Christian Century, Vol. LXXIV, p. 975 (August 14, 1957).
[73] Gustafsson, Svensk Kyrkogeografi, pp. 20, 22.

received the rite. As might have been expected, the proportion of those attending church was higher in the smaller than in the larger parishes. But early in the 1950's in parishes of less than 500 residents it was only 9.2 per cent. while in those having from 15,000 to 20,000 residents it was only 1.1 per cent. Farmers had a somewhat better record of frequent attendance than members of other occupations. In 1948 the proportion of non-attendants was highest in the 20- to 29-year age group and the proportion of those who attended regularly increased with age, until among those over 50 it was 26 per cent.[74] The larger percentage of church attendance in the South and the South-west seems in part to have been a heritage from the Shartau, Hoof, and Sellergren awakenings in the nineteenth century.[75] Thought-provoking was the insufficient number of theological students to fill the demand even of existing parishes, not to speak of the new ones which were urgently required by the shifts in the population and the growth of cities.

How did the Christian bodies fare who were not embraced in the Church of Sweden? The largest had emerged out of the awakenings of the nineteenth century.[76] In general their growth slowed or they declined. The National Evangelical Association (*Evangeliska Fosterlandsstiftelsen*), with most of its members in cities of medium size, nearly doubled the number of its congregations between 1930 and 1955, but between 1940 and 1955 its membership shrank by about a third—from 100,000 to 68,275.[77] The Bible Believing Friends (*Bibeltrogna Vänner*), who had their inception shortly before 1914, displayed a rapid growth after that year and in 1950 counted more congregations than the *Evangeliska Fosterlandsstiftelsen,* but subsequent to 1930 the increase was not as marked as at the outset.[78] The Swedish Mission Covenant (*Svenska Missionsförbundet*) had had a striking development in the nineteenth century, but after 1920 its numbers remained almost stationary and declined slightly between 1950 and 1955—from 104,101 to 100,694.[79] The much smaller Swedish Missionary Alliance (*Svenska Alliansmissionen*) showed a much greater loss —from 825 units in 1940 to 493 in 1955.[80] The Swedish Baptist Union, which had counted 51,259 members in 1910, 60,913 in 1920, and 63,399 in 1930, in

---

[74] *Ibid.,* pp. 27–34. For a study covering one diocese from the mid-eighteenth to the mid-twentieth century, with extensive statistics, see Ernst Enochsson, *Den Kyrkliga Seden med Särskild Hänsyn till Västerås Stift* (Stockholm, Svenska Krykans Diakonistyrelses Bokförlag, 1949, pp. 382), *passim,* especially the statistical tables on pp. 333 ff.

[75] Volume II, pp. 170, 171.

[76] Volume II, pp. 172–175. On the Free Churches see Gunnar Westin, *Den Kristna Friförsamlingen i Norden, Frikyrklighetens Uppkomst och Utveckling* (Stockholm, Ernst Westerbergs Boktr.- och Förlags, 1956, pp. 392), pp. 233 ff.

[77] Gustafsson, *op. cit.,* pp. 39–41.

[78] *Ibid.,* pp. 46–49.

[79] *Ibid.,* p. 63.

[80] *Ibid.,* p. 73.

1955 could report only 34,953.[81] The Pentecostals (*Pingströrelsen*), of more recent introduction (1907), who had risen from 25,000 in 1925 to 50,000 five years later, added to their numbers in each succeeding decade, and late in the 1950's were said to have 160,000 adherents and to have sent missionaries to 29 countries.[82] The Methodists, less numerous, declined by about a third in the four decades after 1914—from 17,404 in 1910 to 11,643 in 1955.[83] The Salvation Army added to its membership—from 22,000 in 1930 to 39,932 in 1955[84]—and the Roman Catholic Church had a striking increase—from 3,070 in 1910 to 21,000 in 1955.[85] Numerically the other churches represented were negligible. In general the bodies dissenting from the Church of Sweden shared in the drift from Christianity which that body displayed. Together in the mid-1950's they enrolled only about 5 per cent. of the population and that proportion was dwindling.

The tie between the Church of Sweden and the state remained and the Church had little freedom. The Church Assembly appeared to afford the Church a larger collective voice in its affairs than that possessed by its sister bodies in Denmark and Norway, but it could only ratify or veto the legislation passed for it by Parliament. Its clergy had much of their time taken by recording vital statistics for the government, and many of their parishes were too huge to free them from such duties as baptisms, weddings, funerals, preaching, and pre-confirmation instruction to give adequate attention to their other pastoral functions. Sweden was a welfare, socialist state with general physical well-being, little poverty, and few slums. The state carried on most of the social services traditionally performed by the Church. When in 1951 the Swedish bishops issued a pastoral letter, the first such in recent times, on family life and dealing with divorce, artificial insemination, adultery, and other social problems it was greeted with a storm of protest in the secular press. On January 1, 1952, a law came into effect which granted each citizen the privilege "freely to exercise his religion" and to withdraw from the Church of Sweden without joining another religious body. By that time teachers in public schools were not required to be members of the state church.[86]

Although measured by statistics Protestantism in Sweden seemed to be waning, and although the pastors of the Church of Sweden were burdened with too many formal duties to enable them to give adequate pastoral care to the hugh parishes which were customary, the post-1914 years had many evidences of vitality in the Christian forces. The Roman Catholic Church, still

81 *Ibid.*, p. 81.
82 *Ibid.*, p. 94. Du Plessis, *A Brief History of Pentecostal Assemblies.*
83 Gustafsson, *op. cit.*, p. 118.
84 *Ibid.*, p. 124.
85 *Ibid.*, p. 131.
86 Herman, *op. cit.*, pp. 85, 86, 89.

represented by a minute minority, was growing rapidly. Protestantism, enlisting the loyal support of a much larger minority, was displaying vigour in various ways. Late in the 1950's the number of theological students was increasing—from fifty at the opening of the decade in each of the two universities, Lund and Uppsala, to from sixty-five to eighty in the former and seventy-five to a hundred in the latter. To ease the shortage of clergy some men were being ordained after an abbreviated theological course and without a university degree. A liturgical revival was seen in the Church of Sweden and a few communities were coming into being which followed a monastic rule and observed canonical hours.[87] In 1917 the Sigtuna Foundation was brought into existence in a town which had been a strong monastic centre before the Protestant Reformation. Its purpose was to provide an opportunity for intellectuals, not all of whom might be committed to the faith, to work in a Christian environment and thus to penetrate Swedish culture with Christianity and to make possible conferences for the discussion of social and cultural problems.[88] Conferences were organized of students and labourers to bridge the gulf between the two groups and also of employers and employees to allay or prevent strikes. Physicians, teachers, and pastors also met to discuss their respective problems. As one of the fruits of Sigtuna, in 1955 FLOD (*Forbundet fur Liturgie och Dramatik*—Foundation for Liturgy and Dramatics) came into being to produce plays which could appropriately be shown in the churches.[89] In several dioceses study centres were developed, partly on the pattern of Sigtuna, with conferences for youth and also to establish contact with members of various professions. Other foundations were maintained for retreats and fellowship among women who were active in the Church. In the 1930's a Christian labour movement was begun.[90] In the 1950's new churches were being erected in Stockholm—more, it was said, than in seven hundred years.[91] In 1958 after much heated discussion the Church of Sweden through its Church Assembly agreed to accept women as ordained ministers.[92] In the 1950's a distinguished Swedish churchman whose memories went back to the 1890's said that in his judgement the Church of Sweden was in better condition then than in his youth, that the quality of theological students had improved, and that the opposition to the Church was less outspoken than formerly.[93]

Swedish Christians were active in the Ecumenical Movement. Söderblom,

[87] *The Christian Century*, Vol. LXXVI, pp. 704, 705 (June 10, 1959).

[88] Yngve Brilioth, *Svensk Kyrkokunskap* (Stockholm, Svenska Kyrkans Diakonistyrelses Bokförlag, 1946, pp. .xii, 282), pp. 415, 416; Weber, *Signs of Renewal*, pp. 12–14; Siegmund-Schultze, *Die Kirche in Schweden*, pp. 138–142.

[89] *The Christian Century*, Vol. LXXV, pp. 1082, 1083 (September 24, 1958).

[90] Weber, *op. cit.*, pp. 14, 15; Horton, *Contemporary Continental Theology*, p. 150.

[91] *Church News from the Northern Countries*, October 30, 1958.

[92] *Ecumenical Press Service*, October 3, 1958.

[93] To the author, March, 1954.

of whom more in a moment, was outstanding, but others shared and the Ecumenical Centre for the Northern countries was set up in Sigtuna, separate from the Foundation.[94] In a related but somewhat different way, beginning in the 1930's Gunnar Rosendal, a pastor in Osby, stimulated prayers for the unity of Christians and through travel in 1951 established friendly contacts with Roman Catholics.[95]

Although tied to the state, the Church of Sweden possessed a nearer approach to autonomy than its sister churches in Denmark and Norway, for, unlike them, it had an assembly through which it could act. Like them, it had parish councils through which the inhabitants could make their voices heard in the affairs of the Church. Although some pastors regretted the universal membership in the Church and wished, as did the dissenting bodies, to make a sharper distinction between Christians and non-Christians, the existing situation in which the vast majority of the population were embraced in the folk church was defended on the ground that through the connexion all became acquainted with Christian teaching and that very few took steps to dissociate themselves from the Church. In 1957 a poll disclosed that only 18 per cent. of those interviewed wished the tie between the Church of Sweden and the state severed, but, significantly, 30 per cent. of the regular attendants of the national church and an equal proportion of the Free Church members desired that that step be taken.[96]

In the 1950's a movement was on foot better to acquaint pastors with the problems and attitudes of labourers to make more effective their contact with that growing section of society.[97] In 1958 far more Protestant foreign missionaries went from Sweden than from any other country on the Continent, even from Germany with its much larger number of Protestants. The total was 1,568, as against 975 from Germany.[98]

These various illustrations, picked almost at random and not arranged in logical order, are evidence of marked vitality of Christianity in Sweden. Although active Christians were only a minority among a majority who were nominal Christians but were too indifferent even to be hostile, in the aggregate they numbered many thousands and were seeking to meet the problems of the revolutionary age.[99]

The effort of Swedish Christians to face up to the problems of the age was seen strikingly in two areas, one that of the collective social and political prob-

---

[94] Visited by the author, March, 1954.
[95] Villain, *L'Abbé Paul Couturier*, pp. 197–206.
[96] *Church News from the Northern Countries*, March 21, 1957, March 24, 1960.
[97] *Ibid.*, September 7, 1955.
[98] *Occasional Bulletin from the Missionary Research Library*, December 8, 1958.
[99] For a comprehensive study of religious attitudes in the early part of the post-1914 years see Otto Bolling, *Svenskt Fromhetsliv av i Dag* (Stockholm, Svenska Kyrkans Diakonistyrelses Bokförlag, 1931, pp. 324), *passim*.

lems of mankind and the other that of the intellect. Nathan Söderblom (1866–1931) was an outstanding pioneer in the one and prominent in the other. We have already noted his early career—his rearing as a son of a Pietist pastor, his loyalty to that tradition, his early contacts through missions, the Young Men's Christian Association, and Moody with the world outreach of Christianity and movements which transcended denominational borders—his outstanding scholarship, the way he had been influenced by Ritschlianism, and his appointment (1914) as Archbishop of Uppsala.[100] Sanguine, eager, courageous, widely inclusive in his friendships, with an engaging joyousness and sense of humour, radiating physical vitality, and inclined to believe well of all with whom he came in contact, he became primate of the Church of Sweden (May, 1914) on the eve of World War I. He saw in that tragedy a challenge and concerned himself not only with the immediate holocaust but also with the complex economic, social, and political factors of the revolutionary age with which the war was inextricably intertwined. Living as he did in neutral Sweden, he was free from commitments to either of the belligerent camps and saw in that circumstance an opportunity and an obligation.

As one of his early official acts as Archbishop of Uppsala, in November, 1914, Söderblom declared that the war could not sever the ties which bound Christians together. In that month he sought to have the leaders of the churches in both belligerent and neutral countries sign an appeal for peace, but did not obtain sufficient support on either side of the warring line. Undaunted, he laboured indefatigably to promote unity among all Christians and maintained relationships with outstanding churchmen and church organizations in belligerent and non-belligerent lands. In the spring of 1917 he issued a manifesto signed by leaders of Protestant churches in Denmark, Norway, Switzerland, and the Netherlands standing for a "righteous and durable peace." In 1917 in connexion with the Scandinavian committees of the World Alliance for Promoting International Friendship through the Churches (formed almost simultaneously with the outbreak of the war) he sought to bring about a Christian conference to contribute to the termination of the war. Again he failed to enlist the coöperation of churchmen in the belligerent countries, but in December, 1917, a Neutral Church Conference met in Uppsala with about thirty-five participants from Denmark, Norway, Sweden, Switzerland, and the Netherlands. It stood for the unity of Christians, took up the principles underlying the Church's attitude to social and international problems, insisted that the Church must consider every sphere of human life in the light of the Gospel and with the Gospel as judge, and advocated the solution of international conflicts through the development of international law. In 1918 Söderblom again sought to convene an international Christian conference and invited

[100] Volume II, pp. 179–181.

not only Protestants but also the Roman Catholic and Orthodox Churches. Once more he was unsuccessful.

After the war, in 1920, at Söderblom's instance a widely representative group convened in Geneva. It prepared the way for the Universal Conference on Life and Work which met in Stockholm in August, 1925. Some of the Orthodox Churches and a large proportion of the Protestant churches were represented. The Conference adopted a message which affirmed the obligation of the churches to bring the Gospel to bear on "all realms of human life—industrial, social, political, and international"—and said that the mission of the churches was to state principles and to leave to individuals and communities their application. Fittingly, Söderblom was made chairman of the Continuation Committee. Out of it was born the Universal Christian Council for Life and Work, formally constituted in 1930, which became one of the two main bodies to join in the World Council of Churches eighteen years later. Söderblom also gave his support to the World Conference on Faith and Order, the other movement which joined in bringing into being the World Council of Churches, but his death (1931) came too early to permit him to see that consummation.[101]

After World War I a marked awakening was seen in Swedish theology. Einar Billing (1871–1939) was an early spokesman. From a professorship in Uppsala, in 1920 he was made Bishop of Västerås. In his initial pastoral letter he said that revelation is the operation of the living God in history, that the continuing act of God is the basis for the functioning of the Church, and that the Church must carry on the work of God through the proclamation of the Word. The function of theology, then, is to set forth the revealed Word of God, to state the Gospel clearly, and to trust to it to win its way.[102] The main leaders in the awakening, who gave it distinctive forms, were at Lund, not Uppsala. Like much of the Protestant theology of the period, the movement was a reaction against the liberalism of the immediate pre-1914 decades. However, it accepted the methods of the historical criticism of the Scriptures. It was aware of Barth but was more influenced by Althaus than by him and took independent lines. Its chief representatives were Gustav Aulén (1879——), Anders Nygren (1890——), and Gustav Wingren (1906——).

101 For a life of Söderblom see Tor Andrae, *Nathan Söderblom* (Uppsala, J. A. Lindblads Förlag, 1932, pp. 333), translated into German by E. Groening and A. Volklein as *Nathan Söderblom* (Berlin, Alfred Topelman, 1938, pp. 232). For his activities in World War I and his share in the formation of the Universal Christian Council for Life and Work see Rouse and Neill, *A History of the Ecumenical Movement, 1517–1948*, pp. 519–555. For a Dutch doctoral dissertation see Jan Mari Van Veen, *Nathan Söderblom: Leven en Denken van een Godsdiensthistoricus* (Amsterdam, H. J. Paris, 1940, pp. x, 251). For a bibliography of his writings, see Tor Andrae and others, *Nathan Söderblom in Memoriam* (Stockholm, Svenska Kyrkans Diakonistyrelses Bokförlag, 1931, pp. 459), pp. 392–451.
102 Siegmund-Schultze, *Die Kirche in Schweden*, p. 70.

Aulén first taught at Uppsala but in 1913 he went to Lund and with him the centre of Swedish theological thought moved to that university. In 1933 he was made Bishop of Strängnäs, not far from Uppsala and Stockholm, but he continued to be influential in Lund[103] and lived there after his retirement (1952). As Aulén conceived it, the task of the systematic theologian is to elucidate the content of the Christian faith. He was critical of a philosophy of religion which, bearing the impress of German Idealism, sought to set a pattern for religion in general and then to fit Christianity into it. This, he declared, was to be the victim of subjectivism. It failed to understand the Christian faith. Nor has faith, in the Christian sense, so he held, anything to do with metaphysics. To him faith is the expression of the relationship between God and man and is the result of God's action, of being subdued by God. Faith, he maintained, originates and is nourished in revelation and revelation is discerned only by the eye of faith. Christian faith discovers the revelation of God in both nature and history. In Christ the Divine will becomes incarnate and victorious. In *Christus Victor* Aulén attempted to go beyond the two approaches to the atonement associated with the names of Anselm and Abélard. He held that the one interpreted atonement in legalistic terms and the other in human terms—that Anselm viewed Christ in His human capacity as satisfying God's justice and that Abélard stressed the effect of Christ's sacrifice on man. Whereas, so Aulén maintained, the classical view is that the victory was accomplished by God, that in the atonement God alone acted and His love overcame His wrath. Christ as victor fights against and conquers the evil cosmic powers. The dualism represented by this view is not final. What opposes God is part of His creation and is used by Him for good. He both reconciles the world to Himself and is reconciled. This view, which Aulén regarded as classical, is obviously the one which he himself esteemed as Christian and as consistent with the New Testament.

Nygren was a pastor from 1912 to 1920 and then went on the Lund faculty. In 1949 he was appointed Bishop of Lund. He was active in the Ecumenical Movement, especially in the World Council of Churches.[104] In his *Agape and*

---

[103] A full bibliography of Aulén on his sixtieth birthday is in *Till Gustav Aulén. Forskaren, Läraren, Vännen mid Tacksam Myllning På 60 Arsdagen*, by a large number of authors (Stockholm, Svenska Kyrkans Diakonistyrelses Bokförlag, 1939, pp. 413), pp. 366–409. Some of his more important books were *Christus Victor. An Historical Study of the Three Main Types of the Idea of the Atonement*, translated by A. G. Hebert (New York, The Macmillan Co., 1937, pp. 479); *Church, Law, and Society* (New York, Charles Scribner's Sons, 1948, pp. xvi, 114); *För eder Utgiven; en Bok om Nattvarden Offermotiv* (Stockholm, Svenska, Kyrkans Diakonistyrelses Bokförlag, 1956, pp. 240), translated by Eric H. Wahlstrom as *Eucharist and Sacrifice* (Philadelphia, Muhlenberg Press, 1958, pp. xiv, 212); *The Faith of the Christian Church*, translated from the fourth edition of *Den Allmänneliga Kristna Tron* by Eric H. Wahlstrom and G. Everett Arden (Philadelphia, Muhlenberg Press, 1948, pp. 457); and *Den Kristna Gudsbilden genom Seklerna och i Nutiden en Konturteckning* (Stockholm, Svenska Kyrkans Diakonistyrelses Bokförlag, 2nd ed., 1941, pp. 400).

[104] Among Nygren's writings were *Den Kristen Kärlekstanken genom Tiderne: Eros och Agape*

Eros he contrasted the two. As he saw it, *Agape* is the downward moving of the divine love manifested in the Son of Man Who came to seek and to save that which was lost and especially disclosed in Christ's death on the cross; whereas *Eros*, as described in Greek thought, notably in Plato, is the upward striving of the human soul to seek the Divine. According to Nygren's study of the *Epistle to the Romans*, Paul was saying in that letter that in Christ and the Kingdom of God announced by Christ a new aeon was beginning, marked by a new righteousness which is not ours, earned by obedience to the law, but is a gift of God to be received through faith. Nygren rejected the distinction between the religion of Jesus and the religion about Jesus of which some theologians on the eve of 1914, notably Harnack, were making much, a view which said that Paul created the latter and in doing so did violence to the former, and that Hellenism had quite transformed the Gospel as proclaimed by Jesus. Nygren insisted that no contradiction existed between the Gospel as seen in the Synoptic writings and the Gospel as set forth by Paul. Nygren gave much weight to religious experience as an independent source of knowledge. He held that all other roads to knowledge—categories in the Kantian sense—depended on the religious if they were to give valid insight. Here he resembled Schleiermacher but was not identical with him.

In general Aulén and Nygren looked upon their function as descriptive rather than apologetic. As theologians they did not seek to establish the validity of the Christian faith or to compare Christianity with other religions. They regarded theology as the systematic history of the development of Christianity. They viewed revelation as dynamic and impossible to be captured permanently by the intellectual formulations of any era. Revelation, they were convinced, is an act and a deed. It is always defined by the deed which is the living Christ. God continues to act, and through Christ. They held that Christianity, rightly understood, is radically theocentric and is focussed not on man but on God. They contrasted human sin and egocentricity with God's grace. To them the cross is the focus of the cosmic struggle between evil and God's love and marks the decisive victory of God's love. They viewed the Church not as an institution with authority over its members nor as a voluntary association of like-minded people for mutual support, but as part of the redemptive activity of God. They conceived of the Church as always becoming, a fellowship of creative activity. It is invisible yet is always becoming visible, and the institu-

(Stockholm, Svenska Kyrkans Diakonistyrelses Bokförlag, 3rd ed., 2 vols., 1947), translated by A. G. Hebert as *Agape and Eros, a Study in the Christian Idea of Love* (New York, The Macmillan Co., 2 vols. in 3, 1937–1939); *Christ and His Church*, translated by Alan Carlsten (Philadelphia, The Westminster Press, 1956, pp. 125); *Commentary on Romans*, translated by Carl E. Rasmussen (Philadelphia, Muhlenberg Press, 1949, pp. 457); *The Gospel of God*, translated by L. J. Trinterud (London, S.C.M. Press, 1951, pp. 104); *Filosofisk och Kristen Etik* (Stockholm, Svenska Krykans Diakonistyrelses Bokförlag, 2nd ed., 1932, pp. 331); and *Filosofi och Motivforskning* (Stockholm, Svenska Kyrkans Diakonistyrelses Bokförlag, 1940, pp. 225).

tional church is not incidentally but essentially related to the invisible Church. They were convinced that the institutional church is best represented by the folk church taking in the total community and that through it the Gospel enters all society. Aulén thought of the state as being made necessary by sin but as an instrument of God's love and held that the Church has the duty to call the state to its true function—ensuring justice and giving expression to the love of God.

Wingren, much younger than Aulén and Nygren, and also of the Lund faculty, differed from Nygren, Barth, and Bultmann. He held that Nygren in stressing *Agape* had neglected law. He made much of the dialectic between law and *Agape* and emphasized God's forgiveness. In this he regarded himself as being in accord both with Luther and with the New Testament. He criticized Barth for not making the relationship between God and man one of antithesis in the sense of hostility and held that Barth did not speak enough of law. Bultmann, so Wingren held, over-accentuated law and starting with the assumption that man is guilty stressed Christ's death and resurrection as the centre of the *kerygma*.[105]

Yngve Torgny Brilioth (1891–1959) was not primarily in the theological field and did not have as wide an influence beyond the borders of Sweden as Söderblom, Aulén, Nygren, or Wingren. But he was prominent not only in his native country but also in the Ecumenical Movement. A son-in-law of Söderblom, he was a Church historian and for much of his mature life was in ecclesiastical administration. In his early manhood he was a university teacher, but from 1937 to 1950 he was Bishop of Växjö and in 1950 was created Archbishop of Uppsala. His historical studies were primarily concerned with Christianity in Sweden, but he had an important work on the Oxford movement and a historical survey of Eucharistic faith and practice in both the Protestant and Catholic branches of the faith.[106]

SUMMARY

In Scandinavia as in much of Western Europe after 1914 the striking con-

[105] Among Wingren's works were *Luthers Lära om Kellelsen* (Lund, C. W. K. Gleerup, 1942, pp. viii, 272), translated into German by Egon Franz as *Luthers Lehre von Beruf* (Munich, C. Kaiser, 1952, pp. 217) and into English by Carl C. Rasmussen as *Luther on Vocation* (Philadelphia, Muhlenberg Press, 1957, pp. xii, 256); *Theologiens Metodfråga* (Lund, C. W. K. Gleerup, 1954, pp. 223), translated by Eric A. Wahlstrom as *Theology in Conflict. Nygren, Barth, Bultmann* (Philadelphia, Muhlenberg Press, 1958, pp. xxii, 170); *Man and the Incarnation. A Study in the Biblical Theology of Irenaeus*, translated by Ross Mackenzie (Philadelphia, Muhlenberg Press, 1959, pp. xxii, 233).

[106] Yngve Torgny Brilioth, *The Anglican Revival: Studies in the Oxford Movement* (New York, Longmans, Green and Co., 1925, pp. xv, 357); *Nattvarden in Evangeliskt Gudstjänstliv* (Stockholm, Svenska Kyrkans Diakonistyrelses Bokförlag, 1926, pp. 488), translated by A. G. Hebert as *Eucharistic Faith and Practice Evangelical and Catholic* (London, S.P.C.K., 1953, pp. xvi, 295). On other studies in Church history by various authors see *Church History*, Vol. XXIII, pp. 267 ff.

trast continued between what appeared to be the waning of Christianity as a force in the lives of the majority of the population and marked vigour of the faith among minorities. In each of the four countries a Lutheran church was still established by law, and instruction in the tenets of the faith as taught by Lutheranism was part of the curriculum of the state schools. Most of the population were baptized, and the large majority were confirmed in the state church and received instruction by the pastor in preparation for the latter rite. Yet church attendance declined, notably in the cities, and, as in Protestant Germany, many parishes were too large and staffed by too few clergy to permit adequate pastoral care. But less protest was heard against the Church-state tie than at times in the preceding century. Greater leeway was accorded to dissent, but the Free Churches enrolled only small minorities and several of them had ceased to grow and had even declined in numbers. However, through the folk churches some knowledge of Christianity was transmitted from generation to generation. In the loyal minorities much vitality was seen, a large proportion of it through movements of Pietist background. In some cities additional churches were being erected to care for the urban influx. Here and there were new movements. Hundreds of missionaries were sent to countries outside the Occident. Especially in Sweden, where de-Christianization seemed to have proceeded further than in its sister Scandinavian countries, leaders emerged who were prominent in the Ecumenical Movement and creative theological scholarship appeared which had repercussions far outside the borders of the country.

CHAPTER XIII

Protestantism in the Baltic Countries
and Central Europe

W E NOW move into regions where the political changes of the post-1914 decades confronted Christianity with varied challenges. Here were lands which as an outcome of World War I achieved their independence. Then, following the triumph of Communism in Russia and World War II, with the exception of Finland and Austria, they came under Communist regimes which were satellites of Russia or, in the case of Finland, lost territory to Russia, or, in Jugoslavia, were Communist but independent of Moscow. We have already sketched the course of the Roman Catholic branch of the faith in these lands. We now turn to the Protestant record.

FINLAND

Because of its long Swedish connexion as well as its geography, Finland belonged with Scandinavia. In the 1950's it had a population between that of Norway and Denmark in size, and nearly a tenth were Swedish by race and culture.[1] The political separation from Sweden came in 1809 and in that year Finland was transferred to the tsar as grand duke but with much internal autonomy. Late in the nineteenth century the Russians attempted to assimilate Finland to the rest of the empire. They met with dogged resistance and on the outbreak of the abortive revolution in the empire in 1905 for a time the bear's grip was partly eased. In the revolution of 1917 the tsar abdicated, and Finland became independent. Civil war broke out between the Socialists and the bourgeoisie in 1918 and when, with the aid of German armies, the Whites triumphed, a war with Communist Russia ensued (1919-1920) and was ended by a treaty in which the Kremlin recognized Finland's independence. The Republic of Finland came into being in 1919, with a constitution and a single-chamber diet. Relations with the U.S.S.R. were chronically strained and in

---

[1] On the nineteenth-century story see Volume II, pp. 188–196. For a bibliography of Finnish church history see *The Journal of Ecclesiastical History*, Vol. VII, pp. 226–237 (October, 1956).

November, 1939, the Russians invaded the country. In spite of the condemnation of Russia by the League of Nations as the aggressor and of aid from abroad, Finland was forced to conclude a peace (March, 1940) by which she ceded part of her territory to her huge neighbour. Not unnaturally she sided with Germany during the latter's war with Russia. In 1944 the Germans, retreating, looted much of the North and the humiliating peace with Russia cost Finland territory, a heavy indemnity, and the task of caring for several scores of thousands of refugees who were moved out of the lands ceded to Russia. Yet the country rose to the challenge, restored the devastated areas, and paid off the exacted reparations. National renaissance and independence were accompanied by a burst of cultural activity of which the music of Jean Sibelius was an outstanding expression.

In spite of the political vicissitudes of the nation, Christianity showed marked vigour. The population was overwhelmingly Lutheran. Slightly less than two out of a hundred were affiliated with the Orthodox Church, and still smaller minorities were in dissenting Protestant groups and the Roman Catholic Church. Currents from the outside made themselves felt, among them the pessimistic reaction from the optimism of the pre-1914 decades, the thought of Barth and Brunner, and the Oxford Groups.[2] The Church of Finland was a state institution but it had greater freedom than its sister churches in Scandinavia. In 1922 legislation was passed which granted complete religious liberty —to belong to any religious body or to no religious body—but very few availed themselves of the opportunity to withdraw from the Church of Finland. As in Scandinavia, a folk church persisted.[3] Bishops were appointed by the president of the republic from nominations made by the Church, the diet had the power to approve or disapprove of legislation passed by the Church, and after World War II at the request of the Church the state began to levy and collect a church tax to fill the gap brought by the utilization of much ecclesiastical property for the resettlement of refugees. Aside from these qualifying conditions the Church of Finland governed its own affairs. Its highest organ was the synod, which met every five years and which enacted legislation; it had authority over forms of worship, hymnals, Bible translations, and catechisms. Each diocese had a synod composed of the clergy, and the individual congregations enjoyed much autonomy in local affairs.[4]

The effects of the nineteenth-century awakenings continued and the Church of Finland was more permeated by Pietism than were the state churches of Scandinavia. For some years divisions were seen between the Pietists and the

[2] Siegmund-Schultze, Die Kirche in Finnland, pp. 27–33. On the resistance during World War II see Hoffmann, Les Églises du Nord dans la Crise Mondiale, pp. 1–40.

[3] Siegmund-Schultze, op. cit., pp. 60, 83.

[4] Ibid., pp. 83–94; Herman, Report from Christian Europe, pp. 87, 88; Paasio, The Church of Finland through Eight Hundred Years, pp. 8, 10, 13, 14.

elements which held to Christianity as a cultural force. Divisions also existed among the adherents of the awakenings. For instance, the followers of Hedberg separated on theological grounds from the main body of Pietists and in the 1950's the Laestadians, who sprang from a nineteenth-century Swedish movement, numbered about 300,000 and were fifteen times as numerous as they were in Sweden. After World War I the antagonism to Pietism waned, partly because its adherents founded educational institutions, thus proving themselves not to be hostile to culture, partly because of the loyalty of the Pietists to the nation in the struggle with Russian Communism, and partly through membership of Pietists in the diet.[5]

Religious instruction was required in the primary and secondary schools for all pupils—in Lutheran doctrine for children of members of the state church, in an inclusive coverage of religion for those of other communions, and in ethics and the history of religion for those with no church connexion. In addition, Sunday Schools were found in almost every village; in some sections, especially in the eastern part of the country, they enrolled almost all the children.[6]

On the achievement of Finnish independence after World War I the Swedish minority became more self-conscious. In the urge of resistance to the Russian connexion in the nineteenth century the Swedes had been caught up in the tide of Finnish nationalism and tended to be assimilated to the Finnish majority. Now that independence had been achieved, Swedish particularism was strengthened and with it came not only a political structure for the Swedes but also a diocese for them with a bishop of their own (1923) and services employing the Swedish language. In the 1930's the diocese embraced over 400,000 souls.[7] In 1918 a Swedish university was founded at Åbo, to which in 1924 a theological faculty was added.[8]

Efforts were put forth to win or to hold special groups or classes. For the enlistment of youth, movements which were begun late in the nineteenth century were continued, such as the Young Men's and the Young Women's Christian Associations, the Student Christian Movement, and Christian folk schools. In 1925 and 1930 the Church of Finland took steps to make each congregation responsible for the care for its youth and to give to the pastors the direction of efforts to carry out the programme.[9] Late in the nineteenth century attempts were made to reach members of the labouring classes who were drifting away from the Church and being won to socialism. After 1914 they were

[5] Siegmund-Schultze, *op. cit.*, pp. 71–74; Gustafsson, *Svensk Kyrkogeografi*, p. 53; *Church News from the Northern Countries*, December 18, 1956.
[6] Siegmund-Schultze, *op. cit.*, pp. 96, 97; Paasio, *op. cit.*, p. 10.
[7] Siegmund-Schultze, *op. cit.*, pp. 123–133; Schmidt, *Finlands Kyrka genom Tiderna*, pp. 290, 291.
[8] Siegmund-Schultze, *op. cit.*, p. 134.
[9] *Ibid.*, pp. 152–160.

augmented by Christian social settlements, schools, appropriate buildings, religious services, discussion groups, and a society for the evangelization of labourers. In the 1950's young clergymen were being prepared through a three months' seminar, entailing labour in factories, to reach the industrial workers.[10] The Inner Mission, dating from the second half of the nineteenth century and seeking to touch society helpfully through a number of channels, was continued and beginning in 1918 reached out to the workers in industry. Deaconesses were a feature of church life. The Central Union of the Parish Work of the Church of Finland led in social work, directed marriage guidance, and raised funds for people in need.[11]

After World War II additional movements and institutions were created to meet the challenges of the revolutionary age. In 1945 the People's Bible Society (*Kansanraamattuseura*) was founded to conduct evangelistic services and to reach individuals by counselling, confession, and absolution. Early in the 1950's it employed twelve evangelists and forty other workers and was touching about three hundred parishes.[12] Late in the 1940's the Layman's Training Institute was begun at Järvenpää, a few miles north of Helsinki, in a building erected by gifts from American Lutherans. It trained youth workers and Sunday School teachers, held conferences for pastors' wives, prepared cantors and church organists to share in catechetical instruction, sought to widen the Church's interests in social issues, and, like the Evangelical Academies in Germany, provided opportunity for members of various professions to meet and exchange views. It also became a centre for research in adult education. A similar institution was developed at Karis for the Swedish-speaking Lutherans.[13] With financial help from Lutherans in the United States the churches in the North destroyed by the Germans were rebuilt.[14]

Finnish Christians sent missionaries to other countries. However, in proportion to the population they were only about as numerous as those from Denmark and not nearly as many as those from Norway and Sweden.[15]

In spite of the vigour in Finnish Christianity, here as in much of the rest of European Protestantism statistics revealed a decline in church membership and attendance at church services. On January 1, 1957, 93.34 per cent. of the

10 *Ibid.*, pp. 167–173; Schmidt, *op. cit.*, pp. 288, 289; Paasio, *op. cit.*, pp. 22, 23; *Church News from the Northern Countries*, October 29, 1959.

11 Siegmund-Schultze, *op. cit.*, pp. 174–179; Paasio, *op. cit.*, pp. 26–29, 31.

12 Herman, *op. cit.*, p. 25.

13 *Ibid.*; Weber, *Signs of Renewal*, pp. 18–21; Paasio, *op. cit.*, pp. 30, 31; the author's personal observation, March, 1954. For a description of a variety of activities, religious and social, see Simo Palusuo, editor, *Raivatkaa Uudispelto. Suomen Kirkon Seurakuntaopiston Säätiö 1946–1955* (Helsinki, Suomalaisen Kirjallisuuden Kirjapaino Oy, 1957, pp. 93), *passim*.

14 Paasio, *op. cit.*, p. 18.

15 In 1959 Finnish missionaries totalled 250 as against 280 from Denmark, 967 from Norway, and 1,568 from Sweden. *Occasional Bulletin from the Missionary Research Library*, December 8, 1958.

population were members of the Church of Finland as against 95.16 per cent. in 1950. In the five years 1952–1956 an average of 2.92 per cent. of the population went to church on Sundays as against 3 per cent. in the preceding five-year period. In the five years 1952–1956 a total of 81,397 resigned from church membership as against 11,460 who applied for membership. The percentage of civil marriages grew in that period. Yet in 1956 Sunday Schools had increased by about a tenth and their pupils by about a fifth since 1951, and in 1958 more students were entering the theological faculty of the University of Finland than at any time since World War II.[16] In 1958 it was said that the number of clergymen had grown by 40 per cent. since World War I.[17]

Finnish twentieth-century theology was aware of movements in Protestant thought in other countries, yet, partly because of the language barrier, did not have much effect upon the main stream of Protestant theology. For a time it continued to show the influence of Beck[18] but eventually moved away from it. Gustav Johansson (1844–1930), the last prominent representative of the Beck tradition, held firmly to the Bible against the scepticism rampant in intellectual circles, spoke out against Schleiermacher and Söderblom, and, espousing a particular view of eschatology, criticized the Life and Work movement for seeking to improve society. G. O. Rosenqvist (1893———), of the Swedish minority, displayed traces of the views of Beck, took a mediating view towards the historical criticism of the Bible, differed from Ritschl, was concerned with the philosophy of religion, wrote on ethical and social questions, disagreed with the contemporary Swedish theology associated with Lund, wrote prodigiously, held a pessimistic view of history and of the contemporary Western world, stoutly differed from Barth, and in his later years addressed himself more to exegetics than to theology. Like Johansson he was a bishop and was active in ecclesiastical affairs. Antti J. Peitilä, called the most important Finnish systematic theologian of the first half of the twentieth century, had as his chief book his *Kristillinen Dogmatiikka* (*Christian Dogmatics*), in three volumes, completed in 1932. He denounced Ritschlianism, disapproved of both Söderblom and dialectic theology, and sought to unite theology with a practical life of faith which he saw in the piety of the common man. After his death (1932), the leading theologians were Yrjö J. E. Alanen (1890———) and Eino Sormunen. Alanen concerned himself chiefly with social ethics. Sormunen first centred on Luther but later felt constrained to devote himself to social ethics to offset the strong secularizing trends in the revolutionary age in which he was set. Some of the younger Finnish theologians were attracted by Aulén and Nygren, others specialized on Luther, and at least one wrote important studies on

---

[16] *Church News from the Northern Countries*, October 30, 1958.
[17] *Ibid.*, February 28, 1958.
[18] Volume II, pp. 191, 192.

Barth. Both Church historians and theologians were deeply impressed with the awakenings which shaped Finnish Christianity in the nineteenth and twentieth centuries and wrote extensively on them.[19]

Protestant denominations which dissented from the Church of Finland were very small minorities. In 1936 their numbers scarcely reached ten thousand. Of them what were called Free Churches constituted more than half, with Methodists next and Baptists third.[20]

ESTONIA

The half-century which began in 1914 proved to be a stormy time for Estonia. Its people, long victims of the rivalries of their large neighbours, again became spoils of conquest. Estonia was dragged into World War I by its Russian overlords and about a sixth of its population were drafted into the tsar's armies. In 1917, after the collapse of the tsar's regime, Estonia declared its independence, but in February, 1918, it was occupied by the German forces and late that year was invaded by the Bolsheviks. In 1919 it achieved its independence and the following year the Russians formally recognized it as having that status. For two relatively quiet decades it enjoyed a place among the nations. Then, after attempting in vain to remain neutral in World War II, in 1940 it was seized by the Soviets and incorporated into the U.S.S.R., from 1941 to 1944 it was in German hands, and in 1944 it was once more maneuvered into the Union of Soviet Socialist Republics.

In spite of disrupting political vicissitudes, Estonia remained overwhelmingly Lutheran. During the little over twenty years of independence the Estonians sought, with some success, to free the Lutheran Church from the German domination which had prevailed since the Protestant Reformation. A close tie existed between Church and state and the latter subsidized the Church. Relationships were sought with the Lutherans of Scandinavia and in 1921 Söderblom consecrated a bishop for the country. A revival was experienced in religious activities and the study of the Bible. In 1938 formal ties were established with English Protestantism. Largely through North American assistance, the Young Men's Christian Association had a rapid growth. The theological faculty in the University of Tartu/Dorpat flourished, successive church congresses convened, the separation of Church and state was effected, the Lutheran Church became legally a free, autonomous folk church—the church of the nation—with a centralized administration, and after a struggle religious instruction in the schools was regularized.[21]

[19] Osmo Tiililä, *A Hundred Years of Systematic Theology in Finland (Theologica Fennica* IV. Helsinki, Kirjapaino Oy. LAUSE, 1949, pp. 48), *passim.*
[20] Siegmund-Schultze, *op. cit.,* p. 144.
[21] Tobias, *Communist-Christian Encounter in East Europe,* p. 312; A. Torma, *The Church in*

With the Russian occupation in 1940 anti-Christian measures began. All religious education was forbidden, the broadcasting of religious services was terminated, religious gatherings such as Bible camps were prohibited, Christian youth organizations were banned, the theological faculty in the University of Tartu was suppressed, an anti-religious campaign was vigorously prosecuted, ecclesiastical property was confiscated, the clergy were denounced as "enemies of the people," and many churches were closed or turned into cinemas or dancing halls.[22]

The German rule (July, 1941–October, 1944) brought only partial relief. The Church regained most of its property, legal status, and ecclesiastical structure, and it was permitted to carry on religious education, but in general it suffered almost as much as it had under the Russians. When the Germans retreated many Estonians either were deported with them or fled.[23]

With the return of the Russians restrictions were renewed. Taxes were levied on church buildings and on such church functions as weddings, baptisms, and confirmations, and the proceeds were said to have been applied to finance anti-Christian propaganda.[24] In the mid-1950's about 70 per cent. of the population seem still to have belonged to the Church and full liberty was reported to have been given either to join the Church or to leave it. At the same time we hear that church buildings were the property of the state, that five new church buildings had been erected since World War II, that congregations were permitted to use them without charge, and that church dues were voluntary and those who did not pay them for three years were dropped from the church rolls. After the extinction of the theological faculty of the University of Tartu special provision was made for the training of the ministry. Several independent churches arose and in the mid-1950's the number of Christian congregations was more than before World War II. But in the 1950's Sunday Schools and Bible study classes were impossible and few youths from thirteen to thirty years of age attended church services.[25]

LATVIA

In the post-1914 storms Latvia suffered even more than Estonia. During part of World War I that country, then part of the Russian Empire, was occupied by German troops. Invaded by German, Russian, and Bolshevik armies, the prosperity which it had enjoyed in the latter part of the nineteenth century

Estonia (New York, World Association of Estonians, 1944, pp. 20), pp. 18, 19; Latourette, *World Service*, pp. 407–409; Wittram, *Baltische Kirchengeschichte*, pp. 243–266.
[22] Tobias, *op. cit.*, pp. 312–316; H. Perlitz, *The Fate of Religion and Church under Soviet Rule in Estonia 1940–1941* (New York, World Association of Estonians, 1944, pp. 32), *passim*.
[23] Tobias, *op. cit.*, p. 316.
[24] *Ibid.*, p. 316; Wittram, *op. cit.*, pp. 265, 266.
[25] *Church News from the Northern Countries*, September 7, 1955, November 23, 1956.

evaporated. Its population fell off by about two-fifths, from approximately 2,500,000 to roughly 1,600,000. But it proclaimed its independence and that status was recognized by the powers. During the ensuing two decades partial recovery was effected. Like Estonia, Latvia attempted to preserve its neutrality in World War II, but in 1940 it was occupied by the Russians and constrained to become a member of the U.S.S.R. It was seized by the Germans in 1941 and subjected to terrorization by the Gestapo. Then, in 1944–1945, freed from the Germans, it was once more absorbed into the Union of Soviet Socialist Republics. Since in 1949 its population was only about half that in 1914, a loss partly caused by the deportation of tens of thousands to other parts of the U.S.S.R. and the exodus of tens of thousands, much of it compulsory, to West Germany, several hundred thousand Russians were moved in and the Russian language was taught in the schools.

At the outset of the two decades of independence, religiously the population of Latvia was slightly more than half Protestant by profession, about a fourth Roman Catholic, about a seventh Orthodox, of whom Old Believers constituted roughly a third, and nearly one in twenty were Jews. The Germans, who had been dominant since the Middle Ages, attempted to continue their control of the Lutheran Church against the rising tide of Latvian nationalism.

Under independent Latvia religious liberty was accorded to all. Religious instruction was part of the curriculum of the schools, and although the state exercised no control over the Church it subsidized the Lutheran and Roman Catholic theological faculties and gave financial aid to smaller parishes. A concordat was concluded with the Vatican in 1922, and the Roman Catholic Church, under disabilities since the Protestant Reformation, was revived, partly through the activity of religious orders and lay societies. The Orthodox Church became autonomous as against the Russian Orthodox Church and submitted to the Ecumenical Patriarch of Constantinople. The German Lutheran minority separated from the Latvian Lutheran Church, elected their own bishop, and were unreconciled to the use of the ancient church structures by the Latvians. The Latvian Protestant Church, Lutheran by creed, organized a synod which in 1920 elected a Latvian as bishop. He was consecrated by Söderblom. The synod gave his successor the rank of archbishop. Church buildings destroyed during the war were reërected, the depleted ranks of the clergy were reinforced, literature was produced, and education was furthered. Yet the number of clergy was insufficient to care for the parishes, in many parishes only a minority of the registered members came to the Communion, and a large proportion of the weddings were without Christian rites.

As in Estonia, the Russian occupation that began in 1940 was accompanied by anti-Christian measures. The teaching of religion was forbidden, the theological faculties were abolished, the denominational schools were closed, all ecclesiastical properties were nationalized, religious publications were suppressed, some of the clergy were killed or put to hard labour in concentration camps, several church structures were diverted to secular purposes, and religious services were restricted to a few churches.

The Nazi rule brought some relaxation of the Soviet strictures on religion but was emphatic that the Church must be subordinate to the purposes of the state: the German occupation meant persecution in a somewhat less drastic form.[26]

Under the renewed Russian mastery of the country no religious instruction was allowed, children below the age of eighteen were forbidden to go to church, in broadcasts religion was called a superstition propagated by the bourgeois elements to deceive the working people, and pastors were labelled lackeys of the exploiting classes—servants of the bourgeois reaction. Some pastors were deported, the rebuilding of churches was forbidden, and permits were required to attend church services. Yet the Roman Catholic Church founded a theological seminary, in 1948 over two thousand lay delegates elected a Lutheran archbishop, and a committee on religion and worship was created within the cabinet of the state.[27] In 1959 a visitor reported that twenty Lutheran churches were open and that the archbishop estimated the number of Lutherans to be 700,000 and said that although many churches damaged during World War II had not been repaired, several new ones had been opened.[28]

LITHUANIA

Since in 1940 Lithuania was four-fifths Roman Catholic and less than a tenth Protestant, and since in an earlier chapter we have said something of the Roman Catholic Church within its borders, it need not here long detain us.

In the stormy decades which followed 1914 Lithuania had even less of peace than its neighbours. Under Russian rule at the outbreak of World War I, it was compelled by its Russian masters to provide draftees for labour and military service and in the course of the struggle thousands perished. Lithuanian nationalists took advantage of the collapse of the Russian armies to proclaim the independence of the country, but a period of confusion ensued in which Russians and Poles struggled for control. Although in July, 1920, Russia recognized the independence of Lithuania, conflict with the Poles continued. In 1922 a constitution was proclaimed which declared the country to be a republic and guaranteed freedom of assembly, religion, speech, and the press. Lithuanians and Germans clashed over the possession by the former of

[26] Alfred Bilmanis, *The Church in Latvia* (New York, Drauga Vēsts, 1945, pp. 35), pp. 18–35; Tobias, *op. cit.,* pp. 303–306; Wittram, *op. cit.,* pp. 266–298.
[27] Tobias, *op. cit.,* p. 307.
[28] *The New York Times,* February 22, 1959.

Memel, and Nazis and their sympathizers were active. In 1940 the Russians came and in 1941 they were displaced by the Germans. German farmers were brought in and many Lithuanians were taken prisoner. Thousands of Jews were killed. In 1944 the retreating Germans wrought much destruction and added to the previous slaughter. Then came the Russians and the reincorporation of Lithuania into Russia as one of the Union of Soviet Socialist Republics. Great numbers of Russians were settled on Lithuanian soil.

In the years which immediately followed the Russian re-occupation the state gave a degree of liberty to Roman Catholics. Because of their attachment to Rome and their intense nationalism, the government questioned their loyalty. Roman Catholics looked upon the Orthodox as Russian spies and agents. Protestants were distrusted by both Roman Catholics and the Communist regime as having Western sympathies and connexions. Most of them left the country and in 1951 they were said to have less than ten churches and only from three to five pastors.[29]

POLAND

Protestants constituted such small minorities in predominantly Roman Catholic Poland that we must devote only a brief summary to their post-1914 record. In the nineteenth century Lutherans and the members of the United Evangelical Church far outnumbered the Reformed and were recruited chiefly from German colonists.[30] The fate of Protestantism, therefore, was closely tied to that of the Germans. Of the political setting we have already spoken.[31] During World War I the Protestants suffered at the hands of both belligerents. The Russians accused the German colonists of being spies for the enemy, deported scores of thousands to Russia, and destroyed much church property. The German invaders burned many buildings and even whole villages. At the close of the war numbers of the returning deportees, disheartened, sought haven in Germany. To those who continued in Poland help came from fellow Lutherans in the United States. In the years of peace some progress was made. A Protestant theological faculty was created in the University of Warsaw. Several of its students were converts from the Roman Catholic Church. Under the regime which followed the war full religious freedom was given, instruction in the faith was required in the schools and was by teachers approved by ecclesiastical officials, congregations were accorded the right to levy a church tax, and church property was exempt from taxation. Germans and Poles shared equally in the Lutheran governing synodical commission.[32] Many Germans

[29] Tobias, *op. cit.*, pp. 308–311.
[30] Volume II, pp. 200, 201.
[31] Chapter VII.
[32] Siegmund-Schultze, *Die evangelischen Kirchen in Polen*, pp. 67–77.

left the territories transferred to Poland at the close of the war, but those who remained profited by the guarantee of the constitution of 1921 which enabled them to conserve their nationality and their language and set up a synodical administration.[33] The Reformed also took advantage of the freedom guaranteed by the constitution and came together in a synod.[34] The United Evangelical Church, originally an extension of the Prussian Union, lost a large proportion of its membership through the war and the peace settlement but survived.[35] Following World War I a Protestant movement was seen among the Roman Catholic Ukrainian Uniates.[36] The Polish National Catholic Church, of American origin, seized the opportunity afforded by the religious liberty of the interval between the two world wars to begin a mission (1919) and by 1939 had gathered about 50,000 members, mostly in the South and West.[37]

World War II and its aftermath brought marked changes to non-Roman Catholic Christians in Poland. On the eve of hostilities and in the first days of the war the Poles took violent measures against the Germans and their churches in Posen and West Prussia. Church buildings and institutions were destroyed and thousands were killed—not because they were Protestants but because they were Germans.[38] When the Nazi armies stormed in, both Lutherans and Reformed suffered and the two were compelled to unite in one ecclesiastical structure. Partly as a result of Nazi measures, the number of Lutherans was said to have been reduced from 470,000 to 150,000, or by a full two-thirds.[39] At the end of the war many German-speaking pastors, both Nazi and anti-Nazi, were expelled from the territory acquired by Poland, and their churches, parish houses, and hospitals were taken over by Roman Catholics.[40] In Stettin, annexed to Poland as a result of the war and formerly predominantly Protestant, members of that branch of the faith dwindled to a few hundred. Yet in other parts of the country in 1959 about four hundred Lutheran churches and chapels survived.[41] The war brought about the near collapse of the Mariavites, a splinter movement from the Roman Catholic Church late in the nineteenth century.[42] However, perhaps because the Communist rulers favoured it in their attempt to foster a Catholic church independent of

[33] *Ibid.*, pp. 81–89.
[34] *Ibid.*, pp. 105–109.
[35] *Ibid.*, pp. 114–126, 144–146.
[36] *Ibid.*, pp. 183–195.
[37] Andrews, *The Polish National Catholic Church in America and Poland*, pp. 81–85.
[38] Richard Kammel, *The Fate of the German Protestant Parishes in Posen and West Prussia during the Polish Campaign. A Book in Commemoration of the September Days 1939* (Berlin, Verlag des Evangelischen Bundes, no date, pp. 114), *passim*.
[39] Polish Research and Information Service, November, 1948, *Religious Life in Poland* (mimeographed).
[40] Tobias, *op. cit.*, p. 386.
[41] *Ecumenical Press Service*, August 14, 1959.
[42] Andrews, *op. cit.*, pp. 85, 86.

Rome, after 1945 the Polish National Catholic Church increased its adherents from about 50,000 in 1939 to about 250,000 in 1950.[43] In 1947 the Lutherans were unified under a law of the state. Nearly two years earlier the Methodists were granted liberty of worship and equality with other religious communities.[44] Subsidized by their denomination in the United States, they grew in numbers. Possibly in them the government thought that it had another check on the Roman Catholic Church.

CZECHOSLOVAKIA

In Czechoslovakia as well as Poland Protestants were a small minority. As we have seen,[45] in the second half of the nineteenth century they began to emerge from the disabilities and persecutions which had been visited upon them since their incorporation into the Hapsburg domains by the Thirty Years' War and increased in numbers. We have already summarized the historical setting of the four and a half post-1914 decades and the varied Roman Catholic record.[46] Here we must content ourselves with the briefest possible account of Protestantism during those years.

In Czechoslovakia Protestants were in several bodies, partly because of confessional differences and partly because of the rival nationalities encompassed in the state which arose after the dismemberment of the Hapsburg empire. The Bohemian or Czech Brethren Church was predominantly Czech in membership and held to the Augsburg and Helvetic Confessions. The adherents of the two confessions united in 1918 and at that time totalled about 159,000. The departure from the Roman Catholic allegiance which issued in the Czech National Church[47] added a few thousand to the Czech Brethren—slightly over 55,000 in the two years 1921–1922, the high-water mark of the accessions, and about 120,000 in 1919–1936. The gain was partly offset by 14,498 who left the Czech Brethren in the years 1919–1931.[48] The clergy of the post-1918 years had their theological training in the John Hus Faculty in Prague (beginning with 1950 the John Amos Comenius Faculty) and felt the influence of Karl Barth and of the inherited indigenous tradition.[49] The emergence of Czechoslovakia after World War I brought problems to the Germans (the *Sudetendeutsch*) who were included within its borders and who were incorporated into Hitler's realm in 1938. While they were a part of the Hapsburg domains the Protestants among them were affiliated with their brethren in Austria. In 1919 they drew

---

[43] *Ibid.*, pp. 81–85.
[44] Tobias, *op. cit.*, pp. 406, 407.
[45] Volume II, pp. 202, 203.
[46] Chapter VII.
[47] *Ibid.*
[48] Siegmund-Schultze, *Die Kirchen der Tschechoslowakei*, pp. 126, 130.
[49] *Ibid.*, p. 133.

together in a German Evangelical Church which in 1935 numbered about 123,000.[50] Before World War I the Lutherans in Slovakia were in one ecclesiastical structure with their fellow Lutherans of Hungary. When, as an aftermath of that war, Slovakia became part of the independent Czechoslovakia, the Lutherans within its borders organized a separate church (1919–1921). In 1934 it counted 401,600 members, or about an eighth of the population, a larger proportion of Protestants than in the remainder of the Czechoslovak Republic. About 85 per cent. were Slovaks and the rest were Germans and Magyars. Each element preserved its language in its literature and services. The Lutherans in Slovakia had their own schools, with financial aid from the state, and in them religious instruction was required.[51] Prior to the collapse of the Hapsburg empire the Reformed in what became Czechoslovakia were in the same church with those of Hungary. Indeed, it was said that although they included a small Slovak minority they were more Magyar than Reformed. Severing the tie with Hungary was, therefore, a traumatic experience. Yet they made the transition, set up their own organization, in 1930 numbered 219,000 adherents, and in spite of the financial stringency of the first post-war years achieved progress in founding the needed educational institutions.[52] Several smaller bodies existed—among them the *Unitas Fratrum,* affiliated with the Moravians, the Congregationalists, the Baptists, the Methodists, and the Lutherans in East Silesia—but their total membership did not equal that of any one of the larger Protestant bodies.[53]

World War II and its aftermath, first the Nazi occupation and then the capture of the government by the Communists, brought striking changes. Under the Nazis the Protestants suffered persecution.[54] In Slovakia the Roman Catholics were in control, more than a score of Protestant periodicals were suppressed, several Protestant pastors and bishops were imprisoned or ousted, and the schools were required to use textbooks acceptable to the Roman Catholic-dominated state. In Bohemia and Moravia many Protestant halls, chapels, and institutions were confiscated, but their constituencies carried on privately and with much lay leadership.[55] In the first few months of liberation the Czech Brethren gave their support to the progressive realization of a socialist democracy and to the elimination of class privileges and the nationalization of natural resources and industry. In May, 1947, the Protestants formed a national council of Evangelical churches which included all non-Roman Catholics but the Unitarians and the Czech National Church. When the Com-

[50] *Ibid.,* pp. 160–163.
[51] *Ibid.,* pp. 186–191.
[52] *Ibid.,* pp. 197–206.
[53] *Ibid.,* pp. 207–246.
[54] Nemec, *Church and State in Czechoslovakia,* p. 163.
[55] Tobias, *Communist-Christian Encounter in East Europe,* p. 489.

munists took control, the Czech Brethren pledged their support to the government so long as it did not violate Christian principles. In June, 1948, a new constitution guaranteed freedom of religion in public and private, the equality of all religious bodies, and compulsory religious education under church direction for children from six to fifteen years of age except when parents requested exemption. In September of that year, over the objection of most of the Protestant churches and the Roman Catholic Church, the state decreed the cessation of voluntary contributions to the churches, insisted on a decisive voice in the approval of ministerial candidates, and assured the churches of its financial support. Its grants were made not to a church as a whole, but to individual ministers, thus ensuring its direct control. Several church buildings were requisitioned, in some areas pastors were denied ration cards which entitled them to a share in the distribution of clothing, and a few of the minority churches were denounced for their "Western orientation." A number of pastors were arrested for alleged "illegal activities." In 1949 all church property was nationalized. The following year the Mormon missionaries were ordered to leave the country.[56]

In general the Protestant churches acquiesced in the measures of the Communist regime. Their leading theologian and their spokesman in Ecumenical circles was Josef Lukl Hromádka (1889——). Hromádka had studied in Austria, Switzerland, Germany, and Scotland and from 1939 to 1947 had taught in Princeton Theological Seminary in the United States. A member of the Czech Brethren, beginning in 1950 he was dean of the faculty in Prague in which most of the Protestant clergy were prepared. He held that the Gospel is eternal, but that the Western, so-called Christian nations had failed to ensure peace or to provide acceptable living standards for the underprivileged masses. He saw Communism as leading the contemporary world in achieving these objectives, criticized the Central Committee of the World Council of Churches for supporting the United Nations' assistance to the Republic of Korea in its resistance to the Communist effort to unify the country, on a visit to the mainland of China viewed with enthusiasm the achievements of the Communists, and endorsed the peace conferences held from time to time in Prague under Communist auspices.[57] The second of the Christian Peace Conferences convened in Prague in April, 1959.[58]

---

[56] Tobias, *op. cit.*, pp. 490–512; Gsovski, *Church and State behind the Iron Curtain*, pp. 20–34, 42–45.

[57] Of the many instances of the attitude of Hromádka see as examples Tobias, *op. cit.*, pp. 492, 493, 500; Herman, *Report from Christian Europe*, pp. 141, 142; J. L. Hromádka, *The Church and Theology in Today's Troubled Times: A Czechoslovak Contribution to Ecumenical Discussions* (Prague, The Ecumenical Council of Churches in Czechoslovakia, 1956, pp. 94), *passim;* Horton, *Contemporary Continental Theology*, pp. 204, 205.

[58] *Protestant Churches in Czechoslovakia* (Prague, The Foreign and Information Department of the Ecumenical Council of Churches in Czechoslovakia, mimeographed, 1952 ff.), July–September, 1959.

Austria

In the Austria left by the dismemberment of the Hapsburg empire the overwhelming majority were Roman Catholics. Among the Protestant minority were both Lutherans and Reformed. In the mid-1930's they totalled about 300,000 in a population of approximately 6,700,000.[59] Between 1918 and the outbreak of World War II their numbers were swelled by the accession of about 75,000 from the Roman Catholic Church. The joining of Austria to the National Socialist realm was followed by the alteration of the ecclesiastical structure by government action and the severance of the tie with the state. With the restoration of Austrian independence in 1945 came a change in the constitution of the Protestant *Landeskirche* and the separation of Church and state was only partial.[60] In 1959 a national council of churches was constituted by the Lutherans, the Reformed, the Old Catholics, and the Methodists.[61]

Hungary

In Hungary a much larger proportion of the nation were Protestants than in Lithuania, Poland, Czechoslovakia, or Austria. In 1910, out of a population of 18,264,533, 2,603,381 were Reformed, 1,306,384 were Lutherans, 74,275 were Unitarians, and 17,066 belonged to smaller Protestant groups, such as Baptists and Methodists.[62] On the eve of World War I the Protestant churches were autonomous, but representatives of the three largest bodies sat in the upper house of the diet and state subsidies partially met the expenses of the churches.[63]

Earlier we saw the drastic shifts in the political setting in the four and a half decades which followed 1914—the separation from Austria which followed the defeat of the Hapsburgs, the brief Károlyi regime (October, 1918–March, 1919), the few weeks of rule by the Communist Béla Kun (March–July, 1919), the conservative regime of Nicholas Horthy, a Protestant, under a succession of premiers into World War II, the participation in World War II on the German side, the occupation by the victorious Russians, the devastation wrought by retreating German armies and the invading Russians, the setting up of a republic (1945) under Ferenc Nagy, the seizing of control by the Communists, the revolt of 1956, and the Russian intervention which issued in a regime supported by Russian arms.

[59] Siegmund-Schultze, editor, *Die evangelische Kirche in Österreich* (Gotha, Leopold Klotze Verlag, 1935, pp. 168), p. 88.

[60] Grete Mecenseffy, *Geschichte des Protestantismus in Österreich* (Graz-Cologne, Hermann Böhlaus Nachf., 1956, pp. 232), pp. 219–223.

[61] *The International Review of Missions*, Vol. XLIX, p. 66 (January, 1960).

[62] Emeric Révész, Stephen Kováts, and Ladislaus Ravasz, *Hungarian Protestantism, Its Past, Present and Future* (Budapest, Bethlen Gágor Literary and Printing House Co., 1927, pp. xiv, 222), pp. 9 ff.

[63] *Ibid.*, pp. 68, 69.

In the transfer of territory by the Treaty of Trianon, which for Hungary ended World War I, the Protestant churches came out with badly diminished numbers on account of the cessions to Czechoslovakia, Rumania, and Jugoslavia. Transylvania, which went to Rumania, had thousands of Reformed, Lutherans, and Unitarians. The Reformed lost slightly more than half and the Lutherans over half their parishes. However, in 1938 about a fifth of the population of Hungary were Reformed and about 6 per cent. were Lutherans.[64] Between the two world wars all denominations recognized by the state were placed on a basis of equality and, in addition to seventeen dignitaries of the Roman Catholic Church, six Calvinists, four Lutherans, and one Unitarian were members of the upper house of the diet.[65]

World War II and its aftermath brought grave problems. For a time the war years appeared to be marked by a renewal of the inner life of the churches. Revival movements were followed by the founding of deaconesses' homes and retreat and training centres, the opening of folk schools, the ordaining of laymen for religious work, the extension of evangelism through preaching and the press, and the intensification of religious instruction. Yet a Lutheran pastor was expelled from his post by his bishop for joining a Nazi organization, another was court-martialled for praying for the victims of Fascism,[66] and hundreds of churches and other church properties were destroyed or badly damaged, some of them by air raids but most of them by the Nazi forces during evacuation. Post-war inflation meant impoverishment, and land reform deprived the churches and their institutions of a large proportion of the holdings from which much of their support had been derived. To help to make good the loss, the state contributed to the salaries of the clergy and of parochial school teachers and to the expenses of a number of students in Protestant schools. Partly with aid from the World Council of Churches but chiefly through the sacrifices of Protestant constituencies much re-building was accomplished, both of churches and of denominational schools. In the administration of relief Protestants and Roman Catholics frequently coöperated.[67] Before long increasing restrictions were placed on religious instruction in the schools, and the number of denominational schools was greatly reduced—the Reformed from 1,117 in 1938 to 5 in 1952, and the Lutherans from 406 in the former year to 2 in the latter year. Clergy were forced to take an oath of loyalty to the government.[68] The appointment of bishops was subject to government approval. The press of the Reformed Church was suppressed and the youth

---

[64] Keller, *Church and State on the European Continent*, p. 187; Leiper, *Christianity Today*, pp. 120, 121.
[65] Gsovski, *op. cit.*, p. 83.
[66] Tobias, *op. cit.*, pp. 431, 432.
[67] *Ibid.*, p. 433; Leiper, *op. cit.*, pp. 121–129; Herman, *op. cit.*, p. 134.
[68] Gsovski, *op. cit.*, pp. 86, 87.

organizations of that church were dissolved. In 1948, because he opposed these measures Laszlo Ravasz, Bishop of the Reformed Church and chairman of the Ecumenical Council and the National Council, was forced to retire. That same year Bishop Lajos Ordass and Baron Albert Radvanszky, Supervisor General of the Lutheran Church, were arrested on the charge of engaging in the black market.[69] Yet some leaders of both the Reformed and Lutheran Churches came out with emphatic statements that the Hungarian Government was not curtailing religious liberty and insisted that the condemnation of the Roman Catholic Archbishop Mindszenty was brought about by his political activities and was not because he stood for freedom of religion.[70] For a brief time in the 1950's the pressure of the state on the churches appeared to be relaxed. As one example, Bishop Ordass was restored to his official functions. However, the uprising of 1956 was followed by a tightening of controls. Ordass was again removed from his position as the leading bishop of the southern diocese of his church, and Bishop Turocsy, also a Lutheran, was stripped of his office and that in spite of the earlier approval by the government of his election. These actions evoked a formal protest from the ranking bishops of Denmark, Norway, Sweden, and Finland, given as the result of an appeal from Ordass. To it the Hungarian Government gave a tart reply.[71] Presumably to create a better impression in Scandinavia, in August, 1959, Bishop Emil Koren of the Lutheran Church in Hungary visited Denmark and stated that the educational work of the Church was not hampered, that the state paid a third of the salaries of the clergy and subsidized church repairs, that the collections voluntarily given in the churches surpassed the amounts collected from the church taxes in earlier years, and that the ten graduated annually from the clergyman's training college in Budapest were sufficient to meet the demand for pastors.[72] Yet in 1959 the first Communist "name-giving," a substitute for baptism, was reported,[73] obviously another step towards de-Christianization.

Jugoslavia

Jugoslavia had few Protestants. In 1954 they were said to number about 100,000, of whom about 60,000 were Reformed and about 40,000 Lutherans, and in addition were some very small groups. Before World War II their institutions were supported by a church tax with the assistance of the state. Under the Tito regime they were granted liberty of worship but were required to depend on voluntary contributions and forbidden to engage in evangelism,

[69] *Ibid.,* pp. 88, 102.
[70] Tobias, *op. cit.,* pp. 474–476.
[71] *Church News from the Northern Countries,* November 23, 1956, February 29, 1958; *Ecumenical Press Service,* July 4, 1958.
[72] *Church News from the Northern Countries,* September 29, 1959.
[73] *Ecumenical Press Service,* July 3, 1959.

to gather in homes, or to train their clergy. Yet attendance at their services and in their Sunday Schools was reported to be good.[74]

SUMMARY

In general Protestantism lost ground in the Baltic countries and Central Europe in the four and a half decades which followed 1914. The loss was caused partly by the advance of the secularization which was operating elsewhere in the former Christendom. Primarily, however, it was due to the two world wars and to the capture of most of the region by Communist governments. The devastation wrought by the armies of the belligerents, the vast shifts of population, partly forced and partly by refugees fleeing hostile regimes, and the programmes of the Communist regimes operated adversely. Exceptions were seen, notably in Finland. There the Lutheran folk church displayed remarkable vigour, first through traditional channels and the continuation of the nineteenth-century awakenings, second through new movements and institutions, and third in the maintenance of its foreign missions. In Austria Protestantism gained in numbers. A striking evidence of vitality was the fashion in which Protestantism survived. In all the countries except Finland it had long been confronted by severe handicaps. In Estonia and Latvia it had been subject to Russian control and to the domination of the German elements over the non-German majorities. In Poland it had had to contend with the Roman Catholic majority and with the prejudice against it as predominantly German and therefore alien. In Czechoslovakia, Austria, and Hungary it had laboured under disabilities imposed by the Roman Catholic Hapsburgs, disabilities which had been only partially removed by liberalizing measures in the eighteenth and nineteenth centuries. Protestantism displayed surprising vigour in the fashion in which it blossomed in the brief interval of peace and freedom between the two world wars and in its persistence under Communist regimes.

---

[74] *Information Service*, December 11, 1954.

CHAPTER XIV

Protestantism in Switzerland

WHAT was the condition of Protestantism in Switzerland in the four and a half decades which were introduced by the outbreak of World War I? Switzerland maintained its neutrality in both world wars, escaped capture by Communism, and during most of the time was economically prosperous. As in much of the former Christendom, the secularization of society and of the outlook of a large proportion of the population continued. Although their numerical strength varied from canton to canton, in spite of the proportionately more rapid increase of Roman Catholics, in the country taken as a whole Protestants were still in a substantial majority. They were overwhelmingly of the Reformed branch of the faith. As previously, their organization was by cantons: each canton had its own ecclesiastical structure.

One trend was observable which we have found elsewhere in much of Europe—towards a separation of Church and state, with the increasing autonomy of the Church. In cantons which had been traditionally Protestant, the Reformed Church was still that of the large majority and was a folk church. In a few cantons the state contributed substantially to the financial support of the Church and paid the salaries of the clergy—Reformed, Roman Catholic, and Christian Catholic. In at least four cantons a church tax was levied on all the inhabitants. However, in several of the cantons the state assumed no responsibility for the Church but still maintained a kind of supervision.[1]

To aid Protestant churches in predominantly Roman Catholic cantons societies existed in the prevailingly Protestant cantons. The first was organized in Basel in 1842 and in the course of the years others sprang up. They held annual national conferences for joint planning and action. Assistance was also given to Reformed congregations outside Switzerland.[2]

In 1920, developing from steps taken in the second half of the nineteenth century, the Federation of Swiss Evangelical Churches was formed. It had as members all the twenty-two cantonal churches and the Methodist Church. It

[1] Siegmund-Schultze, *Die evangelischen Kirchen der Schweiz*, pp. 40 ff.
[2] *Ibid.*, pp. 90 ff.

355

operated through a variety of commissions which addressed themselves to various aspects of the churches' life and work—such as home and foreign missions, social service, and theology.[3]

Pulsing life in Swiss Protestantism found expression in a variety of ways. Much vigour was seen in individual congregations, for they tended to be self-governing and to assume much initiative.[4] As neutrals in the two world wars, Swiss Protestants were active in relief of the sufferers from these tragedies; the Federation of Swiss Evangelical Churches had an important part. A Christian youth movement which sprang up first in the German-speaking cantons became integrated in a federation known as the Young Church (*Junge Kirche*) and was paralleled by a similar movement in French-speaking cantons. The Federation of Swiss Evangelical Churches helped to institute youth centres in various parts of the country. The chief focus was the *Heimstätte* ("home") established in 1932 at Gwatt on the Lake of Thun.[5] The *Junge Kirche* joined with the YMCA, the YWCA, and other agencies in assisting in relief of youth in the belligerent lands and, among other projects, had camps in Switzerland for refugees. The Christian youth movement drew much of its inspiration from the study of the Bible and sought to deepen the faith and promote the growth in Christian character of the many whose connexion with the Church was merely formal.[6] Swiss Protestants continued to share in the world-wide missionary enterprise. The chief agency was still the Basel Mission, with its more than a century of history, but other organizations participated, the Swiss Missionary Council made for coördination, and in 1958 the number of Swiss missionaries in other lands was reported to be 544. While in proportion to the Protestant population this was less than the total from Norway, it was considerably more than from Germany.[7]

As in several other countries, chiefly after World War II, and paralleling the lay movements in the Roman Catholic Church, institutions were opened for penetrating every aspect of life with the Christian faith. Of these the most prominent was at Boldern in the canton of Zürich and was begun at the suggestion of Emil Brunner. It was called not an "academy," as were similar centres in Germany, but a *Heimstätte*, following the precedent at Gwatt. Contributions towards its support came from the synod, individual parishes, and the state. Conferences were held for particular occupational groups—among them farmers, housewives, agronomists, foremen, accountants, engineers, contractors, architects, lawyers, physicians, retailers, office secretaries, and, notably,

[3] *Ibid.*, pp. 122, 123; Leiper, *Christianity Today*, pp. 66, 67.
[4] Leiper, *op. cit.*, p. 61.
[5] Weber, *Signs of Renewal*, p. 40.
[6] *Ibid.*, p. 40; Leiper, *op. cit.*, pp. 64, 65.
[7] *Occasional Bulletin from the Missionary Research Library*, December 8, 1958, p. 29.

workers and secretaries from the trade unions to reach organized labour, which in Switzerland as elsewhere tended to drift away from the Church.[8]

Switzerland was the chief seat of international Protestant organizations. Here were the headquarters of the World's Student Christian Federation, the World's Alliance of the YMCA, the World's YWCA, and the World Council of Churches.

SWISS PROTESTANT THEOLOGY

Twentieth-century Swiss Protestant theology was vigorous and multiform and in some of its expressions had marked repercussions at home and in other lands, not only on Protestantism but also on Roman Catholicism. Here were earnest attempts to come to grips intellectually with the surging currents of the revolutionary age. The influence of Vinet persisted, chiefly but not exclusively in French-speaking Switzerland.[9] A strong liberal element was seen which was aroused to fresh insistence by the dialectic, "neo-orthodox" theology. In contrast was a conservatism strong in Pietist circles and rejecting some features of Biblical historical criticism and all efforts to mould political life.[10]

The Religious Socialists were prominent, akin to similar groups in England, Germany, and the United States. Like the others, they had their heyday on the eve of World War I, but for a time they persisted after that disillusioning catastrophe.[11] Their pioneers and chief figures were Hermann Kutter (1863–1931) and Leonhard Ragaz (1868–1945). Kutter, a pastor, gave a major impulse to Swiss Christian Socialism, was known outside Switzerland as well as in his native land, and at one time made an impression on Karl Barth.[12] Ragaz was a pastor in Basel and then a professor in Zürich. He was convinced that the Church was not coming to grips with the social movements of the age, with the class struggle, or with the problems brought to the masses by capitalism but had departed from Christ and was intent on preserving its organization and power. In his frank criticisms and his espousal of socialism he aroused much opposition.[13]

[8] Weber, *op. cit.,* pp. 39–42.

[9] Volume II, pp. 213, 214; Siegmund-Schultze, *op. cit.,* p. 156.

[10] Leiper, *op. cit.,* p. 63.

[11] Siegmund-Schultze, *op. cit.,* pp. 218–237.

[12] As a sample of his writing see his *They Must: or God and the Social Democracy, a Frank Word to Christian Men and Women,* American editor, Rufus W. Weeks (Chicago, Coöperative Printing Co., 1908, pp. 232). For a brief bibliography see *Twentieth Century Encyclopedia of Religious Knowledge,* Vol. II, p. 634.

[13] For a brief sketch of the life of Ragaz see Emil Fuchs, *Leonhard Ragas, Prophet unserer Zeit* (Oberursel/Ts., Kompass Verlag, no date, pp. vi, 119). Among the writings of Ragaz are *Der Kampf um das Reich Gottes in Blumhardt, Vater und Sohn und Weiter* (Erlenbach-Zürich, Rotapfel-Verlag, 1925, pp. 337), and *Von Christus zu Marx—von Marx zu Christus: ein Beitrag* (Wernigerade am Harz, H. Harder, 1929, pp. 203).

KARL BARTH GIVES A DECISIVE LEAD IN PROTESTANT THEOLOGY

The most widely recognized Swiss theologian of the post-1914 decades was Karl Barth (1886———). It is no exaggeration to say that Barth was the most influential Protestant theologian after Schleiermacher. He was generally esteemed as the outstanding figure in what was variously called the theology of crisis, dialectic theology, and neo-orthodoxy.[14]

The chronological facts of Barth's career can be quickly summarized. He was born in Basel. He studied in Bern, Berlin, Tübingen, and Marburg. In 1909 he served as vicar in a German Reformed Church in Geneva. Then, from 1911 to 1921, he was pastor in Safenwil, a mountain village in North-western Switzerland. He was professor in Göttingen from 1921 to 1925, in Münster in Westphalia from 1925 to 1930, and in Bonn until he was expelled by Hitler (1935). Beginning in 1935 he was professor of theology in his native Basel and there spent the rest of his teaching career.

These bald facts hint at the intellectual and spiritual pilgrimage from which emerged the Barth who became the prophet and leader for thousands of his contemporaries. Here was a first-class mind, deeply religious, courageous, bold, and uncompromising, caught up in a segment of the revolutionary age which entailed adjustment to a traumatic transition. He vigorously denounced not only his critics but also former friends and collaborators with whom he developed disagreement. His literary style was not always easy reading, but it was often pungent. He had a robust sense of humour which from time to time illuminated his pages. His adjustment to the era ushered in by World War I made of him the voice for which many, engulfed as was he in the changes, were eagerly, almost desperately longing. Reared, as were many of his contemporaries, in a theologically conservative home, in his student days he was deeply impressed by Christian Socialism with its condemnation of the apparent blindness of the Church to the challenge of industrialized society and with its radical and hopeful programme. At Marburg he was under the influence of Hermann, with the latter's combination of personal piety and Ritschlian outlook. In general, he then reflected the liberalism which was shattered for many by World War I. During World War I he was preaching to a congregation in neutral Switzerland, where he had sufficient detachment to meditate on the tragedy sweeping away Europe as he had known it. Yet he was not sufficiently remote to escape the agonizing reëxamination of the postulates on which he had been nurtured. The Germany where he had spent his student days and which he had come to love was being shaken to its foundations, and the the-

14 For a bibliography of Barth's writings through 1955 see the Festschrift in his honour on his seventieth birthday: Antwort. Karl Barth zum siebzigsten Geburtstag am 10 Mai, 1956 (Zollikon-Zürich, Evangelischer Verlag, 1956, pp. xi, 963), pp. 945–960.

ologies popular on the eve of the disaster were clearly inadequate to answer the questions forced on Christians by the disappearance of the nineteenth century. Week after week as he prepared his sermons while the echoes of the storm reverberated in his mountain valley, he found that what he had previously held to be the Gospel sounded hollow and met neither his own needs nor those of his flock. Could he or they be sure of God in a Europe, professedly Christian, where nations were tearing at each other's throats? Out of the struggle issued Barth's initial writing that caught the attention of Protestants, especially German-reading Protestants. Then came a period of teaching in the Weimar Republic, the changes in his thought which accompanied that teaching, the rise of the Nazi power, prominence in the emergence of the *Bekennende Kirche,* the expulsion by Hitler, the years of teaching and writing in Basel within sight of the Germany which was being racked by the Nazis, World War II, the advance of Communism, and vivid awareness of the triumph of Communism in Russia and Central Europe.

It was in this Europe that Barth was engulfed. Aside from trips to the British Isles he never ventured outside the western edges of that continent. He met scholars from other countries, and students from many lands flocked to his lectures and his seminars, but he remained essentially a child of Continental Western Europe and its Protestantism, especially that of Germany, and had no first-hand contact with other sections of the shrinking globe. He was intimately familiar with the great sixteenth-century Reformers and with the Continental European cultural heritage—including especially its music, notably Mozart. Here were his strength and his weakness. He was only slightly if at all aware of theological writings in English. Yet increasingly, chiefly by contacts through the Ecumenical Movement, he showed appreciation of a wider range of ideas. His thought was never static but was marked by successive stages. Yet it was circumscribed by the Europe of which he was the heir and in whose twentieth-century convulsions he was inextricably caught.

Barth first attracted attention by his *Commentary on the Epistle to the Romans (Der Römerbrief)*. It came out in 1918, and in its second edition, issued in 1921, it was drastically revised. Later editions were not subjected to thorough rewriting.[15] The 1921 revision frankly acknowledged the influence of Franz Overbeck (1837–1903), professor of critical theology in the University of Basel from 1872 to 1897, who in two pamphlets, one published in 1873 and the other, posthumous, in 1919, attacked all Christian theology from the patristic age as un-Christian and satanic, as denying the eschatological character of Christianity, and as seeking to domesticate the faith in human civilization. The second edition also embodied changes due to a growing acquaintance

[15] An English translation of the sixth edition, by Edwyn C. Hoskyns, is *The Epistle to the Romans* (New York, Oxford University Press, 1933, pp. xxi, 547).

with Plato, Kant, Kierkegaard, and Dostoyevsky.[16] Barth did not reject the critical method of the study of the Bible, but he denounced what he held to be the superficiality of much that was associated with it—absorption in the establishment of the original texts, seeking the present equivalent of the Greek and Hebrew words, and missing the real message. He saw in the Epistle to the Romans an eschatology which was not lineal, going on to a climax in time. Rather he believed eschatology to be vertical, a continuous impinging upon time. His approach was dialectic, referring in part to God's conversation with man and in part to the paradox inherent in life. From Kierkegaard he derived a distinction between time and eternity. He declared that no way existed to pass from the finite to the infinite and that all points in history are equidistant from eternity. To Barth God was the *totaliter alter,* the wholly Other.

After 1927 and especially after 1930 Barth modified the convictions set forth in *Der Römerbrief.* Although he held that man by his own efforts cannot bridge the gulf between himself and God, that did not mean that God cannot move to man. Yet he maintained that God's act is always miraculous—His nature is such that He is free to act and is not bound by what man deems His laws. Accordingly Barth insisted that God does not operate within time but only upon time. He emphasized that nature and history have no kinship with God—such a disjunction exists between history and Christianity that we must say: if history, then not Christianity; and if Christianity, then not history.

Barth's major work, his multi-volume *Dogmatik,* not completed when these lines were penned, compelled its author to be more systematic than he had been as he exploded in his class lectures.[17] Yet it, too, was based upon lectures prepared for the classroom and its style was more rhetorical than literary. It was the largest theological treatise ever produced by Protestants—perhaps by Christians of any branch of the faith. Written over a number of years, it exhibited stages in Barth's thought. The first section, dating from 1927, bore the title *Christliche Dogmatik.* But the study of Anselm, published in 1931,[18] marked what Barth regarded as a shift in his approach and he altered the title to *Kirchliche Dogmatik.* Barth hesitated to call himself a Christian theologian but thought of himself as a Church theologian. He called attention to the diverse views of theology within the Church and especially the differences between Protestants and Roman Catholics. In so doing he addressed himself to what he regarded as error and held that his chief service was to the Church. He cut short what might be described as his flirtation with existentialism and

16 *Ibid.,* p. 3.

17 Karl Barth, *Kirchliche Dogmatik* (Munich, C. Kaiser Verlag, 1932 ff., later Zollikon-Zürich, Evangelischer Verlag a.g., 4 vols. in 11 parts, 1942–1959), put into English by various translators as *Church Dogmatics* (New York, Charles Scribner's Sons, 4 vols. in 7, 1936–1958).

18 Karl Barth, *Fides Quaerens Intellectum: Anselms Beweis der Existenz Gottes im Zuzammenhang seines theologischen Programms* (Munich, C. Kaiser, 1931, pp. x, 199).

attempted to eliminate dependence on philosophy. He maintained that he worked in a framework—the Word of God—and that theology, to be true, must be elaborated within that framework. He broke with Gogarten and Brunner, with whom he had collaborated in the 1920's. He held that Gogarten was moving too far towards anthropology—as though theology and the knowledge of God were dependent on man—and accordingly was becoming too sympathetic with the German Christians. His denunciation of Brunner (of whom we are to hear more in a moment) came after the latter's *Divine Imperative* and *Nature and Grace*. Brunner, he maintained, held that the Christian faith depended on God's command *and* human reason. He emphatically objected to the *and* as implying that it compromised the sovereignty of God and declared that we could never rightly say *and*. The opening salvo of his attack on Brunner was in an article headed *Nein*. The revolutionary course of events in the 1930's led Barth to take account of the political and social movements of the tragic years. He denounced the Nazis and held that although the Church must be slow in applying radical Christian principles to social questions, it must judge the state.

Through all the developments in his thought, Barth never departed from some central themes. They constantly governed his theology. He based theology on the Word of God. He held that the mission of theology is to examine what the Church has said about the Word of God, and that God has spoken and the Church must proclaim His Word. He held that liberal Christianity had failed because it stressed man's word about God. He saw in the Bible a word which to man is entirely strange and in which God is the centre. The Bible, he insisted, tells us not what man says about God but what God says to man, and it is what God says to man which must be the ground and core of faith. God alone is God, the world exists, but a great gulf of sin and death separates God and the world. Barth did not deny the immanence of God or that God is related to the world, but he said that the relationship is one way—from God to the world—and that God is always sovereign. He was emphatic in pointing out that God is above and apart from the object-subject relation; He is never one subject among other subjects of thought; He is always utterly free and we are completely dependent on Him. Barth held that in revelation, or the Word of God, we discern the relation of God to man, that no way exists from the finite to the infinite, but that in the incarnation God has opened the way. Although he denounced the philosophical approach to theology, Barth had been influenced by Plato and Kant and used philosophy. But he felt that the knowledge of God which God gives through revelation is primary. Barth did not begin, as did Kant, from the limitations of human knowledge, but from the self-revelation of God. He declared that men could not establish criteria by which revelation could be verified; revelation is and must be self-authenticating, and if men could set up such criteria they would place them above revelation and so deny the validity of revelation.

Barth was clear that God's revelation is unique, utterly new, irrevocable, and unrepeatable, and that when once we have apprehended it, it is impossible to think of ourselves as without it. It occurs in the historical process but is not of it. Because the revelation has been accomplished in Him, Jesus Christ is unique. Revelation is not for an individual until it is recognized by an individual in faith, and that faith is the gift of God. Barth viewed revelation as being both in memory and in hope, and held that the hope is here but has not yet been made perfect. He maintained that the Christian proclamation is compounded of the recollection of the past and the hope of the future—the hope that God will come again in Christ. Revelation is always contemporary, it is true and is coming to be true, it took place once for all, and the same Christ through which it came is both here and to come. To Barth revelation and grace are identical. Revelation makes possible the hearing of revelation. God, he insisted, is love, and what He does must be consistent with His love and righteousness: God cannot deny Himself.

A term which Barth found in the Epistle to the Romans for the Word of God is *crisis*, by which is meant judgement. Through the Word of God we perceive God to be God and sin to be sin. Through this *crisis*, this judgement, are God's *yes* and *no*. God, so Barth maintained, says not only *no* but also *yes*. God's *yes* reveals His *no*. Because of sin the world is under judgement, God's *no*. Total depravity means that man of himself can never be anything but sinful. Man is created in the image of God, but because man has turned away from God he can neither reflect nor discern the image of God. However, God's image is seen through God's act in the revelation through Jesus Christ. Grace and sin are not correlative but are reciprocally exclusive. Sin is not a springboard from which a man moves into grace, but grace obliterates sin.

To Barth, Christianity has as its sole centre Jesus Christ. In Christ God comes to redeem man. Our knowledge that we are lost is inseparable from our salvation. God is hidden, the *Deus absconditus,* and only through Christ do we know Him. The revelation of God in Christ is to be seen only through the eyes of faith, and faith is given by God. Jesus was the intersecting of time by revelation, but the Christ in Jesus is veiled and is recognized by faith. The resurrection of Christ is more than history. It is a victory in history. We now live between the time of victory and the final capitulation of the enemy.

Inevitably Barth, stressing grace as he did, had to face the issue of election. He held that because the Word of God is Jesus Christ it is wholly a word of grace—of election. Barth was emphatic in his criticism of existing teachings of election. He insisted that to regard election as derived from the secret will of God is to view it as a lifeless decree from a lifeless God and makes of God sheer power. He held that belief in determinism arises from a wrong view of eternity. Eternity is not chronological, not temporal, not endless continuation, not the opposite of time, but is inclusive of time. God's time, Barth declared, is different from our time. It runs along with our time and is also post-temporal. He scorned the individualistic approach by which some are said to be pre-destined to eternal happiness and others to eternal woe. To Barth God's elec-tion is an election of grace. It is a real choice by God, for God says both *yes* and *no* but in His *yes* overcomes His *no*. In His *yes* He rejects reprobation. In His election God does not abandon His judgement and His wrath against sin but negates the reprobation of man by taking the judgement and wrath upon Himself. In Christ God shouldered the guilt of human sin, became the reprobate man, and took away the reprobation. Grace triumphed over judge-ment. Election is of a divine community around Jesus Christ, Who is God electing. The Gospel comes to a particular individual, but always as a mem-ber of an elect community. Barth said that there are not two spheres of elec-tion, as Calvin would have it—the elect and non-elect. The only isolation from God is through a man's rejection of grace. But is a man free to reject God's grace? Barth taught that man is free to do so and if he does so reverts to the chaos from which God rescued the world at the creation. But God will not be defeated, for His freedom is greater than man's freedom and He will not permit sin, which is a reversion to primeval chaos, to triumph. This seems to mean that Barth held to universal salvation, but he said that that conclusion did not necessarily follow and that the outcome is shrouded in mystery. In speaking of God's election and grace, so Barth maintained, we are speaking of God Himself. God is will, and we cannot separate God's acts from His being.

Barth emphatically rejected natural theology—a basic conviction which led to his denunciation of Brunner. He held that revelation is centred in Christ and that revelation in Christ is not a confirmation of what our reason would lead us to expect but contradicts it. He insisted that we do not know God through His creation but only as He is seen in Jesus Christ. He declared that natural theology is not true theology. Later he went further, maintaining that we cannot even say that there cannot be a natural theology, for to say so im-plies that we are able to use our reason apart from revelation.

Barth saw the Word of God in the Bible, as given to the Church, and in the sacraments. As written, the Word of God is in what he regarded as the strange new world of the Bible. He believed the Scriptures to be the Word when God speaks through them. In his *Dogmatik* he again and again refers to the Bible. He did not take the Bible literally as did some conservatives: he held that the critical study of the Scriptures is essential but that it does not help to discern the Word within the Word. Nor did he agree with the liberals, for he maintained that they had set up some other standard than the Bible by which to judge the Bible. The Bible, he maintained, is a witness to God's revelation in which God asserts Himself, but witness and God's self-assertion are not identical. God only uses witness to assert Himself. Only God is authoritative, not the Bible, but God exercises His authority through the Bible. The proclamation of the Word through the Church, Barth held, is a human act and so is subject to error, but it is also God's act. In the sacraments, too, are both the human element and the divine activity.

The acceptance of the Word of God, Barth taught, is by faith; faith entails decision; and the Word of God confronts us with the necessity of decision. Our faith is in the faithfulness of God and is dependent on God's faithfulness. It is, therefore, an element of human experience. Man must open the door to Christ, but Christ passes through closed doors.

As a summary description of Barth, it must be said that his theology was based entirely upon grace. He regarded himself as a Reformed theologian and tended to hold to the Heidelberg catechism, but always with a difference. He was not strictly a Calvinist, especially in his attitude towards baptism, for he came out for believers' baptism. Yet in some respects he was nearer to Calvin than to Luther. He really marked a new beginning by basing theology exclusively on grace.[19]

Eduard Thurneysen (1888——), a contemporary and close friend of Barth, was long a pastor in Switzerland. He taught practical theology in Basel and interpreted Barth on the pastoral level. Barth was deeply indebted to him, especially for emphasis on a Church theology. They had been neighbours in their rural parishes and had criticized each other's sermons. Like Barth, Thurneysen had been influenced by Hermann Kutter and his Social Democ-

---

[19] Of the extensive body of Barth's writings, in addition to those we have mentioned, the following are useful as throwing light on various aspects of his thought: *Die protestantische Theologie im 19 Jahrhundert, ihre Vorgeschichte und ihre Geschichte* (Zollikon-Zürich, Evangelischer Verlag a.g., 1947, pp. vii, 611); *Wolfgang Amadeus Mozart 1756/1956* (Zollikon-Zürich, Evangelischer Verlag a.g., 1956, pp. 50); *The Knowledge of God and the Service of God According to the Teaching of the Reformation: Recalling the Scottish Confession of 1560*, the Gifford Lectures in the University of Aberdeen in 1937 and 1938, translated by J. L. M. Haire and Ian Henderson from *Gotteserkenntnis und Gottesdienst nach reformatischer Lehre. 20 Vorlesungen über das schottische Bekenntnis von 1560* (New York, Charles Scribner's Sons, 1939, pp. xxix, 254); *Das Wort Gottes und die Theologie. Gesammelte Vorträge* (Munich, C. Kaiser, 7th and 8th thousand, 1929, pp. 212), translated by Douglas Horton as *The Word of God and the Word of Man* (Boston, Pilgrim Press, 1928, pp. 327); *Credo. A Presentation of the Chief Problems of Dogmatics with Reference to the Apostles' Creed*, lectures at the University of Utrecht in 1935, translated by J. Strathearn McNab (New York, Charles Scribner's Sons, 1936, pp. xi, 203); *Dogmatik im Grundriss im Anschluss an das apostolische Glaubensbekenntnis* (Munich, C. Kaiser, 1947, pp. 181), translated by G. T. Thomson as *Dogmatics in Outline* (New York, Philosophical Society, 1947, pp. 155); *The Christian Life*, translated by J. Strathearn McNab from *Vom christlichen Leben* (London, Student Christian Movement Press, 1930, pp. 64); *Die kirchliche Lehre von der Taufe* (Zollikon-Zürich, Evangelischer Verlag, 2nd ed., 1943, pp. 48).

racy. Thurneysen was also indebted to Dostoyevsky as a theologian and, with Barth, had been profoundly impressed by Christoph Blumhardt.[20]

BARTH THE CONTROVERSIALIST

Rejoicing in controversy and characteristically emphatic as he was, Barth tilted with numbers of his contemporaries. We have already mentioned his debates with Roman Catholics.[21] Inevitably he came out in criticism of Bultmann.[22] As we have hinted, his most notable differences were with his fellow Swiss, Brunner.

EMIL BRUNNER AND NATURAL THEOLOGY

Heinrich Emil Brunner (1889——), better known as Emil Brunner, was only a few years Barth's junior. He had his theological education in Zürich, Berlin, and Union Theological Seminary in New York City. For a time he taught languages in Leeds and Yarmouth, England, from 1916 to 1924 was pastor of a Reformed mountain parish in Obstalden in the canton of Glarus in his native Switzerland, and beginning in 1924 was professor of systematic and practical theology in the University of Zürich. He was visiting professor in Princeton Theological Seminary 1938–1939, was Gifford lecturer in Scotland in 1947 and 1948, and for several years beginning in 1953 was professor of Christian ethics and philosophy in the International Christian University on the outskirts of Tokyo.

From this brief chronological sketch it must be obvious that Brunner had a far wider first-hand contact with other peoples and lands and with theological and religious currents throughout the world than had Barth. Like Barth, he knew Germany, although his residence there was less prolonged, and in his years as a village pastor in neutral Switzerland he lived through the storm of World War I and could not but be affected by the shattering of the Europe in which he had been reared. As with Barth, the stage of the age of revolution which was ushered in by that war forced Brunner to think through afresh the theological foundations of his faith. For some years the two shared in formulating the dialectic or crisis theology. But perhaps because of a more irenic temperament, possibly because of his wider international experience, Brunner was more inclusive in his sympathies and in his theological outlook than was

[20] Thurneysen and Barth had several joint collections of sermons, among them *Die Grosse Barmherzigkeit* (Munich, C. Kaiser, 1935, pp. 236). Thurneysen had several books of which he was the sole author, among them *Die Lehre von der Seelsorge* (Zollikon-Zürich, Evangelischer Verlag, 1946, pp. 327). See, on Thurneysen, James D. Smart in *Theology Today*, Vol. XVI, pp. 74–89. On Blumhardt see Volume II, p. 68.
[21] Chapter VI.
[22] Karl Barth, *Rudolf Bultmann: ein Versuch ihn zu Verstehen* (Zollikon-Zürich, Evangelischer Verlag, 1952, pp. 56). See also Heinrich Fries, *Bultmann-Barth und die katholische Theologie* (Stuttgart, Schwabenverlag, 1955, pp. 172).

Barth. For example, for a time he spoke favourably of the highly controversial Oxford Groups and saw in them a hopeful lay movement for evangelism,[23] and in Japan he was friendly with the Mukyokai ("no church church") begun by Uchimura Kanso.[24] He exerted a wide influence in Protestantism, but he did not make as deep an impression or mark a new era in Christian theology, as did Barth.

In view of the contrasts in temperament and geographic background of the two men, the break between Barth and Brunner marked by the former's Nein might have been expected. It revealed not only the differences between the two but also something of the distinctiveness of Brunner's theology.[25] Brunner believed that Barth had drawn erroneous corollaries from the sola gratia of the Scriptures and the Reformers in maintaining that in sinful man no traces remain of the image of God; in holding that every attempt to discover a general revelation is false; in implying that in God's creation and in the preservation of the world no act of grace is to be seen; and in not granting that saving points of contact for grace exist. He insisted that man continues to be responsible for his conduct and retains enough of the image of God to respond to God's grace; that there can be no sin except through a knowledge of the commandment of God and since the commandment is given by God the knowledge of the commandment means a knowledge of God, although not saving knowledge; that through God's grace the worst consequences of sin are cancelled, but sin itself is not abolished; that within the sphere of preserving grace the orders exist—such as marriage, the family, and the state—and through grace they are known by the natural man; that in the persistence of the image of God a point of contact exists through which the grace of redemption operates; that through grace a repairing of the damage done by sin is accomplished in such manner that a new creation comes into being; that the recognition of the orders through natural theology is essential to true social ethics; and that if the Church is to proclaim the Gospel in terms intelligible to the natural man her point of contact must be discerned, and in natural theology, the use of unregenerate man's reason, that point of contact exists. In support of these views he appealed to Calvin.

In reply Barth exploded in his Nein and prefaced it with an angry introduction. He emphatically rejected Brunner's concessions to natural law and maintained that to grant them would entail going much further and would

[23] Emil Brunner, The Church and the Oxford Groups, translated by David Cairns from Die Kirchen, die Gruppenbewegung und die Kirche Jesu Christ (London, Hodder and Stoughton, 1937, pp. vii, 109).

[24] Volume III, Chapter XXII.

[25] Natural Theology, Comprising "Nature and Grace" by Emil Brunner and the Reply "No" by Karl Barth, translated from the German by Peter Fraenkel, with an Introduction by John Baillie (London, G. Bles, 1941, pp. 126); Emil Brunner, Natur und Gnade zum Gespräch mit Karl Barth (Tübingen, J. C. B. Mohr, 2nd ed., 1935, pp. 60).

lead to a position not substantially different from that of the Roman Catholic Church.

Brunner's continuing concern was apologetic, namely, to establish an approach to the thoughtful, cultured unbelievers whose religious faith had been eroded by the currents of the revolutionary age. He was convinced that to win the unbelievers common ground must be found, and that this was in the basic presupposition of thousands shaped by that age: confidence in man's reason. The approach, he was convinced, was through natural theology.[26]

OSCAR CULLMANN AND THE NEW TESTAMENT FAITH

Barth also differed from one of his colleagues on the theological faculty of Basel, Cullmann. Oscar Cullmann (1902——) was born in Strasbourg during the period when it was a part of Germany. He was educated there and for a time taught in its university. Beginning in 1938 he was professor of New Testament exegesis and early Christianity in Basel. He also lectured in the Sorbonne and the Waldensian seminary in Rome. His first important book was on Gnosticism and its relation to Christianity, and he wrote several other books in the fields covered by his chair which attracted wide attention among Biblical and theological students in Europe and America. He defended the "sacramentarianism" of John's Gospel and regarded the author as relating the cultic life of the Church to the life and teaching of Jesus.[27]

---

[26] A selection of the more important works of Brunner is as follows: *Das Gebot und die Ordungen: Entwurf einer protestantisch-theologischen Ethik* (Tübingen, J. C. B. Mohr, 1932, pp. xii, 696), translated by Olive Wyon as *The Divine Imperative, a Study in Christian Ethics* (London, Lutterworth Press, 1937, pp. 728); *Der Mensch im Widerspruch* (Berlin, Furche-Verlag, 1937, pp. xv, 572), translated by Olive Wyon as *Man in Revolt: a Christian Anthropology* (New York, Charles Scribner's Sons, 1939, pp. 564); *Der Mittler: zur Besinnung über den Christusglauben* (Tübingen, J. C. B. Mohr, 1927, pp. x, 565), translated by Olive Wyon as *The Mediator, a Study in the Central Doctrine of the Christian Faith* (New York, The Macmillan Co., 1934, pp. 621); *Offenbarung und Vernunft: die Lehre von der christlichen Glaubensverkenntnis,* translated by Olive Wyon as *Revelation and Reason: the Christian Doctrine of Faith and Knowledge* (Philadelphia, The Westminster Press, 1946, pp. xii, 440); *The Divine-Human Encounter,* translated by Amandus W. Loofs (Philadelphia, The Westminster Press, 1943, pp. 207); and *Dogmatik* (Zürich, Zwingli-Verlag, 2 vols., 1946–1950), translated by Olive Wyon as *Dogmatics* (Philadelphia, The Westminster Press, 2 vols., 1950–1952).

[27] Among Cullmann's more important books are *La Problème Littéraire et Historique du Roman Pseudo-Clémentin: Étude sur la Rapport entre Gnosticisme et le Judeo-Christianisme* (Paris, F. Alcan, 1930, pp. viii, 271); *Die Christologie des Neuen Testaments* (Tübingen, J. C. B. Mohr, 1957, pp. viii, 352); *Urchristentum und Gottesdienst* (Zürich, Zwingli-Verlag, 2nd ed., 1950, pp. 120), translated by A. Stewart Todd and James B. Torrance as *Early Christian Worship* (Chicago, Henry Regnery Co., 1953, pp. 124); *Christ et le Temps: Temps et Histoire dans le Christianisme Primitive* (Neuchâtel, Delachaux & Niestlé, 1947, pp. 182), translated by Floyd V. Tilson from the German as *Christ and Time: the Primitive Christian Conception of Time and History* (Philadelphia, The Westminster Press, 1950, pp. 253); *Petrus, Jünger, Apostel, Märtyer: das historische Petrus-Problem* (Zürich, Zwingli-Verlag, 1952, pp. 285), translated by Floyd V. Tilson as *Peter, Disciple, Apostle, Martyr: a Historical and Theological Study* (London, S.C.M. Press, 1953, pp. 252).

Swiss Protestantism and Psychology

Besides placing its stamp on theology and New Testament studies Swiss Protestantism made notable contributions in the field of psychology and especially of psychiatry. The study of psychology and its application to the treatment of mental disturbances was one of the outstanding features of the twentieth century. Psychiatry and psychoanalysis became familiar terms. In the Western world particularly, thousands sought to resolve the inner tensions and conflicts which arose from the complex pressures of the day by resorting to psychiatrists and to those trained in the application of psychology to personal problems. Conflicting schools developed. From Swiss Protestantism some men issued whose influence was felt beyond the borders of the country. Of them the most prominent was Carl Gustav Jung (1875-1961). The son of a pastor, he was intimately familiar with the Bible and the Christian faith. Although he departed far from orthodoxy, he regarded Christ as unique, the psychological prototype of the only meaningful life.[28] He had once been a disciple of Freud but broke with him and developed his particular approach to the subject, making less than Freud did of sex as a factor in the shaping of personality, and coining terms which became clichés—such as "introversion" and "extroversion." Paul Tournier was less widely known but consciously and sincerely held to the Christian faith and found in it a key to much of his practise as a psychiatric physician.[29]

Summary

Switzerland, neutral in both world wars, but with peoples on all its borders who were victims of the conflicts, could not but be profoundly affected by the stage of the revolutionary age which followed 1914. Swiss Protestantism did not display such marked deepening of its life as came to it through the *réveil* and the Pietism of the nineteenth century. However, it had a vitality which found expression in a variety of ways, some of them new, and which exerted an influence far outside the borders of the country. Its cantonal churches formed a federation which enabled them to make a coöperative approach to the problems of the day. Through several channels Protestants exerted themselves to give relief to the sufferers from the wars. Lay movements developed for the penetration of all aspects of life with the Gospel. Geneva became the headquarters for several of the world organizations which arose from the Ecumenical Movement. Swiss Protestant missionaries were numerous. The most prominent theologian in the entire Church of the day was Karl Barth.

28 C. G. Jung, *The Development of Personality,* translated by R. F. C. Hull (New York, Bollingen Foundation, 1954, pp. viii, 235), p. 181.
29 As an example see his *The Meaning of Persons* (New York, Harper & Brothers, 1957, pp. 238).

His books were read throughout much of the Protestant and even the Roman Catholic world, and students from many countries thronged to his seminars and lectures. Emil Brunner and Oscar Cullmann, although less widely and profoundly influential than Barth, helped to shape thought in land after land. Both indirectly and directly Swiss Protestantism entered into the psychology and psychiatry which had a wide vogue. Here was a vigorous Protestantism.

CHAPTER XV

Protestantism in Latin Europe

IN OUR survey of twentieth-century Protestantism Latin Europe need not long detain us. Here, as we have repeatedly reminded ourselves, were the chief centre and the main strength of the Roman Catholic Church. Here had emerged the majority of the monastic movements and congregations of the religious, both in earlier centuries and in the nineteenth century. Here most of the great Roman Catholic theologians had been born and reared. In the twentieth century, in spite of the trends towards de-Christianization, here much of the theological activity in the Roman Catholic Church took place and such vital developments as the Liturgical Movement and the lay apostolate were potent. From Latin Europe still came the majority of the missionaries who were propagating the Roman Catholic branch of the faith outside the Occident. Moreover, in Latin Europe Protestants were minorities—and, except on the northern fringes of that region, small minorities. Until the spread of secularism with its religious indifferentism in the nineteenth century, Protestantism was subject to severe persecution by the Roman Catholic authorities, persecution which recurred in some quarters even after 1914. In spite of the lessening of the restraints in the nineteenth and twentieth centuries, Protestantism did not enjoy a large numerical growth and such increase as it displayed came partly through contagion from outside and with some exceptions was not purely indigenous. In contrast with the Middle Ages, when, notably in Italy and France, wave after wave of religious awakenings emerged which the Roman Catholic Church deemed heretical, no fresh movements of substantial dimensions akin to Protestantism but not out of its historic stream arose spontaneously in Latin Europe. The absence of such movements may have been due to the decline in religious conviction—evidence of the continued fading of historic religion—and perhaps to the absence of the rampant corruption in the Roman Catholic Church which had formerly stimulated revolt. Whatever the reasons for its minority status, the record of post-1914 Protestantism in Latin Europe must be compressed into a very few pages.

ITALY

The post-1914 strength of Protestantism in Italy was in the Waldensians, the Baptists, the Methodists, and the Pentecostals. The Waldensians traced their origin to Peter Waldo in the twelfth century. As the Protestant Reformation spread, through their proximity to Switzerland they adopted much from the Reformed branch of that movement. Severe and continued persecution drove their remnants into remote Alpine valleys, but in the revolutionary year of 1848 they were granted civil rights and, substituting Italian for French as their language, adopted a programme for the evangelization of Italy. By 1914 they had been officially recognized by the Italian Government (1891) as the *Chiesa Evangelica Italiana* (Italian Evangelical Church) and had congregations in several cities and theological seminaries (one of them in Rome almost under the shadow of the Vatican). Before 1914 Protestant churches had also arisen as the fruit of missions by English Wesleyans, American Methodists, and Southern (American) Baptists.[1]

The four and a half decades which followed 1914 brought an increase in religious liberty. In the Vatican treaties of 1929 between Mussolini and the Vatican, Protestant bodies were declared to be *i culti ammessi* ("admitted" or "permitted" cults). Some Protestant leaders regarded this as an advance over the previous toleration,[2] but others viewed it as reducing them to judicial inferiority.[3] The constitution of the republic which came into being after World War II and which went into effect January 1, 1948, while continuing the concordat of 1929 with its recognition of the special status of the Roman Catholic Church, also declared all faiths to be equally free before the law and said that they could form religious organizations. Struggles ensued to ensure the status accorded by the constitution, for some Roman Catholics presented determined opposition. However, by successive steps Protestants won government support for the implementation of what they regarded as their constitutional rights.[4]

In addition to the denominations represented in the nineteenth century, after 1914 other Protestant groups gained footholds in Italy. Among them were the Church of Christ, from the United States, the Seventh Day Adventists, the (Plymouth) Brethren, the Christian Scientists, the Salvation Army, and notably the Pentecostals, who were affiliated with the Assemblies of God, with headquarters in Springfield, Missouri. The Pentecostals seem to have sprung (about 1908) from emigrants who returned after a long stay in the United States. They were especially numerous in the South and Sicily, where economic and

---

[1] Volume II, pp. 218, 219.

[2] Keller, *Christian Europe Today*, pp. 30, 31.

[3] Leiper, *Christianity Today*, p. 79.

[4] Herman, *Report from Christian Europe*, pp. 101, 102; *The New York Times*, November 12, 1954.

social unrest associated with the poverty of those areas afforded fertile soil to a movement which here as elsewhere won adherents chiefly among the underprivileged and from lower educational and economic levels. In 1955 the Assemblies of God reported 399 groups, of which 365 were in Southern Italy.[5]

Advances were made towards closer coöperation among some of the Protestant bodies. In 1945 four—the Waldensians, the Baptists, the Methodists, and the Wesleyan Methodists—joined in forming the Federal Council of the Evangelical Churches in Italy.[6] The two Methodist bodies, that having its origin in aid from the Methodist Church in the United States and the Wesleyan Methodists, of British provenance, united.[7] After World War II a youth centre, Agape, sprang up in the northern mountains. It was begun by the Waldensians, but to the construction of its buildings youth from many lands and communions—Protestant and Roman Catholic—contributed labour and money. It was completed in 1952 and was used for international conferences—for Bible study and the discussion of social issues, and of various professional groups.[8] It resembled, with important variations, post-World War II Protestant centres which we have met in several countries and others of which we are to speak later. Help came to the Protestant churches in Italy in the form of relief after the destruction wrought in World War II. It was from several organizations.[9]

Accurate figures of the numerical strength of Protestantism in Italy were lacking. The government census of 1901 gave the totals as 65,595, that of 1911 as 123,253, and that of 1931 as 82,569. But the apparent sharp decline between 1911 and 1931 was said to have been due to a method of gathering data which in the latter year counted as Roman Catholics all who had been baptized in that church, even though they had later left it. An estimate made by a Protestant in the mid-1940's gave the total as about 350,000 and said that if it were made to include all those not yet in full communion but in active sympathy it would be approximately 500,000.[10]

From the Waldensian Church came a theologian who attracted attention beyond the borders of his country, Giovanni Miegge (1900——). Accepting much of the new orthodoxy, Miegge valued reason as well as grace and was inclined to believe the heart of revelation to be in the Synoptic Gospels. He dwelt on the central themes of Christianity in the light of the problems and difficulties of contemporary man. He was of the opinion that the current drift from Christianity in the erstwhile Christendom would continue but, far from

[5] Mario Miegge in *Background Information for Church and Society. Department of Church and Society, Division of Studies, World Council of Churches* (mimeographed, Geneva, Switzerland, June, 1956); Leiper, *op. cit.*, p. 74; Du Plessis, *A Brief History of Pentecostal Assemblies.*
[6] Leiper, *op. cit.*, pp. 78, 79.
[7] *Ibid.*
[8] Weber, *Signs of Renewal*, pp. 46–51.
[9] Leiper, *op. cit.*, pp. 77, 78.
[10] *Ibid.*, pp. 74, 75.

despairing, sought so to present the Gospel that its relevance to the revolution-ary age would be manifest.[11]

SPAIN

Protestantism in Spain suffered from the political vicissitudes of the post-1914 decades. In 1914 Protestants constituted a very small minority.[12] Nor did they increase much in the next fifteen years. Early in the 1930's they were said to total 6,259 communicants in 166 local churches with a community of about 22,000. Most of the congregations were small and much of the financial support came from abroad. Indigenous workers were only slightly more numerous than foreign missionaries.[13]

Then, from 1931 to 1936, Spain was a republic. In the main the government was anti-clerical and in principle religious liberty was granted. Under these favouring circumstances Protestantism grew. A national committee for evange-lism was formed, large public meetings were held to present the faith as Protes-tants understood it, and attendance at church services markedly increased. Protestant schools were opened and at least one was thronged. A Protestant became a member of the government and strove to create a network of schools to end illiteracy. Protestants availed themselves of the freedom of the press to print and circulate Bibles and other literature. A reaction which began in 1933 curtailed the freedom enjoyed in the preceding two years.

When, in 1936, civil war broke out, the opponents of the republic instituted persecutions of Protestants in the areas under their control. Many Protestants were imprisoned, exiled, or executed. In 1939 Franco gained full control of the country and the measures against Protestants were accentuated. The reasons given were as much political as religious, for Protestants were accused of sup-porting the republic. It was said that of the approximately 200 halls, churches, or rooms licensed for Protestant services 180 were closed and in the districts where they were located Protestants were forbidden to hold meetings, either publicly or in private. The circulation of Protestant literature, including Protes-tant translations of the Scriptures, was prohibited. In a few places, notably Seville and Madrid, Protestant churches were permitted to remain open. In the interval from 1933 to 1945 many Protestant meetings were secretly held and accessions of members were reported. Among them were at least some youths.

[11] See especially his *Christian Affirmations in a Secular Age,* translated by Stephen Neill from *Per Una Fide* (New York, Oxford University Press, 1958, pp. xiii, 170). Among other writings of Miegge were *The Virgin Mary: the Roman Catholic Marian Doctrine,* translated from the Italian by Waldo Smith (Philadelphia, The Westminster Press, 1955, pp. 196), and *L'Évangile et la Mythe dans la Pensée de Rudolf Bultmann,* translated by Hélène Naef from *L'Evangelo a il Mito* (Neu-châtel, Delachaux & Niestlé, 1958, pp. 130).

[12] Volume II, pp. 220, 221.

[13] C. Araujo Garcia and Kenneth G. Grubb, *Religion in the Republic of Spain* (London, World Dominion Press, 1933, pp. 109), pp. 83–92.

After Mussolini and Hitler, with whom he had sympathized, were eliminated (1945), Franco had 'the subservient Cortes pass a measure which gave a guarded recognition of human rights and which said that no one should be condemned on account of his religious convictions or the practice of divine worship in private. In October, 1945, the provincial governors were ordered to facilitate the re-opening of Protestant places of worship.[14] In 1952 the existence of 20,000 Protestants was admitted by the government, although formerly the number officially given by the state was 2,000.[15]

However, under the Franco regime severe restrictions were imposed on Protestantism. No Bibles issued by Protestants could be printed or imported—although some were circulated clandestinely. Protestant schools were closed. Some church buildings which had been constructed before 1936 were permitted, but even at private services police were present to see that nothing defamatory of the government was said. Protestant theological education, which flourished under the republic to render the churches independent of foreign clergy, for a time was forbidden and then was resumed under severe limitations.[16] Beginning in 1947 more drastic measures were adopted. In pastoral letters bishops, led by Cardinal Segura of Seville, protested the existence of Protestant chapels. As a result many chapels were closed and obstacles were placed in the way of opening those which had been closed. The Roman Catholic Church claimed all who had been baptized into it and sought to have the state declare null and void marriages of such persons under Protestant ceremonies. In 1955 the number of Protestant communicants was said to be about 10,000.[17] The efforts of the Roman Catholic hierarchy were directed towards keeping the country solidly of their faith, and while some Roman Catholics would have wished more religious freedom to be granted, the conservative integralists were in control.

PORTUGAL

Although a small minority, in the mid-twentieth century Protestants in Portugal constituted a larger percentage of the population than in Spain and were not subject to as severe persecution. In 1932 Protestant communicants were said to number 3,316 and the Protestant community was estimated as being about 10,000. Approximately a fifth were members of the Lusitanian

---

[14] Leiper, *op. cit.*, pp. 85–95; Hallström, *Secret Journey Through Spain*, pp. 18–20.

[15] Herman, *op. cit.*, p. 99.

[16] Hallström, *op. cit.*, pp. 38–42, 50–62.

[17] John David Hughey, *Religious Freedom in Spain, Its Ebb and Flow* (London, Carey Kingsgate Press, 1955, pp. vii, 211), pp. 138–164. For a report less favourable to Protestants and claiming that of the 25,000 Protestants about half were foreigners, see an official report by a government office, *The Situation of Protestantism in Spain* (Madrid, Diplomatic Information Office, 2nd ed., 1955, pp. 165, mimeographed), especially pp. 65–67. For an account of a trial arising from a Protestant marriage, see *The Christian Century*, Vol. LXXVI, pp. 1080, 1081 (September 23, 1959).

Church, a body with Anglican connexions, and not far from the same proportion were in the Evangelical Church of Portugal, a union of Presbyterians and Congregationalists. Protestants were chiefly from the middle-income strata rather than from the highly educated or the very poor.[18] Beginning in 1928 the government which came to power in 1926 had Antonio de Oliveira Salazar as its strongest man, first as finance minister and then as prime minister and dictator. Although he had once intended to study for the priesthood and had had as his room-mate in the university the later Cardinal-Patriarch of Lisbon, Salazar did not adopt restrictive measures against Protestants. One of his major objectives was the improvement of education—on the primary and secondary school level and among adults—and his programme of promoting popular literature included a life of Christ which, written by a Roman Catholic priest, was acceptable also to Protestants. The constitution of 1951 maintained the separation of Church and state and, while declaring the Roman Catholic religion to be that of the nation, did not prevent the guarantee of freedom of worship to other faiths. Except in a few remote rural districts, Protestants experienced no persecution. Although they were not permitted to have open-air meetings and only rarely could obtain permission to hold a public gathering in a religiously neutral hall, Protestants had full freedom of worship. In the 1950's the Pentecostals, introduced from Sweden in the 1930's, displayed a phenomenal growth, paralleling what was taking place in Italy and what we are to see in Brazil and some other countries in Latin America. In 1957 they were said to have about 3,000 communicants, more than a fourth of the estimated Protestant communicant membership (11,160). The next largest were the (Plymouth) Brethren, with approximately 2,000 communicants. *Simpatizantes,* who attended Protestant services more or less regularly, were estimated to total between 35,000 and 50,000.[19]

FRANCE

French Protestantism was augmented by the outcome of World War I. The restoration of Alsace-Lorraine (which had been ceded to Germany in 1871) brought under the Tricolour a substantial number of Reformed and Lutherans. They constituted about a fourth of French Protestantism after that year. The separation of Church and state effected in 1905 did not apply to Alsace-Lorraine, for at that time these provinces were not in France. After the change in political alignment the churches in them continued their connexion with the state. By the end of World War II those in France who were sufficiently aligned with Protestantism to conform to its baptismal, marriage, and burial

---

[18] Eduardo Moreira, *The Significance of Portugal: a Survey of Evangelical Progress* (London, World Dominion Press, 1933, pp. 71), pp. 41 ff.

[19] *World Dominion,* Vol. XXXV, pp. 235–238 (October, 1957).

rites totalled approximately 700,000 or 800,000. About 65 per cent. were Reformed, about 25 per cent. were Lutherans, and about 10 per cent. belonged to
groups who were not affiliated with the Protestant Federation of France
(formed in 1905). Protestants were widely scattered but were more numerous
than elsewhere in Alsace, the periphery of the Central Massif (West, South,
and South-east), and the region of Montbéliard, not far from the north-west
corner of Switzerland. They were also in some of the large cities. Many were
in places of importance in the government, education, and business.[20]

In the interval between World War I and World War II French Protestantism, like French Roman Catholicism, experienced a revival. More than before
it stressed the unity of the Biblical message with Christ as the centre. The
laity took a larger share in the life of the congregations than previously.[21]
Theological movements, including the influence of Barth, helped to heal the
divisions among the Reformed which had developed in the nineteenth century.[22] In the 1920's negotiations for the closing of the rift were initiated, early
in the 1930's a joint committee of the two main branches of the Reformed was
set up, and, after prolonged negotiations, in 1939 a union was achieved under
the name of the Reformed Church in France which included the overwhelming majority of the Reformed, the Methodists, and some of the Free Churches.
A minority of the Reformed, led by pastors who believed the purity of the
faith not to have been guaranteed by the formulas of the merger, kept aloof
and came together in the Union of Reformed Evangelical Independent
Churches.[23]

Shifts in population posed problems to Protestantism. In the nineteenth
century Protestants were predominantly in the rural areas. Towards the close
of that century a city-ward movement was noticeable and was accentuated as
the twentieth century progressed. Here was a phenomenon akin to what we
have found elsewhere. In France it meant that many nominal Protestants were
lost to their hereditary churches, so that in Paris in 1950 an estimated 50,000
had ceased to identify themselves with any church. The exodus to the cities
also brought the depletion of rural parishes, the closing of many, and the difficulty of giving adequate pastoral care to the scattered remnants.[24]

Various attempts were made to meet the situation. The McCall Mission,
begun in the nineteenth century to reach the de-Christianized urban proletariat,[25] shrank in the twentieth century.[26] As was true of the Roman Catholics,

20 Leiper, op. cit., pp. 3, 4; Evangelism in France, p. 12.
21 Leiper, op. cit., p. 5.
22 Volume II, p. 230.
23 Rouse and Neill, A History of the Ecumenical Movement, 1517–1948, pp. 464–466.
24 Evangelism in France, pp. 12, 45.
25 Volume II, p. 232.
26 Evangelism in France, pp. 8, 9.

when labourers in the factories were reached they tended to withdraw from that environment rather than to permeate it with Christian ideals.[27] Protestant churches were inclined to be bourgeois ghettos, characterized by a type of mind associated with the bourgeoisie and making difficult entrance of outsiders to church membership.[28] But through societies organized in the mid-nineteenth century both Reformed and Lutherans sought to win those outside the churches. After World War II, among other methods, use was made of the cinema, mass meetings, dramatic presentations through travelling theatrical teams, and colporteurs who circulated the Scriptures and other Christian literature, not only by going from door to door but also by being at fairs and markets where people were disposed to loiter, listen, and engage in conversation. In 1947 a special effort was put forth to reach the people of predominantly Roman Catholic Brittany, where Protestants were a tiny minority. Elsewhere stations for evangelism were opened in summer resorts and correspondence was carried on with isolated Protestants.[29] *Associations Familiales Protestantes,* founded in 1941 and ten years later having a membership of 20,000, sought through teams of from eight to ten families each to approach those alienated from the Church, to organize coöperatives, to found social service centres, and to bring together working-class and bourgeois elements.[30] The Protestant Professional Association strove to win the estranged intellectuals. *La Main Tendue* (The Outstretched Hand) also attempted to regain the de-Christianized.[31] Begun in 1935 by three young women who dedicated themselves to sharing the life of the most poverty-stricken masses in Paris, it spread and in 1949 became a recognized instrument of the Reformed Church.[32]

A response of French Protestant youth to the challenge of World War II was the *Comité Inter-Mouvements auprès des Evacués,* better known by its initials, CIMADE. It was organized in 1939, and the French Protestant youth organizations which were associated under the *Conseil Protestant de la Jeunesse* (C.P.J.) shared in it. It first (1939) aided the homeless Alsatians who had taken refuge in the South of France. Later it extended its activities to concentration camps in which other groups were confined, especially Jews, helped many to escape to neutral Switzerland, and saved others from deportation to Germany for extermination. After the war it established houses for displaced persons and for foreigners without identification papers. It also served in prison camps in which collaborators with the Germans were confined. CIMADE assisted and was assisted by other groups—the Quakers, *Secours*

[27] *Ibid.,* p. 10.
[28] *Ibid.,* pp. 25, 26.
[29] *Ibid.,* pp. 12–23.
[30] *Ibid.,* pp. 31, 32.
[31] Herman, *op. cit.,* p. 21.
[32] *Ibid.,* p. 71; Bishop, *France Alive,* pp. 188–190.

Suisse, the World Council of Churches, and Jewish organizations.[33]

In the 1950's French Protestants created centres somewhat akin to the Evangelical Academies and for the purpose of enlisting the laity—a phase of the lay movement in the Roman Catholic Church and Protestantism. In 1952 one was begun near Paris for preparing church members for service, especially through correspondence courses. Monthly laymen's days were arranged in some districts. The year 1953 saw the opening of a centre in Gary, a small industrial town in the Montbéliard district. It learned much from Bad Boll. The next year a group founded the community of Villemétrie in a manor house about forty miles from Paris in which it arranged for small gatherings of men influential in various lay occupations.[34]

A striking development, not large numerically but unique and widely heralded, was the Taizé Community. Its centre was in Taizé, a rural village between Lyons and Dijon, not far from Switzerland. It had its inception in 1939 through Roger Schutz, a young theologian, a member of the Swiss Student Christian Movement. Having harboured in Taizé some Jews and other political refugees, to escape the Nazi police he went to Geneva and was joined by another theologian and an engineer. When peace came, they returned to Taizé and, their numbers slightly augmented, undertook the rebuilding of the village, then in ruins, and restored a twelfth-century church erected by Cluny monks. In 1947 the first seven took life vows. A rule was developed which was put into writing in 1952. It included celibacy, the community of property, and obedience to the community. The members were drawn from more than one Protestant confession. At Taizé the public worship was designed to restore to Protestantism the pre-Reformation liturgical treasures of the Church and gladly learned from the Liturgical Movement in the Roman Catholic Church. All the brothers engaged in some form of labour—several with their hands in Taizé, one as a physician for the village and its neighbourhood, a few as artists (in pottery and painting), others as pastors of parishes, one in youth work in Africa, and still others in a centre in the Ruhr where they did heavy industrial work. The community published a quarterly theological and ecclesiastical review (Verbum Caro). It had as an ideal the expression of the Christian life not only in worship but also in day-by-day participation in the work of the world. It sought to take the Gospel seriously and let it speak to men living in the world. Each brother was to do what he believed Christ would have him do in the vocation which He had chosen for him. Close contact was maintained with the World Council of Churches and the World's Student Christian Federation. Fellowship was also sought with Roman Catholics in an effort to

[33] Bishop, op. cit., pp. 183–188.
[34] Weber, op. cit., pp. 36–38.

bridge the gap between the two great branches of the Church.[35] In 1959 the community had forty members. They were from Calvinist and Lutheran backgrounds in France, Switzerland, the Netherlands, and Germany. Some were lay and some ordained. Their rule stressed interior silence, meditation on the beatitudes, and prayer three times a day, accenting intercession for the Church and the world. The community had among its concerns the renewal and unity of the Church. Brothers were living in such centres of tension and need as the Ivory Coast, among the Moslems in Algeria, and with the working classes in Marseilles.[36]

By some Roman Catholics friendly Protestant advances were met more than halfway and even anticipated. Thus following the tradition of Paul Couturier with its centre in Lyons, the priests' weekly *La Semaine Religieuse* of that city urged their fellow Roman Catholics to join in prayer with Protestants in the latters' celebration of the four hundredth anniversary of the inception of the French Reformed Church. It thanked God that the celebration was "in the climate of mutual respect, positive charity, and sincere humility which everywhere gradually enfolds Christians seized with the hope of the full unity in love and truth."[37] Whether consciously or without design, Protestant organizations such as the *Associations Familiales Protestantes* and the *Conseil Protestant de la Jeunesse* paralleled movements within the Roman Catholic Church.

Something of a movement of Roman Catholic priests into Protestantism was seen. In 1960 more than forty were said to be ministers or lay members in the French Reformed Church, twelve were reported to be in other Protestant churches, and several had entered the Old Catholic and Orthodox Churches. A group of ex-priests meeting in April, 1960, estimated the number of priests leaving the Roman Catholic Church in France since World War II to be more than a thousand; they believed that even more had left it in Italy and a smaller number in Spain. Former priests in the French Reformed Church organized to aid those leaving the Church of Rome in France or seeking haven there from Italy and Spain.[38]

In proportion to their numerical strength French Protestants, with the exception of Belgium and Norway, had a larger share in the spread of the faith outside the Occident than had Protestants of any other country on the Continent of Europe. In 1956 they were said to have 350 missionaries, but of these about 100 were not of French nationality.[39]

[35] W. S. Taylor in *Theology Today*, Vol. XV, pp. 488–506; Bishop, *op. cit.*, pp. 175–183.
[36] *Ecumenical Press Service*, November 20, 1959.
[37] *Ibid.*
[38] *Ecumenical Press Service*, April 15, 1960.
[39] *Occasional Bulletin from the Missionary Research Library*, December 8, 1958, p. 29.

BELGIUM

Protestants constituted a small minority in Belgium, approximately 100,000 in 1950. In proportion to the population they were about half as numerous as in France but more numerous than in Italy, Spain, or Portugal. We have seen that they were encouraged by the constitution of 1830, which granted liberty of worship, teaching, the press, and association, and that one body, the *Union des Églises Protestantes Evangéliques de Belgique,* or, in the Fleming section of the nation, the *Belgische Nationaal Protestante Kerk,* was given financial support by the state.[40] It was Reformed in its theology and structure and many of its ministers were of Dutch origin. In 1950 it opened a theological seminary with aid from the Netherlands Reformed Church (*Nederlandse Hervormde Kerk*). A free church, somewhat smaller, was formed in the nineteenth century primarily to spread the Gospel among labourers and miners and won many from the Roman Catholic Church. It was known as the *Église Chrétienne Missionnaire Belge* or the *Belgisch Christelijke Zendingskerk.* After World War I the conservative *Gereformeerde Kerk* of the Netherlands created a few congregations. Early in the 1950's the liberals among the intellectuals had the *Église Protestante Libérale,* and a few Methodist and Baptist congregations added to the variety of the ecclesiastical scene.[41] In 1958 at least sixty-one missionaries were sent to other countries by the Protestant minority—proportionately to the numbers of Protestants more than from any other country on the Continent of Europe.[42] This paralleled what was being done in foreign missions by Belgian Roman Catholics and in proportion to the numbers of the two branches of the faith in Belgium quite equalled the latter.

SUMMARY

In that portion of Western Europe where was the historic main centre of the strength and life of the Roman Catholic Church, in the four and a half decades after 1914, Protestantism, although still represented only by minorities, in most countries grew both in vitality and in numbers. Some of the increase was through contacts with Protestantism outside Latin Europe, but some sprang from the Protestant bodies already in existence. In Italy the major numerical expansion was through Pentecostalism, mostly among the economically and socially underprivileged in the South and in Sicily and at the outset largely through leaders of Italian birth and ancestry who came from the United States. The indigenous Protestantism, that of the Waldensians, grew slowly and produced at least one notable theologian. In Spain Protestantism attracted friendly interest among hundreds during the brief years of the Republic, but

40 Volume II, pp. 235, 236.
41 *Twentieth Century Encyclopedia of Religious Knowledge,* Vol. I, p. 122.
42 *Occasional Bulletin from the Missionary Research Library,* December 8, 1959, p. 29.

the civil war and the reaction under Franco gave conservative elements in the Roman Catholic Church the opportunity to renew the persecution through which, beginning in the sixteenth century, they had endeavoured to hold the country solidly to their faith. Spanish Protestantism depended for its existence upon continuing transfusions from abroad. In Portugal under the Salazar regime Protestantism suffered little persecution and grew, mainly through the missions of Swedish Pentecostals. French Protestantism, which, with the cessation in the nineteenth century through secular liberalism of the persecution that had long reduced its numbers, had revived, in the post-1914 years augmented by the restoration of Alsace-Lorraine, displayed marked vigour. As in many other countries and in both Roman Catholicism and Protestantism, many classed with the latter in France were only nominally of that heritage. Yet among the actively loyal old movements were revived, some nineteenth-century divisions were healed, and new movements arose. Several of the latter had as their purpose reaching the de-Christianized. In spite of the impoverishment and disruption wrought by the disasters in the two world wars, efforts were made to win the mounting urban population, to serve the sufferers of the wars, to deepen the interior life, and to contribute to the world mission of the Church. In Belgium the Protestant minorities grew, partly through contagion with larger Protestant groups in neighbouring countries.

CHAPTER XVI

Protestantism in Holland
(The Kingdom of the Netherlands)

W HAT was the course of Protestantism in the Netherlands in the decades
after 1914? We have earlier summarized the developments in the nineteenth century.[1] We have noted that Protestants were in the large majority
in the North and constituted more than half the population of the country.
We saw that the main branches were the Netherlands Reformed Church (*De
Nederlandse Hervormde Kerk*), by far the largest; the Reformed Churches
in the Netherlands (*De Gereformeerde Kerken in Nederland*), representing
a conservative reaction against what they deemed the departure of the former
from true doctrine and with a membership about a fifth as numerous as the
older body; a still more conservative and much smaller group, the Christian
Reformed (*De Christelijke Gereformeerde Kerken*), whose members had refused on theological grounds to enter into the union represented by the
Gereformeerde Kerken; the Remonstrants, going back to the theological controversies of the seventeenth century and extremely liberal theologically; two
branches of the Lutherans; the Mennonites; and some other minorities.

The currents of the revolutionary age played on all these forms of Protestantism—the intellectual ferment, industrialization, the growth of cities, socialism,
and war. An agricultural, industrial, and commercial people, the Dutch presented a variegated economic and social picture. With a high standard of
education and on the whole prosperous, near the centre of the erstwhile Western Christendom, they felt to the full the forces which were impinging upon
that portion of mankind. In World War I they managed to preserve their
neutrality but could not remain completely aloof from the storm raging on
their borders. In World War II their country was occupied by the Germans
(May, 1940) before the end of the first year and they were subjected to the
anti-Jewish and other measures imposed by the Nazis. As a consequence of

[1] Volume II, pp. 237–251.

World War II and the recession of the tide of Western European imperialism, they lost their chief colonial possession, Indonesia.

An obvious early result of the revolutionary age was the mounting secularism. It was reflected in the increasing percentage of the population who declared themselves dissociated from any religion. In 1909 it was 4.97, in 1920 it had grown to 7.77, and in 1930 it was 14.42. The chief sufferer from the loss appears to have been the Netherlands Reformed Church, for the proportion of its membership to the population of the country fell from 44.18 per cent. in 1909, to 41.17 per cent. in 1920, and to 34.43 per cent. in 1930, a decrease almost exactly paralleling the increase of those who described themselves as "without religion." The decline was even more marked when compared with the mid-nineteenth century. In 1859 the Netherlands Reformed Church embraced over half—54.94 per cent.—of the population. However, the loss between 1859 and 1909 was to be attributed not so much to an increase in secularism as to the separation of the elements which followed Kuyper into the *Gereformeerde Kerken*. The falling off may have been more apparent than real and due more to a desire to escape the church tax levied through the state for the support of churches officially recognized than to the advance of secularization. At least it was proof of a lack of commitment to the faith. In the twenty-one-year interval between 1909 and 1930 the Netherlands Reformed Church registered an increase of about 5 per cent. in its membership, even though its share in the total population decreased. In that same period the number of Lutherans sharply declined, the Christian Reformed and the Mennonites fell off, although less markedly, the Remonstrants showed a slight increase, the *Gereformeerde Kerken* increased by about a fourth but included a progressively slightly smaller percentage of the total population (8.42 in 1909, 8.33 in 1920, and 8.04 in 1930), and the Roman Catholics grew by a third (from 2,053,021 in 1909 to 2,444,583 in 1920 and to 2,850,022 in 1930) and percentagewise to the total population showed a slight increase (from 35.02 in 1909 to 35.61 in 1920 and 36.42 in 1930).[2] The favourable Roman Catholic record appears to have been due more to a high birth rate than to conversions.

The increase of those who were unaffiliated with organized religion, largely from the nominal adherents of what might be called the folk church of the Netherlands, must not be interpreted as due to a lack of vitality in that body. The Netherlands Reformed Church embraced many schools of theological thought, in themselves indications of vigour. The leaders recognized the danger of additional schisms and in the 1920's and the 1930's devised measures for preserving a unified ecclesiastical structure which permitted diversity.[3]

The creative vitality in Dutch Protestantism in the years of and following

[2] Siegmund-Schultze, *Die evangelischen Kirchen der Niederlande*, pp. 6, 100.
[3] *Ibid.*, pp. 42–44.

World War I made itself felt in several other ways. Two somewhat different examples may be regarded as typical. In 1917 the Mennonites began holding annual gatherings, and in 1924 an organization (*Algemene Doopsgezinde Societeit*) was formed which brought into continuing coöperation a denomination made up of congregations historically accustomed to individual autonomy.[4] A leader of the Dutch Student Christian Movement, which came into being in 1896 through contagion with the World's Student Christian Federation, reported that, in contrast with the 1890's when professors and students in the universities were almost entirely alienated from the Church, by the 1930's a substantial number among both groups were outspokenly Christian. The membership was originally chiefly from the theological faculties, but the Movement eventually gained rootage in all the other faculties. It had groups in the several universities and through study circles and conferences both deepened the faith of its members and gave them a sense of unity in reaching out to draw others into its fellowship.[5] Efforts were made, increasingly successful, to enlist and train youth, not only in the universities but also outside them. Several national organizations of Protestant youth were formed and prospered.[6] Labour unions existed on a Christian basis. In 1932 the largest was Roman Catholic, but one, nominally inter-confessional but predominantly Protestant, also enrolled several scores of thousands. In that year the Roman Catholic and Protestant movements had 37.11 per cent. and the Social Democrats and Communist bodies, based upon the principle of class warfare, had 41.62 per cent. of organized labour.[7] In the lower house of parliament in the early 1930's out of the one hundred members the Roman Catholic and Protestant parties had fifty-seven, or more than half.[8]

THE CHURCH RISES TO THE CHALLENGE OF WORLD WAR II

World War II, bringing with it occupation by the Nazis, presented a challenge to the Church in the Netherlands. Within a few days after the German invasion, the Dutch army was cut to pieces, the queen and her government took refuge in England, and the land seemed prostrate. By the end of 1944 the suffering was said to be greater than in any other country in Western Europe. The reduction of food rations brought near starvation, fuel was lacking, many public systems of water supply had been destroyed, partly because of the resistance movement railroads had ceased to run, about a hundred thousand Jews were murdered in concentration camps, and thousands of men

[4] *Ibid.*, p. 77.
[5] *Ibid.*, pp. 102–107.
[6] *Ibid.*, pp. 110–117.
[7] *Ibid.*, p. 129.
[8] *Ibid.*, pp. 131, 132.

had been deported for forced labour in Germany.[9] We have seen the fashion in which the Roman Catholic Church rose to the challenge. The Protestant churches were not behind in their response. Indeed, they slightly anticipated the Roman Catholics. In spite of the indications of vitality to which we have called attention and the good work being done by many pastors, it was said that in the 1930's the Netherlands Reformed Church was "without spiritual leadership and without a voice," a bureaucratic organization "without a clear message or purpose," "pastor-centred . . . often theologically divided, very bourgeois," and with a decreasing influence in the country.[10] Yet it and the other Protestant bodies soon demonstrated that they were far from dead or even supine. As in Norway, the Church became a sturdy centre of resistance. An outstanding leader was Koens H. E. Gravemeyer, secretary of the General Synod of the Netherlands Reformed Church. In the early autumn of 1940 the General Assembly of the Netherlands Reformed Church came out with a public confession of Christian faith in regard to the people and the state.[11]

Because of their outspoken denunciation of the measures of the Nazis, many of the pastors were imprisoned or put in concentration camps. To maintain the continuing life of the congregations laymen came forward and thus prepared the way for the active part which they were to take in the post-war years.[12]

As the months wore on, Protestants increased their protests against actions of the German masters. In October, 1940, representatives of the Netherlands Reformed Church, the Christian Reformed Churches, and the Remonstrants spoke out against the Nazi government on its removal of Jews from the civil service.[13] The following March these bodies, with the addition of the Reformed Churches and one of the Lutheran bodies, again raised their voices against the anti-Jewish measures, the deterioration of public life, and the attacks upon liberties which were necessary for the fulfilment of the obligations of a Christian.[14] That same year the Netherlands Reformed Church circulated throughout its membership a confession of faith which in addition to positive affirmations emphatically rejected the belief associated with the Nazis that the voice of the race is the voice of God, denounced anti-Semitism as "one of the most stubborn and deadly forms of rebellion against the holy and merciful God Whose Name we confess," repudiated as "sinful idolatry which results in the most hideous tyranny that something or someone can in a total sense be 'Lord' over us or a total power over us," branded as "a fatal error . . . that

[9] A. L. Warnshuis, *The Church's Battle for Europe's Soul* (New York, American Committee for the World Council of Churches, 1945, pp. 36), pp. 11, 12.
[10] Boas, *Resistance of the Churches in the Netherlands*, p. 12.
[11] *Ibid.*, p. 22.
[12] *Ibid.*, p. 38.
[13] *Ibid.*, p. 70.
[14] *Ibid.*, pp. 71, 72.

it is proper to speak of a 'rebirth' of the Dutch people where the introduction of a new ideology is concerned, which can only divert us from the Holy Spirit," maintained that no one "has the right to set limits to the freedom of the preaching of the Gospel or to the freedom of obedience to it," insisted that no authority could "lay claim to any young person before his majority," and labelled "as anti-Christian doctrine that all things must be subordinated to the welfare of the nation" or that the state has "the right to make demands that are in conflict with the commandments of Christ" or can "be an absolute authority over the citizen."[15] On January 5, 1942, Protestants and Roman Catholics in a joint memorandum protested arrests without stated charges, imprisonment without a hearing, confinement in camps or elsewhere for an undetermined duration without due process of law and without a conviction, the treatment of the Jews, and the imposition of National Socialist ideology upon the Dutch people as a whole.[16] On February 21, 1943, in separate documents the Roman Catholic bishops and the Netherlands Reformed Church simultaneously spoke out against the persecution and execution of Jews, the forced labour of Dutch workers in Germany, the killing of hostages, the imprisonment of Church officials, and the alarming death rate in the concentration camps.[17] The following May the General Synod of the Netherlands Reformed Church lamented the deportations and forced labour which had continued and called for prayer. On the same day the Roman Catholic bishops issued a pastoral letter to much the same effect.[18] Also on the same day (May 21, 1943) the Roman Catholic archbishop and the heads of most of the Protestant bodies spoke out against the sterilization of the husband and wife in mixed marriages of Jews and Christians.[19]

RENEWED VIGOUR AFTER WORLD WAR II

The shock administered by the German occupation and the fashion in which the Protestant bodies rose to the challenge were followed by a renewed vigour which had continuing manifestations after the coming of peace. In contrast to some other countries where the revival of religion during the war proved to be temporary, the leadership of the Netherlands Reformed Church became aware that a large proportion of its traditional constituency had been lost and took measures to put its house in order and if possible to win them back, or at least to make itself felt more effectively in the life of the nation.[20] Plans towards

[15] *Ibid.*, pp. 82–87.
[16] *Ibid.*, pp. 88, 89.
[17] *Ibid.*, pp. 89–93.
[18] *Ibid.*, pp. 93–96.
[19] *Ibid.*, pp. 96, 97.
[20] Herman, *Report from Christian Europe*, p. 24.

that end were developed in part in the concentration camps during the war. There pastors had the leisure for discussion and for joint thought on how to better the structure and work of the Church. They were also thrown into intimate contact with fellow prisoners who were active in political life and in labour organizations.

An important early development was the creation of a new General Synod which gave to the Netherlands Reformed Church a more effective structure than it had possessed. Steps in this direction had been taken, mainly in the first decades of the twentieth century, but the opportunity afforded by the war and the obvious need for a better organization brought about the consummation for which many had hoped.[21] The new structure, put into full operation in 1951, eliminated weaknesses which had handicapped the church. It brought in representatives of the laity and ensured an abler clerical participation. It dealt not only with doctrine but also with action and brought into the heart of the church's concern and organization home and foreign missions, church extension, and efforts to reach the de-Christianized. To facilitate better pastoral care it divided some of the larger parishes. In contrast with the other Protestant bodies the Netherlands Reformed Church sought to be the church for the entire nation—corresponding to the *Landeskirchen* in Germany, the state churches of Scandinavia and England, and the Church of Scotland.[22] That the new organization gave to the Netherlands Reformed Church an instrument for a united voice was seen in the measures taken in the next ten years through the General Synod and its committees and commissions. Such varied issues were dealt with as the thorny problems posed by the successful struggle of Indonesia for independence, Communism, pastoral relations to matrimony, the Church and culture, the Church and the state, the Church and social questions, international relations, colonial problems, the Church and labour, and the Church and the farmers. In 1946 Egbert Emmen became general secretary of the Netherlands Reformed Church and under his leadership not only were these actions taken but ecumenical contacts with churches in other countries were fostered.[23]

For a time the coöperation between the various Protestant bodies and the Roman Catholic Church that had been a feature of the occupation years continued. Almost all joined in a statement of policy towards those who had coöperated with National Socialism during the Nazi period.[24] However, basic

---

[21] For a summary of the history beginning with the General Synod of 1816 to the eve of the General Synod of 1945 see A. J. Bronkhorst, *Op Weg naar een Nieuwe Kerkorde. De Beteekenis van de komende Generale Synode voor de Nederlandsch Hervormde Kerk* (Amsterdam, W. Ten Have N.V., 1945, pp. 80), *passim.*

[22] Count S. C. van Randwijck to the author, July 16, 1952.

[23] *Documenten Nederlandse Hervormde Kerk . . . 1945-1955, passim.*

[24] *Ibid.,* pp. 46–50.

differences could not long be glossed over. In 1950 the General Synod authorized a statement that had been formulated through months of work by a specially appointed commission which stated frankly its position on controversial features of Roman Catholic belief and practice such as Mariology, revelation, the Scriptures, justification, grace, the sacraments, the position and function of the clergy, the place of Peter and the authority of the Pope as his alleged successor, apostolic succession, works, relation to social questions, and the attitude towards the Reformation. No ground was left for compromise. The statement was not entirely unfriendly and thanked God that He had not forsaken the Roman Catholic Church. It noted gratefully the appreciation of the Gospel by Roman Catholics, especially in France and Germany, the study of the Bible by them, the Liturgical Movement, and the deep devotion of many Roman Catholics, but it recalled that some of the Popes had condemned the Protestant Bible societies and saw no possibility of Christian unity on Roman Catholic premises. Yet it expressed the hope that through the power of the Holy Spirit the unity of Christians, now seemingly unattainable, would sometime be achieved.[25] Moreover, informal conversations continued between Roman Catholics and Protestants.

A similar reëmphasis on distinctive convictions and corporate life characterized the relations between the various Protestant bodies and partly nullified the steps towards unity which had been taken in face of the menace confronting all Christians during the German occupation. To be sure, a council of churches existed (the Ecumenical Council of Churches in the Netherlands). It was formed in 1935 to combine the Life and Work and Faith and Order interests and in 1946 its organization and doctrine were brought into conformity with those of the World Council of Churches. But the second largest Reformed body, *De Gereformeerde Kerken in Nederland,* was not a member and the Council embraced only about three-fourths of the Protestants of the country.[26] Each Protestant church, like the Roman Catholic Church, had its own newspaper, its own schools (they received financial aid from the state), and a tendency to develop its distinct community life. Many Protestants and Roman Catholics deplored the barriers but did not succeed in removing them.[27] In 1944 a fresh division was added to those inherited from pre-1914 days. About a fourth of the congregations and slightly over a third of the clergy of *De Gereformeerde Kerken in Nederland* withdrew in 1944 and formed *De Gereformeerde Kerkonderhovdende Art. 31 k.o.* (the Reformed Adhering to Article

[25] *Ibid.,* pp. 129–197.

[26] Rouse and Neill, *A History of the Ecumenical Movement, 1517–1948,* pp. 627, 628.

[27] Paul Minear, from residence in the Netherlands in 1958–1959, to the author, December 8, 1959.

XXXI of the Church-order of Dordrecht). The issue was over the federal theology.[28]

An encouraging development arising from the impetus given by World War II was provision for the better preparation of the clergy of the Netherlands Reformed Church. Heretofore they had received their training exclusively in the theological faculties of the unversities supported by the state, which stressed theology, the Bible, and Church history. Now an institution was created in Driebergen, near Utrecht. To supplement his university course, every graduate of a university who planned to go into the parish ministry was required to attend it for several months before ordination. Through informal small groups in which students lived on intimate terms with the rector and teachers and by discussions which lasted from morning to night the prospective pastors were prepared for their duties and were counselled in their personal and devotional life. At first experimental, the seminary so proved its usefulness that it became an official and permanent part of the Netherlands Reformed Church's programme.[29]

A continuing and mounting movement which had been given encouragement during the occupation was the prominence of the laity in the Protestant churches. Here a parallel was seen to what was taking place in the Roman Catholic Church and in some other countries in Protestantism. One evidence was the attention given the laity by one of the outstanding leaders of the Netherlands Reformed Church, Hendrik Kraemer.[30]

Intimately related to the enlistment and training of the laity was *Kerk en Wereld*. This, too, began at Driebergen, in the autumn of 1945. Its founder was a former YMCA secretary who while in a concentration camp had dreamed of enlisting the laity and training them in theology and methods of evangelism. Conferences were held on a variety of subjects and *Wikas*—youth workers and social workers—were trained for leadership in social and cultural relations and for the promotion of good relations in industry. Meetings were held for lay people who were prominent in law, industry, or other occupations and professions. Some of the gatherings were for more than a few days and were for spiritual refreshment as well as discussion of the bearing of the Christian faith on problems pertinent to those in attendance. Driebergen also became a centre for international work camps. The latter were not peculiar to the Netherlands but were a post-World War II development and were found in many countries under Protestant auspices. They brought together small groups

[28] *Twentieth Century Encyclopedia of Religious Knowledge,* Vol. I, p. 522. On the federal theology, see Vol. I, pp. 81, 82.
[29] Paul Minear to the author, December 8, 1959.
[30] See, for example, Hendrik Kraemer, *A Theology of the Laity* (Philadelphia, The Westminster Press, 1958, pp. 192), *passim.*

from different countries to help by manual labour much needed re-building or fresh construction, and in the intimate fellowship in living, work, and worship they contributed to a realization of Christian community. In the 1950's several centres similar to that in Driebergen were opened in various parts of the country. One, in the North-east, specialized on the problems of the rapidly changing rural life. Another, in an old castle, concerned itself mainly with European problems and was the host to annual summer ecumenical European youth conferences. To coördinate the various centres the Federation of Lay Training Centres in Holland was organized. Aid was received from the government but care was taken that it did not entail control by the state. The leaders sought to delve into the theological and sociological issues pertinent to their work. Attention was also given to such forms of group activity as socio-drama, story-mime, handicrafts, and the presentation of original plays.[31] *Kerk en Wereld* was chiefly maintained by the Netherlands Reformed Church but was not confined exclusively to that body. Here was an unusually creative phase of the movement which we have found in Germany, Scandinavia, Finland, and Switzerland, akin to Catholic Action and the "century of the laity" in the Roman Catholic Church. The *Kirchentag* which originated in Germany was the inspiration for regional *Kerkdagen,* on a smaller scale than in Germany.[32]

Partly as a result of these various developments and partly as an accompaniment of the high general level of education in the Netherlands, in the 1950's a fairly large proportion of the laity were deeply interested and well informed on theological questions. They could listen intelligently to preaching with a solid theological content and to expository sermons centred on the Bible.[33]

In the extensive lands which were being reclaimed from the Zuider Zee in the 1950's systematic plans were being carried through to erect churches to care for the population that was moving in to cultivate them. Care was taken to keep the proportion of Roman Catholics and Protestants the same as in the country as a whole.[34] Many of the churches destroyed in World War I were rebuilt. In the 1950's various denominations were erecting churches, some of them in radically new architecture, in the rapidly growing suburbs of Amsterdam.[35] Fresh experiments were being made in reaching the urban population, especially after the destruction in World War II had made possible new methods.[36]

[31] Weber, *Signs of Renewal,* pp. 31–34; *The Christian Century,* Vol. LXXVL, pp. 289, 290 (March 11, 1959).
[32] W. F. Dankbaar to the author, February 29, 1960.
[33] Paul Minear to the author, December 8, 1959.
[34] *Ibid.*
[35] *The Christian Century,* Vol. LXXV, pp. 1300, 1301 (November 12, 1959).
[36] *A Monthly Letter about Evangelism,* January, 1958.

Dutch Protestants were aware of the currents of the revolutionary age which were sweeping across the country. In addition to what was being done through *Kerk en Wereld* they were making significant efforts at industrial evangelism —the winning of alienated workers in the factories and related enterprises.[37] Protestants were promoting social welfare. Like the Roman Catholics, they were active in forming organizations of labourers. The *Christelijk Nationaal Vakverbond* (C.N.V.) (Christian National Labour Union) was part of an inter-confessional international federation which included both Roman Catholics and Protestants. In 1910 the Lutherans organized a strictly confessional association for social action.[38]

THEOLOGICAL AND BIBLICAL STUDIES

Dutch Protestants were displaying much and varied activity in seeking to meet the intellectual currents of the revolutionary age. The Remonstrants appear not to have shared greatly in it. The Reformed Churches (*Gereformeerde Kerken*) showed marked vigour, chiefly within the bounds of the revived Calvinism which had characterized them in the nineteenth century. They sought to translate into contemporary terms what they believed Calvinism had to say to the men of their day.[39] Barth was widely read but was not always accepted. The Reformed and Christian Reformed Churches, for example, regarded him as deviating from true Calvinism.

One of the most prolific of the theologians was Gerrit Cornelis Berkovwer (1903——) of the *Gereformeerde Kerken;* some of his books were translated into English.[40] He noted that emphases in theology had changed from time to time and tended to reflect the attitude of the age in which they were evolved. He valued Barth but believed him to have over-stressed grace to the neglect of man's part in faith. Yet he also said that faith is the gift of God and that to give man credit for it would make for works righteousness. Perseverance, he held, depended on preservation by God. Gerardus van der Leeuw (1890–1950) of the Groningen faculty specialized on the phenomenology of religion and traced its development from primitive forms through the great historic re-

---

[37] *The Christian Century*, Vol. LXXV, pp. 1300, 1301 (November 12, 1958).

[38] Hagoort, *De Christelijke-Sociale Beweging*, pp. 5–8; Gestel, *Het Religieus-Socialisme*, pp. 226 ff., 243 ff., 253 ff., 281 ff.

[39] See a description of trends in *Gordon Review*, May, 1955, pp. 57 ff.

[40] See, for example, his *Faith and Justification* (Grand Rapids, Mich., W. B. Eerdmans Publishing Co., 1954, pp. 207); *Faith and Perseverance* (Grand Rapids, Mich., W. B. Eerdmans Publishing Co., 1958, pp. 256); *General Revelation* (Grand Rapids, Mich., W. B. Eerdmans Publishing Co., 1955, pp. 336); *The Person of Christ* (Grand Rapids, Mich., W. B. Eerdmans Publishing Co., 1954, pp. 368); *De Triomf der Genade in de Theologie van Karl Barth* (Kampen, J. H. Kok, 1954, pp. 397), translated by Harry Boer and published in the United States by W. B. Eerdmans Publishing Co., 1956, pp. 414.

ligions culminating in Christianity.[41] His treatment was purely factual and objective. That, indeed, was his approach in his *Introduction to Theology*.[42] Yet he was prominent in a liturgical movement in the Netherlands Reformed Church.[43] Arnold Albert van Ruler (1908———) in a large work reflected a current interest when he dealt with the relation of revelation to existence.[44] Jan Nicolaas Sevenster and Gerhard Sevenster specialized on the New Testament. In Church history Hendrik Berkhof had a widely used survey.[45] Other outstanding theologians were Theodor Haitjema (1888———), Oepke Noordmans (1871–1956), Kornelis Heiko Mickotte (1894———), and Gerard C. van Nifbuk (1904———). Jan Nicolaas Bakhuizen van der Brink (1896———) was noted as a Church historian.

The world mission of the Church was the chief interest of Hendrik Kraemer (1888———). He had been a missionary in Indonesia, was a specialist in the religions of the world and was on the Leiden faculty when the German invasion for a time diverted him. He was a leader in the resistance, was imprisoned, then became outstanding in the Ecumenical Movement, especially as the head of the Ecumenical Institute near Geneva, and lectured in many countries. His first widely read book was written for the International Missionary Council and was a forthright presentation of the uniqueness and validity of the Christian Gospel in contrast with the non-Christian religions.[46] A later book returned to the same theme and with the same convictions, but from a slightly different angle.[47]

The Share in the World Mission

In spite of the outstanding share of Kraemer in formulating a Protestant theology of missions, the Protestants of the Netherlands did not increase the personnel which represented them among non-Occidental peoples as rapidly as did their Roman Catholic fellow countrymen. Although a larger proportion of the population than the Roman Catholics, in 1956 Dutch Protestants had only about six hundred missionaries in other countries.[48] In relation to their

[41] See his *Phänomenologie der Religion* (Tübingen, J. C. B. Mohr, 1956, pp. xii, 808), translated by J. E. Turner as *Religion in Essence and Manifestation, a Study of Phenomenology* (London, G. Allen and Unwin, 1938, pp. 709).

[42] *Inleiding tot de Theologie* (Amsterdam, H. J. Paris, 2nd ed., 1948, pp. 274).

[43] Bogler, *Liturgische Erneuerung in aller Welt*, p. 43.

[44] Arnold Albert van Ruler, *De Vervulling van de Wet; een Dogmatische Studie over de Verhouding van Openbaring en Existentie* (Groningen, pp. 539).

[45] Hendrik Berkhof, *Geschiedenis der Kerk* (Nijkerk, G. F. Callenbach, 3rd ed., 1946, pp. 356).

[46] Hendrik Kraemer, *The Christian Message in a Non-Christian World* (New York, International Missionary Council, 1938, pp. xviii, 458).

[47] Hendrik Kraemer, *Religion and the Christian Faith* (Philadelphia, The Westminster Press, 1957, pp. 461). On Kraemer see A. Th. van Leeuwen, *Hendrik Kraemer, Dienaar der Wereldkerk* (Amsterdam, W. Ten Have N.V., 1959, pp. 174).

[48] *Occasional Bulletin from the Missionary Research Library*, December 8, 1958.

numerical strength this was a smaller number than were sent by the Protestants of Norway, Switzerland, or France. The seeming lack of missionary dynamic was to be ascribed to the fact that Dutch Protestants had long concentrated most of their overseas effort on the Netherlands East Indies, where they were faced with teeming peoples in a vast area under the Dutch flag. World War II and its aftermath forced most of the Dutch, including missionaries, out of that archipelago. In contrast, Dutch Roman Catholics had not centred their missionary efforts so exclusively on those islands but were represented in several other parts of the world, and the Norwegian, Swiss, and French Protestant missions had been directed to countries where the changing political situation was not so adverse.

SUMMARY

Like the Roman Catholic Church, the Protestant bodies in the Netherlands were subjected to unusual stresses in the forty-five years which began with the outbreak of World War I. In addition to the revolutionary forces which ante-dated the year 1914 and which were augmented after that year, the Netherlands suffered unusually severely during World War II. Yet, like Dutch Roman Catholicism, Dutch Protestantism showed fresh vigour after that testing. Laity came to the fore as they had not for many years, extensive efforts were made to enlist and train them in permeating all life with the faith, many churches damaged or destroyed in the war were restored, and in the new areas reclaimed from the sea and in the rapidly growing suburbs of the cities church buildings were erected. Theology and Biblical studies were vigorous. Although the faith of thousands was nominal, devoted and growing constituencies were seeking to check de-Christianization and to make Protestantism an increasing factor in the life of the nation and of the world.

CHAPTER XVII

Protestantism in the British Isles

GENERAL PERSPECTIVE

W HAT developments in Protestantism were seen in the British Isles in the first half of the twentieth century? In an earlier volume we noted the remarkable vitality displayed in the nineteenth century.[1] We summarized the setting with its challenge to Christianity. The British Isles were the home of the Industrial Revolution. Mining towns and industrial and commercial cities grew apace. With the large increase in population, not only did the urban centres expand but a vast migration to the cities disturbed the traditional patterns of rural and village life. As a result the churches were confronted with the problem of increasing their facilities to care for throngs for whom the existing provisions for worship, nurture in the faith, and pastoral care were palpably insufficient and to adjust to the changes in the country-side. The Christian conscience was also confronted with the evils attendant upon the early stages of an industrialized society with its exploitation of labour, its grinding poverty, and its festering slums. Intellectual currents which were features of the revolutionary age appeared to be undercutting the Christian faith and making it an anachronism. It was in England that Darwin formulated the theory of evolution and that Herbert Spencer, following him, propounded a view of the development of society that made religion, including Christianity, a contingent feature corresponding to no ascertainable reality apart from man's subjective consciousness. To thousands the Christian faith appeared to be untenable by informed and honest minds. In London Karl Marx elaborated the form of socialism which, militantly atheistic, was to sweep much of the world in the following century. Following the defeat of Napoleon and enriched by the long near-monopoly of the processes of the Industrial Revolution, Great Britain was in command of the seas: the British navy was without a serious rival, British ships were the commercial carriers of the world, and British merchants ransacked the planet for raw materials and markets for

[1] Volume II, pp. 252–431.

their factories. The British Empire burgeoned until it embraced much of Asia, Africa, the Americas, the islands of the sea, and all of Australia.

In spite of the fact that at the outset of the nineteenth century it seemed ill prepared to rise to the challenge and to many observers appeared moribund, British Protestantism experienced awakenings which not only revivified it but made it more of a force at home and abroad than it had ever been. That was true of the Church of England, the Nonconformist bodies in England, the churches in Wales and Scotland, and the churches of British provenance in Ireland. Needed reforms were made in the Church of England, in Scottish Presbyterianism, and in the (Anglican) Church of Ireland. Nonconforming bodies, whether in England, Wales, Ireland, or Scotland, had a phenomenal growth. New church buildings were rapidly erected in the cities, such new instruments as the Salvation Army, social settlements, and the Young Men's and Young Women's Christian Associations were created to serve the diverse elements in the urban populations, and the Student Christian Movement sprang up to reach the oncoming generations in the universities. The Christian conscience placed measures on the statute books to remedy some of the crying social evils, and private philanthropy inspired by the Christian faith gave birth to movements and institutions to allay or remove the suffering and degradation which were features of the emerging society. Protestants wrestled with the problems posed by the intellectual currents of the day and made notable contributions in philosophy, theology, and Biblical studies. The growth of the empire was accompanied by the geographic expansion of British Protestantism both in the new nations which were arising from the migrations in North America, Australia, New Zealand, and South Africa and by missions to non-Christian peoples in the British possessions and in areas touched by British commerce.

During the decades ushered in by the fateful events of 1914 many of the movements which had marked the nineteenth century were intensified. The world wars which punctuated the twentieth century impinged heavily on the British Isles, and the wave of revolt against Western imperialism brought about the independence of the majority of the populations which had comprised the British Empire. Although still within the family of nations called the Commonwealth, and retaining the British Crown as the formal tie, they avoided the designation "British."

The mechanization and urbanization of society, the growth of socialism and the welfare state, and the intellectual currents which appeared to make the Christian faith irrelevant continued and mounted. Industrialization was accelerated. This meant that the daily routine of the employees in factories and mines rendered difficult if not impossible participation in what had been the normal worship and activities of the churches. The churches did not keep pace with the growth of the cities with their sprawling suburbs and their new housing estates. The bicycle and then the motor car made for week ends in the country which did not include attendance at church services. Open hostility to Christianity was not as marked as in some portions of the nineteenth century, but a larger proportion of the population, especially of the labouring classes, drifted away from the Church, and what amounted to de-Christianization proceeded fairly steadily, as in much of the neighbouring Continent. A study of York, which may not be typical of all England, showed that in 1901 attendance at church services was 35.5 per cent. of the adult population (over seventeen years of age), in 1935 the proportion had sunk to 17.7 per cent., and in 1948 it was 13 per cent. The Anglicans had suffered more than the Nonconformists, and the Roman Catholics had shown a slight gain. As on the Continent, women constituted a slight majority of those frequenting the churches.[2] With modifications, the decline the country over was similar. Until about 1900 the churches had been growing since at least the middle of the nineteenth century—in attendance, church membership, and buildings. Their strength was in the middle classes. From about 1900 on, the Christian faith was being eroded in those classes. To the decline a number of factors contributed. Some were intellectual. Periods of economic depression in the 1920's and 1930's with the pressure of poverty and with widespread strikes gave stimulus to steps towards socialism and the welfare state, promoted first by the Liberal Party and then by the Labour Party. The demands of welfare measures and the burdens of the two world wars brought greatly augmented taxation with steeply graded levies on incomes and on the transmission of wealth by inheritance. They bore especially heavily on the upper and middle classes, from which much of the financial support of the churches had come.

The British Isles were deeply involved in the two world wars. From the outset of each Great Britain was a belligerent, and while in World War II Éire, now independent, maintained its neutrality it could not but be affected and during World War I was engrossed in the struggle which issued in its autonomy and later in the full severance of its tie with the United Kingdom. How far the wars hastened de-Christianization is uncertain for by 1960 that movement had proceeded fully as far and perhaps farther in Sweden, which had preserved its neutrality in both struggles. The trend appears to have been due primarily to the factors which were common to both Sweden and Britain and which we summarized in the preceding paragraph. Yet in the British Isles active participation in the wars reinforced these factors.

The transformation of the British Empire into the Commonwealth seems not to have affected seriously if at all the course of Christianity in the British Isles. As we are to see, the missionary outreach persisted in all the portions

2 Rowntree and Lavers, English Life and Leisure, pp. 342, 343.

of the empire which achieved independence. Increasingly the churches in these areas became autonomous, but that was a move long desired by missionaries and was common throughout the non-Occidental world regardless of the political environment. It was hastened by the rising tide of nationalism but was not solely a result of it.

Swept into the currents of a shrinking world, British Protestantism was affected by Protestant movements in thought and action in other lands. In Biblical studies *Formgeschichte* had repercussions. Kierkegaard, Barth, Berdyaev, and Reinhold Niebuhr influenced theology. The Ecumenical Movement was accepted by the churches which enrolled the overwhelming majority of the Protestants.

THE CHURCH OF ENGLAND: ITS CONDITION IN 1914

We have seen that in the nineteenth century the Church of England had experienced a variety of awakenings and came to the summer of 1914 more vigorous than at any previous time.[3] The quality of its clergy had risen and was never higher than in that year. More effective service to the constituency had been obtained by the creation of additional dioceses and parishes, an approach to an equalization of clerical and episcopal stipends, the reduction of sinecures, pluralism, and absenteeism, better episcopal supervision, and the erection of new churches in the growing cities. Public worship had been improved, church fabrics which had been allowed to fall into disrepair had been restored, the Evangelical wing was active, the emphasis upon the Catholic heritage had been revived, and through a variety of channels, some of them new, efforts had been made to permeate in a Christian fashion the society which was arising from the Industrial Revolution and the attendant developments. The intellectual currents of the day were being faced, and in spite of resistance from conservatives fearless efforts were seen to re-think the Christian faith in the light of the findings of science and to apply to the Bible the methods of current historical scholarship. The rapid growth of the British Empire and of British commerce had been paralleled by the phenomenal expansion of the Anglican Communion. Through migrations and missions, in contrast with the situation in 1815 when it was limited to the British Isles, the United States, and a few British colonies, the Anglican Communion had become a fellowship, largely of autonomous churches, which was almost world-wide and which found visible expression in a common ministry through the historic episcopate, the Book of Common Prayer, the creeds and sacraments, acceptance of the Scriptures, and the decennial meetings of the bishops in the Lambeth Conferences.

[3] Volume II, pp. 256–313.

Vigorous though the Church of England was, it was not keeping pace with the challenge of the changing society in which it was set. Such statistics as were available appeared to show that in spite of the growing population, by the year 1914 attendance at church services had fallen off from the mid-century and even from the 1880's.[4] Yet an increase by a fourth in the number of communicants in the 1890's[5] seemed evidence of what we have found elsewhere in the historic Christendom—the mounting loyalty of a large core of the faithful in contrast with the drifting away from more than nominal connexion with the Church of an increasing proportion of the population. Efforts to remedy the situation by the division of ancient parishes in urban areas had sometimes weakened the Church: many of the parishes, both old and new, were poorly equipped with physical facilities and had in them so few who were committed to the Church that both the latter and their clergy were frustrated and discouraged.[6] In retrospect a prominent clergyman declared that the historic parish system which on the whole had been adequate was now becoming ill adapted to the altered social structure.[7] Moreover, in the decline in the number of men seeking ordination was forecast a shortage of enough clergy not only to halt the de-Christianization of large elements of the population but even to give adequate care to the faithful. In most of the nineteenth century the number of ordinations had mounted, although not in proportion to the population. But by the latter part of the 1890's the annual number of ordinations had fallen off sharply—from 2,324 in 1886–1888 to 1,994 in 1896–1898. The quality had probably not declined and perhaps had improved, but the body of clergy was clearly insufficient fully to rise to the challenge of the day.[8]

THE CHURCH OF ENGLAND AND WORLD WAR I

The storm of World War I broke suddenly upon the Church of England as it did upon the country as a whole and found it quite unprepared for the ordeal.[9] However, a variety of measures were improvised to meet the emergency. In August, 1914, Randall Davidson (1848–1930), Archbishop of Canterbury, aided by others, prepared prayers for use in the churches asking for the removal of arrogance and feebleness and for the gift of courage, loyalty, tranquility, and self-control, but not directly for victory.[10] Offers by the clergy for the chaplaincy poured in beyond the immediate demands. Davidson discour-

---

[4] Volume II, pp. 353, 354; Lloyd, *The Church of England in the Twentieth Century*, Vol. I, pp. 59–62.

[5] Lloyd, *op. cit.*, Vol. I, p. 60.

[6] *Ibid.*, pp. 61, 62.

[7] Iremonger, *William Temple*, pp. 204, 205.

[8] Lloyd, *op. cit.*, Vol. I, pp. 62, 63.

[9] Bell, *Randall Davidson*, Vol. II, p. 731.

[10] *Ibid.*, pp. 736, 737.

aged priests who wished to enlist as actual combatants on the ground that such service was "incompatible with the position of one who has sought and received Holy Orders."[11] The number of chaplains was augmented, those in France were placed under the able direction of Llewellyn H. Gynne, bishop in Egypt and the Sudan, as deputy chaplain-general, and although the change from their usual parish duties entailed major readjustments, the large majority of the chaplains rose to the challenge. Many ministered to the troops under fire and others served in novel ways behind the lines.[12] Their task was made the more difficult by the moral disintegration among the men under arms which was the customary accompaniment of war and by the religious illiteracy and low moral standards which many of the troops brought from civilian life.[13] Later (1916) when a military service act was passed introducing conscription and the clergy were exempted, the exception was not made at the request of the bishops, and in 1918, when the need for troops became more acute, the bishops, led by Davidson, permitted and even encouraged the clergy to enlist.[14]

In England itself during the war, in the main the leadership of the Church of England sought to restrain hate and reprisals. In Davidson the Church of England had one of its greatest Archbishops of Canterbury. He commanded the respect of much of the public and many of the men prominent in public life. He consistently stood out against letting righteous indignation degenerate into hatred of the enemy.[15] Cosmo Gordon Lang (1864–1945), like Davidson of Scottish birth and reared in the Church of Scotland, who succeeded him in Canterbury, was then Archbishop of York. Although in the early days of the war he had urged men to enlist, a remark in a public address in which he said that he did not believe that the kaiser would have lightly embarked on a war with England brought him great unpopularity.[16] In an attempt to check the drunkenness that accompanied the war, Davidson and Lang joined with Cardinal Bourne, Roman Catholic Archbishop of Westminster, and Joseph Compton-Rickett, the President of the Free Church Council, in urging the nation as part of the self-sacrifice and self-discipline demanded by the times to follow the example of the king and abstain from all alcoholic liquor during the duration of the hostilities.[17] The step aroused criticism even from some high in the clergy and was not widely successful.[18] When legislation was enacted conscripting men for the armed services, Davidson, while not sharing

---

[11] *Ibid.*, pp. 738, 739.
[12] Lloyd, *op. cit.*, Vol. I, pp. 225–234; Bell, *op. cit.*, Vol. II, pp. 761–763, 848, 849.
[13] Lloyd, *op. cit.*, Vol. I, p. 232.
[14] Bell, *op. cit.*, Vol. II, pp. 887–890.
[15] *Ibid.*, pp. 755–757.
[16] Lockhart, *Cosmo Gordon Lang*, pp. 248–251.
[17] Bell, *op. cit.*, Vol. II, p. 749.
[18] Henson, *Retrospect of an Unimportant Life*, Vol. I, pp. 182–186.

their convictions, supported conscientious objectors in their refusal to conform and, when the war was over, protested against official acts which denied to those who had done alternative work reinstatement in their previous posts in the civil service.[19] As the war dragged on its exhausting way and the Germans began to use poison gas, Davidson protested against retaliation in kind.[20]

Early in the war leaders in the Church of England endeavoured to stimulate that body, as the national church, to stir the people of the country to a Christian dedication. For a time early in the war churches were thronged and many anticipated a revival of religion. Pilgrimages of prayer were started by women, and the League of the Spiritual War was inaugurated. In 1916 the National Mission of Repentance and Hope was undertaken. Cardinal Bourne and the heads of the Nonconforming churches were informed of the plan with the hope that they would take parallel action, but they were not invited to collaborate. Here was an attempt "to call the men and women of England to earnest and honest repentance of our sins and shortcomings as a nation and to claim that in the Living Christ, in the loyal acceptance of Him as the Lord of all life, individual and social, lies the one sure hope." Arthur Foley Winnington-Ingram (1858–1946), Bishop of London from 1901 to 1939, was made chairman of the central council and with characteristic enthusiasm threw himself wholeheartedly into the project. Retreats of the clergy were held to prepare them spiritually for participation. But national repentance did not follow. Here and there individuals and groups were stirred and Davidson attempted to follow the Mission with a dedication of the Church of England to evangelism, greater efficiency, and the application of the Gospel to industrial problems. But the people as a whole were unmoved. Controversy between the various parties in the church partly nullified the effort.[21]

Although the National Mission of Repentance and Hope did not issue in the desired fruits, another movement, bearing the name of Life and Liberty, had continuing and positive results in giving the Church of England an approach to independence and a structure which had in it something of democracy. Impetus was given by the National Mission and the conviction, which it strengthened, that the Church of England badly needed reform. Groups had been at work to formulate proposals. One was a committee appointed by Davidson,[22] and another had Charles Gore, the Bishop of Oxford, as its chairman.[23] In 1903 the Representative Church Council had been initiated with

[19] Bell, *op. cit.*, Vol. II, pp. 817–822, 952, 953.
[20] *Ibid.*, pp. 757–761.
[21] *Ibid.*, pp. 767–774; Lloyd, *op. cit.*, Vol. I, pp. 239–245; Iremonger, *op. cit.*, pp. 204–219; Henson, *op. cit.*, Vol. I, pp. 176–182; Reckitt, *Maurice to Temple*, pp. 159–164.
[22] Bell, *op. cit.*, Vol. II, pp. 957–960.
[23] Prestige, *The Life of Charles Gore*, p. 387.

houses of bishops, clergy, and laity.[24] In spite of the advances that had been made in the preceding century[25] great inequalities still existed in the stipends of the clergy, and advowsons—the right to present a clergyman to a living— were regarded as personal property to be bought and sold. For the repentance urged in the National Mission to be real, it must begin in the national church if that church was to make the Gospel more of a force in the post-war world. Since the Church of England was established, changes could be only by acts of Parliament, and that body was too crowded with other pressing business and too many of its members were indifferent to give adequate attention to what was required. Some of the more ardent urged disestablishment to free the church from the shackles inseparable from the connexion with the state. More moderate counsels prevailed and a Parliamentary measure was sought which would concede to the church more power to govern its own affairs and set up machinery through which the church could act. The outstanding leaders were Hugh Richard Lowrie Sheppard (1880–1937), better known as "Dick" Sheppard, William Temple (1881–1944), and Frederic Athelwold Iremonger. Sheppard, son of a clergyman and a graduate of Cambridge, had served in Oxford House among the underprivileged of London, for a time in 1914 had been a chaplain in France, and from 1914 to 1927 was vicar of St. Martin's in the Fields, in one of the busiest centres of London. There his fiery eloquence and his radiant, selfless devotion attracted throngs. Temple, son of the Frederick Temple who had been Bishop of London and Archbishop of Canterbury, extraordinarily versatile and able and equally devoted, resigned the lucrative living and distinguished pulpit of St. James Piccadilly (London) to give full time to the chairmanship of the movement. Iremonger was later Dean of Lichfield. The movement was launched in 1917. Mounting support came from clergy and laity. Late in 1919 what was called the Enabling Act was passed and received the royal signature. Through it the laity in every parish were accorded a voice in the management of their church, and not merely as citizens but as members of the Church. Under it elected church councils were required to be set up in all the parishes. Their functions were limited, for they could not appoint or even recommend a man to be their pastor: that was still left to the patron. Nor could they decide what form of service could be used: that remained within the power of the priest. However, they gradually developed in the laity a sense of responsibility. Their powers were defined (1921) as being "to coöperate with the incumbent in the initiation, conduct, and development of church work both within the parish and outside." Moreover, the Enabling Act gave sanction to the National Assembly of the Church of England. That

[24] Bell, *op. cit.*, Vol. II, p. 959.
[25] Volume II, pp. 282–284.

body met for the first time in 1920. It had three houses—the bishops, the clergy (the lower houses of the convocations of Canterbury and York), and the laity, made up of communicant members of the Church of England elected by lay representatives in diocesan conferences. The Assembly could "debate and formulate its judgement by resolution upon any matter concerning the Church of England or otherwise of religious or public interest," but it could not define the doctrines of the Church of England or theology.[26] Here was progress towards permitting the Church of England to speak out and act unitedly. It paralleled what we have seen in several other countries and churches in the nineteenth and twentieth centuries—for example, ultramontanism with the enhanced power of the Papacy in the Roman Catholic Church, disestablishment of the Protestant *Landeskirchen* in Germany following World War I, movements towards the separation of Church and state in Switzerland, and the reorganization of the Netherlands Reformed Church after World War II.

The pressure of the national emergency did not quiet controversy in the Church of England. Indeed, by setting nerves on edge it may have intensified it. Inclusive as it sought to be, embracing all the nation, the Church of England could not hope to escape internal dissensions over convictions conscientiously held. During World War I two issues aroused major storms. One was the reservation of the consecrated elements in the Communion, a practice of some Anglo-Catholics and vigorously opposed by many. Even among the Anglo-Catholics were those who feared that, unless safeguarded, reservation might lead to adoration and a cultus akin to Roman Catholic practice and to belief in transubstantiation.[27] The other storm was over the appointment of Henson to the see of Hereford. Herbert Hensley Henson (1863–1947) was from a middle-class family and his father was an ardent Evangelical. He had had a brilliant career at Oxford, had served briefly as head of Oxford House, then in several posts, including a canonry in Westminster Abbey and concurrently as Rector of the adjacent St. Margaret's, and (1912–1918) as Dean of Durham. He was a notable preacher, had written a number of books, and, charming and with a sense of humour, forthright and often provocative, was at times a controversial figure. He had moved from a high-church to a broad or modernist position. The announcement of his designation as Bishop of Hereford was greeted by numerous and determined protests, particularly from the members

---

[26] Bell, *op. cit.*, Vol. II, pp. 956–980; Iremonger, *op. cit.*, pp. 220–281; Lloyd, *op. cit.*, Vol. I, pp. 246–253; Neill, *Anglicanism*, pp. 391–394. For the part of a young clergyman—Edward Woods (1877–1953), who died as Bishop of Lichfield—in furthering the Life and Liberty Movement, see Oliver Tomkins, *The Life of Edward Woods* (London, S.C.M. Press, 1957, pp. 160), pp. 54–63. For a critic of the Life and Liberty Movement see Henson, *op. cit.*, Vol. I, pp. 206–211, 302. On the structure provided by the Enabling Act see Marchant, *The Future of the Church of England*, pp. 107–115.

[27] Bell, *op. cit.*, Vol. II, pp. 795–815; Iremonger, *op. cit.*, pp. 189, 190; Lockhart, *op. cit.*, p. 213; Prestige, *op. cit.*, pp. 379–381, 390–394.

of the English Church Union, a fellowship of Anglo-Catholics, and from those of similar views. Although he was outspokenly committed to the incarnation, Henson was said to have denied the virgin birth and resurrection of Jesus. His appointment was sustained by a large majority of the prebends of the Hereford cathedral, yet Davidson was urged to refuse him consecration. The controversy caused the archbishop great pain, but Henson declared emphatically that he repeated the Apostles' Creed without any desire to change it, and Davidson went ahead with the consecration. Henson won the confidence of his diocese and after two years was translated to the see of Durham.[28]

THE CHURCH OF ENGLAND BETWEEN WORLD WARS

The interval of slightly less than two decades between World War I and World War II brought England and the Church of England grave problems. The Victorian era and its brief and lush Edwardian postscript were now history. The great efforts of World War I had taken their heavy toll. The disintegration of the British Empire which had been foreshadowed by the South African War (1899–1902) was in the offing. The industrialization of the country with its attendant urbanization and social revolution was mounting. Organized labour was increasingly potent. The Labour Party was on its way to power. The general strike of 1926 threatened to disrupt the British economy and was evidence of the direction in which the English social and political structure was moving. Much of the current literature reflected dissatisfaction and rebellion against inherited standards which had been accentuated by the war. The prolific and widely read Herbert George Wells (1866–1946) was temporarily shocked out of his easy-going utopian optimism but the God whom he discovered and set before his readers was not the God of the Church of England or of any form of orthodox Christianity.[29] Giles Lytton Strachey (1880–1932) was an extreme example of those who cynically appraised figures regarded as heroes by the preceding century. The extensive circulation of his most talked-of book was evidence that he spoke for many.[30] The popularity of David Herbert Lawrence (1885–1930) and Aldous Huxley (1894———) showed a similar repudiation of Victorian standards. The hardy perennial George Bernard Shaw (1856–1950) continued to tilt against complacency. Bertrand Russell (1872———), a brilliant philosopher, had reacted against a Christian family background and was openly an atheist.

Several of the clergy sought to awaken the Church of England and its con-

---

[28] Bell, *op. cit.*, Vol. II, pp. 851–890; Henson, *op. cit.*, Vol. I, pp. 215–284; Prestige, *op. cit.*, pp. 394–403.

[29] H. G. Wells, *Experiment in Autobiography. Discoveries and Conclusions of a Very Ordinary Brain (since 1866)* (New York, The Macmillan Co., 1934, pp. xi, 717), pp. 568–578; H. G. Wells, *God the Invisible King* (New York, The Macmillan Co., 1917, pp. xvii, 174), *passim*.

[30] G. L. Strachey, *Eminent Victorians* (New York, G. P. Putnam's Sons, 1918, pp. xi, 351).

stituency. Serving, as some of them had, as chaplains with the troops they had become vividly aware that that church was failing to reach many of the rank and file. They viewed it as too bound by convention and outdated practices and sought to stab it into reform. "Dick" Sheppard by his direct preaching and his self-giving love for all whom he touched filled St. Martin's in the Fields to over-flowing. St. Martin's in the Fields had been the centre of a family parish of Victorian Evangelicalism but, as its environment changed, had declined. Sheppard abolished the reserved seats and the allotted pews, opened it to all and sundry and made it the church for the soldiers, the down-and-outs, the young and the old, the classes and the masses. He centred his message on Christ, wished the churches more nearly to exemplify His life, and called upon the Church of England to lead the other churches in forming the real body of Christ, removing the barriers which separated the adherents of one church from those of another and especially the barriers which prevented fellow Christians from kneeling together at the Communion. He urged the ordination of all ministers in one Church Universal. He had the true pastor's deep concern for individuals, particularly for those in any kind of trouble—physical, mental, moral, or spiritual. Although he wondered whether the authorities would allow him to remain in the Church of England, Sheppard was later made Dean of Canterbury and a canon of St. Paul's. He chronically drove himself beyond his physical strength, was often ill, and died in middle life. An ardent pacifist, he became the chief promoter of the Peace Pledge Union, which for a time in the 1930's in the reaction against war enrolled thousands.[31]

Another voice which attracted wide attention was Geoffrey Anketell Studdert-Kennedy (1883-1929), popularly known by the nickname "Woodbine Willie," embodying much affection, given him by the soldiers during the war. Ordained in 1908, Vicar of St. Paul's Worcester from 1914 to 1921, during much of that incumbency he was with the troops in France and devoted himself unstintedly to them. In 1922 he became Rector of St. Edmund, King and Martyr, on Lombard Street in London, one of the old parishes in the heart of the metropolis. He moved about the country, preaching and attracting great audiences. A loyal priest of the Church of England, he believed the Eucharist to include the real presence, sacrifice, and communion. He had as a major

[31] Charles H. S. Matthews, Dick Sheppard: Man of Peace (London, James Clarke & Co., no date, pp. 93); R. Ellis Roberts, H. R. L. Sheppard: Life and Letters (London, John Murray, 1942, pp. xi, 356), passim; H. R. L. Sheppard, The Impatience of a Parson. A Plea for the Recovery of Vital Christianity (New York, Doubleday, Doran and Co., 1928, pp. xviii, 227), passim, especially pp. 60, 70, 94, 104, 150, 182–189, 202–212; Halford E. Luccock, editor, The Best of Dick Sheppard (H. R. L. Sheppard) (New York, Harper & Brothers, 1951, pp. xx, 162), passim; R. J. Northcott, Dick Sheppard and St. Martin's (London, Longmans, Green and Co., 1937, pp. xvii, 309), passim; William Paxton and others, Dick Sheppard. An Apostle of Brotherhood (London, Chapman and Hall, 1938, pp. 117), passim; H. R. L. Sheppard, a Note in Appreciation (London, Cobden-Sanderson, 1937, pp. 87), passim; Harold Anson, Looking Forward (London, William Heinemann, 1938, pp. vii, 295), pp. 212–215, 267–271.

interest the economic phases of society and held that the Gospel offered the way to end the injustices of the social order, but he was also deeply concerned for individuals and was sought by many for counsel in the difficulties of their spiritual and moral life. Intensely sensitive to the evil in the world, he saw in the cross the clue to its solution and the centre of the Gospel, the way in which God suffers in and with His children and yet triumphs so that His name stands for power and joy. He also supported the Industrial Christian Fellowship, which had arisen in part from the National Mission.[32]

A striking personality came out of the war years with a distinct movement. Philip Thomas Bayard Clayton (1885———), better known as "Tubby," a cousin of "Dick" Sheppard and an Oxford graduate with a first in theology, when World War I broke out was a curate in Portsea under Cyril Garbett, later Archbishop of York. He became a chaplain in the mud and blood of the deadly Ypres salient in Flanders. There he and his senior chaplain, the gigantic Neville Talbot, later Bishop of Pretoria, opened a social centre for the troops which they called Talbot House, after Neville Talbot's brother Gilbert, the youngest son of the Bishop of Winchester, who had been killed in the early months of the war. Under Clayton's ministry Talbot House acquainted uncounted thousands of men with the meaning of fellowship in Christ. When the war ended, Clayton was put in charge of a school to train for the priesthood several hundred men who while in service had decided to enter the ministry. Within a few months, with the help of Sheppard and the encouragement of William Temple, he refounded Talbot House in London as Toc H. He meant it to reproduce Talbot House and to serve returning veterans who had known it at the front; but he also wanted to spread its spirit throughout the country to teach the younger generation class reconciliation and unselfish service. In 1922 it received a royal charter and in that year Clayton was appointed by Randall Davidson vicar of one of the old churches in the heart of London, All Hallows Barking-by-the-Tower. All Hallows became the guild church of Toc H. The Toc H movement spread, with centres in Britain, Canada, and elsewhere. Clayton travelled prodigiously, partly because he enjoyed the sea, but chiefly to promote the movement. From 1932 to 1939 Toc H supported the British Empire Leprosy Relief. In the neighbourhood of All Hallows, Tower Hill Improvement was carried through and Tower Beach was opened for children. Although All Hallows was wrecked by a bomb during World War II, the damage did not prevent Clayton from creating the

[32] *The Best of G. A. Studdert-Kennedy (Woodbine Willie) Selected from his Writings by a Friend* (London, Hodder and Stoughton, 1947, pp. 238); G. A. Studdert-Kennedy, *Lies!* (London, Hodder and Stoughton, preface 1919, pp. x, 267); G. A. Studdert-Kennedy, *I Believe. Sermons on the Apostles' Creed* (New York, George H. Doran Co., preface 1921, pp. xvi, 316); G. A. Studdert-Kennedy, *The Hardest Part* (New York, George H. Doran Co., no date, pp. xxiii, 195); Reckitt, *op. cit.*, pp. 164–166.

Winant Volunteers, inaugurated in 1948, and the Osler Volunteers, begun in 1950, to recruit young people to come at their own expense to help in clubs and settlements in London's East End. Clayton formed a close friendship with George MacLeod, whom we are to meet later as the inspirer of a somewhat similar movement with its centre on the island of Iona off the coast of Scotland.[33]

A quite different development in the years following World War I was the revision of the Book of Common Prayer and its rejection by Parliament. Here was an experience which showed that in spite of the Enabling Act the Church of England was still so closely bound to the state that it was not free to control its forms of worship. The war had witnessed an increasing emphasis upon the Eucharist, a practice which had helped to raise the thorny issue of the reservation of the consecrated elements. Revision of the Prayer Book had been under consideration for some time. In 1920 the convocations of both York and Canterbury agreed that it should be undertaken, and in 1922 the Church Assembly authorized by the Enabling Act gave its approval. Many and varied suggestions came to the committee set up for the purpose. Controversy chiefly centred on the order of Holy Communion, the opponents fearing that an alteration or an alternative order would open the gates to Anglo-Catholic practices, including reservation. The revision prepared by the committee was finally agreed upon by both convocations and the Church Assembly. The old Prayer Book was to be continued unaltered and the use of the new one was to be optional. Much public interest had been aroused. Many Evangelicals opposed the revised Prayer Book as moving in the Catholic direction, while extreme Anglo-Catholics were critical because, in their judgement, it did not go far enough. The issue then went to Parliament, for favourable action by that body was essential before the measure could be presented for royal approval. The House of Lords acted in the affirmative, but the House of Commons voted adversely by a substantial majority. The bishops decided to try again after making changes to remove some of the objections and allay misapprehensions. But the amended version (1928) was rejected by the House of Commons. Intense feeling was aroused. In the Commons were many who were not communicants of the Church of England and some who were not even Christians. Could the Church of England conscientiously submit to having its forms of worship, a purely spiritual matter, determined by such a body? Although extremists favoured disestablishment as a solution, the bishops approved as a *modus vivendi* the use of the Prayer Book of 1928 as well as the old Prayer Book (of 1562), but

[33] Melville Harcourt, *The Impudent Dreamer: the Story of Tubby Clayton . . . who had the impudence to believe that under God's hand he could make dreams come true* (New York, Oxford University Press, 1953, pp. 260), *passim*; *Who's Who, 1955*, p. 563.

ordered that deviations from them should cease.[34]

That conditions in the post-war years called for serious effort by the Church of England could not be questioned. A survey of the crowded industrial and mining district of Tyneside, in and around Newcastle, made in 1925 showed that 70 per cent. of all the babies born were baptized in the Church of England and 18 per cent. were baptized in the Roman Catholic Church. Yet of the children only 19.5 per cent. were in the Sunday Schools of the Church of England, 4 per cent. in those of the Presbyterians, and 8.4 per cent. in those of the Wesleyans, and only about 30 per cent. of the eligible adolescents were confirmed. On Easter Sunday and during Easter week perhaps 6 per cent. of the adult population made their Communion. It was estimated that in Tyneside as a whole about an eighth of the population were regular church-goers and of those slightly less than a third could be counted as Anglicans, a larger proportion were Nonconformists, and Roman Catholics had more than the Anglicans but less than the Nonconformists.[35] In some of the sprawling suburbs of the great cities, especially London, the lack of a sense of community was chronic and church life was non-existent or low.[36] In spite of the large number of returning veterans from World War I who prepared for the priesthood and were ordained, the totals of clergy in the country as a whole declined —and that in the face of the greater need posed by the growth of the population and the advancing secularization. The year 1905 had seen 19,053 clergy in active service. By 1914 the total had fallen to 18,180, in 1922 to 17,162, and in 1930 to 16,745.[37] For the men who entered the priesthood the financial outlook was progressively darker. Although in 1921 the average stipend of incumbents was £426, of members of cathedral staffs £850 to £900, and of bishops over £4,000, a survey made in 1927 showed that the purchasing power of the income from the average benefice had fallen by 16 per cent. since 1914.[38] Moreover, in 1925 the historic tithe was fixed once for all at a declining figure which would abolish it completely in less than a hundred years, and its proceeds went to Queen Anne's Bounty as a common fund administered through special commissioners.[39] Here was a grim picture which was paralleled in other churches and in other parts of Europe.

Yet, as elsewhere in much of Europe, indications of vigorous life were seen.

[34] Bell, *op. cit.*, Vol. II, pp. 1325–1360; Lockhart, *op. cit.*, pp. 299–309; Prestige, *op. cit.*, pp. 503–509; Henson, *op. cit.*, pp. 151–200; Iremonger, *op. cit.*, pp. 347–358; Harvey, *The Church in the Twentieth Century*, pp. 51–106; F. L. Cross, *Darwell Stone, Churchman and Counsellor* (Westminster, Dacre Press, 1943, pp. xxvi, 467), pp. 163–202.

[35] Lloyd, *The Church of England in the Twentieth Century*, Vol. II, pp. 199, 200.

[36] *Ibid.*, p. 212.

[37] *Ibid.*, p. 144; Marchant, *op. cit.*, pp. 81–104, 115–120.

[38] Lloyd, *op. cit.*, Vol. II, p. 149.

[39] Siegmund-Schultze, *Die Kirche von England*, pp. 80–84.

Successful efforts were made to improve the use of the cathedrals by more people. Even as late as the middle of the nineteenth century the cathedrals had been little frequented, some of their deans discouraged entrance to them, and they were more like museums than houses of worship. Frank Selwyn Macaulay Bennett (1866-1947), whose undergraduate years were in Keble College, Oxford, and who was Dean of Chester Cathedral from 1920 to 1937, completed repairs on the Chester edifice which were already under way, abolished the tipping of vergers, in various ways encouraged the use of the building for worship, both in its services and in individual prayer, assigned its chapels to boys' clubs and men's and women's organizations, restored the ancient refectory so that inexpensive meals could be served to visitors and to groups, and by his personal charm and interest made the building a centre for pastoral care.[40] In the 1920's a somewhat similar transformation was wrought in several other cathedrals.[41] In 1934 in the midst of the vast unemployment and its attendant distress which were a phase of the world-wide depression, a mass pilgrimage was organized to the cathedrals in which tens of thousands participated, headed by the king and queen. Prayers were said for the lifting of the depression, and the gifts offered were used for the unemployed.[42] The erection of new cathedrals was undertaken, notably of a large one in Liverpool. The cathedral clergy were kept so busy with diocesan activities that most of them had no leisure for the kind of scholarship which was once thought to be associated with canons.[43] Numbers of new churches were erected to serve the housing estates rising in the suburbs of the cities. In some the styles of architecture differed decidedly from the Gothic of the Middle Ages and the neo-Gothic of the Victorian era and sought to give to congregations and clergy a sense of community in worship.[44]

Forms of ministry were devised to seek to reach labourers in factories and mines whose daily occupations kept them from attending the services in the churches and from sharing in the life of the parish. Factory chaplains became a growing but still not numerous feature of the Church of England. Several of them sought, like the later worker-priests in France, to share the lives of those to whom they ministered, to speak their language, to conform to their standards of comfort—or discomfort—and to fight their battles. One of the pioneers was Hugh Lister (1901-1944). A Cambridge graduate, for a time he was employed by a railway and through living in the dormitories of railwaymen developed a deep interest in the industrial workers. He came to believe it was his vocation to serve them as a priest, prepared himself at Cuddesdon,

40 Lloyd, *op. cit.*, Vol. II, pp. 237-244; *Who Was Who, 1941-1950*, p. 89.
41 Lloyd, *op. cit.*, Vol. II, p. 238.
42 *Ibid.*, pp. 243-247.
43 *Ibid.*, pp. 235, 236, 247, 248.
44 *Ibid.*, pp. 228-230.

a theological college near Oxford where Anglo-Catholic influences were strong, was ordained, and for four years before the outbreak of World War II lived in Hackney, an underprivileged industrial section of London. There he identified himself with the labourers, gathered a few of them around him, with them organized trade unions, and promoted strikes to obtain better conditions for factory workers. At the beginning of World War II he enlisted in the army and he was killed in France in 1944.[45] Small groups or cells of laymen had been begun before Lister became active and by the time World War II broke out were multiplying, some in parishes and others in factories. The movement spread even more rapidly during that war and found association through such informal fellowships as "the Nails" and "the Servants of Christ the King."[46]

In April, 1924, soon after World War I, the Conference on Christian Politics, Economics, and Citizenship, briefly known as COPEC, was held in Birmingham, one of the great industrial centres of Britain. It was indebted to interest which antedated World War I and was said to have been the direct outgrowth of a Student Christian Movement conference of 1909 which had for its subject "Christianity and Social Problems." Among its predecessors were annual meetings, begun in 1911, of denominational bodies concerned with social issues. In its preparation members of several denominations joined, including Roman Catholics, but it was predominantly Anglican. Temple, then Bishop of Manchester, was its chairman and chief figure. In the meetings in Birmingham the Roman Catholics, for theological reasons, declined to be represented. Careful preparations were made by commissions and from them twelve volumes emerged on such topics as the home, the relations of the sexes, leisure, crime, war, industry, property, politics, and citizenship. Here was a courageous attempt of British Christians to face up to the crucial social questions of the revolutionary age. The conference was based on "the conviction that the Christian faith, rightly interpreted and consistently followed, gives the vision and the power essential for solving the problems of today, that the social ethics of Christianity have been greatly neglected by Christians, with disastrous consequences to the individual and society, and that it is of the first importance that these should be given a clearer and more persistent emphasis."[47]

Under devoted men some villages and towns were profoundly influenced through the traditional channels of parish life. Alton, in Hampshire, south-west

[45] *Ibid.*, pp. 222–224.
[46] *Ibid.*, pp. 224, 225.
[47] *The Proceedings of C.O.P.E.C., Being a Report of the Meetings of the Conference on Christian Politics, Economics and Citizenship held in Birmingham April 5–12, 1924* (London, Longmans, Green and Co., 1924, pp. xi, 295), p. xi. See also *C.O.P.E.C. Commission Reports* (London, Longmans, Green and Co., 12 vols., 1924); *A Summary of the Reports of the Commissions* (London, Student Christian Movement Press, 1924, pp. vii, 111); Iremonger, *op. cit.*, pp. 328–336.

of London, was one of them. Here Charles Bond (1876-1931) spent his life. When he was a butcher's errand boy an accident had cost him a leg. He became a carpenter, gave himself to boys, as a lay reader held crowded men's services on Sunday afternoons, managed to take a theological course, was ordained (1914), became a curate and then a vicar in Alton, devoted himself without stint to the community, and was trusted and loved as an informal preacher, as one who saw that the poor were fed, and as confessor and counsellor.[48]

In a generation which was drifting away from the Bible and to whom that book was increasingly unfamiliar, in 1922 the Bible Reading Fellowship was organized. It began in a parish in South London as the Fellowship of St. Matthew, and its members were held together by a monthly publication which contained Bible passages for reading and subjects for intercession. At first it grew slowly, but by 1930 the circulation of its leaflet had jumped to 20,000, and those who used it were encouraged to formulate their own subjects for intercession rather than have them suggested. So rapidly did the movement spread that in 1930 headquarters were moved to Westminster and a full-time staff was set up to handle the circulation. It continued to grow and at the end of twenty-five years had a membership of 351,000.[49] Contemporaneously somewhat similar and much larger enterprises were seen in the United States, such as the Upper Room of the Methodists and the Secret Place of the Baptists.

THE CHURCH OF ENGLAND AND WORLD WAR II

World War II did not take the Church of England quite as much by surprise as had World War I. Yet it was more dislocating than its predecessor. Enemy bombings destroyed or damaged far more churches—along with other buildings—than in the earlier war.[50] To escape the danger of bombing, large elements in the population were moved to small towns or rural districts and this entailed a more serious disruption of church attendance and normal parish life than that brought by World War I. In both wars the pressures of defense measures and of war industries cut into the observance of Sunday. The evacuations revealed to the clergy in whose parishes the evacuees were placed the colossal religious ignorance of many of the youth.[51]

As in the earlier war, many looked to the Church for leadership and heard a mixture of voices. William Temple, who had followed Lang as Archbishop of York in 1929 when the latter was translated to Canterbury and who in 1942 was enthroned as Archbishop of Canterbury after Lang's resignation and

---

[48] Lloyd, *op. cit.*, Vol. II, pp. 209-219.
[49] *Ibid.*, pp. 64-71.
[50] About 15,000 ecclesiastical buildings suffered.—Spinks, *Religion in Britain since 1900*, p. 217.
[51] Spinks, *op. cit.*, p. 216.

who died in October, 1944, on the eve of victory, repeatedly had the ear of the nation. He looked upon the second war, as he had the first, as a divine judgement but held that England was right and against "the deified nation of the Nazis" had taken its stand "as a dedicated nation." Although far from being a pacifist, he championed the conscientious objectors, more numerous than in the earlier struggle.[52] While declining to speak out, as many wished him to do, against some of the forms of fighting, such as the bombing of the Ruhr dams, he vigorously condemned suggestions for reprisals on the civilian population of Germany in retaliation for the flying bombs launched by the Germans against England.[53] He refused to draw up or sanction prayers for victory and regretted that Garbett, his successor at York, and Lang, while Archbishop of Canterbury, were unable to share that conviction.[54] He joined with the Archbishop of Canterbury, the Archbishop of Westminster (Cardinal Hinsley), and the Moderator of the Free Church Council in a public statement which endorsed Pope Pius XII's "Five Peace Points" and added to them five standards "by which economic situations and proposals may be tested."[55] He sought to alleviate the famine in the lands occupied by the German armies, to aid refugees, to succour the Jews, and to prevent reprisals against prisoners of war.[56] Lang, as Archbishop of Canterbury, induced the king to ask that May 26, 1940, be observed as a day of prayer.[57] Cyril Forster Garbett (1875–1955), who was translated from Southwark to Winchester in 1932 and then to York in 1942 when Temple was translated to Canterbury, was deeply concerned over the fate of Poland and the Jews, held that the war was a crusade against unrelieved evil, and publicly supported the bombings of German and Italian cities as a protest against the treatment of Poland and the Jews.[58]

George Kennedy Allen Bell (1883–1958), who had been chaplain to Davidson and Dean of Canterbury (1924–1929) and in 1929 had been made Bishop of Chichester, had long been active in international affairs. A friend of Söderblom and for a time chairman of the Universal Christian Council for Life and Work, when National Socialism became dominant in Germany he aided the pastors who were refugees from the Nazis, assisted the *Bekennende Kirche,* and was close to Bonhoeffer. He spoke out fearlessly against the obliteration bombings of German cities and is said so to have incurred the displeasure of Churchill thereby that the latter would not recommend him to the king for the Archbishopric of Canterbury. Partly through his friendship with Bonhoeffer he

---

[52] Iremonger, *William Temple,* pp. 540–544.
[53] *Ibid.,* pp. 544–546.
[54] *Ibid.,* pp. 555, 558.
[55] Koenig, *Principles for Peace,* pp. 632–640; Iremonger, *op. cit.,* p. 560.
[56] Iremonger, *op. cit.,* pp. 562–568.
[57] Lockhart, *Cosmo Gordon Lang,* p. 427.
[58] Margaret, *Archbishop Garbett,* p. 55.

learned of the resistance movement which sought to unseat Hitler and urged the British Government, vainly as it proved, to support it. On the eve of the invasion of Norway he had come to know Berggrav and did what he could to uphold him in the ensuing ordeal. During the war he chaired the Famine Relief Committee and on the coming of peace led in mobilizing the British churches for the reconstruction of the devastated countries. It was natural that he should be present at the meeting in Stuttgart soon after the war in which leaders of the German churches met with those from other countries in the successful effort to reëstablish fellowship. He was later the first chairman of the Central Committee and then an honorary president of the World Council of Churches.[59]

Henson, who was called out of his retirement from the see of Durham to a canonry in Westminster Abbey (1940), there by his preaching to help in the war emergency, publicly opposed reprisals.[60] In 1940 Temple and Bell joined with two Nonconformists and representatives of the Church of Norway in setting forth what they deemed to be the conditions on which Britain could properly enter negotiations with Germany.[61]

Efforts were made as in World War I, but now more in association with other churches, to bring about a revival of religion in the country. Thus the Sword of the Spirit movement, launched by Hinsley, in which only Roman Catholics could be full members, was supported by both Anglican archbishops and the Nonconforming churches. Committees arranged for parallel action in religious matters and joint action in social and international concerns.[62] Temple and Garbett set on foot a campaign—the Church Looks Forward—in conjunction with the Religion and Life movement, initiated by the recently formed British Council of Churches, in which the Church of England and the other Protestant bodies coöperated.[63]

In 1941 in the midst of the war what was known as the Malvern Conference was convened. Its purpose was to prevent the kind of post-war slump that had brought great suffering after World War I. The suggestion came from P. T. R. Kirk, an Anglican clergyman, the general director of the Industrial Christian Fellowship. That movement, Anglo-Catholic in leadership, had been seeking for some years to render the social message of the Gospel effective in industry and had won the support of many of the manufacturers and the leaders in the trade unions. Among other achievements, it had made "Industrial Sunday" an annual event in a number of churches. To prepare for post-war reconstruction Kirk persuaded Temple to be convener and chairman of a conference "to

[59] *The Ecumenical Review,* Vol. XI, pp. 133–142; *Who's Who, 1955,* p. 533.
[60] Henson, *Retrospect of an Unimportant Life,* Vol. III, p. 153.
[61] Spinks, *op. cit.,* p. 218.
[62] *Ibid.,* p. 218; Iremonger, *op. cit.,* p. 423.
[63] Spinks, *op. cit.,* p. 219.

consider from the Anglican point of view what are the fundamental facts which are directly relevant to the ordering of the new society that is quite evidently emerging, and how Christian thought can be shaped to play a leading part in the reconstruction after the war is over." Approximately four hundred met for about three days in January, 1941, and listened to addresses by distinguished speakers. Malvern was more concerned with theology than what was in some ways its predecessor—COPEC. In contrast with COPEC it was exclusively Anglican. Its results were hard to measure, but it at least provoked and facilitated thinking on the social and economic issues presented by current society.[64]

World War II was the occasion for the Education Act of 1944. In it both the Church of England and Nonconformists shared and its passage would not have been possible but for that coöperation. For many years dissatisfaction had existed on the state of education and we have seen the various efforts made in the nineteenth century to bring improvement.[65] The war, with its evacuation of numbers of children from the large cities to towns and rural districts, brought vividly to the attention of many the religious illiteracy as well as other ignorance and the lack of discipline and decency of many youths who had been reared in the slums. The result was a bill which raised to sixteen years the age of compulsory attendance in the elementary and secondary schools. In these schools it required religious teaching, the daily opening of the schools by corporate worship, and the giving of religious teaching at any hour of the school day and not simply at the beginning. It made religious knowledge a prerequisite for teachers' certificates from teachers' colleges. The inspection of religious teaching in the schools by government officials was provided for. The dual system inherited from the nineteenth century was continued—of state and denominational schools. The latter were to be aided to the extent of half their construction and maintenance and the former were to use a religious syllabus which was undenominational but based upon the Bible. Parents, if they so formally requested, might have denominational instruction given their children.[66]

The Church of England: The Post-War Decade and a Half

In a number of ways the fifteen years which followed World War II appeared to be discouraging for Protestantism in England, including the Church

---

[64] Iremonger, *op. cit.*, pp. 428–440; *Malvern, 1941. The Life of the Church and the Order of Society. Being the Proceedings of the Archbishop of York's Conference* (New York, Longmans, Green and Co., 1941, pp. xv, 235), *passim*.

[65] Volume II, pp. 355–358.

[66] Spinks, *op. cit.*, pp. 216, 217; Iremonger, *op. cit.*, pp. 569–576; Lockhart, *op. cit.*, pp. 368, 369; *Information Service*, October 18, 1952, November 15, 1952.

of England. In general one effect of the war was to quicken movements already in motion which made for de-Christianization.

One such movement was the continued falling off in the number of clergy. It was said that in 1951 the total was 13,000.[67] This represented a fairly steady decline from 18,180 in 1914 and 16,745 in 1930. The root cause was ascribed to the inadequacy of the parsons' pay.[68] Another set of figures, only slightly less disturbing, noted that in 1905 the Church of England had 19,053 clergy serving a population of 34,000,000 and in 1958 it had 15,500 clergy serving 40,000,000; the average age was at least 52 and 29 per cent. were 65 years of age or over; about 600 ordinands were required annually if the total was to be maintained at its then figure, and in 1957 only 479 were ordained and a quarter of these were over forty years of age. The cost of training was considered excessive, for much was carried on in small theological colleges.[69] Late in the 1950's it was reported that in the North there was one clergyman to every 4,115 of the population, while in the South the ratio was one to every 2,919 of the population.[70] In the mid-twentieth century as in much of the past, appointment to a large proportion of the livings was in the hands of the crown (which meant, as with the naming of bishops, the government in power) and to many others rested with individuals, the two ancient universities, the cathedrals, or the bishops. The clergy deficiency was in part, but only in part, covered by the ordination of men in middle life who had retired from the civil and colonial service or from business and who were ordained after a theological course of two years. Although they were not profound scholars, they were said to know how to deal with men.[71] Stipends were so low that many of the clergy sought part-time employment in other occupations.

A falling off was also seen in the numbers vitally connected with the Church of England. In 1939 Easter communicants totalled 2,245,102, in 1947, 1,859,115; in 1950, 1,995,573; and in 1953, 2,068,829.[72] As far as could be ascertained—the statistics were not entirely reliable—the body of full-time women workers also slumped, from 2,041 in 1913 to 1,547 in 1923 and to 832 in 1953. The totals of lay readers even more sharply declined, from 4,060 in 1913 to 4,044 in 1923 and to 1,139 in 1953. The number of infants baptized also decreased, strikingly as compared with the mounting population. In 1913 the total was 559,976, in 1923 it was 494,063, in 1939 it was 384,992, in 1940 it was 361,461, and, while in 1950 it mounted to 450,611, in 1953 it was 398,146. Adult baptisms fell from 15,629 in 1913 to 12,352 in 1923, to 10,271 in 1933, to 9,502 in 1939, to 9,454 in

[67] Information Service, November, 10, 1951.
[68] Ibid.
[69] Frontier, Vol. I, p. 298.
[70] The Christian Century, Vol. LXXVI (October 28, 1959).
[71] Norman Sykes to the author, June 25, 1952.
[72] Rhodes, The New Church in the New Age, p. 18.

1940, and to 8,496 in 1950. But they rose to 10,623 in 1953. The number of persons confirmed had a somewhat similar record. In 1913 it was 239,018, in 1923 it was 233,427, in 1933 it was 184,616, in 1939 it was 157,627, in 1940 it was 134,159, but in 1950 it rose to 142,294 and in 1953 to 154,548.[73] In one parish with a vicar and two curates and a population of about 80,000, most of whom left school at the age of fifteen or less, the combined congregations in the two churches on a Sunday morning in the 1950's was seldom as many as fifty.[74] In Sheffield, a growing manufacturing centre with a population of about half a million in 1950, the attendance at Anglican services on an average Sunday in 1881 was said to have been 33,835, and in 1956 from 12,000 to 13,000. In 1916 Easter communicants were 13,456 and in 1950 about 11,000.[75]

In general, late in the 1940's it was reported that if all denominations were taken into account about 15 to 20 per cent. of the population went fairly regularly to church, another 40 per cent. did so occasionally, and many listened to religious broadcasts. In England church attendance was lower than in Wales or Scotland and in the industrial cities lower than in rural areas. For example, one study showed that in London 28 per cent. had been in church within a month, in large towns the corresponding percentage was 38, in small towns 40, and in rural areas 50. Of those who never attended church nearly six out of ten were members of the Church of England, two out of ten were Nonconformists, and one in ten was a Roman Catholic.[76] A Gallup poll taken in 1957 showed that of 2,261 men and women interviewed 14 per cent. had been to church the preceding Sunday, 28 per cent. said that they went once a month or more, 32 per cent. denied ever going to church, and 7 per cent. reported listening only to radio and television services. Of those who never went to church, a third stopped going before the age of fifteen, and a half between sixteen and twenty years of age. Yet of those interviewed nine-tenths declared it to be the duty of parents to teach their children to pray and nearly all said that children should be baptized.[77] Late in the 1950's about half the marriages were solemnized in the Church of England and two-thirds of the population were baptized in that church.[78] On the whole these figures are higher than those which we have found in several countries on the Continent.

Bleak though some of the statistics were, the Church of England was still very much alive. Here and there "house churches" were seen with celebrations of the Eucharist on the kitchen table.[79] Village evangelism constituted a move-

---

[73] J. N. F. Earle, an Anglican clergyman, manuscript used by permission, January, 1958.
[74] *Ibid.*
[75] Wickham, *Church and People in an Industrial City*, p. 168.
[76] *Information Service*, April 30, 1949.
[77] *Ecumenical Press Service*, May 31, 1957.
[78] *The Christian Century*, Vol. LXXVI, p. 1252 (October 28, 1959).
[79] Earle, *op. cit.*

ment which came into existence after World War II. Founded by two clergy-men, it included men and women and laymen and clergymen and had no tight organization. The evangelists came to a parish or a group of parishes on the invitation of the local clergy and were there usually for two weeks. Prepa-ration was made a year in advance by correspondence and perhaps by a per-sonal visit. The missioners systematically called in homes, distributing literature, and after a preliminary week addresses were given in the church. The mission was followed up by efforts of the pastor and the parish council. Eventually the evangelists extended their efforts to suburban areas.[80]

A similar yet different movement was the Servants of Christ the King. It was born during the war, in 1942, continued to grow, and in 1948 outlined its purposes more specifically than at its foundation. A purely Anglican society, it gathered together, without publicity, small groups of men and women who sought through close fellowship to live to the full the Christian life in their daily occupations, to infiltrate the secular communities in factories, mines, and the professions, and to win others to discipleship. They worked in close co-operation with the clergy and by annual conferences encouraged an inclusive fellowship.[81] Here was another instance of what we have found among both Roman Catholics and Protestants, a lay movement of dedicated minorities in the midst of a secularized society, endeavouring to permeate it while living within it and seeking to win others to the faith.

Although some pessimists maintained that the traditional parish system was completely outmoded, wherever the pastor had imagination and vigour ways were found to make it effective, at least in rural communities. While fewer were present at church services than in the nineteenth century, those who came did so out of conviction. That was especially true of youth, and in Oxford and Cambridge the attendance at chapel was improving.[82] Numbers of the ancient church fabrics, including cathedrals, were badly in need of repair, but new churches were being erected in several cities.[83] Partly because of the shortage of ordinands, some parishes were being combined, and the need was said not to have been as acute as the decline in numbers might indicate. The quality was reported to be good. About 60 per cent. of the men applying for ordination were university graduates and the non-graduates coming from the army and the colonial service were declared on the whole to be able.[84]

An attempt to find a solution to the challenge presented by the industrialized city was the Industrial Mission, with its centre in Sheffield. Its major figure

---

[80] A Monthly Letter about Evangelism, No. 9, November, 1957.

[81] Roger Lloyd, An Adventure in Discipleship. The Servants of Christ the King (London, Long-mans, Green and Co., 1953, pp. 127), passim.

[82] G. K. A. Bell to the author, July, 1952.

[83] W. Greer, Bishop of Manchester, to the author, July, 1954.

[84] George F. Woods to the author, October, 1958.

was E. R. Wickham, a clergyman. It was based upon the conviction that a church whose structure was mapped on a wholly geographic and territorial pattern, as was the traditional parish, could not impinge effectively upon a highly industrialized, urbanized society. Sheffield was an example, for in the twentieth century the Church there had progressively lost ground. The Industrial Mission proved that it was possible through ministers specially trained and giving their full time to the enterprise to make and maintain continuous contact with the personnel of the heavy steel industry. When confidence had been won and after negotiations with management, works' councils, and shop stewards' committees, the men were regularly visited, and talked with during the lunch hour and other breaks in the working day. Informal groups met after working hours. The companies asked the staff of the Mission to help in the whole range of training their employees for the increasingly specialized and mechanized processes of the mills. Laymen in the daily work in the mills were encouraged to organize their fellows to further the objectives of the Mission: the mission was designed to be a lay enterprise.[85] Here was still another phase of a mounting tide of lay action which we have found among both Roman Catholics and Protestants in a variety of the occupations and aspects of life.

Several other novel approaches were made by Anglicans to permeate the revolutionary age with Christian principles. Thus after World War II Marcus Morris, who while in charge of a village parish had begun experimenting in ways of conveying the Christian faith through the printed word, from a publishing office on Fleet Street in London developed a new form of the popular "comic books" in order to reach the children. Some of the "comics" portrayed Biblical characters and other Christian heroes and heroines. Others were not avowedly Christian but endeavoured to treat their themes in a Christian manner. The "comic books" had an enormous circulation. Clubs were organized in connexion with them, with hostels, cricket and football coaching, outings, and Christmas carol services. Morris also edited a mass circulation women's periodical. He sought not to present Christian doctrines directly but to relate Christian values to every-day life.[86]

In William Temple College, in Rugby, labourers and employers were brought together to be instructed in Christianity and to discuss the bearing of the faith on their occupations.[87] Its head had been a member of the Labour government. It had an excellent library and it sought to combine sound theology with practical application to economic and labour problems. An enterprise called the Missions to Seamen, organized in 1856, under its symbol "the Flying Angel" ministered for over a century to men in Britain's widely flung

[85] Wickham, *op. cit.*, pp. 243–254; *Information Service*, May 14, 1955.
[86] Malcolm Boyd in *Religion and Life*, Vol. XXVI, pp. 62–67.
[87] W. Greer to the author, July, 1954.

merchant marine. Through centres in the British Isles and in ports in many countries, during and after the two world wars it helped sailors with lodgings, wholesome recreation, chapels, literature, and personal friendship.[88] St. Catherine's, in Cumberland Lodge not far from Windsor Castle, had features similar to Sigtuna. Here points of contact were sought with intellectuals, but not obviously in a Christian way or with religious services—although a chapel was available for those who wished to use it. The Christian Frontier Council, with a membership of about forty men and women prominent in various activities and occupations, met monthly in London and issued the quarterly *Christian News-Letter,* which was followed by *The Christian Frontier.* It was based upon the conviction that a frontier existed between Christian theology and the many spheres in which men must act and that new methods must be found for exploring it. The Dons' Advisory Group, made up of university teachers, was supported by the Christian Frontier Council and the Student Christian Movement. St. Anne's House, in London, of which the Bishop of London was the president, had as its objective "the recovery of the prophetic ministry of the Church" alongside its traditional sacramental and pastoral ministries and tried to develop a strong body of active and intelligent Christians to make the Church "incarnate" in the revolutionary age and thus to illuminate the latter's social complexities.[89]

THE CHURCH OF ENGLAND: THE CONTINUATION OF THE MONASTIC MOVEMENT

The revival of the monastic life in the Church of England which had begun in the nineteenth century continued[90]—another evidence of vitality. Some of the older communities expanded their operations. Thus the Society of St. John the Evangelist, its members better known as the Cowley Fathers, grew, especially outside England. In 1914 the branch in the United States became autonomous and in 1939 that status was achieved by the Canadian province. In 1933 the American congregation founded a province in Japan.[91] The Community of the Resurrection had its headquarters in Mirfield in the heart of an industrial and mining section of Yorkshire. Its members conducted a theological college, had a deep concern for social problems, served away from Mirfield in a variety of capacities—pastoral, evangelistic, scholarly—and from time to time returned to Mirfield to maintain the community life. They sought to develop the religious life, to effect the union of Christendom, and had extensive missions in Africa, one of which, in Southern Rhodesia, was inaugu-

---

[88] L. A. G. Strong, *Flying Angel. The Story of Missions to Seamen* (London, Methuen & Co., 1956, pp. x, 189), *passim.*
[89] Malcolm Boyd in *Religion in Life,* Vol. XXVI, pp. 62–67.
[90] Volume II, pp. 274–277.
[91] Anson, *The Call of the Cloister,* pp. 87, 88.

rated in 1919. An older mission, in the Union of South Africa, was expanded. To further Christian unity, in 1928 the Fellowship of St. Alban and St. Sergius was begun to foster understanding between Anglicans and the Eastern Orthodox.[92]

The Society of the Sacred Mission, with its centre at Kelham, near Newark, whose members were celibate and took the vow of poverty, gave itself to worship, to the preparation of clergy, to pastoral care, and to the spread of the Gospel in other lands. In the 1950's its chief work was the training of ordinands to help make good the deficiency in the body of clergy. It had charge of industrial parishes, possessed a growing province in South Africa, and opened a house in Australia (1947) for the training of clergy in that country. It encouraged the movement known as Parish and People, which sought to foster the idea of the Church as the family of God, partly by furthering corporate liturgical worship and building up groups which would think of themselves as worshipping communities. Parish and People was another instance of what we have found repeatedly in the twentieth century in Roman Catholic and Protestant circles—earnest and devoted minorities, largely lay, within a society which was drifting from its earlier Christian moorings.[93]

The Society of the Divine Compassion was an attempt to embody the manner of life of the initial followers of Francis of Assisi. It first established itself in poverty-stricken Plaistow on the lower Thames, where were great docks. As the physical conditions of the neighbourhood improved with national health insurance and old age pensions the Society remained, although in World War II its superior held to his pacifist position and the bombings all but destroyed its church. Between the two wars a mission was begun (1926) in Southern Rhodesia, and in 1921 the Society of St. Francis was inaugurated by a former novice and made the care of travellers its special object.[94]

From the Society of the Divine Compassion came William Sirr, who had been its superior but felt himself called to a life of prayer and in 1918 began to live in complete poverty as a hermit. He made his home in a stable in Worcestershire and until 1936, the year before his death, drew pilgrims, both Christian and non-Christian, from many walks of life. He sought to exemplify the law of love and, like a Russian *starets,* gave counsel to all who wished it.[95]

Several of the sisterhoods of nineteenth-century inception continued to flourish. Thus the Community of St. Mary the Virgin, from its main centre in Wantage, Berkshire, stressed worship, the training of teachers, and rescue work for wayward girls or girls who were in grave danger. It opened houses

---

[92] *Ibid.,* pp. 122–139.
[93] *Ibid.,* pp. 139–148.
[94] *Ibid.,* pp. 148–162, 200–208.
[95] Geoffry Curtis, *William of Glasshampton: Friar: Monk: Solitary* (London, S.P.C.K., 1947, pp. xi, 176), *passim.*

of mercy or assumed responsibility for houses of mercy which other agencies invited it to undertake. It had missions in India and South Africa and its vitality was seen, among other ways, in the societies which sprang from it after 1914.[96] The Community of Nursing Sisters of St. John the Divine, begun in 1848, soon after World War I seemed about to expire, but about 1932 it was placed under the direction of Cowley and it revived and opened new homes.[97] The Society of St. Margaret, founded in 1855 by John Mason Neale, had as its original purpose nursing the poor, but later enlarged it to include the care of orphans and the aged. In the mid-twentieth century it had more than a score of houses in England, Wales, South Africa, and Ceylon and about ten houses in a branch in the United States and Canada.[98] The Sisters of the Church, begun in 1870, gave themselves to the service of the poor and down-trodden, expanded to India, Burma, Australia, New Zealand, and Canada, and in the mid-twentieth century had more than a score of houses, the majority of them in England.[99] Most of the other communities of women which had their inception in the nineteenth century persisted beyond 1914.

Several communities were founded in the four decades which began with 1914. At least five of them were of men—one of them of contemplatives and another of seculars. The latter, the Company of Mission Priests, was made up of autonomous houses, each with a common purse. The rule was flexible. The members did not take life vows but remained unmarried as long as they continued in the company. The company was governed by a council.[100] About a dozen communities of women were founded between 1914 and 1953. One, the Society of the Sacred Cross, was of enclosed nuns who devoted themselves to prayer, study, and manual work. Another, the rapidly growing Order of the Holy Paraclete, organized during World War I, took its inspiration from Whitby Abbey, then in ruins but centuries earlier a centre of learning, Christian education, and missions. The members specialized in educational, maternity, and medical work and branch houses were opened in at least three places in Africa.[101]

A unique community was that of St. Julian's, conceived by Florence Allshorn (1887-1950). Sent by the Church Missionary Society to Uganda in 1920, she was prevented by ill health from returning after furlough in 1924. In 1928 she was placed in charge of a hostel for training missionaries. In 1940 she began a community of women who developed a centre to which missionaries could come for rest and further training, especially in the spiritual life. She

[96] Anson, op. cit., pp. 242-259.
[97] Ibid., pp. 280-285.
[98] Ibid., pp. 336-355.
[99] Ibid., pp. 439-445.
[100] Ibid., pp. 209-219.
[101] Ibid., pp. 508-528.

herself was marked by a remarkable spiritual insight and a completely un-selfish devotion which proved contagious.[102]

The Church of England deemed it advisable to provide for comprehensive supervision of the religious communities of men and women. In 1920 and 1930 the Lambeth Conference took formal cognizance of them. In the latter year a joint committee of bishops and superiors of the religious communities met and in 1935 an advisory council for the provinces of Canterbury and York was approved. As its name suggests, the council's functions were largely consulta-tive.[103]

THE CHURCH OF ENGLAND: WORSHIP AND THE DEVOTIONAL LIFE

A feature of the Church of England in the first half of the twentieth century was a growing emphasis upon corporate worship and the devotional life of the individual. The faith of the majority of the population was being eroded, but among the loyal minority more use was made of both public and private worship. Here was a parellel to the Liturgical Movement in the Roman Catho-lic Church.

Much of the trend was due to the Anglo-Catholic movement. Part of the expression was through the religious communities that we have briefly de-scribed. They set an example which could not but be contagious among the circles in intimate contact with them. Clergy who had had their theological training through the Community of the Resurrection and the Society of the Sacred Mission carried out in their parishes much of what they had learned in their seminary days. No longer did the liturgical forms introduced by the Anglo-Catholics provoke the riotous opposition that had been common in much of the nineteenth century. Some extreme practices were still viewed with lifted eyebrows and even met vocal criticism. But several of the clergy, safely en-sconced in parishes where they had life tenure and were not amenable to the wishes of their flocks, said mass in Latin and in other ways conformed to what they regarded as the Catholic tradition. In a few instances they were rebuked by the bishop. Many of the practices which were formerly suspect spread to parishes that were not controlled by Anglo-Catholics. In 1922 an optional lec-tionary was authorized to be used at the discretion of the minister and in 1955 it was modified. The lectionary of the Book of Common Prayer as com-piled in the sixteenth century and in use since that time had reacted against Roman Catholic practices and had reduced the number of holy days and saint's days with the lessons proper for those days, paid more attention to the calendar year than to the ecclesiastical year, and made possible the reading of almost

---

[102] J. H. Oldham, *Florence Allshorn and the Story of St. Julian's* (London, S.C.M. Press, 1951, pp. 168), *passim*.

[103] Anson, *op. cit.*, pp. 482, 483.

all the Bible in the course of the year. The lectionary of 1922 and its 1955 revision more nearly followed an early Roman model with more emphasis upon the ecclesiastical year and readings from the Scripture deemed fitting for the special periods of that year. It was, therefore, largely an Anglo-Catholic creation.[104] Retreat centres multiplied to which laity and clergy came for worship and for training in the life of prayer. It was said that in 1913 the Church of England had only one retreat house and that in 1932 it had twenty-two diocesan houses for that purpose and over thirty which belonged to religious communities. Some of these houses received over a thousand retreatants a year.[105]

Among those who were much in demand for the direction of retreats was Evelyn Underhill (1875–1941). She also wrote many books on worship, mysticism, and the life of prayer, which were widely read. The daughter of a lawyer and married to a childhood friend who was also a lawyer, she had a keen analytical mind which did not find faith easy. Although confirmed in the Church of England, at one point in her spiritual pilgrimage she gave serious thought to becoming a Roman Catholic. But she remained in the Anglican Communion and regarded herself as an Anglo-Catholic. For some time she had Von Hügel as her spiritual director and owed much to him, especially for her transition from a somewhat cold theism to a profound and heart-warming acceptance of the incarnation. Indeed, she said that "under God," she was indebted to him for her "entire spiritual life." Highly intellectual, a lover of art and beauty, a skilled yachtswoman, much travelled, she also gave herself to the poor and was counsellor to many, both high and low, in personal interviews and through correspondence. Chronic ill health increasingly harassed her. Yet in spite of physical weakness and times of severe depression she compassed an enormous amount of writing and speaking.[106]

Among the many other books issued to promote the devotional life one by William Temple on the Gospel of John must be mentioned. The fact that it went into a number of printings was evidence of the existence of thousands who responded to its deep spiritual insight.[107]

---

[104] Geoffrey G. Willis in *The Journal of Ecclesiastical History*, Vol. IX, pp. 73–86.

[105] Evelyn Underhill, *Worship* (New York, Harper & Brothers, 1936, pp. xvii, 350), p. 338.

[106] Margaret Cropper, *Life of Evelyn Underhill* (New York, Harper & Brothers, 1958, pp. xxii, 244), *passim*. Some of the more important books by Evelyn Underhill were *Mysticism. A Study in the Nature and Development of Man's Spiritual Consciousness* (New York, E. P. Dutton and Co., 4th ed., 1912, pp. xv, 600); *Worship* (New York, Harper & Brothers, 1937, pp. xxi, 350); *The Life of the Spirit and the Life of Today* (New York, E. P. Dutton and Co., 1922, pp. xi, 311); *The Essentials of Mysticism and Other Essays* (New York, E. P. Dutton and Co., 1920, pp. vii, 245). See also *Collected Papers of Evelyn Underhill*, edited by Lucy Menzies (London, Longmans, Green and Co., 1946, pp. 240), and *The Letters of Evelyn Underhill*, edited by Charles Williams (London, Longmans, Green and Co., 1944, pp. 344), *passim*, especially pp. 195, 196.

[107] William Temple, *Readings in John's Gospel* (*First and Second Series*) (London, Macmillan and Co., 1945, pp. xxxiii, 412).

THE CHURCH OF ENGLAND: THE VARIATIONS EMBRACED BY ITS INCLUSIVE STRUCTURE

Seeking as it did to be the church of the nation, the Church of England permitted a wide variety of beliefs and practices within its ample fold. If anything, in the twentieth century they were accentuated rather than diminished. They were kept together by the historic episcopate, the creeds, baptism and the Lord's Supper (the two sacraments acknowledged by all), and the sixteenth-century Book of Common Prayer, still the only one authorized by Parliament. Effective machinery was lacking to enforce uniformity. The mounting diversities may have been another evidence of vitality. In the loyalty of the minority of the nation who held firmly to the Church in the face of the progressive de-Christianization of the majority was a depth of conviction which partly expressed itself in conscientiously held but far from uniform emphases. Here, too, was evidence of the urge to achieve the unity of all who bore the Christian name. It impelled leaders of the Church of England to take an outstanding part in the Ecumenical Movement and in efforts to attain the re-union of what had been the Catholic Church of early centuries.

The main trends in nineteenth-century Anglicanism which were labelled Evangelical, Broad, and Catholic persisted in the twentieth century, but the lines which separated them were increasingly blurred and they tended to penetrate one another.[108] Each developed variations within itself with the result that the Church of England became more and more a Joseph's coat of many colours. To attempt to describe or even to name all the facets would extend our narrative quite beyond its proper dimensions. We can take the space to mention only a few.

Within the Evangelical wing what was akin to the extreme fundamentalism seen in the United States drew a minority away from the Church Missionary Society, begun as that organization had been by Evangelicals and depending for support chiefly upon those of Evangelical traditions, and formed (1922) the Bible Churchmen's Missionary Society.[109] Following World War II conservative Evangelicalism displayed a revival in Britain, mainly in the Church of England. It was strong among youth and in the Inter-Varsity Fellowship. Rejecting some forms of the inerrancy of the Scriptures held by many fundamentalists and moving away from strictly individualistic Pietism with its despair of society, it held that when the Bible is judged by its own standards it is the Word of God and that Evangelicals must concern themselves with society as Wilberforce and Shaftesbury had done.[110] We are to find a similar

108 Lloyd, *The Church of England in the Twentieth Century*, Vol. II, p. 58.

109 Strong and Warnshuis, *Directory of Foreign Missions*, p. 11.

110 James I. Packer in *Christianity Today*, Vol. II, pp. 3–6 (September 29, 1958); *Religion in Life*, Vol. XXIX, pp. 154, 155 (Winter, 1959–60).

trend among some conservative Protestants in America. Contrary to this trend, some Evangelicals were seeking to make a radical adjustment to the intellectual currents of the day. They associated themselves in the Anglican Evangelical Group Movement. Begun in 1905, it brought together those in sympathy with it and in 1923 publicly declared its principles and invited applications for membership.[111]

Ernest William Barnes (1874-1953), Bishop of Birmingham, represented what might once have been described as an extreme Broad Church position. In 1947 he caused something of a sensation by a little book meant for a popular constituency[112] in which he traced the beginnings of Christianity and paid special attention to Jesus and the early Church. He rejected the virgin birth of Jesus and, while accepting some of His recorded sayings as approximately authentic and acknowledging the fact of the crucifixion, held that the accounts of the trial and death of Jesus had so many varied and contradictory statements that only a rough outline could be determined with any assurance of accuracy. He cast doubt on the physical resurrection and ascension of Jesus and questioned whether Jesus at the Last Supper instituted the Eucharist. Although both archbishops openly dissented from the book, one of them privately insisted that that particular school of thought had a right to be represented in the episcopate. Moreover, in his Gifford Lectures a few years earlier Barnes had frankly stated his belief in God as ruling the world and, since the laws of nature are His laws, as not permitting those laws to constrain His freedom. He held that God is goodness, beauty, and truth, and that His guidance of the world is purposive. He spoke of Jesus as "having matchless religious understanding," believed in and practised petitionary prayer, and maintained that belief in God and in personal immortality must stand or fall together. Earlier he had stoutly insisted that he was an Evangelical, maintained that central in Evangelicalism was the incarnation, that Jesus Christ was both God and man and that Christ had the words of eternal life, held to belief in the atonement and the authority of the Bible, and insisted that Evangelicalism had its most powerful allies in literary criticism, natural science, and philosophy.[113]

The term "Broad Church" was passing out of favour. Instead "English Modernism" was preferred, for the Broad Churchmen were said to be placing too little emphasis on the Church and the English Modernist was moving towards what he called a liberal Catholic position, stressing the Church as the

[111] Harvey, The Church and the Twentieth Century, pp. 364-366.
[112] Ernest William Barnes, The Rise of Christianity (London, Longmans, Green and Co., 1947, pp. xx, 356.
[113] Ernest William Barnes, Scientific Theory and Religion. The World Described by Science and Its Spiritual Interpretation (Cambridge University Press, 1933, pp. xxiv, 685), pp. 638, 639, 644, 653; Liberal Evangelicalism. An Interpretation by Members of the Church of England (London, Hodder and Stoughton, 4th ed., 1924, pp. x, 304), pp. 287-304.

"beloved community."[114] Yet whether as Broad Church or English Modernism, the movement still provoked violent criticism. For example, a great outcry greeted the conference of the Modern Churchmen's Union held in Cambridge in 1921.[115]

Further variety was seen in a volume of essays by men of broadly Catholic convictions,[116] and intended to be in the tradition of *Lux Mundi*, edited by Gore, to which Anglo-Catholics had contributed.[117] Its authors were quite aware of the historical method and of the problems which it posed both for the authenticity of the Gospel records of Jesus and for the nature of the Church. They were frankly Catholic, as they understood that term, but rejected the distinctive features of the Roman Catholic Church. They believed in the authority of the Catholic Church in its continuing tradition but made room for individual judgement. They rejected the picture of Jesus which the Liberals had drawn from the Gospel narratives and believed that these narratives contained incontrovertible evidence that Jesus thought of Himself as the Christ, uniquely the incarnate God. They faced up to the difficulties presented by the New Testament accounts of the resurrection but maintained that Christ was raised from the dead, that His tomb was empty, and that He appeared to His disciples. They pointed out that the other evidence was reinforced by the transforming effect upon the disciples. They knew the objections urged against the traditional belief that Christ had instituted the two sacraments baptism and the Communion, but they held to that conviction. Here, clearly, was an approach to what had been called the Broad Church position, which many of their contemporaries preferred to call English Modernism.

The Church of England Faces the Intellectual Currents of the Time

From what we have said in the last few paragraphs it must be evident that many in the Church of England were seeking to think through their faith in full cognizance of the intellectual currents of the twentieth-century stage of the revolutionary age. Their answers were not uniform, but they did not attempt to dodge the challenge and they believed that they could honestly remain within the Anglican Communion.

We must now go on to note some similar efforts and to speak of a few of the other outstanding theologians and Biblical scholars in that church. Obviously they could not and did not work in a vacuum. The world in which they lived was being racked by wars in which England was deeply involved.

---

[114] H. D. A. Major, *English Modernism, Its Origin, Methods, Aims* (Cambridge, Mass., Harvard University Press, 1927, pp. 274), *passim*.

[115] Lloyd, *op. cit.*, Vol. II, pp. 38–48; Henson, *Retrospect of an Unimportant Life*, Vol. II, p. 144.

[116] Edward Gordon Selwyn, editor, *Essays Catholic & Critical* (New York, The Macmillan Co., 1926, pp. x, 452).

[117] Volume II, pp. 297, 298.

Communism was threatening, the world-wide depression was bringing distress, and the Labour Party was stepping up the adoption of socialist measures. Some acquaintance was had with philosophical, theological, and Biblical thought on the Continent and in the United States. Logical positivism, which was being changed to logical analysis, had its advocates. Barth was read, although he did not have as profound an effect as on the Continent. Berdyaev was known. Reinhold Niebuhr's voice was heard. The list might be lengthened of the men of other lands who made an impress. Yet, as in earlier years, Anglican theology and Biblical scholarship were to some degree insular, as was English life in general. Here, too, we must content ourselves with brief mention of only a few of the many whom a full coverage would include.

Some of the men who had been prominent in the latter part of the nineteenth century lived beyond 1914, but their major contributions had been made before that year. H. Scott Holland died in 1918. E. S. Talbot, slightly older, lived until 1934, to the ripe age of ninety. Hastings Rashdall, much younger, provoked controversy at the Modern Churchmen's Conference of 1921 but three years later passed from the earthly scene.[118] Charles Gore (1853–1932), who had come to prominence as the editor of *Lux Mundi* (1889), continued to be active well past 1914. Although repudiating the charge that he was a Broad Churchman, he was critical of the Anglo-Catholics and called himself a "liberal Catholic." During the years when he was engrossed in his duties as a bishop (Worcester, 1902–1904, Birmingham, 1905–1911, and Oxford, 1911–1919) he had little leisure for writing. After his resignation from Oxford book after book poured from his pen, and that in spite of many other occupations. They had a wide reading. In them both his theological and social concerns were evident.[119]

William Temple was even longer occupied in administration and in organizations than was Gore. He was more a prophet than a theologian. However, he had a first-class mind, read widely, possessed a tenacious memory, and wrote with clarity. His Gifford Lectures were his major scholarly work.[120] He was indebted to many thinkers, but especially to Plato. He had as a basic conviction from which he never wavered a profound belief in God. It was from this starting point that he approached life and theology. He maintained that a divine purpose exists in the universe. To a certain point this conviction can be supported by reason, he held, but ultimately an act of faith is required.

[118] Volume II, pp. 297, 304; Lloyd, *op. cit.*, Vol. II, p. 38; Prestige, *Charles Gore*, pp. 455, 456.
[119] Among the many in this period the following are typical: *The Epistles of St. John* (New York, Charles Scribner's Sons, 1920, pp. xiii, 237); *Belief in Christ* (New York, Charles Scribner's Sons, 1922, pp. x, 329); *Belief in God* (New York, Charles Scribner's Sons, 1922, pp. xvi, 300); *Christ and Society* (New York, Charles Scribner's Sons, 1928, pp. 218); *The Holy Spirit and the Church* (New York, Charles Scribner's Sons, 1924, pp. xiv, 366); *Jesus of Nazareth* (London, T. Butterworth, 1929, pp. 256).
[120] William Temple, *Nature, Man and God* (London, Macmillan and Co., 1934, pp. xxxii, 530).

William Ralph Inge (1860-1954) was strikingly different from Gore or Temple, and, indeed, from Barnes. His theological outlook is indicated by the fact that he was president of the Modern Churchmen's Union. He first attracted the attention of the religious world by a series of lectures on Christian mysticism (1889) which continued to come out in successive editions until 1925.[121] In 1911 he left the Lady Margaret Professorship of Divinity at Cambridge to become Dean of St. Paul's, in London. The prime minister in recommending the appointment, it was said, wished to revive the tradition of making that office the most literary post in the Church of England. Inge preached and lectured widely and wrote many books. He had a warm admiration for Greek philosophy and regarded Plotinus as its culmination. Anglican Modernist that he was, he was extremely critical of the Roman Catholic Church and regarded it as a survival of Roman imperialism and ancient paganism infiltrated by Christianity. Yet he had no use for the Roman Catholic Modernists, opposed Loisy and Tyrrell, and, while welcoming much in Harnack, did not agree with him on the doctrine of Christ. To Inge, not only was Christ the supreme moral teacher, but in Jesus the divine Logos was incarnate. Inge was sometimes called "the gloomy dean." He certainly looked with sombre eyes upon his time, held that the Victorian and the Elizabethan ages were the greatest in human history, and, while glad that individuals could progress, took a very dim view of human progress as a whole and held that the human race had exterminated several species more beautiful and less vicious than itself and had devastated the loveliness of the world. He welcomed science and the challenge that it gave to theology. Because of age he resigned his deanship in 1934 but he lived twenty years longer.[122]

Clement Charles Julian Webb, a slightly younger contemporary of Inge, attracted less popular attention but was a theologian of high rank. In his Gifford Lectures he spoke of the personality of God, with Whom His worshippers can enjoy direct intercourse.[123]

Inge's successor as Dean of St. Paul's was Walter Robert Matthews (1881——). A graduate of King's College, London, he had been dean of that college (1918-1932) and, briefly (1931-1934), Dean of Exeter Cathedral before

[121] W. R. Inge, *Christian Mysticism* (London, Methuen & Co., 6th ed., 1925, pp. xiv, 379).

[122] W. R. Inge, *Diary of a Dean, St. Paul's 1911-1934* (London, Hutchinson & Co., pp. 228), *passim.* Some of his other books were *The Church in the World. Collected Essays* (London, Longmans, Green and Co., 1927, pp. xi, 275); *Christian Ethics and Modern Problems* (New York, G. P. Putnam's Sons, 1930, pp. ix, 427); *God and the Astronomers* (London, Longmans, Green and Co., 1933, pp. xiii, 308); *The End of an Age and Other Essays* (New York, The Macmillan Co., 1949, pp. vii, 288); *The Things that Remain* (New York, Harper & Brothers, 1958, pp. xx, 140), published in Great Britain under the title *Goodness and Truth.*

[123] C. C. J. Webb, *Divine Personality and Human Life* (London, G. Allen· and Unwin, 1920, pp. 291). See also his *Problems in the Relations of God and Man* (London, J. Nisbet and Co., 1915, pp. xvi, 288); *Studies in the History of Natural Theology* (Oxford, The Clarendon Press, 1915, pp. vi, 363).

being transferred to St. Paul's. Like Inge he wrote extensively, but mostly rather brief books. One on *God in Christian Thought and Experience* went into several editions.[124] In *The Purpose of God*[125] he maintained that God has a purpose in history—the establishment of the Kingdom of God. He did not believe that the culmination of the Kingdom of God means the end of time, for while the order in which we now live may end in time, there will always be men and orders in which the purpose of God will find fulfilment.

Very different from Gore, Temple, Inge, and Matthews, Charles Earle Raven (1885——) too faced honestly the issues which challenged Christians and gave his answers, some of them hammered out in the midst of the acutest stresses of the day.[126] Raven was reared in a lawyer's home, was educated in a public school and in Cambridge, was confirmed and outwardly conformed, boldly discussed with friends the questions raised by science and philosophy, and was familiar with at least one aspect of patristic learning. In his early twenties, quite unexpectedly to Raven, Jesus became a living reality and companion. Raven thereupon felt himself impelled to seek ordination. He regarded the Church of England as the freest of all communions to men of diverse views. As a chaplain in World War I in hazardous positions on the front lines under fire he found Jesus a continuing presence. He became a convinced pacifist. Much of his life he spent in Cambridge—as Dean of Emmanuel College, later Regius Professor of Divinity, Master of Christ's College, and Vice Chancellor. He was also court preacher and canon of the Liverpool Cathedral and then of Ely. Deeply interested in science and a specialist in some of its aspects, he was vividly aware of the questions which it raised. Early experience had made him familiar with the slums of England's cities. His writings reflected his wide-ranging interests, the answers which he had made to the problems of the age, and his deep sympathy for those enmeshed in them, even when their answers did not seem to him valid.[127]

Arthur Gabriel Hebert, of the Society of the Sacred Mission, took the attitude towards the Church and the sacraments which could be expected from

---

124 In its American edition it was *God in Christian Experience* (New York, Harper & Brothers, 1930, pp. xix, 283). Its seventh London edition was published in 1942.

125 (New York, Charles Scribner's Sons, 1936, pp. 182).

126 For an autobiography see Charles E. Raven, *A Wanderer's Way* (New York, Henry Holt and Co., 1929, pp. 220).

127 Among his books, reflecting his interests, were *Appolinarianism* (Cambridge University Press, 1923, pp. viii, 312); *Christ and Modern Education* (London, Hodder and Stoughton, 1929, pp. 223); *Christian Socialism, 1848–1854* (London, Macmillan and Co., 1920, pp. xiii, 396); *The Creator Spirit. A Survey of Christian Doctrine in the Light of Biology, Psychology and Mysticism* (Cambridge, Mass., Harvard University Press, pp. xv, 310); *Jesus and the Gospel of Love* (New York, Henry Holt and Co., 1931, pp. 452); *War and the Christian* (New York, The Macmillan Co., 1938, pp. 185); *Natural Religion and Christian Theology* (the Gifford Lectures) (Cambridge University Press, 2 vols., 1953).

that connexion.[128] Somewhat similar positions were held by Oliver Chase Quick (1885–1944). He viewed the sacraments as an extension of the incarnation. Recognizing the debates which had raged over the exact words used by Christ in the institution of the Lord's Supper and not seeking to ascertain precisely the relation of Christ to the elements in the Eucharist, he believed in the actual presence in them of the risen Lord.[129] Arthur Michael Ramsey (1904——) was clearly in the Anglo-Catholic tradition. He was moved rapidly from the Regius Professorship of Divinity in Cambridge (1950–1952) to the Bishopric of Durham (1952), to the Archbishopric of York (1955) and to the Archbishopric of Canterbury (1961). These transfers left little time for substantial writing.[130] Lionel Spencer Thornton (1884——), of the Community of the Resurrection, a Cambridge graduate, taking account of Alfred N. Whitehead, endeavoured to show how the incarnation could be harmonized with emergent evolution and held that it was the culmination of that process at the highest level.[131] He also set forth an Anglo-Catholic view of the Church.[132]

Oxford and Cambridge continued to produce theological scholarship of high quality. Leonard Hodgson (1889——) won a respectful hearing.[133] Austin Farrer (1904——) gave the Gifford Lectures under the title *The Freedom of the Will*[134] and also wrote on the Gospels. Eric Lionel Mascall (1905——), a Cambridge graduate, had several books which attracted attention.[135]

Some lay theologians were widely read. For example, Dorothy Leigh Sayers (Mrs. Fleming) (1893–1957), early known for her detective stories in admirable literary style, later turned to books on the Christian faith in which she intelligently espoused it.[136] Clive Staples Lewis (1898——), long fellow and tutor

---

[128] Arthur Gabriel Hebert, *The Form of the Church* (London, Faber and Faber, 1944, pp. 126); *Liturgy and Society. The Function of the Church in the Modern World* (London, Faber and Faber, 1936, pp. 267).

[129] Oliver Chase Quick, *The Christian Sacraments* (New York, Harper & Brothers, 1927, pp. xv, 264). See also his *Catholic and Protestant Elements in Christianity* (London, Longmans, Green and Co., 1924, pp. ix, 118).

[130] See his *The Gospel and the Catholic Church* (London, Longmans, Green and Co., 1956, pp. xiv, 234) for an indication of his views.

[131] Lionel Thornton, *The Incarnate Lord* (London, Longmans, Green and Co., 1928, pp. xxxiv, 490).

[132] Lionel Thornton, *The Common Life in the Body of Christ* (London, Dacre Press, preface 1941, pp. xiii, 470); *The Form of the Servant. Revelation; Dominion of Christ; Christ and the Church* (Westminster, Dacre Press, 3 vols., 1950–1956).

[133] Among other books see his *And Was Made Man. An Introduction to the Study of the Gospels* (London, Longmans, Green and Co., 1928, pp. xiii, 216); *The Doctrine of the Trinity* (London, Nisbet and Co., 1943, pp. 237); *For Faith and Freedom*, the Gifford Lectures, Volume I on natural theology and Volume II on Chistian theology (Oxford, B. Blackwell, 2 vols., 1956, 1957).

[134] (London, A. and C. Black, 1958, pp. xi, 315).

[135] *He Who Is: a Study in Traditional Theism* (London, Longmans, Green and Co., 1943, pp. xiii, 210); *Via Media: an Essay in Theological Synthesis* (Greenwich, Conn., Seabury Press, 1957, pp. xvi, 171); *The Recovery of Unity: a Theological Approach* (London, Longmans, Green and Co., 1958, pp. xiii, 242).

[136] See her *The Mind of the Maker* (London, Methuen & Co., 1941, pp. xi, 186); *Creed or Chaos*

in Magdalen College, Oxford, and later holding the chair of medieval and Renaissance English in Cambridge, had a spiritual pilgrimage which led through boyhood conformity to Christianity and confirmation in adolescence in the Anglican Communion, through scepticism, and then by way of the Hegelian Absolute to theism, where he felt that God had pursued him and forced him to surrender, to a deep Christian faith with belief in the incarnation.[137] He wrote a number of books in unconventional form setting forth various aspects of the Christian faith as he understood them.[138]

Anglicans made notable contributions to the scholarly study of the Bible. Robert Henry Lightfoot (1883-1953) welcomed *Formgeschichte* as a fresh approach but did not accept all the results of its German exponents.[139] Francis Crawford Burkitt (1864-1935), somewhat older and holding a chair of divinity in Cambridge, was the author of many books on early Christianity, especially on its Syrian forms. Although classed as a liberal, he believed that liberal Christianity had failed.[140] Burnett Hillman Streeter (1874-1937), long connected with Oxford, specialized on the New Testament but was also interested in other religions and in mysticism, particularly that of India. He was sceptical of the findings of many of the source critics of the Bible. He maintained that Christianity contained a synthesis of all that was best in the other high religions.[141] Sir Edwyn Hoskyns (1884-1937), the thirteenth baronet, son of a Bishop of Southwell, in contrast with Bultmann held to the continuity of the *kerygma* of the early Church with Jesus, both in teaching and in conscious intent. He recognized the impossibility of writing a life of Jesus akin to the biographies to which the modern age was accustomed and said that critical research did not bring the New Testament into accord with current humanitarianism and humanistic thinking. He was convinced that Jesus believed that He was bringing in a new order—of complete obedience to the will of God— that on Him rested the unique and creative obedience to the will of God, and

---

and Other Essays in Popular Theology (London, Methuen & Co., 1947, pp. vii, 88). She also wrote sacred drama.

[137] C. S. Lewis, *Surprised by Joy. The Shape of My Early Life* (London, Geoffrey Bles, 1955, pp. 224), *passim*.

[138] Among his books were *The Screwtape Letters* (London, G. Bles, 1942, pp. 160); and *The Pilgrim's Regress: an Allegorical Apology for Christianity, Reason, and Romanticism* (London, J. M. Dent & Sons, 1933, pp. 255).

[139] Robert Henry Lightfoot, *History and Interpretation of the Gospels* (London, Hodder and Stoughton, 1935, pp. xvii, 236).

[140] As examples of Burkitt's writing see his *Church and Gnosis. A Study of Christian Thought and Speculation in the Second Century* (Cambridge University Press, 1932, pp. ix, 153); *Early Eastern Christianity* (London, J. Murray, 1904, pp. viii, 228).

[141] Among Streeter's writings were *The Four Gospels. A Study of the Origins, Treating of the Manuscript Traditions, Sources, Authorship, and Dates* (New York, The Macmillan Co., 1925, pp. xiv, 622); *The Buddha and the Christ. An Exploration of the Meaning of the Universe and of the Purpose of Human Life* (New York, The Macmillan Co., 1933, pp. xiii, 336); *The God Who Speaks* (New York, The Macmillan Co., 1936, pp. vii, 223).

that His life and death were an achievement of God. He maintained that the critical method could disclose this but that it could not decide between the acceptance and the rejection of the convictions which underlay the New Testament.[142] In his study of the Fourth Gospel Hoskyns developed the thesis that that book was later than the other three Gospels, assumed in its readers a knowledge of the story which they presented if not of the books themselves, and supplemented that knowledge with additional first-hand material and with meditations on the meaning of the act of God in Christ.[143]

THE CHURCH OF ENGLAND HAD NOTABLE AND ABLE LEADERSHIP

A striking feature of the Church of England in the half-century after 1914 was the high quality of the leadership which endeavoured to guide it through the storms of those decades. Even though much of its traditional constituency was drawn away from it by the currents of the revolutionary age, never had the Church of England possessed abler and more devoted men in its chief offices and in many of its subordinate posts.

We have already had occasion to mention the Archbishops of Canterbury of that period. Randall Davidson (1848-1930)[144] spanned the transition from the nineteenth to the twentieth century. He came to the office in 1903 in the heyday of the opulent prosperity of the Edwardian era and held it through the trying years of World War I and the mass unemployment and poverty which followed it. Because of advancing age he resigned in 1928—the first in the long succession to do so. The esteem in which he was held was made evident by the widespread regret with which the announcement of the step was greeted and the fact that he was at once created Baron Davidson of Lambeth and so continued to sit in the House of Lords. By his integrity, courage, and sound judgement he commanded the respect and confidence of men of affairs in all walks of life.[145] He was ably supported by his wife, a daughter of Archbishop Tait. She was ten years his junior and outlived him by six years.[146]

As we have noted, Davidson was succeeded as Archbishop of Canterbury by Cosmo Gordon Lang (1864-1945). Lang's father and grandfather had been ministers in the Church of Scotland and his father had been Moderator of that church, an office which a brother was to hold. After Glasgow University the future archbishop had gone to Oxford, had attained distinction as an under-

---

[142] Edwyn Hoskyns and Francis Noel Davey, *The Riddle of the New Testament* (London, Faber and Faber, 1931, pp. 322), *passim*.

[143] Edwyn Clement Hoskyns, *The Fourth Gospel*, edited by Francis Noel Davey (London, Faber and Faber, 2 vols., 1940).

[144] Volume II, p. 292.

[145] The standard life has been cited again and again—G. K. A. Bell, *Randall Davidson, Archbishop of Canterbury* (London, Oxford University Press, 2 vols., 1935). See also Sidney Dark, *Archbishop Davidson and the English Church* (London, Philip Allan & Co., 1929, pp. ix, 249).

[146] Mary C. S. Mills, *Edith Davidson of Lambeth* (London, John Murray, 1938, pp. xii, 249).

graduate, had no great interest religiously, and was about to be admitted to the bar when he suddenly felt that he must enter the clergy. He was confirmed, went to a theological college, and was ordained. He sought to combine the best of the Oxford Movement with the freedom of Maurice, Kingsley, and Robertson. After a few years of experience in a parish interrupted by a period as chaplain of Magdalen College, Oxford, he was made Bishop of Stepney and Canon of St. Paul's As Bishop of Stepney he was suffragan to the Bishop of London and his see was in one of the depressed areas of the metropolis. From there, in 1908, at what was thought an early age for that dignity, he was translated to the Archbishopric of York. A warm friend of Davidson, he collaborated with him in facing the problems that confronted the Church of England in the difficult years which followed. By conviction he remained unmarried the better to give himself to his work. Dignified, handsome, a master of ecclesiastical ceremony, he was also an able and conscientious administrator and a gracious and charming host to both high and low. He had a warm admiration for the monarchy, was deeply loyal to it, and had known personally both Victoria and Edward VII. He was intimate with George V, who had consulted him on his apprehensions about the Prince of Wales, and he was deeply troubled by the determination of that young man, as Edward VIII, to marry a divorcee and wondered whether he could officiate at the coronation. He was relieved of the necessity of making that decision by the abdication, a step which was taken without the slightest initiative on his part and purely on the advice of the prime minister and with the support of the party of the opposition and the prime ministers of the Dominions. Yet his broadcast after the step brought him severe criticism. He was a close friend of George VI. Because of his advancing years, in 1941 he resigned, and, like Davidson, was created a baron.[147] If Davidson was the statesman, Lang was the churchman.

Of William Temple, who followed Lang, both as Archbishop of York and as Archbishop of Canterbury, we have spoken so often that we need say little more. Extremely able, intellectually and in other ways, a man of high courage and deep devotion, whose social concerns had led him for seven years to be a member of the Labour Party, above commitment to any party in the Church of England, and outstanding in the Ecumenical Movement, his simple goodness, his hearty humour, his broad sympathies, which did not compromise his loyalty to the Church of England, and his unaffected kindness won the affection of thousands. His early death (1944) brought grief both in Britain and in many nations and communions.[148] Son of an Archbishop of Canterbury, a

---

[147] We have already cited his standard biography, J. G. Lockhart, *Cosmo Gordon Lang* (London, Hodder and Stoughton, 1949, pp. xi, 481).

[148] We have also cited his standard biography—F. A. Iremonger, *William Temple, Archbishop of Canterbury. His Life and Letters* (New York, Oxford University Press, pp. xv, 663).

graduate of Oxford, for a time he was a resident fellow in Queen's College in that university. With his charm, his intellect, and his inherited social position, he could easily have settled into a life of ease. But he early developed socialist convictions and became active in the Workers' Educational Association, seeking to bridge the gulf between the intellectuals and the men who worked with their hands. In his Oxford days he had been caught up in the Student Christian Movement, a beginning of his association with the Ecumenical Movement. In an early visit to Australia at the instance of John R. Mott in behalf of the World's Student Christian Federation he gave impetus to the Student Christian Movement in the universities of that continent. Through that Movement he also became committed to the world mission of the Church. Convinced that the Church of England must have men of high intellectual character in its clergy if it would fulfil its mission, he felt constrained to seek ordination. In 1910 he became Headmaster of Repton, an ancient public school for boys. From there, in 1914, he became Rector of St. James, Piccadilly, where we first met him. From Life and Liberty he moved to a canonry in Westminster Abbey; then, early in 1921, he became Bishop of Manchester, a see which appealed to him as a centre where the problems of the industrial age were acute, and from Manchester he was translated to York and then to Canterbury.

Geoffrey Francis Fisher (1887——) succeeded Temple in Canterbury. Like Temple he was the son of a clergyman and a graduate of Oxford. At Oxford he had a brilliant career as a scholar. He followed Temple as Headmaster of Repton, but for a longer period than Temple—from 1914 to 1932. From 1932 to 1939 he was Bishop of Chester and from 1939 to his translation to Canterbury he was Bishop of London—during the difficult years of World War II. He came, then, to the primacy with extensive experience in administration but with none in a parish. Because of the progressive secularization of the state, he did not exert the political influence which had marked the pontificates of several of his predecessors, even some of recent years, but his voice in the House of Lords was listened to, and as the ranking Anglican bishop he had an important place in the leadership of that communion, now world-wide, and was on the presidium of the World Council of Churches.[149]

We have also had occasion to mention Cyril Forster Garbett. He had been Vicar of Portsea, where Lang had preceded him by several years and where he showed ability and devotion in directing a large staff, in evangelism, and in attacking social evils. From there he was appointed Bishop of Southwark, in South London, largely a slum area. A celibate, an indefatigable worker, widely and deeply read, he came to know his diocese thoroughly, its clergy and

[149] Edward Carpenter, editor, *The Archbishop Speaks. Addresses and Speeches by the Archbishop of Canterbury, the Most Reverend Geoffrey Francis Fisher* (London, Evans Brothers, 1958, pp. 231); *Who's Who, 1955*, pp. 466.

many of its people, and concerned himself with its social problems. An inveterate pedestrian, as Bishop of Winchester, a largely rural see, he covered much of the diocese on foot, with a walking staff shaped like a crosier. As Archbishop of York he was caught up in national and ecumenical affairs as well as the responsibilities of the northern province of his church. He worked on into his eighty-first year and, although because of ill health he was about to resign, he died, as he had wished, in harness.[150] Forthright, an Anglo-Catholic but never attached to any one church party, he was keenly aware of the threats to the faith in his day, especially Communism. He subscribed to the findings of a commission appointed by the two archbishops and published in 1945 under the title *Towards the Evangelization of England,* which pointed out the decline in church-going and the collapse of Christian moral standards, and which said that the Church had a divine commission of evangelism and made practical suggestions as to how it could be effectively carried out. Yet his experience in evangelism, Garbett held, had shown that for the most part only those once in active touch with the Church were reclaimed and that very few were won who had had slight or no previous contact with it. He maintained that the Church must take a practical interest in the work of the factory, the mill, the shop, the mine, and the fields. While he respected sincere Christian pacifists but did not agree with them, he pointed out that the Lambeth Conference of 1948 had declared war incompatible with the teaching and example of Christ. He said that the Christian must pray for peace and work for the removal of causes which lead to war and insisted that war is not inevitable.[151]

The Bishop of London during a long period which spanned 1914 was Arthur Foley Winnington-Ingram (1858–1945).[152] He was the son of a clergyman of the Church of England, and his mother was the daughter of a bishop. He was graduated from Oxford with a good but not distinguished record as a scholar. After a period of doubt through which he was helped by reading Gore, he was ordained. From a brief experience in two other posts, in 1888 he became head of Oxford House, which five years earlier had been opened in underprivileged East London. In 1897 he became Bishop of Stepney, over an area which included that served by Oxford House. Four years later (1901) he was consecrated Bishop of London and held the post until his resignation, because of

---

[150] See a short, appreciative biography, by Margaret, the Prioress of Whitby, *Archbishop Garbett, a Memoir* (London, A. R. Mowbray & Co., 1957, pp. vii, 109). A full-length, able biography is Charles Smyth, *Cyril Forster Garbett, Archbishop of York* (London, Hodder and Stoughton, 1959, pp. 536).

[151] See the views, expressed near the end of his life, in his book *In an Age of Revolution* (New York, Oxford University Press, 1952, pp. 318), *passim.*

[152] Arthur Foley Winnington-Ingram, *Fifty Years' Work in London (1889–1939)* (London, Longmans, Green and Co., 1940, pp. xi, 249), *passim;* C. S. Carpenter, *Winnington-Ingram. The Biography of Arthur Foley Winnington-Ingram, Bishop of London 1901–1939* (New York, Oxford University Press, 1949, pp. 358), *passim.*

age, in 1939. A man of rare charm, complete devotion, whether in the pulpit or in personal contact he drew to him those about him, of all stations in life and especially the young men. He was neither a scholar nor a statesman, but an evangelist. He was a pastor at heart—a shepherd of souls—and brought that passion into his preaching, his relations with his clergy, and his care for thousands of individuals. He fought vice in its various forms as it flourished in his huge diocese, especially in the centre of London. A loyal son of the Church of England, after his early doubts untroubled in his faith, he was above party strife in the Church. A prodigious worker, with a schedule which allowed for no waste moments, a celibate who gave himself unstintedly to his calling, he was not primarily an administrator, but during his episcopate, such was his zeal for adequate care for the burgeoning metropolis, seventy-nine new churches were consecrated and thirty-eight were rebuilt or enlarged.

Also a celibate, a bishop, and completely devoted to his calling, Walter Howard Frere (1863–1938) was in many ways a contrast to Winnington-Ingram.[153] A scholar by family background and temperament and with a zest for music, an aristocrat by inheritance and bearing, a graduate of Cambridge, a Christian socialist, and an Anglo-Catholic, he was one of the early members of the Community of the Resurrection and in time became its Superior. In 1923 he was created Bishop of Truro, a diocese which embraced Cornwall and the Scilly Isles. He was a liturgist, a historian, and a hymnologist, and had a deep spiritual life. He sought to bridge the gulf between the Russian Orthodox and the Anglicans. With advancing years and physical infirmities, in 1935 he resigned his bishopric and retired to Mirfield, the headquarters of his community.

Another celibate bishop was St. Clair George Alfred Donaldson (1863–1935).[154] Born into a family of wealth, social standing, and an Evangelical atmosphere, a graduate of Eton and Cambridge with a university record distinguished for scholarship and athletics, in 1904 he went to Australia as Bishop of Brisbane and was soon archbishop of a new province with that city as its centre. He was appointed Bishop of Salisbury in 1921 and served in that see until his death. In Salisbury he made the cathedral and its clergy a spiritual power house for the diocese. Missionarily minded from his young manhood, he was chairman of the Missionary Council of the Church of England and vice-chairman of the International Missionary Council—in the latter office succeeded by Garbett.

A quite different kind of bishop, but also able, was Nugent Hicks (1872–

---

[153] C. S. Phillips and others, *Walter Howard Frere, Bishop of Truro* (London, Faber and Faber, 1947, pp. 216), *passim*.

[154] C. T. Dimont and F. de Witt Batty, *St. Clair Donaldson* (London, Faber and Faber, 1939, pp. xix, 271).

1942).[155] A graduate of Harrow and Oxford, he had a good record in scholarship, was ordained, and from 1897 to 1909 was on the staff of Keble College, Oxford, a position which is sufficient evidence of his churchmanship—Catholic in the Anglican sense of the term and akin to that of Gore. He was the first principal of a new theological school, Bishop's College, at Cheshunt (or Cestrehunt), an institution which he sought to make inclusive of the parties in the Church of England. For a time he had parish experience. In 1927 he was consecrated Bishop of Gibraltar, a see that covered much of the Mediterranean. During his years there he cultivated friendly relations with Roman Catholics and Orthodox. In 1933 he was enthroned as Bishop of Lincoln and at the service dignitaries of the Orthodox Church were present. As Bishop of Lincoln he came to know his clergy, some of them intimately, saw to the improvement of the schools and to the erection of churches in new housing areas, and kept in touch with colleges at Oxford and Cambridge with which he had official connexions.

There is no space to enlarge on what we have already said of Henson and Bell, bishops of Durham and Chichester respectively and with differences which characterized the Church of England.[156]

Here, in the twentieth-century episcopate of the Church of England, were men with a wide variety of convictions and talent, but one in their sedulous performance of the duties of their office, in their high intelligence, and in their uncompromising integrity.

THE CONTINUED AND GROWING OUTREACH OF THE CHURCH OF ENGLAND

In the face of the drifting away of a large proportion of the population of England from the national church, the contrast offered by the vigour of the large minority which remained faithful was heightened by the fashion in which the Church of England displayed added initiative in reaching out beyond its borders both in enhancing the unity of those who bore the Christian name and in seeking to win non-Christians in other lands.

Within the British Isles the Church of England was seeking increasing fellowship with other Protestants. In 1920 the Lambeth Conference issued *An Appeal to All Christian People* urging the visible unity of the Church and suggesting as a basis the Holy Scriptures, the Nicene or the Apostles' Creed, baptism, holy Communion, and a ministry acknowledged in every part of the Church with the episcopate as the "one means of providing such a ministry."[157]

[155] Maurice Headlam, *Bishop and Friend. Nugent Hicks, Sixty-Fourth Bishop of Lincoln* (London, Macdonald & Co., no date, pp. 158), *passim*.

[156] On Henson in addition to his *Retrospect of an Unimportant Life*, which we have already cited, see Evelyn Foley Braley, editor, *Letters of Herbert Hensley Henson* (London, S.P.C.K., 1951, pp. 255).

[157] Bell, *Documents on Christian Unity, 1920–4*, pp. 1–14.

The National Assembly of the Church of England welcomed the appeal (1920) and the upper and lower houses of Canterbury and York approved (1921), but with reservations about the exchange of pulpits between episcopally ordained and non-ordained ministers. The two bodies representing the majority of the Nonconforming churches in England, namely, the Federal Council of the Evangelical Free Churches, composed of delegates appointed by the annual assemblies and conferences of the Free Churches, and the National Council of the Evangelical Free Churches, consisting of delegates chosen from the local Free Church councils, welcomed the proposals but pointed out unresolved difficulties. The official bodies of several Free Churches took similar action. High among the difficulties were disagreement over the nature of the Church and the validity of non-episcopal ordinations.[158] During the years 1921–1925 conferences were held in Lambeth Palace between representatives of the Church of England and of the Federal Council of the Free Churches for the purpose, not of negotiating a union, but of exploring the issues which divided the churches in hopes of reaching a common mind. The conferences agreed that ordination should be through a "representative and constitutional episcopate," but the Free Churches believed that this term needed further explication and that elements from the congregational and presbyterial order should more clearly be combined with it than had yet been done. While much cordiality was shown on both sides, the conversations came to an impasse over the issue of episcopal recognition of the validity of the ordinations of the Free Churches and were suspended.[159] Archbishop Davidson conveyed the *Appeal* in person to the General Assemblies of the Church of Scotland and the United Free Church of Scotland, but the two bodies were too much absorbed in the negotiations which led to their reunion to do more than give him a courteous hearing.[160] However, Davidson's appearance at the General Assemblies was without precedent, as were the conversations between the Church of England and the Free Churches of England.

As a result of the Lambeth Conference of 1930 the conferences with the Free Churches were resumed, at first on an informal basis. A document thus prepared and setting forth an elaborate and comprehensive structure on an episcopal basis was taken over by an official joint group and published in 1938, but the near approach of World War II prevented further serious consideration.[161] Soon after the war, in 1946, Fisher, then Archbishop of Canterbury, in a

---

[158] *Ibid.*, pp. 100–169.

[159] *The Church of England and the Free Churches. Proceedings of Joint Conferences held at Lambeth Palace, 1921–1925* (London, Oxford University Press, 1925, pp. xii, 91), *passim;* Bell, *Randall Davidson*, Vol. II, pp. 1115–1123; Lockhart, *Cosmo Gordon Lang*, pp. 264–278.

[160] Lockhart, *op. cit.*, pp. 278, 279.

[161] Bell, *Documents on Christian Unity, Third Series, 1930–48*, pp. 6, 7, 71–101; Rouse and Neill, *A History of the Ecumenical Movement, 1517–1948*, p. 484.

sermon preached before the University of Cambridge suggested a fresh approach towards re-union with the Free Churches by proposing that they adopt episcopacy as a step towards common sacraments and a commonly accepted ministry. The sermon was followed by conversations between Anglicans and Free Churchmen and a report (November, 1950) which recommended terms on which Fisher's proposals might be adopted. Yet not all Free Churchmen or all Anglicans were satisfied with it.[162]

In 1957 a document unanimously adopted by representatives of the Church of England, the Episcopal Church of Scotland, the Church of Scotland, and the Presbyterian Church of England suggested as a basis for closer relations between the four bodies the election of bishops by the Church of Scotland who would receive apostolic succession through the Anglican episcopate and the institution by the Anglicans of lay officers corresponding to the elders in the Church of Scotland.[163] In 1958 the Church of England and the Methodist Church began conversations looking towards intercommunion on the basis of the reciprocal acceptance of each other's ministries.[164]

In the meantime closer coöperation was achieved through the creation in 1942, as a result of steps taken in 1937, of the British Council of Churches. It included Anglican as well as non-Anglican Protestant churches in the British Isles and some non-ecclesiastical bodies such as the Salvation Army and the YMCA and the YWCA. Its purpose was to facilitate common action through a wide variety of channels. One of its initial undertakings was the sponsoring of the Religion and Life movement during World War II.[165]

Increasingly the Church of England reached out to churches in other parts of the world. We have already spoken of the Malines Conversations with the Roman Catholics.[166] With their emphasis upon their Catholic heritage and their continuity from the Church of the first centuries, the Anglicans were particularly eager to establish contacts with others of that background and to work for what they regarded as the reunion of the several branches of the early Church. Barely to mention all the efforts would unduly prolong this paragraph. We can simply mention a few. As Archbishop of Canterbury Davidson took steps to relieve the distress from which the Russian Orthodox Church and members of its hierarchy suffered during the transition of Russia to Communist rule.[167] In the 1920's as a result of conversations with the Orthodox Churches as a step to full intercommunion the Ecumenical Patriarch formally

[162] Rouse and Neill, *op. cit.*, pp. 483–486.
[163] *The Ecumenical Review*, Vol. IX, pp. 449–459.
[164] *The Ecumenical Review*, Vol. IX, p. 298.
[165] Rouse and Neill, *op. cit.*, pp. 624, 625; Leiper, *Christianity Today*, p. 135.
[166] Chapter IX.
[167] Bell, *Randall Davidson*, Vol. II, pp. 1067–1086.

recognized the validity of Anglican orders.[168] In 1925 the Old Catholic Church of Utrecht also declared that the apostolic succession had been preserved by the Church of England.[169] In the 1930's a joint theological commission of Anglicans and all the Orthodox Churches except that of Russia met, but without producing significant findings; the Rumanian Church joined the churches of Constantinople, Jerusalem, Cyprus, and Alexandria in acknowledging the validity of Anglican orders and ministrations; correspondence was had with the Syrian Orthodox Jacobite Church;[170] and intercommunion was established with the Old Catholics.[171] Also in the 1930's negotiations between the Church of England and the Church of Finland led to the admission of communicants of the Church of Finland to Communion in the Church of England and to the same privilege for members of the Church of England in the Church of Finland.[172] The 1940's and 1950's witnessed visits to the Russian Orthodox Church by successive Archbishops of York. In the next volume we shall see the prominence of Anglicans in the creation and leadership of the World Council of Churches.

Increasingly the Lambeth Conferences, with the Archbishop of Canterbury as the ranking prelate, brought into fellowship the various national members of the Anglican Communion. In 1959, to make that fellowship effective a bishop from the United States was appointed the full-time executive officer.

The numerous organizations through which members of the Church of England maintained missions among non-Christians were continued and some were added to them. To coördinate them, in 1921 the Missionary Council of the National Assembly of the Church of England was created.[173]

THE SOBERING PLIGHT OF THE FREE CHURCHES

A striking feature of the half-century of Christianity which followed the eventful summer of 1914 was the declining role of the Nonconformist Protestant or Free Churches in the life of England and the world. It was partly indicated by a loss in church membership, the more sobering because the population of England was growing: the Free Churches not only lost in actual numbers but were percentage-wise a much smaller proportion of the population in 1960 than in 1914. As we have seen, in the nineteenth century the Nonconformist or Free Churches had enjoyed a growth which was little less

---

[168] *Ibid.,* pp. 1104–1114.
[169] Lockhart, *op. cit.,* pp. 356, 357.
[170] *Ibid.,* pp. 362, 363; Bell, *Documents on Christian Unity, Third Series, 1930–48,* pp. 37–55.
[171] Lockhart, *op. cit.,* pp. 364, 365.
[172] Bell, *Documents on Christian Unity, Third Series, 1930–48,* pp. 146–153.
[173] Strong and Warnshuis, *Directory of Foreign Missions,* pp. 10–22.

than spectacular.[174] By the end of the century they counted about two million members, or approximately six out of a hundred of the population. Between the years 1900 and 1910 the increase continued—about 13.5 per cent. in that decade, as compared with the 10.89 per cent. growth of the population in those years. By 1910 the peak had been reached. Even before the outbreak of World War I the total of the Methodists, the largest of the Free Church families, had experienced a sharp slump and the other numerically major Nonconformist denominations, the Congregationalists and the Baptists, had suffered a slight loss. The Presbyterians, much smaller, remained about stationary. The Methodist recession continued through the war but was stayed by 1919, and numbers once more mounted until about 1930, but not to the peak attained in 1910. During the war years Congregationalists and especially Baptists seemed to be recouping their losses and shortly after the coming of peace were approximately where they had been in 1910. Indeed, the Baptists were more numerous than in that year. However, the 1930's witnessed a marked decline in the Methodist and Congregational ranks and one only less striking in the Baptist fold. It continued during World War II and although by 1950 it was levelling off, in that year the total Free Church membership was approximately a million and a half, or about 4 per cent. of the population. The loss in attendance at church services appears to have been even greater, for in 1910 many frequented the Free Church services who were not members, but forty or fifty years later the attendance was said to have been mainly of those who were already members. The decline in the Sunday School enrolment was still more ominous, for it was from the Sunday Schools that most of the church members were recruited. In 1907 the enrolment was reported as being 3,436,000 and in 1947 it was said to be 1,473,000. However, beginning in 1947 a sharp increase was seen.[175]

The picture varied from section to section of the country and within zones in the cities. It was less favourable in the North than in the South. In Yorkshire, for example, the decrease was larger than in Sussex and Dorset. Indeed, in the latter in the fore part of the 1950's more congregations showed gains than losses. In London in the older, central boroughs the churches were in a worse plight than in the suburbs which had been developed between the two wars. In general, in the mid-1950's the Free Churches were fairly strong in the middle-class areas, were weak elsewhere, and had little contact with the workers in industries.[176]

The reasons for the losses were complex and were more difficult to ascertain than were the statistics. The suggestion was made that among them was nineteenth-century science, now for the first time making a decided impact upon

---

[174] Volume II, pp. 314–351.
[175] *The British Weekly,* March 10 and 17, 1955.
[176] *Ibid.*

the constituencies from which the Free Churches drew most of their members. Another contributory factor was the small size of many of the local congregations. A large proportion had fifty members or less and the pastors who served them could not be given adequate financial remuneration, with the result that many, discouraged, went into other occupations. The proliferation of congregations of competing denominations in communities where the numbers were insufficient to support them was also held responsible. In the latter part of the 1950's the Methodists appeared once more to be gaining, and one reason ascribed was their emphasis upon Sunday Schools and other ways of reaching youth.[177] Another cause of the losses might be found in the weakening of the middle class, from which the Free Churches had drawn their chief strength. Taxes, made ever more burdensome by wars and the demands of the welfare state, had reduced the incomes of the sturdy element which had flourished under the individualistic economy of the nineteenth century. It may be significant that in the 1950's the Free Churches seemed on the whole to prosper most in the suburbs, where the social conditions of the nineteenth century more nearly prevailed. Here, however, were conjectures which did not take into account the similar decline of the active constituencies of churches, both Roman Catholic and Protestant, which we have found elsewhere in Western Europe and not simply the Free Churches of England.

As we go on to a brief summary of the record of the larger Nonconformist or Free Churches we shall find, as we have elsewhere, evidences of both losses and vitality.

THE CONGREGATIONAL RECORD

Congregationalism, with its high intellectual standards and its freedom, was susceptible to the currents of thought, especially within Protestantism, which were sweeping across the world in the stormy half-century which began in 1914. It also had a background of evangelism, for through that its growth of the nineteenth century had been largely accomplished.[178] Seven developments and features of the fifty years introduced by the outbreak of World War I can be pointed out. One was the decline in membership to which we have just now called attention. In 1913 the Congregational churches in England and Wales reported 452,489 members.[179] In 1927 the corresponding total was 453,814, of whom 138,131 were in Wales.[180] In 1947 it was 367,774, of whom 128,571

---

[177] *Ibid.*
[178] Volume II, pp. 321–328.
[179] *The Statesman's Year Book, 1914*, p. 27.
[180] *Congregational Year Book, 1929* (London, Congregational Union of England and Wales, 1929, pp. 650), pp. 551, 552.

were in Wales.[181] In 1958 the total had shrunk to 218,000.[182]

A second development was a growing centralization in organization. In 1831 the Congregational Union of England and Wales had been constituted. It was an assembly for consultation and advice, for in principle each church was independent of every other. Indeed, that was one connotation associated with the word "Congregational" and with the older term "Independent." In theory Congregationalism did not permit a central organization. In practice the Congregational Union of England and Wales became a federation, with more functions increasingly assigned to it. The country was being divided into provinces presided over by moderators. An approach was being made to a Presbyterian organization.[183]

A third development was the series of efforts to stem the retreat. English Congregationalists did not supinely surrender to changing conditions but made heroic attempts, some of them successful, to meet the rapidly changing environment in the post-1914 stage of the revolutionary age. The institution of provinces and moderators was a coöperative approach to the problem. Soon after World War I a "forward movement" was launched to provide larger financial resources for the varied needs of the denomination and raised over half a million pounds. As was true in the Church of England, men were recruited for the ministry from the returning veterans of World War I. New churches were erected in rapidly growing towns and suburbs. Lay preachers were trained. The stipends of ministers were increased, even though not sufficiently to keep pace with the rising cost of living.[184] Yet advance was hampered by the lack of funds to erect churches in the new housing areas—even where these had been assigned by coöperative religious agencies to Congregationalists. The heavy income and estate taxes had reduced the number of wealthy men such as those who had made possible much of the material growth in the nineteenth century.

A fourth feature (rather than a development) was the comparative lack of outstanding preachers and laymen in contrast with the nineteenth century. Some who had come to prominence before 1914 did not complete their course until after that year, but most of their main achievements had been earlier. Among them were Robert Forman Horton (1855–1934), man of prayer, scholar, preacher, author, with a deep concern for foreign missions and for the under-

---

181 *Congregational Year Book, 1948* (London, Congregational Union of England and Wales, 1948, pp. 528), pp. 353, 354.

182 *The Statesman's Year Book, 1959*, p. 70.

183 Grant, *Free Churchmanship in England, 1870–1940*, pp. 310–322; Albert Peel, *These Hundred Years. A History of the Congregational Union of England and Wales, 1831–1931* (London, Congregational Union of England and Wales, 1931, pp. 424), pp. 377–380; Robinson, *A History of the Lancashire Congregational Union 1806–1956*, pp. 104, 105.

184 Robinson, *op. cit.*, pp. 95, 104, 115, 139–150.

privileged at home;[185] Halley Stewart (1838–1937), son of a Congregational minister, a sturdy Liberal in politics, a member of Parliament, advocate of equal suffrage for men and women, opponent of hereditary legislators, a successful business man, a journalist, and a lay pastor;[186] William Hesketh Lever (1851–1925), the creator of Sunlight Soap and a model factory and village at Port Sunlight near Liverpool, the chief figure in Lever Brothers, with its wide financial empire, a generous benefactor of Congregational churches, who died a viscount;[187] Alfred E. Garvie (1861–1945), of Scottish parentage, reared in the United Presbyterian Church, who became a Congregationalist because he could not conscientiously subscribe to the Westminster Confession, pastor, scholar who first made his reputation in a study of Ritschlianism, teacher, principal of a theological college in London, president of the National Free Church Council, and active in the Ecumenical Movement;[188] George Buchanan Gray (1865–1922), professor of Old Testament in Mansfield College, Oxford, from 1891 until his death, and outstanding in the field of his specialization;[189] Arthur Adlington Haworth (1865–1944), born to wealth, active in the family business in Manchester, who helped to modernize old churches in the heart of the city to serve the slum areas, was prominent in creating two institutional churches, aided the erection of churches in new areas, contributed to the establishment of headquarters for Congregationalism in the city, as a Liberal served in Parliament, was made a baronet, and was an ardent supporter of the League of Nations;[190] Bertram Smith (1863–1943) and Francis Wrigley (1868–1945), who were joint ministers in Leeds, a city grown large through the Industrial Revolution, and there, resisting invitations to move, in a lifetime of service, by adopting new methods made their church the centre of a throbbing congregational life;[191] William Boothby Selbie (1862–1944), an attractive preacher to students, long principal of Mansfield College, whose major scholarly work on Schleiermacher appeared in 1913 on the eve of World War I;[192] John Daniel Jones (1865–1942), a native of Wales but for many years pastor in Bournemouth where he built up a great congregation, who was known as the outstanding ecclesiastical statesman of the Free Churches of his time and took the lead in raising a large fund to augment the stipends of rural ministers;[193] John

---

[185] Volume II, p. 324; Albert Peel and J. A. R. Marriott, *Robert Forman Horton* (London, George Allen and Unwin, 1937, pp. 381), *passim*.

[186] Peel, *The Congregational Two Hundred, 1530–1948*, p. 223.

[187] *Ibid.*, pp. 246–248.

[188] Alfred E. Garvie, *Memories and Meanings of My Life* (London, George Allen and Unwin, 1938, pp. 274), *passim*.

[189] Peel, *op. cit.*, pp. 276, 277.

[190] *Ibid.*, pp. 277, 278.

[191] *Ibid.*, pp. 273–275.

[192] *Ibid.*, pp. 271, 272.

[193] *Ibid.*, pp. 280, 281.

Henry Whitley (1866–1935), inheritor of the family cotton-spinning business, active in the Sunday Schools and in evening schools, long a member of Parliament, and speaker of the House of Commons from 1921 to 1928;[194] and George Campbell Morgan (1863–1945), who by his expository, theologically conservative preaching filled the huge Westminster Chapel not far from the Abbey, and whose numerous books had a wide circulation.[195] Giants they were, examples of the rugged individualism of the nineteenth century inspired and controlled by the Christian faith. To them must be added the name of Peter Taylor Forsyth (1848–1921),[196] whose wrestling with the basic Christian verities in light of the intellectual currents of the revolutionary age had an even more profound effect in the 1940's and 1950's than during his lifetime.

As a fifth feature we must hasten to say that although not as many outstanding figures emerged in English Congregationalism in the first half of the twentieth as in the nineteenth century, they were by no means completely lacking. Some were noted preachers. Thus Frederick William Norwood (1875——), born and educated in Australia, was minister of City Temple in London from 1919 to 1936 and helped to revive that outstanding pulpit of English Congregationalism after the furor aroused by its late pastor, R. J. Campbell, through his "new theology." Norwood had been preceded, briefly (1916–1919), by the American Joseph Fort Newton (1876–1950).[197] Maude Royden (Mrs. G. W. H. Shaw, 1876——), who had been a leader in the woman's movement, was assistant preacher in City Temple (1917–1920).[198] William Edwin Orchard, of lowly birth, reared first in the Church of England and then in the Presbyterian Church of England, in his middle teens was converted in an evangelistic meeting, had a theological but not a university course, read prodigiously, was ordained a Presbyterian, and eventually became pastor of King's Weigh House in London. Since that was a church with Congregational affiliations he joined the Congregational Union. During World War I he was an outspoken pacifist and assisted in organizing the Fellowship of Reconciliation. He became a liberal, both theologically and politically. Increasingly he adopted Catholic practices, with vestments, the mass, and confession. In 1932, following what he believed to be the logic of his development, he became a Roman Catholic.[199]

Some Congregational laymen were prominent, even though without the wealth that had marked many of their denomination in the nineteenth century.

[194] Ibid., pp. 283, 284.

[195] Who Was Who, 1941–1950, p. 812.

[196] Volume II, pp. 327, 328.

[197] Who's Who, 1955, p. 2206; Clare, The City Temple, 1640–1940, pp. 179–188, 194–224.

[198] Who's Who, 1955, p. 2574; Clare, op. cit., pp. 191–193.

[199] W. E. Orchard, From Faith to Faith. An Autobiography of Religious Development (New York, Harper & Brothers, 1933, pp. 310), passim.

William Wedgewood Benn (1877–1960), created the first Viscount Stansgate in 1941, was a leader in the Labour Party and among other offices had been secretary of state for India (1929–1931) and secretary of state for air (1945–1946).[200]

From Congregationalism, too, came scholars who helped to re-think the faith in terms of the intellectual currents of the revolutionary age. Among them were James Vernon Bartlet (1863–1940), a graduate of Oxford and professor of Church history in Mansfield College, who shared in COPEC and wrote extensively on Church history, theology, and the New Testament.[201] Cecil John Cadoux (1883–1947), grandson of a Congregational minister and son of a merchant, educated in King's College, London, professor of Church history and vice-principal of Mansfield College, gained wide recognition by his historical work on Christian pacifism.[202] Charles Harold Dodd (1884——), educated in Oxford and Berlin, became professor of divinity in Cambridge (1935–1949). His chief work was on the New Testament and he attracted notice by what was called "realized eschatology," an attempt to solve the eschatological issue.[203] After his retirement from Cambridge Dodd gave his chief time to the editorship of a fresh translation of the Bible into modern English.

A sixth feature was the fact that in the four decades after 1914 English Congregationalism had marked doctrinal shifts which paralleled those in some other forms of Protestantism. In the 1920's and 1930's English Congregationalism seemed to be moving far in the direction of liberalism, minimizing historic Christian doctrine and stressing experience and the re-stating of the faith in terms of the thought of the day. The climax came in the Blackheath Group late in the 1920's and early in the 1930's. The Group was composed of men akin to Modernists in Anglicanism and in other denominations. The more extreme among them looked upon Jesus as leader rather than Lord. A reaction came towards the historic Reformed positions. In it Nathaniel Micklem (1888——) was outstanding. A product of Rugby and Oxford, after teaching in the Biblical field in England and Canada, in 1932 he became principal and professor of dogmatic theology in Mansfield College.[204] The revival of the

---

[200] *Who's Who, 1955*, p. 2807.

[201] *Who Was Who, 1929–1940*, p. 73.

[202] *Who Was Who, 1941–1950*, p. 177.

[203] Charles Harold Dodd, *The Apostolic Preaching and Its Development. Three Lectures with an Appendix on Eschatology and History* (London, Hodder and Stoughton, 1936, pp. vii, 240); *The Parables of the Kingdom* (London, Nisbet and Co., 1935, pp. ix, 214). See also his *The Epistle of Paul to the Romans* (London, Hodder and Stoughton, 1932, pp. xxxv, 246); *The Interpretation of the Fourth Gospel* (Cambridge University Press, 1953, pp. xi, 477); and *The Authority of the Bible* (New York, Harper & Brothers, 1929, pp. 310).

[204] Grant, *op. cit.*, pp. 292 ff.; *Who's Who, 1955*, p. 2035.

theology of P. T. Forsyth made for the same emphasis—akin to that stressed by Barth and by others on the Continent.

A seventh feature of English Congregationalism was persistence in the historic efforts to spread the Gospel outside the Occident. The London Missionary Society, the chief agency through which this was accomplished, celebrated its sesquicentennial in 1945. It suffered from a decline in the number of wealthy men in its constituency and from recurring and embarrassing deficits, but in spite of those handicaps it registered some increase in income. Moreover, between 1895 and 1945 it appointed about 800 missionaries as compared with 548 in the preceding fifty years and 475 in the first five decades of its history. Significant, too, was the progress made in the autonomy of the younger churches in Asia, Africa, and the islands of the sea for whose founding and nourishment it had been chiefly responsible.[205]

THE BAPTIST RECORD

Entering the post-1914 decades with fewer members than the Congregationalists, by 1959 the Baptists outnumbered them by about 50 per cent. Yet that did not indicate growth. Rather, the decline in membership had simply been smaller. On the eve of 1914 Baptists were said to total 392,034.[206] World War I and the immediate aftermath saw a shrinkage—to 388,252 in 1919.[207] In the next few years the losses were slightly more than recouped—to a total membership in 1929 of 414,000. But in 1958 the number reported was 327,000.[208] Another set of figures showed a loss between 1925 and 1939 of over 30,000 members and more than 148,000 in the enrolment in Sunday Schools, and between 1939 and 1951 of 50,000 members and 57,000 pupils in Sunday Schools.[209] How far if at all the contrasts in losses between the Congregationalists and the Baptists were due to the different economic and educational levels from which the two denominations drew their members and to what extent to theological factors would be impossible to determine. On the whole, Baptists did not have as high a level of income or of education as did Congregationalists but, like the latter, they were predominantly from the middle classes. Presumably their faith was not as badly eroded by the intellectural currents of the day as was that of the Congregationalists. They did not display as marked a trend towards liberalism in the 1920's and 1930's as did the Congregationalists, nor was the

205 Norman Goodall, A History of the London Missionary Society, 1895-1945 (New York, Oxford University Press, 1954, pp. xv, 640), passim, especially pp. 529 ff.
206 The Statesman's Year Book, 1914, p. 27.
207 Ibid., 1920, p. 28.
208 Ibid., 1930, p. 21, 1959, p. 70.
209 Payne, The Baptist Union. A Short History, p. 194.

rebound towards the historical Reformed position represented by Barth as extreme.

Again like the Congregationalists, the Baptists adopted a more centralized comprehensive administration and methods of ensuring more professional training for their ministry. They divided the country into ten areas, over each of which a general superintendent was appointed. One of the purposes of the new structure was to put into effect the Sustentation and Ministerial Settlement programme for maintaining a minimum stipend for the clergy. In connexion with the plan increased control over the individual churches accepting help was placed in the Baptist Union, a national organization which dated from early in the nineteenth century.[210]

The two world wars and Britain's involvement in them brought challenges to Baptists. During World War I the council of the Baptist Union called on their fellow Baptists in the Empire to join in "a war to end war." The Baptist Union also provided huts and institutes for the troops for recreational and religious purposes and its secretary joined with others in insisting, successfully, that Free Churchmen, including Baptists, be appointed chaplains.[211] World War II made for much dislocation or suspension of normal church life, and the enemy bombings destroyed or damaged many church structures. Baptists again officially supported the government in the war. Their representatives coöperated with other religious leaders in suggesting peace terms and a programme for a new social order. Following both wars Baptists raised a special fund to meet pressing needs, partly to increase the stipends of the clergy and partly, after World War II, to aid in the reconstruction or repair of church buildings. After World War II, in contrast with its predecessor, which was succeeded by a dearth of candidates for the ministry, numbers of returning service-men sought training for it. With the increasing religious interest among university students, in 1947 a Baptist Students' Federation was organized, followed a little later by a Baptist Theological Students' Union.[212]

Between the wars some important developments were seen. A large sum was collected for new buildings and paralleling the campaign to raise it a special effort on evangelism was made.[213] John Howard Shakespeare (1857–1928), for twenty-eight years (1898–1926) secretary of the Baptist Union, was eager for an inclusive union among Protestants. President of the National Free Church Council during part of World War I, he was chiefly responsible for the formation (1919) of the Federal Council of the Evangelical Free Churches and was its first moderator. He was also willing to go further and

---

[210] *Ibid.*, pp. 182–184.
[211] *Ibid.*, pp. 180, 181.
[212] *Ibid.*, pp. 191, 214–216, 224, 227.
[213] *Ibid.*, p. 203.

accept some kind of reordination by Anglican bishops and was happy when Lang, as Archbishop of York, presented the Church of England's *Appeal* to the Baptist Union Assembly. However, to his great grief, most Baptists were unwilling to follow him that far. English Baptists, moreover, returned a courteous negative to Archbishop Fisher's suggestion that the free churches accept the principle of the episcopacy as a basis for full intercommunion. Yet the Baptist Union coöperated in the Ecumenical Movement. Moreover, John Clifford (1836–1923) was the first president of the Baptist World Alliance, organized in London in 1905.[214]

Representing, as they did, diverse theological positions, some of General and others of Particular background, it was to be expected that British Baptists would find it difficult always to agree. For a time the "down grade" controversy led by Spurgeon over the acceptance of higher criticism[215] seemed about to reawaken over the doctrine of the substitutionary atonement, but dissent was quieted by the presentation in official publications of both the challenge to it and the defense of it. Controversies also arose over the views taught by some members of the faculties of the theological colleges. However, no such major rifts occurred as among Baptists in North America.[216]

We have already had occasion to note two outstanding English Baptist scholars who led in the re-thinking of the faith in terms of contemporary intellectual currents, for both had risen to prominence before 1914.[217] Terrot Reaveley Glover (1869–1943), of Scottish ancestry, English-born in a Baptist minister's family, was graduated from Cambridge and after a brief teaching experience in Canada was long on the faculty of that university. He combined scholarship with a readable literary style and lectured and wrote vividly on New Testament characters and the world into which Christianity was born.[218] Henry Wheeler Robinson (1872–1945), honest, fearless, acquainted with Continental scholarship from study in German universities, loyal to his Baptist heritage, had had experience as a pastor but came to prominence as a teacher and scholar. His major writing was on the Old Testament. As principal of Regent's Park College he transferred that institution from London to Oxford, thus placing prospective Baptist ministers in the midst of a university.[219]

The 1950's witnessed some improvement in the condition of the Baptists. An increase, although slight, was registered in church membership. It was said to have been due chiefly to the creation of new churches—more than seventy

[214] *Ibid.,* pp. 166, 167, 185–187, 200, 203, 219, 292–303.
[215] Volume II, pp. 331, 332.
[216] Payne, *op. cit.,* pp. 205, 206.
[217] Volume II, p. 333.
[218] H. G. Wood, *Terrot Reaveley Glover. A Biography* (Cambridge University Press, 1953, pp. xii, 233), *passim.*
[219] Ernest A. Payne, *Henry Wheeler Robinson, Scholar, Teacher, Principal* (London, Nisbet and Co., 1946, pp. 212).

in the ten years which followed World War II. True to its promise, the government through its War Damage Commission gave extensive sums to the repair of buildings which had suffered from the bombings, and Baptists received from it at least £1,500,000. The minimum stipend for ministers and deaconesses was raised, although not sufficiently to meet the rise in prices, and many pastors' wives sought supplementary employment to maintain their families. Moreover, a shortage of ministers was reported; in 1951 the total of the clergy was 329 less than in 1910 and many were caught up in administrative and teaching posts both within and outside the denomination. An effort was made to ease the situation by a re-grouping of churches, postponing the age of retirement, and an increased use of deaconesses. In spite of gains, late in the 1950's the over-all picture was still sombre.[220]

As did the Anglicans and the Congregationalists, the Baptists had their missions in other lands. The vision which had inspired William Carey was still cherished by the society whose founding he had stimulated. Yet mounting costs, the failure of income fully to meet them, the shortage of personnel, and the closing by the Communists of areas long served in China were sobering developments.

THE SOCIETY OF FRIENDS

The Society of Friends, popularly known as the Quakers, remained, as in the nineteenth century, a small minority, but in contrast to the decline in the larger denominations their numbers grew. In 1913 their total was said to have been 17,466[221] and in 1958 it was reported to be 21,400.[222] The two world wars and the sufferings attendant on each, both during the hostilities and after them, presented a challenge to a people whose historic witness had been against war and for the victims of man's inhumanity to man. During and after both wars the English Friends joined with those in other countries, especially in the United States, in widespread efforts for relief and reconstruction, both by funds and by personal service, the latter often in positions of extreme danger.[223]

Out of World War I and largely from the English Friends came the Fellowship of Reconciliation, which eventually had an international coverage. Its

[220] Payne, *The Baptist Union. A Short History*, pp. 240–243.
[221] *The Statesman's Year Book, 1914*, p. 27.
[222] *Ibid., 1959*, p. 60.
[223] On what was done during and after World War I, especially by the English Friends, see A. Ruth Fry, *A Quaker Adventure. The Story of Nine Years' Relief and Reconstruction* (London, Nisbet and Co., 1926, pp. xxxii, 389), *passim*. On the record during and after World War II, see Roger C. Wilson, *Quaker Relief. An Account of the Relief Work of the Society of Friends, 1940–1948* (London, George Allen and Unwin, 1952, pp. xii, 373), *passim*. For the experiences of one Friend in World War I as a conscientious objector and in dangerous relief work which cost him his life, see *George Lloyd Hodgkin, 1880–1918* (printed for private circulation, The Edinburgh Press, 1921, pp. vii, 268), pp. 45–61, 137–175.

chief creator was Henry Theodore Hodgkin (1877–1933). Born to wealth, of old and devout Quaker stock, Hodgkin had his university course in Cambridge and was caught up in the Student Christian Movement and the World's Student Christian Federation. He prepared in medicine, was a missionary in West China, and from 1910 to 1920 was secretary of the Friends' Foreign Missionary Association. In England on that assignment when World War I broke out, in 1915 he joined with other pacifists, among them Maude Royden and W. E. Orchard, in founding the Fellowship of Reconciliation. Large of body, striking in personal appearance, and with marked gifts of leadership, he became its first chairman and helped to spread it not only in Britain but also in other lands. Its purpose was indicated in its name—to work for reconciliation, not only negatively by opposing war, but also positively, by seeking to remove the causes of war and of conflicts between races and classes. It was distinctly Christian, but enrolled members from many communions.[224]

The limitations of space forbid even the listing of the groups of Friends who travelled to various storm centres in the international scene in efforts to prevent war and to promote reconciliation. Nor can we do more than mention such Quaker scholars as H. G. Wood, who contributed to Christian thought in the face of the intellectual and social currents of the revolutionary age. We must content ourselves with barely naming the Selly Oak Colleges, which arose from the initiative of the Cadburys near their chocolate works and model community at Bournville on the outskirts of Birmingham and in which several denominations coöperated in advanced training for Christian service. Here in the English Friends was one of the creative Christian minorities which exerted an influence far out of proportion to its numerical strength.

THE METHODISTS

Methodism entered the twentieth century divided into several branches which together outnumbered in membership the total of all the other Free Churches of England. In 1960 it still enrolled the majority of Nonconforming Protestants but in the meantime important developments had taken place.[225]

One was the coming together of the large majority of English Methodists into a single ecclesiastical body. In this a parallel was seen in the centralization among the Congregationalists and Baptists and in unions in Scotland, Canada, the United States, and several countries in Asia and elsewhere. The movement towards union had begun shortly before 1914. In 1907 the Methodist New Connexion, the Bible Christian Methodists, and the United Methodist Free Churches had joined to form the United Methodist Church. That step left the

224 H. G. Wood, *Henry T. Hodgkin, A Memoir* (London, Student Christian Movement Press, 1937, pp. 281), *passim*, especially pp. 153–176.
225 On Methodism in the nineteenth century see Volume II, pp. 335–342.

overwhelming majority of English Methodists in three bodies. The largest, the Wesleyan Methodists, had 522,721 members; the next largest, the Primitive Methodists, reported 207,034 members; and the United Methodists, the smallest of the big three, had 159,095 members—all figures for 1908.[226] In 1932 the three bodies came together in one Methodist Church, the culmination of many years of discussion and negotiation.[227]

The uniting of the Methodist forces did not prevent the numerical decline of Methodism to which we have called attention. In 1913 the three bodies which merged in 1932 reported a total of 959,494 members,[228] in 1919 of 818,581 members,[229] and in 1929 of 861,000 members.[230] In 1932 the corresponding figure was 859,652 and in 1949 it was 749,703.[231] The number then rose, and in 1958 it was 1,081,000,[232] but although the tide seemed to have turned, in proportion to the population Methodists were fewer than in 1913.

Earnest efforts to stay the decline were made and in the 1950's they were attended by encouraging results. Late in the 1940's what were called "Christian commando campaigns" were instituted in which many Methodists shared and through which laymen and clergy visited factories, cinemas, and other places where people gathered, forthrightly presenting the Gospel. At the climax of the campaign about three thousand centred their efforts on London.[233] An efficient programme for reaching youth through Sunday Schools and other media also contributed to the improvement.[234]

Agonizing appraisals were made of the causes of the Methodist recession. Clearly some factors applied to the other Free Churches and to the Church of England and operated elsewhere in Western Europe. Within Methodism itself the sense of urgency in evangelism was said to have dwindled, with less zeal in winning the unconverted. Such typical Methodist customs as the class meeting, the love feast, the Sunday night prayer-meeting, the open-air meeting, the camp-meeting, and the personal appeal to decide for Christ were said to have disappeared, and lethargy among church members, especially youth, with a lack of conviction of the meaning and importance of conversion, was reported to be general.[235] This was simply saying, however, that the corrosive forces

[226] Volume II, p. 341.
[227] Wearmouth, *The Social and Political Influence of Methodism in the Twentieth Century*, pp. 69–76.
[228] *The Statesman's Year Book, 1914*, p. 27.
[229] *Ibid., 1920*, p. 28.
[230] *Ibid., 1930*, p. 21.
[231] Wearmouth, *op. cit.*, p. 54.
[232] *The Statesman's Year Book, 1959*, p. 70.
[233] Wearmouth, *op. cit.*, pp. 54, 55; C. A. Roberts in *World Dominion*, Vol. XXXIII, pp. 138, 139 (May/June, 1955).
[234] *The British Weekly*, March 17, 1955.
[235] Wearmouth, *op. cit.*, pp. 56, 57.

operating on Western society as a whole were eroding Methodism as they were other denominations.

That Methodism was neither dead nor moribund was abundantly clear. The numerical gains late in the 1950's and the devotion and conviction which helped to bring them about were encouraging. Institutions and methods developed in the nineteenth century to meet the distinctive needs of the revolutionary age were continued. The Central Halls in London and Manchester and projects such as the West London Mission were maintained. Between 1947 and 1955 approximately 190 churches and churchhalls were erected. Deaconesses still served churches and communities.[236] Great preachers continued to emerge who turned to advantage the interests and mores of the day to present the Gospel in ways which would make it clearly relevant to the needs of their hearers. Among others, Leslie Dixon Weatherhead (1893———), who beginning in 1936 was the minister of the City Temple, came out of a devout home in which the father was a Scottish Presbyterian, served as a minister in India, then as an officer in the armed forces in World War I, and later as a chaplain in Mesopotamia, and, while stressing the central verities of the faith, also sought to utilize the psychology of the day in the spiritual and physical cure of souls. He had rejuvenated a down-town Methodist church in Manchester, had attracted great throngs in a Methodist church in Leeds, and by his numerous books, personal counselling, and an enormous correspondence had reached many thousands, when he was called to the City Temple. That church's building was bombed during World War II, but its congregation was offered the hospitality of other churches and he continued to fill them until City Temple could be equipped with a new physical plant.[237] Donald O. Soper (1903———), educated in Cambridge and the London School of Economics, had varied experiences in London: as a member of the South London Mission (1926–1929), in the Central London Mission (1929–1936), and then as superintendent of the West London Mission. He was skilled in out-door preaching in London in such places as Tower Hill and Hyde Park and in the repartee which thrived in them.[238]

Wilfred H. Bourne, called "the telephone parson," came into the Methodist ministry after service in World War I. As a result of notices in the daily press, thousands called him for a "tonic thought" which was read to them by Bourne or his wife. Although they were not asked to tell their names or their story,

236 Volume II, pp. 235, 236; C. A. Roberts, *op. cit.*, p. 141.

237 Clare, *The City Temple, 1640–1940*, pp. 245–286. Among Weatherhead's many books were *His Life and Ours: the Significance for Us of the Life of Jesus* (Nashville, Abingdon-Cokesbury Press, 1933, pp. 361); *Discipleship* (New York, The Abingdon Press, 1934, pp. 152); *Psychology and Life* (New York, The Abingdon Press, 1935, pp. xix, 280); and *Psychology, Religion, and Healing* (London, Hodder and Stoughton, 1951, pp. 544).

238 *Who's Who, 1955*, p. 2772.

many later sought counsel by telephone, in writing, or in person.[239]

In 1954 William Gowland, minister in Albert Hall in Manchester, with a constituency of fifteen hundred, resigned to take over a broken-down church in the heart of an industrial district. Within five years he built it up from a congregation of sixty to a membership of five hundred, growing at the rate of a hundred a year, drawn largely from the factories. He sought to encourage the members to work at their faith in their daily occupations. He also founded an industrial college to train shop stewards, apprentices, managers, and industrial chaplains. By 1959 it had graduated about three hundred, ministers and laymen, and in 1958 had over three thousand applications for admission. Gowland's purpose was to bring Christian principles to bear on labour relations and to stimulate Christians to be active in their unions and save the latter from falling into the hands of Communists and thugs.[240]

Some Methodist laymen who were enlisted in labour organizations in the second half of the nineteenth century continued to be prominent after 1914. Among them were William Straker (1855–1941), who, in his youth a Primitive Methodist lay preacher, became the leading official in the Northumberland Miners' Association,[241] and John Cairns (1859–1923), Labour member of Parliament (1918–1923), an active trade unionist, outstanding in furthering provision of homes for aged mine workers, who obtained his training in public speech as a Primitive Methodist local preacher and found in his Christian faith his abiding inspiration.[242] The list could be largely extended of coal miners in Northumberland who were lifelong Methodists, acquired facility in public speech as local preachers, and were active in labour organizations and in public affairs well into the twentieth century.[243] The same was true of coal miners in the neighbouring Durham and in Yorkshire and the Midlands. Among them were younger men who did not reach maturity until after 1914.[244] The Labour Party owed much of its early leadership to Methodists, some of whom continued to be prominent in its counsels in the twentieth century.[245] The most prominent was Arthur Henderson (1863–1935). To the end of his life he retained his standing as a local Methodist preacher. More than any other one man he was responsible for the creation and solid growth of the Labour Party. He was its secretary from 1911 to 1918, served in Parliament and in more than one post on the cabinet, and in 1931 became head of the party. Of unflinching

[239] *A Monthly Letter about Evangelism*, May, 1959.
[240] J. G. Ferry in *The Christian Century*, Vol. LXXVI, pp. 847–849 (July 22, 1959).
[241] Wearmouth, *op. cit.*, pp. 85, 86.
[242] *Ibid.*, pp. 86, 87.
[243] *Ibid.*, pp. 90–108.
[244] *Ibid.*, pp. 120–161.
[245] *Ibid.*, pp. 185–210.

courage and high integrity, he won the respect of opponents as well as supporters.[246]

Methodism did not develop as many outstanding theologians and Biblical scholars as did some other denominations. Yet in its post-1914 years it had men who were esteemed for their competence in these fields. Such was Robert Newton Flew (1886——). Educated in Oxford, Marburg, and Fribourg, a chaplain in World War I, during most of his working life he was in Wesley House in Cambridge, as its principal until his retirement.[247]

As did the other major Free Churches, British Methodism continued to share in the world mission of the faith, both by enterprises in Asia and Africa and through the Ecumenical Movement.[248]

THE SCHOLARLY PRESBYTERIANS

The Presbyterian Church of England was never a large body, but in the post-1914 years in proportion to its numerical strength it produced more scholars who helped in the adjustment of theology and Biblical studies to the intellectual climate of the day than did any other English denomination. In its membership it suffered losses. In 1913 it reported 86,848 communicants,[249] in 1919 the total had risen to 88,166,[250] but by 1929 the corresponding number was 84,000,[251] and in 1958 it had sunk to 70,940.[252] Yet from that minority had come a number of men to whom all English-speaking Protestantism was deeply indebted. Among those who stood out were John Wood Oman (1860–1939), who studied in Edinburgh, Erlangen, and Heidelberg, who after a long pastorate in Northumberland (1889–1907) became professor of systematic theology (1907–1935) and was as well principal (1922–1935) of the theological college of his church, and whose most widely read book was *Natural and the Supernatural;*[253] Patrick Carnegie Simpson (1865–1947), a native of Australia, educated in Edinburgh, who was pastor in Scotland and England, who from 1914 to 1938 was on the faculty of Westminster College in Cambridge, and whose *The Fact of Christ* was translated into several languages;[254] Herbert Henry Farmer (1892——), a graduate of Cambridge who after a few years of teaching in the United States became a member of the faculty of Westminster

[246] *Ibid.*, pp. 246, 247.
[247] *Who's Who, 1955,* p. 1003.
[248] Strong and Warnshuis, *Directory of Foreign Missions,* p. 24. For glimpses through the eyes of one long connected with Methodist missions in these years see W. J. Noble, *Something to Remember* (London, Cargate Press, pp. 182), *passim.*
[249] *The Statesman's Year Book, 1914,* p. 27.
[250] *The Statesman's Year Book, 1920,* p. 28.
[251] *Ibid., 1930,* p. 21.
[252] *Ibid., 1959,* p. 70.
[253] *Who Was Who, 1929–1940,* p. 1023.
[254] *Ibid., 1941–1950,* p. 1057.

College and among other honours was a Gifford lecturer;[255] and Thomas Walter Manson (1893–1958), educated in Glasgow and Cambridge, who was long professor of Biblical criticism and exegesis in the University of Manchester and whose *The Teaching of Jesus: Studies in Its Form and Content,* was widely used.[256] In spite of its small size, the Presbyterian Church of England had a continuing share in the world mission in India, Malaya, and China.[257]

THE SMALLER FREE CHURCHES CONTINUE

Unfortunately we cannot take the space to do more than hint at the twentieth-century record of the smaller Free Churches. All of those mentioned as in being in the nineteenth century survived[258]—the Unitarians, the Moravians, the Churches of Christ, the Catholic Apostolic Church, and the Brethren. The Salvation Army also continued, although, strictly speaking, it was not a church. Unitarianism was not as prominent as in the nineteenth century. Two of its great figures of that period, Joseph Estlin Carpenter (1844–1927) and Lawrence Pearsall Jacks (1860——), lived well beyond 1914 but were already in middle or late life when World War I introduced a new stage in the revolutionary age.[259] No Unitarians of similar intellectual and moral stature emerged to take their places. Nor did the other smaller churches produce figures equal to those who were associated with them in the nineteenth century.

THE FREE CHURCHES ACHIEVE INCREASING MUTUAL COÖPERATION

We have already called attention to the increase of coöperation among the Free Churches which the post-1914 decades witnessed. It was not an isolated phenomenon but was part of a widespread movement which we have found in Continental Protestantism and of which we are to hear much more as, in the next volume, we move to the Americas and the non-Occidental world. It was also within the framework of the Ecumenical Movement, that mounting trend of Protestants to come together in a global unity which permitted wide variation and into which some of the Eastern Churches were drawn.

The stages of the British effort can be quickly summarized. In 1892 the first Free Church Congress met, in Manchester. In 1893 a Free Church Council was created in Birmingham as the climax of a city-wide house-to-house canvass to increase church attendance. In 1896 the first National Council of the

---

[255] *Who's Who, 1956,* p. 968.
[256] *Who's Who, 1955,* p. 957.
[257] Strong and Warnshuis, *op. cit.,* p. 25.
[258] Volume II, pp. 316–320, 343, 345.
[259] C. H. Herford, editor, *Joseph Estlin Carpenter, a Memorial Volume* (Oxford, Clarendon Press, 1929, pp. vi, 128); L. P. Jacks, *The Confession of an Octogenarian* (London, George Allen and Unwin, 1942, pp. 272); L. P. Jacks, *Near the Brink. Observations of a Nonagenarian* (London, George Allen and Unwin, 1952, pp. 120).

Evangelical Free Churches convened, as the fourth annual Congress, and adopted a constitution which had as its purpose an advance in coöperation and the formation of local councils. In 1901 it undertook an evangelistic mission to England. In 1919, largely at the instance of J. H. Shakespeare, the Federal Council of the Evangelical Free Churches was formed of official representatives of the member bodies. For twenty years the National Council and the Federal Council worked side by side in friendly association. In 1940, partly under the pressure of the emergency created by World War II, the two merged in the Free Church Federal Council.[260]

As we have seen, increasingly friendly relations arose between the Free Churches and the Church of England. Free Church agitation for the disestablishment of the Church of England subsided. On some official state occasions representatives of the Free Churches were given status along with those of the Establishment.

THE YOUNG MEN'S CHRISTIAN ASSOCIATION ENLISTS LAYMEN IN NEW WAYS

although initiated by a Free Churchman, was the Young Men's Christian Association. As we have seen, it was begun in London in 1844 by George Williams, a Congregational layman, and grew rapidly, both nationally and internationally.[261] As a lay enterprise it continued after 1914, devising new

A form of coöperation, unofficial, and not confined to the Free Churches, methods to meet the challenges of the changing revolutionary age. One was the creation of colleges for the training of laymen. They arose from the joint initiative of the Student Christian Movement, the Christian Frontier Council, and the English National Council of the YMCA's. The first college was opened in 1945 and in the next ten years was followed by six others. The colleges were for boys and men and sought to show to the skilled technician in industry the bearing of the Christian faith on his work and thought. Five were under the auspices of the YMCA and brought men to them for a period of weeks. A sixth, William Temple College, as we have noted, was begun by Anglicans, and a seventh, Moor Park College, also predominantly Anglican, dated from 1950. Obviously they were akin to what we have found in several countries on the Continent.[262]

Somewhat different kinds of coöperative movements were the Student Christian Movement and the Cambridge Inter-Collegiate Christian Union (CICCU). Both began in the nineteenth century and thrived in the post-1914 decades. Both drew students from the Church of England and the Free Churches. The Student Christian Movement was widely inclusive and had membership in the

260 Jordan, Free Church Unity, passim.
261 Volume II, pp. 361, 362.
262 Weber, Signs of Renewal, pp. 26–30.

World's Student Christian Federation.[263] The Cambridge Inter-Collegiate Union was conservative theologically, in line with earlier Evangelicalism and in active sympathy with the Keswick Conferences,[264] and was part of the Inter-Varsity Fellowship—also an international organization.[265]

EVANGELICAL MOVEMENTS FROM THE UNITED STATES HAVE REPERCUSSIONS

Closely related in history, language, and tradition, it is not surprising that the Protestant churches of Anglo-Saxon provenance of the British Isles and the United States interacted on each other. As we have seen and are to see, much from Great Britain came to the United States both before and after 1914. We have noted the profound influence which two American evangelists, Charles G. Finney and Dwight L. Moody, had in the British Isles.[266] After 1914 two other men, like them Evangelicals, made a wide and deep impress on England.

The older was Frank N. D. Buchman (1878——). Born in Pennsylvania, a Lutheran, with strong Evangelical convictions, he sought by novel methods to bring about the conversion of individuals, making Christians out of pagans and better Christians out of Christians. At the outset he used what were called "house parties" in informal settings, holding up the standards of absolute unselfishness, purity, honesty, and love which he found in the Sermon on the Mount, stressing confession, the power of Christ to change lives, and the guidance of the Holy Spirit in "quiet times." Before World War I he had travelled widely, but the movement, at first known as Buchmanism, grew rapidly after the coming of peace. In England Buchman concentrated on the universities, especially the oldest, and the movement came to be known as the Oxford Groups. Later it adopted the title Moral Rearmament, or MRA, seeking to further a programme of life which would issue in personal, social, racial, and national supernatural change. It was often met by outspoken criticism and as often won loyal adherence from both high and low. Emil Brunner for a time aided it and B. H. Streeter gave it his unqualified allegiance. It spread to many countries.[267]

[263] Tissington Tatlow, *The Story of the Student Christian Movement of Great Britain and Ireland* (London, Student Christian Movement Press, 1933, pp. xv, 944), *passim;* J. Davis McCaughey, *Christian Obedience in the University. Studies in the Life of the Student Christian Movement of Great Britain and Ireland, 1930–1950* (London, S.C.M. Press, 1950, pp. 228), *passim.*

[264] Volume II, pp. 281, 282.

[265] J. C. Pollock, *A Cambridge Movement* (London, John Murray, pp. xv, 288), *passim.*

[266] Volume II, p. 323.

[267] Of the enormous literature, friendly and unfriendly, the following are samples: Emil Brunner, *The Church and the Oxford Group* (London, Hodder and Stoughton, 1937, pp. 109), friendly; Herbert Hensley Henson, *The Oxford Group Movement* (New York, Oxford University Press, 1933, pp. 82), fairly friendly but calling it a middle-class movement which could not be brought into working harmony with the Church of England; R. H. S. Crossman, editor, *Oxford and the Groups* (Oxford, Blackwell, 1934, pp. xiv, 208), embodying various attitudes; Marjorie Harrison, *Saints Run Mad. A Criticism of the "Oxford" Movement* (London, John Lane: The Badley Head, 1934,

The younger, William Franklin Graham (1918———), usually known as Billy Graham, was more nearly in the tradition of Finney and Moody. Born in North Carolina, a Baptist, educated in what were usually known as fundamentalist schools and colleges, handsome, well-mannered, deeply in earnest, transparently humble and sincere, Graham had already held evangelistic meetings in many cities in North America and was backed by the well-organized and financed Billy Graham Evangelistic Association when in 1954 and 1955 he was in the British Isles, with great meetings in London in 1954. In London he was assisted by more than a thousand churches, the majority of them Anglican, preached to hundreds of thousands, in the final meeting was supported by the Archbishop of Canterbury, and also preached to the queen and her consort at Windsor Castle. Both praise and criticism were evoked.[268]

THE CONTINUING ALTHOUGH WANING EFFECT OF PROTESTANTISM ON ENGLAND

Any attempt to appraise the impact of Protestantism upon the life of England must be faulty or at least incomplete, no matter what era is considered. Yet as we seek to determine what the effect was in the four and a half decades which followed 1914 we are impressed by what appear to be two valid generalizations. First, it was not as striking as in the nineteenth century. Second, it was still very considerable and because of it England more nearly conformed to Christian standards than it did at the outset of the nineteenth century.

That the effect of Protestantism was not as pronounced as in the nineteenth century seems fairly obvious. At the beginning of that century, with the exception of significant minorities, from the Christian standpoint the life of England was on a low level. That was true of public life and of high society under the regency and then the reign of George IV. It was also true of the rank and file of the nation. In the course of the nineteenth century, as we have seen,[269] a marked improvement was registered, largely traceable to a conscience inspired by Protestantism. It was conspicuous in education, in legislation for the protection of labourers in industry, the mines, and agriculture, in the abolition of the African slave trade and of Negro slavery, in better prisons, in improved care of children, in contributions to the labour movement, in a more benevolent colonial policy, in literature, and in a general advance in private morals.

After 1914 no such striking effects were seen. Yet effects there were, and

---

pp. viii, 151), very critical; Walter Houston Clark, *The Oxford Group: Its History and Significance* (New York, Bookman Associates, 1951, pp. 268), seeking objectivity.

[268] For a favourable report, well written, see Stanley High, *Billy Graham. The Personal Story of the Man, His Message, and His Mission* (New York, McGraw-Hill Book Co., 1956, pp. 275), *passim*. For a somewhat critical appraisal see *The British Weekly*, February 10, 1955. For a moderately favourable appraisal see Cecil Northcott in *Religion in Life*, Vol. XXVIII, pp. 181–189 (Spring, 1959).

[269] Volume II, pp. 352–388.

public and private life did not sink as low as in the closing years of the eighteenth and the opening decades of the nineteenth century. Moreover, thanks to the social legislation of the post-1914 years the standard of living of the lower-income groups was still more improved, so that much less abject poverty existed than at the beginning of the nineteenth century. Much of the contrast between the beginning of the nineteenth and the first half of the twentieth century can be attributed to the momentum gained in the nineteenth century, but not a little was due to the continued impact of Protestantism. Part of this we have already seen. To single out only a few examples, some of which we have mentioned and others which we can take the space simply to name, it was obvious in the public sentiment which acquiesced in the independence of major portions of the Empire, in the adoption of measures which characterized the welfare state, in contributions to the growth and strength of the Labour Party and to a sense of public trust in the Conservative Party, in the Education Act of 1944, and in the support given to the government in its opposition to the proposed marriage of Edward VIII to a divorcee. Not all these could be fully ascribed to the Protestant conscience but in them that conscience had a part, even if it was not readily measured. Although moral practices were often far from those inculcated by Christianity and conditions in many quarters could not but be deplored by Protestants,[270] at least the Protestant conscience protested against them and led many to abstain from them. Much of Protestantism stood solidly behind the League of Nations as a hoped-for means of bringing order into chaotic international relations,[271] and endorsement of the United Nations came from the same quarter. Lord Robert Cecil, a devout Anglican, was outstanding in arousing public sentiment in support of the League of Nations. COPEC was a prominent land-mark in the prolonged concern of Anglicans and Free Churchmen for the betterment of social conditions.[272] Much writing indicated the continuing interest of Protestants in the economic and social life of the nation.[273]

In contrast with much of the nineteenth century, when many of the Anglican clergy were pronouncedly conservative politically, growing numbers of the

---

[270] As disclosed in Rowntree and Lavers, *English Life and Leisure, passim*, especially pp. 122–227.

[271] Jordan, *op. cit.*, p. 181.

[272] Reckitt, *Maurice to Temple, passim*.

[273] To give simply two examples, Vigo Auguste Demant (1893———), an Anglican priest, wrote many books, of which the following were typical: *God, Man and Society. An Introduction to Christian Sociology* (London, Student Christian Movement Press, 2nd ed., 1934, pp. 224) and *Religion and the Decline of Capitalism* (London, Faber and Faber, 1952, pp. 204); Maurice Benington Reckitt (1888———), a layman, editor of several journals, a central figure in an attempt to construct a Christian society, was the author of *Faith and Society: a Study of the Structure, Outlook, and Opportunity of the Christian Social Movement in Great Britain and the United States of America* (London, Longmans, Green and Co., 1932, pp. xii, 467) and *Militant Here on Earth: Considerations on the Prophetic Function of the Church in the Twentieth Century* (London, Longmans, Green and Co., 1957, pp. xi, 160).

clergy of the Church of England were sympathetic with the Labour Party. Gore and Temple especially influenced the Church of England. How much effect the changing attitude had upon the country as a whole could not be accurately determined. If literature did not have exemplars of the Christian ideal as outstanding as Tennyson and Browning, such poets as W. H. Auden and T. S. Eliot were authentically Christian and had a wide reading. Although he who was briefly Edward VIII departed from Christian standards in his personal life, others of the royal family who wore the crown had an unwavering sense of duty derived at least in part from Christian nurture.[274] Not only did private citizens espouse pacifism because of their Christian conscience and organize the Fellowship of Reconciliation, but some high in public life, inspired and sustained by their Christian faith, laboured indefatigably for disarmament and other measures to promote peace.[275] George Lansbury (1859–1940), a leader of the Labour Party, to the end of his long life was a sturdy pacifist. Reared in underprivileged East London, in his teens he was won to an active Christian commitment by an Anglo-Catholic priest. For a time in his middle years he dropped his Christian faith and sent his children to an Ethical Sunday School. But in later middle life he rejoined the Church of England and remained loyal to it. An ardent socialist, he was said to have equated socialism with Christianity. He believed profoundly in prayer and testified that it strengthened him in his arduous labours and in standing true to his principles. His grief over the outbreak of World War II is said to have shortened his life.[276] Richard Stafford Cripps (1889–1952), who did much at one period to shape the policies of the Labour government, was a devout churchman, governed by his Christian conscience and upheld by his Christian faith. John Edwards (1904–1959), for a time a secretary of the Student Christian Movement, a Labour member of Parliament, private secretary to Cripps, a leading figure in the Council of Europe, had earlier contemplated entering the Community of the Resurrection but came to believe that his Christian vocation must be through these other channels.[277] How much the effort of Neville Chamberlain, as prime minister, to avert World War II by sharing in the Munich Pact of 1938 was due to his Unitarian background would be difficult if not impossible to determine.

Significantly, the mid-twentieth century saw the return to the Christian faith of several intellectuals who had previously derided it. Such a one was C. E. M.

[274] On George V see Harold Nicolson, *King George the Fifth, His Life and Reign* (London, Constable & Co., 1952, pp. xxiii, 570), pp. 4–6, 146.

[275] See, as one example, the Quaker Philip John Noel-Baker, as described in *The New York Times*, November 6, 1959.

[276] Raymond Postgate, *The Life of George Lansbury* (London, Longmans, Green and Co., 1951, pp. xiii, 332), *passim*, especially pp. 54 ff.

[277] Alan Booth in *Frontier*, Vol. I, pp. 52, 53 (Spring, 1960).

Joad, who with his trenchant pen had long tilted against Christian beliefs and moral principles. In his closing years he wrote of his recovery of belief and he died in communion with the Church of England.[278] Clearly Protestantism was far from being a spent force in the life of England.

THE WELSH STORY

In previous volumes we have seen something of the pre-twentieth-century course of Protestantism in Wales.[279] We noted that until the coming of the Industrial Revolution the country, largely mountainous, was rural, sparsely settled, and poverty-ridden. The Industrial Revolution brought about the exploitation of the great coal fields, the lesser ones in the North-east and the major ones in the South. For a time the proximity of iron ores and coal enabled the South to become the major iron-producing region of the world. Although that supremacy was lost, the smelting of copper ores and the manufacture of tin plate continued to make the South both a mining and an industrial centre, with the many human problems brought by those occupations. Concurrently with the development of mining and industry, although not necessarily with a causal connexion, marked religious awakenings brought to Welsh Protestantism the greatest vigour it had known. The Anglican Communion, established by law, displayed decided improvement. The Nonconforming churches especially flourished, partly, it was said, because they used the Welsh language in their preaching and services, an accompaniment of the revival of Welsh nationalism. The bodies which grew to substantial dimensions were the Independents (Congregationalists), the Calvinistic Methodists, the Baptists, and the Wesleyan Methodists.

In the post-1914 decades the economic situation underwent important changes, with profound repercussions in the life of the people. Between the two world wars Wales passed through grim years of depression in mining and industries. Although Wales was still the chief coal-exporting region of the United Kingdom, the output declined and the smelting of copper ore fell off. The processing of nickel ore, imported from Canada, was partly a substitute, and the production of steel and tin plate continued. But unemployment was rife and with it went extreme suffering and unrest. After World War II the coal mines were nationalized (1947) and the output of coal rose. The manufacture of both steel and tin plate was modernized, new industries were stimulated by the government, and the standard of living improved. Yet unemployment, although lessened, continued, and thousands of youth left the country.

[278] *The Christian News-Letter*, July, 1953, pp. 137–142.
[279] Volume I, pp. 62, 182; Volume II, pp. 389–394.

Protestantism in Wales experienced striking changes and on the whole, as in England, a loss of numbers was seen. Yet, like Protestantism in England, it continued to display vitality. A development which took place not far from the outbreak of World War I was the disestablishment of the Church of Wales —a branch of the Anglican Communion. In support of disestablishment was the fact that only a minority of the people of Wales were adherents of the Church of Wales and that Nonconformists outnumbered that minority. Many of the Welsh resented the Establishment and the large majority of the members of Parliament returned from Wales in the two elections which followed 1909 were known to favour disestablishment. The bill to effect disestablishment was introduced in April, 1912. Some in Wales opposed it. The Archbishop of Canterbury and the Archbishop of York, together with a majority of the bishops of the Church of England, were against it and it was rejected by the House of Lords. Several English Nonconformists regarded its terms as too ungenerous to the Church of Wales. However, the House of Commons carried it over the adverse votes of the Lords. The ancient endowments were taken from the church and were devoted to other purposes in behalf of the Welsh people, largely education. Because of the outbreak of the war, disestablishment was not put into effect until the close of hostilities. When, in 1919, it was accomplished, the financial provisions were softened. In contrast with the original measure some endowments were left to the church. Even then Lord Salisbury and Lord Robert Cecil felt aggrieved, so much so that in protest the latter resigned from the cabinet. The Welsh dioceses were divorced administratively from the Church of England and became a separate province of the Anglican Communion.[280]

The Church of Wales survived disestablishment. It was crippled financially and its poverty constituted a handicap. However, by the late 1950's two additional dioceses had been created. Fellowship was retained with the Church of England, and the Welsh bishops were regularly invited to meetings of the bishops of the larger body. In the participation of the laity—including women —in its government from the parish to the national level (partly under a new constitution adopted in 1922) the Church of Wales became more nearly identified with the life of the people than it had been. Although some of the clergy moved to the Church of England, attracted by larger salaries and enhanced prestige, on the whole the Church of Wales gained by disestablishment and ceased to be handicapped by the accusation that it was imposed by an alien power.[281]

---

[280] Lockhart, *Cosmo Gordon Lang*, pp. 221, 238; Bell, *Randall Davidson*, Vol. I, pp. 640–644, Vol. II, pp. 980–990; J. Scott Lidgett, *Reminiscences* (London, The Epworth Press, preface 1928, pp. 95), pp. 72–75.

[281] Neill, *Anglicanism*, pp. 316–318; *The Encyclopædia Britannica*, 1954 printing, Vol. XXIII, p. 298.

In the post-1914 decades the non-Anglican Protestant bodies in Wales shared with the Free Churches of England the experience of declining membership. To be sure, the Calvinistic Methodists had a slight gain—to 201,000 in 1958 as compared with 183,647 in 1913.[282] But unemployment and World War II were said to have broken the hold of the non-Anglican churches upon many of the youth.[283] A study in the mid-1950's showed that Baptists, Congregationalists, and Wesleyan Methodists were giving ground and had been doing so since 1945. The Calvinistic Methodists were losing the gains they had made in the 1920's and 1930's. As was to be expected from what we have found in other countries, in general the losses were most marked in the industrial South. In the North the Wesleyan Methodists were the chief sufferers and the other denominations did not decline as sharply as in the South.[284]

Yet in the 1950's the picture for the non-Anglican bodies, like that of the Church of Wales, was not entirely bleak. The Calvinistic Methodists, renamed the Presbyterian Church of Wales by act of Parliament in 1927 in recognition of their distinctly Welsh character, remained a stronghold of the Welsh language—important in a day when the current of Welsh nationalism was running strong.[285] After 1952 enrolment in the Sunday Schools, which had been in a long decline, mounted sharply, giving promise of an increase in church membership.[286] The years which followed World War II witnessed the founding of the Welsh League of Youth (Urdd) by Ifan ab Owen Edwards, in an effort to combine Welsh patriotism with Christian brotherhood under the slogan "Wales, fellow-men, and Christ."[287] Some laymen prominent in the preceding century lived well past World War I and were honoured and exerted an influence for the faith. For example, John Edward Lloyd (1861–1947), knighted in 1934, a noted expert in Welsh history and language, served as chairman of the Welsh Congregational Union in 1934 and in 1941 was made a freeman of Bangor.[288]

PROTESTANTISM IN DIVIDED IRELAND

The political tensions and turmoil in Ireland during the decades introduced by the outbreak of World War I had their repercussions upon Protestantism as they had on Roman Catholicism. As we have seen,[289] in the Irish Free State, which later (1948) as the Republic of Ireland (Éire) became completely inde-

[282] *The Statesman's Year Book, 1959*, p. 76, *1914*, p. 27.
[283] Spinks, *Religion in Britain since 1900*, p. 71.
[284] *British Weekly*, March 10, 1953.
[285] *The Encyclopædia Britannica*, 1954 printing, Vol. XXIII, p. 298.
[286] *British Weekly*, March 10, 1955.
[287] Spinks, *op. cit.*, p 71.
[288] Peel, *The Congregational Two Hundred, 1530–1948*, p. 269.
[289] Chapter VII.

pendent, Roman Catholics were in the overwhelming majority. Out of its population in the 1950's of a little short of 3,000,000, Roman Catholics totalled 2,786,264, Protestant Episcopalians (members of the Church of Ireland) 124,829, Presbyterians 23,870, Methodists, 8,355, and 12,020 belonged to other bodies. In Northern Ireland, with a population (1946) of 1,370,921, 471,460 were Roman Catholics, 410,215 were Presbyterians, the Church of Ireland enrolled 353,245, the Methodists had 66,639, and others were 69,362.[290]

Of the Protestant bodies, the Church of Ireland was the largest. It was in communion with the Church of England and for many years had been a phase and symbol of the tie with England. We have noted[291] that in 1869 it was disestablished. The financial measures which accompanied that act of Parliament were more generous than those given the sister Church of Wales on the severing of the latter's tie with the state. Although the church of a minority, the Church of Ireland survived the shock and in time gained in vitality. In it, as in the disestablished Church of Wales, laymen were prominent in the administrative structure which was set up, from the parish to the highest level. But, unlike the Church of Wales, women were denied an official share in that structure. The Church of Ireland insisted that it had an unbroken history going back to the first planting of the faith in the island and that no doubt clouded the validity of the apostolic succession of its bishops such as could be urged against those of England. Partly to differentiate it clearly from the Roman Catholic Church it emphasized its Protestant features. For example, at the celebration of the Communion the priest was required to stand at the north end of the Holy Table, the placing of a cross on or behind the table was strictly forbidden, and any departure from the sober vestments used by the priest in a public service was prohibited. Part of the endowments were in land, and with the breaking up of the large estates in the effort to further peasant proprietorship the Church of Ireland suffered some loss of income. The unrest and civil strife which preceded the full independence of Éire led to the exodus of many of the members. The rapid increase in the cost of living reduced numbers of the clergy to poverty. To meet the situation a sustentation fund was raised, as in some of the churches in England, to prevent stipends from going below a standard minimum, and several of the parishes were amalgamated. With the rapid growth of Belfast, new churches and a great new cathedral were erected in that city. A second revision of the Prayer Book was completed in 1926 (the first had been in 1879). Among other changes, a holy day was added for St. Patrick, thus emphasizing the continuity of the Church of Ireland from the introduction of Christianity. Friction developed with the Roman Catholic Church over the insistence of the latter that to be valid all marriages

[290] *The Statesman's Year Book, 1958*, pp. 120, 1155.
[291] Volume II, pp. 396–398.

between Roman Catholics and Protestants must be solemnized by a Roman Catholic priest. In general, attendance at the services of the Church of Ireland was better than at those of the Church of England and in proportion to the total membership was higher in Éire, especially in the rural districts, than in the North. The consciousness of being a minority group made for loyalty.[292]

Of the other Protestant churches in Ireland in the decades after 1914 there is no need to add much except to note their numerical status. In 1911 the Presbyterians in all of Ireland totalled 440,525; in 1945, 419,000;[293] and in 1951, 434,085.[294] These figures indicate a slight loss since 1911 but a gain after 1945. Significant, however, of the political tensions between Northern Ireland and Éire was the fact that while between 1945 and 1951 the total in the former had mounted from 390,931 to 410,215, in the latter it had shrunk from 28,067 to 23,870. Methodists, next to the Church of Ireland and the Presbyterians the largest of the Protestant bodies, showed an increase—from 62,382 in 1911[295] to 64,784 in 1945[296] and to 74,994 in 1951.[297] They, too, dwindled in Éire between 1945 and 1951. The membership of the Church of Ireland declined from 576,611 in 1911[298] to 490,474 in 1945[299] and to 478,074 in 1951.[300] Between 1945 and 1951 it also, while gaining in Northern Ireland, had lost in Éire. Since the North was growing in population and Éire was losing, in proportion to the population the three main Protestant communions were about holding their own, receding slightly in the latter and advancing in the former. In other words, numerically the twentieth-century record of Protestantism was better in Ireland than in England.

Irish Protestants were also continuing to share in the world-wide spread of the faith. The Church of Ireland did so chiefly through the two great societies of the Church of England—the Society for the Propagation of the Gospel in Foreign Parts and the Church Missionary Society. The largest of the Presbyterian bodies had its own society.[301]

THE CHANGING SCENE IN SCOTLAND

In Scotland as in the other portions of the British Isles the twentieth-century

[292] Neill, *Anglicanism*, pp. 294–298; Walter Alison Phillips, editor, *History of the Church of Ireland from the Earliest Times to the Present Day* (New York, Oxford University Press, 3 vols., 1933, 1939), Vol. III, pp. 387–424; Thomas J. Johnston, John L. Robinson, and Robert Wyse Jackson, *A History of the Church of Ireland* (Dublin, A.P.C.K., 1953, pp. vii, 313), pp. 263–270.

[293] *The Statesman's Year Book, 1915*, p. 28, *1946*, p. 75.

[294] *Ibid., 1959*, pp. 122, 1141.

[295] *Ibid., 1915*, p. 28.

[296] *Ibid., 1946*, p. 75.

[297] *Ibid., 1959*, pp. 122, 1141.

[298] *Ibid., 1915*, p. 28.

[299] *Ibid., 1946*, p. 75.

[300] *Ibid., 1959*, pp. 122, 1141.

[301] Strong and Warnshuis, *Directory of Foreign Missions*, pp. 40–42.

stage of the revolutionary era brought marked changes, both in the setting and in Protestantism.

Scottish Protestantism shared most of the changes in the setting with the Protestantism of other countries, but with variations peculiar to itself. The two world wars exacted their toll in lives, but the second was not accompanied by as much destruction by bombing as had taken place in the neighbour to the south. The urban-ward movement of the population, common to much of the world, for Scotland meant, among other developments, the depletion of large areas in the Highlands and the outlying islands with the dwindling or disappearance of the constituencies of many of the parishes that had long constituted an important part of the religious life of the country. The intellectual currents of the revolutionary age impinged on Scotland as they did elsewhere. The manifold social currents, the automobile, and new forms of amusement contributed to the breakdown of customs, including Sunday observance and church attendance, which had characterized the older Scotland.

A striking feature, paralleled by what we have found in some other lands, was a spectacular movement towards unity in the Protestant forces and the weakening of the tie with the state. We have already called attention to the fact that the Church of Scotland, a Presbyterian body, was the Established Church of the country and at the dawn of the nineteenth century enrolled the large majority of the population. We have also noted the Presbyterian bodies which split off from it—some before the nineteenth century and in 1843 the major division, the Disruption, which resulted in the formation of the Free Church of Scotland. We have seen that in the nineteenth century the process of reunion had begun—in the formation of the United Presbyterian Church in 1847 by the merging of the United Secession Church and the majority of the Relief Church, by the adherence to the Free Church of a portion of the Secession Church (1852) and of the Cameronians (1876), and by the formation of the United Free Church of Scotland in 1900 through the coalescence of the United Presbyterian Church and the large majority of the Free Church of Scotland.[302] Suggestions looking towards the reunion of the Church of Scotland and the Free Church of Scotland had been made in the last quarter of the nineteenth century.[303]

Following the formation of the United Free Church of Scotland efforts were put forward, ultimately successful, to heal the breach of 1843. From the side of the United Free Church the chief impediments were the establishment of the Church of Scotland and the endowments which contributed to the support of the latter rather than the full dependence on voluntary gifts. In 1909 the General Assemblies of the two bodies appointed committees to confer on pos-

---

[302] Volume I, pp. 102, 103; Volume II, pp. 406–409, 415.
[303] Black, *The Scottish Church*, p. 249.

sible union. The urgency of united action to meet the religious needs of the country was made painfully obvious by a census of 1911 which disclosed that the members and adherents of the two churches did not include one-half the people of the country, that because of the movement to the cities from rural areas, especially the Highlands, the old parish system had broken down, and that the provision for worship and pastoral care was largest where the population was sparsest and smallest where the population was densest. Clearly a united approach to the challenge was needed rather than the competition which had previously led to the duplication of churches in particular areas. These sobering facts, together with the decline in Sunday School enrolments and in church attendance and the increased neglect of Sunday observance, were emphasized by findings of the Scottish Churches' Council published in 1927.[304]

World War I suspended the conferences on union but made for closer co-operation. The two churches shared in providing chaplains and in maintaining huts to care for the social, moral, and spiritual welfare of the troops, and to compensate for the absence of pastors on the warring fronts congregations began worshipping together. Coöperation also advanced in education, in promoting temperance, in seeking to solve social problems, and in meeting the needs of youth.[305]

With the coming of peace the steps towards union went forward. In 1921 Parliament formally assented to a new constitution for the Church of Scotland which met the minds of both churches. The document gave the freedom of interpretation to the doctrinal statement which was desired by the United Free Church. It was emphatic that the Church of Scotland was part of the Holy Catholic or Universal Church, declared Christ to be its Divine King and Head and that from Him alone, subject to no civil authority, it received the power to legislate and adjudicate finally in all matters of the doctrine, worship, government, and discipline of the Church, and said that the civil authority had no right to interfere with the proceedings and judgements of the Church within the sphere of its spiritual government and jurisdiction. It acknowledged the divine appointment of the civil magistrate in his own sphere and held that the nation had a duty acting in its corporate capacity to render homage to God, to acknowledge the Lord Jesus Christ to be King over all nations, to reverence His ordinances, to honour His Church, and to promote in every appropriate way the Kingdom of God.[306] The document thus both freed the Church of Scotland from control by the state in its spiritual affairs and affirmed the duty of the nation, acting through the state, to give official recognition to Christ and His Church. The issue of endowments—although the sums entailed

---

[304] Fleming, *The Story of Church Union in Scotland*, pp. 65–70.
[305] *Ibid.*, pp. 86–97.
[306] See the document in Fleming, *A History of the Church in Scotland, 1875–1929*, pp. 310–312.

were not nearly as large as those involved in the disestablishment of the Church of Ireland and the Church of Wales—was settled by act of Parliament in 1925 which made provision for the claims of the Church to the "teinds" (the ancient tithe, although actually much less than a tenth, which since the reign of Charles I had made the maintenance of the ministry a first charge on the tax paid by the landowners to the crown) and which gave the Church full control over the proceeds of the teinds and other endowments.[307] The obstacles having been removed, in 1929 the union of the two churches was formally completed. A small minority of the United Free Church dissented.[308]

The Church of Scotland, as the reunited body was officially known, was by far the largest Protestant church in the country and had many more communicants and still more adherents than the Roman Catholic Church. By history and present fact it was even more the church of the nation than was the Church of England that of England. A few small Presbyterian bodies were not in it and the largest Protestant body not included was the Episcopal Church. Although the Church of Scotland was now fully independent of the state, each year the sovereign sent to its General Assembly a representative as lord high commissioner. He was treated with great respect and was given a seat in the gallery immediately behind the moderator, but he was not a member of the Assembly, came in by a side door and not through the main entrance, could read the address from the crown only with the permission of the Assembly, and could neither officially convene nor dissolve the body as his predecessors had done in the days of the establishment. But by his presence the recognition of the state was given to Christianity as the religion of the Scottish nation and to the Church of Scotland as the representative of that faith.[309]

The Church of Scotland, with its unity more nearly restored than at any time since the fore part of the eighteenth century, maintained its place as the national church. In numbers of communicants it continued to enrol about the same proportion of the population as the two bodies which joined in it together had had on the eve of World War I. In 1913 the Church of Scotland was said to have 714,000 communicants and the United Free Church of Scotland 507,000 communicants—a total of 1,221,000.[310] In 1937 the membership of the Church of Scotland after eight years of union was reported as 1,284,450 besides adherents.[311] That indicated a slight increase in the percentage of the population. In 1945, at the conclusion of World War II, the total had fallen to 1,259,925 and the number of pupils in the Sunday Schools had shrunk badly,

[307] Ibid., pp. 107–111, 161; Fleming, The Story of Church Union in Scotland, pp. 109–120.
[308] Fleming, A History of the Church in Scotland, 1875–1929, pp. 126–134, 142, 143.
[309] Highet, The Churches of Scotland To-day, p. 11.
[310] The Statesman's Year Book, 1915, p. 28.
[311] Ibid., 1939, p. 23.

from 320,344 in 1937 to 239,481 in 1945.[312] By the end of 1958 the reported membership had risen again, to 1,315,466 besides adherents, and the enrolment in Sunday Schools was said to be 307,218,[313] a partial but incomplete recovery of the losses during the war years. In proportion to the population the membership in 1958 was slightly lower than in 1913—a gain of about 7.7 per cent. as against that of about 8.6 per cent. in the population.[314] In 1947 the Church of Scotland included in its membership about 36.1 per cent. of the adult population and 64.1 per cent. of all the church membership in the country. The other Presbyterian churches had 1.15 per cent. of the adult population and 2.04 per cent. of the church membership of the nation. The corresponding figures for the non-Presbyterian churches were 5.47 per cent. and 9.74 per cent., and of the Roman Catholic Church 13.55 per cent. and 24.12 per cent., indicating that 56.18 per cent. of the adult population were members of some church.[315] Of the remainder many would be counted as adherents. Indeed, in 1946, 60.3 per cent. of the marriages were performed in the Church of Scotland, 12.6 per cent. in the Roman Catholic Church, 3 per cent. in the Episcopal Church, 7.6 per cent. in other churches, and only 16.5 per cent. were by civil rites.[316] Presumably the distribution of the population by baptism in the respective denominations was about the same, for that sacrament appears to have been almost universal. The proportion of the adult population who were members of the Church of Scotland seems to have fallen from 43 per cent. in 1926 to 39.3 per cent. in 1936 and to 36 per cent. in 1947.[317]

Although in the interval between 1913 and 1958 percentage-wise the membership of the Church of Scotland had only slightly fallen behind the population, doubt existed as to whether in attendance at its services it had done as well. Early in the 1950's the complaint was heard that while young people joined the church in considerable numbers, the public practice of religion was becoming confined to the elderly and middle aged, and that thousands partook of the Communion only frequently enough to keep their names on the membership rolls but remained away from most of the other services. Church attendance fell off strikingly during World War II and although after the coming of peace it revived, it was much less than in the early years of the twentieth century.[318] In 1947, for example, 908,414 members of the Church of Scotland took the Communion at least once—72.7 per cent. of the membership of the congregations which made a return. This was the highest proportion

---

[312] *Ibid., 1946*, p. 23.
[313] *Ibid., 1959*, p. 70.
[314] In 1911 the population was 4,760,904 and in 1958 it was 5,169,000.—*Ibid.*, pp. 65, 67.
[315] Highet, *op. cit.*, p. 75.
[316] *The Statesman's Year Book, 1950*, p. 69.
[317] Highet, *op. cit.*, p. 76.
[318] Black, *op. cit.*, p. 258.

since 1932, when it was the same.[319] In the 1950's the numbers of students in the four university theological faculties of the Church of Scotland were quite inadequate to meet the requirements of the churches. Some relief was found in consolidating overlapping parishes of the former Church of Scotland and United Free Church and in combining others in which migration to the cities had reduced the constituencies, but these devices did not eliminate the need for more clergy.[320] The Church of Scotland did not fully keep pace with the shifts and growth in population, but its record was better than that of the Church of England and the Free Churches of England and of the Protestant churches in Wales.

In the 1950's the attitudes of the Scottish people towards Christianity varied from class to class and from occupational group to occupational group. It was said that in the eyes of the workers in the industries the Church belonged to the world of the bankers, managers, and teachers. Yet a larger percentage of the workers were reported as being in the Church than a century before, and in the older and less wealthy areas the proportion of those claiming a connexion with the Church was higher than in the new housing areas. A smaller proportion of the middle class and especially those of wealth and power were in the Church than the mid-nineteenth century had seen, but the largest and most prosperous congregations were drawn from this class. In the universities rationalism was less strong than in the 1930's, but while the interest in religion had grown, dissatisfaction with the Church as an institution was general.[321] Clearly, too, as in much of the rest of the British Isles, the ancient parish structure, designed at the outset to cover the entire population, was not adequate for the urban society of the twentieth century. Moreover, although seeking to meet the challenge of the urban areas, the Church of Scotland did not solve the problem of the depleted rural districts, where the existing parishes could not be sufficiently staffed to care for the dwindling population.

The Church of Scotland was not content to mark time or to engage in a defensive rear-guard action against the advancing secularism. In a variety of ways it strove not only to regain lost ground but also to make the Christian faith more of an effective force in the changing life of the nation.

Multiform programmes of evangelism were among the channels through which advance was sought. Significantly, many of them were in the decade and a half following World War II. The Church of Scotland was endeavouring to meet head on the forces released or accentuated by that struggle. In 1946 it issued a booklet, *Into All the World,* in which a committee appointed by the General Assembly outlined procedures "that Scotland may be won back to

[319] Highet, *op. cit.,* p. 77.
[320] The author's observations, 1954.
[321] *Ecumenical Studies. Evangelism in Scotland,* pp. 22–25.

the faith." The same year saw the appointment of special missioners to travel about the country "preaching the paramount need of the personal witness of the Christian." Before the end of the year plans for lay visitation had been carried out in some city parishes and open-air inter-denominational meetings had been conducted. In Glasgow, the largest city of the country, in 1945, 1946, and 1947 evangelistic meetings were held in the public parks. In Edinburgh in 1947 a "commando" campaign was put through by joint action of several denominations to reach in various public places the 100,000 to whom Christianity was said to mean nothing. A press bureau, broadcasting, and the cinema were employed. In spite of the post-war shortage of building material, additional churches were erected in new housing areas in sections allocated by an inter-denominational committee.[322] A "mission of friendship," begun in 1935, became the precursor to similar missions in many parishes in the 1940's and 1950's in which all the residents within the boundaries of the parish were visited by members of the church as a part of the normal evangelistic activity of the congregation.[323] Beginning in 1952 a somewhat similar movement was seen, country-wide in its scope and inter-denominational, under the designation "tell Scotland." It sought to enlist lay folk to reach their neighbours.[324] Industrial chaplaincies, begun by a parish minister during World War II, were launched by the Home Board of the Church of Scotland in 1942 and rapidly assumed large dimensions. In 1952 the Scottish Christian Industrial Order was founded in Edinburgh at a conference of over one thousand laymen "to advance the knowledge and understanding of the Christian faith and its practice; to promote the best human relations in industry on the basis of the Faith and to further the application of its principles throughout industrial life and society."[325] In the spring of 1955 "Billy" Graham spent six weeks in Scotland and he and members of his team conducted an "all-Scotland crusade" in which several denominations coöperated. Over a million people attended the meetings, some of them held in the largest stadiums and auditoriums.[326]

A movement which centred in the island of Iona attracted wide attention. Iona was the island off the west coast, made famous by Columba, from which much of the original conversion of Scotland had been accomplished. It had long ceased to be the home of monks and of its monastic buildings only ruins

[322] *Ibid., passim;* Highet, *op. cit.,* pp. 82–112; *British Weekly,* May 26, 1960.

[323] *Ecumenical Studies. Evangelism in Scotland,* pp. 38, 39.

[324] *The Christian Century,* Vol. LXXVI, p. 1046 (September 16, 1959); *World Dominion,* Vol. XXXIII, pp. 175–180.

[325] *The Scottish Industrial Chaplain,* issued by the Home Board of the Church of Scotland, mimeographed, January, 1953; *SCIU News* (Home Board of the Church of Scotland, mimeographed, January, 1952———); *Scottish Christian Industrial Order: the Necessity for SCIO* (Edinburgh, Home Board of the Church of Scotland, pamphlet, no date, ca. 1952); William MacIntyre in *World Dominion,* Vol. XXX, pp. 297–300 (September/October, 1952).

[326] Tom Allan, editor, *Crusade in Scotland . . . Billy Graham* (London, Pickering & Inglis, 1955, pp. 128), *passim.*

remained. The Iona Community was the creation of George Fielden MacLeod (1895———), later Sir George MacLeod, the fourth baronet, grandson of the Norman MacLeod who had been the most outstanding minister of the Church of Scotland in the third quarter of the nineteenth century. During the depression years of the 1930's when in some areas as high as four-fifths of the male population were out of employment, he was minister of a church in one of the worst hit districts. He became impressed with the need for a ministry which would reëstablish the relevance of the Church and its faith to the whole of life. To that end, in 1938 he initiated the Iona Community. He wished it to be a working laboratory to express that relevance. The members spent their summers on Iona and there with skilled craftsmen restored the ancient abbey. During the rest of the year the workmen returned to their usual occupations on the mainland and the members, giving two years or more after their theological course, went out in teams of two to work under the direction of the parish minister in housing schemes, in industrial works and dock areas, in down-town churches in depressed districts, or in the central church of a country town. The Iona Community sponsored the Christian Workers' League, which arose from a group of industrial workers in 1943 to study the relevance of the Christian faith to their daily lives. The Community's full members were few, only about a hundred, but associates numbered several hundred and for the financial support late in the 1950's contributions came from thousands in many churches and countries. The Iona Youth Trust was set up (1943) to strengthen Christian conviction among the Scottish youth and to further the principles of the Community. An important phase of the programme of the Iona Community was the furtherance of worship, both individual and corporate. During the summers corporate worship, including the Communion, took place in the abbey church on the island. The members, both full and associate, followed a discipline which included individual prayer and Bible-reading throughout the year.[327] Here was a project which, with variations, paralleled others we have found in Protestantism in most of the countries of Western Europe. Like them, too, and like what we have seen in the Roman Catholic Church, it emphasized the participation of the laity. For a time many in the Church of Scotland looked at it askance as not fitting into the accustomed ecclesiastical pattern. Eventually, however, it was domesticated without compromising its vision, and MacLeod became moderator of the church.

Kirk Week, inspired by the *Kirchentag* of Germany and sponsored by the "tell Scotland" movement, was first held in Aberdeen in 1957. A second con-

---

[327] Highet, *op. cit.*, pp. 129–140; George MacLeod, *We Shall Re-build. The Philosophy and Program of the Iona Community in Scotland* (Philadelphia, Kirkridge, 1945, pp. 140), *passim; The Coracle* (the periodical of the Iona Community, published irregularly from more than one centre, 1938 ff.); T. Ralph Morton, *The Iona Community Story* (London, Lutterworth Press, 1957, pp. 96), *passim.*

vened in Dundee in 1959. Each had as a purpose the promotion of local action by the laity and each was attended by over a thousand delegates.[328]

To meet the problems of the revolutionary age the Church of Scotland engaged in a wide variety of activities through its committee on social service. It had homes for children, homes for working lads, one of them a lads' club and hostel opened in 1947, hostels for young women, projects to provide care for delinquent girls, homes for elderly people, hostels for miners, employment offices for women, hospitals, and rest homes for deaconesses, missionaries, and church workers.[329]

Changes were made in the public worship of the Church of Scotland. In 1940 the Book of Common Order was issued by the authority of the General Assembly. Although its use was not compulsory, increasingly it became standard. *Prayers for the Christian Year* was also issued (1935, revised 1952), Communion services were more frequent, and many buildings were kept open weekdays for private prayer.[330]

The Church of Scotland also continued the extensive foreign missions which had been begun in the nineteenth century by the several churches whose union was consummated in 1929. They were in China, India, Arabia, the New Hebrides, the West Indies, and several sections of Africa.[331]

None of the other Protestant churches in Scotland approached the Church of Scotland in numerical strength. The largest was the Scottish Episcopal Church, which in 1957 had 55,764 communicants.[332] It seems to have suffered a loss in the post-World War II decade, for in 1945 57,113 communicants were reported.[333] What were called its permanent members, which included communicants, totalled 106,000 in 1957,[334] 2,000 less than in 1950 and 10,000 less than at the beginning of the century. This was in spite of the creation of a number of new congregations in the expanding housing areas and the erection of additional church buildings. Many of the clergy—about two-fifths in 1949—came from England and other countries.[335] After World War I a social service board was organized and a friendly attitude was adopted towards the Industrial Christian Fellowship.[336] The Scottish Prayer Book, following closely the Eng-

---

[328] *Ecumenical Press Service,* August 23, 1957; *The Christian Century,* Vol. LXXVI, p. 1284 (November 4, 1959).

[329] Highet, *op. cit.,* pp. 112–119.

[330] William D. Maxwell, *A History of Worship in the Church of Scotland* (New York, Oxford University Press, 1955, pp. 190), pp. 183, 184; Evelyn Underhill, *Worship* (New York, Harper & Brothers, 1937, pp. xxi, 350), p. 295.

[331] Strong and Warnshuis, *Directory of Foreign Missions,* p. 43.

[332] *The Statesman's Year Book, 1959,* p. 70.

[333] *Ibid., 1946,* p. 23.

[334] *Ibid., 1959,* p. 70.

[335] Goldie, *A Short History of the Episcopal Church in Scotland,* pp. 124–130; Highet, *op. cit.,* pp. 64, 65.

[336] Goldie, *op. cit.,* p. 132; Highet, *op. cit.,* p. 103.

lish Book of Common Prayer but with its own history and distinctive features, was revised in 1929. Foreign missions were also maintained.[337]

The Congregational Union was said to have 35,314 members in 1947. In 1948, soon after World War II, it expressed itself as feeling an obligation to help in the re-Christianizing of Scotland and in the revival of the churches and the maintenance of Christian faith and culture on the Continent. It also urged the government to be more active in providing housing to preserve the sanctity of family life and came out against the continuation of military conscription in peace time.[338]

In 1947 the Baptists counted 20,602 members,[339] a decline from 22,815 in the mid-1920's and a recession from the rapid growth which had characterized the second half of the nineteenth century.[340]

Several small Presbyterian bodies remained aloof from the Church of Scotland. Of these, in 1947 by far the largest was the United Free Church, which was composed of those who refused to acquiesce in the union of 1929. In 1948 it had 24,606 members, with a steady although not a large increase in each of the preceding four years. It opposed all connexion with the state, stood for greater theological liberty, and insisted upon the support of the Church by free-will offerings alone. In Scotland it stressed youth work and abroad it had a mission in South Africa.[341] The Free Church, often called the "Wee Frees," was made up of those congregations that had refused to go into the union of 1900 from which had issued the United Free Church of Scotland. It was particularly strong in the Highlands—in the North and West—and especially in the Western Isles. There it outnumbered the Church of Scotland. In 1950 its communicant membership was estimated as 10,000 and its adherents as about 50,000.[342] The Free Presbyterians, who withdrew from the Free Church of Scotland in 1893 in protest against what they deemed the slackening of confessional standards, in 1947 were said to number about 3,000.[343] The Original Secession Church, also known as the United Secession Church, in 1946 had 1,876 members.[344] The Reformed Presbyterians, going back to the fore part of the eighteenth century and springing from the Cameronians, in 1947 had only 800 members.[345]

A variety of denominations accounted for other small minorities. They in-

[337] Goldie, op. cit., pp. 131, 136–139.
[338] Ibid., pp. 74, 206–211.
[339] Ibid., p. 74.
[340] George Yuille, editor, History of the Baptists in Scotland from Pre-Reformation Times (Glasgow, Baptist Union Publications Committee, preface 1926, pp. 312), pp. 76–87.
[341] Highet, op. cit., pp. 28, 29.
[342] Ibid., p. 25.
[343] Ibid., pp. 23, 74.
[344] Ibid., p. 74.
[345] Ibid., p. 74.

cluded the Methodists, with 12,472 members in 1947; the Churches of Christ, with 1,956 members in 1947, a sharp decrease from the preceding year; the Unitarians, with four congregations in 1948 and with about 800 members in that year; the Assemblies of God, with seven congregations in 1933; the Society of Friends, with nine meetings in 1948; the Elim Four Square Gospel Alliance, begun in Ireland in 1915 and with seven churches in 1947 with 1,180 members; the Church of the Nazarene, successor to the Pentecostal Church, with seventeen churches in 1947; the Christian Scientists, with a growing membership; the Assemblies of Christian Brethren, usually known as the Plymouth Brethren, with an estimated membership in 1947 of about 30,000; the Catholic Apostolic Church, with about 2,000 members in 1947; the Spiritualist Churches, with approximately 2,000 members in 1947; two groups of the Churches of God; a few hundred Jehovah's Witnesses; the Apostolic Church with fifty assemblies; two churches of the Seventh Day Adventists; and two or three other groups, all small. The Salvation Army, not officially a church, counted about 19,000 members in 1947.[346]

As in most other countries, a progressive growth of coöperation was seen among the Protestants of Scotland and of the share of Scottish Protestants in friendly relations with churches in other parts of the British Isles and in the world at large. We have noted some examples of the trend. Another was what was called the Christian Front in Glasgow, when in 1945 men prominent in the ecclesiastical life of that city and from several denominations issued a joint statement in which they stressed the importance of safeguarding the family by more and better housing, the extension of social services, and the training of young people for marriage and parenthood; greater public control of capital reserves and means of production; the curtailment of national sovereignty by the jurisdiction of a world organization of peace; and full freedom for all peoples in the world without discrimination on racial grounds.[347] The Scottish churches were included in the British Council of Churches which came into being in 1942. The Church of Scotland was deeply involved in the proposal (1957) for closer relations between the Church of England, the Church of Scotland, the Presbyterian Church of England, and the Episcopal Church of Scotland. Opposition in the Church of Scotland quickly developed and made unlikely the adoption of the plan, at least in the immediate future.[348] Scottish churchmen were active in the Ecumenical Movement and representatives of the Church of Scotland were prominent in both the World Council of Churches and the International Missionary Council.

Through preaching and scholarship Scottish Presbyterianism continued to

[346] *Ibid.*, pp. 47–66, 74, 75.
[347] *Ibid.*, pp. 145–152.
[348] *The New York Times*, May 1, 1957.

seek to meet constructively the intellectual currents of the revolutionary age. As was to be expected from their dominant numerical position, the leadership was held by the Church of Scotland and the two bodies which united to form it.

An outstanding churchman, more a statesman than a preacher, John White (1867–1951), for forty years minister of the famous Barony Church in Glasgow, Moderator of the General Assembly of the Church of Scotland in 1925, was the chief architect of the union of the Church of Scotland and the United Free Church of Scotland and was the Moderator of the General Assembly of 1929 in which the union was consummated. He deplored the passing of the parish as the administrative unit of the state and its waning importance in the Church, but in many ways he was prominent in advocating adjustment to the changing conditions of the revolutionary age. He was a leader in promoting the erection of new church buildings to care for the shifting population in the growing cities. He wished to recognize the increasing place of women in public life by bringing them into the official structure of the Church with membership in its courts. He supported MacLeod and the Iona Community, he was one of the presidents of Toc H, and he believed that the Church should restate its unchanging faith in terms of the needs of the day.[349] Among the great preachers were Norman MacLeod (died 1952), pastor of St. Cuthbert's in Edinburgh from 1915, a Moderator of the Church of Scotland, who preached the sermon at the opening of the League of Nations;[350] Arthur John Gossip (1873–1954);[351] and James Stuart Stewart (1896——), educated in St. Andrews and New College, Edinburgh, minister successively in several churches, chaplain to George VI and Elizabeth II, and after 1947 professor of New Testament language, literature, and theology in the University of Edinburgh.[352]

The list of theologians and Christian philosophers was also impressive. Several exerted an influence far beyond the borders of Scotland. We can take the space to mention only a few of the more important. Alfred Edward Taylor (1869–1945) after teaching in Canada was on the faculty of St. Andrews from 1908 to 1924 and was professor of moral theology at Edinburgh from 1924 until his retirement in 1941. A specialist on Plato, he early attracted attention by a work on metaphysics and was best remembered by his Gifford Lectures on *The Faith of a Moralist*. He was unabashedly a Christian, with a philosophical approach.[353]

---

[349] Augustus Muir, *John White* (London, Hodder and Stoughton, 1958, pp. xv, 478), *passim*.

[350] Norman Maclean, *The Years of Fulfilment*, third volume of an autobiography, *The Former Days* (London, Hodder and Stoughton, 1953, pp. 315).

[351] See as typical his *The Secret Place of the Most High. Some Studies in Prayer* (New York, Charles Scribner's Sons, 1947, pp. 210).

[352] See his *A Faith to Proclaim* (London, Hodder and Stoughton, 1952, pp. 160).

[353] Among his books were *Plato, The Man and His Work* (New York, Dial Press, 1927, pp. xi,

With Taylor should be bracketed Arthur Seth Pringle-Pattison (1856–1931), who had his education in Edinburgh and Germany and whose Gifford Lectures of 1912 and 1913 dealt with a similar problem: the relation of philosophy to the Christian faith. He had a vast knowledge of Western philosophy and theology and held that theology should stress the implication of the incarnation. He believed that the secret of the universe was God, Who lives in the perpetual giving of Him Who shares the life of His finite creatures and that His omnipotence consists in the all-compelling power of goodness and love to enlighten the grossest darkness and to melt the hardest heart.[354]

George Galloway, who died in 1933 as principal and professor of theology in St. Mary's College of the University of Aberdeen, stressed the philosophy of religion and to some extent followed Robert Flint (1838–1910), whom we have already met.[355] He held that Christianity is the fullest entrance of the Divine Spirit into human history and regarded Jesus Christ as the supreme creative personality. He held that the historic creeds were not adequate as expressions of the growing spiritual consciousness. He displayed something of the dislike of the Ritschlians for the association of metaphysics with theology. Yet he had the idealistic tradition as a background.[356]

Hugh Ross Mackintosh (1870–1936) based his theology squarely on the Bible, held to the validity of the knowledge of God possessed by faith, had sympathy with Schleiermacher but could not fully agree with him, both commended and criticized Kierkegaard, and while adhering to the historic Catholic doctrine of Christ found fault with the definition given by Chalcedon. He made much of joy as inherent in the Gospel.[357]

William Paterson Paterson (1860–1939), educated in the Universities of Edinburgh, Leipzig, Erlangen, and Berlin, for some years a parish minister, professor of systematic theology in Aberdeen 1894–1903, professor of divinity in Edinburgh from 1903 to his retirement, and at one time moderator of his church, refused to regard man, although fallen, as completely without a knowledge of God and maintained that evidence in support of the existence of God could be had from nature, man, and history. Yet he believed in the sovereignty

522); *The Problem of Conduct. A Study in the Phenomenology of Ethics* (New York, The Macmillan Co., 1901, pp. viii, 501); *A Commentary on Plato's Timmaeus* (Oxford, Clarendon Press, 1928, pp. xv, 700); *The Faith of a Moralist* (London, Macmillan and Co., 2 vols., 1930).

354 Andrew Seth Pringle-Pattison, *The Idea of God in the Light of Recent Philosophy* (New York, Oxford University Press, 2nd ed., pp. xvi, 443).

355 Volume II, p. 420.

356 Mozley, *Some Tendencies in British Theology*, pp. 136–138; George Galloway, *The Philosophy of Religion* (New York, Charles Scribner's Sons, 1914, pp. xii, 602); George Galloway, *The Ideal of Immortality* (Edinburgh, T. & T. Clark, 1919, pp. vii, 234); George Galloway, *Religion and Modern Thought* (Edinburgh, T. & T. Clark, 1922, pp. vii, 342).

357 H. R. Mackintosh, *Types of Modern Theology. Schleiermacher to Barth* (New York, Charles Scribner's Sons, 1937, pp. vii, 333); H. R. Mackintosh, *The Doctrine of the Person of Christ* (New York, Charles Scribner's Sons, 1912, pp. xiv, 540); H. R. Mackintosh, *The Christian Experience of Forgiveness* (New York, Harper & Brothers, 1927, pp. xv, 290).

of God and in the ability of God to act in and through natural causes as the Controller and Disposer of all events. He maintained that God had as His guiding purpose the highest good of the soul that puts its trust in Him. Paterson, like many another Scot, was influenced by the common-sense theology which was formulated in the eighteenth century.[358]

David Smith Cairns (1862–1946) was reared in a manse of the United Presbyterian Church. During his student days in a secondary school and in the University of Edinburgh he went through a period of extreme and painful doubt of the basic tenets of Christianity which for a time wrecked his health. From those unhappy months he emerged with faith that had been refined in the furnace. He completed his university course, studied theology, had a period in Marburg where he came under the spell of Wilhelm Herrmann, was ordained, served for some years as minister in a rural parish on the Scottish border, and used the time to read widely, especially in New Testament criticism with emphasis upon the Gospels, and further hammered out his convictions. Because of his long pilgrimage to a clear faith he almost inevitably became an apologist. He began to write, especially on the Kingdom of God as seen in the teachings of Jesus. After refusing several offers of professorships in the United States, Canada, and Australia and a large city pastorate, he joined the faculty of the United Free Church College, later known as Christ's College, in Aberdeen and remained there, part of the time as principal, until his retirement because of age. He interpreted the Christian faith not as one of resignation and acceptance but as rebellion against evil, importunate confidence in God, and unconquerable hope for the victory of His kingdom on earth where the evils must be fought. His optimism was later tempered by the tragedies of the two world wars, but he never became a pessimist. He was prominent in the missionary thinking of the period and as a trusted speaker and writer for the Student Christian Movement. He lectured widely in America and the Far East.[359]

The brothers John Baillie (1886–1960) and Donald MacPherson Baillie (1887–1954) were sons of a Free Church manse on the western shore of the Highlands. John studied under Herrmann, graduated from the University of Edinburgh and New College, Edinburgh, with high honours, for fifteen years taught in theological seminaries in the United States and Canada, from 1934 to his retirement because of age followed Paterson as professor of divinity in the University of Edinburgh, after 1950 was principal of New College and

[358] W. P. Paterson, *The Nature of Religion* (New York, George H. Doran Co., pp. xii, 506), his Gifford Lectures; Mozley, *op. cit.*, pp. 143–145.

[359] David Cairns, *An Autobiography . . . with a Memoir by Professor D. M. Baillie* (London, S.C.M. Press, 1950, pp. 220), *passim*. Among his several books the one which did most to spread his fame and which was his most distinctive contribution to theology was *The Faith that Rebels* (London, Student Christian Movement Press, 1928, pp. 260).

dean of the faculty of divinity in the University of Edinburgh, was Moderator of the Church of Scotland, and was a president of the World Council of Churches. An independent thinker, he believed profoundly in the incarnation but differed from the Chalcedonian statement of the relation of the human and divine in Christ. He held that Jesus Christ was not another name for God but the name of a Man in Whom God was and through Whom God came to meet man, that we can know God in a satisfying way only through Jesus Christ, that in one form or another religious experience has been universal, and that religion has had its consummation in the soul of Jesus Christ.[360] The most widely used of his books were *A Diary of Private Prayer*[361] and its accompanying *A Diary of Readings*[362]—evidence of a deep devotional life. Donald also had a brilliant record as a student. He was for a time a parish minister and from 1935 to his death was professor of systematic theology in St. Andrews. He did not write as much as his brother, but he lectured and preached extensively, in his quiet way devoted himself to his students and was beloved by them, and in his few books exerted a wide influence.[363]

John Baillie was followed in his Edinburgh chair by Thomas Forsyth Torrance (1913———). The son of missionaries to China, Torrance had his early education in that country, later studied in Edinburgh, Oxford, Basel, Athens, and Jerusalem, and after briefly teaching Church history came to the important professorship in the University of Edinburgh and New College. A pupil of Barth, he represented a variation of Barthian neo-orthodoxy. He was particularly expert in Calvin's writings and theology and made a deep impression not only on theological students from Scotland but also on the many scores who came to New College from other countries.[364]

James Moffatt (1870–1944) represented a different field of scholarship from the theologians. Educated in Glasgow, for a few years he taught the New Testament in Mansfield College, Oxford. During most of his academic life he had a chair of Church history in Glasgow and then one in Union Theologi-

---

[360] Among his books were *The Interpretation of Religion* (New York, Charles Scribner's Sons, 1928, pp. xv, 477), *Our Knowledge of God* (New York, Charles Scribner's Sons, 1939, pp. ix, 263), *And the Life Everlasting* (New York, Charles Scribner's Sons, 1933, pp. xvi, 350), and *The Belief in Progress* (New York, Oxford University Press, 1950, pp. viii, 240).

[361] (New York, Charles Scribner's Sons, 14th impression, 1947, pp. 135).

[362] (New York, Oxford University Press, 1955, pp. ix, 385).

[363] See his *God Was in Christ* (New York, Charles Scribner's Sons, 1948, pp. 213), in which he dealt critically with various christologies and approaches to religion and came out positively with his own convictions. As he saw it, in Jesus the grace of God is present in fullest measure. See also his *To Whom Shall We Go?* with a biographical introduction by John Dow (Edinburgh, Saint Andrew Press, 1955, pp. viii, 199).

[364] In addition to a joint editorship of a Church dogmatics and providing extensive notes and an introduction to a translation of Calvin, Torrance wrote sermons collected into volumes and *Calvin's Doctrine of Man* (London, Lutterworth Press, 1949, pp. 183), *The Doctrine of Grace in the Apostolic Fathers* (Edinburgh, Oliver and Boyd, 1948, pp. vii, 150), and *Kingdom and the Church. A Study in the Theology of the Reformation* (Fair Haven, N.J., Essential Books, 1956, pp. viii, 168).

cal Seminary in New York City. Most of his books were on the New Testament.[365] His work which had the largest circulation was a fresh translation of the Bible into current and felicitous dignified English.[366]

SUMMARY

In the four and a half decades which were ushered in by the fateful summer of 1914 the Protestantism of the British Isles, like that on the Continent of Europe, did not display as much vigour as it had in the nineteenth century. Here, as on the Continent, a contrast was seen between the rising strength of the forces making for de-Christianization and the marked vitality in the Protestant churches. On the one hand the economic expansion which had characterized the Britain of the nineteenth century slowed, and the colonial empire, which had displayed a phenomenal growth in that era, first had additions only in the form of mandates which did not carry absolute sovereignty and then moved out from under the British flag with mounting momentum. The British navy and British commerce no longer dominated the seven seas. In the two world wars Britain was on the defensive, suffered great losses in life and treasure, and became a debtor rather than a creditor nation. Although after World War II it made a remarkable recovery, the sense of a boundless future which had given zest to the British people had waned and the change was reflected in the Protestant churches. Largely because of the increase of its constituency in Great Britain by immigration from Ireland, the Roman Catholic Church did not share that loss of morale, but was growing and in its leadership was confident. The continued industrialization, the persistent movement from rural districts to the cities, the mobility of the population, and the further disintegration of the inherited patterns of society confronted the Protestant forces with challenges which were not new—for in the preceding century they had become familiar features of the revolutionary age—but were intensified. The intellectual currents, the seemingly boundless achievements of science, the concentration on the winning of the wars, the moral retrogression which accompanied those struggles, and the absorption in the measures which made for the welfare state appeared to thousands to render the Christian faith either untenable or irrelevant.

The combined impact of the multiple adverse forces brought about a decline in the hold of the Protestant churches on the population. As on the Continent in the historic Roman Catholic and Protestant constituencies, baptism was still almost universal. However, in contrast with their growth in much of the nine-

---

[365] See his *An Introduction to the Literature of the New Testament* (New York, Charles Scribner's Sons, 1911, pp. xli, 630) and *The General Epistles. Peter and James* (London, Hodder and Stoughton, 1928, pp. viii, 246).

[366] *The Holy Bible, Containing the Old and New Testaments, a New Translation* by James Moffatt (Garden City, N.Y., Doubleday, Doran, 1926, pp. xiv, 1031, iii, 340).

teenth century, communicant membership and attendance at church services fell off. The decline was more marked in England and Wales than in Ireland and Scotland, and in the 1950's in some churches recovery had begun. But in few places was the hold of the churches as strong as it had been at the height of the awakenings of the nineteenth century. The efforts to plant the faith outside the British Isles which in that century appeared to be endlessly accelerating also declined.

Yet British Protestantism was far from moribund and in some of its aspects was showing fresh life. In the Church of England able leadership continued to come forward. Never had its quality been better religiously, morally, or intellectually and seldom if ever had it been as high. Among the faithful minority, still very considerable in its total numerical size, devotion in worship increased, both in public services and in individual and group retreats. Fresh attempts to meet the challenge of industrialized society were made both by Anglicans and by Free Churchmen. The participation of the laity, never absent, mounted. In many localities successes were seen in solving the problems presented by the changes of the day. In the new housing districts in all four countries—England, Wales, Ireland, and Scotland—new churches were erected to care for the shifting populations. Scholarship was seeking to deal both with the perennial problems presented by human life and with those peculiar to the twentieth-century stage of the revolutionary age. Increasingly Protestants were seeking to unite their forces not merely to conserve their existing place in the life of the world but as well to reach out coöperatively to bring the world to conform to the Christian faith. Here and there, as in Scotland where after the mounting fissiparousness of the eighteenth and nineteenth centuries the vast majority of Protestants coalesced in the one Church of Scotland, severed branches of denominational families came together and projects for more inclusive unions were discussed. In a more comprehensive way local and national councils of churches were formed; the British Council of Churches came into being, and participation was general in the global Ecumenical Movement. In the British Isles as a whole, in the 1950's, in spite of the rising intensity of the revolutionary age, Protestant Christianity was in a far healthier state than it had been a hundred and fifty years earlier.

CHAPTER XVIII

The Old Catholic Minorities

IN A survey which is as comprehensive and yet as limited in the pages allotted to it as ours must be, we can do no more than dismiss with the briefest mention the Old Catholic Churches of Europe. In 1951 their total adherents in Western and Central Europe probably numbered less than 150,000. The Old Catholic movement arose chiefly from two sources. The first dated from early in the eighteenth century and centred in the Netherlands. It sprang mostly from resistance by some of the Dutch clergy to what they deemed the usurpation by Rome of their historic liberties and was complicated by the dispute over Jansenism, in which the attack on that movement was led by the Jesuits and won the support of Rome. Administratively the Old Catholic Church had its headquarters in Utrecht. Its archbishop had that city as his see and professed to trace his succession through Willibrord, the English missionary of the seventh and eighth centuries, the first Archbishop of Utrecht. The second main source was the dissent from the endorsement of Papal infallibility by the Vatican Council of 1869-1870. It issued, as we have seen, in Old Catholic Churches in Germany, Austria, and Switzerland. Since no Roman Catholic bishop went with them, they obtained episcopal consecration through an Old Catholic bishop of the Netherlands for the bishop whom they elected.[1]

In 1889 the Utrecht Union was formed of the Old Catholic bishops of the Netherlands, Germany, and Switzerland and was later joined by the Old Catholics of the Austro-Hungarian Empire (after World War I they were separated administratively into those of Austria and Czechoslovakia), the Mariavite bishops of Poland, and a Croatian bishop. These Old Catholics were in communion with one another and held biennial conferences. The conference of 1931 approved of intercommunion with the Anglicans and to this some Catholic Churches in North America separated from Rome assented. Friendly relations were also established with the Orthodox.[2]

---

[1] Volume I, pp. 285-287.

[2] Fried. Siegmund-Schultze, editor, *Die altkatholische Kirche* (Gotha, Leopold Klotz Verlag, 1935, pp. 151), *passim*, especially pp. 48, 49, 84-113.

During World War II many buildings of the Old Catholics were damaged or destroyed. In 1951 it was reported that the Old Catholics of the Utrecht Union numbered 15,000 in the Netherlands under three bishops, totalled 25,000 in Germany under one bishop, had 30,000 in Austria of whom 25,000 were in Vienna, in Czechoslovakia had 20,000 communicants, in Switzerland numbered 28,000 under the name of the Christian Catholic Church, in Jugoslavia enrolled several thousand, and counted 10,000 in Poland. In addition there were a few thousand Old Catholics in several countries who were not connected with the Utrecht Union.[3]

[3] *Twentieth Century Encyclopedia of Religious Knowledge*, Vol. II, p. 814.

CHAPTER XIX

Christianity in Revolutionary Russia

I N NO major country of Europe did the twentieth-century stage of the revolutionary age bring such sweeping and basic changes as in Russia and in none was Christianity more handicapped as it faced the challenge. Yet here, although it suffered severe reverses, Christianity survived and by the mid-1950's was beginning to recover.

THE CHALLENGE OF THE SETTING

The main outline of the setting is quickly sketched. At the very beginning of World War I Russia was drawn into the struggle. Indeed, it is said that the general mobilization of the Russian armies was the step which kept the hostilities between Austria-Hungary and Serbia from being localized and gave the war European dimensions. Owing chiefly to incompetent leadership, including that of the tsar, the Russian armies were badly defeated early in the conflict. Loss of morale followed with mounting unrest, and in March, 1917, a revolution broke out, the tsar was forced to abdicate, and a temporary government was installed. In July, 1917, Alexander Kerensky became the leader in this government but proved unable to meet the crisis. In November, 1917, the Communists took over the government and the following March signed a peace treaty with Germany. The Communist regime was headed by Lenin and under it all means of production, distribution, and transport were confiscated and made state institutions and the land was nationalized. The reign of terror which accompanied the revolution was accentuated by the intervention of foreign powers, first in the continued war with Germany and then by the Western Allies who in their endeavour to restore the Russian front against Germany gave aid to the "white" armies in opposition to the "reds." Civil war broke out. In July, 1918, the tsar, the tsarina, and their children were killed. Many officers and private owners of property under the old regime suffered a similar fate or left the country. By 1921 the Communists had obtained full control. They organized the Empire into the Union of Soviet Socialist Republics (the U.S.S.R.), which eventually numbered twelve states. Of these three were in Europe—Russia proper embracing the "Great Russians," Ukrainia, and Byelorussia (White Russia). The others were in the lands of the Caucasus and Asia. In theory the government was a democracy, but actually it was tightly controlled by the Communist Party. Lenin died in 1924 and Stalin followed as the masterful dictator. Bureaucratic state socialism was enforced under a succession of five-year plans. In World War II Russia first sided with Hitler under an agreement which called for the division of Eastern Europe into Russian and German spheres. Late in September, 1939, Poland was partitioned between the partners and in 1940 Russia seized Estonia, Latvia, and Lithuania and obtained part of Rumania. In 1941 Hitler attacked Russia. The German armies quickly moved into West and South Russia but were balked before they could take Leningrad, Moscow, and Stalingrad. The war cost Russia several million lives before the Germans were driven back and defeated. The German collapse was followed by the Russian occupation of most of Central Europe and the setting up of governments under Communist control and friendly to the U.S.S.R. Stalin died in March, 1953. An intra-party struggle for power followed from which Khrushchev emerged as the new dictator. By the mid-1950's Russia had made a remarkable recovery, its standard of living was rising, and it was taking an attitude of confidence towards the West and continuing its efforts to extend its system throughout the world.

Christianity in Russia was singularly ill prepared to rise to the challenge of the revolution. The revolution was dominated and guided by the Communist Party and the controlling ideology was the Marxist brand of socialism. That ideology, formulated in Western Christendom and in London, the metropolis which owed its outstanding position chiefly to the Industrial Revolution, was a secularized and atheistic distortion of the Christian hope. In it Christian eschatology became the promise of a classless society in which each member would be assured of having his needs met and to which each would give according to his abilities. Through it Christian apocalypticism was perverted into a determinism by which the course of history was interpreted as making inevitably for that consummation. And yet sufficient freedom of the will was accorded to men to enable them to hasten the consummation. In Russia, for the large majority Christianity was represented by the Orthodox Church and that Church appeared to be an obstacle to the realization of the Communist dream. It was tied hand and foot to the tsarist state. Peter the Great had allowed its patriarchate to lapse and had replaced it with the Holy Synod dependent on the throne. Many of the intellectuals were sceptical or hostile, an attitude going back at least as far as the Enlightenment with the influx of its ideas and reinforced by many currents from the West in the nineteenth century. As we have noted, the Russian Orthodox Church experienced a marked revival in the nineteenth century, paralleling what was taking place in the Roman

Catholic Church and Protestantism.[1] But Pobedonostsev, the Chief Procurator of the Holy Synod from 1880 to 1905, attempted to make it a bulwark against the revolutionary ideas which were entering from Western Europe and it was, accordingly, regarded as a major enemy by all who, like the Communists, were committed to those ideas. During World War I antagonism to the official church was heightened by the baleful influence in affairs of state in the name of religion by the dissolute Rasputin (1872–1916) through his domination of the tsarina.[2] Communism was opposed to all religion, but the intimate association of the Orthodox Church with the old regime made that church peculiarly vulnerable.

Indigenous bodies which dissented from the establishment, among them varieties of the Old Believers, were even less prepared to meet the drastic revolution which entered from the West than was the Orthodox Church.[3] However, indigenous movements with Biblical roots similar to those of Western Protestantism proved to have considerable vitality in surviving the ideological flood which stemmed from the West.

THE ORTHODOX CHURCH REORGANIZES TO MEET THE CHALLENGE: THE RESTORATION OF THE PATRIARCHATE

During the brief months between the collapse of the monarchy and the seizure of power by the Communists the leaders of the Russian Orthodox Church endeavoured to adjust themselves to the new situation. During the liberal days which followed the abortive revolution of 1905 a movement had developed to restore the patriarchate and to make the Holy Synod resume its canonical place. The Kerensky regime was not unfavourable to the Church. It granted religious liberty, facilitated plans to reform the Church, wished to separate the Church from the state, transferred the 37,000 parochial schools to the Department of Education, and made religious instruction in the schools optional rather than compulsory as heretofore. It authorized the Church to convene an all-Russian sobor, or national assembly to enable the Church to make its adjustment to the new order. The need for such a body was urgent, for disorder was already appearing in the Church. In some dioceses congresses of clergy had deposed their bishops. The sobor met in Moscow in August, 1917. Its members included conservatives, liberals, and a centre group. It opposed the disestablishment of the Church but wished to have the Church autonomous in its internal affairs. Some desired an elected holy synod as the

[1] Volume II, pp. 452–467.

[2] René Fülop-Miller, *Rasputin, the Holy Devil,* translated from the German by F. S. Flint and D. F. Tait (New York, The Viking Press, 1928, pp. xii, 386), *passim;* John Shelton Curtiss, *Church and State in Russia—the Last Years of the Empire—1900–1917* (New York, Columbia University Press, 1940, pp. xxi, 787), pp. 366 ff.

[3] For a list see Volume II, pp. 470–472.

directing body, but the majority stood for a restored patriarchate. In the disorder which occurred during the fighting in Moscow and which led to the assumption of power by the Communists, what remained of the sobor decided on the latter measure and chose the patriarch by lot. The lot fell on Tikhon, Archbishop of Moscow, whose secular name was Vasily Ivanovich Bellavin. Born in 1866, the son of a priest, he had been popular with his fellow students, became a monk, was consecrated Bishop of Lublin in 1897, and from 1898 to 1907 administered the Orthodox Churches in North America. He then became bishop of Yaroslavl, where he was well liked, was next Bishop of Vilna in Russian Poland until he was driven out by the German armies, and as Archbishop of Moscow was host to the sobor. He was enthroned as patriarch just as the Communists were taking over Moscow.[4]

The Head-On Collision Between Communism and the Church

The Communists proved far more difficult than the Kerensky regime. Lenin was outspoken in his hostility to religion. However, for many months they were so engrossed in confirming their power that the full development of their anti-religious programme was delayed. Yet in December, 1917, they nationalized all the land of the country, including that of the churches and monasteries. Early in 1918 they formally separated the Church from the state and eliminated all religious ceremonies and objects from government offices and functions; state financial support of the churches was stopped, religious teaching in the schools ceased, and the cash reserves and financial investments of the Church were confiscated. By the constitution of 1918 priests and other ministers were declared to be non-workers and servants of the bourgeoisie and as such, along with the latter, were disfranchised. Church marriages were refused recognition: only the civil ceremony had legal status.[5] The purpose of the government was obviously so to weaken the Church that it would wither away. But it sought not to do such personal violence to the clergy and monks as would win popular sympathy for them as martyrs. In theory freedom of religion existed—either to profess it or to deny it. Here and there priests were killed and one bishop perished, but by local violence and not with the approval of the central government.[6]

---

[4] Spinka, *The Church in Soviet Russia*, pp. 3–14; Curtiss, *The Russian Church and the Soviet State, 1917–1950*, pp. 10–38; A. Wuyts, *Le Patriarcat Russe au Concile de Moscou de 1917–1918* (Rome, Pont. Institutum Orientalium Studiorum, 1941, pp. xvi, 244), *passim*; Hecker, *Religion under the Soviets*, pp. 46–62.

[5] Curtiss, *The Russian Church*, pp. 45–47; Spinka, *op. cit.*, pp. 14–19; Hecker, *op. cit.*, pp. 67–71; Timasheff, *Religion in Soviet Russia, 1917–1942*, pp. 24–28; Kischkowsky, *Die sowjetische Religionspolitik und die Russische Orthodoxe Kirche*, pp. 27 ff.

[6] Curtiss, *The Russian Church*, p. 47.

The Russian Orthodox Church at first denounced the Communist regime and did what it could to overthrow it. In his first message to the Church (January, 1918) the newly elected patriarch excoriated the attacks on the Church, threatened those who would harm it with excommunication and hell fire, labelled as "the monsters of the human race" those who secularized ecclesiastical property and the schools, and called upon the faithful to rise to the defense of their Holy Mother.[7] For a time his stand was a real menace to the Communists. Not only were thousands fully in sympathy with the Church, but many more who on other grounds were hostile to the new regime might make common cause with the clergy. Leagues of laymen were organized in support of the Church, and inflammatory pamphlets against the government were circulated.[8] Tikhon condemned the peace of Brest-Litovsk which the Soviets negotiated with the Central Powers (March, 1918) and celebrated a requiem mass for the murdered imperial family.[9]

CIVIL WAR INTENSIFIES THE COLLISION

During the civil war, which lasted from the summer of 1918 to the end of 1920, when the Communist regime was fighting for its life against the "white" armies, the clergy were divided. Some sought to remain neutral, some sided with the Communists, and others ardently supported the "whites." In general, Tikhon was neutral, but, especially in areas controlled by the "whites," numbers of the bishops and their clergy gave unqualified support to the latter. Some of the clergy even fought in the "white" armies. During these months the Communist government progressively stepped up its action against the Church. In March, 1919, it forbade teaching religion to youths under eighteen years of age, although the next year it permitted theological education for those over that age in preparation for the priesthood. Church marriages were allowed, but divorce was made a purely civil affair. The rule against ikons in public buildings was strictly enforced. The Church's diocesan factories for the manufacture of tapers, incense, and oil for sacramental use were nationalized and their products were to go directly to the churches and monasteries and were not for re-sale. Thus the Church was deprived of a source of revenue. By 1920, 673 monasteries were reported by the government to have been dissolved, their capital and other property nationalized, their lands distributed among the peasants, and their buildings devoted to non-ecclesiastical purposes. In the course of the closing of the monasteries the Soviet authorities widely publicized what they declared were frauds revealed in revered relics. Numbers of the

[7] *Ibid.*, pp. 49, 50; Hecker, *op. cit.*, pp. 62, 63.
[8] Curtiss, *The Russian Church*, pp. 54–57.
[9] Spinka, *op. cit.*, p. 19.

clergy were arrested for agitation against the Soviet regime and given sentences of varying severity.[10]

Antagonism between the Orthodox Church and the Soviets was further intensified by the action of clergy who sought refuge abroad. In November, 1921, bishops who had fled on the defeat of the "white" armies and had been granted haven in Karlovtsi in Jugoslavia organized what they called the Supreme Russian Ecclesiastical Administration Abroad, a continuation of what they called the Temporary Higher Church Administration formed in Tomsk in 1918. They held a conference of clergy and laity—to which they gave the designation of sobor, thus seeking to accord it ecclesiastical sanction as speaking for the entire Russian Orthodox Church. The Karlovtsi Sobor adopted a resolution praying that God would restore to the throne of Russia a member of the house of Romanov. Although this action was repudiated by Tikhon, it could only intensify the antagonism of the Soviet authorities towards the Church.[11]

The Orthodox Church came through the civil war both weakened and strengthened. Many among the masses derided it and its services, numbers of priests either refused to submit to its traditional discipline or openly renounced their profession, and many of the lower clergy expressed loyalty to the new regime. On the other hand, thousands from the masses thronged the churches, hundreds of the educated, formerly sceptical or indifferent, flocked to them as offering stability and hope in a time of suffering and uncertainty, and a few sought admission to the priesthood. For a time a revival of religion appeared to be in progress. Most of the children were still baptized, the majority of the marriages were by religious as well as civil ceremony, and of those who turned away from the Church about two-thirds were said to be Communists, who still constituted a small minority of the population.[12]

FAMINE FURTHER HEIGHTENS THE COLLISION

In 1921 and 1922 a famine swept across much of Russia, especially in the normally productive Ukraine and the valley of the Volga. The causes were the civil disturbances aggravated by a severe drought. The famine became the occasion of intensified Communist action against the Orthodox Church. Ostensibly for the purpose of obtaining funds to help relieve the suffering, the Communist government ordered the sale of the vessels, ornaments, and vestments and the precious metals and jewels in the ikons of the churches. In principle they had already been nationalized but had been permitted to be retained for their original purposes. At first leading churchmen were willing to

[10] Curtiss, *The Russian Church*, pp. 71–101.
[11] Spinka, *op. cit.*, pp. 24–26; Hecker, *op. cit.*, p. 78; Curtiss, *The Russian Church*, p. 95.
[12] Curtiss, *The Russian Church*, pp. 101–105.

have non-sanctified objects devoted to the relief of the famine. But Tikhon secretly circulated an order disapproving the diversion of consecrated articles in this fashion. The government and its supporters publicized this refusal as evidence of the callousness of the Church to the desperate needs of the starving. Critics of the government said that the latter did not put the extremely valuable crown jewels on the market but instead plundered the Church. The government's wrath against the Church was heightened by the appeal of the Karlovsti Sobor to the peoples of the world to assist the refugees from the Communists in their efforts to overthrow the "red" rule. In a large proportion of the parishes the priests and the faithful coöperated in the use of the Church's treasures for famine relief and were supported by some of the bishops. However, in a number of localities violent opposition developed to the execution of the measure. A total of 1,414 "bloody" clashes were reported. The state arrested some of the leading churchmen who were charged with complicity with the opposition, had several of them executed, among them the aged Metropolitan of Leningrad, and exiled others to the far North or Siberia. Tikhon was placed under house arrest.[13]

THE CHURCH IS WEAKENED BY DIVISION:
THE RISE OF THE LIVING (RENOVATED OR RENOVATIONIST) CHURCH

In 1922 a movement within the Orthodox Church led to a widening of a rift which had already appeared over the attitude towards the Communist regime. It was furthered by the opposition of Tikhon to the sale of ecclesiastical treasures for famine relief. Contributing to it was the long-smouldering resentment of the parish clergy, who were married, against the bishops and the monks and the exclusion of the married clergy from high office in the Church. What was called the Living or Renovated or Renovationist Church arose, led by clergy who favoured coöperation with the Communists and wished to adjust the Church to the new day. While Tikhon was under arrest the dissidents called a new sobor which in turn set up in place of the patriarchate the Supreme Church Administration, presbyterial in form. The government, nothing loath to do whatever would weaken the Church, gave the dissidents active assistance and in 1925 the Living Church claimed 12,593 parishes, 16,540 clergy, and 192 bishops—ostensibly about half the strength of the Russian Orthodox Church. Among the clergy of the Living Church were clearly some who were sincerely devoted to the Orthodox Church, were convinced that it must be reformed, and believed that a *modus vivendi* with the Soviet regime could be devised. But others were seeking for power, while many simply took

[13] *Ibid.*, pp. 106–128; Hecker, *op. cit.*, pp. 78–82; Spinka, *op. cit.*, pp. 28–30; McCullagh, *The Bolshevik Persecution of Christianity*, pp. 5–8; Anderson, *People, Church and State in Modern Russia*, pp. 74–76; Kischkowsky, *op. cit.*, pp. 32–35.

the course of least resistance. Possibly all motives were present in many individuals. In the West were those who hoped that the movement would lead to a re-vitalization of the Russian Church. The leaders of the Living Church could not agree among themselves and the movement soon broke up into sections called the Living Church, the Ancient Apostolic Church, and the Renovated Church. Although they soon (1923) came together in a single holy synod, in 1925 recognition was given to an autonomous Ukrainian Church. The second sobor of the Living Church (April, May, 1923) denounced the 1918 sobor and declared Tikhon deposed. In June, 1923, Tikhon was reported to have issued a confession repenting of his anti-Soviet acts, acknowledging the correctness of the accusations under which he had been arrested, and asking for release. He refused reconciliation with the Living Church and died (May, 1925). By his death the Orthodox Church was further thrown into confusion, for several ecclesiastics contended for leadership and not until May 31, 1927, would the government recognize the Patriarchal Church administration which professed to succeed him. The Orthodox Church, accordingly, appeared to be hopelessly divided.[14]

For a time the Living or Renovated Church seemed to have a promising future. By a decree in April, 1923, the state allowed all religious organizations to call provincial and national conventions and to elect executive boards, but only with the permission of the Soviet authorities. That permission was given to groups which had been persecuted under the tsars and to the Living Church but not to the portion of the Orthodox Church which held to the patriarchal form of government. The state turned over to the Living Church many church buildings and to make room for the clergy of that body expelled eighty-four bishops of the Patriarchal Church from their sees and more than a thousand priests from their parishes.[15] In 1924 the Ecumenical Patriarch of Constantinople as the ranking ecclesiastic in the Orthodox Church suggested that Tikhon resign as a way of bringing peace in the Russian Orthodox Church. When Tikhon indignantly refused and denounced the Ecumenical Patriarch for meddling in the internal affairs of the Russian Church, the Ecumenical Patriarch retorted by declaring Tikhon removed from the administration of that body and recognized the synod of the Living Church as its true head. The other patriarchs of the Orthodox Church at first backed Tikhon but eventually sided with the Living Church.[16]

[14] Anderson, *op. cit.*, pp. 76–87; Hecker, *op. cit.*, pp. 81–119; Spinka, *op. cit.*, pp. 30–47; Curtiss, *The Russian Church*, pp. 129–174; Kischkowsky, *op. cit.*, pp. 36–42.
[15] Timasheff, *op. cit.*, p. 31.
[16] Curtiss, *The Russian Church*, p. 173. For a picture of the situation in 1923 by a bishop of the Methodist Episcopal Church who took an unfavourable view of the Living Church and including some interesting documents and the opinions of some other American churchmen, see Richard J.

THE PATRIARCHAL CHURCH HAS A LEADER IN SERGIUS

In spite of its name, the Living Church did not have sufficient vitality to retain the loyalty of the rank and file. The large majority of the laity held to Tikhon, especially after he declared that he was no longer an enemy of the Soviet government. The latter eventually found it wise to compromise and in 1927 recognized Metropolitan Sergius, the acting Guardian of the Patriarchal Throne, as the administrator of the Russian Orthodox Church. Sergius (1867–1944), the monastic name of Ivan Nikolaievich Stragorodsky, was a scion of a priestly family. An able student, he was graduated from the theological academy of St. Petersburg, became a monk, and at his own request was sent to the Orthodox mission in Japan. After two brief terms of service in Japan he returned to Russia, was rapidly promoted, won the respect of intellectuals, became known as a liberal, was created bishop and then archbishop, was made a member of the Holy Synod and later, in spite of his alleged defense of one who was accused of leniency towards the notorious Rasputin, became head of the Holy Synod and was retained by Tikhon on that body and appointed a metropolitan. For a short period he sided with the Living Church but penitently returned to allegiance to Tikhon and again became a member of the Holy Synod. After a complicated succession of events which followed Tikhon's death and a period in prison, Sergius emerged (1926) as the leader of the Patriarchal Church and was accepted by the majority of the hierarchy as Deputy to the Guardian and then as Guardian of the Church.[17] By his unwavering loyalty to the Soviet government he sacrificed the support of the *émigré* bishops and clergy, but he was tolerated by the government and was able to hold together the majority of the Orthodox in the U.S.S.R. The Living Church seems to have reached its apex in 1925. Thereafter the number of parishes which adhered to it declined. Its main centres were not in the heart of Russia but in the outlying republics. At the end of 1928 it was still strong. It possessed theological academies in Moscow and Leningrad with about one hundred students in each, had fifty students in a theological school in Kiev, maintained pastoral training courses in several other cities, and issued three periodicals and several diocesan organs.[18] Not until after the vastly improved condition of the Patriarchal Church in the 1940's and the election of Sergius as Patriarch did the leaders of the Living Church make their peace with the main body. Then several of its metropolitans and bishops asked for re-admission to the parent church. They were accepted, but often with reduced rank.[19]

Cooke, *Religion in Russia under the Soviets* (New York, The Abingdon Press, 1924, pp. 311), pp. 156 ff.

[17] Spinka, *op. cit.*, pp. 52–61; Curtiss, *The Russian Church*, pp. 178–190.

[18] Curtiss, *The Russian Church*, pp. 189–191.

[19] *Ibid.*, pp. 294, 295.

FURTHER DIVISION: THE AUTOCEPHALOUS UKRAINE

The story of the attempt to create an autocephalous Orthodox Church in the Ukraine is complicated and we can pause only for the barest summary. The Ukraine was the scene of the beginnings of Russian Christianity, for there was Kiev, and the baptism of Kiev's prince, Vladimir, late in the tenth century is usually regarded as the decisive act in the conversion of Russia. Here, too, had long been the chief centre of the Russian Orthodox Church. Ukrainian particularism was strong, and it is not surprising that in the chaotic conditions which followed the overthrow of the Romanovs the Ukrainian nationalists attempted (1917) to set up their own church. In 1921 they held a sobor in Kiev in which they chose a bishop and proclaimed him metropolitan of that city and head of the Ukrainian autocephalous church. They circulated the Bible in a Ukrainian translation and their services were in Ukrainian. Some of the clergy dissented and held to the old ways and to the bond with the Russian Orthodox Church. The Living Church was also strong, but by May, 1927, the Ukrainian Church was said to have 36 bishops, 2,300 priests, and about 3,000 congregations. Tensions with the Patriarchal Church were frequently acute. The Soviet authorities looked with suspicion on the autocephalists because of their alleged support of anti-Soviet Ukrainian nationalism and took measures to prevent them from taking over parishes against the wishes of the parishioners. In spite of its attempt to set up an autocephalous section the Living Church had only a transient existence in the Ukraine. The hostility of the Soviet government led to the dissolution (1930) of the original autocephalous church. Yet some of its bishops and clergy held out until suppressed.[20]

THE COMMUNISTS INTENSIFY THEIR ATTACK

In the mid-1920's the Communists intensified their anti-Christian campaign. Always frankly anti-Christian, during the period when they were establishing themselves and were engrossed in civil wars to maintain their existence, they only incidentally paid attention to ecclesiastical affairs. Some Communists were of the opinion that, left to itself, the Church would lose the support of its constituency and feared that to attack the Church too openly would be premature and might arouse widespread opposition at a time when the Soviet government was not the secure master of the country. In 1922-1923 the Komsomol (Young Communist League) launched an aggressive campaign with anti-

[20] *Ibid.*, pp. 145, 191, 235, 291; Heyer, *Die orthodoxe Kirche in der Ukraine von 1917 bis 1945*, pp. 34-227; *Dossier Américan de l'Orthodoxie Panukrainienne. Dix-huit Documents Inédits*, translated from the Ukrainian by Pierre Volkonsky and Michel d'Herbigny (Rome, Pontificio Instituto Orientale, 1923, pp. 129-224), *passim; Documents Inédits. "L'Église Orthodoxe Panukrainienne." Crée en 1921 à Kiev. . . . Introduction, Traduction et Notes* (Rome, Pontificio Instituto Orientale, 1923, pp. 73, 126), *passim.*

religious carnivals, processions, slogans, and plays. Here and there a priest was ducked in a well and debates were held in churches. Although the latter attracted crowds and reduced the attendance at church services, the more cautious among the Communists feared that such measures would provoke the faithful and stir up propaganda for religion.[21] Late in 1922 the newspaper *Bezbozhnik* (the Godless) was begun. Around it sprang up a society dubbed Friends of the Newspaper *Bezbozhnik* which in 1925 was re-named the League of the Militant Godless. It grew rapidly, from a reported 87,033 members in 1925 to 465,498 in 1928. It was supported by the dues of the members and the income of the *Bezbozhnik* publishing house. It had paid workers—instructors, lecturers, and organizers—who were maintained by funds from a variety of sources. Numbers of Communists criticized the League of the Godless as unwise. They believed that materialist education and the proven success of socialism would in time wean the populace from religion. However, in 1926 a Communist Party conference endorsed a more radical programme and the first five-year plan, adopted in 1928, included anti-religious objectives and was followed by the intensification of the attack on the Church.[22]

Sergius Attempts Accommodation

Within the Patriarchal Church Sergius led in an effort to placate the Soviet government. By a declaration issued in 1927 after his release from prison he expressed gratitude to the Soviet government for its "attention to the spiritual needs of the Orthodox population" in granting him permission to set up a temporary holy synod and thus giving formal recognition to a central organization for the Patriarchal Church. On behalf of the Orthodox he recognized the Soviet Union as the "civil fatherland whose joys and successes" were their "joys and successes and whose misfortunes" were their "misfortunes" and called on the *émigré* clergy to take a written pledge of loyalty to the Soviet government on pain of expulsion from the Moscow Patriarchate. Although by this submission to the Soviet regime Sergius obtained the authorization for the central administration of his church, in doing so he further divided the Orthodox Church and thus weakened its resistance. Many in high ecclesiastical office resigned rather than approve and were either imprisoned, exiled (to Siberia or to desolate islands in the North), or shot; their posts were filled by men who supported Sergius. Some of the bishops sent to an island in the White Sea accepted what they called the "purely political part" of Sergius's declaration but protested against the expression of gratitude for the government's care for the spiritual needs of the Orthodox population as ignoring the sweeping actions

[21] Curtiss, *The Russian Church*, pp. 202, 203.
[22] *Ibid.*, pp. 205–216.

of the state in closing monasteries, forbidding catechetical instruction of the children, profaning churches, removing religious books from the libraries, and in effect surrendering the ecclesiastical autonomy granted by the constitution.[23]

THE COMMUNIST ATTACK IS CONTINUED

By his submission Sergius may have saved some semblance of the structure of the Patriarchal Church, but he did not prevent an intensification of the campaign against religion. For prudential reasons the Soviet government was willing to grant a degree of toleration to those in the Orthodox Church who sided with Sergius, but in its campaign for the thorough re-making of Russia it included religion and took violent methods looking towards its elimination from the life of the people. Legislation enacted in 1929 forbade religious associations to use property at their disposal for any other purpose than satisfying religious needs; to hold meetings for children, youth, and women for prayer and other purposes, or groups for literary, Biblical, or religious study; to open libraries or reading rooms; or to organize excursions, children's playgrounds, sanatoria, or medical aid. Only books needed for the performance of services were permitted in church buildings or houses of prayer. The text of the constitution was altered from "freedom for religion and anti-religion is granted to every citizen" to "there is freedom for religious confession and anti-religious propaganda," and the new form was interpreted as forbidding religious propaganda and limiting the activity of religious associations to holding services. A six-day working week eliminated Sunday or any other day as a common weekly holiday, ministers of religion were classified among non-productive members of society and deprived of civil rights, including residence in a communal house and bread cards, and their children could not attend institutions for higher education. By 1929, 150 bishops had been arrested or exiled and in some districts only about a fifth of the pre-revolutionary number of priests remained. Heavy taxes and other assessments were placed on the churches. The Patriarchal Church was not permitted to have higher theological courses or a publication. The chief sufferers were priests and Baptist groups in rural sections and villages and towns, for the decade was that of the socialization of agriculture and the cities were already deeply affected.[24] Indeed, an order promulgated in 1928 had closed a large number of churches in the cities and in the country, had destroyed them or turned them to other uses, and had forbidden the erection of new churches. Anti-religious museums were set up. In 1930 they were said to number forty-four and several of them were in once-famous churches and

[23] Spinka, *op. cit.*, pp. 66–73; Kischkowsky, *op. cit.*, pp. 49 ff.
[24] Anderson, *op. cit.*, pp. 101–113.

monasteries.[25] Organized labour was enlisted in the anti-religious campaign and in 1929 the eighth congress of trade unions adopted a resolution endorsing the struggle against religion.[26] In that year locals of the trade union of printers refused to print religious publications, and locals of transport workers put a ban on carrying works or articles intended for religious ceremonies. Individuals known to be Christian were dismissed from teaching posts and from employment in industries. Text-books teaching the incompatibility of religion with science and the association of religion with the bourgeoisie and the ruling class were introduced in the schools.[27] By January, 1930, the membership of the League of the Militant Godless is said to have leaped to 2,000,000.[28] In 1932 it was reported to be 5,500,000. The large majority of the members were between fourteen and forty years of age and about two-thirds were reported to be men. In addition the junior organization for children below fourteen years of age was reported to be 2,000,000 strong. Significantly, however, only about a tenth of the huge membership were estimated as being engaged in active propaganda. The army was long a centre of anti-religious education.[29]

The Attacks Reach a Peak

In the mid-1930's the organized anti-religious campaign seems to have attained its peak. The anti-religious five-year plan adopted in 1932 had as its programme the removal of all religious symbols from the churches, the cessation of education for the priesthood, the elimination of all literature with a religious content, the termination of religious elements in the life of the family, the spread of anti-religious propaganda throughout the entire country, the concentration of that propaganda on youth, the liquidation of the remaining houses of worship, and the uprooting of underground remnants of religious life.[30] Yet in 1932 the membership in the League of the Militant Godless fell short by two-thirds of the goal set for it in 1929. Similarly the circulation of the periodicals of the League attained only a third of the dimensions planned for them in that period. Many members of the League were indifferent or inactive and some of the local units went out of existence. In 1932 Emil Yaroslavsky, president of the League, denied that that movement was engaged in a campaign but said that its method was merely propaganda. He said that a systematic attempt was being made to use the state schools for that propaganda and to create institutions with a two-year course for leaders in the anti-religious

25 Kischkowsky, op. cit., pp. 56 ff.; Curtiss, The Russian Church, p. 255; Hecker, Religion and Communism, pp. 257 ff.
26 Curtiss, The Russian Church, p. 236.
27 Timasheff, op. cit., pp. 42–44.
28 Curtiss, The Russian Church, p. 237.
29 Hecker, Religion and Communism, pp. 218–224.
30 Kischkowsky, op. cit., p. 62.

education. In these institutions religion and religious organizations were labelled as the "worst foes of socialistic advance," doubt was thrown on the historical existence of Christ, and similarities were pointed out between the cult of Christ and the mystery cults.[31] Moreover, in 1937 as in part a reaction against the liberalism which had been permitted in the preceding five or six years a great purge took place in which many churchmen were condemned for alleged counter-revolutionary fascist activities. Among them were bishops, archpriests, deacons, former nuns, and former landowners. Leaders of both the Patriarchal Church and the Living Church were accused of unbecoming acquisition of wealth. Peasants were arrested for reading the Bible as a group and two were sentenced to from eight to ten years in prison.[32] It was said that in the first half of 1937, 612 churches were destroyed and 2,900 churches and 63 monasteries were closed.[33] Another set of figures declares that in the entire year of 1937, 1,100 Orthodox churches, 240 Roman Catholic churches, 61 Protestant prayer houses, and 110 mosques were closed.[34] As we have suggested, the measures taken in 1937 all but extinguished the autocephalous Orthodox Church in the Ukraine: the remaining bishops and almost all the surviving priests were exiled. The Patriarchal Church in the Ukraine was also seemingly erased. Its hierarchy was liquidated, partly by deportation and partly by imprisonment and death. Its churches were closed and most of its priests were imprisoned or in other ways suppressed.[35]

THE ATTACK ONLY PARTLY SUCCEEDS

Precisely how effective these measures were would be difficult to determine. In 1932 Yaroslavsky told a group of American teachers that of the trade union members in Moscow 80 per cent. were "Godless" and in the country as a whole the percentage was over 40. He said that of those living on collective farms not less than ten millions were in that category, that in some villages all the population would call themselves "Godless," that in the cities only the children of religious families held to the faith, and that while about two-thirds of the population of the U.S.S.R. were still religious, less than half of the rising generation remained Christian.[36] If this statement reflected the facts, an increasing proportion of the youth who had been born and reared since the disestablishment of the Orthodox Church were growing up without religion

[31] Anderson, *op. cit.*, pp. 115–149; Curtiss, *The Russian Church*, pp. 254–256.

[32] Anderson, *op. cit.*, pp. 149–158; Timasheff, *op. cit.*, pp. 50, 51. For a narrative of a man who suffered as a Christian see V. Ph. Martzinkovski, *With Christ in Soviet Russia*, abridged and translated by Hoyt E. Porter (published by the author, no place or date, preface 1933, pp. 364).

[33] Kischkowsky, *op. cit.*, p. 65.

[34] Timasheff, *op. cit.*, pp. 52, 53.

[35] Heyer, *op. cit.*, pp. 124–126.

[36] Anderson, *op. cit.*, pp. 115, 116.

and the trend away from Christianity was strongest in the cities and among the labourers in industry. After the state adopted a milder policy, such figures as could be obtained appeared to show that between 1917, the eve of the beginning of Communist rule, and 1941 the number of Orthodox churches had fallen from 46,457 to 4,225, of Orthodox priests from 50,960 to 5,665, of Orthodox deacons from 15,210 to 3,100, of Orthodox bishops from 130 to 28, and of Orthodox monasteries from 1,026 to 38.[37] In other words, the outward structure and official personnel of the Russian Orthodox Church had shrunk to about one-tenth of its dimensions at the beginning of the revolution. But another set of statistics seemed to indicate a much less marked decline and a persistence of religious customs with an increase during part of the anti-religious campaign of the 1920's. In 1925 government figures showed in the 48 provinces of the Russian Soviet Federated Socialist Republic (embracing most of Russia and Siberia) 28,381 Orthodox parishes, of which 81 per cent. were of the Patriarchal Church. In 1927 a "Godless" periodical reported 8,324 churches (presumably Orthodox) in the Ukraine, 23 per cent. less than in 1914. If Byelorussia had the same proportion to the population as the Ukraine, in 1927 it had about 1,000 churches. That would mean a total of about 39,000 churches in the U.S.S.R. in 1928 as against 40,437 parishes in the same area in 1914. Early in 1927 nearly all the 460 churches in Moscow were in use. In 1928, with its intense anti-religious campaign, in the entire U.S.S.R. 354 churches and 28 monasteries ceased to function. In 1927 a periodical of the Karlovsti Synod gave the names and locations of 272 bishops in Russia, of whom 35 were said to be in exile within the country and 9 in prison. In the same year an anti-religious journal declared that the Ukraine had 95 bishops and 10,647 priests. Both figures of 1927, if reliable, indicate an increase since 1914. In 1930 Sergius said that the Patriarchal Church had 30,000 parishes, 163 bishops, and several tens of millions of believers. Obviously the discrepancies in the figures forbid dependable conclusions. The destruction of ecclesiastical discipline led to the consecration, or uncanonical consecration, of many bishops. This may account for the higher number in 1927 and 1930 as against the number in 1917. The Moscow registry office showed that in 1925, 41.6 per cent. of the births were without religious ceremony, but that in 1928 the percentage had shrunk to 38.1, that 55.9 per cent. of the births in 1925 were with religious ceremony and that in 1928 the percentage had risen to 57.8 per cent.; that of the burials 40.7 per cent. were without religious ceremony in 1925 and in 1928 only 33.3 per cent. were in that category, whereas the percentage of burials with religious ceremony had risen from 57.5 in 1925 to 65.7 in 1928. Of the marriages, on the other hand, the proportion without religious ceremony had grown from 77.3 per

[37] *Ibid.*, p. 159.

cent. in 1925 to 86.3 per cent. in 1928, and those with religious ceremony had fallen from 21.1 per cent. in 1925 to 11.8 per cent. in 1925.[38]

THE COMMUNISTS BLOW COLD AND HOT

Towards the end of the 1930's the policy of the Soviet government underwent a sharp change. The government seems never formally to have sponsored the League of the Militant Godless. Its persecution of the Church had ostensibly been on political and not religious grounds. Its alleged reasons had been that the churchmen, both clergy and laity, but especially the clergy, were counter-revolutionaries and were either directly conspiring with the enemies of the regime or perpetuating attitudes which were basically hostile to Communism. Here in the churches was a force which was not fully amenable to the Soviet government and in the latter's interests must either be liquidated or induced to coöperate. By 1936 the government apparently found it wise to be conciliatory, either because it had found religion too well entrenched to be eradicated or because it was now so weakened that it need no longer be feared. In 1936 a new constitution was adopted which, while retaining the earlier recognition of freedom of worship and of anti-religious propaganda, abolished the disabilities imposed on priests, noblemen, former police officers, kulaks, and ex-capitalists.[39] By that year the government permitted the children of clergymen to enrol in institutions of higher learning. In the same year the ringing of church bells and the collection of funds for churches were permitted, and in 1938 the mass observance of Christmas and Easter was recognized and it was ordered that workers were not to be penalized for absenteeism during those seasons. Not far from the same time the manufacture and sale of objects connected with worship were allowed and ikon painters in one of the districts were given liberty to practise their trade for at least a year. In 1940 the seven-day week was restored with Sunday as a compulsory legal holiday. In 1938 blasphemous plays and films and anti-Christmas and anti-Easter carnivals were prohibited and history texts ridiculing Russian Christianity were removed from the schools. Films, plays, and books lauded the churchmen of early centuries as patriots and portrayed the constructive role of Christianity in the formation of Russian culture.

At the same time executions of the clergy were continued and in 1938 more than eight bishops were accused of being spies and were shot, fifty other prelates were imprisoned, and many more priests, monks, and laymen were shot. In 1937, 1,900 places of worship were closed, including 1,100 Orthodox churches, 115 synagogues, 110 mosques, 240 Roman Catholic churches, 61 Lutheran

---

[38] Curtiss, *The Russian Church*, pp. 222–224.

[39] Bolshakoff, *The Christian Church and the Soviet State*, p. 54; Curtiss, *The Russian Church*, pp. 272, 273.

churches, and buildings belonging to other faiths.[40] The admittedly imperfect statistics appear to indicate that the pressures of the 1930's had brought an added decline in religion.[41]

THE GERMAN INVASION BRINGS A PARTIAL TRUCE

The attack which Hitler launched against the U.S.S.R. in 1941 brought a partial truce between Church and state. During the early months of the invasion the Communists were forced back and for a time it looked as though they would be erased. The common danger brought the Orthodox to the defense of Mother Russia. Russian patriotism proved stronger than the chronic clash between the Communist government and its now weakened domestic enemy. Through vigorous propaganda the Germans made a bid for the support of the Church against the Soviet regime. The latter was quite willing, at least for the time being, to bury the hatchet if the Church would reciprocate. Sergius and the rank and file of the Patriarchal Church did not wait for the proffered olive branch. On June 28, 1941, six days after the Nazi onslaught, Sergius, supported by more than a score of priests, sang a service of intercession for Russia and her armies in a crowded cathedral in Moscow. His example was followed throughout Russia as a pastoral letter from him exhorted the faithful to rise to repel the invasion and called on the clergy to pray and to minister to the sufferers from the war. Although the advancing Germans closed the anti-religious museums and invited the Orthodox clergy to hold thanksgiving services, very few priests, if any, complied. In the United States the Russian Orthodox supported the Soviets in their resistance to the Germans.[42]

A few exceptions were seen to the loyalty of the Orthodox to the Soviets. The most notable were in the Ukraine where under the German occupation Archbishop Polikarp renounced his allegiance to Sergius and attempted to revive the autocephalous church. Indeed, two rival attempts were made, one to restore the autocephalous church and the other to create an autonomous church. Efforts to unite the two failed, partly because of the opposition of the Germans. The language issue also entered into the division, for the autocephalous advocates wished to use Ukrainian in the services. To both branches the recruitment and education of a body of clergy was a pressing problem. Both also endeavoured to provide religious instruction for the young to offset the prolonged anti-religious propaganda. By the close of the year 1942 considerable

---

[40] Bolshakoff, *op. cit.*, pp. 55, 56; Curtiss, *The Russian Church*, pp. 274, 276–282; Anderson, *op. cit.*, pp. 202, 203.

[41] Curtiss, *The Russian Church*, pp. 284–289.

[42] Bolshakoff, *op. cit.*, pp. 69–71; Kischkowsky, *op. cit.*, pp. 75 ff. For propaganda by Orthodox churchmen in behalf of the Soviet government during the German invasion see *The Truth about Religion in Russia, issued by the Moscow Patriarchate (1942)*, English translation under the supervision of E. N. C. Sergeant (London, Hutchinson & Co., no date, pp. 175), *passim*.

progress had been made, and the life of the Orthodox Church in the eparchy of Kiev had been rebuilt to about two-thirds its strength on the eve of the revolution. Varying progress was seen elsewhere in the Ukraine. The German administration, while distrusting the Roman Catholics, was quite willing to aid the Orthodox. However, it was tactless and alienated both wings of that church. Ukrainian nationalists were no more willing to submit to the Germans than they had been to the Moscow-centred Soviet government. However, when in 1943 the Russian armies drove out the Germans, most of the autocephalous clergy left with the retreating Nazi forces and some of the autonomous clergy fled southward through Odessa to Rumania or found refuge in Germany. On the capitulation of Germany many of both the autocephalous and the autonomous clergy were in the American and British zones and several eventually made their way to North or South America.[43] We also hear of an archbishop on the Baltic who collaborated with the Germans.[44]

In the course of the war the Soviet regime took an increasingly lenient attitude towards the Orthodox and the latter reciprocated by supporting the government. At Easter, 1942, the government lifted the curfew in Moscow to enable those who wished to do so to attend the midnight services. It appointed a metropolitan to a commission to investigate the crimes committed by the invaders. In September, 1943, Stalin received Sergius and others of the hierarchy and said that the government did not object to the calling of a sobor by the Patriarchal Church to elect a patriarch. A few days later nineteen bishops met in a sobor in Moscow and chose Sergius for the office. The sobor thanked the government for its care for the Church and called on the Christians of the entire world to oppose Hitlerism. It also decreed excommunication of laymen and unfrocking of ecclesiastics who collaborated with the Germans. That same month Garbett, the Archbishop of York, and two Anglican priests were permitted to enter the country and were welcomed by Sergius. They were invited to the chancel of the Patriarch's cathedral and Garbett made a brief address urging the unity of the Church of England and the Russian Orthodox Church against the common foe. In the course of the war congregations and religious associations raised substantial funds to assist in the national defense. In October, 1943, the government created a council for affairs of the Orthodox Church to direct relations between the Church and the state. In June, 1944, the Orthodox Church was permitted to open a theological institute and a theological course in Moscow. Priests were allowed to give religious instruction to children and might do so in groups in the priests' homes. Medals were awarded by the government to several of the clergy for their assistance in the defense of Leningrad, Moscow, and Tula. In 1943 the publication of the leading anti-religious

[43] Heyer, *op. cit.*, pp. 170–227.
[44] Curtiss, *The Russian Church*, p. 291.

journals was discontinued, professedly because of the shortage of paper. That same year the League of the Militant Godless was dissolved and anti-religious propaganda was suspended.[45]

Sergius died (May 15, 1944) before the war was over. His temporary successor as head of the Patriarchal Church, Alexius (Simansky), Metropolitan of Leningrad, later Patriarch, pledged his allegiance to the country on behalf of himself and his colleagues. Early in 1945, obviously with the full consent of the government, a sobor met in Moscow attended by several scores of clergy and laity, the Orthodox Patriarchs of Alexandria and Antioch, representatives of the Patriarchs of Constantinople and Jerusalem and of the Serbian and Rumanian churches, the Patriarch and Catholicos of Georgia, and Metropolitan Veniamin, who headed the parishes of the Patriarchal jurisdiction in North America. Here was clearly an attempt of the Soviet regime not only to enlist the support of the Orthodox but also to use the Russian Orthodox Church to further Russian interests in the Balkans and the Middle East. After the collapse of Hitler Alexius officiated at a service of thanksgiving. He also publicly thanked God for sending Stalin as the leader of the country.[46]

THE ORTHODOX CHURCH CONTINUES ITS RECOVERY

In the fifteen years after World War II the Russian Orthodox Church continued the recovery which had begun late in the 1930's and had been accelerated during the war. That recovery was due both to the decrease of the hostility of the Soviet government and to the inner vitality of the Church.

The waning of official hostility did not arise from the conversion of the leaders of the state or of the Communist Party which controlled the state. The Communist Party still adhered to the atheism of Karl Marx to which it was formally committed. Nor was any mass movement to Christianity seen. However, the League of the Militant Godless was not revived nor was the anti-religious campaign renewed for several years, and then not with its erstwhile fervour. The majority of the population were more indifferent than hostile. In practice they were committed to the materialism for which Marxism stood. That attitude stemmed partly from the anti-religious propaganda of the 1920's and 1930's. Presumably more responsible for the failure of the Church to win the majority was the absorption of the latter in other interests—in obtaining a livelihood and in achieving advance in comfort and in social and official recognition. Some of the forces were at work which were also responsible for the de-Christianization of large elements in Western Christendom.

The recovery of faith was ascribable in part to inner vitality in the Church

[45] Ibid., pp. 292–295; Kischkowsky, op. cit., pp. 75–83.
[46] Curtiss, The Russian Church, pp. 296–299; Kischkowsky, op. cit., pp. 83–93.

and to the fact that the Christian faith met the needs of men and filled a gaping void which nineteenth- and twentieth-century secularism could not close. In addition was a growing interest in Russia's history associated with the rising tide of nationalism and an increasing appreciation of the contributions which the Church had made to Russian culture.

Because of the fragmentary nature of the information coming from the U.S.S.R. a complete picture could not be obtained. For example, with the exception of the Baptists, little was known of the Old Believers or of most of the other pre-revolutionary movements which bore the Christian name but did not conform to the Orthodox Church. Yet enough data were available to reveal a decided growth of the Patriarchal Church.

The several statistical reports still displayed marked discrepancies. One declared that in the three years between the close of World War II in 1945 and 1949 the number of parishes had risen from 16,000 to 22,000 and that in the latter year monasteries totalled 89. A visitor in 1947 said that 25,500 churches and 3,500 houses of prayer were open.[47] In 1957 the Moscow Patriarchate told a group of Christian youth visitors from the West that there were 20,000 Orthodox churches, 35,000 priests, 8,000 monks in 50 monasteries, and 8 seminaries and 2 academies for preparing priests, and said that the Church did not suffer from a shortage of clergy. The 1957 figures showed advances of over 4,225 churches and 5,665 priests. It was also affirmed that the majority of churchgoers were young and were made up of workmen, peasants, and intellectuals, both men and women.[48] A Quaker who was briefly in Russia in 1957 or 1958 reported that about a quarter of the population of the U.S.S.R. were regular attendants at church services.[49] The following year an American Methodist after being in Russia said that the lowest figures given for Christians in the U.S.S.R. was 30,000,000 Orthodox, 520,000 Baptists, 20,000 Mennonites, and 25,000 Seventh Day Adventists. He also said that a few new churches were being erected in the suburbs of cities, that young people were present in the services, that young men were becoming clergymen, and that the enrolments in theological seminaries were rising. He also gave it as his judgement that Moslems were suffering more than Christians and noted that two new atheistic universities had opened, one in Leningrad and the other in Ashkhabad (in Asia on the Trans-Caspian Railway).[50] Another report for 1957 had it that the attendance at services was largely of adults, but that in the summer of 1957, 400,000 young people were expelled from the Komsomol (Young Communist League) for "immorality" and attending church services.[51] Confirmation of

[47] Curtiss, *The Russian Church*, p. 305. See also, on statistics, Spinka, *op. cit.*, pp. 118–120.

[48] *Ecumenical Press Service*, August 23, 1957; Jackson, *The Eternal Flame*, p. 102.

[49] *The Christian Century*, Vol. LXXV, pp. 304–306 (March 12, 1958).

[50] Otto Nall in *The Christian Century*, Vol. LXXVI, pp. 261, 262 (March 4, 1959).

[51] H. H. Barnette in *Christianity Today*, Vol. II, No. 6, pp. 3–5 (December 23, 1957).

this trend was seen in complaints by Communist organs that members of the Communist Party were participating in religious ceremonies and rituals, that Party members had been married in the Church and had had their children baptized, and that a Komsomol group in Moscow had called a special meeting to discuss the case of one of its number who had had his child christened. Moreover, the Central Committee of the Communist Party was directing Party members to restrain their zeal in anti-religious efforts and to reduce it to propaganda.[52]

In 1945 a new body of statutes was adopted by the Russian Orthodox Church. Although the separation of Church and state was continued, the Church was controlled by the state from the highest level to the local parish and could operate only with its consent. Under the structure of the Orthodox Church during the earlier stages of the Soviet regime no effective centralized supervision by the ecclesiastical authorities was possible. Any group of as many as twenty believers could ask the civil authorities for the use of a building and the vessels required for worship and if the request was granted could hire a priest. The tenure of the priest was subject to the will of the parish. By the new statutes the property of the Church was, as heretofore, vested in the state and granted to the Church for its use. A structure was authorized with the patriarch at the top, with a sobor made up of clergy and laymen. The only mandatory function of the sobor was the election of the patriarch. Below were the bishops, each with his diocese. Each diocese was divided into deaneries. The bishop appointed the parish priest and the priest was made the head and leader of the parish and the parish council. The state created the Council for Orthodox Church Affairs. No patriarch could be chosen or bishop appointed without the consent of the Council, nor could action be taken on the diocesan level without the approval of the commissioners of the Council. The sobor could meet only with the permission of the chairman of the Council. All acts of the Holy Synod were issued in the name of the "Patriarch of Moscow and All Russia." Here was a structure which gave hierarchical discipline and a sense of unity to the Russian Orthodox Church and served to eliminate the chaos which existed between World Wars I and II. It also provided for control by the state through the Council and its commissioners.[53] Although the separation of Church and state was technically maintained, actually the control of the social and civil position of the Church by the state was even more thoroughgoing than under the tsars and the forms developed by Peter the Great. The separation was seen in the fact that the state did not concern itself with doctrine and the sacraments.

The Russian Government was as willing and eager to use the Russian Ortho-

[52] *The New York Times*, November 12, 1954.
[53] *St. Vladimir's Seminary Quarterly*, Vol. II, No. 3 (Summer, 1958), pp. 23–39.

dox Church to consolidate its rule in the U.S.S.R. and to extend Russian influence abroad as the tsars had been. In 1946 about five million Galician Uniates in what had been Eastern Poland but was now Soviet territory, in spite of the protests of Rome, resumed the allegiance of their ancestors to the Orthodox Church. That connexion had been lost when in 1596 as the result of pressure from their Polish overlords they had submitted to Rome. Now, under Russian rule, they were induced to swing into the orbit of the Russian Orthodox Church. Similarly in 1949 the Sub-Carpathian Ruthenian Uniates were brought under the Patriarch of Moscow.[54]

Shortly before the end of the war and soon thereafter, with the approval of the Soviet government, delegations from the Moscow Patriarchate sought to establish the leadership of that office over the Orthodox in East Europe and the Balkans. In March, 1945, the Archbishop of Pskov was sent to Estonia to bring the Orthodox of that country to acknowledge the jurisdiction of the Moscow Patriarchate. In April of that year a delegation went to Bulgaria to establish relations with the Orthodox of that land. A delegation to Jugoslavia was given a cordial reception by Marshal Tito and one of the bishops of the Jugoslavian Orthodox publicly expressed the wish that the Russian Orthodox Church would take the leadership of the Slavic Orthodox churches. A delegation dispatched in May, 1945, to Rumania made fraternal contact with the Patriarch of the Rumanian Orthodox Church. Efforts to persuade the Russian Orthodox in Western Europe to submit to the Moscow Patriarchate were only fleetingly successful. Nor did success attend the attempt to attract all the Orthodox in the United States into that relation.[55]

In 1945 Patriarch Alexius and his entourage were flown by a Soviet plane to the Middle East and there visited the Orthodox Patriarchs of Antioch and Alexandria and the Russian Orthodox in Jerusalem. The small Orthodox Church in Czechoslovakia was taken under the wing of the Patriarch of Moscow and was accorded the dignity of an exarchate and autocephalous status by Alexius. Autocephaly was similarly granted to the Orthodox Church of Poland —although the Ecumenical Patriarch held that this position could be canonically conceded only by the Phanar. In the 1940's the Hungarian Orthodox Church was brought under the jurisdiction of the Patriarch of Moscow. Official visits to Moscow were made in the 1950's by heads of the Rumanian, Bulgarian, and Albanian Orthodox Churches.

In 1948 a conference of the Orthodox autocephalous churches was held in Moscow in connexion with the celebration of the five hundredth anniversary of the autocephalous status of the Russian Orthodox Church. To it came the heads of several of these churches and representatives of some others. It was

[54] Curtiss, *The Russian Church*, p. 307; Spinka, *op. cit.*, pp. 128–131.
[55] Kischkowsky, *op. cit.*, pp. 97, 98.

the most inclusive gathering of the Orthodox Churches which had been held for many years and was obviously a bid by the Russian Orthodox, as the largest of them, for a kind of hegemony. The abstention of the representatives of the Ecumenical Patriarch and of the Orthodox Church of Greece from signing the findings of the gathering was presumably due partly to the strained relations between the U.S.S.R. and Turkey and Greece and partly to the unwillingness of these churches to acquiesce in what they deemed the pretensions of the Russian Orthodox Church. The conference adopted resolutions which were in accord with U.S.S.R. policies—among them a condemnation of the Roman Papacy and a refusal to take part in the Ecumenical Movement.[56]

The Russian Orthodox Church also hewed to the line of U.S.S.R. policy in speaking for peace and in condemning what it held was American aggression in Korea and calling for the removal of foreign troops from that country. In accord with the quite understandable desire of the Russian people for peace after the sufferings from the German invasion in World War II, several international conferences in support of peace were held under Soviet auspices or with Soviet support. In most of them and in other peace efforts Russian Orthodox churchmen joined.[57] By many on the outer side of the "iron curtain" these projects were interpreted as being part of the Russian propaganda to lull the West into a false sense of security and to reduce its armaments, that Soviet aims of achieving world-wide dominance through Communism under Russian leadership might be attained. It was suggested that by peace conferences and peace declarations the Soviet government hoped to gain the sympathy of liberals in the West and to weaken the opposition in the "free world."

The seeming reconciliation of the Russian Orthodox Church and the Soviet government did not prevent the resurgence of the anti-religious movement. In 1944 an active campaign was begun to eliminate "the remnants of ignorance, superstition, and prejudice." In 1949 the Komsomol and the schools inaugurated a vigorous attack on religion as being unscientific. In 1950 the Society for the Dissemination of Political and Scientific Knowledge undertook a campaign against "the medieval Christian outlook," to be waged on a purely scientific basis. In 1954 a new anti-religious periodical was launched. Late in 1954 the anti-religious propaganda in the press subsided. But extensive efforts continued to indoctrinate teachers in primary and secondary schools in atheist convictions. Museums were also employed to give a religiously sceptical slant to education —among them museums of anthropology and ethnology.[58] For years, moreover, Christians of all denominations seem to have been singled out for arrest and for imprisonment in labour camps. They included Lutherans from East

---

[56] Curtiss, *The Russian Church*, pp. 308, 314–316; Spinka, *op. cit.*, pp. 131–143.
[57] Curtiss, *The Russian Church*, pp. 317–319; Kischkowsky, *op. cit.*, pp. 113 ff.
[58] Curtiss, *The Russian Church*, pp. 321–323; Kischkowsky, *op. cit.*, pp. 105–112, 126–132.

Prussia, Estonia, and Latvia, Orthodox, Mennonites, Roman Catholics, Mormons, Baptists, and Seventh Day Adventists.[59]

In spite of the continued attacks on Christianity, late in the 1950's the Russian Orthodox Church was very much alive. Infants were being baptized and at the baptism the officiating priest laid on the parents the responsibility for rearing the children in the Christian faith. No figures were available as to the number of children to whom that sacrament was administered, but one well-informed foreign observer was told that most of the infants were baptized. Church services in the cities were reported to be thronged, particularly on the high days of the Christian year. Since, especially in proportion to the population, buildings were fewer than before 1917, this did not necessarily mean that a high percentage of the inhabitants were in regular attendance. Yet attendance was reported to be increasing beginning with World War II.[60] Reports still seemed to indicate that in the congregations the majority were of middle age or older. However, since by 1961 more than forty years had elapsed since the revolution, few "old regime" people were among them. The large majority had been educated under Soviet tutelage. Some social obloquy and even jeopardy to livelihood and professional or occupational advancement might be entailed for those coming with any degree of regularity. Moreover, Sundays were times for many political meetings at which attendance of youth was required. The attraction of the services was not only the religious appeal but also in colour, music, and beauty in what for millions was a grey life. A foreign visitor in 1958 found far more youths in the congregations than in a visit three years earlier and reported that younger married women, the mothers of the on-coming generation, were the dominant element. It was said that many writers and other intellectuals were believers and that a substantial number of students came to the priests for baptism at the end of the academic year.[61]

Little difficulty appeared to be met in obtaining recruits for the priesthood. Attendance at the seminaries was mounting. Before 1914 the enrolments were largely from sons of the clergy and the profession tended to be hereditary. Now students were coming from several social backgrounds—peasants, manual workers, office workers, and professional people. Applicants deemed unworthy were rejected. In 1956 it was reported that about 900 students were in eighteen theological seminaries and four academies and that about 160 were graduated each year. In addition other aspirants for ordination were instructed by priests.[62] Financial support for the clergy was derived from voluntary offerings and

[59] John Noble and Glenn D. Everett, *I Found God in Soviet Russia* (New York, St. Martin's Press, pp. 192), pp. 29 ff.

[60] *The New York Times*, April 3, 1955.

[61] *Frontier*, Vol. III, p. 163 (July, 1958).

[62] *Ibid.*, p. 163; *The New York Times*, April 3, 1955, April 29, 1956; Heyer, *op. cit.*, p. 239; *Ecumenical Press Service*, December 22, 1959; Paul B. Anderson to the author, April, 1956.

from the sale of candles. It appears to have been ample. Preaching was prominent in the services. Because of the shortage of ecclesiastical literature and the absence of religious education in the schools, the sermon became a favoured means of religious instruction.[63] Since the attack on Christianity took every opportunity to hold up to public scorn moral lapses in the priests and what was clearly superstitious, one effect was the purification of the Russian Orthodox Church. The quality of the priesthood improved, the disciplinary power of the hierarchy over the clergy increased, and what in the preaching and services of the Church might rightly be called superstitious was reduced. Since by the Russian Orthodox tradition kenoticism was strong—the spirit of humility and of non-resistance to evil—the Church's teaching still stressed that characteristic. The liturgy was also a means of instruction. It contained many passages from the Bible, and although it was in Slavonic, that language was less removed from the vernacular than was Latin from French or Italian. Those who listened to it learned many of the prayers. In 1956 foreign visitors were told that religious instruction was being given by parish priests in the liturgy, the creed, and the prayers to both adults and children in churches and in a special type of service on Sunday afternoons, and that religious teaching could now be conducted by priests for children in their homes if the parents approved.[64]

THE PERSISTENCE OF CHRISTIAN BODIES OUTSIDE THE RUSSIAN ORTHODOX CHURCH

Some Christian bodies and movements which dissented from the Russian Orthodox Church persisted, and at least one, the All-Union Federation of Baptists and Evangelicals, had a marked growth. For the supervision of all religious bodies other than the Orthodox the Soviet government set up an office parallel to the Council for the Orthodox Church. Information reaching the outside world was at best fragmentary. In 1957 the Old Believers were known to have a church in Moscow.[65] The branch of the Old Believers which had priests was said to be in process of integration with the Patriarchal Church, but little information could be obtained about the priestless.[66] In 1955 several branches of the Old Believers were reported to exist and to be chiefly in Central Russia, Moscow, Moldavia, Latvia, and Lithuania. In a volume of the Soviet Encyclopaedia published in 1948 several sects were listed which bore the name

[63] For some of the sermons see Alexius, *Sermons, Speeches, Pastoral Letters, Articles* (all in Russian, 3 vols., covering 1941–1957, Moscow, The Moscow Patriarchate, 1948, 1954, 1957); Nicolas, *Sermons,* translated into French by Nicolas Poltoratsley and Georges Kaminka (Paris, Éditions de l'Église Orthodoxe Patriarcale Russe, 1956). See reviews of the above in *The Ecumenical Review,* Vol. X, pp. 461–473.

[64] *The New York Times,* March 15, 1956.

[65] *Sobornost,* Winter, 1957–1958, p. 524.

[66] Paul B. Anderson to the author, April, 1956.

of Red Dragon, because they identified the Soviet regime with the red dragon mentioned in Revelation XII:3-9. Some of their number refused to touch Soviet newspapers or Soviet money, others boycotted the Soviet authorities and all who supported them, and still others held that a Messiah would liberate the world from the Communist Anti-Christ.[67] We have noted the continuation of Lutherans in Estonia and Latvia. Apart from them, in 1959 in the entire U.S.S.R. only two Lutheran churches were officially recognized by the government.[68] The other Lutheran churches had been forcibly dissolved in 1938 and their members were imprisoned or scattered over the country, but reports reaching *Hilfswerk* in West Germany in 1958 indicated that several thousand Lutherans were in Siberia and had been able to practice their faith freely since an amnesty granted in 1955. But they could not organize churches. They held their services in private homes and cellars and were allowed to receive Bibles and other religious literature sent them by *Hilfswerk*.[69] The Armenians in the U.S.S.R. were mostly south of the Caucasus, where we shall see them in the next volume, but a few were in European Russia and in 1957 an Armenian church existed in Moscow.[70] The Mennonites, dating from settlements in tsarist days, numbered several thousand. Meeting in homes and with few if any houses of worship, they were permitted and attracted little public attention.[71] The same seems to have been true of the Seventh Day Adventists. The Plymouth Brethren were reported to have a number of groups, also convening privately. They appear to have been a continuation of what was begun by Lord Radstock in the 1870's.[72] The Mennonites, Seventh Day Adventists, and Plymouth Brethren were incorporated into the All-Union Federation of Baptists and Evangelicals. The same was true of the Pentecostals, of whom about 400 congregations were said to exist in 1945. The Free Christians were also included—a movement in the Carpathian Ukraine. Indeed, the Baptist-Evangelical groups seem to have been strongest in the Ukraine. Jehovah's Witnesses were treated as counter-revolutionaries and the few Mormons were sent to prison camps for hard labour.

The largest movement of Protestant background was that of the Baptists and Evangelicals. It was of nineteenth-century origin and traced its history to several influences—Mennonite, Stundist, Molokan, Plymouth Brethren, and German Baptist. The various currents which entered into it had not fully

---

[67] *Sobornost*, Summer, 1955, pp. 243, 252, 253.

[68] *Ecumenical News Service*, April 17, 1959.

[69] *The New York Times*, January 1, 1959.

[70] *Sobornost*, Winter, 1957–1958, p. 524.

[71] On the Mennonites in the early years of Communist rule see T. O. Hylkema, *De Geschiedenis van de Doopsgezinde Gemeenten in Rusland in de oorlogs- en Revolutiejaren 1914 tot 1920* (Steenwijk, Commissie voor Buitenlandsche Nooden van de Doopsgezinden in Nederland, no date, pp. 103), *passim*.

[72] Volume II, pp. 176, 177, 473.

coalesced by 1914.[73] They constituted a problem for the Communists. Some were pacifists and the government permitted alternative service in a labour army. However, later their official spokesmen found Scriptural basis for departing from strict pacifism. In the early days of collective farms Baptists and Evangelicals founded ones with Biblical names, introduced a more egalitarian programme than did the state enterprises, and morally and in economic achievement outdistanced the latter. For ideological reasons in the 1920's the state closed most of them on the ground that they were not in accord with the Marxist principle of class struggle.

The All-Union Federation of Baptists and Evangelicals was created largely at the instance of the government (1944). The step paralleled the permission given by the state to the Orthodox to elect a patriarch. Presumably it was taken for much the same purpose, namely, to bring under a single official or set of officials movements which the government could not easily exterminate and found it the part of prudence to tolerate in such fashion that they could not be actually hostile to the objectives of the Soviets. In 1955 the All-Union Federation had under its jurisdiction about 5,000 congregations scattered over the vast reaches of the U.S.S.R. from the Baltic to Sakhalin and from Leningrad and Moscow to Transcaucasia. It claimed to have 500,000 adult baptized members and to exert an influence over at least 3,000,000. It had no paid ministry. In 1951 the church in Moscow was reported to have 4,000 members and since its building seated only 1,500, five services were held weekly. The services were deeply devotional with prayers and addresses interspersed with singing and with anthems by a choir. In the first half of 1951 about 350 applied for membership in the Moscow church, approximately a third of them young people. Less than half were accepted and the rest were held for further examination. Youth organizations and Sunday Schools were forbidden, and religious education was given in the homes and through attendance at the regular public services.

Partly to undercut the suspicion that they were an infiltration of Western influence, the Baptist-Evangelicals claimed as their spiritual ancestors the Molokans, an indigenous religious movement, and stressed their Slavic heritage from Jan Hus and Peter Chelchitsky. Their congregations appear to have had more women than men and not a large proportion of youths. They were strongly Biblical and emphasized high moral standards. They encouraged their members to be diligent in their daily labour, thus to "glorify our Lord and Saviour through our good deeds." Many of the members were awarded medals for "excellence of labour" and "labour prowess." In 1947 they were

---

[73] Volume II, p. 473.

zealous participants in the Soviet regime's programme of tree-planting, declaring that thus they were performing a Christian duty.[74]

CONTACTS INCREASE BETWEEN THE CHRISTIANS OF THE U.S.S.R.
AND THE CHRISTIANS OF THE WEST

Following World War II contacts were established between the Christians in the U.S.S.R. and the Christians of the West. The initiative was from the latter but would have been frustrated had it not been for the coöperation of the Christians of Russia and the permission of the Soviet government. Contacts mounted as the years passed. So numerous were they that we can take the space to mention only a few. In 1951 a small group of English Quakers spent several days in Russia, chiefly with the object of promoting peace. They had conferences with government officials but took the occasion to see something of the churches.[75] In 1956 the Anglicans sent a theological deputation headed by the Archbishop of York. It discussed with the Russian Orthodox their points of agreement and disagreement. Delegations came from the Baptist World Alliance and from the Baptists of the United States to visit their fellow believers. In 1956 a return visit was made by Russian Baptists to the Baptists of the United States. In March, 1956, a deputation from the National Council of Churches in the U.S.A. went to Russia. A few weeks later a group came from Russia to the United States, representing the Orthodox Church, the Armenian Church, the Lutherans, and the Baptists.[76] In December, 1959, representatives of the World Council of Churches went to Russia. They met with the Moscow Patriarchate, the Lutheran Archbishops of Latvia and Estonia, Baptist leaders, and the Supreme Catholicos of the Armenian Church.[77] They may have succeeded in allaying the resentment of the Russian Orthodox Church at what the latter charged as support of the Western imperialism and at the admission of the Greek Orthodox Church to membership in the World Council of Churches without previous consultation with the Moscow Patriarchate in disregard of the claims of that office to leadership in the family of Orthodox Churches. Slowly misunderstandings were being removed and better relations were being created. In 1961 the Russian Orthodox Church applied for membership in the World Council of Churches.

THE RUSSIANS OF THE DISPERSION

The civil wars through which the Communists achieved their mastery of

[74] *Sobornost*, Summer, 1955, pp. 243–256; Lonsdale, *Quakers Visit Russia*, p. 25.
[75] Lonsdale, *op. cit., passim.*
[76] *The Christian Century*, Vol. LXXIII, pp. 480–482, 733, 742, 743, 751 (April 18, June 13, June 20, 1956); Jackson, *The Eternal Flame, passim.*
[77] *Ecumenical Press Service*, December 22, 1959.

Russia were accompanied and followed by the exodus of hundreds of thousands of the defeated, both adherents of the tsarist regime and of the temporary government. They included many members of the churches of Russia. Some found refuge in South America and groups of both Baptists and Old Believers settled there. We have noted the creation of the Karlovtsi Synod in Jugoslavia. The majority sought asylum in Western Europe. There the main centre of the Orthodox was in France. Here, in Paris, the Orthodox Theological Institute, popularly known as the St. Sergius Theological Academy, was set up. It was made possible by financial assistance from North America and by gifts from various sources in England. In the course of time the chief financial load was carried by the World Council of Churches and the Episcopal church of the United States.[78] Paris was the eventual location of the YMCA Press, which found a home in that city in 1924. Supported by the North American YMCA's, from it issued the cream of Russian Christian literature for which there was no room in the U.S.S.R. It was also the chief focal point for almost all currents in Russian Orthodox thought. Its editors became acquainted with nearly every religious thinker in the Russian Orthodox Church and later made contact with most of the scholars in the other autocephalous Orthodox Churches. It printed new editions of commonly used Orthodox service books and furthered Orthodox religious education. Through translations of its publications into Western languages it helped to acquaint the Western world with the richness of Russian Orthodox thought.[79] In France, too, a vigorous Orthodox Student Christian Movement arose. Among other achievements, in 1959 Syndesmus, the international organization of Eastern Orthodox youth, founded a Pan-Orthodox missionary society.[80] Other centres of Russian Orthodox *émigrés* were in the Netherlands: in the 1950's congregations existed in The Hague and Rotterdam. They were also in England and Germany.[81]

INDIAN SUMMER IN RUSSIAN THEOLOGICAL THOUGHT

We have hinted at the remarkable religious awakening among the Russian intelligentsia on the eve of 1914.[82] In the intense and varied ferment in Russian thought which was rising when it was overwhelmed by World War I, the revolution, and the Communist victory were several first-class minds who had come to the Christian faith after a period of doubt and negation. Familiar with the many intellectual and social currents irrupting from the West, they

---

[78] Donald A. Lowrie, *Saint Sergius in Paris. The Orthodox Theological Institute* (New York, The Macmillan Co., preface 1951, pp. ix, 119), *passim*.
[79] Latourette, *World Service*, pp. 377, 378.
[80] *Ecumenical Press Service*, April 17, 1959.
[81] *Novoe Missionerskoe Obozrenie*, Nos. 11–12 (12–13), 1957.
[82] Volume II, pp. 463, 464.

were seeking to think through the Orthodox heritage in ways which would take cognizance of them.

The storm of revolution swept most of these thinkers into the dust-heap. The majority perished, either by natural death hastened by the privations of the times or forcibly liquidated by execution, imprisonment, or hard labour. Under the Soviet government thought which did not conform to the ideology of the leaders was promptly nipped in the bud and all who hoped for advancement were constrained to conform to the line laid down by the new masters.

However, a few who had dared to think boldly were silenced or banished, or managed to escape to the West and there continued to write. Theirs was an Indian-summer blooming which reflected some of the brilliance of the passing age and had in it a foretaste of the winter which was soon to end it. Like their contemporaries in the West they sought to maintain their integrity as the world they had known toppled about them. Out of that traumatic experience they continued their struggle with spiritual and mental agony. Some of their books were translated into Western languages and had a wide circulation among those who were seeking answers in the revolutionary age.

Serge Nikolayevich Shestov (1866–1938) was one of those whose works were put into French, German, and English. Although several of them had been written before 1914, for the most part the translations were made after World War I and even after World War II. The primary interest of Shestov was philosophy, and among his earlier works were studies of Nietzsche, Tolstoy, and Dostoyevsky. He later wrote on Kierkegaard and existentialism. His literary style was marked by clarity, a lack of affectation, and a combination of elegance and simplicity. His dominant concern was religious and he represented the Russian conflict with secularism. Suffering from no religious doubts and believing firmly in revelation, he fought rationalism, whether in Christian theology or in other systems, ancient and modern. He had great respect for Pascal, Plato, Plotinus, and Spinoza, even when he differed from them. He held that the basic question of life was whether God exists, viewed man as being surrounded by mystery, and maintained that the function of philosophy was to teach man to live in uncertainty. Yet he accepted the Old and New Testaments and Christian revelation and held that faith required the construction of a philosophy which took as its basic conviction the existence of God.[83]

Leo Platonovich Karsavin, born in 1882, who was lost sight of by the West when he was obscured by the "iron curtain," wrote especially on Western European history. Influenced by Solovyev and the Slavophiles, he had little but scorn for the West and, elaborating a philosophy of history, declared that

[83] Zenkovsky, *A History of Russian Philosophy,* Vol. II, pp. 780–791.

it must be Orthodox. He held that faith is the basis of knowledge, but defended rationality and freedom in theology.[84]

Paul Aleksandrovich Florenski, born in 1882, was long imprisoned and then exiled by the Soviet government, eventually to Siberia, and presumably perished there. Early a specialist in mathematics, after graduating from the university, instead of preparing for a professorship in that subject he entered the Moscow Theological Academy and joined with others in forming the Union of Christian Struggle, which had as its object the re-making of the social order. He became a priest, abandoned his radical social views, and put forth a theological thesis which was congenial to the romantic and mystical tendencies in much of Russian society and criticized Western philosophy as being too rationalistic. He emphasized personal religious experience and particularly the experience of the soul of the people. He declared that he did not know whether truth exists but felt that he could not live without it. He regarded the cosmos as a living whole and saw a unity behind the visible diversity of created being. Following Solovyev he viewed Sophia (Holy Wisdom) as the mystical basis of the cosmos. He quoted extensively from the Church Fathers and sought from them support for his position of a total unity.[85]

Serge Nikolayevich Bulgakov (1871-1944), like Florenski, was a priest, but he had a different history. The son of a priest, at the age of thirteen he entered a theological seminary. Rebelling against the enforced piety of that institution, he gave up his faith, for a time was a nihilist, left the seminary, and as a student in Moscow University was an ardent Marxist. His research led him to give up Marxism as out of accord with economic facts. He became a Social Democrat and for five years held a chair of political economy. Still unsatisfied and seeking, partly under the influence of Solovyev he turned from materialism to idealism and moved towards a Christian world view. He became an intimate of Florenski and was one of the circle who marked a religious renaissance among the intellectuals. By the end of World War I his spiritual pilgrimage had led him from philosophy to theology. In 1918 he was ordained. Expelled by the Soviet government in 1923, for a time he was in Prague and then, in 1925, aided in the founding of what became the Orthodox Theological Institute in Paris. He spent the rest of his life as its dean. To the end he held to the canons of science with their conviction of the reality of the visible world. Philosophically he was a transcendental idealist, stressing the importance of intuition and identifying the latter with faith. He was firm in his adherence to the free search for truth as "the most sacred possession of philosophy." He believed that philosophy had as its unique problem the search for God and God alone. His philosophy entered into his theology. He sought

[84] *Ibid.*, pp. 843-852.
[85] *Ibid.*, pp. 875-890.

and found a path through the contemporary world to Orthodoxy. To him Sophia—which he derived from Solovyev—stood between the Absolute and the cosmos, a kind of third being. He viewed the cosmos as a living, animate whole and maintained that the world-soul contains all things in itself and unites the whole. He said that the creation of the world was an act of God in each of His hypostases—and he viewed Sophia as a fourth hypostasis. Sin was the actualization of nothingness. He was convinced that man has full autonomy and freedom and as such actualizes nothingness, but that he also collaborates with God in creation.[86]

In His creation of the world, Bulgakov taught, God revealed His wisdom and reflected in it His image. The fullness of that image is seen in man. Man, having God's image, is godlike and God is manlike. The relation between God and man, Godmanhood, is the image of God in Himself or His holy Sophia. Sophia has two kinds of revelation, being in God as His divine life and glory, and being the creation in man and through him in the world. Sophia, Godmanhood, is the foundation for the incarnation. Jesus Christ united the two natures, divine and human, in His own person, not as two alien natures but as two kinds of existence of the same Sophia of God, of the Uncreated and the created. He is the true Godman and in His humanity manhood has its complete achievement. The humanity was overshadowed by the Holy Spirit. The incarnation can be understood only in the light of redemption as the restoration of fallen man and as the achievement of creation. Christ vanquished the world and therefore the world has become the Church, which is His body. The Church is called to new tasks, to new achievements, and has as its general task the realization of the true Godmanhood. The end of the world is the inscrutable will of God and is also an end to be prepared for and reached by human history. Christian humanism is the answer to the atheistic humanism of Communism. The Church must penetrate the whole of life. Here is a Christian communism, a Christian socialism. The kingdom of Christ has to be won by common work, the creative effort of mankind as well as the creative work of God. This was Bulgakov's philosophy of history.[87]

In a more comprehensive and yet summary view of Christian theology, Bulgakov spoke of revelation as taking for granted the existence of something which is being disclosed, a mystery which manifests itself to us. Mystery remains above human understanding, can never be exhausted by reason, and can never be penetrated by logical thought. In revelation the transcendent discloses itself but is not exhausted by that disclosure. Revelation is a divine-human

---

[86] *Ibid.*, pp. 890–916.
[87] Sergius Bulgakoff, *Social Teaching in Modern Russian Orthodox Theology* (Evanston, Ill., Seabury-Western Theological Seminary, 1934, pp. 28), *passim.*

communion, an act of God within man. It is going on all the time. It will never stop and is life eternal. Christ revealed God in a new way. There exists a natural revelation of God. It goes on in nature and in the moral law in man. But it has been obscured by original sin. Original sin was a barrier but not an insuperable barrier, and a true knowledge of God was gradually implanted in and deepened in the chosen people. The incarnation and Pentecost were further steps in that revelation. Revelation constitutes the history of mankind in its surrender to God. Here is tradition and the need for it. Holy Scripture and Holy Tradition are not two forms of revelation but are features of the whole. Tradition is the life of God through the life of the Church. The Church, the body of Christ, safeguards the truth and bears witness to it. The Church is not merely an organism but is also an organization and as such is necessarily hierarchical. Revelation is not complete, but history is continually expanding revelation. The Church must overcome her tendency to ascetic and eschatological indifferentism in the face of the mounting secularization of life. The whole of life must belong to her and be sanctified by her. The second coming of Christ, the *parousia,* will constitute the revelation which will complete our aeon.[88]

Nicolai Berdyaev (1874–1948) exerted a much wider influence than did any other Russian theologian in the half-century after 1914, partly because of the power of his thought and partly because of the number of books which poured from his prolific pen and were translated into several European languages.[89] Born of aristocratic stock, with Russian, French, Tatar, Polish, and Lithuanian ancestors, Berdyaev was reared in Kiev in a partially impoverished family. With an almost complete absence of early religious teaching, with no boy companions, self-disciplined but resentful of external discipline, in his youth and to the end of his days Berdyaev was an individualist, committed to personal

---

[88] Sergius Bulkagoff in John Baillie and Hugh Martin, editors, *Revelation* (London, Faber and Faber, 1937, pp. xxiv, 312), pp. 125–180.

[89] For lives of Berdyaev see Matthew Spinka, *Nicolas Berdyaev, Captive of Freedom* (Philadelphia, The Westminster Press, 1950, pp. 220), and Donald A. Lowrie, *Rebellious Prophet. A Life of Nicolai Berdyaev* (New York, Harper & Brothers, 1960, pp. x, 310). For an autobiography see Nicolas Berdyaev, *Dream and Reality. An Essay in Autobiography,* translated by Katherine Lampert (New York, The Macmillan Co., 1951, pp. xv, 332). Among Berdyaev's many works were *The Destiny of Man* (New York, Charles Scribner's Sons, 1937, pp. vi, 377); *Dostoievsky, an Interpretation,* translated by Donald Attwater (New York, Sheed and Ward, 1934, pp. 227); *The End of Our Time, together with an Essay on the General Line of Soviet Philosophy* (New York, Sheed and Ward, 1933, pp. 258); *Freedom and the Spirit,* translated by Oliver Fielding Clarke (New York, Charles Scribner's Sons, 1935, pp. xix, 361); *The Meaning of History,* translated by George Reavey (New York, Charles Scribner's Sons, 1936, pp. x, 224); *Spirit and Reality,* translated by George Reavey (New York, Charles Scribner's Sons, 1939, pp. 203); *Slavery and Freedom,* translated by R. M. French (London, G. Bles, 1943, pp. 268); *The Divine and the Human,* translated by R. M. French (London, G. Bles, 1949, pp. ix, 204); *The Beginning and the End,* translated by R. M. French (London, G. Bles, 1952, pp. xi, 256); *Truth and Revelation,* translated by R. M. French (London, G. Bles, 1953, pp. 156); *The Meaning of the Creative Act,* translated by Donald A. Lowrie (New York, Harper & Brothers, 1955, pp. 344).

liberty. In the university he had an intellectual awakening, was for a time attracted by Marxism but gave it up, associated with the Social Democrats, and with a group of them was arrested, imprisoned, and exiled to a small city in the North. There he began writing. After his release he was for a time in Kiev and in Heidelberg. He spent many months in St. Petersburg in the intellectual circles which were throbbing with discussions of a wide variety of ideas. At one time or another he was influenced by Kant, Ibsen, Nietzsche, Plato, and Kierkegaard. He came in contact with Bulgakov and others of the latter's circle and they helped him to see that Christianity did not run counter to his concern for social conditions. By the summer of 1907 he was well on the way to becoming a Christian and believed that in doing so he had not ceased to believe in man, his dignity and creative freedom, but was seeking a deeper and surer basis for that faith. He read some of the Church Fathers and in Dostoyevsky's Christ of the legend of the grand inquisitor found the Christ Whom he accepted, the Christ of the free spirit. He had a period in Paris and on returning went to Moscow where he was again in touch with Bulgakov and the others of the group who were loyal to Orthodoxy. There in addition to the Church Fathers he read the mystics Boehme and Tauler. He steeped himself in the writings of Solovyev. While not accepting all the dogmas or conforming to the hierarchy of the Russian Orthodox Church, he held to the Eucharistic, Trinitarian, and Christological convictions of Orthodoxy. When the Communist flood overwhelmed Russia, he was frankly a member of the Orthodox Church and thereafter never wavered from that allegiance. Banished in 1922, he first went to Berlin and then, assisted by the North American YMCA, to Paris. There he became editor-in-chief of the YMCA Press and in that capacity was supported by the North American YMCA. He wrote prodigiously and led a disciplined life of devotion, nourished by the Bible and the Orthodox prayer book. He had contacts with Maritain and Gilson and assisted the Russian Student Christian Movement and the Orthodox Theological Institute. Although in touch with thousands and brilliant in conversation, he remained essentially a lonely man.

As a philosopher, Berdyaev classed himself as an existentialist. He recognized inconsistencies in his thought but regarded them as expressions of spiritual conflict, of contradictions which lie at the very heart of existence. Berdyaev has been called a Gnostic, but a Gnostic who was essentially Christian. He made much of freedom, a position reinforced by his individualism. He held that true existence is the freedom of non-being. To him, the primary fact was not *being,* which he regarded as enslavement, but *non-being.* He believed that God, an inexpressible mystery and not an object of knowledge, is eternally born out of non-being and becomes super-being without becoming being. Man was created by God and is primarily spirit. Man possesses some-

thing of God. God becomes man and man becomes God. The two are inter-
dependent and are from the same uncreated substance. Creation is the
objectivization of primary substance and therefore a corruption. This, he said,
is evil. Here was a Gnostic. But, unlike the Gnostics, Berdyaev had a strong
sense of history.

Berdyaev found in the God-man the meaning of life. He maintained that all
men participated in the work of Christ. He thought of God as love even before
the foundation of the world and believed that He was universally incarnated
before Christ came in the flesh. He viewed God as not static, but as active, as
self-sacrificing love which is always involved in tragedy. Tragedy arises from
the freedom of man and from the fact that God does not curb that freedom.
As self-sacrificing love, God suffers. The spirit of evil, Berdyaev held, and
not God, rules the world. He saw man as enslaved by himself, individualism,
nature, society, civilization, cultural values, the state, especially the totalitarian
state, nationalism, war, aristocracy, the bourgeois spirit with its emphasis on
property and money, the lure of revolution, utopianism, collectivism, and
aestheticism. Redemption, he contended, is the restoration of freedom and
emancipation from slavery to objectivization. Berdyaev's fundamental ethical
principle was personalism, based on the conviction that the entire world is
nothing compared with a single person. He condemned collectivist socialism
but advocated a personalist socialism which while obtaining bread for all men
would do so without curtailing freedom. Man, personality, freedom, creative-
ness, the eschatological-messianic resolution of two worlds—the worlds of objectivization and subjectivization—were Berdyaev's main themes.

Berdyaev's eschatology was bound up with his hope of the attainment of
perfect freedom, a transformation of the world by de-objectivization. As he
watched the progress of the Russian revolution he became less hopeful, but he
held that in realizing de-objectivization the Russian people had a unique role,
for they had inherited the true Messianic hope. He believed that mankind was
now on the edge of a new era, the era of the Spirit, an era which is to come
within history. As a prophet he looked on history in the light of God's eternal
purpose, and although civilization and modern culture were threatened by
bankruptcy, he was not discouraged. Like Paul in viewing the whole creation
as awaiting the revelation of man's sonship to God, Berdyaev looked forward
to the redemption of all creation, to the eventual restoration to perfection of
every creature and of all nature. But he held that men should not sit passively
by, waiting for God to work the change, but should assert their creative capacities, directing all the powers of their spirits towards bringing the Kingdom
of God to realization in the world.

In both Bulgakov and Berdyaev something akin to the optimism in several
Protestant circles in the late nineteenth century was seen, but it was in a dis-

tinctively Orthodox form. Nor did they, in spite of the violent destruction of the culture in which they had been reared, retreat into an other-worldly eschatology, with despair of realizing the Kingdom of God in history, as did many Protestants in the West. They were convinced that God rules and because it comes through His *kenosis,* His self-emptying and suffering, His triumph is sure. Men, through the Church, can and must have a part in that creative victory.

SUMMARY

To many who attempted to view the record objectively, the half-century which was introduced by the fateful summer of 1914 seemed to be witnessing the approaching death of Christianity in Russia. The vast majority of Russian Christians of tsarist days were communicants of the Orthodox Church. That church had apparently been inseparable from the regime which was destroyed by the explosions accompanying World War I. It had been dominated by the state and in the latter half of the nineteenth century had been used as a bulwark against the tides of the revolutionary age which were surging in the West. The great Pobedonostsev had viewed those tides as a threat not only to the Russian way of life but also to all civilization. Those committed to the tides regarded the Church as the enemy of all they hoped to achieve. Some had been reared in the Church and had rebelled against it. Joseph Stalin, for example, had had his formal education in an Orthodox seminary in his native Georgia and had been dismissed from it at the age of seventeen for "unreliability and lack of a religious vocation." The Orthodox Church appeared also to be handicapped in facing the revolutionary age by its form of piety—its emphasis upon attendance at its services and upon a passive non-resistance symbolized by *kenosis* idealized in its *startsi,* or elders, men who had retreated from the world. The forms of Christianity which dissented from the official church seemed to hold out even less hope, for at best they were tolerated minorities.

The regime which succeeded in mastering Russia embodied many of the forces which had their origin in the West and were either directly or indirectly anti-Christian. They included Marxism, aggressively anti-religious, the religiously sceptical attitudes associated with Western science, and the industrialization which in the West was undercutting the Church and the traditional expressions of Christianity. By 1961 they appeared to be justifying the claims made for them by the improvement of the physical standards of living of the masses and in bringing the forces of nature into subjection to man through the harnessing of the atom and the spectacular penetration of outer space. Although theoretically granting freedom for religious services for the cult, the Soviet government permitted and at times encouraged anti-religious propaganda and stressed atheism in its education. Moreover, although frankly anti-religious in contrast with the ostensibly Christian tsarist regime which it displaced, organizationally it brought the external relationships of the churches, both Orthodox and dissenting, quite as fully under its control as had that regime and induced them, especially the Orthodox Church, to be a tool in its aspirations in international affairs.

But by a contrast even more marked than that which we have seen in Western Europe, Christianity survived in Russia and by 1961 was recovering from the blows dealt it in the initial impact of the revolutionary forces of the West. The Russian Orthodox Church enrolled a substantial minority of the population. So far as figures could be obtained, a large percentage, perhaps a majority, of the infants of Orthodox ancestry were baptized. Church buildings were fewer than in 1914 but were filled and new ones were being erected. No dearth was seen of young men preparing to enter the priesthood. In contrast with pre-1914 years when most of the clergy were sons of priests, the postulants for the priesthood were from several different social classes and industrial occupations and secular professions. Of the dissenting bodies the largest was that into which the Baptists and Evangelicals had come together at the behest of the government and into which some other kindred groups had been merged. It was growing rapidly, recruited from the young as well as from the middle aged and elderly. How long the growth of the Orthodox and the Baptists-Evangelicals would continue no one could safely predict. If the Soviet government instituted or encouraged a vigorous anti-religious campaign, losses might again be experienced. The churches could not mix in politics or conduct social programmes but were compelled to confine themselves to worship and to such forms of religious instruction as were permitted by the state. Only when they reinforced Soviet international policies, such as the Communist-inspired forms of the campaign for peace or the support of Russian nationalism, as in World War II, could they express themselves on political issues. Yet even here they were no more subservient to the state than they had been in the tsarist days.

An interesting comparison could be made between the position of the churches in Russia and in Western Europe. In Western Europe the churches were much freer to express convictions on social, moral, economic, and political issues. But that had been true at least as far back as the nineteenth century. They still had a greater share in education and in shaping youth than did the Russian churches. They were far more actively engaged in spreading the faith throughout the world, but that had been the case before 1914. So far as statistics could be obtained, however, in proportion to the population of Christian ancestry attendance at church services in 1961 was higher in Russia than in Sweden or Denmark and in parts of France, especially in the cities, and may even have been higher than among the Protestant elements in England. It was certainly higher in Moscow than in Copenhagen, Stockholm, Hamburg, Berlin, and Paris. In Western Europe most of the forces working against Christianity were not as outspokenly opposed to the faith as in Russia. With some exceptions, they were not as markedly so as in the nineteenth century, and in several regions the Church was still espoused by the state. But in Western Europe corrosive currents associated with the revolutionary age were almost if not quite as potent as in Russia. Here is a thought-provoking parallel for the appraisal of the effect of the revolutionary age on Christianity and of the vitality of the faith.

CHAPTER XX

The Stormy Course of Christianity in Greece and the Balkan Countries

I N THE nineteenth century the Orthodox Churches in Greece and the Balkans had been freed from the domination of the Moslem Turks and, winning their independence of the alien Phanariots by whom they had been exploited during the Turkish days, had become autocephalous with decreasing subordination to the Ecumenical Patriarch. Gradually, and in varying degrees, their life had improved. Although some other branches of the faith were represented by minorities, the Orthodox Churches were folk churches, in Greece and most of the Balkan countries enrolling the large majority of the population and closely associated with the rising tides of nationalism.[1]

From the eve of 1914 and through the half-century which followed, the region was disturbed by wars and foreign invasions. In 1912 Bulgaria, Serbia, Greece, and Montenegro attacked Turkey, weakened by a war with Italy. They were victorious, and Turkey was compelled to yield all its European territory except Constantinople, Eastern Thrace and a small section bordering the Dardanelles. The Allies fell to fighting over the division of the spoils, Rumania joined in the fray, and the Turks entered the resulting war in an attempt to recoup their losses. The region had scarcely settled down into an uneasy peace when it was engulfed in World War I. That war arose out of the attack of Austro-Hungary on Serbia. Before it was terminated, Bulgaria, Rumania, Greece, and Turkey were sucked into the maelstrom. As an aftermath of World War I Greece and Turkey fought (1921–1923) and as a sequel an "exchange" of populations transferred more than a half-million Greeks from Asia Minor to Greece and freed Greece from all but a small minority of Turks. Scarcely two decades of troubled peace had elapsed when World War II brought fresh turbulence. Italy and then Germany invaded Greece, Jugoslavia was overrun by the Germans, Bulgaria was brought under German tutelage, and Rumania suffered losses of territory while under German occupation. Although in the peace settlement after World War II Rumania regained Tran-

[1] Volume II, pp. 479–492.

sylvania, it was burdened by reparations and lost territory to Russia and Bulgaria. In the 1940's Albania, Bulgaria, and Rumania were drawn into the Russian sphere by the erection of Communist governments with the aid of Russian troops. Jugoslavia went Communist, but its dictator, Tito, eventually broke with Moscow. Under these circumstances, Christianity could not but have a troubled course. The churches would do well to survive and retain some semblance of life.

CONTINUED RECOVERY IN DISTRAUGHT GREECE

In spite of wars, domestic political unrest, and foreign invasions which brought turmoil and suffering, in Greece the Orthodox Church continued the recovery which had been begun in the nineteenth century.[2] During the long years of subjection to the Turk, it had been a symbol and bond of Greek nationalism, and it was still intimately associated with the life of the people. The census of 1951 recorded that of the total population of 7,632,801, 7,472,559 were members. Most of the remainder were Moslems.[3] The Greek Orthodox Church was augmented by the annexations which followed the wars of the fore part of the century. They swelled the number of metropolitanates by thirty-four as against the thirty-three which had previously been under the Greek flag. By an agreement of 1929 with the Ecumenical Patriarchate, to which they had previously been subject, the additional metropolitanates were transferred provisionally to the Holy Synod of Greece for administrative purposes.[4] Part of the numerical gain was also from about 1,500,000 who entered the country following World War I. Approximately 1,250,000 of them were Greeks from Asia Minor, and others were from Bulgaria and the U.S.S.R.

The Church's problem was complicated not only by the annexations and the refugees, but also by political disturbances. The political factors were serious during the Balkan Wars which immediately preceded World War I and during World War I and its aftermath. They were made particularly acute by World War II. The Italian onslaught (1940), although the Greek armies drove out the invaders, was destructive, and the German incursion (1941), reinforced by Bulgars and Italians, was more so. Greek guerrillas harried the occupation forces but were almost as destructive as the latter. Famine stalked the land. The Greek guerrillas and the British drove out the Germans in 1944, but five years of civil strife followed in which government troops fought Communist guerrillas, who received aid from Russian satellites on the north. Although extensive relief came from the outside, the suffering was severe and recovery was only slowly achieved.

[2] Volume II, pp. 480–482.
[3] *The Statesman's Year Book, 1959*, pp. 1070–1072.
[4] *Ibid.*, p. 1072.

In the invasions and internecine strife of the 1940's the Greek Orthodox Church paid a heavy toll. Scores of priests and monks were killed by the Germans, Bulgars, and Italians, and at least 239 priests and monks were done to death by the Communists. Churches were burned and monasteries were pillaged. Hundreds of clergy fled before the Communists.[5] The bishops and clergy took a prominent share in administering relief, and at a crucial period in 1944 Archbishop Damaskinos became regent for the absent king. But the extensive damage could not be quickly repaired.

A continuing movement making for the regeneration of the Greek Orthodox Church was the Zoë Brotherhood of Theologians. Begun in 1907 or 1911 by an itinerant preacher, Eusebius Matthopoulos,[6] in 1958 it had a membership of approximately 130, about a fourth priests and the remainder laymen, most of them graduates of the theological faculty of the University of Athens. Its members were celibates and took the three monastic vows of chastity, poverty, and obedience but did not bind themselves permanently to them. They accepted the principle of not seeking high office in the Church and refusing if it was offered. Their purpose was to teach the Gospel as interpreted by the Orthodox Church and to penetrate every class with the written and oral word of God. Late in the 1950's their weekly publication, Zoë, had a circulation of more than 170,000, said to be larger than that of any other periodical in the Greek language. A minority of the Zoë Brotherhood were centred in Athens, but the majority were serving as chaplains in the army or elsewhere or were dispersed throughout the country, preaching, training catechists and preachers, supervising seminaries for the rural clergy, hearing confessions, and directing youth movements. In 1958 they conducted over 2,100 out of the approximately 7,800 Sunday Schools in Greece. Once a year the Brotherhood gathered for a retreat on the outskirts of Athens. Many movements sprang up which were more or less closely connected with the Zoë Brotherhood. Among them were the Christian Union of Educators (begun in 1947); the Christian Education Panhellenic Union of Parents (founded in 1934); the Christian Union of Working Youth (started in 1945); and the Saint Eunice Christian Union (founded in 1940), through which young women gave themselves to nursing. Eusebia (established in 1938) enlisted unmarried young women who were graduates of university schools and endeavoured to inculcate Christian principles of family life. The School of General Christian Studies (founded in 1943) sought to relate science and the Christian faith and had as an offshoot the Institute of Hygiene and Medical Psychology. A number of other movements, quite independent of Zoë, sprang up in various centres. Among them were *Anaplasis* and *Christianiki*

---

[5] Hammond, *The Waters of Marah,* pp. 94, 95.
[6] Volume II, p. 482.

Enoseis. Several were viewed with suspicion by the more conservative and attempts were made by the latter to restrict their activities. Here and there were extreme liberals. But radical open anti-clericalism was not prominent. A few village school teachers sought to propagate atheistic Communism.[7]

Much effort was made to further the awakening by producing and distributing literature. The Bible was published in many forms and editions. Books of theological and religious content were issued, besides other books on many subjects and with a Christian character. Illustrated novels for children attained a circulation of over one million. A series of popular pamphlets dealing with doctrine, faith, and ethics had an even larger sale. After World War I Zoë took the lead in organizing the Christian Union of Scientists and Professional Men which in 1958 had 1,450 members and in 1938 began a periodical, *Antikes.* In 1945 Zoë founded the Student Christian Union, preceded (1933) by the Academic Social Association. In 1958 its membership numbered 2,400. In the 1950's a liturgical movement was under way to enable the laity to participate intelligently in the Eucharist and to encourage more frequent Communion.[8]

In 1930 the Apostolic Diaconate of the Church of Greece was founded in an effort to coördinate the various movements which were endeavouring to deepen the Christian life of the country. It was directed by a council composed of members of the Holy Synod and of professors of the theological faculty of the University of Athens: the archbishop was president. It had headquarters in Athens and an office in each diocese. It conducted a school for preachers and confessors, furthered evangelistic work, and maintained a printing press which published the official journal of the Church of Greece and periodicals for the clergy and the family.[9]

Some improvement was seen in the education of the clergy. The majority of the latter could do little more than read the service. In 1920 out of about 4,500 priests only 805 had education beyond the elementary schools. The priests in the rural parishes were generally chosen by the elders and presumably had the respect of their flocks. The town clergy were usually not looked upon with as much deference. In the years which followed World War I a number of ecclesiastical seminaries were instituted. Their students were largely parish clergy. The course of study was two years in length and consisted of lectures on the Bible, especially the Gospels, doctrine, catechising, canonical law, the liturgy, training in the ecclesiastical chant, and some rudiments of medicine (for in the rural districts the priest was also the physician). As in the other Eastern Churches, the parish clergy were married and the higher clergy were

[7] Hammond, *op. cit.,* pp. 95, 125–138; Littell and Walz, *Weltkirchen Lexikon,* pp. 515, 516; Demetrios J. Constantelos in *St. Vladimir's Seminary Quarterly,* Vol. III, pp. 11–25 (Spring, 1959).

[8] Hammond, *op. cit.,* pp. 137, 138; *Information Service,* January 15, 1955.

[9] Hammond, *op. cit.,* pp. 138, 139; Eric Baker in *The Christian Century,* Vol. LXXVI, p. 850 (July 22, 1959).

celibate. The latter were educated in the theological faculty of the University of Athens, or in the older days in the theological academy of Halki, near Constantinople, and more recently in the new theological faculty of the University of Salonica. The university course generally required four years. Numbers of theological students went to Western Europe for further training. In spite of the progress that had been made, in the 1950's scores of rural parishes were without resident priests. The deficiency was partly supplied by the bishops. The average diocese had about 85,000 of the faithful and somewhat less than 100 parishes. The bishop generally attempted to visit each parish and to preach (for the local pastor was usually required to confine his preaching to reading a homily sent him by his bishop). In his preaching the bishop might be supplemented by one of his staff and by laymen who went out Sunday by Sunday to deliver sermons.[10]

In spite of the improvement during recent decades, in 1959 it was said that of the 7,000 priests scarcely one in twenty had full university and seminary training, and that of the 800 students in the theological faculties of the Universities of Athens and Salonica not more than 10 per cent. were expecting to be priests; the others would teach. With the rising level of general education, more and more it was true, as in the West, that other leaders of the community were better educated than the clergy.[11]

Theological, historical, and Biblical studies experienced the awakening which was seen in other aspects of the life of the Greek Orthodox Church. Notable contributions were made, although few of them found their way into Western European languages.[12] In 1958 a new constitution (a set of statutes) was adopted for the Orthodox Church of Greece.

Monastic life continued but did not loom as prominently in the consciousness of the average Greek as in earlier centuries. The main centre was still on Mt. Athos, where it had been for hundreds of years. With the spread of Communism and the barrier between Greece and the countries under Communist rule, the number of monks from Russia, Bulgaria, and Serbia fell off sharply and Mt. Athos became mostly Greek in its personnel. Because of its isolation and rugged terrain, it was very little affected by the wars of the twentieth century, but some other monasteries were not as fortunate and were either destroyed or severely damaged.[13]

The non-Orthodox Christians in Greece constituted small minorities. By the census of 1951 they included 28,430 Roman Catholics, 1,205 Armenians, 7,034 Protestants, 1,205 Monophysites, and 4,438 other Christians.[14]

---

10 Hammond, *op. cit.*, pp. 28–30, 141–153.
11 A. C. McGiffert, Jr., in *The Christian Century*, Vol. LXXVI, p. 639 (May 27, 1959).
12 Demetrios J. Constantelos, *Greek Orthodox Theological Scholarship Today* (typescript, 1957).
13 Hammond, *op. cit.*, pp. 83–88.
14 *The Statesman's Year Book, 1959*, pp. 1071, 1072,

JUGOSLAVIA AND ITS ORTHODOX

Jugoslavia emerged as a state from World War I and was composed of territorial elements which had long been distinct politically but which had in common a Slavic ethnic heritage. Into it were brought what had been Serbia, Montenegro, Bosnia-Herzegovina, Croatia-Slovenia, Slovenia, and Dalmatia. Internal conflicts were inevitable and the insistence of the Croats on autonomy was particularly troublesome. In 1941 Jugoslavia was overrun by the Nazis and was soon divided among the Germans, Italians, Hungarians, and Bulgarians into occupation zones. Puppet governments were set up in Serbia and Croatia.

As we have seen,[15] one of the fruits of World War I and associated with the bringing together of the South Slavs in Jugoslavia was the reërection of the Patriarchate of Pech (1920). Under it were united the long-separated fragments of the Orthodox Serbian Church—not only Serbia proper but also the Serbs in Hungary who were under the primate of Karlovac, those in Montenegro (Crnagora) under the Metropolitan of Cetinjeh, those in Bosnia and Herzegovina whose ranking bishop had his seat in Sarajevo, those in Bukovina, and those in the sub-Carpathian region of Czechoslovakia. In 1922 the Ecumenical Patriarch formally recognized the renewed Patriarchate and in doing so surrendered the suzerainty of his see over the Serbian eparchies in Macedonia and Bosnia and Herzegovina. The incumbent of the revived post was known as "his Holiness the Archbishop of Pech, Metropolitan of Belgrade and Karlovac, Serbian Patriarch" and had his residence in Belgrade.[16] During the brief years of relative peace some signs of fresh life were seen in the Orthodox Church. For example, in the 1920's Bishop Nicolai Velimirovitch led a peasant Christian movement which appeared to offer promise.[17]

World War II was a rude interruption. The foreign invaders and the conflicts between the domestic aspirants for power and among the different nationalities brought intense suffering. The Ustachi (Ustaši), Croatians, sought to exterminate the Serbs in Croatia or to force them to submit to the Roman Catholic Church. About 600,000 Serbs were said to have been killed. Hungarian troops joined in the massacres. Many priests were put to death. Hundreds of churches and other ecclesiastical buildings were destroyed.[18]

Under the Communist government set up by Tito Church and state were separated and although it occasionally gave financial help the latter confiscated much of the Church's property. In the schools and universities, as was to be expected under a Communist regime, materialism was taught and Christianity was declared to be outworn. Although some of the intelligentsia were dissatis-

---

[15] Volume II, pp. 484–487.
[16] Attwater, *The Christian Churches of the East*, Vol. II, p. 98.
[17] Donald A. Lowrie, in a mimeographed letter from Belgrade, December 9, 1930.
[18] Attwater, *op. cit.*, p. 98; *St. Vladimir's Seminary Quarterly*, Vol. II, No. 4, p. 39 (Fall, 1958).

fied with Communism and were open-minded towards Christianity, they were grossly ignorant of it.

Under these adverse circumstances the Orthodox Church had to be reconstructed. It suffered from no great shortage of clergy, but recruits for the priesthood were largely from the rural districts and had little of the kind of education which prepared them to meet the new challenges. Yet here and there were leaders who sought to bring about a revival. Some of them had been in England and directed their efforts chiefly against the barren formality in the religious life.[19] Bishop Nicolai, who lived into the 1950's, wrote a series of homilies centring about the prologue to the Gospel of John which were designed for readers who had little knowledge of the faith as well as for theologians.[20]

At times the leadership of the Orthodox Church stood out against Tito. In 1946 a pastoral letter of the Holy Synod protested against the curtailment of religious instruction, the secularization of marriage, and the materialistic propaganda of the state. In 1948 Bishop Barnabas of Sarajevo was put on trial for saying publicly that the enemies of God would perish. A minority of the priests sided with the government and sought to induce their fellow clergy to join the professional "union of priests." They had an organization which was part of the national front and subject to the Communist Party. Yet they seem not to have won the main body of the clergy.[21]

During some of the difficult years the Orthodox Church had able leadership in the person of him whose monastic name was Vikentije (1890–1958). Born in a village, educated in the theological faculty of Belgrade University, he became a monk in 1917 and was consecrated deacon in that year. He had extensive experience as an administrator, part of the time as a bishop, and was markedly successful in rehabilitating church life in a diocese which had suffered severely from the German and Hungarian invaders. In 1950 he was elected patriarch and in that post showed skill in furthering the settlement of thorny problems in the relations of Church and state, complicated as they were by suspicion and misunderstanding on both sides.[22]

In the main the Orthodox Church in Jugoslavia suffered more from the Tito regime than the Russian Orthodox Church did under Khrushchev. The "union of priests" with the moral support of the civil authorities sought to make the Church a political body. The faithful, the Holy Synod, and the patriarch were helpless.

In spite of the difficulties, in the course of the twentieth century the Orthodox

19 From an anonymous refugee to the author.
20 St. Vladimir's Seminary Quarterly, Vol. II, No. 4, p. 41 (Fall, 1958).
21 Shuster, Religion Behind the Iron Curtain, pp. 121, 122.
22 Ibid., pp. 39, 40.

Church made some progress. For example, in Belgrade Orthodox churches were said to number twelve in 1957 as against five in 1900.[23]

In the later months of his patriarchate Vikentije was faced with a serious problem in the portion of Macedonia which was embraced in the Jugoslavian domains. Bulgaria claimed that the Macedonians were in fact Bulgars and should be united with that country. The Orthodox in Macedonia wished to have an autocephalous church, independent of the Patriarch of Pech. In an effort to hold them politically to his rule, Tito sided with them. Yet he wished to avoid a clash with the Serbian Church. In 1958 a compromise was reached by which the Archbishopric of Ochrida was restored but the Church of Macedonia recognized the authority of the Serbian patriarch.[24]

By the census of 1953, out of a population of 16,936,573 in Jugoslavia, 41.4 per cent. were Orthodox, 31.8 per cent. were Roman Catholics, 12.3 per cent. were Moslems, 0.9 per cent. were Protestants, and 12.3 per cent. declared themselves to be without religion.[25]

TROUBLED BULGARIA

Politically Bulgaria fared badly in the half-century which followed 1910. In the first Balkan War (1912–1913) it joined with its neighbours in attacking Turkey. But in the division of the territory wrested from that state it was defeated (1913) by Serbia, Greece, Turkey, and Rumania and lost most of Macedonia, Adrianople, and the Southern Dobruja. In an effort to recoup its losses Bulgaria joined forces with the Central Powers in World War I. It was defeated, lost more territory, and was saddled with the payment of a huge indemnity. Internal disorder followed, with agrarian-Communist agitation. In World War II Bulgaria sided first with Germany. In 1944 it was invaded by Russia. Under Russian auspices the Fatherland Front, predominantly Communist, set up a government. In 1946 the monarchy was abolished and a Communist regime was organized under a constitution (1947) modelled on that of the U.S.S.R. By the peace treaty of 1947 Bulgaria's boundaries were reduced and the country was placed under obligation to pay reparations to Greece and Jugoslavia.

Under these circumstances Christianity could not but have difficulties. It entered into the half-century both aided and handicapped by its history. It was represented mainly by the Orthodox Church, although in the nineteenth century Protestantism had entered and had won small minorities. Minorities, also minute, of Roman Catholics and Uniates existed. The Orthodox Church was a symbol and bond of Bulgar nationality and it had revived the Bulgarian

23 *Ecumenical Press Service*, February 15, 1957.
24 *The New York Times*, October 6, 1958.
25 *The Statesman's Year Book, 1959*, p. 1569.

language as a literary medium. But during the long Turkish domination it had been ruled by Greek bishops. In the second half of the nineteenth century the Bulgars expelled the Greek bishops and a schism followed. The Bulgars, with Russian support, set up an exarchate. The Ecumenical Patriarch condemned the adherents of the exarchate for phyletism (allowing nationalism to divide the Church) and for a time rival bishops—of the exarchate and of the patriarchate—were found in the same city. Yet seminaries were instituted by the exarchate to train clergy, and a faculty of theology was organized in the University of Sofia. The branch of the Orthodox Church under the exarchate was the religion of the state. As the state religion it was given financial subventions by the government, and the clergy officiated on public occasions.[26] Identified as it was with the Bulgarian nation, the Orthodox Church entered the post-1914 decades with the advantage of that alliance.

The Balkan Wars and World Wars I and II, with their heavy toll of life and property, brought problems to the Orthodox Church as to other phases of Bulgarian culture. Between the two wars the Bulgarian Orthodox Church displayed remarkable vigour in producing periodicals and books, in higher education for the clergy, in reaching youth, and in participating in inter-confessional bodies which eventually joined in the World Council of Churches. Following World War II the Church was confronted by a Communist regime. However, in accord with its policy of using the churches to further its political aims, the U.S.S.R. was not unwilling to enlist the Bulgarian Church for that purpose, and an accommodation was reached between the Bulgarian puppet regime and the leaders of the Church which subordinated and limited the latter and yet permitted it to exist.

Before the Communists took over, the Bulgarian Orthodox Church continued to show signs of a mind of its own as contrasted with the state. In July, 1940, its annual assembly adopted a plan for the development of religious education in the schools and the promotion of youth groups in the parishes. During the Nazi occupation it collected funds to send liturgical books to the portions of Russia in German hands, but it rejected pressure to denounce the election of Sergius to the Moscow Patriarchate as a Communist manoeuvre and in July, 1944, before Nazi domination had entirely ended, it spoke out against all forms of totalitarianism.[27]

In the period between the expulsion of the Germans and the full establishment of a Communist regime some advances were made by the Bulgarian Orthodox Church. Stefan, chosen exarch in January, 1945, asked Patriarch Alexius of Moscow to request the Ecumenical Patriarch to recognize his election and end the schism. This a delegation from Moscow to Constantinople

[26] Volume II, pp. 487, 488; Shuster, *op. cit.,* pp. 218, 219.
[27] Tobias, *Communist-Christian Encounter in East Europe,* p. 354.

was able to effect. Although the government terminated prayers and religious instruction in the public schools, abolished church services in the army, declared dialectical materialism to be the correct educational philosophy, and limited Church activities to public worship under the eyes of government agents, parents were permitted to engage private tutors to teach their children religion and in some places Sunday Schools were begun to replace the religious education formerly given in the public schools. In June, 1946, the League of Orthodox Clergy met and sought to call a general council of the Bulgarian Church to draft a "democratic" constitution for the Church, to seek to introduce religious teaching in the public schools with priests as instructors, to oppose the threatened closing of the theological faculty of the University of Sofia, to promote social work to counter the government's secularization of social agencies, and to promote the unity of the churches. The Holy Synod also protested the proposed separation of Church and state.[28]

The constitution of the state adopted in December, 1947, brought the relations of Church and state into line with those in the U.S.S.R. with some modifications which favoured the Church. It guaranteed freedom of conscience, religion, and the performance of religious rites, forbade the preaching of racial, national, or religious hatred, separated Church and state, and prohibited the use of the Church or religion for political ends. The government assured the Church that the latter would continue to receive state subsidies. In return the Orthodox Holy Synod urged its people to back the government in "all useful undertakings" such as charities, justice, and social and economic progress.[29] In September, 1948, the Holy Synod authorized the clergy to join pro-Communist organizations and to support the collective farms, and endorsed state decrees forbidding priests to teach religion in the schools. In December, 1949, it urged the clergy to conduct services honouring the seventieth birthday of Stalin. Yet many of the clergy were slow to conform and some were sent to slave-labour camps. The pro-Communist Union of Orthodox Priests long had difficulty in recruiting members. One theological school remained open and the two theological journals were permitted.[30]

Control of the churches by the state was progressively tightened. Priests and Evangelical pastors were urged to become members of the Fatherland Front. Although Orthodox priests extended their Sunday School activities and the Orthodox Christian Brotherhood for a time enlarged its evangelistic, educational, and social welfare activities, a Union of Democratic Clergy pledged support to the Fatherland Front, denounced Protestantism, the Roman Catholic Church, and the Ecumenical Movement as under the influence of imperialists,

[28] *Ibid.*, pp. 355, 356.
[29] *Ibid.*, pp. 357, 367.
[30] Shuster, *op. cit.*, pp. 223, 224.

and approved placing all education under the state and the large-scale participation of the clergy in labour brigades. Exarch Stefan resigned, ostensibly because of ill health but presumably under pressure from the government, the Orthodox theological faculty added courses in Marxism to its curriculum, many Protestant pastors were imprisoned, and the official bodies of the Bulgarian Orthodox Church and of the Baptist, Methodist, and Congregational Churches denounced "traitorous pastors." Protestants fared worse than in the U.S.S.R., possibly because of their alleged Western connexions and because they were made up of educated and therefore non-Communist elements. In 1949 a law was enacted which named the Orthodox Church as "the traditional religion of the Bulgarian People" and permitted state subsidies where these were necessary, but placed all activities of the churches under state control, expropriated all ecclesiastical institutions and youth activities, terminated the Roman Catholic mission, and closed all churches with headquarters abroad. Baptists and Methodist assemblies severed their ties with their mother churches, the senior secretary of the Holy Synod was dismissed, and the leader of the Orthodox Brotherhood, which had been promoting church renewal, religious education, and welfare, was arrested, probably because the movement had been growing since it had narrowly escaped liquidation in 1944. The theological faculty was detached from the University of Sofia.[31] In 1955 the Union of Orthodox Priests (or Union of Clergy Brotherhood) was disbanded.[32] In close association with the Communist regime, in 1953 the Bulgarian Orthodox Church revived the patriarchate which had lapsed in the fourteenth century and elected the Metropolitan Kiril to the post.[33] But the election was not accepted by the Phanar.

In 1949, in spite of the measures of the Communist regime, of the estimated population of 7,200,000 Bulgaria was said to have 6,000,000 Orthodox, 761,000 Moslems, 123,000 Roman Catholics, 23,000 Armeno-Greeks, 20,000 Jews, and 15,744 Protestants.[34]

ALBANIA

Albania, predominantly Moslem, had Christian minorities. In the 1950's, out of a population of about 1,400,000, Moslems constituted about half, Orthodox about 15 per cent., and Roman Catholics about 7 per cent.[35]

A small, rugged country, inhabited by mountain folk, Albania was long under Turkish rule and did not obtain its independence until 1913, on the eve of World War I. It suffered from internal turbulence, from a variety of re-

[31] Tobias, *op. cit.*, pp. 360–362, 367–379.
[32] *The Statesman's Year Book*, 1959, p. 861.
[33] *Ibid.*, p. 860.
[34] *Ibid.*, p. 861.
[35] *Ibid.*, pp. 799, 800.

gimes, and from an Italian-German invasion during World War II. In 1945 it passed into the control of Communists.

At the time Albania achieved its political independence its Orthodox were under Greek bishops appointed by the Ecumenical Patriarch. Led by an Albanian priest from the United States, after World War I the Orthodox demanded that their church be autocephalous. The Greek bishops fled. The Ecumenical Patriarch seemed disposed to comply, but complications ensued in which the Italian and Greek governments and the Jugoslav patriarch were involved. In 1929 a holy synod was formed and pronounced the church independent. The Jugoslav patriarch approved the step, but the Ecumenical Patriarch demoted the members of the synod from the episcopal office, the Albanian Government expelled his representative, and in 1937 he resigned himself to the *fait accompli* and recognized the autocephaly of the Albanian Orthodox Church.[36]

Under the Communist regime the Church's lands were nationalized and the clergy were dependent financially upon the state. In 1949 the archbishop was deposed and arrested and two other bishops were placed under arrest, presumably for resistance to the state.[37] Some attempt was made to establish friendly relations with the Moscow Patriarchate and a delegation to Moscow in 1948 declared that the Russian Orthodox Church was the defender of the Albanian Orthodox Church. In 1951 the latter sent a delegation to Czechoslovakia for the ceremony by which the Archbishop of Prague was invested with the metropolitanate of the Orthodox Church of that country.[38]

The Communist government dealt much more harshly with the Roman Catholics than with the Orthodox. By the 1950's ties with Rome had been compulsorily severed, the Papal nuncio had been expelled, the Roman Catholic press had been suppressed, all religious youth organizations had been banned, Catholic Action had been liquidated, ecclesiastical property had been expropriated, and many of the clergy and laity had been executed. The severity was due at least partly to the memories of the Italian invasion and the fear of future Italian aggression.[39]

THE RUMANIAN STORY

Rumania, in the 1950's with a population about as large as that of Jugoslavia, had not fully emerged from the Ottoman Empire until 1878 but had been moving towards independence since the latter part of the eighteenth century. During World War I she came out for the Allies against the Central Powers

[36] *Ibid.*, p. 800; Attwater, *The Christian Churches of the East*, Vol. II, pp. 136, 137.
[37] Shuster, *op. cit.*, p. 203.
[38] Tobias, *op. cit.*, pp. 381, 382.
[39] Shuster, *op. cit.*, pp. 203–205.

and in March, 1918, was overrun by the Germans and was forced to sign a humiliating treaty. Later in the year she came back into the struggle and invaded Hungary. As a return the Allies awarded her Transylvania (from Hungary) and Bukovina and Bessarabia (from Russia). In 1921 a programme of land reform was instituted which expropriated the large estates and distributed them among the peasants. Various shifts in the government marked the interwar years. In World War II Rumania was first compelled to yield large portions of her territory to Russia, Hungary, and Bulgaria. In 1940 she cast in her lot with the Axis and joined in the invasion of the U.S.S.R., but in 1944 she entered the war on the side of Germany's foes. In the peace settlement she was required to recognize the incorporation of Bessarabia and Bukovina into the U.S.S.R. and of Southern Dobrudja into Bulgaria, but she retained all Transylvania and Northern Dobrudja. Following the war, supported by Russia, the Communists seized power, and in 1948 they instituted the Rumanian People's Republic with a constitution modelled on that of the U.S.S.R. Before long typical Communist measures were put through, with the abolition of private schools and the organization of collective farms. Rumania was predominantly agricultural and four-fifths of her population were rural.

Following World War I with its gains of territory, the Rumanian Orthodox Church, having the majority of the population, was reorganized and in 1925 was given a structure which was comprehensive of the areas that had been added as well as those within the pre-war boundaries. It permitted the preservation of some features of the Orthodox Church in Transylvania, but it brought all the Orthodox under the Rumanian flag into one ecclesiastical body and, as in Jugoslavia three years earlier, a patriarchate was set up. The patriarchate was promptly recognized by the Ecumenical Patriarch. Some of the Rumanian Orthodox, under the spur of nationalism and the augmentation of numerical strength, believed that their church must now take the leadership of all Eastern Christianity, for Constantinople had long since fallen into the hands of the Moslems and now the Russian Orthodox Church was disrupted and under the Communist thumb.[40]

In other ways the Rumanian Orthodox Church made advances in the years which immediately followed World War I. Steps were taken to improve the quality of the rank and file of the clergy—a quality which the bishops acknowledged to be inferior. Faculties of theology existed in four universities and in the 1930's a score of seminaries were maintained in other places. In 1932 the Holy Synod ordered that only licentiates in theology be admitted to the priesthood. Among the clergy were able men who worked for reform. In 1932 religious instruction was made compulsory in all primary and secondary schools,

---

[40] Attwater, *op. cit.*, pp. 104, 105; Janin, *The Separated Eastern Churches*, translated by P. Boylan (London, Sands & Co., 1933, pp. 243), pp. 153–162.

thus raising the level of a knowledge of the main tenets of the faith among the rank and file of the population. Efforts were seen to improve the monasteries. In 1939 those for men were said to number 44 with a total enrolment of 1,584, and those for women, 24. A college for young monks was founded in 1930. It was in addition to an earlier one. Attempts, not very successful, were initiated by the episcopate to induce the monasteries to carry on publishing enterprises and to become training centres for missionaries. Orthodox Action, inspired by the example of Catholic Action, was undertaken, members of a society of student missioners gave themselves to the instruction of children and the holding of retreats, movements akin to the Greek Zoë sprang up, and the *Oastea Domnului* (Lord's Army) followed the pattern of the Salvation Army.[41]

The reorganization of the Rumanian Orthodox Church in the 1920's was paralleled by legal provisions for other churches, especially for those in the recently annexed territories—Roman Catholic, Uniate, Reformed, Lutheran, and Unitarian—notably in Transylvania. Equal freedom was granted to all denominations provided they did not endanger public order, law, or morals. However, clergymen or heads of religious organizations were required to be Rumanian citizens or to have applied for naturalization.[42]

World War II with the subsequent coming to power of the Communists inevitably brought grave complications to the Rumanian churches. Although, in conformity with the terms of the treaty of peace with the Allied and Associated Powers, the constitution of 1948 guaranteed freedom of conscience and of religious worship, the state quickly tightened its controls and limited ecclesiastical activities. All denominational schools except a few theological seminaries were abolished and their properties were confiscated. Much of the land belonging to the churches was expropriated and divided among the peasants.[43] During the German occupation many Baptists and Seventh Day Adventists had been arrested and sentenced to long imprisonment.[44] Soon after the Germans were expelled a number of Lutheran pastors and laymen and several Uniate priests were deported to Russia.[45]

Although in 1946 an Orthodox publication hailed the World Council of Churches as making for international friendship and Patriarch Nicodim expressed his desire for ecumenical contacts, the increasing power of the Communists moved Rumania away from the West and fully into the Russian orbit. Orthodox clergy who could be trusted to work with the Communists were

[41] Attwater, *op. cit.*, pp. 106–109; Gsovski, *Church and State behind the Iron Curtain*, pp. 265, 266.
[42] Gsovski, *op. cit.*, pp. 259–271.
[43] *Ibid.*, pp. 271–281.
[44] Tobias, *op. cit.*, p. 321.
[45] *Ibid.*, p. 322.

placed in high governmental posts, and the International Red Cross was expelled and subsequent relief was distributed through the Rumanian Red Cross. After the death of Nicodim, Justinian, Metropolitan of Moldavia, was elected to the vacant patriarchate. On his enthronement (June 6, 1948) Justinian came out strongly for coöperation with the new political regime and called on the Uniates to sever their ties with Rome and to rejoin their Orthodox brethren. He appointed priests to agitate against Anglican, Roman Catholic, and ecumenical relations. In 1948 the concordat of 1927–1929 with Rome was abrogated. The Vatican and American imperialism were represented as working hand in hand. Against the protest of Uniate bishops and many of their clergy the reunion of the Uniates with the Orthodox was carried through and their bishops either disappeared or were imprisoned. Lutheran, Reformed, and Unitarians—strong elements in Transylvania—were compelled to establish a joint seminary in which the professors were to be approved and partly supported by the state. The Lord's Army and leaders of other Christian lay movements were imprisoned. The Bible Society was closed. In 1949 the YMCA was dissolved and its property confiscated. In 1950 Justinian in a pastoral letter accused the Vatican and the World Council of Churches of joining with Western forces in preparing for a new war. That same year the Papal nuncio was expelled from the country and steps were taken to create a national Catholic church divorced from any connexion with the Holy See. Late in 1950 the leaders of the Baptists, Seventh Day Adventists, Pentecostals, and Gospel Christians declared that they would not maintain contacts with bodies or individuals outside Rumania which would be harmful to the state. By the end of 1950 churches were forbidden to engage in general educational activities or social welfare, religious publications were sharply curtailed and controlled, all priests were required to attend a two-month course of "missionary and social instruction," and the Orthodox Church was limited to two theological institutes and one theological faculty for the training of its clergy. The Roman Catholics still had two monasteries for men and three for women, but their members were required to learn a trade to contribute to the work of the community.[46]

Although the Rumanian Orthodox Church had through its patriarch coöperated with the Communist regime and praised it for its religious policy, in the 1950's further strains developed. In 1958 hundreds of priests and more than a score of bishops were said to be in prison or under house arrest.[47] Other bodies were also under adverse pressure. In 1959 the government was attempting to prevent youths from being confirmed in the Lutheran Church by re-

[46] *Ibid.*, pp. 322–351; Shuster, *op. cit.*, pp. 230–246.
[47] *The Journal-Courier*, Louisville, December 9, 1958, through the United Press.

fusing to permit those receiving confirmation to graduate from school, and thus closing to them opportunities for a livelihood.[48] Yet in Rumania, owing so it was said to the efforts of the patriarch, 520 nuns were in convents, twice the number to be found in the U.S.S.R. and many times the total in Jugoslavia or Bulgaria.[49] In 1958 the Rumanian Orthodox Church was reported to have twelve dioceses, 10,165 priests, and 5,814 monks and nuns, and a Holy Synod and a National Ecclesiastical Assembly.[50]

THE ECUMENICAL PATRIARCHATE

The Ecumenical Patriarchate, since 451 the ranking see of the Orthodox Churches, suffered severely in the loss of population directly subject to it but continued to hold its place of dignity among the other patriarchates of the Eastern Churches. It was still located in Constantinople, a city now bearing the Turkish name of Istanbul, and by 1961 the flock in Turkey over which it had primary jurisdiction had shrunk to less than 100,000. The decline was due to the dwindling of the territory in Europe controlled by the Turks, the near-disappearance of the Greeks in the domains which remained to Turkey, and the full attainment of autocephaly of the Orthodox Churches which formerly were ruled by bishops from the Phanar or which received their holy oil from the Ecumenical Patriarch. In the strained Turkish-Greek relations which followed World War I the Turks for a time insisted that the Ecumenical Patriarchate as a centre of pro-Greek intrigue be abolished. It was saved by the insistence of a British diplomat, but the civil jurisdiction which it had exercised for centuries over the Greek community was ended and its functions were limited to purely ecclesiastical matters.[51] In 1955 riots in Istanbul against the Greeks which resulted in loss of life and the destruction or desecration of Orthodox church buildings again jeopardized the continued residence of the Ecumenical Patriarch in that city and its removal was seriously discussed.

In the 1950's the post was filled by Athenagoras I, a Greek of marked ability and high character, who through long residence in the United States had acquired a broad perspective and was friendly to the World Council of Churches and the entire Ecumenical Movement. One evidence of the spiritual activity of the office and yet of its close association with the Greeks was the canonization decreed in 1955 of Nicodemus the Hagiorite (1748 or 1749–1809), a monk of Mt. Athos, the most prolific of modern Greek monastic writers.[52]

[48] *Ecumenical Press Service*, July 3, 1959.
[49] *Ibid.*, February 15, 1957.
[50] *Statesman's Year Book*, *1959*, p. 1353.
[51] Matthew Spinka in *Church History*, Vol. IV, pp. 104, 105.
[52] *Sobornost*, Summer, 1955, p. 256.

SUMMARY

The wars and the revolutions through which Greece and the Balkan peoples passed in the half-century which began with the explosion of 1912, followed as they were by Communist domination in all the countries but Greece, constituted a heavy handicap to churches which had only recently emerged from centuries of Moslem Turkish rule. Christianity, represented chiefly by the Orthodox branch of the faith, had the advantage of being traditionally associated with the life of the various peoples. In most regions the Orthodox Church was a symbol and bulwark of national loyalty. On the whole it retained the allegiance of its historic flocks. In some countries, notably Greece, it experienced a marked revival. Except Greece, in every country that revival was sharply curtailed by the emergence of Communist governments after World War II—all but Jugoslavia subordinate to the U.S.S.R. Although the ties of the Roman Catholic minorities with the Vatican were weakened or severed and Uniates were constrained to return to the Orthodox fold, the government of the U.S.S.R., officially atheist though it was, was disposed to strengthen its hold on its satellites by encouraging such of the Orthodox as would coöperate with the Moscow Patriarchate.

CHAPTER XXI

By Way of Summary and Transition

To HARDY souls who have made their way through the preceding chapters the many details may have seemed to obscure any sense of general direction. Even the summary paragraphs and the occasional attempts to point out correlations of country with country and of church with church may not have relieved the impression of bewildering confusion. Some sense of order may be achieved if we pause before leaving Europe to put into perspective what we have attempted to recount, to suggest some generalizations growing out of the narrative, and to point to the connexion with the rest of that global coverage which we are to essay in the final volume.

To those who are acquainted with the story which we endeavoured to cover in the first two volumes of our series it must be obvious that Christianity in Europe came to the close of the nineteenth century on a rising tide. In the face of the challenge of revolutionary movements which had their inception in Western Christendom, which in part owed their existence to Christianity, and which appeared to imperil the continuation of that faith, and in spite of the fact that it seemed so closely integrated with the age which was passing that to many observers it appeared moribund, Christianity had a remarkable revival. At the close of the nineteenth century it was much more vigorous in the historic Christendom than it had been at the outset of that era and had spread more widely beyond the borders of its traditional centre than in any previous period. By the year 1914 it was more nearly global than it or any other religion had ever been. The revival had been in all three of the main branches of Christianity—Roman Catholic, Protestant, and Orthodox. It was most outstanding in Protestantism, was marked in the Roman Catholic Church, and, while less striking, was also apparent in various Orthodox bodies.

In the half-century which was ushered in by the fateful summer of 1914 Christianity was confronted with greater threats than it had known for many centuries. Two world wars racked the planet and were followed by the frightening possibility of a third holocaust which would dwarf its predecessors and possibly wipe out civilization and even human life in great portions of the

539

globe. The two world wars and the menace of the third had their centres in the region in which Christianity had longest had a near approach to full opportunity and among peoples which by tradition had for centuries professed that faith. They were fought with weapons developed in that region, and the fear with which the future was faced arose from the harnessing of the atom which had first been achieved in a geographic extension of that region. A potent cause of the wars was an intensified nationalism, first apparent in Christendom and a force setting rival peoples at one another's throats. Accompanying the wars were political revolutions which swept into the discard ancient ruling houses and the governments associated with them. Some of the successor regimes were openly hostile to Christianity. The ideology incorporated in most of them was Communism, and Communism had been given its classic formulation by two men—Marx and Engels—who had once been Christians and had been reared and had spent their lives in Western Europe surrounded by a professedly Christian society. In addition to the wars and political revolutions forces were working which were slower and less dramatic but which also had their sources in the heart of the historic Christendom and were fully as grave a challenge to Christianity. They included the continuation and acceleration of the Industrial Revolution with its attendant growth of cities and alterations of the patterns of life to which the churches with their parish organizations had been accustomed. Among them were also the rapidly expanding knowledge of the physical universe and the problems of adjusting to it the intellectual expressions of the Christian faith.

As a result of these threats and challenges, Christianity was losing whatever hold it had possessed on many millions in what had been known as Christendom. In Western Europe anti-clericalism was less rampant and anti-Christian voices were less strident than in the nineteenth century. More by neglect and absorption in other interests than by vocal opposition Christianity was fading out of the lives of countless persons of Christian ancestry. The overwhelming majority of the children were still baptized into one or another of the churches. But that rite was increasingly a social convention inherited from a previous stage of culture and its religious significance was more and more disregarded. In several countries confirmation either in the Roman Catholic Church or in one of the Protestant bodies was nearly universal and instruction in the tenets of the faith was part of the curriculum of the elementary schools subsidized by the state. But attendance at church services and participation in the Communion were falling off. The decline was most marked in the cities—whether London or Paris, Stockholm or Madrid, Hamburg or Marseilles, Berlin or Rome. It characterized many mining communities. But it was also apparent in numbers of rural areas. The Roman Catholic Church, Protestantism, and the Eastern Churches suffered. In countries under Communist rule—Russia, much of Central Europe, and the Balkans—active anti-Christian propaganda and measures curtailing the churches or harnessing the churches to the purpose of secular totalitarian governments were universal. To those who viewed only this side of the picture Europe appeared to be entering the post-Christian era. By contributing to forces which were destroying it Christianity was presumably digging its own grave.

This, however, was only one part of the picture. By a seeming paradox Christianity was very much alive. It was giving birth to new movements or strengthening old ones. In contrast with the nineteenth century, this pulsing life was more immediately obvious in the Roman Catholic Church than in Protestantism. Unlike the record in the nineteenth century when more congregations were created than in any previous hundred years of that church's history, few new ones appeared. Here would seem to be evidence of stagnation but for the fact that other movements rose to prominence. Catholic Action, organizations which were the expression of Christian democracy, the Liturgical Movement, and Eucharistic Congresses flourished. They had in common the enlistment of the laity. Indeed, the twentieth century was called the century of the laity and much talk was heard of the priesthood of the laity. Here was an attempt to present to a hostile world a united front of loyal, practising Catholics. Nor was it a defensive, rear-guard strategy. It was part of a programme for making Christ King in all mankind and in all aspects of life. One of its features was the enlargement of the missionary outreach into all the world. From Western Europe still went the overwhelming majority of Roman Catholic missionaries. In several portions of the globe, notably in Africa South of the Sahara, the Roman Catholic Church was experiencing a rapid growth and was becoming deeply rooted in many peoples through indigenous clergy and hierarchies. It had an able succession of men on the throne of Peter. It had purged itself of Modernism, for it held that here was a dangerous compromise with the deceptive currents of the revolutionary age. But the purge had not discouraged those who within the limits set by the Pope as the Church's central authority sought to think through afresh the relevance of the eternal Gospel to the problems of the day and to the rapidly expanding horizons of mankind. Geographically the vigour in the Roman Catholic Church was most noticeable in a belt which ran from the British Isles through Belgium, the Netherlands, the Rhine Valley, portions of France, and Switzerland into North Italy, but it was not confined to that area.

In some ways the Protestantism of Europe appeared to have responded less successfully to the challenge of the twentieth century than had Roman Catholicism, possibly because many of the movements which constituted the challenge had first arisen in areas which were deemed Protestant. The Industrial Revolution had had its beginnings and earliest development in Protestant Britain,

Das Kapital had been written by former Protestants in supposedly Protestant London, some of the anti-Christian intellectuals of the nineteenth century who had repercussions in the post-1914 decades, among them Nietzsche and Strauss, had Protestant backgrounds, the most daring and disturbing studies of the Bible had been by Protestant scholars, and the convulsive nationalism of the twentieth century had had its most assertive initial expression in the predominantly Protestant Germany of the nineteenth century. In spite of its great burst of creativity in that century, European Protestantism might seem at last to be succumbing to the forces which it had helped to evoke. Undebatable was the fact that, in contrast with the Roman Catholicism of Europe, its share in the world-wide spread of the faith was much less than in the nineteenth century. That torch, as we are to see, had passed across the Atlantic.

On a more careful survey, far from being dead or dying, European Protestantism was seen to be responding to the challenge by fresh movements. As in the Roman Catholic Church, these were in part either stemming from the laity or enlisting them. We have noted them in the Confessing Church (although more among the clergy than the laity), the Evangelical Academies, and the *Kirchentag* in beleaguered Germany—and in Germany the most acute challenge had come not from Protestantism but from a nominal Roman Catholic, Hitler. Indeed, it may be significant that the other outstanding totalitarian leaders were not Protestant but of Roman Catholic or Orthodox background —notably Mussolini, Franco, Tito, Stalin, and Khrushchev. To mention only a few other Protestant movements, we have found them in Sigtuna in Sweden, in *Kerk en Wereld* in the Netherlands, in the "tell Scotland" movement and in the support given to the Iona Community in Scotland, in the many retreat centres in England, in CIMADE in France, and in *Agape* in Italy. They were minorities, but creative minorities. From European Protestantism fresh attempts were being made on the intellectual level to rise to the twentieth-century phase of the revolutionary age. Again to name only a few of the many and varied examples, they included such diverse approaches as those of Heim and Bultmann in Germany, Nygren and Wingren in Sweden, Barth and Brunner in Switzerland, Temple and Dodd in England, and the Baillie brothers and Torrance in Scotland. In several places in the major industrial centres, notably in England and Scotland, new approaches were being made to reach the elements which under the exigencies of the altered patterns of life had drifted away from the Church. In the various aspects of the Ecumenical Movement at which we have hinted and of which we are to hear more in the next volume, European Protestants were outstanding. In that quite novel and promising approach to the realization of the dream of Christian unity which had troubled and inspired Christians since the first century the geographic headquarters were in Europe, and European Protestants were more nearly unanimous in their coöperation than were Protestants in any other part of the world.

Within countries dominated by Communism both Roman Catholics and Protestants were about equal in their staunch adherence to the faith in the face of pressures and persecution—in the German Democratic Republic, Poland, and Hungary. Indeed, while some in both wings of the faith endeavoured to make their peace with the Communist regimes, in the main both Roman Catholics and Protestants were again proving that the blood of the martyrs was the seed of the Church. In the U.S.S.R. it was the government-enforced federation of Baptists and Evangelicals that was having the most impressive growth of any of the European Protestant bodies.

The Orthodox Churches appeared to have less resilience than did the Roman Catholic Church and Protestantism. By long tradition they had been subordinate to the state, and the revolutionary currents from Western Christendom swept aside the regimes with which they had been identified. Yet, far from vanishing with the political structures which had dominated them, they survived. By mid-century the largest of them, the Russian Orthodox Church, was recovering and the hard-hit Greek Orthodox Church, escaping Communist control, was putting out fresh shoots.

We next move to the world beyond Europe. Much of our attention must be devoted to the larger Occident in the Americas and Australasia. There we shall find all branches of the faith displaying a striking vitality in the face of the challenges of the twentieth-century stage of the revolutionary age. In the non-Occidental world—in Asia, Africa, and the islands of the sea—we shall witness even more phenomenal growth of both the Roman Catholic Church and Protestantism. Although in most of these areas Christians were still minorities—usually small minorities—as never before Christianity was becoming world-wide.

BIBLIOGRAPHY

As in previous volumes, to save space the following bibliography is confined to works which have been cited more than once. For those cited only once—and they are probably twice or three times the number which are included below—the necessary data are given in the footnotes in which they are utilized.

Acta Apostolicae Sedis Commentarium Officiale (Rome, Typis Polyglottis Vaticanis, 1909 ff.).

Allen, Yorke, *A Seminary Survey* (New York, Harper & Brothers, 1960, pp. xxvi, 640). A highly competent factual survey of Roman Catholic, Protestant, and Eastern Orthodox seminaries in Asia, Africa, and Latin America.

Ammann, Albert, *Abriss der ostslawischen Kirchengeschichte* (Vienna, Herder, 1950, pp. xvi, 748). By a Jesuit. Comprehensive, from the beginning to 1945.

Andersen, J. Oskar, *Survey of the History of the Church in Denmark* (Copenhagen, L. Lohse, 1930, pp. 79). A useful summary.

Anderson, Paul B., *People, Church and State in Modern Russia* (New York, The Macmillan Co., 1944, pp. 240). By an expert.

Andrews, Theodore, *The Polish National Catholic Church in America and Poland* (London, Society for Promoting Christian Knowledge, 1953, pp. ix, 117). Carefully done.

Anson, Peter F., *The Call of the Cloister. Religious Communities and Kindred Bodies in the Anglican Communion* (London, S.P.C.K., 1956, pp. xvi, 641). Comprehensive, sympathetic, based on extensive research.

Årbok for den Norske Kirke (Oslo, Land og Kirke, 1951 ff.). An annual publication.

Attwater, Donald, *The Christian Churches of the East, Vol. II. Churches not in Communion with Rome* (Milwaukee, Bruce Publishing Co., 2nd ed., 1948, pp. xii, 290). Factual, by a Roman Catholic.

Aubert, Roger, *La Théologie Catholique au Milieu du XXe Siècle* (Tournai, Casterman, 1954, pp. 101). An excellent survey by an expert.

Baptist Work in Denmark, Finland, Norway, and Sweden (Stockholm, Baptistmissionens Bokförlags ab Sweden, 1947, pp. 87). By various authors.

Beck, George Andrew, editor, *The English Catholics, 1850–1950. Essays to Commemorate the Centenary of the Restoration of the Hierarchy of England and Wales* (London, Burns Oates, 1950, pp. xix, 640).

Bell, G. K. A., editor, *Documents on Christian Unity, 1920–4* (London, Oxford University Press, 1924, pp. 20, 382). Comprehensive, by an expert.

Bell, G. K. A., editor, *Documents on Christian Unity Third Series 1930–48* (New York, Oxford University Press, 1948, pp. xii, 300). Comprehensive, by an expert.

Bell, G. K. A., *Randall Davidson, Archbishop of Canterbury* (London, Oxford University Press, 2 vols., 1935). The standard life, by a close personal friend.

Bendiscioli, Mario, *Nazism versus Christianity,* translated from the Italian by Gerald Griffin (London, Skeffington & Son, no date, pp. 256). Covers both Protestants and Roman Catholics. Moderate, factual, on the side of Christianity.

Binchy, Daniel A., *Church and State in Fascist Italy* (New York, Oxford University Press, 1941, pp. ix, 774). A careful study.

Bishop, Claire Huchet, *France Alive* (New York, The Declan X. McMullen Co., 1947, pp. xi, 227). A sympathetic account, chiefly of Roman Catholic activities, but also of Protestants.

Black, Charles Stewart, *The Scottish Church. A Short Study in Ecclesiastical History* (Glasgow, William Maclellan, 1952, pp. 276). A popular survey of the history from the beginning into the 1950's.

Blanshard, Paul, *The Irish and Catholic Power: An American Interpretation* (Boston, Beacon Press, 1953, pp. viii, 375). Critical of the Roman Catholic Church, but with many facts.

Boas, J. H., *Resistance of the Churches in the Netherlands* (New York, Netherlands Information Bureau, 1944, pp. 99). Contains important documents in translation.

Bogler, Theodor, editor, *Liturgische Erneuerung in aller Welt. Ein Sammebericht* (Maria Laach, Verlag Ars Liturgica, 1950, pp. 174). A country-by-country survey by various authors.

Bolshakoff, Serge, *The Christian Church and the Soviet State* (London, Society for Promoting Christian Knowledge, 1942, pp. ix, 75). By an eminent Russian Orthodox émigré scholar.

Bolshakoff, S., *New Missionary Review (Novoe Missionerskoe Obozrenie)* (Oxford, 1952 ff.). Mimeographed, by a Russian Orthodox scholar, having chiefly to do with Russian Orthodox missions but embracing reports on other churches gleaned from the author's travels.

Boulard, F., *Essor ou Déclin du Clergé Français* (Paris, Éditions du Cerf, 1950, pp. 479). Based on a very careful study, with many statistical tables.

Boulard, F., with the collaboration of A. Achard and H.-J. Emerard, *Rencontres 16 Problèmes Missionnaires de la France Rurale* (Paris, Cerf, 2 Parts, 1945).

Bouyer, Louis, *La Vie de la Liturgie. Une Critique Constructive du Mouvement Liturgique* (Paris, Éditions du Cerf, 1956, pp. 332). A thoughtful essay by a member of the Oratory.

Brémond, Henri, and others, *Manuel de la Littérature Catholique en France de 1870 à Nos Jours* (Paris, Éditions Spes, new ed., 1939, pp. 493). By various authors, two of them priests.

British Weekly. A Journal of Social and Christian Progress (London, 1886 ff.).

Browne-Olf, Lillian, *Pius XI, Apostle of Peace* (New York, The Macmillan Co., 1938, pp. xiv, 257). A readable, admiring biography.

Brugerette, J., *Le Prêtre Français et la Société Contemporaine Sous le Régime de la*

Séparation. Le Reconstitution Catholique (*1908–1936*) (Paris, P. Lethielleux, 1937, pp. vi, 793). A standard work, well documented, sympathetic with the Roman Catholic Church.

Burrows, Millar, *The Dead Sea Scrolls* (New York, The Viking Press, 1955, pp. xv, 435). Standard.

Cahiers d'Histoire Mondiale. Journal of World History. Cuaderos de Histoire Mondial (publication of the *Commission Internationale pour une Histoire du Développement Scientifique et Culturel de l'Humanité*. Neuchâtel, Éditions de la Baconnière, 1956 ff.).

Carpenter, S. C., *Winnington-Ingram. The Biography of Arthur Foley Winnington-Ingram, Bishop of London 1901–1939* (New York, Oxford University Press, 1949, pp. 358). Based on careful research.

The Catholic Encyclopedia (New York, Robert Appleton Co. and the Encyclopedia Press, 16 vols., 1907–1914).

The Catholic Historical Review (Washington, D.C., The Catholic University of America Press, 1914 ff.). The organ of the American Catholic Historical Association.

The Catholic World (New York, 1865 ff.).

Causton, Bernard, editor, *Kirchentag Calling. The Story of the Protestant Laymen's Rally* (Frankfurt/Main, Ecumenical Committee of the *Deutscher evangelischer Kirchentag*, no date, pp. 24).

Cazelles, Henri, *Église et État en Allemagne de Weimar aux Premières Années du IIIe Reich* (Paris, Rousseau et Cie, 1936, pp. 283). A doctoral dissertation.

The Christian Century (Chicago, 1898 ff.). From May to December, 1901, two papers were published by the Christian Century Company—*The Christian Century* and *The Christian Century of the Disciples of Christ*. In January, 1902, the American Weekly Company continued *The Christian Century* as *The American Weekly. The Christian Century of the Disciples of Christ* was continued as *The Christian Century*.

Christianity and Crisis. A Christian Journal of Opinion (New York, 1951 ff.). Connected with Union Theological Seminary.

Christianity Today (Washington, D.C., 1957 ff.). A fortnightly journal of moderately conservative Protestant evangelicalism.

Church History (the journal of the American Society of Church History, 1932 ff.).

Church News from the Northern Countries. Edited by the Northern Ecumenical Institute (Sigtuna, Sweden, 1955 ff.).

Civardi, Luigi, *Compendio di Storia dell' Azione Cattolica Italiana* (Rome, Coletti Editoire, 1956, pp. 285). A useful survey.

Clare, Albert, *The City Temple, 1640–1940. The Tercentenary Commemorative Volume* (London, The Independent Press, 1940, pp. xxiv, 286).

Clonmore, Lord, *Pope Pius XI and World Peace* (New York, E. P. Dutton and Co., 1938, pp. xi, 303). Admiring, based on fairly extensive published material.

The Commonweal (New York, 1890 ff.). A Roman Catholic journal.

Confrey, Burton, editor, *Readings for Catholic Action* (Manchester, N.H., Magnificat Press, 1937, pp. xxi, 1699). Compiled from various sources and authors.

Congar, M.-J., *Chrétiens Désunis. Principes d'un "Œcuménisme Catholique"* (Paris, Éditions du Cerf, 1937, pp. xix, 403). Translated by M. A. Bousfield as *Divided Christendom. A Catholic Study of the Problem of Reunion* (London, Geoffrey Bles, 1939, pp. xv, 298). By a Dominican.

La Continuité Pontificale. Conférences Prononcées à l'Institut Pie XI (Sixième Session) (Paris, Maison de la Bonne Presse, 1935, pp. 282). Sketchy, semi-popular, apologetic.

Copleston, Frederick, *Contemporary Philosophy. Studies in Logical Positivism and Existentialism* (Westminster, Md., The Newman Press, 1956, pp. ix, 227). A useful introduction.

Curtiss, John Shelton, *The Russian Church and the Soviet State, 1917–1950* (Boston, Little, Brown and Co., 1953, pp. x, 387). Based on careful research.

Daniel, Yvan, *Aspects de la Pratique Religieuse à Paris* (Paris, Éditions Ouvrières, 1952, pp. 134). Careful statistical studies and a thoughtful analysis.

Daniélou, Jean, *Advent,* translated by Rosemary Sheed (New York, Sheed and Ward, 1951, pp. 181).

Dansette, Adrien, *Destin du Catholicisme Français (1926–1956)* (Paris, Flammarion, 1957, pp. 493). Largely on the attempts to win back the de-Christianized.

Dansette, Adrien, *Histoire Religieuse en France Contemporaine* (Paris, Flammarion, revised ed., 2 vols., 1948, 1951). Lacking in footnotes, but with a bibliography for each chapter.

Delcacroix, S., editor, *Histoire Universelle des Missions Catholiques.* Vol. III. *Les Missions Contemporaines (1800–1957)* (Paris, Librairie Grund, 1958). By several contributors.

Delattre, Pierre, *La Vie Catholique en Allemagne. Études et Récits* (Paris, Éditions Spes, 1932, pp. 176). An excellent semi-popular survey of conditions near the end of the Weimar Republic.

Deroo, André, *L'Épiscopat Français dans la Mêlée de son Temps 1930–1954* (Paris, Bonne Presse, 1955, pp. 430). Sympathetic, by a Roman Catholic.

Descola, Jean, *Histoire de l'Espagne Chrétienne* (Paris, Robert Laffont, 1951, pp. 359). A comprehensive historical survey.

Documenten Nederlandse Hervormde Kerk. Verklaringer, Kanselkondigingen, Boodschappen, Digd Door of Namens de Generale Synod der Nederlandse Hervormde Kerk in de Jaren 1945–1955 (The Hague, Boekencentrum N.V., no date, pp. 637).

Douglass, Paul F., *God among the Germans* (Philadelphia, University of Pennsylvania Press, 1935, pp. xiii, 325). Based upon an extensive use of the sources.

Drummond, Andrew Landale, *German Protestantism Since Luther* (London, The Epworth Press, 1951, pp. x, 282). Competent, comprehensive.

Duncan-Jones, A. S., *The Struggle for Religious Freedom in Germany* (London, Victor Gollancz, 1938, pp. 319). By a Dean of Chichester.

Du Plessis, David J., *A Brief History of Pentecostal Assemblies,* manuscript 1960. By courtesy of the author.

Eberdt, Mary Lois, and Schnepp, Gerald J., *Industrialism and the Popes* (New York, P. J. Kenedy and Sons, 1953, pp. xxii, 245). A useful survey.

Ecumenical Press Service (Geneva, World Council of Churches, 1934 ff.).

The Ecumenical Review (Geneva, 1948 ff.). An official organ of the World Council of Churches.

Ecumenical Studies. Evangelism in Scotland (Information Bulletin published by the Secretariat for Evangelism of the World Council of Churches, Geneva, April, 1954, pp. 54).

Einaudi, Mario, and Goguel, François, *Christian Democracy in Italy and France* (Notre Dame, Ind., University of Notre Dame Press, 1952, pp. x, 228). A sympathetic, scholarly treatment by Roman Catholics.

The Emory University Quarterly (Atlanta, 1944 ff.).

Le Encicliche Sociali dei Papi da Pio IX a Pio XII (1864–1956). Edited by Igino Giordani (Rome, Editrice Studium, 1956, pp. 1191). Italian translations.

Enciclopedia Cattolica (Vatican City, Enciclopedia Cattolica e per Libro Cattolico, 12 vols., 1948–1954). An official publication.

The Encyclopædia Britannica (14th ed., London, The Encyclopædia Britannica Co., 1929, 24 vols.).

Evangelism in France (one of a series, *Ecumenical Studies;* information bulletin issued by the Secretariat for Evangelism of the World Council of Churches, Geneva, 1951, pp. 58).

Fides Service. See *Worldmission Fides Service.*

Fleming, J. R., *A History of the Church in Scotland, 1875–1929* (Edinburgh, T. & T. Clark, 1933, pp. x, 338). A competent survey.

Fleming, J. R., *The Story of Church Union in Scotland: Its Origins and Progress, 1560–1929* (London, James Clarke & Co., preface 1929, pp. 176). Friendly, authoritative.

Fogarty, Michael P., *Christian Democracy in Western Europe, 1820–1953* (Notre Dame, Ind., University of Notre Dame Press, 1957, pp. xviii, 461). A thoughtful, detailed, comprehensive study by a Roman Catholic. Covers both Roman Catholics and Protestants, and objectively. First published in England.

Foreign Affairs. An American Quarterly Review (New York, 1922 ff.).

Franks, J. D., compiler, *European Baptists Today* (Rüschlikon-Zürich, Baublatt A.G., 2nd ed., 1952, pp. 132).

Frey, Arthur, *Cross and Swastika. The Ordeal of the German Church* (London, Student Christian Movement Press, 1938, pp. 224). Translated by J. Strathearn McNab with an introduction by Karl Barth. A semi-popular survey by the head of the Swiss Evangelical Press Service in Zürich.

Frontier (London, 1958 ff.).

Gade, John A., *The Life of Cardinal Mercier* (New York, Charles Scribner's Sons, 1934, pp. ix, 312). An admiring biography based on extensive research.

Gerhardt, Martin, *Ein Jahrhundert Innere Mission. Die Geschichte des Central-*

Ausschusses für die Innere Mission der Deutschen Evangelischen Kirche (Gütersloh, C. Bertelsmann Verlag, 2 vols., 1948). A standard account.

Gestel, P. C. van, *Het Religieus-Socialisme* (Louvain, De Vlaamsche Drukkerij, 1932, pp. 388). A scholarly survey by a Dominican of both Roman Catholic and Protestant socialism in Europe.

Goldie, F., *A Short History of the Episcopal Church in Scotland from the Restoration to the Present Time* (London, S.P.C.K., 1951, pp. x, 168). Written for members of the Episcopal Church in Scotland.

Graham, Robert A., *Vatican Diplomacy. A Study of Church and State on the International Plane* (Princeton University Press, 1959, pp. xii, 442). A scholarly study by a Jesuit based on extensive research.

Grant, John W., *Free Churchmanship in England, 1870–1940, with Special Reference to Congregationalism* (London, The Independent Press, no date, pp. vii, 424). Chiefly an historical survey of the conceptions of the Church.

Gsovski, Vladimir, editor, *Church and State behind the Iron Curtain. Czechoslovakia, Hungary, Poland, Romania, with an Introduction to the Soviet Union* (New York, Frederick A. Praeger, 1955, pp. xxxi, 311). A publication of the Mid-European Studies Center of the Free Europe Committee. Largely documents and statistics.

Guerry, *L'Église Catholique en France sous l'Occupation* (Paris, Flammarion, 1947, pp. 379). By the Archbishop-Coadjutor of Cambrai.

Guilday, Peter, editor, *The Catholic Church in Contemporary Europe 1919–1931. Vol. II. Papers of the American Catholic Historical Association* (New York, P. J. Kenedy and Sons, 1932, pp. xiv, 354).

Guriàn, Waldemar, and Fitzsimons, editors, *The Catholic Church in World Affairs* (Notre Dame, Ind., University of Notre Dame Press, 1954, pp. ix, 420). A survey of uneven quality, by several authors, of various aspects of the Roman Catholic Church in the early 1950's.

Gustafsson, Berndt, *Svensk Kyrkogeografi med Samfundsbeskrivning* (Malmö, Gleerups Vorlag, 1957, pp. 195). A careful statistical study.

Gwynn, Denis, *The Catholic Reaction in France* (New York, The Macmillan Co., 1924, pp. xii, 186). By an Irish Roman Catholic journalist after three years of residence in France.

Hagoort, R., *De Christelijke-Sociale Beweging* (Hoorn, Drukkerij Edecea, 1933, pp. 226). Carefully done, by a Protestant, primarily on the Protestant phase of the Christian Social Movement, especially in the Netherlands.

Halecki, Oscar, in collaboration with James F. Murray, Jr., *Eugenio Pacelli, Pope of Peace* (New York, Farrar, Strauss and Young, 1951, pp. viii, 355). An admiring treatment of the efforts of Pius XI to promote peace.

Hales, E. E. Y., *The Catholic Church in the Modern World. A Survey from the French Revolution to the Present* (Garden City, N.Y., Hanover House, 1958, pp. 312). A sympathetic, popular account.

Hallström, Björn, *Secret Journey Through Spain* (London, Lutterworth Press, 1948, pp. 76). Report of a journey by a Swedish Protestant in 1947.

Hammond, Peter, *The Waters of Marah. The Present State of the Greek Church*

(London, Rockliff Publishing Corp., 1956, pp. ix, 186). Largely from personal observation.

Hansson, Kristian, *Stat og Kirke. Fredstiger og Kampar i Norge* (Bergen, John Griegs Forlag, 1945, pp. 150). Mostly on the nineteenth and twentieth centuries by a state official closely related to the Church.

d'Harcourt, Robert, *The German Catholics,* translated from the French by Reginald J. Dingle (London, Burns Oates & Washbourne, 1939, pp. xiii, 274). Sympathetic with the Roman Catholic Church as against the Nazis.

Harvey, G. L. H., editor, *The Church and the Twentieth Century* (London, Macmillan and Co., 1936, pp. xviii, 448). By several authors.

Hayes, Carlton J. H., *Contemporary Europe since 1870* (New York, The Macmillan Co., 1953, pp. xiii, 785). A standard survey.

Hecker, Julius F., *Religion and Communism. A Study of Religion and Atheism in Soviet Russia.* (New York, John Wiley and Sons, 1934, pp. xii, 303). A conscientious objective study.

Hecker, Julius F., *Religion under the Soviets* (New York, Vanguard Press, 1927, pp. xi, 207). By a Christian, well informed, with some sympathy for the Soviets.

Henson, Herbert Hensley, *Retrospect of an Unimportant Life* (New York, Oxford University Press, 3 vols., 1942–1950). An uninhibited autobiography.

Herman, Stewart W., Jr., *It's Your Souls We Want* (New York, Harper & Brothers, 1943, pp. xv, 315). By an American Lutheran, pastor of the American Church and then of the American Embassy in Berlin.

Herman, Stewart W., *The Rebirth of the German Church* (New York, Harper & Brothers, 1946, pp. xviii, 297). A sympathetic account by an American Lutheran. Especially valuable for its first-hand observations.

Herman, Stewart Winfield, *Report from Christian Europe* (New York, Friendship Press, 1953, pp. 211). By an American Lutheran, from first-hand observation.

Hermelink, Heinrich, *Das Christentum in der Menscheitsgeschichte von der französichen Reformation bis zur Gegenwart* (Stuttgart, J. B. Metzler, and Tübingen, Rainer Wunderlich Verlag Hermann Leins, Vol. I, 1951, Vol. III, 1955). Utilizes a manuscript by Karl Holl.

Hermelink, Heinrich, *Geschichte der evangelischen Kirche in Württemberg von der Reformation bis zur Gegenwart. Das Reich Gottes in Württemberg* (Stuttgart, Rainer Wunderlich Verlag Hermann Leins, 1949, pp. xx, 528). Comprehensive, but lacking in references to sources and in a bibliography.

Hermelink, Heinrich, *Die katholische Kirche unter den Pius-Päpsten des 20. Jahrhunderts* (Zollikon-Zürich, Evangelischer Verlag, 1949, pp. 144). By a Protestant Church historian. Objective, succinct.

Heuvel, J. van den, *The Statesmanship of Benedict XV,* translated by J. C. Burns (London, Burns Oates & Washbourne, 1923, pp. 59). A useful, favourable summary.

Heyer, Friedrich, *Die orthodoxe Kirche in der Ukraine von 1917 bis 1945* (Cologne-Braunsfeld, Verlagsgessellschaft Rudolf Müeller, 1953, pp. 259). Based on extensive research.

Highet, John, *The Churches in Scotland To-day. A Survey of Their Principles, Strength, Work and Statements* (Glasgow, Jackson Son & Co., 1950, pp. xi, 257). Careful, comprehensive, objective.

Hoffmann, J. G. H., *Les Églises du Nord dans la Crise Mondiale* (Geneva, Éditions Labor, no date, pp. 143). By the pastor of the French Church in Stockholm.

Hofinger, Johannes, and Kellner, Joseph, *Liturgische Erneuerung in der Weltmission* (Innsbruck, Tyrolia Verlag, 1956, pp. 455). Based on careful research, friendly.

Hogg, William Richey, *Ecumenical Foundations. A History of the International Missionary Council and Its Nineteenth Century Background* (New York, Harper & Brothers, 1952, pp. xi, 466). The definitive account.

Hoog, Georges, *Histoire du Catholicisme Social en France 1871–1931* (Paris, Éditions Domat Montchestien, rev. ed. 1946). Carefully done. Sympathetic.

Hopper, Stanley Romaine, editor, *Spiritual Problems in Contemporary Literature* (New York, Harper & Brothers, 1952, pp. xvi, 298). By various authors.

Horton, Walter Marshall, *Contemporary Continental Theology. An Interpretation for Anglo-Saxons* (New York, Harper & Brothers, 1938, pp. xxi, 246). By an American theologian with extensive experience in Europe. Covers Russian Orthodox, Roman Catholics, and Protestants, in a semi-popular but expert manner.

Hughes, Philip, *The Popes' New Order. A Systematic Summary of the Social Encyclicals and Addresses, from Leo XIII to Pius XII* (London, Burns Oates & Washbourne, 1943, pp. viii, 232).

Hughes, Philip, *Pope Pius the Eleventh* (New York, Sheed and Ward, 1937, pp. x, 317). An admiring biography, based on a fairly extensive bibliography.

Hughey, John David, *Religious Freedom in Spain, Its Ebb and Flow* (London, Carey Kingsgate Press, 1955, pp. vii, 211). A carefully documented study by a Protestant with experience in Spain.

Information Service (New York, Federal Council of Churches of Christ, later the National Council of the Churches of Christ in the U.S.A., 1922 ff.). A weekly publication, except July and August.

Inge, W. R., *The Diary of a Dean of St. Paul's 1911–1934* (London, Hutchinson & Co., 1949, pp. 228).

The Internationul Review of Missions (London, International Missionary Council, 1912 ff.). The standard Protestant periodical on missions.

Iremonger, F. A., *William Temple, Archbishop of Canterbury, His Life and Letters* (New York, Oxford University Press, 1948, pp. xv, 663). The standard life, sympathetic.

Jackson, Joseph H., *The Eternal Flame. The Story of a Preaching Mission in Russia* (Philadelphia, Christian Education Press, 1956, pp. 125). By the Negro member of a Baptist delegation.

Jarry, A., *L'Église Contemporaine* (Paris, Bloud & Gay, 2 vols., 1935–1936). A useful survery by a French Roman Catholic.

Jemolo, Arturo Carlo in *Chièsa e Stato in Italia negli Ultimo Cento Anni* (Turin, Giulio Einaudi, 3rd ed., 1952, pp. 752). By a Roman Catholic layman, embodying extensive research mostly in published works.

Jordan, E. K. H., *Free Church Unity. History of the Free Church Council Movement, 1896–1941* (London, Lutterworth Press, 1956, pp. 254). Based on an Oxford doctoral dissertation.

The Journal of Ecclesiastical History (London, Faber and Faber, 1950 ff.).

De Katholieke Encyclopaedie (Amsterdam, Joust van den Vondel, 25 vols., 1949–1955).

Keller, Adolph, *Christian Europe Today* (New York, Harper & Brothers, 1942, pp. x, 310). By a distinguished Swiss Protestant churchman, a pioneer in the Ecumenical Movement.

Keller, Adolph, *Church and State on the European Continent* (London, The Epworth Press, 1936, pp. 382).

Kirchliches Handbuch für das katholische Deutschland (Cologne, Gilde-Verlag, 1915 ff.).

Kirchliches Jahrbuch für die evangelischen Landskirchen Deutschlands (Gütersloh, C. Bertelsmann, 1874 ff.).

Kischkowsky, Alexander, *Die sowjetische Religionspolitik und die Russische Orthodoxe Kirche* (Munich, Institut zur Erforschung der Ud SSR, 1957, pp. 136). Based on an extensive bibliography and containing the translation of a number of documents.

Koch, Hal, *Danmarks Kirke gennem Tiderne* (Copenhagen, Gyldendal, 1949, pp. 247). A semi-popular survey by a distinguished specialist.

Koenig, Harry C., editor, *Principles for Peace. Selections from Papal Documents, Leo XIII to Pius XII* (Washington, National Catholic Welfare Conference, 1943, pp. xxv, 894). Useful translations of excerpts.

Koenker, Ernest Benjamin, *The Liturgical Renaissance in the Roman Catholic Church* (University of Chicago Press, 1954, pp. xi, 272). A careful, comprehensive, and sympathetic account by a Lutheran.

Kraemer, Hendrik, *A Theology of the Laity* (Philadelphia, The Westminster Press, 1958, pp. 192). A useful, semi-popular survey.

Lama, Friedrich Ritter von, *Papst und Kurie in ihrer Politik nach dem Weltkrieg. Dargesteldt unter besonderer Berücksichtigung des Varhältnisses zwischen dem Vatikan und Deutschland* (Illertissen, Bavaria Martinusbuchhandlung, 1925, pp. 691). Carefully done, by a Roman Catholic under ecclesiastical imprimatur.

Latourette, Kenneth Scott, *World Service. A History of the Foreign Work and World Service of the Young Men's Christian Associations of the United States and Canada* (New York, Association Press, 1957, pp. xiv, 489). Based on the primary sources.

Latourette, Kenneth Scott, and Hogg, W. Richey, *World Christian Community in Action. The Story of World War II and Orphaned Missions* (New York, International Missionary Council, 1949, pp. 43). Based upon the archives.

Lebret, L.-J., *La France en Transition. Étapes d'une Recherche* (Paris, Éditions Ouvrières Économie et Humanisme, 1957, pp. 165). A careful study of the religious situation largely from a sociological viewpoint.

Leiper, Henry Smith, editor, *Christianity Today. A Survey of the State of the*

Churches, sponsored by the American Committee for the World Council of Churches (New York, Morehouse-Gorham Co., 1947, pp. xvii, 452). By a number of authors.

Littell, Franklin H., and Walz, Hans Hermann, *Weltkirchen Lexikon. Handbuch der Ökumene* (Stuttgart, Kreuz Verlag, 1960, pp. 1755). An extremely valuable comprehensive work of reference.

Lloyd, Roger, *The Church of England in the Twentieth Century* (London, Longmans, Green and Co., 2 vols., 1947, 1950). A competent, sympathetic survey, by an Anglo-Catholic.

Lockhart, J. G., *Cosmo Gordon Lang* (London, Hodder and Stoughton, 1949, pp. xi, 481). The standard biography.

Loewenich, Walther von, *Der moderne Katholizismus Erscheinung und Probleme* (Witten, Luther Verlag, 3rd ed., 1956, pp. 460). A thoughtful and critical description by a Protestant.

Lonsdale, Kathleen, editor, *Quakers Visit Russia* (London, East-West Relations Group of the Friends' Peace Committee, 1952, pp. 145). Reports of a visit in 1951.

McCullagh, Captain Francis, *The Bolshevik Persecution of Christianity* (London, John Murray, 1924, pp. xxi, 401). Antagonistic; based on original documents.

McKnight, John R., *The Papacy: A New Appraisal* (New York, Rinehart and Co., 1952, pp. 437). By a Protestant, well informed, critical but not unfriendly. Especially important on Pius XII.

McLaughlin, Terence P., editor, *The Church and the Reconstruction of the Modern World. The Social Encyclicals of Pope Pius XI* (Garden City, N.Y., Doubleday and Co., 1957, pp. 433).

Magri, Francesco, *L'Azione Cattolica in Italia* (Milan, Editrice la Fiascola, 2 vols., preface 1953). A detailed study. Vol. I, 1775–1939, Vol. II, 1939–1951.

Marc-Bonnet, Henri, *La Papauté Contemporaine (1878–1945)* (Paris, Presses Universitaires de France, 1946, pp. 136). A useful, in the main objective, survey.

Marchant, James, editor, *The Future of the Church of England* (New York, Longmans, Green and Co., 1926, pp. xvi, 244). By various authors.

Margaret, The Prioress of Whitby, *Archbishop Garbett, a Memoir* (London, A. R. Mowbray & Co., 1957, pp. ix, 109). A labour of love.

Mathew, David, *Catholicism in England. The Portrait of a Minority, Its Culture and Tradition* (London, Eyre and Spottiswoode, 3rd ed., 1955, pp. x, 295). Sympathetically objective.

Means, Paul Banwell, *Things That Are Caesar's. The Genesis of the German Church Conflict* (New York, The Round Table Press, 1935, pp. 288). By an American, formerly a student in Germany.

Mendizabal, Alfred, *The Martyrdom of Spain: Origins of a Civil War* (London, Geoffrey Bles, 1938, pp. viii, 277). By a professor in the University of Oviedo, with strong convictions, partly favourable to the Roman Catholic Church.

Michonneau [George], *Revolution in a City Parish* (Westminster, Md., The Newman Press, 1952, pp. xxi, 189). Translation of a book by a French priest dealing with the problems of a modern urban parish.

Micklem, Nathaniel, *National Socialism and the Roman Catholic Church. Being an Account of the Conflict between the National Socialist Government of Germany and the Roman Catholic Church 1933–1938* (New York, Oxford University Press, 1939, pp. xi, 243). By an outstanding English Free Church scholar. Factual, sympathetic with the Roman Catholic Church.

Miller, Basil, *Martin Niemoeller. Hero of the Concentration Camp* (Grand Rapids, Mich., Zondervan Publishing House, 1942, pp. 160). A popular, admiring account.

Missionary Research Library, *Occasional Bulletin* (New York, 1950 ff., mimeographed).

Missions. An International Baptist Magazine (1803 ff., under various titles; has had the name of *Missions* since 1910).

Molland, Einar, *Fra Hans Nielsen Hauge til Eivind Berggrav* (Gyldendal, Norsk Forlag, 1951, pp. 101), translated by Harris Kaasa as *Church Life in Norway 1800–1950* (Minneapolis, Augsburg Publishing House, 1957, pp. vii, 120). By the outstanding authority on the religious history of Norway in the nineteenth and twentieth centuries.

A Monthly Letter about Evangelism (Geneva, World Council of Churches, 1955 ff.).

Moody, Joseph N., editor, *Church and Society, Catholic Social and Political Thought and Movements* (New York, Arts, 1953, pp. 914). By various authors.

Moorman, John R. H., *A History of the Church in England* (London, Adam and Charles Black, 1953, pp. xx, 460). A competent survey, but omitting the Nonconforming bodies.

Morgan, Thomas B., *The Listening Post. Eighteen Years on Vatican Hill* (New York, G. P. Putnam's Sons, 1944, pp. 242). Sympathetic reminiscences by an American newspaper correspondent.

Mozley, John Kenneth, *Some Tendencies in British Theology from the Publication of Lux Mundi to the Present Day* (London, S.P.C.K., 1951, pp. 166). A posthumous publication, very comprehensive, by a brilliant and devout Anglican.

Naurois, Claude, *Dieu Contre Dieu? Drame des Catholiques Progressistes dans une Église du Silence* (Fribourg/Paris, Éditions Saint Paul, 1957, pp. 297). A Roman Catholic account of events in Poland under the Communists.

Neill, Stephen, *Anglicanism* (Harmondsworth, Penguin Books, 1958, pp. 466). A highly competent survey of the history and structure of the Anglican Communion the world over.

Nemec, Ludvík, *Church and State in Czechoslovakia, Historically, Juridically, and Theologically Documented* (New York, Vantage Press, 1955, pp. xi, 577). By a Czechoslovak Roman Catholic clergyman, scholar, and refugee. Chiefly on the Communist period, but with a survey of pre-Communist history.

Neuss, Wilhelm, *Die Kirche der Neuzeit* (Bonn, Bonner Buchgemeinde, 1954, pp. 584). A survey of the history of the Roman Catholic Church beginning with the Protestant Reformation.

Niemöller, Wilhelm, *Die evangelische Kirche im Dritten Reich. Handbuch des*

Kirchenkampfes (Bielefeld, Ludwig Bechauf, 1956, pp. 408). Sympathetic. Based on research in the archives.

Novoe Missionerskoe Obozrenie (edited by S. Bolshakoff, privately mimeographed, Oxford, 1952 ff.).

Occasional Bulletin from the Missionary Research Library (New York, 1950 ff., mimeographed).

O'Connor, Daniel A., *Catholic Social Doctrine* (Westminster, Md., The Newman Press, 1956, pp. xii, 204). Deals chiefly with Pius XII.

Orchard, W. E., *From Faith to Faith. An Autobiography of Religious Development* (New York, Harper & Brothers, 1933, pp. 310).

Paasio, J. K. V., designer, *The Church of Finland through Eight Hundred Years* (Helsinki, Suomalaison Kirjallisuuden Seuran Kirjapainon Oy, 1955, pp. 40). A profusely illustrated popular account.

Palmer, C. H., *The Catholic Church in France. Some Aspects* (London, The Faith Press, 1928, pp. 134). Friendly.

Payne, Ernest A., *The Baptist Union. A Short History* (London, Carey Kingsgate Press, 1959, pp. x, 317). A competent account by a secretary of the Union.

Payne, E. A., *The Free Church Tradition in the Life of England* (London, S.C.M. Press, 1944, pp. 159). A competent historical survey.

Peel, Albert, *The Congregational Two Hundred, 1530–1948* (London, The Independent Press, 1948). Brief biographical sketches by a Congregation official.

Peers, E. Allison, *Spain, the Church and the Orders* (London, Eyre and Spottiswoode, 1939, pp. xi, 219). Sympathetic with the Church.

The Persecution of the Catholic Church in the Third Reich. Facts and Documents translated from the German (New York, Longmans, Green and Co., 1942, pp. x, 565).

Peters, Walter H., *The Life of Benedict XV* (Milwaukee, Bruce Publishing Co., 1959, pp. x, 321). An admiring biography based on diligent research in the printed literature.

Piper, Otto, *Recent Developments in German Protestantism* (London, Student Christian Movement Press, 1934, pp. xvi, 159). By a Protestant anti-Nazi theologian.

Power, Michael, *Religion in the Reich* (London, Longmans, Green and Co., 1939, pp. viii, 240). Semi-popular, by an English observer with personal experience in Germany. Anti-Nazi.

Premoli, Orazio, M., *Contemporary Church History (1900–1925)* (London, Burns Oates & Washbourne, 1932, pp. xvi, 407). A translation from a semi-popular account by a Barnabite, strongly pro-Catholic, and based on an extensive bibliography.

Prestige, G. L., *The Life of Charles Gore, a Great Englishman* (London, William Heinemann, 1935, pp. xi, 547). An admiring biography.

Problèmes du Catholicisme Français (Cahier No. 5, 11e Année Nouvelle Série de *La Nef*) (Paris, Julliard, 1954). By various authors.

Prunskis, Joseph, *Comparative Law, Ecclesiastical and Civil, in the Lithuanian Con-*

cordat (Washington, D.C., The Catholic University of America Press, 1945, pp. viii, 161). A doctoral dissertation of the Catholic University of America.

Reckitt, Maurice B., *Maurice to Temple. A Century of the Social Movement in the Church of England* (London, Faber and Faber, 1947, pp. 245). By a specialist in the field.

Religion in Life. A Christian Quarterly of Opinion and Discussion (Nashville, Abingdon Press, 1930 ff.).

Religion and the Modern World (Philadelphia, University of Pennsylvania Press, 1941, pp. 192). By various authors.

Rhodes, C. O., *The New Church in the New Age* (London, Herbert Jenkins, 1958, pp. 256). A study of the Church of England by the editor of the *Church of England Newspaper* and an organizer of the Modern Churchman's Union.

Ridley, F. A., *The Papacy and Fascism's Crisis of the Twentieth Century* (London, Martin Seeker Warburg, no date, pp. 264). Critical of the Papacy.

Roberts, David E., *Existentialism and Religious Belief* (New York, Oxford University Press, 1957, pp. viii, 344). Covers Pascal, Kierkegaard, Heidegger, Sartre, Jaspers, and Marcel. From a Christian point of view.

Robinson, W. Gordon, *A History of the Lancashire Congregational Union 1806–1956* (Manchester, Lancashire Congregational Union, 1955, pp. 186). An official history.

Rogier, L. J., *Katholieke Herleving. Geschiedenis van Katholiek Nederland sinds 1853* (The Hague, Pax, 1957, pp. 646). A standard work.

Rountree, B. Seebohm, and Lavers, G. R., *English Life and Leisure* (London, Longmans, Green and Co., 1951, pp. xvi, 482). A careful, provocative study.

Rouse, Ruth, and Neill, Stephen Charles, editors, *A History of the Ecumenical Movement, 1517–1948* (London, S.P.C.K., 1954, pp. xxiv, 822). The official history, by various authors.

Rovan, Joseph, *Histoire de la Démocratie Chrétienne II. Le Catholicisme Politique en Allemagne* (Paris, Éditions du Seuil, 1956, pp. 289). Covers the years 1789–1956.

St. Vladimir's Seminary Quarterly (New York, St. Vladimir's Orthodox Theological Seminary, 1957 ff.).

The New Schaff-Herzog Encyclopedia of Religious Knowledge (Grand Rapids, Mich., Baker Book House, 15 vols., 1951–1954). A reprint of the 1908–1914 edition, with two supplementary volumes.

Schmidlin, Joseph, *Catholic Mission History,* a translation edited by Matthias Braun (Techny, Ill., Mission Press, S.V.D., 1933, pp. xv, 862). A standard survey, with important additions by Braun.

Schmidlin, Josef, *Papstgeschichte der neuesten Zeit* (Munich, Josef Kösol & Friedrich Pustet, 3 vols., 3rd ed., 1933–1936). A standard work by an eminent Roman Catholic scholar. The years covered are 1800–1922.

Schmidt, Wolfgang, *Finlands Kyrka genom Tiderna. En Oversikt* (Stockholm, Svenska Kyrkans Diakonistyrelses Bokförlag, 1940, pp. 331). A competent historical survey from the beginnings of Christianity in Finland into the 1930's.

Schuster, Hermann, *Das Werden der Kirche. Eine Geschichte der Kirche auf deutschen Boden* (Berlin, Alfred Töpelmann, 2nd ed., 1950, pp. xix, 569). By a specialist with the aid of other experts.

Schwegler, Theodor, *Geschichte der katholischen Kirche in der Schweiz von den Anfängen bis auf die Gegenwart* (Stans, Josef von Matt, 1943, pp. 426). Comprehensive, carefully done.

Schweitzer, Carl, editor, *Das religiöse Deutschland der Gegenwart. Ein Handbuch für Jedermann* (Berlin, Hochweg-Verlag, 2 vols., 1928, 1929). By several authors. Mostly on Protestantism but also includes the Roman Catholic Church and several non-Christian movements.

Shuster, George N., *Religion Behind the Iron Curtain* (New York, The Macmillan Co., 1954, pp. xxi, 281). By an American Roman Catholic layman.

Shuster, George N., *In Silence I Speak. The Story of Cardinal Mindszenty Today and of Hungary's "New Order"* (New York, Farrar, Straus and Cudahy, 1956, pp. xix, 296). Warmly sympathetic with the Roman Catholic Church.

Siegmund-Schultze, Fried., editor, *Die evangelischen Kirchen der Niederlande* (Gotha, Leopold Klotz Verlag, 1934, pp. 176). One of the *Ekklesia* series. By various authors.

Siegmund-Schultze, Fried., editor, *Die evangelischen Kirchen in Polen* (Leipzig, Leopold Klotz Verlag, 1938, pp. 274). By several authors. One of the *Ekklesia* series.

Siegmund-Schultze, Fried., editor, *Die evangelischen Kirchen der Schweiz* (Gotha, Leopold Klotz Verlag, 1935, pp. 253). One of the *Ekklesia* series. By various authors.

Siegmund-Schultze, Fried., editor, *Die Kirche in Dänemark* (Leipzig, Leopold Klotz Verlag, 1937, pp. 195). One of the *Ekklesia* series, with articles by several Danish experts.

Siegmund-Schultze, Fried., editor, *Die Kirche von England* (Gotha, Leopold Klotz Verlag, 1934, pp. 124). One of the *Ekklesia* series. By several authors, chiefly G. K. A. Bell.

Siegmund-Schultze, Fried., editor, *Die Kirche in Finnland* (Leipzig, Leopold Klotz Verlag, 1938, pp. 203). One of the *Ekklesia* series and by several authors.

Siegmund-Schultze, Fried., editor, *Die Kirche von Norwegen* (Gotha, Leopold Klotz Verlag, 1936, pp. 207). One of the *Ekklesia* series, with articles by several Norwegian experts.

Siegmund-Schultze, Fried., editor, *Die Kirche in Schweden* (Gotha, Leopold Klotz Verlag, 1935, pp. 180). One of the *Ekklesia* series, with articles by several authors.

Siegmund-Schultze, Fried., editor, *Die Kirchen der Tschechoslowakei* (Leipzig, Leopold Klotz Verlag, 1937, pp. 250). By various authors. One of the *Ekklesia* series.

Sobornost (London, Fellowship of St. Alban and St. Sergius, no date of beginning). A semi-annual official publication of the Fellowship of St. Alban and St. Sergius.

Somerville, Henry, *Studies in the Catholic Social Movement* (London, Burns Oates

& Washbourne, 1933, pp. xvii, 162). A sympathetic account of the movement in France, Germany, Austria, Holland, and Belgium.

Spinka, Matthew, *The Church in Soviet Russia* (New York, Oxford University Press, 1956, pp. xi, 179). Highly competent.

Spinks, G. Stephens, editor, *Religion in Britain since 1900* (London, Andrew Dakers, 1952, pp. 256). Comprehensive, by several authors.

The Statesman's Year Book (London, Macmillan and Co., 1864 ff.).

Stephan, Horst, and Leube, Hans, *Die Neuzeit* (Tübingen, J. C. B. Mohr, Paul Siebeck, 2nd ed., 1931, pp. xii, 472). Vol. IV of *Handbuch der Kirchengeschichte*, edited by Gustav Krüger. Useful, especially for Germany.

Strong, Esther Boorman, and Warnshuis, A. L., editors, *Directory of Foreign Missions. Missionary Boards, Societies, Colleges, Coöperative Councils, and Other Agencies of the Protestant Churches of the World* (New York, International Missionary Council, 1933, pp. xii, 278).

The Student World (Geneva, 1907 ff.). The official organ of the World's Student Christian Federation.

Szuldrzynski, J., *The Pattern of Life in Poland. XVI. The Situation of the Catholic Church* (Paris, Mid-European Research and Planning Centre, 1953, pp. 61). From the standpoint of the Roman Catholic Church.

Teeling, William, *Pope Pius XI and World Affairs* (New York, Frederick A. Stokes Co., 1937, pp. viii, 312). Semi-popular, by a Roman Catholic.

Theology Today (Princeton, N.J., 1944 ff.). A quarterly Protestant journal connected with Princeton Theological Seminary.

Timasheff, N. S., *Religion in Soviet Russia, 1917–1942* (New York, Sheed and Ward, 1942, pp. xii, 171). By a Roman Catholic scholar.

Time, The Weekly News-Magazine (New York, 1923 ff.).

Tobias, Robert, *Communist-Christian Encounter in East Europe* (Indianapolis, School of Religion Press, 1956, pp. vi, 567). A factual account of the interaction of Communist governments and Christian churches in East Europe, 1917–1951.

Tragella, P. G. B., *Pio XI, Papa Missionario Ricordo del Giubileo Sacerdotale del S. Padre (1879–1929)* (Milan, Pont. Istituto della Missioni Estere, 1930, pp. 187). Especially important for its documents.

Twentieth Century Encyclopedia of Religious Knowledge. An Extension of the New Schaff-Herzog Encyclopedia of Religious Knowledge (Grand Rapids, Mich., Baker Book House, 2 vols., 1955).

Villain, Jean, *L'Enseignement Social de l'Église* (Paris, Spes, 3 vols., 1953, 1954). A survey of Roman Catholic teaching, especially under Leo XIII, Pius XI, and Pius XII, and of organizations to put it into effect.

Villain, Maurice, *L'Abbé Paul Couturier, Apôtre de l'Unité Chrétienne* (Tournai, Casterman, 1957, pp. 380). A sympathetic biography which includes a number of important documents.

Walker, Reginald F., *Pius of Peace* (Westminster, Md., The Newman Bookshop, preface 1945, pp. 140). A sympathetic account, composed largely of excerpts from Pius XII's utterances during World War II.

Ward, Maisie, *France Pagan? The Mission of Abbé Godin* (New York, Sheed and Ward, 1949, pp. xii, 243). The first part is a life of Henri Godin and the second is a translation of *France, Pays de Mission?* by Godin and Yvan Daniel.

Wearmouth, Robert F., *The Social and Political Influence of Methodism in the Twentieth Century* (London, The Epworth Press, 1957, pp. xiii, 265). Based on careful research, by a Methodist.

Weber, Hans-Ruedi, editor, *Signs of Renewal. The Life of the Lay Institutes in Europe* (Geneva, Department of the Laity, World Council of Churches, 1956, pp. 63). By various authors with first-hand contact with the subjects of their chapters.

Weigel, Gustave, *A Catholic Primer on the Ecumenical Movement* (Westminster, Md., The Newman Press, 1957, pp. x, 79). An excellent, objective summary by a Jesuit of the history of the Roman Catholic attitude.

Who Was Who (London, Adam and Charles Black, 4 vols., covering 1897–1950, 1950–1952).

Who's Who, 1955 (London, Adam and Charles Black, 1955, pp. 3286).

Who's Who in Germany (Munich, Intercontinental Book and Publishing Co., 1956, pp. xv, 1311, 114).

Wickham, E. R., *Church and People in an Industrial City* (London, Lutterworth Press, 1957, pp. 292). An historical and contemporary study of Sheffield by an industrial chaplain.

Wilder, Amos N., *Modern Poetry and the Christian Tradition. A Study in the Relation of Christianity to Culture* (New York, Charles Scribner's Sons, 1952, pp. xviii, 287). By an expert.

Williams, Daniel Day, *What Present-Day Theologians Are Thinking* (New York, Harper & Brothers, 1952, pp. 158). A competent survey.

Wittram, Reinhard, editor, *Baltische Kirchengeschichte* (Göttingen, Vanderhoeck & Ruprecht, 1956, pp. 347). By various authors.

World Dominion (London, 1923–1957). A quarterly review, an organ of the World Dominion Movement.

Worldmission Fides Service (formerly *Fides News Service*) (Rome and New York, ca. 1926 ff.). An organ of the Society for the Propagation of the Faith.

Wylie, Samuel J., *New Patterns for Christian Action. How Christians Here and Abroad Are Meeting the Challenge of Secularism* (Greenwich, Conn., The Seabury Press, 1959, pp. 96). A sympathetic account of Roman Catholic-Protestant *rapprochement,* by an Episcopalian.

Zenkovsky, Vasilii V., *A History of Russian Philosophy,* translated by George L. Kline (New York, Columbia University Press, 2 vols., 1953). A standard survey.

Zubek, Theodoric J., *The Church of Silence in Slovakia* (Whiting, Ind., 1956, pp. 310). By a Franciscan.

INDEX